Applied Social Psychology

Third Edition

Applied Social Psychology

Understanding and Addressing Social and Practical Problems

Third Edition

University of Guelph   **Jamie A. Gruman**

University of Windsor   **Frank. W. Schneider**

L. M. Coutts & Associates   **Larry M. Coutts**

Editors

Los Angeles | London | New Delhi
Singapore | Washington DC | Melbourne

FOR INFORMATION:

SAGE Publications, Inc.
2455 Teller Road
Thousand Oaks, California 91320
E-mail: order@sagepub.com

SAGE Publications Ltd.
1 Oliver's Yard
55 City Road
London EC1Y 1SP
United Kingdom

SAGE Publications India Pvt. Ltd.
B 1/I 1 Mohan Cooperative Industrial Area
Mathura Road, New Delhi 110 044
India

SAGE Publications Asia-Pacific Pte. Ltd.
3 Church Street
#10-04 Samsung Hub
Singapore 049483

Acquisitions Editor: Lara Parra
Editorial Assistant: Zachary Valladon
Associate eLearning Editor: Morgan Shannon
Production Editor: Laura Barrett
Copy Editor: Janet Ford
Typesetter: C&M Digitals (P) Ltd
Proofreader: Jennifer Grubba
Indexer: Rick Hurd
Cover Designer: Candice Harman
Marketing Manager: Katherine Hepburn

Printed in the United States of America

Library of Congress Cataloging-in-Publication Data

Names: Gruman, Jamie A., editor. | Schneider, Frank W., editor. | Coutts, Larry M., editor.

Title: Applied social psychology : understanding and addressing social and practical problems / editors, Jamie A. Gruman, University Of Guelph, Frank W. Schneider, University Of Windsor, Larry M. Coutts, L. M. Coutts & Associates, and Part-time instructor, Sprott School of Business, Carleton University.

Description: Third Edition. | Los Angeles : SAGE, [2016] | Includes bibliographical references and index.

Identifiers: LCCN 2016013695 | ISBN 978-1-4833-6973-0 (pbk. : alk. paper)

Subjects: LCSH: Social psychology.

Classification: LCC HM1033 .S36 2016 | DDC 302—dc23 LC record available at https://lccn.loc.gov/2016013695

This book is printed on acid-free paper.

16 17 18 19 20 10 9 8 7 6 5 4 3 2 1

CONTENTS

PREFACE

This textbook serves as an introduction to **applied social psychology,** which is the branch of the field of social psychology that focuses on understanding social and practical problems and on developing intervention strategies directed at the amelioration of such problems. As editors of this third edition, as with the first two editions, we have two main objectives. One objective is to produce a text for a course in applied social psychology that is compatible with the interests and abilities of students at the advanced undergraduate level. The second main objective is to share with students the promise of applied social psychology and our excitement about the field. That excitement can be traced to a considerable extent to our mutual involvement in the graduate program in applied social psychology at the University of Windsor: Frank Schneider was a co-founder of the program, Jamie Gruman earned his doctorate from the program, and Larry Coutts served as a faculty member in the program. Our excitement also stems from an awareness of the mounting evidence of the applicability of social psychological theory and knowledge to the improvement of the functioning of individuals, groups, organizations, communities, and societies with respect to a wide variety of social and practical problems.

REACTIONS TO EARLIER EDITIONS

Not long after the publication of the first edition our initial vision for the book began to be confirmed by two formal reviews of the book (Boon, 2005; Simpson, 2005) and by the rate of its adoption as a text. Both reviewers had high praise for the book, including how well we were able to maintain consistency of writing style and organization despite the involvement of many authors. An unanticipated reward for us was the pedagogical impact the book had on the reviewers themselves. One reviewer wrote,

> I have a renewed enthusiasm for my field and a much deeper appreciation of the range of situations in which social psychological theory and research may be, and indeed have been, applied, and a fuller understanding of the opportunities, perhaps even the obligation, that I have, as a social psychologist, to do research that positively impacts the world. (Boon, 2005, p. 251)

The second reviewer wrote,

> "This is a refreshing, well-written, inspirational text that suggests that psychology is indeed making progress in making the world a better place. Reading it has revitalized my desire to redirect my formal experimental social psychology training to solve practical problems." (Simpson, 2005)

We also were encouraged by the number of instructors who adopted the book for courses in applied social psychology and related courses (applied psychology, special topics in social psychology, etc.), as well as by the feedback from the psychology editor at SAGE that *Applied Social Psychology* was regarded as among their more successful books. Moreover, we were pleased to learn of the book's adoption in a number of graduate courses, including applied social psychology and the social bases of behavior. We were also delighted to learn that the book is used around the globe. One indication of its global impact was a review of the second edition in the *Journal of the Indian Academy of Applied Psychology* (Team JIAAP, 2014).

ORGANIZATION

As with the two earlier editions, the book maintains a balance between social psychological theory, research, and application. The book is formally divided into three parts.

Part 1: Foundations of Applied Social Psychology includes four chapters that provide readers with bases for understanding the processes by which applied social psychologists develop theories, acquire knowledge, and design and evaluate interventions. Chapter 1 defines the field of applied social psychology and places the field in a historical and intellectual context. Chapter 2 defines and illustrates the nature of theory and the processes of theory development. Chapter 3 reviews basic research designs and data collection methods used by applied social psychologists. Chapter 4 defines and illustrates the steps involved in the design, implementation, and evaluation of programmatic interventions.

Part 2: Applying Social Psychology to Arenas of Life consists of 10 chapters that examine how social psychological theory and research evidence have been applied to understanding and addressing social and practical problems in different topic areas: clinical/counseling (Chapter 5), sports teams (Chapter 6), media (Chapter 7), health (Chapter 8), education (Chapter 9), organizations (Chapter 10), criminal justice (Chapter 11), community (Chapter 12), environment (Chapter 13), and diversity (Chapter 14).

Part 3: Applying Social Psychology to One's Own Life consists of 3 chapters that examine how individuals can draw on social psychological theory and evidence to improve their own lives (i.e., "personal interventions") with respect to selected areas of functioning: interpersonal relationships (Chapter 15), the classroom (Chapter 16), and well-being (Chapter 17).

The book is most appropriate for students with some course work in psychology. However, students with little or no formal background in psychology, including those in allied fields (e.g., sociology, communication studies) should feel comfortable in reading the book because of the instructional approach that it takes. In particular, the instructional features come in the first four chapters which systematically review the basic processes of applied social psychology.

FEATURES

- Central role of intervention strategies. The content and emphases are guided by the assumption that at the core of applied social psychology is the development and implementation of intervention strategies directed at the improvement of individuals, groups, organizations, communities, and societies.
- Personal interventions. The book is unique among applied social psychology books in having chapters that focus on personal uses of social psychology that help to underscore the personal relevance and utility of the field.
- Focuses on research and intervention. The chapters in Part 2 include at least one *Focus on Research* and one *Focus on Intervention*, which are boxed sections that review in greater detail and depth research studies and social psychologically based interventions, respectively.
- Culture capsules. The chapters in Parts 2 and 3 include a *Culture Capsule* that reports empirical data that serve to illustrate that theoretical principles, research findings, and/or intervention

practices that are well established in the North American context do not necessarily hold true or prove effective in other cultural contexts.

- Other pedagogical elements. All chapters include an opening outline, highlighting of key terms, and a final summary. Also, chapters in Parts 2 and 3 begin with a vignette that sets the stage for the content that follows.

NEW TO THE THIRD EDITION

- Content has been updated in all chapters resulting in over 270 new citations.
- Consistent with the growth in popularity of qualitative research methods, new detailed examples of research using qualitative methods have been added to *all* content chapters.
- Chapter 1 incorporates a new discussion of the different approaches adopted in the field of applied social psychology.
- Chapter 2 includes an entirely new section drawing on the *Theory of Planned Behavior* to explain the nature of social psychological theory.
- Chapter 3 incorporates an expanded discussion of qualitative research methods and notes where examples of specific methods can be found in the text.
- Chapter 4 includes a detailed example of incorporating qualitative methods to design and evaluate interventions.
- Chapter 6 introduces the concept of shared mental models in teams.
- Chapter 7 presents an updated account of video games and aggression, and how the Internet influences the way we consume news media.
- Chapter 8 includes a new section on health literacy and how people evaluate health claims on the Internet.
- Chapter 9 presents new material on procrastination, bullying, and cyberbullying, new Focus on Research and Focus on Intervention sections, and an expanded discussion of intrinsic motivation and goals.
- Chapter 10 includes new material on persuasiveness in communication.
- Chapter 11 incorporates an elaborated discussion of false confessions.
- Chapter 12 includes a new discussion of virtual sense of community, introduces the concept of intersectionality, and includes a new section on activism in research.

- Chapter 13 includes an expanded discussion on how to effectively craft messages to promote environmentally friendly behavior.
- Chapter 14 contains a new section on the social axioms approach to cultural analysis.
- Chapter 16 includes an expanded discussion of cognitive errors and tendencies.
- Chapter 17 includes an expanded discussion of optimism and pessimism, positive social psychology, and introduces a balance framework for conceptualizing how social phenomena promote "the good life."
- In sum, new sections and/or substantially revised sections permeate the entire book.

IN APPRECIATION

We greatly appreciate the contributions of the many individuals who helped us accomplish this revision. We certainly extend our gratitude to the contributing authors who sustained their commitment to our vision for the book by agreeing to revise their chapters for a third edition. SAGE commissioned reviews of the second edition in preparation for the revision. We were very impressed with the reviewers' thoughtful comments and suggestions and drew on many of their ideas to improve the new edition. We thank Reid Hester, our initial editor, who encouraged us to produce a third edition of the book, and Lara Parra who took over from Reid and saw the book to completion. Special thanks go out to Morgan Shannon, her editorial assistant, whose professionalism and timeliness made managing this large project much easier. We would also like to thank the faculty in the applied social psychology area of the University of Guelph for offering valuable insight into recent developments in the field and changes to the book that might best improve it. In particular, we thank Drs. Paula Barata, Benjamin Giguère, Ian Newby-Clark, and Kieran O'Doherty. We would especially like to thank Dr. Jennifer Dobson, who stepped up to assist with much of the research, writing, and administrative details involved with this revision. Her experience teaching applied social psychology using the text in addition to her keen judgment allowed her to offer valuable suggestions about changes, and implement many of those changes. Jennifer's contributions cannot be overstated and are partly recognized with an authorship of one of the chapters. Finally, we'd like to thank all of the instructors around the globe who have chosen to use and continue to use this book in their courses. It is because of your continued willingness to select this book from among all of those available that a third edition was warranted and has allowed this text to be born anew. We hope this third edition lives up to your expectations of it as the "go to" textbook on applied social psychology.

Jamie A. Gruman

Frank W. Schneider

Larry M. Coutts

PART I

FOUNDATIONS OF APPLIED SOCIAL PSYCHOLOGY

1

Defining the Field of Applied Social Psychology

Frank W. Schneider

Jamie A. Gruman

Larry M. Coutts

CHAPTER OUTLINE

SOCIAL PSYCHOLOGY

The purpose of this book is to introduce you to the field of applied social psychology. Before reviewing some of the contributions of the field in various domains of life (e.g., education, health, sports), it is important to define the field of applied social psychology, including placing it in the context of its parent field, social psychology. We begin by considering a series of social interactions described to one of the chapter authors by friends who live in a city in the

U.S. Midwest. The interactions occurred in early fall of 2010. The events were similar to those that commonly occur in people's lives—a first-time meeting of two couples, the development of friendship between the couples, and a party hosted by one of the couples—and as most social interactions do, they reflected a great variety of social psychological phenomena. These phenomena enable us to illustrate first the focus of the science of social psychology and then the focus of applied social psychology, which we define as a branch of social psychology.

A family moved in across the street from Ken and Kim (all names altered). They first met their new neighbors when the husband (Scott) came across the street with jumper cables to help Ken start his car. Ken thought that Scott seemed quite friendly. After the car was started, Ken and Kim invited Scott and his wife Jen in for coffee. The couples liked each other right away, discovering they had many interests in common. Over the following weeks a strong friendship began to develop as they spent more and more time together. The two men took in a number of sports events, and Ken interested Scott in taking up kayaking. The two women began to go to garage sales and flea markets. The couples agreed with each other's parenting practices and began to watch the other couple's children on occasion.

Kim suggested to Ken that they introduce their new friends to some of their other friends. So they invited Scott and Jen and three other couples to a pizza and game night at their home. The evening began very well. There was lively conversation and lots of laughter with Scott and Jen readily joining in. However, the pleasant atmosphere quickly evaporated when the conversation turned to the ongoing controversy over the proposal to build a mosque within a few blocks of the site of the World Trade Center disaster. The discussion became increasingly loud and heated as sharp differences of opinion emerged. One of the group, named Russ, forcefully advanced the position that the location of the mosque should be moved farther away from the site of the disaster out of respect for the memory of the victims and sensitivity for their loved ones. As Russ argued his position, Ken began to worry because he knew that Russ had temper control problems. Meanwhile,

Scott strongly disagreed with Russ, believing the mosque should be built as planned as a sign of America's commitment to religious freedom and because it would give an international face to moderate and peaceful Islam. When Scott raised the possibility that negative attitudes toward Arabs may underlie opposition to the proposed location, Russ became enraged and yelled, "I don't have negative attitudes toward Arabs; I just love my country," and then he pointed at Scott and called him "an un-American loser." That triggered louder voices and more accusations about prejudice and racism. Ken and Kim's friendly get-together was clearly in danger of falling apart. Several people tried to settle down the people who were arguing, but unfortunately no matter what they tried, nothing worked. Soon the party ended with Russ and Scott refusing to shake hands and all guests leaving for home.

Defining Social Psychology

So, what about the above series of interactions helps to define the field of social psychology? For one thing, the events were rich in social psychological phenomena. Drawing on the definitions in several social psychology textbooks (e.g., Myers, Spencer, & Jordon, 2009), **social psychology** may be defined as the science that seeks to understand how people think about, feel about, relate to, and influence one another. Given this definition, you should be able to identify many examples of social psychological subject matter in the interactions involving Ken, Kim, and their friends by looking for instances of thinking about others, feeling about others, relating to others, and influencing others. Scott *related* to Ken by helping with his car. Ken *thought* Scott seemed friendly. Ken and Kim invited (*related* to) Scott and Jen into their home. The couples liked each other (*feelings*), and they subsequently *related* to each other by spending time together, including going to various events. Ken *influenced* Scott to take up kayaking. The couples agreed with (*thoughts*) each other's parenting practices and helped (*related* to) each other by watching each other's children. Ken was *influenced* by Kim to have the party. In the beginning, the party went well with the partygoers *relating* positively in lively conversation, but then things turned for the worse. . . .

We want you to recognize that one can do a similar analysis with virtually any kind of social situation. Those processes exemplified in the above social interactions—thinking and feeling about others, relating to and influencing them—are precisely the kinds of processes that comprise the subject matter of social psychology, and thus are what social psychologists focus on in their research. We also can see where the examples of social psychological processes in those interactions can be related to broader areas of social psychological concern and investigation, such as helping behavior (e.g., Scott helping with Ken's car), friendship formation (e.g., relationship between the two couples), person perception (e.g., Ken's view of Russ as having a volatile temper), and interpersonal conflict (e.g., altercation among group members).

Social Psychology as a Science

So, those are the kinds of phenomena that social psychology—as a science—seeks to understand. Do not pass lightly over the phrase "as a science" because the fact that social psychology is a science is fundamental to its meaning. The *essence of science* involves (a) a set of research methods that in combination make up what is known as the scientific method, and (b) a foundation of core values.

Scientific method and core values. The research methods (e.g., correlational, experimental) that fall under the scientific method are those that depend on **empirical tests**, that is, the use of systematic observation to evaluate propositions and ideas. An empirical test of an idea (e.g., people are happier in sunny weather) entails a research study that is (a) set up in such a way as to allow for the idea to be either refuted or supported, and (b) conducted so that what is done can be readily evaluated and replicated by other researchers (Cozby, 2009).

Undergirding and guiding research methods is a set of *core values* (Baron, Branscombe, & Byrne, 2008; Heiman, 2002). The following are some of the most important values that are absolutely essential for scientists to adhere to in their work:

- *Accuracy*: precise, error-free measurement and collection of information (i.e., data)
- *Objectivity*: minimization of bias in data collection and proposition testing
- *Skepticism*: refusing to believe findings and conclusions without rigorous verification
- *Open-mindedness*: readiness to accept as valid evidence that which may be inconsistent with one's initial, and perhaps strongly held, beliefs or theories
- *Ethics*: acceptance of the absolute importance of ethical behavior in conducting research

Adherence to the first four values is necessary to ensure that findings of research validly reflect the phenomenon under study. The fifth value, ethics, also pertains to the validity of findings (e.g., researchers should not wittingly alter or misrepresent their results), but also encompasses the need to safeguard the dignity and well-being of research participants.

Scientific understanding. Thus, to seek an understanding of social psychological phenomena, social psychologists, as scientists, are guided by certain core values and rely on research strategies that fall under the scientific method. But, what is meant by "understanding"? In science, including social psychology, *understanding* involves the accomplishment of four goals: description, prediction, determining causality, and explanation (Cozby, 2009). We define these goals and illustrate them by considering the possible influence that having a pet has on the adjustment of the elderly.

The goal of **description** entails identifying and reporting the details and nature of a phenomenon, often distinguishing between the classes or types of the phenomenon and recording its frequency of occurrence. In the case of the adjustment of the elderly, a researcher might distinguish between emotional adjustment and social adjustment and then measure and record the incidence of older persons in the community who fit this classification. The researcher could also find out whether or not each elderly person has a pet, perhaps listing information about the kind and number of pets. Achieving accurate descriptions of phenomena is one aspect of understanding. Understanding also entails prediction.

The **prediction** form of understanding requires knowing what factors are systematically related (i.e., correlated) to the phenomenon of interest. In our example, if research showed that there is a relationship between adjustment and having a pet—those who have a pet tend to be better adjusted—we would understand that adjustment in the elderly can be predicted in general by the presence or absence of a pet. This relationship would represent an important insight and lead us to consider the third form of understanding: ascertaining whether or not there is a causal relationship between having a pet and adjustment.

Determining causality between two factors means determining that changes in one factor produce (i.e., cause) changes in the other factor. Just because two factors are related does not necessarily mean that they are causally related. For instance, having a pet might have no effect whatsoever on the adjustment of the elderly even though a relationship may exist. A third factor could be responsible for the existence of the relationship. For instance, physical health could influence both how well-adjusted people feel and whether they have a pet (because it is easier to care for a pet if one is healthy). So, it is important not to be misled by a common tendency among people to assume that if two things are correlated, a causal relationship necessarily exists.

Identifying the cause(s) of phenomena is a very important component of understanding. If research were to establish that having a pet does indeed lead to improvements in adjustment (i.e., causes better adjustment), there could be clear-cut practical implications in terms of providing help to the elderly. But, pursuit of understanding does not end with the establishment of causation. Understanding also involves explanation, the fourth goal.

Explanation pertains to establishing *why* a phenomenon or relationship occurs. We may understand that one factor causes another factor without knowing exactly why the effect occurs. If having a pet does lead to improvements in the adjustment of the elderly (and this does seem to be the case [Beck & Katcher, 1996]), what is the explanation? Is it because having a pet reduces loneliness, because it increases feelings of security, because it gives the elderly person a chance to feel needed by nurturing a living thing, or because of some other factor?

Social psychological understanding: The formation of intergroup attitudes. Let us further illustrate social psychology's approach to understanding social psychological phenomena by considering the formation of intergroup attitudes. An attitude may be defined as "a person's overall evaluation of persons (including oneself), objects, and issues" (Petty & Wegener, 1998, p. 323). Thus, an *intergroup attitude* refers to a person's overall evaluation of members of a group to which the person does not belong. One major area of research in the study of attitudes focuses on understanding how attitudes are formed (i.e., how people come to possess their attitudes). Let us focus specifically on intergroup attitudes and consider a small portion of the research that sheds some light on how negative intergroup attitudes develop in people. Note that this is essentially a question of causality. We expect that you are sensitive to the serious social and political consequences that can stem from the existence of negative attitudes (and relations) between various groups (e.g., ethnic, racial, religious, national) in the world. Recall the furor that erupted at Ken and Kim's party when one person simply implied that another person possessed negative attitudes toward Arabs.

One approach that social psychologists have taken in the study of the formation of intergroup attitudes is to examine the role of various agents of socialization. This research indicates that children tend to take on the attitudes of important people around them (e.g., parents, teachers, peers) and that at least part of the explanation is that these people influence the development of such attitudes through the basic principles of learning, such as instrumental conditioning, classical conditioning, and observation (e.g., Banaji & Heiphetz, 2010; Oskamp, 1991). For instance, Castelli, De Dea, and Nesdale (2008) showed that when White preschool-age children observed a White adult nonverbally convey uneasiness toward a Black person, they subsequently expressed more negative attitudes toward Black targets.

So, intergroup attitudes are learned partly from others. But, as is the case with many social psychological phenomena, multiple factors must be recognized when exploring the determinants of intergroup attitudes. Another influential factor that is a salient part of people's lives is the media (Banaji & Heiphetz, 2010). For instance, news reports about terrorism have been linked to increased prejudice toward Arabs (Das, Bushman, Bezemer, Kerkhof, & Vermeulen, 2009). It is especially noteworthy that social psychologists also have found that people's attitudes toward other groups may be influenced by the simple fact that they see themselves as members of a particular group. When people view themselves as belonging to one group (e.g., Americans), that group is referred to as the in-group; nonmembers of the in-group (e.g., non-Americans) are called the out-group. Many investigations confirm the existence of a very robust phenomenon called **in-group/out-group bias**, which means that in-group members tend to evaluate and relate to the in-group favorably and to the out-group less favorably (or unfavorably). This might not seem particularly surprising. What is remarkable, however, is that in-group/out-group bias is such a basic social psychological phenomenon that it can show up even in a situation where there is just the slightest differentiation between the in-group and the out-group. In many laboratory experiments, Tajfel and his colleagues (e.g., Tajfel & Billig, 1974) and others (e.g., Allen & Wilder, 1975) divided participants—all strangers—into two groups on the basis of trivial criteria

(e.g., those who underestimate and those who overestimate the number of dots on slides). Across experiments, participants consistently assigned more favorable rewards and traits to in-group members than to out-group members (see also Paladino & Castelli, 2008). Relatedly, Lyons, Kenworthy, and Popan (2010) recently provided evidence linking negative attitudes and behaviors toward Arab immigrants among Americans to their degree of identification with their national in-group (i.e., being American). So, we know that simply being a member of a group contributes to the development of negative attitudes toward other groups. We also have a glimpse of some social psychological factors that were potentially relevant to whether or not Russ, in fact, did harbor negative attitudes toward Arabs (as intimated by Scott). These factors include the levels of ethnic tolerance, especially toward Arabs, of his significant other; his exposure to media reports about threatening acts associated with Arabs; and the strength of his national identity.

As we consider social psychology's approach to understanding the development of negative intergroup attitudes, let us recognize one more causal factor—competition. Around 1950, Muzafer Sherif and his research team took the investigation of intergroup relations into the field where they studied the role of competition between groups (Sherif, 1966b; Sherif & Sherif, 1953, 1969). The researchers conducted an ingenious series of 3-week experiments with 11- and 12-year-old boys at isolated camp settings. The investigations were conducted in weeklong phases. During Phase 1—group formation—the boys were divided into two groups of approximately 10 each. Each group lived in a separate cabin and, as arranged by the experimenters, engaged in a series of appealing activities that required cooperative interdependence (e.g., camping, building a rope bridge). Members of each group soon developed a sense of "we-feeling" as their group developed a definite role structure (e.g., leaders, followers) and set of norms (e.g., expectations about how things should be done). During Phase 2—group conflict—the researchers investigated conditions that resulted in negative intergroup attitudes and behavior. They implemented a series of competitions (e.g., tug-of-war, skits) in which only the victorious group of boys won a prize. By the end of the week, the relations between the two groups had deteriorated to a very antagonistic situation involving strongly negative stereotypes (e.g., "sneaky," "stinkers") and behavior (e.g., name-calling, food fights, damage to property).

In all of the preceding examples of research on intergroup attitudes, we can see that the social psychologists focused on furthering the understanding of one or more of the following: how people think about, feel about, relate to, and influence each other. All of the research reviewed fits under social psychology's umbrella. Now let us look under the applied social psychology umbrella.

APPLIED SOCIAL PSYCHOLOGY

Sherif's (1966b) field research on intergroup relations involved a third phase. During this phase—reduction of conflict—the researchers developed and evaluated an intervention strategy to improve the relations between the groups of boys. The strategy was designed in accordance with Sherif's understanding of the existing research literature on the determinants of positive attitudes and relations among groups that are divided along racial, political, and industrial lines (Sherif & Sherif, 1953). The strategy was based on the idea that groups in conflict would experience improved relations if they cooperate in the attainment of **superordinate goals**, that is, goals that are highly appealing to both groups, but that can be attained only through their cooperative effort. During this phase, the groups of boys were introduced to a series of superordinate goals (e.g., pulling together on a rope to start a broken-down truck that had been on its way to get food). Over the course of several days, hostile interaction between the groups declined considerably and friendships began to cross group boundaries. Since this early work of Sherif, the utility of superordinate goals in

contributing to the reduction of conflict between a wide variety of groups has been well established (e.g., Kelly & Collett, 2008).

In Sherif's research on breaking down the barriers between the groups of boys, we have an example of the *use of social psychology to effect positive social change*. Notice how his emphasis shifted from trying to understand the causes of a social problem—intergroup antagonism—to trying to come up with a strategy for doing something about the problem. This concern with contributing to positive change brings us more fully into the area of social psychology that focuses on application—applied social psychology.

Applied social psychology refers to the branch of social psychology that draws on social psychological theories, principles, methods, and research evidence to contribute to (a) the understanding of social and practical problems, and (b) the development of intervention strategies for improving the functioning of individuals, groups, organizations, communities, and societies with respect to social and practical problems. In this definition, *functioning* is broadly viewed as encompassing how well people perform or operate with respect to any one of many criteria, including emotional and social adjustment, physical health, and performance in school, work, or athletics.

In our view, it is *the concern with the development of intervention strategies* that is unique to applied social psychology and sets it apart as a branch of social psychology. The remainder of this chapter elaborates on the meaning and focus of applied social psychology, and in so doing defines its position in the context of its parent field, social psychology.

Applied Social Psychology as a Science

As a branch of social psychology, applied social psychology is by definition a science, accordingly it relies on the scientific method, and is guided by the core values of science. Moreover, applied social psychologists likewise are motivated by the aforementioned goals of science: description, prediction, determining causality, and explanation. However, they are distinguished from other social psychologists by also having a strong interest in what may be regarded as the fifth goal of science: control (Christensen, 2004; Goodwin, 2003). In science, **control** means being able to manipulate conditions that will cause changes in a phenomenon. Thus, once scientific research has identified the causes of a phenomenon, the potential for scientific control will have been established. Returning to the example of pets and adjustment, once researchers determine that having a pet frequently improves adjustment in older people, a "pets visit nursing home" program might be implemented as an intervention strategy. Another example is that once the basic principles of attribution theory were formulated, clinical psychologists began to use them to develop interventions designed to alleviate depression (see Chapter 5).

Although their ultimate goal is to effect positive change—to improve the functioning of people—applied social psychologists themselves may conduct research that helps them to understand the nature and causes of phenomena that concern them. This is seen in Sherif's (1966b) research on how competition can negatively affect intergroup relations. As another example, applied social psychologists who are interested in reducing bullying among schoolchildren (see Chapter 9) may investigate the correlates or causes of such antisocial behavior with a view toward using the results of their research to develop effective intervention strategies. However, it is often the case that they will draw on knowledge accumulated by other researchers who may or may not be interested in the direct application of research findings. That is, many social psychologists are very interested in conducting research that will enhance our understanding of social problems, but in their own work do not address how that understanding can be applied. Regardless of the origin of the research evidence, interventions that applied social psychologists are involved in developing,

such as bullying reduction strategies, will have solid scientific bases to them.

Thus, just as research studies designed to enhance the understanding of a phenomenon are guided by the researchers' understanding of the existing theory and research evidence, so too are intervention strategies designed by applied social psychologists based on existing theory and knowledge. Furthermore, applied social psychologists' responsibility does not stop with careful science-based design of intervention strategies, but rather extends for both scientific and ethical reasons to the evaluation of the consequences of the interventions. The scientific obligation stems from our responsibility to test the theoretical rationales and hypotheses underlying intervention strategies. The ethical obligation stems essentially from the need to ensure not only that the intended beneficiaries of interventions gain from them, but also that they (or others) do not experience unintended negative consequences. We return to the design and evaluation of intervention strategies in Chapter 4.

Another ethical implication of applied social psychology further elaborates on the idea of negative consequences. What if there are social psychological findings which can be implemented and which might produce some desirable immediate outcomes, but which might also have longer-term outcomes that could be undesirable? For example, research has shown that when subtle cues of being watched are present in the environment, people's behavior may improve. In one interesting study, researchers examined how much money people would contribute to an "honesty box" to pay for the milk they put into their tea or coffee when a banner placed in clear view of the beverages depicted either flowers or a set of eyes. The results revealed that people paid on average 2.76 times more when the banner depicted eyes (Bateson, Nettle, & Roberts, 2006). Based on findings like these, some people suggest that individuals in certain professions, like policing, should wear body cameras to encourage good behavior. For example, in 2015 the mayor of London initiated a plan to deploy 20,000 body cameras on police officers

(New Scientist, 2015). But, what happens when based on the idea of improving people's behavior, everyone starts wearing body cameras—your teachers, your parents, your friends? What psychological consequences occur among people who know that their every action is being recorded and potentially stored for future review? Might this have a detrimental effect on people's levels of spontaneity, security, or well-being? This example highlights the broad ethical implications of research and application in applied social psychology.

The Role of Personal Values

As we have noted, in conducting research, scientists are guided by a universally agreed on set of core values. We must also recognize the role of personal values in the conduct and application of science. Although one of the core values of science is objectivity, it is widely recognized that the individual's personal values influence many decisions that he or she makes as a scientist. For example, a social psychologist's concerns about racial injustice in society may lead him or her to choose as an area of research one that focuses on the causes of prejudice and discrimination and also to search for evidence that implicates certain political groups or institutions in the perpetuation of prejudice in society.

As social psychologists become involved in implementing control—developing strategies to change people's lives—personal values take on added importance (Mayo & La France, 1980; Sapsford & Dallos, 1998). In contributing to the development of an intervention, the applied social psychologist has determined that a problem exists. However, the determination of what constitutes a social problem cannot ever be purely objective. When someone breaks a leg while skiing, a physical problem unequivocally exists, and the services of a medical professional are clearly required. Unlike the medical professional, the social psychologist's choice of whether or not to intervene in a situation always involves personal values. Consider the example

of affirmative action programs attempting to overcome the historical disadvantages experienced by certain minorities by requiring employers to hire members of these groups. The basic value underlying affirmative action is equality. However, some people argue that affirmative action is unfair because giving preferential treatment to selected groups may exclude more qualified people from consideration. The value underlying this second line of reasoning is merit. Whether or not an employer decides to voluntarily implement an affirmative action program is based partly on his or her values. Similarly, the applied social psychologist who contributes to the development of affirmative action initiatives also is promoting a specific set of values.

So, interventions developed by applied social psychologists are value laden in that the psychologists' values play a role in determining what social and practical problems to address, including which people should be targeted for change and what should constitute change. As Mayo and La France (1980) noted, "Improving quality of life may entail social changes [that are] not always to everyone's liking" (p. 85). For example, not all organizational interventions, such as redesigning people's jobs may meet the needs or wishes of all employees. Thus, the goal of control through intervention is sometimes controversial.

Historical Context of Applied Social Psychology

The scientific foundation of applied social psychology can be traced at least as far back as the 1930s to the thinking and work of social psychologist Kurt Lewin (1936). Lewin conducted research on a variety of practical issues and social problems, such as how to get people to eat healthier diets and how interpersonal relations and productivity are affected by different supervisory styles. For instance, in the latter case, Lewin and his colleagues, Lippitt and White (1939), conducted an experiment in which they had groups of schoolboys work on hobbies under the direction of a male adult who varied his leadership in one of three ways: autocratic (controlling, gave orders, made the decisions), democratic (asked for input, allowed boys to make choices), or laissez-faire (interacted little with boys, mainly observed). The results for interpersonal relations and productivity generally favored the democratic style. For example, compared with boys under the laissez-faire leadership style, boys under autocratic and democratic leaders spent more time working; however, when the leader left the room, the amount of work done by the autocratic groups dropped sharply, whereas this did not happen in the democratic groups.

It is important to recognize that Lewin's goal was not only to further the scientific understanding of these topics, but also to contribute to their solutions. Very important to him was linking psychological theory to application, and the following words of Lewin (1944/1951) represent probably the most commonly cited quotation in social psychology:

> Many psychologists working in an applied field are keenly aware of the need for close cooperation between theoretical and applied psychology. This can be accomplished in psychology, as it has been accomplished in physics, if the theorist does not look toward applied problems with highbrow aversion or with a fear of social problems and if the applied psychologist realizes that there is nothing so practical as a good theory. (p. 169)

Lewin left a solid scientific legacy for applied social psychology in his emphasis on the integration of theory, research, and practice.

Among social psychologists like Lewin, the 1930s and 1940s witnessed a flurry of concern with applied issues and practical problems, much of which stemmed from the rise of Nazism and World War II (Jones, 1998). In fact, Brehm, Kassin, and Fein (1999) went so far as to suggest that Adolf Hitler had more influence on the field of social psychology than did any other person, including leading social psychologists:

> Hitler's rise to power and the ensuing turmoil caused people around the world to become desperate for answers to social psychological questions about what causes violence, prejudice and genocide, conformity and obedience, and a host of other social problems and behaviors. (pp. 12–13)

Reich (1981) observed that the foundation of applied social psychology was set by 1950 because the potential of using scientific methods to address social problems had been demonstrated successfully, for instance, by Lewin and colleagues' (1939) work on the effects of autocratic leadership, and Sherif's (1966b) work on conflict resolution. It seemed as though an applied psychology centered in the field of social psychology was poised to take off. Yet the "takeoff" did not occur for another 20 years or so. In fact, in social psychology, there occurred a backlash to applied developments. The negative reaction emanated largely from a widespread concern that "applied" was synonymous with low quality, and thus threatened the scientific integrity of the discipline (Reich, 1981; Streufert & Suedfeld, 1982). During the late 1940s and the 1950s, social psychology experienced a concerted movement away from applied concerns to a "pure science" emphasis on theory and laboratory experiments focused on basic social processes (e.g., processes of attitude formation and change, group structure, impression formation). In fact, the relationship between research on basic processes and applied research was described with terms such as *estrangement* and *schism*.

Just as the events around World War II sparked interest in applied social psychology, so too did the events of the 1960s. A host of powerful social and political occurrences (e.g., assassinations of John F. Kennedy and Martin Luther King, Jr., war in Vietnam, race riots, campus protests, civil rights movement, women's liberation movement) forced increased attention on a variety of pressing social issues endemic to American society (Ross, Lepper, & Ward, 2010). Many of the problems were the same as those that had come to a focus during the 1930s and

1940s (e.g., violence, prejudice), and some were new (e.g., social injustice). There were increased cries—both within psychology (including from students) and in the broader society—for psychology to become more socially relevant (Jones, 1998; Reich, 1981). At the same time, many social psychologists had begun to criticize the overreliance on laboratory experiments, pointing out that the field would benefit from methodological approaches that also included field research and a variety of nonexperimental research methods. Very instrumental in setting the stage for the emergence of a clearly defined field of applied social psychology was a 1969 series of articles in *American Psychologist* that focused on the interface between science and social issues. Some of the titles of the articles reflected the emerging applied emphasis of the field: "Psychology as a Means of Promoting Human Welfare" (Miller, 1969); "Social Psychology in an Era of Social Change" (Weick, 1969); "Socially Relevant Science: Reflections on Some Studies of Interpersonal Conflict" (Deutsch, 1969); "Experimental Psychology and Social Responsibility" (Walker, 1969); and "Reforms as Experiments" (Campbell, 1969).

In response to such developments, applied social psychology surfaced during the 1970s as a clearly identifiable field (Reich, 1981; Streufert & Suedfeld, 1982). There were several notable benchmarks, including in 1970–1971, the establishment of a journal devoted specifically to applied issues and research, the *Journal of Applied Social Psychology*, as well as the founding of the first doctoral program in applied social psychology at Loyola University of Chicago in 1974 (Bickman, 1981). These soon were followed by other developments that reinforced the identity of applied social psychology, including another journal (*Basic and Applied Social Psychology*) in 1980 and the first textbook in applied social psychology (Fisher's *Social Psychology: An Applied Approach*) in 1982. So, after some delay, the field of applied social psychology finally took off—"an actualization of long-term fundamental trends in the science" (Reich, 1981, p. 65). Now, here we are

some 40 or so years later, and in our view, a lot has happened that has reinforced the initial promise of Lewin's legacy of integrating theory, research, and practice. Applied social psychology is firmly entrenched as a branch of social psychology.

A Problem Focus

Social problems. At the very heart of applied social psychology is a regard for addressing social problems. Morawski (2000) observed that since its very early days around the turn of the 20th century, social psychology has had "an appreciation of its immediate connectedness with pulsing social conditions—crises, dysfunctions, or tensions" (p. 427). In 2002, social psychologist Philip Zimbardo, then president of the American Psychological Association, affirmed the central role of psychology in the solution of many of the most serious problems facing the United States. Zimbardo (2002a) discussed problems such as AIDS, substance abuse, prejudice and discrimination, minority student dropout rates, crime and juvenile delinquency, and "lethal hostility" (e.g., gang fighting, war). According to Zimbardo, the "solutions and prevention require changes in attitudes, values, behavior, and lifestyles" (p. 5). Although Zimbardo was extolling the potential contributions of psychology in general, the centrality of the field of social psychology is readily apparent: In order to ameliorate many of the most serious problems facing us today, changes must occur in the very phenomena that constitute the core subject matter of the field of social psychology—people's attitudes, values, and behaviors/lifestyles.

For instance, for health-related problems, a very big part of the solution often comes down to behavioral (i.e., lifestyle) changes. Here are some behaviors that are serious candidates for modification if one's goal is good health and longevity: live as a couch potato and avoid regular exercise, smoke cigarettes, abuse drugs, overeat, eat unhealthy foods, drive recklessly, ride with drunk drivers, fail to comply with doctors' orders, sunbathe, live in an abusive relationship, survive on little sleep, and do not use sunscreen, seatbelts, life jackets, or condoms.

Let us consider in more detail one of the problems mentioned by Zimbardo (2002a), a problem for which the news now is more optimistic than what we reported in the first edition of this book—AIDS. Without a doubt, the AIDS epidemic is one of the most serious crises facing humanity. Table 1.1 shows some of the terrifying statistics, which are taken from the 2010 UNAIDS report on the global AIDS epidemic (United Nations Global Report, 2010). The table compares 2001 with 2009 on three key criteria for the world as a whole and also for two regions of the world: North America and sub-Saharan Africa (the region that has been most severely devastated by the AIDS epidemic). Table 1.1 reveals that across the world in 2009 alone 1.8 million people—adults and children—died from AIDS and 33.3 million people were living with HIV. This represents a staggering amount of deaths and suffering, yet the figures in Table 1.1, as well as other data collected by UNAIDS, lead to the conclusion that the tide finally has begun to turn in the worldwide multibillion dollar (US$15.9 billion was allocated in 2009) United Nations response to the epidemic: "On the cusp of the fourth decade of the AIDS epidemic, the world has turned the corner—it has halted and begun to reverse the spread of HIV" (United Nations Global Report, 2010, p. 8). For one thing, AIDS-related deaths were no greater in 2009 than in 2001. More important is that the actual peak year was 2004 when 2.1 million died (not shown in Table 1.1), meaning the lower 2009 figure represents a substantial decrease. The increased availability and application of antiretroviral therapy and increased care and support for people who live with HIV are the main factors contributing to the decline in death rates. The same factors also underlie the increase from 2001 to 2009 in the number of people who are living with HIV.

The most telling comparison is the one that indicates a substantial decrease (16%) in the incidence of new infections between 2001 and 2009.

In fact, in 33 countries (22 from sub-Saharan Africa), the rate of new infections declined more than 25%. And while declines in deaths and increases in those living with HIV are primarily attributable to medical treatment and care, the declines in new infections are the result of *prevention efforts*: "HIV prevention works—new HIV infections are declining in many countries most affected by the epidemic" (United Nations Global Report, 2010, p. 8). Moreover, in line with Zimbardo's assertion about the centrality of behavior/lifestyle change, "behavior change is the most important factor accounting for these encouraging declines in new HIV infections" (United Nations Global Report, 2010, p. 64). The most successful prevention efforts have focused on promoting safer sexual behavior in young people, including, for example, increased condom use, delay of first sexual experience, and reduction in number of sexual partners (see Maticka-Tyndale & Brouillard-Coyle [2006] for a review of interventions with young people in developing countries).

Now, let us bring the issue of AIDS prevention closer to the personal lives of many readers—to applied research on the college campus. As the figures in Table 1.1 show, the HIV/AIDS epidemic continues to pillage many lives in our region of the world and represents a potential threat to any sexually active individual. Hodges, Klaaren, and Wheatley (2000) investigated ways in which to increase the likelihood of females engaging in "safe sex" discussions, a critical aspect of AIDS prevention behavior. They noted that college students know the risks of unprotected sex and know that they are supposed to discuss condom use with their partners, but too often fail to carry out such discussions. The researchers observed that students "generally find it easier to have unsafe sex than to discuss safe sex" (p. 332) and noted the paucity of safe-sex role models in the media, where most "couples collapse onto the nearest horizontal surface in the heat of passion without broaching issues of safe sex" (p. 332). In brief, the research of Hodges and her colleagues suggests that the willingness of females to have safe-sex

Table 1.1 Worldwide and Regional HIV and AIDS Statistics, 2001 and 2009

	AIDS-Related Deaths	*People Living With HIV*	*People Newly Infected With HIV*
World Total 2001	1,800,000	28,600,000	3,100,000
2009	1,800,000	33,300,000	2,600,000
Sub-Saharan Africa 2001	1,400,000	20,300,000	2,200,000
2009	1,300,000	22,500,000	1,800,000
North America 2001	30,000	1,200,000	66,000
2009	26,000	1,500,000	70,000

SOURCE: United Nations Global Report (2010). Based on data collected from 182 countries. Figures represent best estimates.

conversations with males would increase if they were provided with a positive experience in actually discussing safe-sex practices with a male, and if they were informed that such discussions become easier with repeated occurrences. The implications of the findings for the development of AIDS prevention campaigns are fairly straightforward.

A point that we wish to underscore with regard to the AIDS issue is that although, at the most basic level, HIV/AIDS is a biological and medical problem, it is also very much a social problem. The virus is spread by people relating to people; therefore, as the work of Hodges and colleagues (2000) suggests prevention efforts necessarily must have a very strong social psychological component. This, of course, applies to many other health-based problems (e.g., smoking is very much a socially precipitated and sustained behavior). There are other critical problems that at one level clearly are the domain of the nonsocial sciences (e.g., biology, geology, physics, and engineering) yet are strongly rooted in social behavior, and thus are amenable to social science-based solutions. As Bjork (2000) affirmed, the answers to many of the most complex problems rest with the behavioral sciences:

Overcoming the problems that beset our schools, for example, does not lie with making computers and associated devices better, faster, and more available. . . . Overcoming the violence in our society does not lie in more and better metal detectors or surveillance cameras. (p. 27)

A prime example is what many people regard as the most serious crisis facing humanity—the continuing devastation of the earth's environment by factors such as acid rain, global warming, ozone layer destruction, and the depletion of forests, fisheries, agricultural land, and water supplies. Many scientists believe that on our current course, our planet will be "irretrievably mutilated" (Union of Concerned Scientists, 1993, p. 1) and the earth "will be nearly uninhabitable for future generations" (Oskamp, 2000, p. 496). These environmental threats can be addressed in part by physical science initiatives (e.g., increasing agricultural productivity, decreasing toxic emissions). Nonetheless, a strong case can be made for the idea that escape from ecological disaster requires social science-based solutions because the causes of the most critical environmental problems are directly traceable to human choice and behavior, particularly to two categories of behavior: overpopulation and overconsumption (Oskamp, 2000). Toward this end, in his 2008 presidential address to the American Psychological Association, Alan Kazdin outlined a variety of ways in which psychology can contribute to fostering environmentally sustainable behaviors through its psychosocial research and knowledge base in the areas of education, message framing, feedback, decision making, the media, incentives and disincentives, the integration and understanding of multiple influences, and social marketing (Kazdin, 2009). As he so aptly stated,

> There are multiple disciplines already participating [in fostering a sustainable environment], and their impact could be enhanced by our participation because, of all things, changing behavior at multiple levels and understanding the domains in which behavior is embedded . . . are our specialty. (p. 353)

Practical problems. Beyond any doubt, applied social psychology has enormous potential in the prevention and reduction of social problems. However, a singular focus on social problems misrepresents the past and current accomplishments and potential contributions of the field. As you will discover as you read this book, the applicability of the field extends well beyond social problems. Applied social psychology addresses other undesirable or unsatisfactory circumstances that do not qualify as social problems in the conventional sense. For example, in Chapter 6, improvements to sports team cohesiveness and communication are considered as a means of dealing with the problem of poor team performance, and in Chapter 10, decision making is addressed in the context of improving both individual work performance and organizational functioning. Although poor team performance and ineffective decision making are not typically defined as social problems, they are certainly social in that they occur in the context of groups, organizations, and people interacting with other people. We refer to such unsatisfactory circumstances that people (e.g., groups, organizations) face as *practical problems* to distinguish them from conventional social problems and to acknowledge their centrality to the field of applied social psychology.

Without wanting to confuse you, we should also put a positive spin on the focus of applied social psychology in that application can be extended to the improvement of an already acceptable or even very favorable situation. For instance in sports, strategies may be implemented to improve the goal-focused communications of a team that already has an outstanding record of wins versus losses. In organizations, measures can be taken to develop flourishing work cultures even in the absence of any performance problems. This take on applied social psychology is consistent with recent developments in psychology that focus more on the positive aspects of life than the negative aspects. We touch on this in Chapter 17 when we discuss *positive social psychology* and how a more "balanced" view of things may be more appropriate than either an exclusively negative or positive view.

Personal uses. Also, with respect to issues in everyday life, individuals can look to social psychology for assistance. Murphy (1998) referred to *personal uses* of social psychology, meaning how each of us can use social psychological knowledge to improve his or her own life. For instance, to improve the size of a tip, a restaurant server might draw on the research on server behavior (e.g., Rind & Strohmetz, 2001; Seiter & Weger, 2010). This research shows that higher tips tend to be given when servers engage in positive verbal communication (e.g., introduce themselves by name, mention that tomorrow's weather is expected to be beautiful, compliment a customer's meal choice) and also engage in positive nonverbal behavior (e.g., smile, draw a smiley face on the check, and briefly touch the customer's shoulder). A customer interested in receiving attentive service might be sure to use the server's name given the evidence that when others use their names, people regard this as a rewarding stimulus—as complimentary—and tend to respond with positive acts in kind (Howard, Gengler, & Jain, 1997). These would be personal uses/applications of social psychology. One can wonder what social psychological theories and knowledge might have been used by someone at Ken and Kim's party to bring the heated argument to a peaceful end and allow the people to return to having a good time together.

Approaches to Applied Social Psychology

Research and practice in all areas of science are influenced by paradigms. Filstead (1979) defines paradigms as a "set of interrelated assumptions about the social world which provides a philosophical and conceptual framework for the organized study of that world" (p. 34). Paradigms reflect the different rationales that underlie the various research methods scientists use (Madill & Gough, 2008), and have a significant influence on the approaches adopted by researchers and practitioners.

As will be demonstrated in this book, work in applied social psychology tends to adopt one of three approaches, each with its own paradigm: 1) the social cognition approach, 2) the engaged research approach, or 3) the critical approach. As an example of the dominance of these three approaches we may note that the program in Applied Social Psychology at the University of Guelph in Canada has structured itself around these three approaches.

The **social cognition approach** is the traditional approach to research in which the researcher is regarded as a dispassionate chronicler of social psychological phenomena whose job is to report generalizable results in a manner that is as impartial, neutral, and objective as possible. The paradigm underlying this approach is positivism, which regards the researcher as separate from that being researched, and which emphasizes the reduction of bias when studying participants and topics (Ponterotto, 2005). Researchers working within this tradition will primarily concern themselves with traditional forms of validity and reliability in their research. That is, they will want to make sure that their work accurately sheds light on genuine social psychological phenomena that can be replicated by other researchers. An example of work within this tradition is a study by Terrier and Marfaing (2015), which demonstrated that hotel guests can be encouraged to reuse their towels by placing cards in their rooms indicating that 75% of guests choose to do so the same. Note that in this study, the researchers were trying to objectively report on an effect that was independent of their involvement.

By contrast, in the **engaged research approach,** the researcher is not regarded as a dispassionate observer neutrally reporting objective data, but is instead regarded as an active agent, enthusiastically engaging with community groups and other parties to address issues that can serve as a basis for social change. The paradigm underlying this approach is the advocacy/participatory worldview (Creswell, 2009), in which the goal is to assist in producing change among marginalized people. Although not ignoring traditional forms of validity and reliability, researchers within this tradition may concern themselves more with impact validity, "the extent to which research has the potential to play an effective role in some form of social and political change or is useful as a tool for advocacy or activism" (Massey & Barreras, 2013, p. 616). An example of work within this tradition is a study by Shura, Siders, and Dannefer (2011) which explored changes that needed to be implemented to improve the living conditions among residents in a long-term care facility. Instead of conducting focus groups and interviews and then offering recommendations based on their own analyses, the researchers worked in conjunction with experts, residents of the facility, and their families to formulate the research questions, goals, and to stimulate needed changes in the facilities. Note that in this study, the researchers were active participants working in close collaboration with those who had a stake in the potential changes.

The final approach, called the **critical approach,** emphasizes power and liberation from oppression. The paradigm underlying this approach is critical theory which focuses on how the distribution of power shapes the way people construct their experiences. Similar in some ways to the engaged research approach, a fundamental goal of the critical approach is emancipation from oppression and the production of a more egalitarian society (Ponterotto, 2005). Researchers within this tradition use their work as a form of social criticism (Ponterotto, 2005). An example of work in this approach is a paper by Prilleltensky (2008) which presents a critical discussion of how subtle forms of power affect wellness, oppression, and liberation.

Although all three approaches to applied social psychology are discussed in this book, consistent with the dominant approach in the field, the social cognition approach is emphasized. It is beyond the scope of this book to delve into the various worldviews adopted by each approach; however, you should be aware that although each approach is based on a different paradigm, the paradigms are not necessarily incompatible (Madill & Gough, 2008). More information about the research methods employed within these approaches can be found in Chapter 3.

Social Influences on Behavior: The Power of the Situation

A core assumption of the field of social psychology is that *the behavior of individuals is strongly influenced by the social situation or context.* Both social psychological theory and research focus on understanding how and why people are influenced by social factors.

Research demonstrations of the powerful influence of situations. Examples of the powerful role of situational determinants abound in social psychological research, including the results of some of the classic and best-known studies. We saw the power of social influence in the work of Sherif (1966b), where competition between groups of campers led to a marked deterioration in relations. In his research on independence and conformity, Asch (1955) demonstrated that on a very simple judgment task (e.g., distinguishing between the lengths of lines) in which the correct judgment was perfectly obvious, many participants chose to go along with the erroneous judgments of others rather than to publicly disagree with them. Depending on the particular study, 50% to 80% of participants

conformed at least once over a series of trials. Dozens of bystander intervention studies—laboratory and field—that contrast the behavior of individual bystanders when alone and when with other bystanders have demonstrated that an individual's tendency to intervene in an emergency is sharply inhibited by the presence of others (Latané & Nida, 1981).

Stanley Milgram's obedience research is perhaps the most widely recognized illustration of the power of the situation. In Milgram's (1974) research, each participant was told by the experimenter that the study was about the role of punishment in learning. The participant had to administer apparently painful shocks to a learner (an experimental accomplice who only pretended to receive the shocks) every time the learner made a mistake on a learning task. The learner (accomplice) made a total of 30 mistakes in 40 opportunities. In a series of studies, Milgram examined the effects of different situational variables on people's compliance with the experimenter's insistent directives to increase the shock intensity with each successive error made by the learner up to the maximum shock level of 450 volts. The 30 shock levels ranged from a low of 15 volts, labeled "slight shock," to a high of 450 volts, which was beyond the label of "danger, severe shock."

Table 1.2 shows that for seven of the situations manipulated by Milgram, the percentages of the participants who obeyed completely by shocking the learner all the way up to the 450-volt maximum. The numbers showing maximum obedience ranged, depending on the situation, from nobody (0%) to a strong majority (65%). This clearly is a striking demonstration of what may be called situational control. Although all of the participants in the situations in the table were adult male volunteers from the community (in Connecticut), a replication of the first situation with females showed exactly the same level of maximum obedience (65%). Further attesting to the power of the situation was a control condition in which participants were not directed by the experimenter to increase the severity of shocks and were free to choose any shock level.

In this situation—with pressure from the experimenter removed—only one participant of 40 (2.5%) chose the maximum shock intensity, and the mean (average) level selected by participants across all 30 learner errors was level 4 of 30 levels (in the slight shock range).

You should be careful not to dismiss Milgram's findings as reflecting a bygone era given that research during the intervening years has indicated similar levels of obedience (Blass, 2004; Burger, 2009). Social psychologists have drawn parallels between the obedient behavior of Milgram's participants and actual examples of "destructive obedience," including military personnel following "orders" in Nazi Germany, in Bosnia, and at Abu Ghraib prison in Iraq. Everyday life abounds with examples of the strong influence of the power of the situation on people's behavior; for example, when we turn on our best behavior when we enter a place of worship or begin a job interview and then may turn the good behavior sharply off when we are horsing around with friends or imbibing at a local bar.

Nonetheless, we must be cautious in interpreting the results of contemporary social psychological studies that attempt to shed light on research conducted decades ago because social conditions change, and the social forces acting on modern participants may be different from those that were acting on participants in prior eras, thus producing results that are not entirely commensurate (Haney & Zimbardo, 2009). For example, people were generally much more deferent to authority in past years. Therefore, the results of research conducted today that examines how people respond to situations demanding obedience are not necessarily equivalent to the results of research conducted in earlier eras. We always need to think critically about what studies reveal to us. For example, some recent research has suggested that in following the orders they were given, participants in Milgram's studies weren't demonstrating obedience so much as identification with the experimenter's goals (Haslam, Reicher, & Birney, 2014). However, this interpretation still underscores the power of social processes on individual behavior. Studies, such as those conducted by Milgram, Sherif, and others demonstrate that when we alter the structure of social situations, we can change people's behavior in striking ways (Reicher, Haslam, & Miller, 2014).

Recognizing the role of individual differences. You may be thinking something like, "Sure, people are influenced by the situations they are in, but not everybody is influenced the same way." If you are, you have a good point. After all, the amount of conformity in Asch's (1955) experiments varied greatly, with some participants showing no conformity at all. Likewise, in each of the other classic studies described earlier, people differed in how they reacted to the situation. For instance, we can see in Table 1.2 that in every condition in the obedience research, there were some participants who resisted the authority of the experimenter. What is being suggested here is the relevance of individual differences. **Individual differences** refer to characteristics or qualities of an individual (as opposed to characteristics of a situation) and include things such as personality variables, attitudes, values, and abilities, as well as demographic variables, such as gender, ethnicity, religion, and age.

Although social psychology is primarily concerned with social determinants and explanations of behavior, the field recognizes the important role of individual difference variables in understanding the behavior of people. The idea that behavior is a function of both the person and the situation was advanced by Lewin (1936): "Every psychological event depends upon the state of the person and at the same time on the environment, although their relative importance is different in different cases" (p. 12). That is, at any given moment, what we are doing usually is a reflection of our personalities and the surrounding social and physical contexts. This position also was expressed aptly by Myers and colleagues (2009): "The great truth about the power of social influence is but half the truth if separated from its complementary truth: the power of the person" (p. 292). Social influences

Table 1.2 The Milgram Experiments: How Variations in the Experimental Situation Influenced Levels of Obedience to Authority

	Experimental Situation	*Percentage of Participants Who Showed Maximum Obedience*
1.	Learner is in adjacent room; participant cannot see learner, but can hear his protests about the shocks and complaints about having a heart condition	65.0
2.	Similar to No. 1 except that there is no mention of the learner having a heart condition	62.5
3.	Participant is a few feet away from learner and can readily see and hear his protests; no mention of a heart condition	40.0
4.	Participant is beside learner and must hold (force) learner's hand onto shock plate; no mention of a heart condition	30.0
5.	Same as No. 1 except that, after giving initial instructions, experimenter departs and directs participant by telephone	20.5
6.	Same as No. 1 except that participant and two other participants (actually accomplices) jointly teach learner; the others begin to defy the experimenter	10.0
7.	Same as No. 1, but involves two experimenters; one begins to direct participant to stop shocking the learner, whereas the other one encourages him to continue	0.0

SOURCE: Based on Milgram (1974).

on behavior and personal influences on behavior should not be viewed as incompatible. Instead, social psychologists commonly view them as demonstrating an *interactive relationship* (Snyder & Ickes, 1985). This interactionism between the person and the situation has become well established in social psychology (Carnahan & McFarland, 2007). One way in which personal and social influences interact with each other is that social situations may have different effects on different people. For example, people with different personalities may react to a situation differently because they do not construe it in the same way (Ross & Nisbett, 1991; Shoda, 2004), as would have been the case if some of Milgram's (1974) participants had viewed the experimenter as a powerful authority figure, whereas others had not.

Generally, personal characteristics are thought to exert a greater effect on behavior in "weak" situations—those that place few constraints on people's behavior—compared to "strong" situations—those that place powerful constraints on behavior (Kenrick & Funder, 1988). For example, your personality is more likely to influence your behavior when you're playing video games at home with your friends (weak situation) than it is when you're participating in a military procession (strong situation). However, as we note above, sometimes even in strong situations personal characteristics exert a powerful influence on behavior. For our purposes, the key point to remember is that the power of situations in influencing behavior can be as strong as the power of dispositions (Funder & Ozer, 1983).

Underestimating the role of situational influences.
When we observe people's behavior, we explain it by making internal attributions, external attributions, or a combination of the two. **Internal** (dispositional) attributions explain behavior by focusing on factors within the person who has been observed. **External** (situational) attributions explain behavior by focusing on factors in the observed person's social environment. Despite the fact that behavior results from both personal and social influences, we have a tendency to underestimate the role of situational factors in influencing other people's behavior. For example, imagine showing up for the first day of class and meeting your new psychology professor. Imagine further that your new professor is dressed in a dirty suit, speaks in a monotone voice, does not seem to care about the lecture material, and is short with you when you ask a simple question about the format of the exams. In this situation, you are likely to infer that the professor is a bitter curmudgeon, and because of that you might even consider dropping the course. Notice that in this situation, you would have made an internal attribution for the professor's behavior; you explained his behavior by inferring something about his personality. However, it is entirely possible that the professor is in fact a pleasant, caring, and helpful individual who had a flat tire and ruined his favorite suit on the way to class. Had you known this, you would have been more likely to make an external attribution of the professor's behavior. You would have chalked up his poor mood to unfortunate circumstances.

This tendency for us to underestimate the influence of situational factors and focus on individual factors in explaining other people's behavior is called the **fundamental attribution error** (Ross, 1977). Because people themselves are more salient to us than their situations when we are observing them, we tend to focus on people rather than situations when explaining their conduct. You can see from the data provided earlier the great extent to which situational factors influenced the behavior of participants in Milgram's (1974) studies. However, if you had been an observer in one of Milgram's sessions, you probably would have made an internal

attribution for the participants' behavior (e.g., that the participants who administer high-voltage shocks are aggressive individuals or perhaps even sadists). If so, such a conclusion would have been inaccurate. As we mentioned earlier, in one version of his experiment, Milgram gave participants the opportunity to administer whatever voltage shock they desired. Under this experimental condition, the vast majority of participants chose to administer very low-voltage shocks. Clearly, situational factors (e.g., the demanding experimenter) played the primary role in prompting participants to administer high-voltage painful shocks. However, if you did not know about the results of Milgram's "free choice" condition, and thus had not been made aware of the power of the situation, you would likely explain participants' cruel behavior in terms of the participants' character rather than the situation.

Haney and Zimbardo (2009) suggest that another reason we tend to focus on people instead of situations when explaining behavior includes the fact that blaming other people for undesirable behavior absolves from blame the people who may have engineered the situational forces that contributed to the behavior. Of course, they go on to note, doing this diminishes any motive for broad-based social change or reform. For example, if a prison warden blames prisoners for bad behavior there is no need for the warden to examine or revise the structures and policies in the prison.

In their treatise on the history of social psychology, Ross and colleagues (2010) identify the general tendency for people to fail to recognize the extent to which situational forces control social behavior as one of four foundational contributions ("insights" or "pillars") "that constitute cumulative lessons and continue to guide contemporary analysis, research, and application" (p. 3). Applied social psychology, by focusing on effecting change in people's social environments as a means of bringing about changes in their behavior, helps us to counteract a person's propensity to fall victim to the fundamental attribution error, and instead helps him or her to be attentive to the importance of social influences on behavior. More will be said about the fundamental attribution error in subsequent chapters.

Intervention strategies as social influence. Consider the intervention strategies that we have mentioned so far: Sherif (1966b) using superordinate goals to reduce intergroup conflict, and Hodges and colleagues (2000) providing positive safe-sex discussion experiences to increase college females' tendencies to engage in such discussions prior to having sex. Notice how each strategy involves introducing the target individuals to a social situation devised for the purpose of effecting changes in their attitudes and/or behavior. Thus, each strategy entails a social influence attempt, that is, an attempt on the part of some social agent (e.g., person, group, organization) to induce changes in behavior that will contribute to more effective functioning (e.g., more harmonious intergroup interaction, safer sex). The focus of this book is on how social psychological understanding of social influence processes can be applied to improving the lives of people. In essence, we are saying that the field of applied social psychology rests on the power of the situation. That is, fundamental to the field is the assumption that the systematic exercise of situational control (i.e., intervention strategies) can be employed to improve the functioning of people.

Levels of Analysis

We have underscored that the social psychological perspective emphasizes the importance of social influences on people—that how we think, feel, and behave is greatly affected by aspects of the social situation or context. To explore further what may be viewed as constituting one's social situation, let us consider your current activity, which is reading this chapter. As you review this section of the chapter, what is the social situation that is possibly causing you to read the material with more or less motivation and diligence? Is it a social stimulus in the immediate situation? For

instance, are you being encouraged by a motivated friend with whom you are reading and studying the material—at this very moment—or perhaps by other students earnestly studying around you in the library? Also, it might be helpful to look beyond your immediate situation to the broader social context to understand your current level of motivation on this task. Are you reading intently because you are concerned that the instructor may call on you during the upcoming class? Or, are the perceived expectations of significant others, in addition to your instructor, having an influence on you? For instance, are you applying yourself because your family or close friends expect this of you, or (conversely) is your heart not really in this task because of the pull of friends who really want you to be out having fun with them? Beyond the influence of significant others, are you working hard (or not so hard) because the academic standards at your school are quite high (or not so high) and you feel a lot of pressure (or little pressure) to do your best?

From this personal example, you can see that the social situation can be conceived broadly, ranging from the direct influence of specific others to the influence of more general factors. The social situational determinants of an individual's behavior may be viewed as falling into the following categories: interpersonal, group, organizational, community, and societal/cultural. Based on categorizations similar to this one, in social psychology we refer to *levels of analysis* (or explanation) that correspond with the various categories of determinants. For example, we seek to explain a person's behavior (e.g., studying) by investigating the effect of individuals on him or her (explanation at the interpersonal level), or by investigating the effect of groups on him or her (explanation at the group level). Of course, what is missing is the possible role of individual difference variables. In the example of studying, a dispositional explanation would suggest that your current level of diligence stems from your personality; for instance, you have (or do not have) a high drive to achieve. It is customary to combine personal determinants with situational determinants to come up with a more complete list of explanatory variables. It is also important to understand that the term *level* does not imply "superior" in any way; all levels may be important in establishing a thorough understanding of a phenomenon, although the relative importance of explanatory levels may vary from phenomenon to phenomenon.

A study by Riksheim and Chermak (1993) allows us to consider further the meaning of the social situation as a determinant of behavior and clearly illustrates the notion of levels of analysis. Riksheim and Chermak were interested in examining factors that lead police officers to engage in various behaviors, such as providing service (e.g., assisting motorists), making arrests, and employing force on suspects. They distinguished among four categories of determinants of police behavior: (a) immediate situational variables like characteristics of the incident (e.g., seriousness of crime) and of the parties involved (e.g., demeanor of the suspect); (b) organizational variables like differences among police units in policing style and enforcement strategy; (c) community variables like the crime rate and ethnic makeup of the neighborhood; and (d) officer individual difference variables like gender and racial attitudes. Riksheim and Chermak's classification of variables divides the determinants of police behavior into three situational categories and one individual difference category.

Table 1.3 summarizes what Riksheim and Chermak (1993) found in their review of 40 studies that examined factors that predict police officer use of force (use of fists, firearms, stun guns, pepper spray, etc.). The researchers pointed out the importance of understanding the determinants of officer use of force because of its potential alienating and inflammatory effects on communities. For each category of variable (level of explanation), Table 1.3 illustrates those variables reported by Riksheim and Chermak that showed a relationship to use of force. For instance, under the immediate situation, use of force was related to the number of officers present (occurring more often with more officers

present) and the suspect's conduct (occurring more often with antagonistic suspects).

Further inspection of Table 1.3 clearly shows that to gain a more complete understanding, it is also necessary to investigate police use of force from the perspective of the three other levels of analysis—individual difference, organizational, and community—because variables at these levels likewise are shown to be related to use of force. The distinction among levels of analysis is an especially important one for applied social psychology because it begs the question of toward what level(s) and toward what variable(s) intervention

Table 1.3 Variables Found to Predict Police Use of Force

Individual differences (officer characteristics)
Gender (male)
Racial attitudes (prejudicial)
Skilled in handling overt conflict (most skilled)
Immediate interpersonal situation
Number of officers (more officers)
Suspect's conduct (e.g., antagonistic, consumed alcohol)
Bystanders (not present)
Weapon (used by citizen)
Organizational
Department policy (less restrictive about use of force)
Assignment/nonassignment to specialized unit (assignment)
Supervisory review process (not in place)
Community
Ethnic composition of community (more non-White)
Racial heterogeneity (more heterogeneous)
Transience of population (less transient)

SOURCE: *Journal of Criminal Justice* Vol 21(4). Riksheim et al. "Causes of police behavior revisited" pp. 371–372. Printed with permission from Elsevier.

strategies should be directed. Given the results in Table 1.3, what do you think? One possibility is to intervene at the organizational level by ensuring the consistent application of supervisory review of questionable incidents involving force, thereby ensuring greater accountability of officers for their actions. We imagine that you can see some other intervention possibilities, perhaps especially at the organizational and individual difference levels.

The Need for a Broad Approach

As we noted earlier, applied social psychology can be relevant to addressing social and practical problems in virtually *all areas of life.* Although the field certainly does not have all of the answers, it already has provided useful information, important insights, and fresh approaches with respect to many different areas of life (Sadava, 1997). It is clear to us that applied social psychology will be more effective in achieving its potential to the extent that the field embraces the value of taking a broad approach to the solution of problems. Here we underscore three interrelated aspects of such a broad approach: the use of multiple research methods, the emphasis on collaboration in research and application with representatives of other disciplines, and the recognition of the potential contributions of other relevant perspectives.

In order to optimally understand and address social and practical problems in diverse groups, organizations, and communities, applied social psychologists must have the expertise and readiness to draw on research strategies and analytical procedures that are particularly suitable for dealing with the relevant problem(s), including those that are more common to allied disciplines. For example, such disciplines include cognitive science, communication studies, sociology, education, political science, criminal justice, program evaluation, marketing, organizational studies, and public health (Crano & Brewer, 2002). Chapter 3 reviews basic research strategies employed by applied social psychologists; additionally, there are examples of a variety of research methods found throughout the book.

With respect to addressing social and practical problems, applied social psychologists limit their effectiveness if they fail to draw on the knowledge and expertise of representatives of other fields. Not only must we be informed about the research contributions and knowledge bases of other disciplines, we must increasingly pursue cross-disciplinary collaboration in research and practice. For instance, the design, implementation, and evaluation of an anti-bullying program in a school system would clearly benefit from the input of several professionals, including teachers, school administrators, school psychologists, police officers, and of course program designers and evaluators. Likewise, recall the earlier observation that many medical conditions (e.g., HIV/AIDS) are also biological, medical, and social problems. By implication, successful intervention efforts require the involvement and collaboration of individuals with expertise in those areas and other pertinent areas, not the least of which is the cultural context (see below) in which an intervention is enacted.

Although social psychologists devote primary attention to the role of the social context/situational factors in understanding and explaining the complexities of human social behavior, we appreciate that a richer and more thorough understanding of many aspects of social behavior must also take into account other relevant perspectives. We noted earlier that individual difference variables (e.g., personality) have a substantial influence on how people think, feel, and behave in a social context. The evolutionary perspective, which focuses on inherited tendencies to respond to the social environment in ways that enabled our ancestors to survive and reproduce, has been used to explain a diverse array of social behaviors and attitudes, including genetic influences on interpersonal attraction, job satisfaction, and aggression.

Moreover, to understand behavior in a social context, we must consider the influence of culture—the attitudes, values, beliefs, and behaviors shared by a group of people. Culture plays a subtle, but powerful role in our lives. As Triandis (1994) pointed out, people are often not aware of their own cultures until they come into contact with other cultures. Arnett (2008) observed that the dominant focus of American psychology is the American population, despite the fact that the American population represents only about 5% of the population of the world. Arnett affirms that American psychology should become less American given the evidence that the conditions (e.g., income, education, physical health) under which the vast majority of the people in the world live differ dramatically from those of Americans (and people in other Western countries). Arnett argues "that American psychology can no longer afford to neglect 95% of the world given that many of the problems psychology can potentially address are worse among the neglected 95% than in American society" (p. 602). In concurrence with Arnett's perceptions about the focus of American psychology, issues in this book are discussed primarily from a North American vantage point. However, also consistent with Arnett's main message—that more attention must be devoted to the rest of the world, we recognize that this perspective may not always be relevant to the consideration of problems in other cultures. Therefore, in order to help all of us maintain awareness of the importance of considering the role of culture in understanding and addressing social and practical problems, most of the chapters include a section called "Culture Capsule" designed to draw our attention to cultural variations in social psychological phenomena.

Various Roles of Applied Social Psychologists

Whereas the goal of social psychology in general is to develop and empirically test theories of social behavior, applied social psychology is concerned more specifically with understanding and finding solutions to social and practical problems by drawing on the knowledge base of existing theory and research, conducting research, and developing intervention strategies.

Within these broad objectives, applied social psychologists may assume many different roles. For example, Sadava (1997) listed several roles, including planner, organizer, evaluator, consultant, advocate, and activist. Fisher (1982) grouped many of these roles into two major categories: applied scientist and professional practitioner. Drawing on the thinking of both Sadava and Fisher, we see at least six major roles for applied social psychologists: researcher, program designer, evaluation researcher, consultant, action researcher, and advocate.

Researcher. The applied social psychologist conducts research on social and practical problems. That is, the applied social psychologist seeks to understand social and practical problems through the application of both the core values and research strategies embodied in the scientific method. Thus, in the role of researcher, the applied social psychologist functions in a manner similar to other social scientists.

Program designer. Using existing theory and research evidence, the applied social psychologist may be involved in developing or improving interventions designed to resolve or ameliorate social and practical problems. As noted by Fisher (1982), this role combines theory, research, and practice; therefore, in the tradition of Lewin and colleagues (1939), it embraces a true scientist/practitioner model. The role of program designer is a central focus of Chapter 4.

Evaluation researcher. As an evaluation researcher (or a program evaluator), the applied social psychologist applies social science research methods to evaluate the process and outcomes of interventions (e.g., social programs and policies). The role of program evaluation also is addressed more fully in Chapter 4.

Consultant. During their careers, many (if not most) applied social psychologists will serve in some capacity as consultants to various groups, organizations, or communities. In the role of consultant, the applied social psychologist provides his or her expertise in social process and social theory to help clients resolve particular difficulties they are experiencing.

Action researcher. In the capacity of action researcher, the applied social psychologist works closely with an organization or a community group to resolve a particular issue or problem. This is accomplished through a collaborative cycle of data collection and interpretation leading to the development of appropriate action strategies. Action research is discussed in Chapter 12 in particular.

Advocate. In the role of advocate, the applied social psychologist functions within the political arena. As stated by Fisher (1982), "The advocate uses his or her expertise to press for social change, usually in collaboration with a specific group, lobby, or institution that is working to change some aspect of the sociopolitical system" (p. 19).

OVERVIEW OF BOOK

This textbook serves as an introduction to the field of applied social psychology, which focuses on understanding social and practical problems and on developing intervention strategies directed at the amelioration of such problems. Part 1 sets the context of the field. In order to examine the nature of social psychological theory, it includes the present chapter and three other chapters that review basic research methods used by social psychologists, and explore the design of interventions and the evaluation of their effectiveness. These chapters help you to more fully appreciate the ten chapters in Part 2 that focus on content areas of the field (e.g., team sports, health, organizations, and criminal justice). Each content chapter introduces you to research that seeks to develop understanding of relevant social and practical problems as well as the application of social psychological knowledge to the design of intervention strategies. Each content chapter covers

a selection of important topics; however, the chapters are not meant to be comprehensive in their coverage of these topic areas. Part 3 includes three chapters that focus on how readers can apply social psychological knowledge to improve their own lives in the following areas: personal relationships, classroom interaction, and well-being.

SUMMARY

Applied social psychology is the branch of the science of social psychology that focuses on (a) developing social psychological understanding of social and practical problems, and (b) drawing on that understanding to design intervention strategies for the amelioration of social and practical problems. As scientists, applied social psychologists are guided by a core set of values (e.g., accuracy, objectivity, skepticism, open-mindedness, ethics), and by the scientific method that includes specific research methods used to provide empirical tests of hypotheses. Scientific understanding of phenomena, including social and practical problems, entails the accomplishment of five goals: description, prediction, determining causality, explanation, and control.

The embracement of the goal of control (manipulation of conditions to cause changes in phenomena) particularly distinguishes applied social psychology as a separate branch of social psychology. That is, at the heart of applied social psychology is a concern with developing social influence strategies (i.e., interventions) to improve people's functioning with respect to social and practical problems. Although the field is particularly concerned with addressing social and practical problems on a general level (e.g., education, environment), individuals also can use social psychology to improve their own lives.

The core assumption of the field of social psychology and applied social psychology is that people's attitudes and behavior are greatly influenced by situational factors. In fact, intervention strategies may be viewed as involving the use of knowledge about social situational influence to effect improvements in people's functioning. However, applied social psychology also recognizes that to understand and address problems, individual difference variables (e.g., personality) must be considered. Moreover, the social situation can be viewed as reflecting different levels of analysis (e.g., interpersonal, group, community); accordingly, interventions may be directed at different levels.

Applied social psychology requires a broad approach to social and practical problems, including the use of multiple research methods, an interdisciplinary orientation, and recognition of the value of other perspectives (e.g., evolutionary, personality, cultural). In his or her work, the applied social psychologist can assume several roles, some of which include researcher, program designer, evaluation researcher, consultant, action researcher, and advocate.

2

SOCIAL PSYCHOLOGICAL THEORY

MICHELLE A. KRIEGER

GREG A. CHUNG-YAN

SHELAGH M. J. TOWSON

CHAPTER OUTLINE

How can we understand the role of theory in applied social psychology? A good place to start is with the realization that we all are applied social psychologists. Although most of us would probably not think of ourselves in this way, all of us are constantly engaged in a process of making observations, constructing theories based on these observations, testing hypotheses derived from our theories, and applying these theories in our lives.

Let us imagine that you are 16 years old again and that you will be taking your driver's test in just a few months. Now, as you see it, the purpose of getting your driver's license is so that you can drive a car, and your reasons for wanting to drive a car are to have increased access to places you cannot get to with public transportation, more opportunities to spend quality time with friends, and greater freedom from parental supervision. Once you have your license, there will be only one obstacle standing in the way of your goal, and that is the fact that you do not have a car, and are unlikely to be able to afford one in the foreseeable future.

You realize that your dream of independence will be fulfilled only if you start now on what you anticipate will be a long and hard campaign to get permission to use the family car on a regular basis. Your first step in this campaign is careful observation of the tactics your friends use with their own families, tactics that include "borrowing" their family cars without actually asking; prolonged begging, whining, and pleading; and, when all else fails, completing homework and assigned responsibilities around the house without having to be nagged to do so, and even volunteering to do some helpful things.

On the basis of your observations, you conclude that some of these tactics work better than others. But, what distinguishes the tactics that work well from those that do not? The "borrowing" first and asking later approach seems to result in severe negative consequences, and begging, whining, and pleading seem to succeed only occasionally. However, more often than not, acting responsibly and being helpful seem to increase your friends' chances of using their family cars. So, putting all your observations together, you construct an "adolescent car acquisition theory" that goes something like this:

1. Parents believe that their primary role as parents is to raise their children to be responsible adults.
2. Because of this belief, parents are always looking for indications that their efforts have been successful, and when they see evidence of positive adult behavior, they reward it.

3. Therefore, parents are more likely to accede to a request allowing the enactment of adult behavior (e.g., borrowing the family car) if the request is preceded by the demonstration of different, but positive adult behavior.

While you are waiting to apply for your license, you design a research study to test your theory. You develop specific hypotheses like the following: Volunteering to babysit younger siblings instead of going out with friends on Friday night results in a higher probability of car acquisition on Saturday night. You subsequently recruit your friends to test these hypotheses with their families. Your hypotheses are supported; when your friends demonstrate responsible adult behavior, their rates of car acquisition increase markedly. Therefore, after you get your driver's license, you apply your theory by becoming a model (at least for a teenager) of adult maturity and responsibility. You take out the garbage without being asked, you leave the bathroom sparkling clean after you use it, and so on. Sure enough, when you pop the question, "May I borrow the car Saturday night?," the answer is usually yes.

But wait, there is more. Based on your observations of its successful application, you revisit your theory and realize that it may apply to more behaviors than just car acquisition. You generate and test additional hypotheses like the following: "If I finish my homework, my chances of having a later curfew will increase," and "If I mow the lawn, my band might be able to practice in the basement." Once more, your hypotheses are supported, and your confidence in your theory grows. You apply the knowledge you have gained, consistently demonstrate adult behavior, and become the envy of your friends for all of the privileges you get. Your parents are happy because they believe that your new maturity is the result of their excellent child-rearing techniques, and you are happy not only because of all the privileges you have gained, but also because you have constructed, tested, and applied your first social psychological theory. (In fact, you might be beginning to contemplate social psychology as a career.)

Would you have gotten to use the family car if there had been no adolescent car acquisition theory? Probably, but without the theory, your opportunities to drive would have occurred less often and would have been chance occurrences rather than planned ones. Your theory helped you to accomplish the five goals of science described in Chapter 1 (description, prediction, determining causality, explanation, and control) by providing you with a better *understanding* of what was going on in your parents' heads, thereby enabling you to exert more *control* over the car acquisition process.

This chapter discusses theory in the context of applied social psychology. First, it examines the role of theory in the scientific process. Then, it describes three functions fulfilled by social psychological theories and some of the characteristics of these theories. Finally, the chapter explores two influential theories—cognitive dissonance theory and the theory of planned behavior—in terms of their functions, characteristics, and contributions to applied social psychology. The intent

is not to provide an overview of major social psychological theories—which is done ably in other chapters in this book—but instead to give you a good understanding of theory and its essential role in applied social psychology.

THE SCIENTIFIC PROCESS

The five goals of science are description, prediction, determining causality, explanation, and control. Fulfilling these goals involves carrying out the steps in the scientific process outlined in Figure 2.1—from the observation of phenomena, to the development of theory, to the deduction of specific hypotheses derived from the theory, to testing these hypotheses through research and interventions. You might be interested in knowing that this was the path you followed, albeit unwittingly, in getting the keys to the family car and other privileges.

The first step in the process is *observation*. For social psychologists, the observation stage

Figure 2.1 The Scientific Process

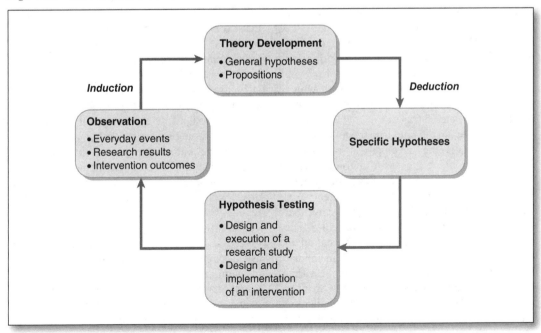

might consist of a single vivid incident from everyday life, a systematic program of descriptive data gathering (such as you used to construct your adolescent car acquisition theory), a review of existing research evidence, or the analysis of intervention outcomes. The bystander behavior theory of social psychologists John Darley and Bibb Latané, for instance, was triggered by their perception of the events surrounding a murder in New York City that took place in front of many witnesses who did not intervene to help the victim (Darley & Latané, 1968).

The next step in the scientific process is *theory development,* with **theory** defined as "a set of interrelated hypotheses or propositions concerning a phenomenon or set of phenomena" (Shaw & Costanzo, 1982, p. 4). In your case, the phenomenon in question was the adolescent pursuit of the family car. You thought about (i.e., analyzed) all of your observations of your friends' behaviors in attempting to get their family cars and their parents' reactions, looked for a common thread, and found it: Parents reward evidence that they have succeeded in their mission to raise responsible adults. On the basis of your observation of many examples of a variety of behaviors and resulting consequences, you constructed a theory that explained all of the examples. This process of moving from the specific to the general is known as **induction** (i.e., inferring general principles from observing specific instances), and it is the way in which the vast majority of social psychological theories are constructed.

The third step in the scientific process outlined in Figure 2.1 is the development of *specific hypotheses* through a process of **deduction** (i.e., deriving specific hypotheses from the general hypotheses and propositions of the theory). A **hypothesis** may be defined as a prediction that specifies the relationship between variables. The relationship that is specified may be causal in nature (i.e., one variable causes change in another variable), or may simply suggest that the variables are correlated, but not in a causal manner (see Chapter 3). Your adolescent car acquisition theory includes the general causal hypothesis that the voluntary enactment of particular adult behaviors by an adolescent will result in parents' granting permission for other adult behaviors (e.g., driving the family car). Based on this general hypothesis, you developed a series of specific hypotheses that attempted to specify the relationship between particular adult behaviors enacted by your friends (e.g., babysitting, washing dishes) and the particular adult behavior for which they would request permission (i.e., borrowing their family cars).

The fourth step in the scientific process is *hypothesis testing.* To test hypotheses, social psychologists use a variety of strategies, including conducting research and carrying out interventions. As indicated in Chapter 1, many social psychologists focus primarily on the goals of science that center on understanding social psychological phenomena. For these psychologists, the goal of control through the application of social psychological knowledge is not a central concern, and hypothesis testing is carried out through the design and execution of systematic research studies. The results (observations) of such research may provide support for the hypothesis, and thus for the theory from which it was derived. Observations that do not support the hypothesis may lead to modifications of the original theory, or to the development of a new one.

However, many social psychologists, particularly those who define themselves as applied social psychologists, are interested in pursuing the fifth goal of science—control. Thus, these social psychologists are interested in the *application* of the knowledge gained through theory development in the design and implementation of interventions. As a teenager who is eager to drive, your careful analysis of the adolescent request–parental resistance phenomenon enabled you to influence your parents so that they would give you the car keys nearly every time you asked. Applied social psychologists use theories in a similar way, that is, as the source of intervention strategies designed to improve the functioning of individuals, groups, or organizations. And as Figure 2.1 shows, the process does not end there.

Intervention strategies derived from theory and research results lead to further observations, to the modification of existing theories or the construction of new ones, to the testing of hypotheses derived from these theories, and to new possibilities for application (through a continuing process of induction and deduction).

THEORY IN SOCIAL PSYCHOLOGY

Functions of Social Psychological Theories

We noted in Chapter 1 that Kurt Lewin, one of the founders of social psychology, believed that there was "nothing so practical as a good theory" (Lewin, 1944/1951, p. 169). Why is a good theory practical? Or, to put it another way, what functions does a theory perform? One way in which to think about the functions of a theory is to see it as the one component of the scientific process outlined in Figure 2.1 that ties the other three components together by providing organization, direction, and guidance for the development of interventions.

The first function of a theory, which is related to observation, is to provide *organization.* Organization refers to the systematic arrangement of observations that demonstrate their relationship to one another. Just as an architect needs a blueprint to turn a heap of stones into a house, the social psychologist needs a theory to discern the pattern that underlies and connects observations of relevant phenomena. The move from observation to theory is a critical one because the most careful compilations of fact—the most detailed descriptions—do not tell us possible ways in which the observed phenomena are interrelated. Referring once more to your adolescent car acquisition theory, some of your friends found that their chances of using their family cars increased if they mowed the lawn, whereas others observed the same result if they volunteered to babysit. However, it was only when you organized these two observations (and others) within the framework of your theory that you were able

to identify a common theme that connected them. It was not solely lawn mowing or babysitting that earned your friends' use of their family cars; it was the meaning of these behaviors to your friends' parents.

The second function of theory, which is related to hypothesis testing, is to provide *direction.* Direction refers to guidance as to where research efforts should be focused. When you are traveling to a new destination, you use a road map to chart your course, perhaps noting alternate routes that you may try on future trips if your initial choice is not satisfactory. In the same way, social psychological theories may suggest possible previously unconsidered relationships between observed phenomena and may provide stimulation and guidance for further hypothesis testing, and the possible alteration of the theory or even the generation of new theories. For example, your adolescent car acquisition theory led you to demonstrate previously untried mature behaviors to your parents in pursuit of permission for other adult behaviors besides driving the car.

The third function of a theory, which is related most directly to application, is to guide *intervention.* Intervention refers to the attempt to bring about a change in the world. The goal of medical science is to identify the causes of disease, not out of idle curiosity, but rather to prescribe actions that will prevent its occurrence. In the same way, theories in social psychology provide prescriptions for the solutions to social and practical problems. So, for example, you used your adolescent car acquisition theory as the basis for an intervention strategy that solved your practical problem of getting access to the family car as frequently as possible.

Characteristics of Social Psychological Theories

Social psychological theories differ in terms of a number of characteristics, including scope, range, testability, and parsimony. The **scope** of a theory refers to the number of different human behaviors that the theory attempts to explain. Social psychology, like other branches of psychology, has been influenced by several broad perspectives that explain most human behaviors by reference to a single central concept. For example, according to psychologist John Watson's (1913) *behaviorist perspective,* all human behaviors are learned responses to external rewards and punishments. Sigmund Freud's (1935) *psychoanalytic orientation* suggests that humans behave as they do because of unconscious motivations, and Lewin's (1944/1951) *phenomenological perspective* advances the notion that human behavior is the result of the way in which we subjectively interpret our environment. Many social psychological theories incorporate some aspects of these perspectives, recognizing the importance of learning (behaviorist), motivation (psychoanalytic), and internal cognitive processes (phenomenological). However, social psychological theories do not claim to be able to explain all kinds of human behavior and thus are more limited in scope than the perspectives they reflect.

Many social psychological theories, such as cognitive dissonance theory and the theory of planned behavior (discussed in more detail later in this chapter) are *midlevel theories* that attempt to explain one way of thinking or behaving that is relevant in a number of different situations. Other theories are *minitheories* that attempt to explain a particular human behavior when faced with a particular set of circumstances. For example, cultivation theory, discussed in Chapter 7, could be described as a minitheory because it focuses on how viewing a lot of television impacts individuals in various ways.

Range refers to whether a theory predicts the behaviors of only a specific group of people or all humans. Until relatively recently, the assumption shared by many social psychologists was that it is possible to identify certain universal principles that shape the behavior of all humans; therefore, the theories they developed were thought to apply to people in general. Social psychologists have come to realize, however, that people's behavior may be influenced by individual differences, such as intelligence and temperament, as well as by group differences, such as gender and cultural background. Therefore for instance, to determine possible limits to a theory's range, increased attention has been paid to testing hypotheses with men and women separately and with people who differ on individual- and group-level attributes.

Another characteristic of a theory, and perhaps the most important one, is its **testability**. Testability refers to the idea that a good theory is capable of being refuted or disproved. In our individualistic culture, the idea that you can accomplish anything you want so long as you try hard enough is a very powerful theory. Unfortunately, it is not a good theory because it is impossible to disprove. Did you accomplish your goal? If so, it must be because you tried very hard. If not, it must be because you did not try hard enough. How does one know that you did not try hard enough? One knows because if you had tried hard enough, you would have succeeded. The theory that anything is possible with enough effort is not testable because it does not specify what "enough" effort means. Many of the variables in which social psychologists are interested, such as values, attitudes, and beliefs, are internal states that are not directly observable, and so for some time theories about these variables were thought to be untestable. Thus, social psychologists were hampered in their theorizing until methods to measure these internal variables were developed (Jones, 1998), and much current social psychological research is devoted to developing new and better measurement methods so that promising theories can be tested.

A theory should also demonstrate **parsimony**, meaning that it should use the fewest possible propositions to explain the phenomenon in question. Perhaps in part because social psychologists have focused on midlevel theories and minitheories rather than attempting to construct and test grand theories (i.e., those that are broad in scope) of human behavior, their theories tend not to include an overabundance of propositions. However, given the complexity of social behavior, social psychologists sometimes have to sacrifice some parsimony to provide adequate theoretical explanations.

Probably the best way in which to understand theories' functions and characteristics, as well as the interplay of observation, theory construction, hypothesis testing, and application, is to look at actual theories. We now consider two influential theories in social psychology—cognitive dissonance theory and the theory of planned behavior—and examine their function in terms of organization, direction, and possibilities for intervention.

COGNITIVE DISSONANCE THEORY

Description

How would you react if you felt the tremors of an earthquake, but fortunately did not suffer any direct injury or property damage? Prasad (1950) observed that, curiously, people in India who were in exactly this situation after a severe earthquake started spreading rumors of even worse disasters to come. When Festinger (cited in Myers & Spencer, 2004) read Prasad's descriptive study, he wondered whether perhaps the people spread these rumors not to provoke more anxiety, but rather to justify the anxiety they still felt, even though the earthquake was over and they had suffered no injuries or damage. Festinger wrote, "From that germ of an idea, I developed my theory of dissonance reduction—making your view of the world fit with how you feel or what you've done" (p. 132).

As indicated in Figure 2.2, the core of cognitive dissonance theory is the idea that humans are motivated to maintain consistency among their cognitions (e.g., opinions, attitudes, knowledge, values) because cognitive dissonance, the situation that exists when two cognitions are psychologically inconsistent with one another, is psychologically uncomfortable. Festinger's cognitive dissonance theory would suggest, in the case of Prasad's (1950) rumor spreaders, that their cognition that "the earthquake didn't hurt me in any way" was inconsistent with the cognition that "I'm still feeling very frightened." For them, apparently the easiest way in which to reduce their dissonance-caused discomfort was to justify their fear by adding new cognitions (Figure 2.2), that is, by generating rumors of impending disasters. They might have taken a seemingly more logical approach (e.g., moving away from the earthquake zone), but an additional key element of cognitive dissonance theory is the proposition that people will reduce dissonance in the easiest way possible. For example, the cognition that "exercising is good for my health" is dissonant with the cognition that "my only exercise is the trip between my couch and my refrigerator." The most logical action for me to take would be to start exercising. However, because breaking old habits and acquiring new ones is very difficult, I probably will reduce my dissonance in one of several other ways. I might change my cognition that exercising is good for my health ("Joggers drop dead from heart attacks every day"), add new cognitions that rationalize my "couch potato" existence ("Relaxing is also good for my health") (Festinger, 1957), or trivialize the importance of my inconsistent cognitions ("What's the big deal? Nobody lives forever") (Simon, Greenberg, & Brehm, 1995).

Organization

Although Festinger (1957) wrote an entire book detailing the definitions, assumptions, and hypotheses of his theory of cognitive dissonance, its essence can be captured in a few sentences. Think about what is implied by this seemingly simple theory: Human inconsistency is not a new phenomenon. Everyone can think of examples when we knew we were behaving in ways that contradicted our attitudes or beliefs, yet we still managed to find ways to rationalize the contradictions. In fulfilling the first function of a theory—organization—what cognitive dissonance theory does is to organize what we know about human inconsistency in such a way that we are led to some nonobvious conclusions about

Figure 2.2   Cognitive Dissonance Theory

Cognitive Dissonance Theory

Central Hypotheses

- Cognitions can be irrelevant to, consonant with, or dissonant with each other.
- Humans are motivated to maintain cognitive consonance.
- The presence of cognitive dissonance is psychologically uncomfortable and creates pressures to reduce dissonance.

Some Dissonance Producing Situations

- *Postdecisional dissonance.* Dissonance almost always exists after a decision has been made between two or more alternatives.
- *Effort justification.* Dissonance almost always exists when a person engages in an unpleasant activity to obtain some desirable outcome.
- *Insufficient justification.* Dissonance almost always exists after a successful attempt has been made to elicit overt behavior that is at variance with private opinion by offering a reward that is just sufficient to elicit the overt behavior.

Some Ways to Reduce Dissonance

- Change one or more of the dissonant cognitions.
- Add new cognitions to make existing cognitions consistent.
- Downplay importance of dissonant cognitions.

SOURCE: Adapted from Festinger (1957) and Aronson and Mills (1959).

the relationship between attitudes and behavior, particularly the idea that we may change our attitudes to match our behavior rather than the other way around.

Direction

The second function of a theory is to provide direction for research, and by this criterion, cognitive dissonance theory is one of the best. Festinger (1957) derived a number of intriguing hypotheses from cognitive dissonance theory that have been tested in hundreds of experiments. Figure 2.2 illustrates the three dissonance situations that have received the most attention. They involve postdecisional dissonance, effort justification, and insufficient justification.

Postdecisional dissonance. Let us start with postdecisional dissonance. Have you ever had to choose between two attractive alternatives? You go back and forth considering the pros and cons of each alternative, but eventually you have to make up your mind. Dissonance theory predicts that whichever alternative you choose (e.g., when purchasing a car), you will feel dissonance because of the two conflicting cognitions: "I bought the BMW" and "Maybe I should have bought the Audi because there are some great things about it." But, it is too late to change your mind; you have already signed the papers and driven the car home. Your decision has been made, so you cannot reverse your behavior. What will you do? The dissonance theory prediction, supported by extensive research (e.g., Brehm,

1956; Heine & Lehman, 1997; Knox & Inkster, 1968; Litt & Tormala, 2010; Shultz, Léveillé, & Lepper, 1999), is that you will reevaluate the chosen and unchosen alternatives so that the chosen alternative appears to be clearly superior to the unchosen alternative. In other words, two cars that were judged to be very close together before you made your decision are now perceived to be much further apart. Note what has happened here and how in some ways it contradicts common sense. We like to think that our attitudes guide our behaviors: "I like BMWs better, so I bought a BMW." But in this instance, your behavior actually contributed to a change in attitude: "I bought a BMW, so I guess I must like BMWs better."

Automobile salespeople are very aware of the practical implications of postdecisional dissonance. They use what is called a *lowball* technique by offering such a good deal on a car that the customer commits to buying it. In some cases, the customer is even allowed to take the car home overnight to reinforce the commitment made. When the customer returns the next morning to pay for the car, just before money changes hands, the salesperson explains that some costs in the total price had accidentally been omitted by the sales manager, so the car will actually cost more than the amount the customer had originally agreed to pay. The logical decision at this point is to refuse the deal (because it is no longer such a great deal). But by now, the customer has had many hours to justify choosing this car instead of any others that had been considered. The chosen alternative now looks so much better than the unchosen ones that the customer does not mind shelling out a little extra cash. After all, it is clearly a superior car (Cialdini, Cacioppo, Bassett, & Miller, 1978).

Effort justification. Cognitive dissonance theorists have also tested the effects of effort justification on attitude change. Have you ever worked very hard to achieve a goal—say, admission to the college you are now attending—only to have a sinking feeling after you attained the goal that all that effort might not have been worth it?

In this case, your two dissonant cognitions are "I worked very hard to get accepted by this college," and "So far, my college experience doesn't seem to be as good as I expected it to be." Cognitive dissonance theory predicts, again with research support (e.g., Aronson & Mills, 1959; Cunha & Caldieraro, 2009; Gerard & Mathewson, 1966), that in this situation, where (once again) you cannot change your behavior (changing schools in midyear is difficult), you will instead reevaluate the goal you have attained and convince yourself that it was in fact a very worthy goal (e.g., "I doubt that I would have a better experience at any of the other colleges I considered").

The idea of effort justification may be applied to practical problems. For example, Axsom and Cooper (1985) recruited overweight female college students to participate in a weight loss experiment in which participants were told that they would be completing a series of cognitive tasks (e.g., reciting nursery rhymes with delayed auditory feedback) designed to increase neurophysiological arousal that supposedly would enhance emotional sensitivity, and in turn lead to increased weight loss. (In actuality, there was no evidence that the cognitive tasks helped with weight reduction.) For some participants, the cognitive tasks were relatively difficult and required considerable effort to complete; for others, the tasks were relatively easy. Participants in a control group completed no cognitive tasks and were simply weighed. After four sessions over three weeks, the high-effort women had lost more weight than had the low-effort and control-group women. The dissonance theory interpretation for the high-effort women goes like this: "After I have expended all this effort to lose weight, I am more convinced than ever that weight loss is a good goal, and so I will try even harder to lose weight." Furthermore, despite the fact that there were no more sessions and the participants were not aware that they would be contacted again, the beneficial effects of the high-effort condition were still apparent a year later. When they weighed in at that time, the high-effort women had lost an average of

6.7 pounds, compared to less than 1 pound for the low-effort women and a gain of nearly 2 pounds for the control-group women. Further research by Axsom and his colleagues (Axsom, 1989; Cooper & Axsom, 1982) suggested that psychotherapy patients who have to work hard at their own treatment are more likely to report feeling better when the treatment is over than are those patients who do not have to work as hard.

Insufficient justification. Insufficient justification is the most difficult dissonance theory hypothesis to understand and is also the most intriguing. Suppose that your friend has just gotten a haircut that makes him look like a badly plucked chicken. When he asks you for your opinion, you can either tell him what you really think and hurt his feelings, or lie and tell him that the new haircut looks great. Normally, your knowledge that you lied would be dissonant with your belief that you are an honest person, and you would feel uncomfortable. However in this case, your concern for your friend's feelings provides you with considerable external justification for your lie, so you do not feel dissonance, and you do not change your real opinion (i.e., you still believe that the haircut was a big mistake). But, what happens if you lie about something and there is very little external justification for doing so? When this happens, cognitive dissonance theory predicts that because you cannot take back the lie (it has already been told), you will provide yourself with internal justification for your behavior. You will convince yourself that you were not really lying by changing your attitude regarding whatever it is you lied about.

In the original test of the insufficient justification hypothesis (one of the classic experimental studies of social psychology), Festinger and Carlsmith (1959) had college students participate in a very boring study and then induced them, for either $1 or $20, to tell another student that the study was very interesting. The participants were then asked to indicate how they really felt about the experiment. Consistent with cognitive dissonance theory predictions, students who

had lied to a fellow student for only $1 evaluated the experiment as more interesting than did students who had lied for $20. Why? According to Festinger and Carlsmith, both the $1 students and the $20 students had two dissonant cognitions: "I thought that the experiment was boring" and "I just told a fellow student that it was interesting; I just told a lie." For the students who had lied for $20, the inconsistency was resolved with the addition of the cognition, "I'm a poor student, and I got paid a lot of money for telling a harmless lie." But, for the students who had lied for $1, the knowledge that they had lied to a fellow student could not be externally justified (who lies for a paltry $1?), so they had to provide internal justification for their behavior by convincing themselves that the study had actually been kind of interesting.

The cognitive dissonance aroused by insufficient justification has been demonstrated in many studies (e.g., Brehm & Cohen, 1962; Hobden & Olson, 1994; Macias et al., 2009; Riess & Schlenker, 1977) and also has been used to change people's attitudes about important issues. Leippe and Eisenstadt (1994) either told (high external justification) or asked (low external justification) White college students at a U.S. university to write an essay in support of doubling the scholarship funds available to African American students, even though this would mean halving the funds available to other students. Consistent with cognitive dissonance theory predictions, only the students who had written the essay voluntarily subsequently expressed more favorable and supportive attitudes toward African Americans than they had before engaging in the attitude-discrepant behavior.

As illustrated, good theories provide direction for research by generating testable hypotheses. The results of hypothesis testing research also can lead to theory modification. One modification of cognitive dissonance theory with significant implications for application is Aronson's (1968, 1992) reinterpretation of cognitive dissonance as always involving some form of *self*-justification. Think about the following cognitions: "I am driving at night on a lonely country road and just got a flat tire," and "I don't have my tire jack with me." In his book, Festinger (1957) argued that a person in this situation, although frustrated would not feel dissonance because the two cognitions are not psychologically inconsistent; that is, the two cognitions do not contradict each other in the way that the following cognitions do: "I smoke," and "I know that smoking is bad for me" (pp. 277–278).

Aronson (1999) disagreed, stating that the dissonance would come from the fact that the driver, like most of us, likes to think that he is a reasonably intelligent individual, but his two cognitions lead him to conclude that he must be a total idiot to drive down a country road in the middle of the night without a jack. This observation led to Aronson's *self-consistency dissonance theory,* which posits that situations evoke dissonance because of an inconsistency between self-concept and awareness of one's behavior. In other words, people experience dissonance when they behave in ways that they view as reflecting negatively on themselves (that they are incompetent, immoral, irrational, etc.). Research supports this idea, and as Aronson (1968, 1992) pointed out, the results of many cognitive dissonance experiments can be interpreted in accordance with his modification of cognitive dissonance theory. Furthermore, Aronson's reworking of dissonance theory provides a good illustration of how cognitive dissonance theory has fulfilled the third function of theory: helping in the design of interventions.

Intervention

Do you believe that we need to do more to conserve our natural resources? Now, do you behave in a way that is consistent with your beliefs? It is quite possible that your behavior is not necessarily consistent with your beliefs. Let us take recycling as an example. How many of us look for the recycling box every time we have something to throw out, and how many of us "cheat" quite often, or at least occasionally, because it is just easier to toss that bottle into the nearest garbage can?

But, what would happen to your behavior if you were asked to write and deliver a speech on the importance of recycling, a speech that would be videotaped and shown to various audiences as part of a community campaign to increase participation in recycling programs? Now, suppose that you do not recycle very much, if at all, even though you think that it is a good idea. You still would probably be able to give the speech, coming up with some pretty good arguments in support of recycling. However, it is unlikely that your own recycling behavior would change much at all. But, suppose that just before you write the speech, you are questioned about your own recycling behavior. Now that you must focus on your behavior, you have two dissonant cognitions: "I will be preaching recycling to my community," and "I don't practice what I preach." In other words, you are now very aware of your hypocrisy.

This is exactly the manipulation that Fried and Aronson (1995) used in their experiment. College students were asked to write and deliver a pro-recycling speech, but prior to writing the speech, half of the participants (the hypocrisy condition) were asked to list examples of recent times when they had failed to recycle. After they had written their speeches, all participants were asked whether they would volunteer to make phone calls for a local recycling organization. Just as predicted, the participants in the hypocrisy condition (who had been reminded that their actual behavior was not consistent with their expressed attitudes) volunteered significantly more often, and for longer periods of time, than did those students who had only written the speeches. Similar results have been reported in experimental studies involving the induction of hypocrisy to increase condom use (Aronson, Fried, & Stone, 1991; Stone, Aronson, Crain, Winslow, & Fried, 1994), to encourage water conservation (Dickerson, Thibodeau, Aronson, & Miller, 1992), and to encourage safe driving (Fointiat, 2004).

A meta-analysis of research using dissonance-based health interventions was conducted by Freijy and Kothe (2013). They found that programs that incorporated hypocrisy, such as having participants talk about the health risks of binge drinking and then reflecting on their own drinking behavior (arousing dissonance), were the most frequently used and also tended to be highly effective. One area that is particularly promising for dissonance-based interventions is in the prevention of body dissatisfaction and treatment of eating disorders. In their meta-analysis, Stice, Shaw, and Marti (2007) reported that eating disorder prevention programs with a dissonance-based component were the most effective in reducing dieting behaviors, body dissatisfaction, and fear of weight gain despite participants being underweight, and exhibiting extreme exercise behaviors.

Naughton, Eborall, and Sutton's (2013) study of smoking cessation provides another example of how theoretically grounded research can drive the development of effective health interventions. The researchers interviewed pregnant women who were experiencing dissonance related to their smoking behavior (e.g., "I smoke even though it can cause birth defects"), which increased their motivation to stop smoking. Consistent with cognitive dissonance theory, women who were unable to quit smoking reduced their dissonance by adopting "disengagement beliefs" that underestimated the likelihood of harm to their babies, such as deciding that the medical evidence was unclear. The results of this study can be used to design interventions that target and debunk these beliefs, thus decreasing their usefulness as dissonance reducers and increasing the likelihood that pregnant women will be able to stop smoking.

Summing Up Cognitive Dissonance Theory

How can we sum up cognitive dissonance theory? Based on the "germ of an idea" triggered by his reading a study about rumors, Festinger (1957) developed a theory that, given its applicability to a number of different situations, could be described in terms of scope as a midlevel theory. As originally proposed, cognitive dissonance theory had a broad range because it was presumed to apply to people in general rather than to particular individuals or groups. Further research on individual and cultural differences has modified this presumption somewhat. The central premise of cognitive dissonance theory is that psychological inconsistency makes people uncomfortable. However, Cialdini, Trost, and Newsom (1995) developed a Preference for Consistency scale and discovered that some people have a low preference for consistency, whereas others have a high preference for consistency. Consistent with cognitive dissonance theory predictions, both high- and low-consistency preference individuals changed their attitudes when they were induced to behave in attitude-inconsistent ways, and had low external justification for doing so. However, contrary to cognitive dissonance theory predictions, people with a low preference for consistency changed their attitudes to match their behaviors even when they had high external justification for behaving as they did and could have avoided attitude change by attributing their behavior to the external pressure.

As discussed elsewhere in this book, cross-cultural psychologists have identified a reliable cultural difference known as individualism–collectivism (Hofstede, 1991). In individualistic cultures, the integrity of the individual is most important, whereas people in collectivistic cultures are expected to behave in ways that preserve the integrity of the group, regardless of their own attitudes. Therefore, Kashima, Siegal, Tanaka, and Kashima (1992) hypothesized that the preference for internal psychological consistency would be stronger in individualistic cultures than in collectivistic cultures. Consistent with their hypothesis, they found that Australians, whose culture is relatively individualistic, had stronger beliefs about the importance of attitude–behavior consistency than did Japanese, whose culture is relatively collectivistic. Recent research also shows that cognitive dissonance operates differently between North Americans and East Asians (e.g., Hoshino-Browne et al., 2005; Imada & Kitayama, 2010; Kitayama, Snibbe, Markus, & Suzuki, 2004).

Without a doubt, cognitive dissonance theory fulfills the criterion of testability. Since its inception, it has inspired many hundreds of studies and continues to influence research (e.g., Abelson et al., 1968; Harmon-Jones & Mills, 1999; Martinie, Olive, & Milland, 2010; West, Jett, Beckman, & Vonk, 2010; Wicklund & Brehm, 1976). Cognitive dissonance theory also provides a good example of parsimony given that the essence of the theory can be captured in a few propositions.

In short, cognitive dissonance theory provides an excellent example of how theory serves three main functions: (a) organizing the existing literature, (b) providing direction for the testing of hypotheses derived from the original theory and for the generation of new hypotheses and new theories, and (c) suggesting many possibilities for intervention. Recapitulating the scientific process (see Figure 2.1) and emphasizing the relationship that should exist between experimentation and application, Festinger (1999) said it very well:

> I think we need to find out about how dissonance processes and dissonance reducing processes interact in the presence of other things that are powerful influences of human behavior and human cognition, and the only way to do that is to do studies in the real world. They're messy and difficult. . . . But out of them will emerge more ideas which we can then bring into the laboratory to clarify and help to broaden and enrich the work. (p. 385)

We turn now to the theory of planned behavior—a younger theory than cognitive dissonance, but one that has generated a large volume of research across many fields.

THEORY OF PLANNED BEHAVIOR

Description

The **theory of planned behavior** emerged as many theories do through a process of observation and reflection. As graduate students in the 1960s, Icek Ajzen and his contemporaries compared strict behaviorist interpretations of human action with their own experiences with complex decision making (Ajzen, 2011b). For example, people deciding which button to press in response to a specific stimulus in order to earn an artificial "reward" in a laboratory experiment hardly seems analogous to people's decisions to join a gym, smoke marijuana, or disobey traffic laws. Ajzen and his colleagues also observed a disconnect between the way people behave, and their general dispositions (Ajzen, 2011a). For example, you may know someone who values environmental causes, but may not always make eco-friendly choices, perhaps choosing to drive to school some days instead of biking or taking the bus.

The foundation for the theory of planned behavior is the theory of reasoned action, proposed by Fishbein and Ajzen in 1975 to explain and predict a variety of volitional behaviors. The theory of reasoned action states that people enact behaviors because they intend to do so, although intentions can change over time as people take in new information. In the theory, **behavioral intentions** result from a combination of a person's attitude toward the behavior and subjective norms. **Attitude** is determined by what a person believes the likely outcome of the behavior will be, and what they think about that outcome. **Subjective norms** are a person's beliefs about what the people they know would think of this behavior, and how motivated they are to do what these significant others would do or approve of. Let us return to your adolescent car acquisition theory. In your quest to gain the use of the family car, you decide to demonstrate responsible behavior, so you take out the garbage without being asked, thus (you hope) making it more likely your parents will lend you the car on a regular basis. According to the theory of reasoned action, you believe that taking out the garbage will probably lead to your parents noticing and approving of this action (outcome), which will be helpful to you (evaluation of outcome) in that it will further demonstrate responsible behavior. On this basis, you form a positive attitude toward taking out the garbage.

You also believe that your parents think you should be helping out around the house by taking out the garbage (subjective norm), and you want to comply with their expectations in order to test your theory. Your attitude toward taking out the garbage combines with your perception of your parents' approval of this activity to produce an intention to take out the garbage, which leads to the behavior. In this example, the subjective norm is related to your attitude toward the behavior, which is often the case with real-life examples. Now, imagine one component of the theory is absent. For example, suppose your parents don't really care whether or not you take the garbage out. The likely result would be that you will not form the intention to take out the garbage, and therefore not perform the behavior. Extensive research continues to support the theory of reasoned action through direct testing of the relationships among attitudes, subjective norms, and behavioral intentions. However, the theory of planned behavior has been found to be

less predictive of intentions when the behavior is not completely under a person's control (Godin & Kok, 1996). In fact, Ajzen (2011b) noted that confining the theory to volitional behaviors "imposed too severe a limitation on a theory designed to predict and explain all manner of socially significant behavior" (p.445).

Ajzen (1985) decided to extend the theory of reasoned action by introducing the variable of volitional control and developed the theory of planned behavior (see Figure 2.3). Ajzen recognized that a multitude of factors under varying degrees of individual control can interfere with the performance of behaviors. You may have planned all week to shop for groceries on Saturday, but when you wake up, it's raining outside and your roommate needs to borrow the car, so you postpone your shopping expedition. As Ajzen put it, "every intended behavior is a *goal* whose attainment is subject to some degree of uncertainty. We can thus speak of a behavior-goal unit; and the intention constitutes a plan of

Figure 2.3 The Theory of Planned Behavior

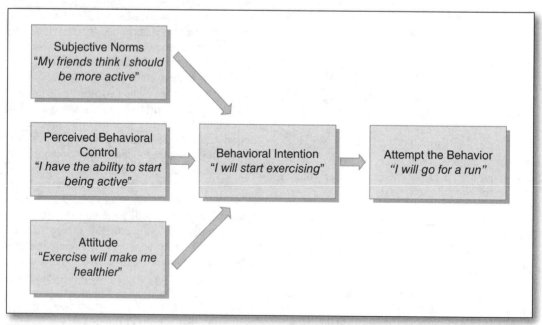

action in pursuit of the behavioral goal" (1985, p. 24). In other words, volitional control, the amount of control a person believes they have over a behavior, and their perception of the probability that there will be obstacles (control beliefs), as well as their evaluation of how much of an impact will occur with facilitating or obstructing factors, will affect a person's intentions to attempt a behavior. These factors can be external, like time, opportunity to perform the behavior, or whether the behavior relies on other people. Or they can be internal factors, such as skills, abilities, emotional state, or beliefs about the ability to perform a specific behavior (self-efficacy). For example, you may believe you can improve your grades by spending more time studying, but you also believe that your role on the soccer team will place significant demands on your time. And since you also believe that you are a much better soccer player than a student, you conclude that there is little point in attempting to study more (no behavioral intention).

Organization

Ajzen (1985) developed the theory of planned behavior based on his analysis of experiments that tested the theory of reasoned action. He noted that although some studies showed a high correlation between intention and attempted behavior, thus supporting the theory of reasoned action, other experiments showed a much weaker relationship between intention and action. The behaviors studied in the experiments with weaker relationships, such as a study of weight reduction in college women (Sejwacz, Ajzen, & Fishbein, 1980), and a study of blood donation (Pomazal & Jaccard, 1976), seemed to involve variables that reduced behavioral control. For example, losing weight depends in large part on an individual's metabolism, and in order to donate blood, potential donors have to be able to pass the screening procedures. The new theory of planned behavior organized these seemingly inconsistent results and formulated a set of relationships to be tested.

It is easy to imagine how the theory of planned behavior can be applied to a variety of behaviors of concern to social scientists who are interested in determining why people decide to act or fail to act, especially in cases where people's stated attitudes and beliefs do not translate into actions. Consider the practice of downloading music or movies from the Internet without paying for them. People who otherwise believe that stealing is wrong sometimes engage in this behavior. Why might this be? The theory of planned behavior can provide a testable framework for the analysis of this attitude-behavior disconnect. For example, you believe that stealing is wrong, but you love music, you know that all your friends are effortlessly downloading free music, and the cyber-police have not come to their houses to arrest them. As a result, your pro music attitude, supported by a high perceived level of behavioral control and a perception of supportive subjective norms, will make it likely that your behavior will not reflect your anti-stealing attitude, and you will download music from the Internet without paying for it. In fact, some researchers have started to apply the theory of planned behavior to issues like illegal downloading and other online behaviors (e.g., Robertson, McNeill, Green, & Roberts, 2012; Sang, Lee, Kim, & Woo, 2015). Other researchers have used the theory of planned behavior to understand and predict attitude-behavior links across diverse fields, such as social psychology, business, information technology, education, and healthcare (Conner & Armitage, 1998; Godin & Kok, 1996).

Direction

Analysis of the available research also indicates that the theory of planned behavior, like cognitive dissonance theory, has fulfilled the second function of a theory—providing research direction by suggesting new relationships among existing phenomena, thereby stimulating hypothesis testing. The theory of planned behavior has been applied to diverse topics, from recycling and eco-friendly tourist behaviors (Cheung & Chan,

1999; Han, Hsu, & Sheu, 2010) to adolescent sexting (Walgrave, Heirman, & Hallam, 2014), and like cognitive dissonance theory has proceeded through the phases of hypothesis testing with direct tests and proposed extensions.

One area where the theory of planned behavior has provided ample direction is behaviors related to health and safety. Researchers have found that perceived behavioral control, in addition to attitude and subjective norms is predictive of intentions to exercise (Blue, 1995), engage in unsafe driving behaviors (Parker, Manstead, Stradling, Reason, & Baxter, 1992), use condoms (Albarracin et al., 2001), attend cancer screenings (Devellis, Blalock, & Sandler, 1990; Montano & Taplin, 1991), quit smoking (De Vries, Backbier, Kok, & Dijkstra, 1995; Norman, Conner, & Bell, 1999), and start smoking (Van De Ven, Engels, Otten, & Van Den Eijnden, 2007). Another study of unsafe driving behaviors by Parker and colleagues (1992) provides an example of how the theory of planned behavior outlines the path from thoughts to behaviors. In this study, drivers who a) had relatively negative views regarding dangerous driving behaviors, such as following closely or drinking and driving (attitude), b) felt that others would disapprove (subjective norm), and c) believed they had control over these behaviors (perceived behavioral control) were less likely to intend to engage in these unsafe behaviors. Interestingly, while many other studies report that attitudes are the strongest predictor of intentions, this study reported that subjective norms were the most influential. This finding has interesting implications for other behaviors that are performed in social contexts like tipping in restaurants, and suggests future directions for social psychological research and intervention.

Direct tests of the theory of planned behavior confirm the predictive value of perceived behavioral control on intentions and goal attainment, but suggest that the theory is more predictive for some types of behavioral intentions than others (Godin & Kok, 1996; Schifter & Ajzen, 1985). Several meta-analyses also suggest that researchers can use parts of the theory, like measures of attitudes, subjective norms, and

perceived behavioral control to predict behavioral intentions indirectly (e.g., Albarracin et al., 2001; Blue, 1995), and that beliefs can predict attitudes, subjective norms, and perceived behavioral control (Armitage & Conner, 2001), providing researchers with different avenues for hypothesis testing.

In addition to providing direction to numerous researchers over the past 30 years, the theory of planned behavior continues to stimulate interest and new directions. For example, Conner and Armitage (1998) have suggested that the theory of planned behavior could be extended to include belief salience (how easily the belief comes to mind), past behavior, self-efficacy, moral norms, and self-identity. Researchers have found support for the inclusion of anticipated affective outcomes, such as guilt or regret in theory of planned behavior models for behaviors, such as gambling and illegal downloading (Robertson et al., 2012; Wang & McClung, 2012). For example, if an individual anticipated they would feel worried and regret for their actions after having unprotected sex, they would incorporate this into their decision making and be less likely to intend to have unprotected sex.

Intervention

One strength of the theory of planned behavior is its fulfillment of the third function of a theory, that is, its application in interventions (see Hardeman et al., 2002 for a review of these applications). As Ajzen (2011a) highlights, the questionnaires developed to test the theory of planned behavior are ideally suited for the development of behavioral interventions. Direct testing of the theory of planned behavior often involves pilot testing to determine which beliefs about a behavior are commonly held by a group of participants in order to develop a survey measure. Similar procedures can be used to identify salient beliefs that can be targeted when developing behavioral interventions. For example, a poverty reduction organization that wants to increase attendance at a job skills program it offers could ask potential clients about the disadvantages and advantages of attending the program (behavioral beliefs), whether they think the significant others in their lives would approve or disapprove of their attendance (subjective norms), and the factors that might make attending the program easier or harder (control beliefs). On the basis of this information, the organization could then develop an intervention to target beliefs or concerns that prevent people from attending, such as an advertising program stressing the value of the outcomes (usable skills), or locating of the program delivery site on a bus route. When developing interventions, researchers can also compare people who engage in the behavior of interest (e.g., exercising regularly) to those who do not, to identify potential differences in salient beliefs regarding the behavior. Returning to the example of the job skills program, if the organization observes that single parents drop out of the program at higher rates than other clients, it could talk to single parents about the barriers they perceive and experience and redesign the program to include additional supports that will increase attendance for this group. If a common concern for the single parents is undependable childcare arrangements, resulting in low perceived behavioral control, then the organization could invite parents to bring their children and provide an on-site caregiver. The theory of planned behavior also provides a theoretical foundation for evaluating interventions. After all, we want to ensure that our interventions are not only grounded in theory, but also that they work! One of the ways the theory of planned behavior can guide these efforts is by providing information about the factors that contribute to the formation of behavioral intentions. Let us say that a large company develops a customer service training program for its staff members. Before management decides to spend money on training every department, they assess the program's effectiveness by comparing several departments that received the training to similar departments that did not. They wisely decide to survey both groups on their attitudes, subjective norms, and perceived

behavioral control in relation to customer service, as well as asking about intention to engage in service behaviors, and actual behavior over the past 30 days. If after six months management finds no difference in the rates of service behaviors between groups, the company could turn to the theory of planned behavior to help figure out why. By assessing any changes (or lack of changes) in the factors that contribute to a behavior of interest, researchers can determine what factors the intervention needs to target and can adjust accordingly. Conversely, if the intervention is successful, the researchers have an idea as to why.

Summing Up the Theory of Planned Behavior

Ajzen's (1985) theory of planned behavior focuses on the way in which attitudes and beliefs interact to create behavioral intentions and action. In scope, the theory of planned behavior can be described as a midlevel theory, designed to predict and explain behavioral intentions in a variety of situations.

The limited body of cross-cultural research suggests that the theory of planned behavior is generalizable to different cultural groups, although the pattern of relationships may be different. For example, Hagger and colleagues (2007) used the theory of planned behavior to compare exercise behaviors among youth in Estonia, Great Britain, Greece, Hungary, and Singapore. The authors hypothesized that the theory would predict behavior for all the groups. The authors found, as predicted, that the attitudes of significant others in the youths' lives (subjective norms) were more influential in the countries characterized as holding highly collectivist values, whereas the youth's own attitudes about exercise were more influential in individualistic countries. However, as predicted, behavioral intentions did predict behavior for youth in all the countries, suggesting that the theory of planned behavior can be adapted to specific cultural groups. The theory has also been applied to understanding people's intention to disobey traffic laws by exceeding the speed limit in Turkish and Swedish samples (Warner, Özkan, & Lajunen, 2009). Given the ever increasing globalization of commerce, other studies have tested the applicability of the theory of planned behavior to topics such as e-commerce (Pavlou & Chai, 2002), environmentally friendly purchasing behaviors in Chinese and U.S. samples (Chan & Lau, 2002), and entrepreneurial intentions among students from Germany, India, Iran, Poland, Spain, and the Netherlands (Moriano, Gorgievski, Laguna, Stephan, & Zarafshani, 2012), all with similar results.

Like cognitive dissonance theory, the theory of planned behavior provides a good example of the three functions of theory—organization, direction, and intervention. Of particular interest to applied social psychologists are the many potential applications of this theory.

What about testability? As indicated previously, the theory of planned behavior deals with the internal processes that may lead to behavioral intentions, which in turn may lead to behaviors—a chain of events that may be difficult to study in its entirety. Researchers have addressed this challenge by testing subsets of the variables included in the theory of planned behavior and tailoring their measures to each population of interest. The theory of planned behavior also treats perceived behavioral control as a proxy for actual behavioral control, which can limit the predictive and explanatory power of the theory when these perceptions are inaccurate. Meta-analyses support the predictive value of perceived

behavioral control, though debate continues on how to measure perceived behavioral control and the extent of its influence (Armitage & Conner, 2001; Conner & Armitage, 1998).

Like cognitive dissonance theory, the theory of planned behavior is a parsimonious theory, even though it explains and predicts all manner of social behaviors. Overall, the theory of planned behavior has admirably fulfilled the three key functions of theory: organization, direction, and intervention.

SUMMARY

The scientific process involves a continuing cycle of observation, theory development, deduction of hypotheses, and hypothesis testing (in research and applications). Theory development is central to this process—organizing our observations, directing our hypothesis testing, and guiding our efforts to intervene in solving real-world problems. The two theories discussed in this chapter—cognitive dissonance and the theory of planned behavior—illustrate the way in which the process works, with the original theory leading to hypothesis testing, observation of results, and theory revision (if needed). As you read through this book, you will discover the many different contexts where social psychology has been applied and the importance of theory to the development and implementation of intervention strategies designed to improve the functioning of individuals, groups, organizations, communities, and societies.

3

RESEARCH METHODS IN APPLIED SOCIAL PSYCHOLOGY

KENNETH M. CRAMER

LOUISE R. ALEXITCH

W e often look at the work of social psychologists and wonder, "Why would anyone study love and communication? Everyone knows they don't go together!" The truth is that although much of what social psychologists study might seem to be common sense, it is clear that we cannot always come up with reliable scientific principles based *solely* on common sense (Babbie & Benaquisto, 2002). Consider the following example.

Years ago, the state of California was suffering severely under an extreme drought. In an effort to conserve water, the state urged large institutions, such as businesses and universities, to come up with strategies to use less water (Dickerson, Thibodeau, Aronson, & Miller, 1992). For instance, officials at the University of California, Santa Cruz, noticed that a good deal of water was consumed in the campus athletic facilities and reasoned that if they could reduce the duration of student showers, significant water savings would result. But, how could that be accomplished? Actually, it seemed rather straightforward. At first, they simply mounted signs on the change room walls urging students to shower in less time. This common-sense strategy had no effect. What if the signs were made more noticeable? To explore this possibility, each sign was mounted on a stand and positioned right in the doorway to the showers so that students would have to notice it. This seemingly reasonable decision would prove to be folly. Not only did the strategy fail to curb shower duration; it actually had the opposite effect. The signs were thrown around, and students took especially long showers in defiance. Despite these noble intentions, the university's efforts were ineffective and costly. What could be done?

The University of California, Santa Cruz, eventually did find a solution (which we share at the end of this chapter) based on research methods and tools often employed by social psychologists to tackle relevant social and practical problems. Problems encountered in areas such as education, health, the environment, and the criminal justice system are addressed using these same research methods and techniques. Specifically, decisions about how to set up and conduct research in applied social psychology are made on the basis of three research dimensions: method of data collection, research design, and research setting. This chapter introduces you to the three research dimensions. Let us begin by considering how we gather information (i.e., data) from the world around us.

METHODS OF DATA COLLECTION

Before reviewing the basic methods of data collection, we should recognize that all research data reflect the researcher's attempt to study and measure specific variables. Accordingly, we first briefly consider the meaning and measurement of variables.

Variables and Their Measurement

All research begins with a research question. For example, Chapter 1 considered research stemming from questions such as whether children learn intergroup attitudes from their parents, and whether competition between groups leads to negative intergroup attitudes. Moreover, Chapter 2 considered what groups can do to reduce groupthink, and the beginning of this chapter considered how a severe drought led to the question of how to get college students to reduce the use of water while taking showers. Researchers often translate their research questions into hypotheses like the following: If "use less water" signs are placed in highly visible locations, water use will decline.

Each research question (and hypothesis) specifies the variables of interest. A **variable** refers to a property of a person, an object, or an event that can vary in quantity (e.g., amount, degree) or in quality (e.g., kind). Some of the variables indicated in the preceding research questions were intergroup attitudes, learning, competition, water use, and groupthink. When researchers investigate research questions, they must measure the variables of interest; thus, an important decision they must make is how exactly they will measure each variable. As an example, a researcher might measure water use by having students themselves time and record the duration of their showers, or by using a mechanical meter that automatically records volume of water used.

The specific way in which a researcher measures a variable is referred to as the **operational definition** of the variable. The choice of an operational definition is very important because some operational definitions will reflect what the researcher means by a variable more closely than will other definitions. A measurement procedure that reflects the meaning of the variable accurately is said to have a form of validity called **construct validity**. For instance, a measure of water use that entails having students monitor and record their shower times may have questionable construct validity because it does not accurately reflect the amount of water consumed, and there is a definite possibility that some students might alter the data they provide to the researcher so as to make a good impression. On the other hand, the mechanical meter accurately calculates water volume and is much less susceptible to distortion; therefore it would have higher construct validity as a measure of water use.

Measurement of variables provides researchers with the data (information) they analyze in trying to answer their research questions. In the water use study, possible data included the students' written reports of how long they showered on each occasion, and the mechanical meter's numerical output of the volume of water consumed.

To address specific research questions, applied social psychologists use a variety of data collection tools. For instance, data may be gathered through mail surveys, face-to-face or telephone interviews, focus groups, and observations of behavior in natural settings. We distinguish between two basic and broad categories of data collection: those that rely on self-report procedures (e.g., surveys, personality scales, aptitude tests, single-item ratings) and those that rely on observational procedures (e.g., visual, auditory, and physiological observations). We begin with an examination of self-report procedures and follow with considerations of observational techniques.

Self-Report Methods: The Special Case of Surveys

Self-report data collection procedures are those that require participants to report (either orally or in writing) on themselves with respect to the variable(s) of interest. Examples of self-report measures include surveys, personality scales, vocational interest inventories, and single-item rating scales. This chapter focuses on surveys because of their versatility and widespread use in applied social psychology.

Surveys involve a series of questions about one's attitudes toward, views on, and behaviors regarding a variable or set of variables. Like face-to-face interviews, surveys have had a long

history in psychological measurement and continue to be a popular option for social researchers. Given that the survey is one of the key tools of the applied social psychologist, it is important to understand how a survey is constructed. The following subsections deal with the issues of question type, wording, sequence, and response formats typically considered in survey development.

Question type. Regardless of how you plan to administer a survey, you must first decide on the question type. There are three basic question types used in surveys: factual, attitude, and behavioral. Each has its strengths and weaknesses. Do you want to find out about a person's current situation or about what has happened to him or her in the past? These are called **factual questions** and are used to collect demographic data (e.g., age, gender, level of education), and information regarding events or circumstances about which a person is knowledgeable. Although these questions aim at tapping objective information, they are susceptible to lapses in memory or even conscious withholding of information. Alternatively, **attitude questions** measure a person's feelings, beliefs, or views that often cannot be easily ascertained from his or her behavior or other sources of information (Ajzen, 1991). Because attitudes are complex, responses to attitude questions are often difficult to interpret. For example, a person might not have an opinion about a topic, but may feel obligated to provide a response, or two people might have the same attitude toward an event (e.g., they are positive about it), but differ in how strongly they feel about it. Attitude questions must be as specific as possible. For example, a study of attitudes toward recycling household products should be tackled using a series of separate questions about the recycling of newspapers, cans, bottles, and so on. Finally, **behavior questions** tap into specific aspects of current or past behavior, such as its frequency, intensity, and timing. Because they are subject to memory gaps and distortions, behavior questions are best asked about recent behaviors (Kraus, 1997).

Question wording. Research shows that even minor differences in the wording of questions can have a significant impact on responses. Questions have to be worded carefully to avoid bias or misinterpretation. Listed below are some general guidelines for developing survey questions. These guidelines are not exhaustive and are only meant to give you an idea of the complexity of question construction in surveys.

1. *Wording should be exact* so that it reflects precisely what you want to measure. For example, it is very common to see the words *frequently, usually,* and *sometimes* in surveys. What if you want to determine the potential demand for public transportation in a city? It might not be enough to know that a person will "sometimes" use the bus because it is uncertain what exactly this means. You would obtain more precise and useful information if you asked respondents to estimate the number of times they would take the bus during a certain period (e.g., a month).

2. *Wording/terminology should be simple* so that even people with poor literacy skills, with little education, or from different backgrounds can understand it. Avoid jargon, abbreviations, acronyms, and terms that may be unfamiliar to respondents.

3. *Loaded questions should be avoided.* **Loaded questions** are questions that are phrased so that respondents are led to choose one response over another (often reflecting the bias of the researcher). Consider the following "yes/no" question: "Should the city council fix the dangerous playground equipment in the public parks?" The word *dangerous* would suggest to respondents that you are looking for a "yes" answer.

4. *Questions should be kept short and relatively simple.* Do not use complex lengthy questions that may be hard to understand. It may be prudent to split such questions into multiple questions. In this regard, avoid **double-barreled questions** that involve having more than one question embedded within a sentence. Consider the following "yes/no" question: "Do you think that the city council should allow skateboarding and rollerblading on public sidewalks?" If an individual responds "yes," does he or she support both skateboarding *and* rollerblading on sidewalks or only one of them?

5. *Questions should not make assumptions* about respondents, such as about their experiences or demographic status. Consider the following example: "How long have you owned a cellular phone?" How could a person respond if he or she does not own a cell phone?

Question sequence. The sequence of survey questions is important for three reasons. First, you want to capture respondents' interest from the beginning and maintain it throughout. One way in which to do this is to start with a general, easy-to-answer question that is both nonthreatening and important to respondents and also is clearly relevant to the topic of study. Unless you are screening for particular respondents (e.g., a specific age group), *never* start your survey or interview with demographic questions. These are boring to respondents and are highly personal. Put demographic questions at the end. Second, one question can affect responses to subsequent questions, a process called a **context effect** (Dillman, 2000; Fowler, 1998). Consider the following example:

Question 1: Indicate how often in an average month you recycle each of the following materials: Newspapers _____ Cardboard _____ Aluminum cans _____ Plastic containers _____

Question 2: In your opinion, what is the most important environment-friendly behavior that an individual can engage in? _____

Do not be surprised if the majority of responses to Question 2 feature recycling. Other possible responses (e.g., using public transportation) will be less likely to be mentioned because Question 1 will *prime* the respondents to think about recycling. It is prudent to present general questions first, followed by more specific questions (i.e., reverse the order of Questions 1 and 2).

Third, questions about sensitive and controversial topics (e.g., mental illness, drug use, abortion) should be presented near the end of the survey. By this time, you have established better rapport with the respondents, and they may feel more comfortable answering such questions. If such questions are presented too early, respondents may choose not to answer them or may provide inaccurate or socially desirable responses. Do not end the survey with sensitive or controversial questions because respondents may complete the survey feeling uncomfortable or embarrassed.

Response format. You need to select the format of your responses. There are two basic response formats: closed-ended (fixed alternatives) response and open-ended (free) response. Each of these formats serves a different purpose and carries unique advantages and disadvantages. **Closed-ended questions** provide respondents with a specified predetermined set of possible responses. Examples include checklists, multiple-choice items, rankings, and rating scales. Here is an example of a multiple-choice question:

Recycling is a worthwhile endeavor.

 a. Strongly disagree

 b. Disagree

 c. Agree

 d. Strongly agree

Closed-ended questions generally can be easily and quickly answered by respondents and easily coded and analyzed by the researcher. However, these questions are relatively time-consuming to design and require (in advance) some knowledge of the possible responses. That is, you need to make sure that all conceivable response categories are presented, often including an undefined alternative, such as "no opinion," "don't know," or "not applicable." Closed-ended questions invite other issues. Consider the same question using a rating scale:

To what extent do you think recycling is a worthwhile endeavor?

Not at all 1 2 3 4 5 6 7 To a great extent

If you use rating questions, should they involve a 7-point scale (as in this example) or a 5- or 9-point scale? How should you label the endpoints? Should you include a middle neutral point? Should you include a "don't know" option? These are the kinds of decisions one has to make in designing rating questions.

One solution to the constraints of closed-ended questioning is to "open up" the questions by using an open-ended format, akin to writing an essay question on a test. **Open-ended questions** allow individuals to respond freely in their own words to survey or interview questions. An example might be the following: "Please describe your views about recycling." The researcher codes responses to open-ended questions in terms of key words, categories, or themes. (This procedure is similar to qualitative research methods, a topic covered later in the chapter.) This format is ideal when you are not familiar with the range of possible responses on a topic or an issue, or when you want to explore fine distinctions in attitudes, opinions, or beliefs among your respondents. But, this approach is not without disadvantages. A major one is that the process of interpreting and coding data from these questions can be time-consuming and difficult.

Internet surveys. In the last decade, we have seen a remarkable increase in the use of the Internet or World Wide Web as a survey mode. There are many types of electronic surveys, each with its own methodological and statistical implications (for reviews of web surveys, see Couper, 2000; Couper & Miller, 2008). Particularly relevant to applied social psychologists are electronic surveys that are employed in research and/or organizational consulting. In a typical procedure, a sample of individuals from a clearly defined population is notified of a survey by e-mail, with the questionnaire accessed through a hyperlink or an attachment. One example is a job satisfaction survey conducted by a human resources department in an organization. Those conducting the survey know the number of employees in the organization, their characteristics, and the number of people who have been asked to participate. Thus, they are able to determine important information, such as *response rates* (i.e., percentage of a sample who complete a survey) and *response bias* (i.e., effect of nonrespondents on survey results).

Issues related to question wording and response format when using mail-out surveys and in-person interviews also apply to Internet surveys. There are, however, special considerations when adapting question formats used in paper-based or interview modes to web or e-mail surveys. For example, Couper, Tourangeau, and Conrad (2004) found that questions using radio buttons (similar to a checklist in paper-based surveys) as a response format produced a significantly different pattern of responses than did questions employing drop-down menus. In the latter case, participants tended to choose the options that were visible rather than those that appeared only after scrolling down the list of options.

Electronic surveys have the advantage of combining the benefits of other survey modes into one format, including being able to reach large numbers of people in a short time (similar to a telephone), a more interactive question format (similar to in-person and telephone interviews), and the use of visual cues to help participants respond accurately (similar to in-person formats). Moreover, because responses are gathered electronically, data coding and entry can be done quickly (Börkan, 2010; Converse, Wolfe, Huang, & Oswald, 2008).

Whereas the use of Internet surveys for data collection has afforded applied social psychologists many advantages relative to other forms of survey administration (e.g., lower costs, less time-consuming, ease of data coding), there are some disadvantages relative to mail-out, telephone, and in-person surveys (Börkan, 2010; Converse et al., 2008; Couper & Miller, 2008). For example, Heerwegh and Loosveldt (2008) found that compared with in-person survey respondents, web-survey respondents produced lower quality of data, including less differentiation on rating scales (i.e., number of different scale points used by respondents), more "don't know" responses, and more item nonresponse (i.e., leaving items unanswered). Also, Heerwegh and Loosveldt found a lower response rate among the web-survey sample, which accords with the results of many electronic surveys. Such lower response rates (sometimes less than 10%) have become a fundamental concern among researchers (Couper & Miller, 2008). Low response rates carry the added problems of lowered representativeness of the final sample and increased sample bias. Some researchers (e.g., Börkan, 2010) have advised using electronic surveys combined with other survey formats (called **mixed-mode surveys**) to improve response rates and sample coverage.

Observational Methods

Self-report approaches, such as surveys and interviews, are common means of data collection, but are not the only ones. Instead of asking participants to report about themselves, the researcher may observe and record some aspect of their functioning. For instance, the researcher may measure physiological processes (e.g., use a polygraph during job interviews for high-ranking security positions). The researcher may audiotape phone conversations (e.g., track how employees deal with customer complaints). Also, the researcher may record actual behavior as it happens (e.g., count the number of cars that run a red light at an intersection), or after it has happened (e.g., measure floor tile erosion in front of various museum exhibits as an index of exhibit popularity).

Indeed, the latter two examples invite discussion of an important measurement problem in both the social and natural sciences—the possibility that measurement of a variable (e.g., a person's attitude) changes that variable. In other words, measuring floor tile erosion in a museum has no bearing on the people who once stood there. However, if you instead measure exhibit popularity by standing with a clipboard and stopwatch at each exhibit, you might well scare off some museum patrons and possibly obtain a biased set of responses about the exhibits. Fortunately, observational techniques that permit the researcher to get close to respondents without unduly influencing their behavior are available.

In the method of **participant observation**, the researcher is an active participant in the social situation that he or she has chosen to observe. In some cases, the researcher may pose as another member of the situation (e.g., joining a street gang to observe how gang members interact). Alternatively, participants may be made aware that the researcher not only is participating in the event, but also is studying their behavior (e.g., attending meetings of an organization's advisory board to study how the group makes decisions). By using participant observation, the researcher still risks changing the behavior under study (especially if people know that they are being observed), or losing objectivity if he or she adopts a role in the setting. For many social situations, however, there is no way in which to remain unobtrusive, and valuable insights may be gained by actively participating in the events of interest.

With a different approach, **nonparticipant observation**, the researcher remains separate from the event being observed so as not to influence (i.e., contaminate) the natural behavior and dynamics of the situation. The researcher can engage in nonparticipant observation either by observing the behavior of interest directly or by gathering observations through indirect means. **Direct (systematic) observation** involves selecting a naturally occurring set of behaviors, making observations of the behaviors using checklists or a coding system (developed ahead of time), and categorizing these observations for analysis. This method has been widely used to study a variety of behaviors, including for example, people's facial expressions when lying, people's reactions to receiving religious pamphlets, and latent prejudice in selecting a checkout line at a cafeteria (Page, 1997). The observer may be hidden or in the open, but he or she usually makes an effort to avoid interfering in any way with the relevant behavior. That way, participants either are entirely unaware of being observed or quickly get used to the presence of an observer.

So, how is systematic or direct observation different from the everyday "people watching" that we do? Direct observations (a) serve a specific research purpose (i.e., address specific questions or hypotheses), (b) are carefully planned ahead of time, and (c) are recorded systematically. Efforts are made to focus on behaviors that are relevant to the variables under study. Suppose that you wished to study playground aggression in children. Many decisions must be made. For instance, you would have to determine exactly what you mean by aggression and define it operationally. Is it the number of times that a child strikes another child? Does it include swiping possessions or name-calling? (All of these observable behaviors are consistent with at least some theoretical definitions of aggression.) In addition, you would have to decide when, where, and how often you would make observations. Would you go to different playgrounds or observe behavior in just one playground? What time of day would you record observations? Would you record behavior continually, every hour, or every 5 minutes? Finally, would you record the behavior using paper and pencil, camcorder, or microphone?

Another type of nonparticipant observation, **indirect observation**, involves recording physical traces of the target behavior, for example, empty alcohol containers in recycling boxes to track drinking patterns, and as mentioned earlier, floor tile erosion to measure exhibit popularity. In addition, one can review previously collected (**archival**) data to examine behaviors that are difficult to observe, occur infrequently, or to determine patterns of behavior over long periods of time (e.g., comparing crime and weather statistics to determine whether tempers rise with temperature).

Social psychologists investigate their research questions and test their hypotheses based on the data they obtain from either self-report or observational methods of data collection. The next section reviews the four basic quantitative research designs used to investigate research questions and test hypotheses. Both self-report and observational methods can be employed with any of the four quantitative research designs.

RESEARCH DESIGNS

The four basic research designs are true experimental, quasi-experimental, correlational, and descriptive. Each of these designs has unique advantages and disadvantages. The researcher's choice of design depends chiefly on the type of research question being asked, and this depends on what the researcher currently knows about the phenomenon. No matter which research design is chosen to investigate a topic, the design will have limitations. Ideally, a research program (i.e., a series of studies) on a topic, including a social or practical problem, should employ different designs. In this way, one design's limitations will be addressed by another design's strengths. Table 3.1 provides an overview of the four designs. You should refer to Table 3.1 as a

guide to the designs as they are reviewed in the following subsections.

True Experiments

Characteristics of true experiments. What leads people to litter? Is lack of awareness the chief reason why people fail to recycle? If governments invest more money in health promotion campaigns, will people choose healthier lifestyles? Note that these questions seek to uncover the reason(s) behind a phenomenon, that is, the *cause* of the behavior. An experimental design enables the researcher to address causal questions. Specifically, a **true experiment** allows the researcher to assess the degree to which and whether a variable (the possible cause) manipulated by the experimenter leads to a change in another variable (the effect). There are three kinds of variables relevant to experiments: independent, dependent, and extraneous.

An **independent variable** is one that is actively *manipulated* (i.e., changed) by the experimenter.

Table 3.1 Comparison of Research Designs

Design Type	Features	Questions Addressed
Experimental	• Manipulation of independent variable(s) • Random assignment of participants to conditions • Comparison of groups on measured dependent variable(s)	• Does one variable affect another variable? • Can demonstrate causality.
Quasi-experimental	• Manipulation of independent variable(s) or distinguish between categories of people • No random assignment • Comparison of groups on measured variable(s)	• Do nonequivalent groups differ on a variable? • May suggest possible causality, especially when manipulation is used.
Correlational	• Measurement of variables without manipulation • Examine relationship between variables	• Is one variable correlated with another variable? • Demonstrates a (noncausal) relationship.
Descriptive	• Measurement of variables without manipulation • Summarize measurements of variables	• How is something described with respect to certain variable(s)? • Summarizes information.

A thermostat dial in a house is like an independent variable in that it can be manipulated to regulate how much heat the furnace generates. Experiments involve at least two *levels* (i.e., variations) of an independent variable, for example, setting the thermostat at either a warm setting or a cool setting. Participants who are introduced (i.e., exposed) to a level of an independent variable are said to be in a particular **experimental condition** (e.g., warm setting condition). Experiments often involve more than one independent variable. For example, you might be interested in the effect of warm and cool temperatures when the furnace fan is on or off. This study would be referred to as a "two by two" design. If you were reading about it in a journal article, it would be represented as a 2 (cool vs. warm) by 2 (fan on vs. fan off) design.

A **dependent variable** is one that is *measured* by the experimenter to determine if it changes in response to the manipulation of the independent variable. Thus, house temperature (dependent variable) would be measured to see if it changed with (i.e., "depended" on) adjustments of the thermostat dial (independent variable). An **extraneous variable** is one that the experimenter wishes to hold constant across levels of the independent variable so as to rule it out as a possible reason why the dependent variable changes in accordance with the manipulation of the independent variable. In the home heating example, extraneous variables might include other heat sources (e.g., open windows, lit fireplace) that could affect house temperature and make it difficult to determine the exact influence of the thermostat setting on house temperature.

Experimenters rule out the possible biasing effects of extraneous variables by using *two basic types of control*. One form of control is **random assignment of participants** to experimental conditions (i.e., levels of the independent variable). This involves using a procedure (e.g., coin toss, table of random numbers) that ensures that all participants have the *same* probability of being assigned to each of the conditions. Random assignment minimizes the likelihood that the participants in one condition differ on average from those in another condition on extraneous

variables (e.g., intelligence, personality factors) that might influence how they respond to the measurement of the dependent variable. The second form of control is **experimental control**, which involves ensuring that participants in the different experimental conditions are exposed to the *same* environmental stimuli (e.g., room, experimenter, instructions) with the exception of the independent variable. Thus, with good experimental control, there will be no uncontrolled environmental stimuli (e.g., an experimenter who is warm and friendly vs. one who is gruff and distant) that might account for differences in behavior across the experimental conditions.

Example of a true experiment: Effect of prosocial video games on helpful behavior. Gentile and his colleagues (2009) conducted research on the effects of prosocial video games on prosocial behavior (i.e., "behavior intended to help others"). Although considerable research has examined the behavioral effects of violent video games, little research has been conducted on the behavioral effects of prosocial video games. The social significance of this line of research is underscored by the fact that almost all U.S. teens play video games; one survey indicated 99% of boys and 94% of girls (Lenhart et al., 2008). An experiment was set up to test the hypothesis (prediction) that playing prosocial video games would increase helpful, prosocial behavior, whereas playing violent video games would increase unhelpful, aggressive behavior. The independent variable was the type of video game, which had three levels: prosocial game, violent game, and neutral game. There were two dependent variables: prosocial behavior and aggressive behavior.

Each type of video game was represented by two actual games as follows: prosocial game (*Super Mario Sunshine* and *Chibi-Robo!*), violent game (*Ty the Tasmanian Tiger 2* and *Crash Twinsanity*), and neutral game (*Pure Pinball* and *Super Monkey Ball Deluxe*). (During the experiment, depending on the condition [e.g., violent game], one of the two games was randomly assigned to the participant to play.) To ensure that the games selected reflected the intended characteristics of the game type (e.g., the two violent games were in fact violent in content), a pilot study was carried out in which 27 college students played the games and rated each game (using a 7-point scale) on a series of dimensions that pertained to how much their character helped/did nice things for, or harmed/shot or killed other characters. The ratings were combined to yield a helpful score and a harmful score. The mean scores are shown in Table 3.2 and confirm that the independent variable was effectively constructed in that the prosocial games and violent games were experienced (rated) by game players to contain relatively high levels of helpful content and harmful content, respectively, and the neutral games were experienced to contain low levels of both helpful and harmful content.

Participants were 161 American college students (66 men, 95 women) who were randomly assigned to one of the three experimental conditions (levels of the independent variable). When a participant arrived, the experimenter explained the main purpose of the study was to investigate how different types of video games influence performance on puzzles. The participant was told that he or she would have a partner, and after each had separately played a video game, they would assign each other 11 puzzles to try to solve. The experimenter explained further that part of the study was to see if motivation to win a reward affects performance. The experimenter added that on a strictly random basis the partner had been chosen to be eligible to win a gift certificate if the partner could later solve

10 of 11 puzzles, whereas the participant would not have such an opportunity.

After receiving the experimental instructions, the participant was asked to wait in a nearby cubicle. Soon afterward, the participant overheard the arrival of another person of the same sex who actually was an experimental confederate pretending to be the participant's partner. The participant heard the experimenter go through the same *cover story* (i.e., stated objectives of the study) and instructions and then ask the partner (confederate) to go to a second cubicle. At no point during the experiment did the participant see or interact with the confederate. Then, the participant played for 20 minutes either a prosocial, a neutral, or a violent video game, depending on the condition. Immediately afterward, the participant selected 11 puzzles for his or her partner to try to solve from a list of 30 puzzles that were classified by difficulty level: 10 easy, 10 neutral, and 10 hard. The experimenter explained that if the partner solved 10 of the 11 puzzles in 10 minutes, the partner would win a $10 gift certificate. Thus, the participant could help the partner by assigning easy puzzles or hurt the partner by assigning hard puzzles. The participant was asked to complete a questionnaire while waiting to receive 11 puzzles from the partner. Once the questionnaire was completed, the experimenter explained that the study was over and debriefed the participant.

There were two dependent variables: helpful behavior and hurtful behavior. Helpful behavior was operationally defined as the number of easy puzzles participants assigned to their partners,

Table 3.2   Pilot Test Mean Ratings of Content of Video Games Used in Experiment

	Prosocial games	Neutral games	Violent games
How often one does nice things to or for other characters	5.6	1.1	2.5
How often one shoots at or kills other characters	1.8	1.1	6.2

SOURCE: Gentile et al. (2009). Note: Ratings were based on a 7-point scale.

whereas hurtful behavior was operationally defined as the number of hard puzzles assigned. The results are presented in Figure 3.1. The heights of the three columns on the left side of the figure reflect the amount of helpful behavior (i.e., number of easy puzzles assigned to the partner) in the experimental conditions. Consistent with the experimental hypothesis, students who had played a prosocial video game were more helpful to their partners than were those who had played a violent video game (also a neutral game). Also in support of the hypothesis, the three columns on the right side of Figure 3.1 show that those who had played a violent game displayed more hurtful behavior than those who played a prosocial video game (also a neutral game). Gentile and his colleagues (2009) concluded that playing video games with prosocial content had caused the players to become more helpful afterward. They pointed out that this cause-and-effect relationship had not been demonstrated previously in the research literature on video games. The researchers also concluded that the finding of a cause-and-effect relationship between violent video games and aggressive behavior replicated that which had been well established in the research literature on video games (Anderson & Bushman, 2001).

Level of confidence that a cause-and-effect relationship has been demonstrated. It is important to note that Gentile and his coresearchers (2009) concluded that the above investigation allowed them to draw causal conclusions about the relationship between playing video games and players' subsequent social behavior. Recall that Table 3.1 indicates that experimental designs surpass the other basic designs in the ability to demonstrate cause-and-effect relationships. Although true experiments may allow us to draw causal conclusions, steps must be taken in conducting an experiment so that our confidence

Figure 3.1   Helpful and Hurtful Behavior as a Function of Type of Video Game

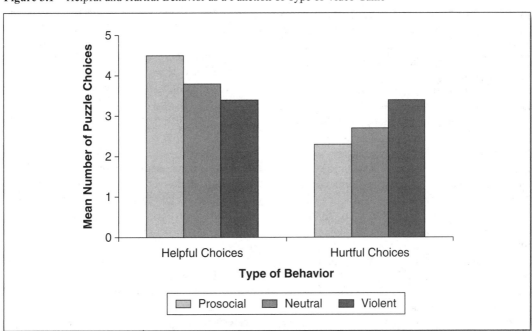

SOURCE: Gentile et al., 2009.

that a cause-and-effect relationship has been demonstrated remains high. The steps involve using extreme care in carrying out the two key types of control: random assignment and experimental control. Actually, when we can be confident that an experiment has demonstrated a causal relationship, the experiment is said to have a type of validity known as internal validity. **Internal validity** refers to the extent to which one can infer that an independent variable has influenced the dependent variable, that is, has caused the difference in behaviors between the participants in the different experimental conditions. Failure to achieve internal validity seriously undermines the value of an experiment because conclusions about causality cannot be made with confidence. Internal validity is directly related to how well the experimenter has nullified the influence of possible extraneous variables through experimental control and random assignment.

If we discern a possible failure to adequately control for an extraneous variable in the Gentile et al. (2009) study, this would constitute a **threat to internal validity**. Fortunately, the experiment seems to have been conducted with proper controls, and we can be confident that causal relationships were demonstrated. First, participants were randomly assigned to the three experimental conditions, thus reducing the likelihood that the differences between the conditions in helpfulness and harmfulness could be due to differences among the participants in factors (e.g., trait of empathy; personal history of playing violent video games) relevant to the dependent variables. Second, there is no evidence of a breakdown in experimental control in that participants in the three experimental conditions seem to have been exposed to the same environmental stimuli (e.g., same physical setting, same oral instructions) except for the type of video game they played. Had there been a difference between the experimental conditions in a potentially relevant experimental variable, confidence in the internal validity of the study would have been undermined, and we rightly would question the conclusions related to causality.

Quasi-Experiments

As we have seen, true experiments permit causal conclusions because they entail randomly assigning participants to the conditions and exerting experimental control, thereby eliminating a host of alternative explanations. However, many events worthy of study are outside of the researcher's control (e.g., people's exposure to a natural disaster). In addition, people are already members of particular groups or categories (e.g., gender, religion, socioeconomic level, right- or left-handedness), and so random assignment to those groups is either unethical or impossible. Finally, in many cases where the researcher may implement a treatment (i.e., independent variable), he or she might not be able to assign participants randomly to the different levels of that treatment because participant assignment is not under the researcher's control (e.g., using humorous examples in teaching one section of a course, but not a second section where students themselves choose their sections when registering). So, how do we address questions involving differential effects on the basis of *preassigned groups*? The researcher may employ any one of a collection of research designs known as quasi-experiments. **Quasi-experiments** allow comparisons to be made in observations across time and among groups with the assumption that these groups may not be equivalent to each other (for a thorough review of these designs, see Cook & Campbell, 1979).

Pretest–posttest design. Drunk drivers are a major concern in many communities. Drunk driving has been linked to serious accidents and traffic fatalities. As a response to this problem, police monitoring programs have been launched in many places in the United States and Canada, and penalties for drunk driving have become more severe. Do these strategies have any effect on the number of people who engage in this behavior? To address this question, we could employ a **pretest–posttest design** (Reichardt & Mark, 1998). Briefly, initial observations are taken (the pretest), the treatment (e.g., an intervention) is implemented, and observations are taken again (the posttest) so that a comparison can be made between what happened before the treatment and what happened after the treatment. This design is depicted as follows:

Observations Before → *Treatment* →
Observations After

Does implementing more severe penalties for drunk driving actually reduce the number of drunk driving incidents? Suppose that a researcher used a pretest–posttest design to evaluate the effect of legislative reforms on alcohol-related fatal and injury accident rates. By determining that rates before the reforms were higher than those after the reforms, the researcher concluded that the reforms had been effective.

Now the question is, based on the research design used in the preceding hypothetical study, can we conclude with confidence that harsher penalties reduced alcohol-related injuries and deaths? Not necessarily. A number of other extraneous factors may have led to the reduction, posing serious threats to the internal validity of the study. For instance, an event in the community may have coincided with the introduction of the new penalties. Perhaps there was a particularly serious traffic accident attributed to drunk driving, and in the aftermath many people may have become more reluctant to drive while intoxicated. In addition, a natural process of time could yield such an effect among drivers. That is, even before the introduction of severe penalties, the people in the community may have already started curbing their drinking and driving behavior. We would then see a decline in the number of drunk driving cases from the pretest to the posttest that had very little, if anything, to do with the new penalties (the treatment).

Interrupted time series design. To address the limitations of pretest–posttest designs, we may want to use a different quasi-experimental design, the **interrupted time series design**, which involves an *expanded* version of a pretest–posttest design. In this case, a number of

observations are taken over time before a treatment (i.e., the interruption) is administered, and then a number of observations are taken afterward. This design is represented as

$$O_1\ O_2\ O_3\ O_4\ \text{Treatment}\ O_5\ O_6\ O_7\ O_8$$

where O = observation. In this way, we can detect any patterns of behavior occurring before the treatment and whether the treatment affected this pattern. So, if drunk driving rates were already declining in the community months (or years) before the new penalties were introduced, we would still be able to determine whether the penalties had any impact on this pattern of decline. For instance, the penalties might speed up the rate of decline in drunk driving. As an added advantage, by including numerous posttest observations, we also can determine whether the treatment has a long-term effect on drinking and driving behavior. In fact, Rogers and Schoenig (1994) employed an interrupted time series design to study the impact of legislative reforms (including stiffer penalties) in California by tracking alcohol-related injury and death rates over several years. They concluded that the reforms did lead to lower rates, and their conclusion could be made with more confidence than would have been the case with a simple pretest–posttest design.

Nonequivalent control group designs. But, what if we simply do not have the time or opportunity to conduct an interrupted time series study? How can we increase the internal validity of a study? An improvement on the pretest–posttest design would be to use a control group. The addition of a control group would be an improvement because we would have a comparison group that was not exposed to the treatment. However, unlike with a true experiment, random assignment is not used; the control group usually is a preexisting group and is not assumed to be equivalent to the treatment group. This approach involves a **nonequivalent control group design** in which the treatment group is compared with a nonequivalent control group. In the drinking intervention study, the researcher could try to match the treatment community with another comparison community on things, such as economic level, population size, and number of drunk driving cases during the pretest period. Whereas both the treatment and control groups receive initial and follow-up observations, only the treatment group receives the unique element (e.g., intervention) that is thought to yield the desired effect. The nonequivalent control group design is shown as follows:

Treatment Group: Pretest → Intervention → Posttest

Control Group: Pretest → No Intervention → Posttest

If the treatment group, but not the control group, displays a decline from pretest to posttest (e.g., in drunk driving incidents), our confidence in internal validity (i.e., that the treatment worked) would be greater than it would with the simpler pretest–posttest design because with this design we have evidence that change did not occur without the treatment.

As you may have guessed, a nonequivalent control group also can be added as an improvement to an interrupted time series design (called a **control time series design**). This involves a series of the same observations for the control as for the treatment group, but without exposure to the treatment.

It is important to remember that although quasi-experiments resemble true experiments, they are more vulnerable to threats to internal validity than are true experiments. Consequently, the baggage of quasi-experimental studies is that they are much more limited than true experiments with respect to being able to make inferences about cause-and-effect relationships.

Correlational Studies

Our research questions often address the relationships among variables. Are home repair stresses more severe if the homeowners are

older? What if they have less money? To address these questions, we can use a correlational study. A **correlational study** involves measuring variables and determining the correlation between them. A **correlation coefficient** is a measure of the degree of association between different variables so that knowing one thing about a person may tell you something else (e.g., knowing a person's height may let you predict his or her shoe size).

Mathematically, correlation coefficients (denoted by r) range from -1 to $+1$. This boundary allows us to compare coefficients and understand both the strength and the direction of the relation between two variables. When two variables are positively correlated ($r > 0$), high values of one variable typically are found among high values of the other variable (and, of course, low values of one variable typically are found among low values of the other variable) so that the values of the variables move together in the same direction. Figure 3.2 shows a positive correlation in a scatterplot graph comparing years of university education and earned income. Each diamond signifies one person and shows both that person's years of university and his or her earned income. Alternatively, two variables can be negatively correlated ($r < 0$), where high values of one variable typically are found among low values of the other variable (and vice versa) so that the values of the variables move in opposite directions. Figure 3.2 shows a negative correlation between number of annual dental problems and income. Note that the sign in front of the correlation coefficient reveals the direction of the relation, whereas the absolute magnitude of the coefficient reveals its strength. That is, larger correlation values signify a greater connection between the variables. For example, whereas a correlation of $+.80$ represents a stronger relationship between two variables than does a correlation of $+.60$, it reflects the same magnitude of relationship as does a correlation of $-.80$.

We can also witness correlations in nature for which there is no observable relation between the variables. That is, high values of one variable may be observed with low values, high values, or moderate values of another variable. In short, we cannot predict the value of one variable just by knowing the value of the other variable. Figure 3.2 shows little or no correlation between the number of churches in a neighborhood and earned income. That is, there may be few, some, or many churches in an affluent neighborhood and likewise in a poor neighborhood.

Correlations are quite useful at uncovering relationships among variables. However, no matter how tempted we might be, we cannot derive causal explanations from a correlation because there could be any number of alternative explanations. Suppose that we found a positive correlation between violent crime and poverty so that the incidence of violent crime was higher in more impoverished neighborhoods. Based on this relationship, can we say that poverty causes violent crime? Not necessarily. It is possible

that the reverse holds true. Can you think of a reason why the incidence of violent crime might promote poverty in a neighborhood? And perhaps we are being overly simplistic to look at only two variables when, in fact, many social problems, such as violent crime and poverty, are far more complex. For instance, a *third* variable might account for the relationship between the two variables. In this case, the variable of crowding might represent such a third variable. With a possible adverse influence on interpersonal relationships and cognitive development, crowding could contribute to both crime and poverty. In other words, by considering a third variable, crowding, we have one possible explanation for why violent crime and poverty might be related, but not necessarily in a causal way. There could, of course, be many other possible third variables not yet considered, such as sanitation, health problems, and drug use. Also, beware

Figure 3.2   Scatterplot of Positive, Negative, and Null Correlations

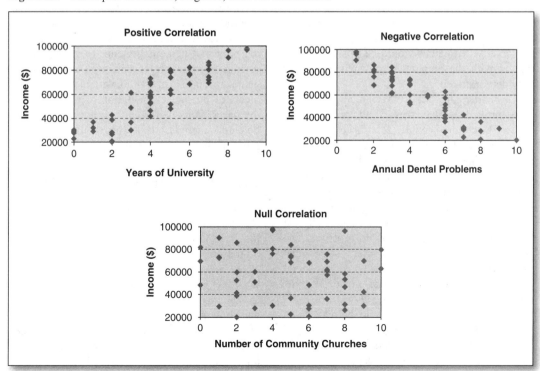

of words/terms such as *influences, leads to, results from,* and *affects* in reference to correlational evidence. This is causal language and misleadingly suggests that one variable causes another; it may do so, but with correlational evidence we just do not know. We should more accurately refer to a correlation as a "relationship," a "linkage," or an "association" between variables. Often correlational evidence of a relationship between variables can serve as a first step in a research process that is designed to determine if the relationship is a causal one (i.e., by the application of experimental and quasi-experimental designs).

To further understand the nature of correlational studies, we return to Gentile and colleagues' (2009) research on prosocial video games and prosocial behavior. As you recall, these authors reported an experiment that demonstrated a cause (i.e., prosocial video games) and effect (i.e., prosocial behavior) relationship. In their article, Gentile and his colleagues also reported a correlational study of the relationship between prosocial video games and prosocial behavior. In the study the researchers hypothesized that the amount of time that children spent playing prosocial video games would be positively correlated with the amount of prosocial behavior they demonstrated.

The participants were 727 Singaporean children enrolled in either the seventh or the eighth grade. The children completed a survey on which they indicated their three favorite video games, ratings of how often the main character in the games would help others, and estimates of the number of hours per week they played video games. Each participant was assigned a score on *prosocial game exposure* based on a formula that combined the three pieces of information. The survey also included multiple-item scales that measured the following aspects of prosocial behavior (first two scales) and prosocial traits (second two scales): *helping behavior* (e.g., "I would spend time and money to help those in need"), *cooperation and sharing* (e.g., "I feel happy when I share my things with others"), *empathy* (e.g., "When I see a student who is upset,

it really bothers me"), and *emotional awareness* (e.g., "I know when I am getting angry").

The results of the research demonstrated that the children's prosocial game exposure was positively correlated with both measures of their prosocial behavior and both measures of their prosocial traits. However, we draw your attention to how Gentile and his colleagues (2009) interpreted the findings of this correlational study. The researchers note that the findings are consistent with the hypothesis that prosocial video games lead to (i.e., cause) increases in prosocial behavior among game players. However, they are also quick to emphasize that such an inference of causality based solely on correlational evidence would be inappropriate and cite the very reasons we have mentioned in exploring the limitations of correlational designs, "because either variable might precede the other (or some uncontrolled third variable might be related to both)" (Gentile et al., 2009, p. 756). That is, because participants were asked to report about their prosocial game experience and prosocial behavior at the same point in time, if a causal relationship did exist it could just as well have been in the direction of prosocial behavior causing prosocial game experience (e.g., prosocially oriented people prefer and seek out prosocial games to play). Or, a third variable, such as the levels of prosocial orientation of the parents of the participants, could have influenced the participants' inclinations toward both engaging in prosocial behaviors and playing prosocial games.

Descriptive Studies

Let us suppose that you want to study home repair stress, but do not quite know where to begin. In fact, yours may be the very first study on the subject. You may not know enough about stress experienced in home repair to suggest what factors either promote or reduce that stress. In that case, an experiment might be premature, and so would a correlational study if you cannot even hypothesize what variables might be related to home repair stress. Therefore, your research aims might be more exploratory in that you wish simply to describe the phenomenon in an effort to identify important variables. In that case, you would conduct a descriptive study. In **descriptive research**, the objective is to observe variables and summarize the observations by using descriptive statistics, such as means, frequencies, and percentages. In your home repair study, you would merely record relevant behaviors, for example, by asking people (using interviews or a survey) about their home repair experiences, observing home repair activity, and measuring stress levels. Of course, with a purely descriptive approach, you would lack the ability to determine *why* the behavior occurs. Nevertheless, the scope of questions that descriptive designs can address is quite vast.

To consider an example of descriptive research, let us return to the issue of drunk driving. Monto, Newcomb, Rabow, and Hernandez (1992) surveyed university students with items that inquired about whether their friends had ever driven drunk, and, if so, whether the students had intervened. The results showed that among those who reported having been in cars with friends who were too drunk to drive, only 65% reported confiscating their friends' keys, driving them home, or calling a taxi.

RESEARCH SETTINGS

One of the first decisions that a researcher makes is whether to conduct the study in a laboratory or out in the "real world" (i.e., the field). Research conducted in a laboratory typically offers more definitive support for theories than does research conducted in the field. This is achieved by getting rid of "noisy," unwanted extraneous influences on the phenomenon. That is why biologists sterilize instruments before adding germs to a petri dish in case unwanted biotoxins get in the dish by mistake.

So, why do we not conduct all research in the laboratory? One answer is simply because laboratories are not typical environments for people, and so people might behave differently in laboratories than they normally do. The alternative,

then, is to conduct studies in the real world to enhance their ecological validity. **Ecological validity** signifies the extent to which the experiences and behaviors we observe in research are genuine in the sense of being similar to those that occur in everyday life. That is, we have more confidence that participants' behavior is not merely an artifact of being in a laboratory, or the result of knowing that they are being observed.

Studies conducted in the natural environment are called **field studies**. In field studies, we typically do not have as much control over unwanted influences as we have in laboratory studies. Let us consider some research on helping behavior. Recall that Chapter 1 refers to the bystander effect in which individuals are more likely (often much more likely) to intervene in an emergency if they witness it by themselves than in the presence of other people (Latané & Nida, 1981). The bystander effect was demonstrated in many laboratory experiments employing a wide variety of staged emergencies; participants were confronted with the decision to help or not in instances involving a potential fire, an injured woman, and a seizure victim. But, how often do people find themselves in a laboratory having to deal with a possible fire, an injured woman, or a seizure victim? What if an incident occurred in the real world? Would more people still help when they are alone than when they are with others? This is a question of another kind of validity, external validity, which is closely tied to ecological validity. **External validity** refers to the extent to which research findings can be generalized beyond a particular study to other people, times, settings, regions, and so forth.

Darley and Latané (1970) investigated the external validity of their laboratory finding on helping by conducting a field experiment in a liquor store. Two men (sufficiently muscle-bound so that one would not tangle with them) waited until there were either one or two customers remaining (independent variable) in the store (this was determined randomly). When the clerk went into the back room to check on price and inventory, the two men picked up a case of beer close to the exit. One loudly announced that "they won't miss this" as they fled the store with the beer. Supportive of the external validity of the laboratory evidence, the likelihood that a customer reported the theft to the store clerk (dependent variable) was higher when the customer was the only witness to the crime.

As this discussion implies, there is a trade-off between laboratory studies and field studies. As noted previously, laboratories allow us to better identify and eliminate the influence of extraneous variables. In experimental research, for instance, this means we can be more confident that the manipulation of the independent variable led to the observed differences in behavior; that is, we can be more confident about internal validity. But, increasing control and hence internal validity may invite problems associated with low ecological validity and low external validity. Therefore, increasing confidence in these two kinds of validity often requires leaving the laboratory setting in favor of a field setting. Of course, this move usually means giving up some control over extraneous variables, thus impairing internal validity.

In short, any good researcher will appreciate that both laboratory studies and field studies have their strengths and weaknesses; therefore, both are needed to get a complete picture of a social psychological phenomenon. As Crano and Brewer (2002) wrote,

> The interplay between laboratory and field research is critical to the development of effective applications in social sciences. Basic experimental research may isolate important causal processes, but convincing demonstrations that those processes operate in applied settings are essential before theory can be converted into practice. (p. 120)

Before concluding this section on research settings, the third major dimension of research, we emphasize that both laboratory research and field research can involve either kind of data collection strategy—self-report or observational—and also can be used with any of the four basic research designs: true experimental, quasi-experimental, correlational, or descriptive. Thus,

the three research dimensions are what may be called *completely balanced*, such that research entailing any combination of the three dimensions, under the appropriate circumstances, is not only feasible, but also potentially very informative (Hendricks, Marvel, & Barrington, 1990).

QUALITATIVE RESEARCH METHODS

The most frequently employed methods of gathering and analyzing data in applied social psychology are quantitative in that they involve the goal of *measuring* constructs (with frequency counts, averages, percentages, totals, etc.) that can serve as a basis for testing theories and relationships among variables. For instance, both the experimental study and the correlational study that Gentile and colleagues (2009) conducted were focused on quantitative data, including, for example, the *number* of easy mazes chosen for the partner (experiment), and scores reflecting the *amount* of prosocial game exposure (correlational study). Such quantitative methods are useful once a research topic is understood sufficiently well that objective data can be gathered and meaningfully interpreted. Sometimes, however, researchers are more interested in probing the interpretations people have of situations and the meanings they attach to them. In these circumstances, qualitative research methods are more appropriate. **Qualitative research methods** represent the "means for exploring and understanding the meaning individuals or groups ascribe to a social or human problem" (Creswell, 2009, p. 4). It is a form of inquiry that focuses more on textual rather than numerical analysis. Since the early 1990's the number of psychology studies that employ qualitative research methods has increased considerably (Carrera-Fernández, Guàrdia-Olmos, & Peró-Cebollero, 2014).

There is no definitive typology of qualitative research methods (Madill & Gough, 2008). In the interest of parsimony, we draw on the work of Creswell (2007) who enumerates five qualitative research methods, and then add one more. **Narrative research** focuses on gathering detailed stories about one individual or a small number of individuals. It involves collecting data on the stories through observation, interviews, letters, and other artifacts, and then *restorying*—reorganizing the stories into a coherent framework—taking context (e.g., personal, cultural, historical) into account. Narrative research would be used, for example, to produce someone's biography. Chapter 8 includes an example of a study that uses narrative research to analyze participants' descriptions of living with chronic pain (see the study by Zheng et al., 2013).

Phenomenological research involves gathering the stories of a group of people in order to ascertain what experiences they have in common when they live through some specific phenomenon (e.g., getting dumped, being bullied at work). The purpose of phenomenological research is to generate an integrated account of the essence of the experience by drawing on textural description (what was experienced), and structural description (the context in which it was experienced). In order to accomplish this, the researcher is expected to try to "bracket out" his or her own experiences, or at least make them explicit so as to minimize their interference with the analysis. Data gathering usually takes the form of multiple interviews, but can also involve observations and various artifacts. Chapter 5 includes an example of a study that uses phenomenology to investigate the experience of depression (see the study by Smith & Rhodes, 2015). Using phenomenology to study depression is useful because it allows researchers to understand what it means to feel depressed from a first person perspective.

The purpose of **grounded theory** is to move beyond people's accounts of their experiences in order to formulate a theory of people's actions, interactions, and social processes as they pertain to a particular topic. The fundamental idea is that the theory is not arbitrarily developed, but instead is "grounded" in the accounts of those who have experienced the phenomenon under investigation. In brief outline, the researcher conducts interviews with people who have experienced a phenomenon and tries to generate

categories that capture the fundamental aspects of the experience. Once categories are developed, the researcher conducts more interviews in an iterative fashion until no new information that helps to clarify the categories is forthcoming, and the theory is fully developed. If desired, the theory can then be tested using quantitative methods. An example of a grounded theory study is presented in Chapter 10. In this study, Gillespie, Chaboyer, Longbottom, and Wallace (2010) used grounded theory to create a model of successful communication in medical operating rooms.

Ethnographic research focuses on the description and interpretation of the shared values, beliefs, behaviors, and language of a specific intact cultural group (e.g., teachers at an elementary school, gang members). This qualitative research method typically involves participant observation, and interviews also are commonly used. The researcher attempts to uncover patterns in events, social relations, and other cultural themes in the lives of the group members in order to produce a cultural portrait of the group. Chapter 14 includes an example of ethnographic research (see the study by Duck, 2012).

Another qualitative research method is the **case study**. Case studies involve the investigation of a particular issue within a specific context, for example, examining why a patient failed to take her medicine as prescribed and became seriously ill. Case studies employ many different data gathering techniques, including interviews, the examination of archival records, observation, and anything else that can elucidate the issue. The ultimate product of a case analysis is a report outlining what has been learned about the issue. Chapter 5 includes a unique case study of one person's experience with the mental health system in the United States (see the study by Goddard, 2011).

A final qualitative method we will mention is **content analysis** (Patton, 1990). Content analysis involves describing, analyzing, and interpreting patterns or themes within data. In content analysis, researchers search the data (which often consists of transcripts of interviews or focus groups, but can also include text, such as newspaper articles or even photographs) for commonalities or themes. Content analysis is often the first step in a more in-depth analysis, such as phenomenological research, but it can also stand alone. An example of a study using content analysis is presented in Chapter 7. In this study, Oswald, Prorock, and Murphy (2014) interviewed participants about their motivations for playing video games.

As suggested in the discussion of grounded theory, one last point we should highlight is that qualitative research methods and quantitative research methods can be used in tandem. This **mixed-method approach** can produce studies that are stronger than what can be achieved by relying on one method exclusively (Creswell, 2009). Although it is argued that the rationale for such designs should be sound, mixed-methods studies may contribute more to researchers' understanding of a phenomenon than even the researchers themselves anticipate (Bryman, 2006). Many issues and problems dealt with by applied social psychologists are complex and multifaceted, and drawing on both qualitative and quantitative methods often enables researchers to achieve a more complete understanding of them.

RESEARCH ETHICS

As psychologists, we want our studies to resemble the real world as much as possible and to be as sound and well controlled as we can make them. Alternatively, we want to avoid causing our participants to endure unnecessary stress. But, these two goals often conflict. We are concerned about the health and welfare of individual participants. However, we also wish to make important discoveries surrounding human social behavior and believe that it would often be immoral *not* to carry out research (see Becker-Blease & Freyd, 2006). Indeed, some studies have caused widespread controversy because people have regarded them as unethical and claim that they should not have been conducted in the first place. Milgram's (1974) experiments on obedience (see Chapter 1), where "teachers" believed that they were giving increasingly

dangerous levels of shock to a "learner," are widely cited in this context. But, even more important is the question, does the pursuit of knowledge condone the means by which it is achieved? At what point do we say that someone is suffering unjustifiable personal harm or mental distress from taking part in a research study?

Suppose that you want to study how people look at each other during conversations. How do you set up your study to measure this looking behavior? One possibility is that you could place two people in a laboratory equipped with concealed, closed-circuit television. When two participants turn up, you escort them to the laboratory and have them converse for 15 minutes. But, suppose that one participant asks, "What's this all about?" Do you conceal the truth and merely satisfy their curiosity (e.g., "I'm studying how two people get acquainted"), or do you tell the full truth and face the consequences (e.g., "It's an investigation about looking behavior between two people in a conversation; a video camera is hidden behind the wall")? If the participants know what the study is about, imagine how their behavior might change as a result. Two people engaged in a conversation will likely be more conscious of how they look at each other, making it difficult for them to act as they normally do. Because they feel self-conscious, they might avoid looking at each other or might look at each other in atypical ways. This example illustrates why it may be necessary to *deceive* participants so that they are not sensitized to the behaviors being observed. That is why Milgram's (1974) participants were led to believe they were giving lethal shocks to a helpless learner and why in the bystander intervention research (Latané & Nida, 1981) participants were led to believe an actual emergency was occurring. Nevertheless, there are major concerns about using deception in research. These concerns include the fact that deception is morally wrong and violates individuals' right to autonomous behavior and that participants can suffer personal harm, for example, to their self-concepts (they can be so easily duped), and to their trust and respect for research and the discipline of psychology. In turn, the discipline suffers because of the damage to its reputation. Notwithstanding such concerns, participants deceived in research typically regard deception as both acceptable and of value (Christensen, 2004).

So, what solutions exist to the problem of deception? Fortunately, the American Psychological Association (2010) has a set of guidelines for researchers to follow with respect to deception and other ethical issues: Ethical Principles of Psychologists and Code of Conduct. Following are some of the main principles:

1. *Respect for the dignity of persons.* As the central ethical principle, psychologists' respect for human dignity underlies all of the others. For instance, note that we refer to those persons who take part in a study as "participants" rather than as "subjects" (which was used for most of the history of psychology) because it reflects the dignity and respect afforded to the people we study.

2. *Minimization of harm and reduction of risk.* Psychologists must take steps to avoid harming participants.

3. *Informed consent.* Researchers should describe the procedures to participants before they take part in a study, including any factors that might affect their willingness to participate, and they should document participants' agreements to take part in the study.

4. *Freedom to withdraw.* Participants must be informed that they are free to withdraw from a study at any point with no negative consequences for doing so.

5. *Privacy and confidentiality.* All information obtained from individual participants must be held in strict confidence. Confidentiality refers to restricting access to the data and to releasing results in such a way that each individual's privacy is not violated.

6. *Minimal use of deception.* Deception may be used only if the research has potential value (scientific, educational, or applied), and if there are no other viable means of investigating the research questions or hypotheses. Also, it can be used only if it does not put participants at undue risk, and if as soon after completion of the study as is feasible, participants are provided with a full description (i.e., debriefing) of the study's true purpose; an explanation of all procedures, including the need for deception, and an opportunity to withdraw their data.

All researchers are responsible for abiding by the ethical guidelines. Furthermore, many institutions require approval of research projects by an institutional review board (e.g., department or university ethics committee). Moreover, at the chapter authors' institutions (University of Windsor and University of Saskatchewan), we follow the APA guidelines as well as the Canadian Code of Ethics for Psychologists (Canadian Psychological Association, 2000), which articulates four principles that both scientists and practitioners are expected to apply in their decision making and conduct. Generally, in a decreasing order of weight in decision making, the principles are (a) respect for the dignity of persons, (b) responsible caring, (c) integrity in relationships, and (d) responsibility to society.

POSTSCRIPT

Having learned more about the tools that applied social psychologists use to address their research questions, we return to our initial question of how officials at the University of California, Santa Cruz, handled their water shortage problem. Recall that at first the officials implemented two strategies based on what they figured would work (i.e., their common sense), but the instituted measures failed to decrease how long students showered. So what strategy was effective? The university invited social scientists to take on the problem (Dickerson et al., 1992).

The researchers hypothesized that students (in this case females) would take shorter showers if they were (a) made more aware of their attitudes about conservation, or (b) asked to commit to the conservation effort. The researchers' reasoning stemmed from the theory of cognitive dissonance (reviewed in Chapter 2), which posits that we are motivated to reduce the discomfort we feel when our attitudes and behavior are inconsistent (e.g., "I favor conservation of resources, yet I use up a lot of water when I shower").

In this field experiment, before students entered the change room, they were approached by a female researcher who identified herself as a representative of a campus water conservation office (deception). She invited them to participate (following informed consent) in a study on water conservation. The students were randomly assigned to one of four conditions that were manipulated by the experimenter. Students in the first condition completed a brief survey about their water use, making them more *mindful* of their water conservation attitudes. Students in the second condition signed a petition as a *public commitment* to the water conservation effort. Students in a joint condition completed the survey and also signed the petition. Students in a fourth condition, the control condition, received no manipulation. A second female experimenter waited in the change room and measured each participant's shower time. Note that after the manipulation of the independent variable, the researcher did not tell the students that the study had not yet ended (another element of deception) because doing so might have cued them to monitor their shower durations. However, this procedure and the rest of the deception were explained to each participant in a debriefing after the participant emerged from the change room.

The results are presented in Figure 3.3. They show that the duration of shower time was lowest among students in the group whose members completed the survey and also signed the petition (so that they were both committed to and mindful of water conservation issues), averaging approximately 3.5 minutes of water use. Employment of either the survey or the petition alone was less effective (averaging less than 4 minutes of water use), but all three manipulations were more effective than the control group (averaging just over 5 minutes of water use). Overall, this study suggests that it is possible to change people's behavior with respect to conserving water (and possibly to change other conservation behaviors) based on sound theory, well-established research tools, and an explicit ethical code of conduct.

The experience of the University of California, Santa Cruz serves as an example of the limitations of relying on common sense and personal intuition when it comes to understanding human social behavior, and developing effective intervention strategies for changing behavior. The university officials' personal intuitions/judgments about how to get students to act in a more environmentally beneficial manner may have seemed quite reasonable and straightforward to them, but their ideas didn't work. The field of social psychology is replete with examples of the failure of commonsense and intuitive reasoning in predicting the outcomes of research and interventions.

In their treatise on social psychology's history, Ross, Lepper, and Ward (2010) identify the "nonobviousness" of experimental outcomes as one of three major themes of social psychological research. Consider that before conducting their research, Milgram (1974) did not at all expect that a majority of his participants would be willing to administer 440 volts of electricity to another person at the direction of a stranger in a lab coat, and Asch (1955) did not at all expect that as many as 70% of his participants would go along with the blatantly incorrect judgments of others. Below are descriptions of two sets of research findings. The findings may surprise you and may not accord with what you would have predicted. They serve to reinforce the message that until you do research (well), you just cannot be certain about the outcome. The findings also have important applied implications.

1. Simply spending a few minutes imagining a positive and comfortable interaction with an unknown member of an out-group will very likely lead an individual to have a more positive attitude toward and less stereotypical view of members of the out-group as well as lower anxiety about the prospect of future interaction with members of the out-group. Found in several studies (e.g., Crisp & Turner, 2009).

Figure 3.3   Shower Duration (in Seconds) as a Function of the Experimental Manipulation

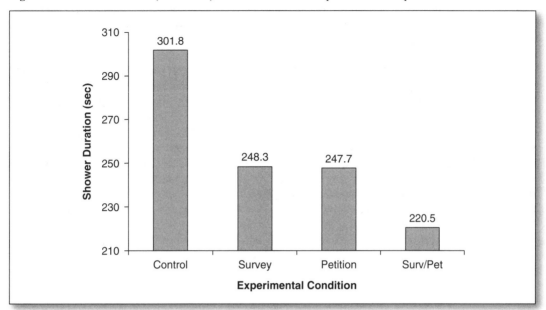

SOURCE: Dickerson et al. (1992).

NOTE: sec = seconds; Surv/pet = Survey and petition.

2. The perception of red in an achievement situation (e.g., seeing a red triangle on the cover page of an IQ test) will very likely cause an individual to perform significantly more poorly (e.g., on an IQ test). Found in several studies (e.g., Maier, Elliot, & Lichtenfeld, 2008).

SUMMARY

Decisions concerning how to conduct research in applied social psychology are made on the basis of three research dimensions: method of data collection, research design, and research setting. Self-report methods represent one category of data collection techniques (e.g., surveys, interviews, attitude scales). Surveys are used to illustrate self-report methods; they consist of a series of questions about a person's attitudes, views, or behaviors regarding one or more topics or issues. Internet surveys are efficient in terms

of time and cost, but have their disadvantages (e.g., low response rates). The other main data collection category is observational techniques, which include, for example, taking physiological, audio, visual, and behavioral measures. Also, researchers can engage in either participant observation or nonparticipant observation in which, respectively, the researcher is an active participant in the situation, or is nonactive and separated from the situation.

One research design entails true experiments, which involve the manipulation of one or more variables (independent variables) so as to observe possible changes in the responses (dependent variable) of participants. Random assignment of participants to conditions and experimental control of extraneous variables allows researchers to infer internal validity, that is, that there is a causal relationship between independent and dependent variables. A quasi-experimental design is an experimental design in which not all extraneous variables are successfully controlled. The internal validity of the simple pretest–posttest design is seriously threatened by the lack of control of external factors. This limitation is addressed by interrupted time series designs and nonequivalent control group designs. Correlational research designs examine the relationship between variables; the relationship is measured by a correlation coefficient, which can vary in both direction and strength. Researchers must be cautious not to draw causal conclusions from correlational evidence because variables can be related yet not in a causal manner. Descriptive designs involve measuring the incidence and magnitude at which specified variables occur. Finally, qualitative methods provide an in-depth, nonnumerical analysis of the themes underlying many social issues.

In terms of the research setting, researchers can conduct a study in a laboratory, which typically allows for more control of extraneous variables (and in the case of experiments, this increases internal validity), or in the field, which typically provides less control, but more external validity (i.e., the generalizability of findings to other settings and groups of participants).

Although understanding and addressing social psychological issues and problems are important, the well-being of research participants is paramount. Researchers in psychology guide their research on the basis of the APA code of ethics. Some of the major guidelines include respect for the dignity of participants; minimization of risk and harm; use of informed consent; freedom to withdraw without penalty; assurance of confidentiality; and minimization of deception.

4

INTERVENTION AND EVALUATION

ADAM LODZINSKI

MICHIKO S. MOTOMURA

FRANK W. SCHNEIDER

CHAPTER OUTLINE

Contributing to the development of intervention strategies that lead to improvements in the lives of people is the defining feature of the field of applied social psychology, and in our view is the most exciting thing about being an applied social psychologist. Imagine the great sense of accomplishment and gratification that Sherif (1966b) and his colleagues must have experienced when they, in fact, did reduce conflict between rival groups of boys by using a strategy that involved having the groups work together toward common goals. Imagine how rewarding it is for those who are involved in designing community-based interventions that influence people to adopt healthier lifestyles (e.g., engaging in regular exercise, employing safe-sex practices), thereby reducing the incidence of serious health problems (e.g., heart disease, sexually transmitted diseases). Throughout the remainder of this book, you will be provided with many examples of successful interventions that are grounded in social psychological theory and research. Likewise in this chapter, several social psychologically based interventions are reviewed. In particular, the chapter focuses on an intervention strategy that has been implemented on many college campuses to deal with the high rates of alcohol abuse.

Given that interventions are so central to the field of applied social psychology, it is important for you, as a student of the field, to have a good understanding of their nature. The major goal of this chapter is to consider how applied social psychologists draw on their understanding of theory, methods, and research evidence in the design and evaluation of interventions. The chapter takes you through the steps involved in developing and evaluating interventions, using examples of actual interventions to illustrate the steps. It also recognizes social psychology's role in influencing social policy, which is another very important way of applying social psychology and is closely related to the application of the field through the implementation of interventions. Near the end, the chapter considers some of the practical and ethical issues that are confronted by people who practice applied social psychology.

DESIGN OF INTERVENTIONS

Nature of Interventions

An **intervention** may be defined as a strategy (or procedure) that is intended to influence the behavior of people for the purpose of improving their functioning with respect to some social or practical problem. Some interventions might not target people's behavior directly; for example, those that are designed to increase knowledge or awareness (e.g., of the environmental benefits of recycling), or are designed to change attitudes (e.g., becoming more supportive of recycling). However, the ultimate goal of most interventions is behavior change (e.g., increased recycling). As pointed out in Chapter 1, interventions can be conducted at different levels of analysis (e.g., individual, group, organization, community). Although interventions can be directed at different levels, it can be argued that ultimately they are directed toward individuals in that for changes to occur, whether in a group or in an organization, the individual members must change in some way.

Moreover, to understand the focus of this chapter, it is helpful to distinguish between two broad types of intervention: personal and programmatic. **Personal interventions** are those that people carry out in the course of their daily lives, that is, when they use their knowledge of social psychology to improve their own circumstances or those of people around them. Examples of personal interventions were provided in Chapter 1 where "personal uses" of social psychology were considered (e.g., waitpersons improving their tips), and will be discussed again in Part 3 of this book. Clearly, all of us can benefit from applying social psychology in our lives. However, personal interventions are not the focus of this chapter, which deals with programmatic interventions.

Programmatic interventions are commonly referred to simply as programs. In this chapter (and in the book as a whole), the terms *intervention* and *program* are used interchangeably. Royse, Thyer, Padgett, and Logan (2006) defined a **program** as "an organized collection of activities designed to reach certain objectives" (p. 5). In the context of applied social psychology, the activities that comprise a program are directed toward addressing a social or practical problem with the objective of preventing, reducing, or eliminating its negative consequences. In some instances, interventions may be directed at reinforcing and strengthening a positive situation (e.g., improving the productivity of an already effective work group). Except for the personal interventions that have been mentioned, all of the interventions discussed so far in this book fall under the category of programmatic interventions. For example, one program involved the procedures and activities that Hodges, Klaaren, and Wheatley (2000) employed in getting female college students to engage in comfortable safe-sex discussions, and another example entailed the set of procedures and activities that Sherif (1966b) used to get groups of boys to work cooperatively toward superordinate goals.

We also can identify some interventions as trial interventions. **Trial interventions** are those that are implemented to determine whether the interventions, as designed, in fact have the intended positive consequences. These are also known as *program efficacy studies* (Crano & Brewer, 2002). Trial interventions typically are associated with programmatic interventions, although theoretically personal interventions can be "tried out" as well. There are two basic kinds of trial interventions. One is when researchers design a study to test out a possible intervention strategy. The interventions of Sherif (1966b), and Hodges and colleagues (2000) represent this type of trial intervention. The second kind of trial intervention is when an organization conducts a pilot program to determine its effectiveness before implementing it on a more permanent basis or before implementing it on a wider scale. For example, as some police departments in North America have attempted to transition to community policing, which is a new model of

policing, they frequently test the efficacy of the model by trying out a community policing unit in one or two neighborhoods. Many interventions considered in this book are trial interventions, particularly those that involve a research test of an intervention design. We now turn to a consideration of the main tasks in intervention design and delivery.

Key Tasks in Intervention Design and Delivery

The process of intervention design and implementation follows four overarching steps that reflect the general problem-solving approach adopted by many areas of applied psychology and are applicable whether the recipient of the intervention is one individual or many individuals. These steps are (a) identifying a problem, (b) arriving at a solution, (c) setting goals and designing the intervention, and (d) implementing the intervention (Oskamp & Schultz, 1997).

Step 1: Identifying a problem. Programs are initiated to address social problems or practical problems. The first step in program design is to identify the existence and severity of a problem. A problem usually is identified and defined by stakeholders. **Stakeholders** are individuals or groups who have a vested interest in the possible development of a program in that they may be affected by it in some way. Stakeholders include not only the potential recipients of the program, but also individuals, such as program funders, administrators of the organizations responsible for delivering the program, program managers, and frontline staff members (i.e., the employees who actually carry out the program activities). As you might imagine, difficulties arise when different stakeholders disagree about whether a problem exists, how serious a problem is, or which problems should be given highest priority.

Needs assessment is the term that is commonly used to refer to the process of establishing whether or not there is a need or problem (these words are used interchangeably) to sufficiently warrant the development of a program. A needs assessment may be *informal* in nature; for example, when a coach determines that a team-building exercise is necessary based on her or his own experience with their team, or when a manager decides that his or her department needs a workshop on sexual harassment after overhearing some of the staff members making sexually inappropriate remarks. In general, we have more confidence in the conclusions of a *formal* needs assessment that relies on systematic research procedures for collecting data that are relevant to problem severity and prevalence. Problems may be investigated using a variety of qualitative and/or quantitative procedures (see Chapter 3); for instance, by means of interviews with representatives of various stakeholder groups, or administering questionnaires to them. Also, a formal needs assessment gauges the availability of existing programs or services as well as possible barriers to or gaps in service.

Step 2: Arriving at a solution. Ascertaining the existence of a problem or need is one thing; determining how best to address it is quite another. To arrive at a solution, it is important to identify the factors responsible for causing the problem. When identifying causal factors, one should distinguish between **precipitating factors** (i.e., those that triggered the problem), and **perpetuating factors** (i.e., those that sustain the problem and keep it from being solved). Making the distinction between precipitating factors and perpetuating factors is critical to the design of an intervention because the factors or events that lead to a problem are not always directly involved in its continuation. For instance, factory employees may be laid off for one reason (the precipitating factor may be a slowdown in the economy), but unable to secure new employment for another reason (the perpetuating factor may be a lack of skills that are demanded by alternative jobs). In this case, one must identify the perpetuating cause—lack of important skills—as the factor to be targeted so as to solve the problem (inability to find new employment).

Once causal factors have been identified, the next step is to find out (often through a literature review) whether interventions that have effectively addressed the same needs already exist. Such interventions can be used to guide the development of a solution to the current problem. If previous interventions cannot be located, then a solution must be developed independently. When possible, solutions should be based on relevant social psychological theory and research evidence as well as theory and evidence from any other field that may contribute to a solution. Recall that Chapter 3 ended by noting that Ross, Lepper, and Ward (2010) identified the "nonobviousness" of experimental outcomes as an important theme of social psychology research. Ross and colleagues also extended this observation to include the nonobviousness of the outcomes of intervention strategies. Some 19 years earlier, Ross and his colleague Nisbett (1991) cautioned against the development of interventions based on conventional lay understanding and intuition because "lay predictions are often both wrong and too confidently made" (p. 18). They added, "The hard won lessons of social psychology . . . constitute a repertoire of strategies with which to supplement the guidance of common sense in constructing interventions" (p. 245).

Consider the following example of an effective smoking prevention intervention that was based on McGuire's (1964) research on the "inoculation effect." McGuire discovered that just as it is possible to be immunized against a disease, such as polio, by being inoculated with a vaccine containing a weak strain of the virus, so too is it possible for people to be immunized against attacks on their beliefs. In a series of laboratory experiments, he demonstrated that if participants are immunized by first receiving a small challenge to their beliefs and have an opportunity to prepare a rebuttal to this weak attack, they are better able to resist a subsequent more powerful attack. In a creative leap from research to application, McAlister, Perry, and Maccoby (1980) wondered whether it is possible to apply the inoculation effect to an actual social problem, namely, helping seventh-grade students resist inducements to smoke. Drawing on

McGuire's (1964) inoculation theory and his innovative methodology, McAlister and colleagues (1980) developed a program involving role-playing that was successful in getting children to resist peer pressure to smoke.

For clarity of conceptualization and communication, solutions to problems should be expressed as intervention hypotheses (Lodzinski, 2003). **Intervention hypotheses** are "if–then" statements that summarize the intervention and the expected outcomes. In the case of McAlister and colleagues' (1980) smoking prevention program, the intervention hypothesis could be stated as follows: "If seventh-grade students are provided the opportunity to rehearse rebuttals to inducements to smoke in realistic role-playing, peer pressure scenarios, then in their daily lives they will be more likely to resist pressures to smoke and less likely to begin smoking."

Step 3: Setting goals and designing the intervention. Once the need and the proposed solution have been determined, it is necessary to develop the **program activities**, which refer to the specific components and procedures of the program. The best place to begin this process is to set the goals and objectives of the intervention. Knowledge of goals and objectives serves to guide the selection of program activities. **Goals** refer to the ultimate or long-term outcomes that one hopes to accomplish through an intervention. For example, a goal for a substance abuse program might be to have the clients abstain from alcohol and other drugs. Once goals have been established, it is important to define the program objectives. **Objectives** refer to short-term outcomes (e.g., during or immediately after an intervention) and intermediate-term changes (e.g., one or two months later) that occur as a result of the intervention and are required for (i.e., support) the attainment of the program goals. In other words, goals refer to the ends, whereas objectives refer to the means or steps by which the ends are achieved. For instance, if the goal is for clients with substance abuse problems to remain abstinent, one objective might be for them to understand why they

use drugs in the first place. The importance of setting appropriate goals and objectives cannot be overstated. All too often program outcomes are vague or impossible to measure. To combat this tendency, stakeholders may use the acronym SMART to develop outcomes that have five criteria: Specific, Measureable, Achievable, Relevant, and Timebound. This not only helps to make the outcomes clear and precise, but also supports an evaluation framework for the intervention which is integral to its success, as we will see in the next section.

Once the goals and objectives have been set, the next step in intervention design is to determine the program activities. When choosing activities, one of the most important questions is the following: What objective (and ultimate goal) will the proposed activity help to meet? For example, for clients to learn the reasons for their drug use (objective), they might need to have individual counseling sessions with a certified counselor (activity). Figure 4.1 illustrates additional examples of intervention activities, objectives, and goals.

The process of specifying the various components of a program—goals, objectives, and activities—requires a sound rationale, often referred to as a program logic model. A **program logic model** is an explanation or a blueprint of how the program activities lead to the attainment of the program objectives, and in turn, how the objectives logically and operationally contribute to the eventual achievement of the program goal(s) (Wholey, 1983). Logic models vary in complexity and detail, but all of them stress a "cause and effect" flow as expressed in the intervention hypothesis. Program logic is the glue that holds the activities, objectives, and goals together.

Fundamental to a program logic model is its theoretical basis (Unrau, Gabor, & Grinnell, 2001). That is, a logic model should be based on a theoretical rationale that explains the causal connections among its various components; for example, why rehearsing rebuttals will induce resistance to peer pressure to smoke. From the point of view of intervention design,

Figure 4.1 Examples of Activities, Objectives, and Goals for Three Programs

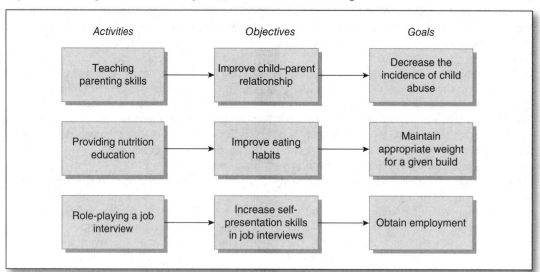

this means that one should be able to point to any component of the intervention and indicate not only what its contribution is, but also why the effect should occur. The use of a program logic model ensures a careful theoretically and empirically based articulation of the program and increases the likelihood of its success. This, of course, helps to ensure that program resources are used as effectively as possible. Unfortunately, in applied settings, too often it is the case that programs are designed without formal articulation of logic models. Some evaluators have begun to employ the notion of a **theory of change model** instead of program logic to underscore the need to make explicit an intervention's underlying theory, including the steps involved along the path to desired change; the assumptions being made; and the preconditions that may enable (or inhibit) the desired change (Mackinnon, Amott, & McGarvey, 2006; Organizational Research Services, 2004).

Step 4: Implementing the intervention. As the term implies, **implementation** refers to the actual process of enacting the intervention activities; that is, of delivering them to the recipients of the intervention. A point worth noting is that there are many practical details that might need to be in place to implement programs properly. Depending on the complexity of an intervention, which is determined by factors like its size and structure, practical details might include securing an appropriate facility, hiring staff members, ensuring adequate training, and developing things, such as operating budgets, management structures, job descriptions, performance appraisal methods, promotional strategies, and cross-agency referral protocols. Moreover, an intervention always should be designed and implemented in such a way that its degree of effectiveness can be evaluated.

EVALUATION OF INTERVENTIONS

As defined in the Encyclopedia of Evaluation, **evaluation** is an applied inquiry process for collecting and synthesizing evidence that culminates in conclusions about the state of affairs, value, merit, worth, significance, or quality of a program, person, policy, proposal, or plan. Conclusions made in evaluations encompass both an empirical aspect (that something is the case) and a normative aspect (judgement about the value of something). It is the value feature that distinguishes evaluation from other types of inquiry, such as basic research, clinical epidemiology, investigative journalism, or public polling (Fournier, 2005, p. 140). In this era of increasing financial constraints and fiscal responsibility, evaluation is essential to ensuring the biggest bang for your buck. All too often interventions are conceived based on paradigms or beliefs that do not hold up under scientific scrutiny. No matter how carefully conceived and convincing a program hypothesis, it is only a proposition until the program is actually designed, implemented, and *evaluated*. Although this chapter considers evaluation in a separate section, be assured that evaluation is an integral part of the process of intervention design and implementation and may be considered a fifth step in the process. In fact, a good intervention design includes a plan for program evaluation (Lodzinski, 1995). Testimony to the importance of evaluating interventions is the existence of a separate field in the social sciences called evaluation research (or program evaluation). It is worth noting that program evaluation recently was cited in the *Monitor on Psychology* as "one particularly hot growth area for psychologists" (DeAngelis, 2008). In fact one author of this chapter (Motomura) defines evaluation research as her main vocational area, and a second author (Lodzinski) regards program design and evaluation as being at the core of his consulting practice; it is noteworthy that both individuals received their graduate degrees in applied social psychology.

Reasons for Evaluating Interventions

The effectiveness of *all* programmatic interventions should be subjected to evaluation. (Actually, this also applies to personal interventions in the case of individuals who want to avoid repeating the same mistakes in their lives.) There are several reasons why programmatic interventions should be evaluated (Lodzinski, 1995).

A major one is *scientific* and stems from the tradition of Lewin (Cartwright, 1951), who viewed all applied work as being guided by theory and as contributing to the development of theory. Specifically, a major reason for evaluation research is to test the theoretical assumptions underlying the intervention (i.e., the foundation of the program logic model or theory of change). If the intervention is implemented as designed, its degree of effectiveness informs those involved in its design of the validity of the theoretical rationale on which the intervention is based. This evaluative feedback is important with respect to attempts to develop theories that have utility in the world of application.

Another important reason for evaluating interventions is an *ethical* one. Royse and colleagues (2006) listed 14 major social problems (e.g., substance abuse, poverty, unemployment, domestic violence, adolescent pregnancy, illiteracy), and suggested that for each problem in the United States, there are hundreds—often thousands—of programs. The existence of that many programs translates into millions of program recipients whose lives are affected by program activities in various ways (e.g., physically, socially, educationally, economically) and to varying degrees. Whereas the goals of such programs are to improve the functioning of their recipients in various ways, the only appropriate means of ensuring that they do so is through evaluation. Those responsible for the implementation of programs have an ethical responsibility to determine whether their recipients are receiving the intended benefits, *and* whether they are experiencing any unintended undesirable consequences. The ethical responsibility also extends to a readiness to modify or even discontinue ineffective programs, and to improve on programs that have been evaluated as effective. Later in this chapter, further ethical issues in the design and evaluation interventions are considered.

The need for *financial accountability* is another reason for program evaluation. Imagine the billions of dollars needed to fund the many thousands of social programs that exist. Most of us likely would say that the money is worth it—if the programs in fact do improve people's lives as intended. On the other hand, most of us would be pretty put off if all those tax dollars (our money) were being wasted on ineffective programs. Royse and colleagues (2006) pointed to a government-sponsored $2 billion antidrug media campaign that was initiated when there were "no well-controlled studies showing that media campaigns are effective in changing behavior" (p. 15). This astonishing example of fiscal irresponsibility very clearly highlights the need for rigorous research on the effectiveness of programmatic interventions. For the sake of the funders of programs, there should be accountability in the sense of convincing demonstrations of program effectiveness. Moreover, even if a program is found to be effective in accomplishing its goals, the program might be too costly. That is, an effective program might cost too much given the available resources that might instead be used for other purposes, including the implementation of other beneficial, yet less expensive, programs.

Finally, *program development* may be viewed as the overriding reason for evaluation research. Programs are evaluated as part of the process of developing the most effective programs possible. In fact, the three reasons for evaluation mentioned previously dovetail into program development by seeking to ensure that programs (a) are based on sound empirically tested theoretical assumptions, (b) are conducted with appropriate ethical safeguards, and (c) have a satisfactory ratio of benefits to costs.

Ineffective Interventions

As suggested, programs must be subjected to evaluation research because their success—even that of the most carefully rationalized and designed ones—cannot be assumed. If we can generalize from the literature on program evaluation, the intervention world is replete with ineffective programs. For example, one systematic review of "Scared Straight" programs that involved organized visits to prison facilities by juvenile delinquents or children at risk of becoming delinquent found that not only do the programs not deter criminal behavior, but they actually lead to an increase in offending behavior (Petrosino, Turpin-Petrosino, & Buehler, 2002).

Now we will discuss in some detail an early dramatic example of a failed intervention, the Cambridge–Somerville project (described in Ross & Nisbett, 1991). What is especially noteworthy about the intervention, as observed by Ross and Nisbett (1991), is the fact that although the program was the "kind of multifaceted intervention that many social scientists would love to see implemented today" (p. 214), it turned out to be a dismal failure. A major goal of the intervention was prevention; that is, to reduce the likelihood of young boys from lower-class backgrounds in a Boston suburb—some of whom were identified as delinquency prone—from going down a criminal path. The program was a model of intervention design, with approximately 250 boys randomly assigned to the program, and another 250 or so randomly assigned to a control group. The boys were involved in the program for five years and received a wide variety of supports (i.e., program activities). For instance, all boys received twice monthly visits to their homes from caseworkers, and substantial percentages received academic tutoring, psychiatric attention, medical attention, and opportunities for involvement with the Boy Scouts and summer camps.

The long-term effects of the program were evaluated in a series of studies for (remarkably) 40 years following the intervention. Two kinds of evaluative data sharply contradicted each other. On the one hand, the subjective impressions of caseworkers and many program participants presented a positive picture of the benefits of the program. On the other hand, the more reliable statistical evidence indicated that the program participants, as compared with the control group, had no fewer juvenile and adult offenses and did not fare better on a number of other indicators, such as health, mortality, and life satisfaction.

Ross and Nisbett (1991) offered several plausible explanations for the failure of the Cambridge–Somerville project, including the fact that the situational factors (i.e., program activities) that were manipulated as the intervention, although impressive in terms of expenditure of time and human resources, were "trivial" compared with the environmental forces that the boys faced on an ongoing basis. They also mentioned the possibility that being identified with the program might have had a stigmatizing effect on the boys, such that they and others would have viewed them as troubled and delinquency prone, with such a view becoming a self-fulfilling prophecy (see Chapter 9). This explanation raises the unfortunate possibility that the intervention actually may have had a harmful effect on the boys. In fact, on several indicators (e.g., multiple offenses, alcoholism, achievement of professional status), the program participants were less well-off than the control participants during adulthood. Another possible reason why the program may have worked to the detriment of the participants is that because the boys could be seen as already receiving help from the program, the usual community sources of help (e.g., clergy, teachers, social service agencies) might have been less likely to provide their assistance. The possibility of unanticipated negative consequences must always be recognized and assessed in the evaluation of a program.

Our main purpose here is not so much to account for the failure of the Cambridge–Somerville project as to underscore that an apparently well-designed and intuitively compelling intervention can fail. If the program evaluation had not been properly designed (i.e., if it had relied solely on the subjective testimonies of key stakeholders), its failure would not have been detected; in fact, it may very likely have been deemed a success and regarded as an exemplary model of prevention. As suggested by the possible explanations for the failure of the Cambridge–Somerville project, there is a wide variety of factors that can contribute to the failure of an intervention to achieve its goal(s).

Here are four more possible reasons for program failure. One is that the theoretical rationale—the program logic model—may be inadequate and require revision. A second is that

the program might not be implemented as designed (see next section on process evaluation) despite a sound theoretical and research basis.

A third cause of program failure can be the operation of reactance in program recipients (Rothman, Haddock, & Schwarz, 2001). **Reactance** refers to the idea that when a source of influence threatens people's sense of freedom to think or behave as they see fit, people will act against the influence to protect their freedom (much like Romeo and Juliet did when their families opposed their love for each other) (Brehm & Brehm, 1981). Thus, even though an intervention is intended to help people, if the people feel pressure to change, they might resist the social influence attempt that the program represents. Therefore for instance, designers of interventions often must take steps to minimize the undermining effects of reactance by avoiding the use of overly strong (i.e., reactance-triggering) persuasive communications, and by helping (as much as possible) to sustain in individuals a sense of choice or control about being exposed to program activities. For instance, one study showed that grade school and high school students who viewed an antismoking video evaluated the message and its source more favorably if the message was implicit as opposed to explicit; that is, if it minimized its persuasive intent and did not impinge on the viewer's freedom of behavior, for example by strongly advising against smoking (Grandpre, Alvaro, Burgoon, Miller, & Hall, 2003). The potential undermining role of reactance speaks to the need for program designers to understand and anticipate how program recipients will define the program's objectives, goals, and activities (Ross et al., 2010).

A fourth reason for program failure may stem from an incompatibility between program design and cultural context. An example of major magnitude occurred during the 1990s when the United Nations came to recognize, after a number of failure experiences, that HIV/AIDS prevention programs that are effective in some countries or regions are less effective or completely ineffective in other countries or regions.

For example, school-based HIV/AIDS prevention programs are regarded as perhaps the most effective way in which to reduce rates of HIV/AIDS (Gallant & Maticka-Tyndale, 2004). However, their potential in some developing countries is curbed enormously by the fact that the majority of children do not attend school and are illiterate, thus would be unable to benefit from information-based program activities in the first place. Also, the goal of condom use, which is a fundamental component of HIV/AIDS prevention programs, is opposed by very powerful cultural forces in many countries where having children is an important symbol of sexual and economic potency as well as a tremendous source of pride and status. The paramount importance of addressing culture in the design of intervention efforts was formalized in UN policy during the late 1990s (e.g., Kondowe & Mulera, 1999).

Types of Evaluation

In assessing the effectiveness of an intervention, there are two main types of program evaluation: process and outcome (Posavac & Carey, 2007). **Process evaluation** (also known as *formative evaluation*) is undertaken to determine whether the program has reached its target audience (as identified in the intervention hypothesis), and whether the program *activities* (as outlined in the program's logic model) have been implemented in the prescribed manner. Basically, one wants to answer the following question: Is the program being implemented in the way in which it was planned? For instance, if an alcohol addiction program's activities include giving addicted people five individual counseling sessions and five group counseling sessions, a process evaluation would ensure that the clients were in fact addicted to alcohol and did indeed receive the prescribed number and types of counseling sessions.

Outcome evaluations typically are conducted after process evaluations. An **outcome evaluation** (also known as *summative evaluation*) assesses how well a program meets its objectives (i.e., short-term outcomes as described in the program logic model), and in a more comprehensive evaluation, it also assesses how well the program is achieving its goals (i.e., long-term outcomes, also part of the logic model). Essentially, the overriding purpose of an outcome evaluation is to determine whether the hypothesized improvement in functioning occurs among the recipients of the program as a result of exposure to its activities. For example, an outcome evaluation of an alcohol treatment program might assess whether participants publicly (e.g., among all other participants) express strong commitment to long-term abstinence by the end of the program. Evaluation of the goal of actual long-term abstinence would occur after a specified period of time (e.g., one year) following completion of the program.

As suggested previously, program evaluation is an integral part of program development. The results of a program evaluation often will lead one to revisit and revise the program logic model, and accordingly make changes in the goals, objectives, and activities. For instance, the logic model for an alcohol addiction program might have to be amended to include the important role of family support, thereby necessitating the inclusion of new program activities (e.g., family counseling) and objectives that emphasize family involvement.

Evaluators also have recognized the important role evaluation can play in supporting the process of innovation and learning within an organization. This type of evaluation has been coined **developmental evaluation** (Patton, 1994) and can be used when interventions are in a stage of early innovation or in situations of high complexity, like poverty or homelessness, where the causes and solutions to the problem are unclear and intervention stakeholders are not on the same page. A developmental evaluation typically involves testing or experimenting with new approaches to a problem—perhaps involving multiple trial interventions—with the intention of developing an innovative solution that can be subjected to process and outcome evaluation approaches (Gamble, 2008; Patton, 2011).

Importance of Research Design in Evaluating Interventions

Chapter 3 stressed the advantages of experimental designs in the study of causal relationships. Heightened confidence in *internal validity* (i.e., the independent variable did in fact cause changes in the dependent variable) comes with sound experimentation. Similarly, as Campbell (1969) and others (e.g., Crano & Brewer, 2002) have argued, if we want to know whether an intervention does indeed result in its intended consequences, evaluators are in a much stronger position to reach a confident conclusion with an intervention that is conducted as an experiment. In such a case, potential program participants are randomly assigned to either the intervention group or a "no intervention" control group. Assuming that all other environmental factors are similar for the two groups (this assumption becomes less tenable with interventions in the field than with those in the laboratory), differences between the groups (e.g., gains in students' self-esteem) can be attributed to the intervention with some confidence. For these reasons, experimental designs or "randomized control trials" have been traditionally considered the "gold standard" in evaluation. However, when it comes to interventions in the "real world," experimentation frequently is not feasible for a variety of practical reasons (e.g., an agency cannot afford to run a program as an experiment, random assignment cannot occur because the evaluator is faced with an intervention group that is preselected), or may not answer the evaluation questions put forward (e.g., why did the intervention work/not work, what parts of the intervention are most valuable/least valuable).

Other approaches to evaluation underscore the value of alternative research designs like quasi-experiments. For example, quasi-experiments exist when random assignment is not used and the outcomes for the intervention group are compared with those of a group of individuals whom the researchers deemed to be similar to the intervention group (e.g., the groups may be matched on a few characteristics, such as income level

and IQ). The use of qualitative research methods has also gained momentum in the evaluation field. As we will elaborate shortly, qualitative methods, such as narrative research or case studies can capture the experience of intervention participants in a much more nuanced way than purely quantitative data. Many evaluators use a mixed-method approach that incorporates both quantitative and qualitative methods providing a more complete picture of the intervention and its effects.

Evidence-Based Interventions

In step with increasing demands on programs and policies for accountability, whether to a program funder, the government, or the general public, is the continually increasing emphasis on the employment of evidence-based interventions or "best practices." For instance, in the field of education, the No Child Left Behind Act of 2001 (2002) required that practices and policies adopted by schools and school districts be "scientifically based," a phrase that is mentioned over 100 times in the legislation. This trend has spawned many books and clearinghouses on evidence-based practices across many disciplines and social problems. Some notable examples of clearinghouses include the What Works Clearinghouse set up by the U.S. Department of Education to provide evidence regarding what works in education; the Cochrane Collaboration that provides systematic reviews of research in human health care and health policy; and the Campbell Collaboration that produces systematic reviews of interventions in education, crime, social justice, and social welfare.

Some organizations have also introduced evidence-based decision-making tools that guide practitioners to critically assess research and apply research findings to their program decisions. In this context, Biglan and colleagues recommended standards that scientific organizations should apply before promoting programs and policies directed toward the prevention of behavior problems in youth (Biglan, Mrazek, Carnine, & Flay, 2003). For example, such organizations include the Center for the Study and Prevention of Violence and the Center for Substance Abuse Prevention. Biglan and colleagues proposed that before an organization recommends adoption of a given prevention program or policy, its positive outcomes for the target group should be demonstrated by at least two well-designed experimental trials or three well-designed interrupted time series experiments (one of the more rigorous quasi-experimental designs, as described in Chapter 3). According to Biglan and colleagues, the use of this

> standard would mean that scientific organizations would put their resources into disseminating the programs and policies that . . . would concentrate the limited resources of scientific, government, and nonprofit organizations on the policies and programs that are most likely to have an impact. (p. 436)

As another example, the Centers for Disease Control and Prevention has a panel of scientists assign HIV/AIDS programs to a four-tiered system that reflects the programs' levels of efficacy and scientific rigor. A program's tier can be adjusted up or down in accordance with the availability of new evidence (Price, 2008). Now, drawing on such systems for rigorously evaluating existing programs, decision makers in many fields have a much greater opportunity to select programs that have scientifically established records of effectiveness.

The following section further clarifies intervention design and evaluation by taking you through each step of the design and evaluation of an actual program.

AN INTERVENTION EXAMPLE: REDUCING ALCOHOL PROBLEMS ON CAMPUS

As noted previously, when designing an intervention, it is important to draw on relevant theory and research to develop the most effective intervention possible. This section describes an intervention that involves the direct application of social psychological theory and research evidence.

The goals of the intervention, which was developed and implemented at Northern Illinois University (NIU), were to reduce high-risk drinking among students and to reduce the incidence of injuries due to alcohol consumption. The intervention was conducted by the Health Enhancement Services Office of the University Health Service at NIU and was initially funded by a grant from the U.S. Department of Education's Fund for the Improvement of Postsecondary Education (Haines, 1996).

Identifying the Problem

Alcohol consumption is a very big problem on many college campuses. The level of alcohol consumption among college students has long been a concern of school administrators, parents, and other community members. The Harvard School of Public Health surveyed students at 119 colleges and universities in the United States (Wechsler, Davenport, Dowdall, Moeykens, & Castillo, 1994; Wechsler et al., 2002). The results showed that overall 44% of students had engaged in "binge drinking" (defined as having five or more drinks in a row) during the two weeks prior to the survey. The survey also showed that a higher percentage of binge drinkers had experienced alcohol-related problems since the beginning of the school year than had non–binge drinkers. Frequent binge drinkers were seven to sixteen times more likely than non–binge drinkers to have reported the following: missed class, fallen behind in schoolwork, engaged in unplanned sexual activity, had sex without protection, found themselves in trouble with campus police, damaged property, and been physically hurt or injured. A survey of NIU students (details reported later) confirmed that NIU was not an exception with respect to having a serious campus-wide alcohol problem.

To deal with problem drinking on campus, many colleges, including NIU have tried "traditional" methods of intervention, such as alcohol education and awareness campaigns, which are based on the idea that increased knowledge of the negative consequences of alcohol consumption will reduce drinking levels. However, there is little research evidence that education-oriented programs reduce alcohol consumption among college students (Moskowitz, 1989). Consistent with the research, NIU found that these traditional methods did not reduce drinking rates or alcohol-related injury rates among its students. It was clear that there was a need for a new kind of intervention to deal with problem drinking among NIU students.

Developing a Solution: Forming the Intervention Hypothesis

To reduce alcohol consumption among NIU students, an intervention that represented an application of **social norm theory** was designed (Berkowitz, 2004; Perkins, 2003). Fundamental to social norm theory is the central role that norms play in people's lives. **Norms** refer to shared beliefs about which behaviors are acceptable and which behaviors are not acceptable for members of a given group to engage in. Essentially, norms are prescriptions for how people should act in particular situations. There is ample research evidence that people do tend to guide their behavior in accordance with what they perceive to be situation relevant norms (Cialdini & Goldstein, 2004). Social psychologists have long recognized the influence of social norms on people. However, what is distinctive about social norm theory is its emphasis on the idea that people often perceive norms incorrectly and use such erroneous perceptions to guide their actions. In fact, social norm theory is based on the following three principles: First, individuals tend to conform to what they perceive to be the norm for a particular behavior. Second, in some instances, individuals may behaviorally conform to misperceived norms. Third, if misperceptions of norms are corrected, individuals will change their behavior to agree with the corrected perceptions.

Research on social cognition has identified some thinking errors that can lead people to misperceive norms. Two are particularly relevant to

the problem of drinking on college campuses. One cognitive error is **false consensus**, which is the tendency for people to believe that others are like them when in fact they are not (Ross, Green, & House, 1977). For instance, heavy drinkers may believe that *most* of their peers (e.g., students at their school) are also heavy drinkers when in fact they are not. We can see how this kind of thinking would allow heavy drinkers to rationalize their own levels of alcohol consumption as normative—socially acceptable—and, thus help to justify and sustain their excessive drinking. Another way in which norm misperception can occur is through **pluralistic ignorance**, which is when the majority of individuals incorrectly assume that others' behavior or thinking is more different from theirs than it actually is (Toch & Klofas, 1984). For instance, students may believe that others drink more than they do when in fact they do not. In fact, survey studies on a variety of college campuses have shown that these two types of misperceptions, especially pluralistic ignorance, are very common. That is, most students think that other students on their campuses drink more than is actually the case (Graham, Marks, & Hansen, 1991; Perkins, Haines, & Rice, 2005). At NIU, similar results were found. A 1988 survey indicated that less than half (43%) of students reported that they drink more than 5 drinks when they "party," whereas 70% of students reported that they believed most NIU students drink more than 5 drinks when they party. Thus, at NIU, the norm was that most students did not drink more than 5 drinks when partying, yet a solid majority misperceived the norm (suggesting the operation of pluralistic ignorance).

As the second principle of social norm theory suggests, not only do college students misperceive the norm for drinking behavior to be higher than it really is (e.g., "everyone is doing it"), but they also behave in ways that conform to this misperception. As evidence of this, studies have determined that if students believe that their peers are drinking more than they themselves are drinking, drinking rates tend to rise (Graham et al., 1991; Prentice & Miller, 1993).

The third principle of social norm theory—that people will conform to corrected perceptions of norms—leads directly to the hypothesis that if misperceptions of the drinking norm are corrected, levels of high-risk drinking will decline. Social norm theory and related research, therefore, led NIU to use the following intervention hypothesis for the design of its program: If NIU students are led to perceive the campus norm for drinking levels more accurately (i.e., the levels are lower than believed), drinking levels among students should decrease.

Goal Setting and Designing the Intervention

The main *goals* of the intervention were to reduce high-risk drinking and alcohol-related injuries among students at NIU. The *objective* of the intervention was to reduce the misperception of the amount of drinking on campus. It was reasoned that reaching this objective would lead to the achievement of the main goals of the intervention. The campaign plan was to target all students who drank alcohol. Because nearly all students (90%) at NIU drank alcohol, a campus-wide intervention was planned. Four rules used to guide the development of the campaign message to the student body were (a) keep it simple, (b) tell the truth, (c) be consistent, and (d) highlight the norm of moderate drinking. Reflecting these rules, the message was that most NIU students (55%) drink five or fewer drinks when they party.

Because of the limited resources available (one full-time staff person) for this project, and the large number of students at NIU (23,000), it was decided that the main program activity would be to use a mass media campaign. Given that most students at NIU reported that the campus newspaper was their primary source of information about campus activities, it was decided that a print media campaign would reach the largest number of students at the lowest cost. The print media campaign included campus newspaper advertisements, a campus newspaper column, press releases, flyers, and

posters (see Figure 4.2). It was also important that students perceived the source of the message as credible. A survey determined that NIU students rated health professionals as more believable than educators and friends. As a result, a print media campaign that was endorsed by health professionals on campus was deemed to be the most effective method of communicating the intervention message to NIU students.

An additional program activity involved a means of increasing the likelihood that students would read and remember the campaign message. This entailed rewarding students who remembered the message and spread the message to others. For example, groups of students were approached at random and asked, "Who knows how many drinks most NIU students drink when they party?" The student with the correct answer received $1. Students also received $5 for putting campaign posters on their dorm room walls.

Implementing the Intervention

The media campaign was first implemented at the beginning of the fall semester in 1989. The long-term intervention strategy was to initiate the media campaign at the beginning of each fall semester and to keep it highly visible until spring break. The messages would taper off after spring break and begin again at the start of the following academic year. Because new students arrive every year bringing their own misperceptions about drinking levels, it was important to conduct the intervention at the start of each school year. This social norm-based intervention has been ongoing at NIU since its inception during the early 1990s.

Evaluating the Intervention

An outcome evaluation of the social norm media campaign at NIU was conducted to determine whether the intervention was able to reach both its main objective and its two key goals. The evaluation sought to answer three questions.

Figure 4.2 One Poster Used for Social Norm Media Campaign at Northern Illinois University

SOURCE: Courtesy of Northern Illinois University.

First, did the perceived rate of high-risk drinking (defined as having more than five drinks when partying) among peers decrease to a more accurate perception? Second, did the rate of actual high-risk drinking decrease? Third, did the rate of alcohol-related injuries decrease? To answer these three questions, baseline information was collected from the students in 1988, that is, before the intervention was implemented. **Baseline information** refers to data that are collected on the target population prior to an intervention (i.e., the pretest) and that are compared with data collected after the intervention has been implemented (i.e., the posttest). A student survey was used in 1988 to collect three pieces of information about NIU students: the perceived rate of high-risk drinking among other students, the actual rate of high-risk drinking, and the rate of alcohol-related injuries. This pretest information was used both to justify the need for the intervention and to compare with data collected after the intervention was implemented (posttest). To rule out other possible explanations

of the evaluation results (i.e., high-risk drinking is reduced because of reasons beyond the intervention), data on national drinking levels among U.S. college students during this same time period were also recorded. This evaluation study demonstrates a quasi-experimental design because a nonequivalent comparison group of U.S. college students was used.

Data were collected at the end of each academic year from 1988 to 1998 (see Figure 4.3). From 1989 to 1990, after the first year of implementation, researchers found that there was a 12% reduction in *perceived* high-risk drinking and an 8% reduction in *actual* high-risk drinking, but no significant reduction in alcohol-related injuries to self or others. Over a span of 10 years using the social norm media campaign, NIU experienced a 37% reduction in perceived high-risk drinking, a 30% reduction in actual high-risk drinking, and a 20% reduction in alcohol-related injuries to self or others (Haines, 2003). In addition, the overall rate of binge drinking among U.S. college students (i.e., the nonequivalent

Figure 4.3   Effects of the Social Norm Media Campaign at NIU on Students' Perceptions of and Actual High-Risk Drinking Behavior

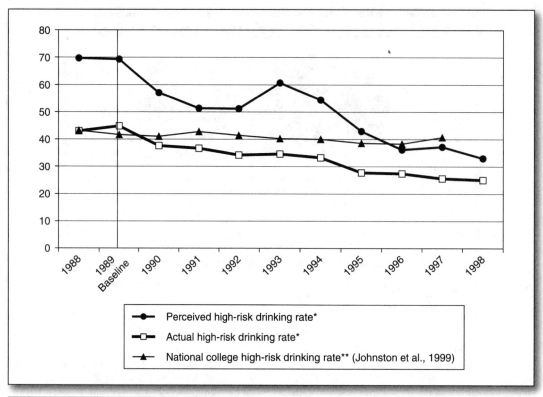

SOURCE: From Haines (2003).

*High-risk drinking defined as having more than five alcoholic drinks when "partying."
**High-risk drinking defined as having five or more alcoholic drinks at a sitting within the past 2 weeks.

comparison group) remained virtually the same over the same time period (Johnston, O'Malley, & Bachman, 1999). These data suggest that the NIU social norm intervention has been very successful in reaching its goals.

INCORPORATING QUALITATIVE METHODS TO DESIGN AND EVALUATE INTERVENTIONS

The NIU social norm intervention was designed and evaluated using quantitative research methods. For example, the researchers used a survey to gauge the credibility of the message source in the design phase, and they collected self-report measures of high-risk drinking and drinking-related injuries in the evaluation phase. Quantitative research is useful for designing and evaluating interventions because it allows researchers to quickly and inexpensively measure attitudes and behaviors of large groups of people, and to test for changes in attitudes or behaviors over time. One disadvantage of using quantitative research to design and evaluate interventions is that the information gathered from participants is often quite basic (e.g., a score on a scale representing attitudes toward drinking). In order to gain more in-depth information about a social problem, researchers sometimes turn to qualitative research methods to help design and evaluate interventions.

To illustrate the benefits of using qualitative research methods for interventions, this section describes an intervention that was designed to address the same social problem as the NIU intervention: high-risk drinking among students. The intervention was conducted by de Visser and colleagues (2015) and took place in England. The goal was to reduce alcohol consumption and alcohol-related harm in young people. Recent research shows that some existing interventions to combat binge drinking may be out of touch with young people's experiences. For example, many social marketing campaigns focus on depicting extremely negative health effects of binge drinking, but research shows that many young people don't worry about these effects or feel that they are irrelevant to their lives. Therefore, de Visser and colleagues (2015) aimed to create a social marketing campaign to reduce binge drinking that would be appealing to young people and also be effective.

The design of the intervention involved both qualitative and quantitative research methods. You may recall from Chapter 3 that mixed-methods studies involve a combination of qualitative and quantitative research methods, and they can produce stronger results than research using only one method. First, to ensure that the intervention would appeal to its target audience, the researchers surveyed approximately 1,400 young people about the strategies that they thought would be effective to combat binge drinking. Participants indicated that an intervention that focused on teaching skills to resist alcohol consumption when others were drinking would be effective. Next, the authors conducted a qualitative study to learn more about the experiences of non-drinkers and moderate drinkers. By asking teenagers about their experiences with drinking and the strategies that they use to avoid drinking too much, the researchers were able to learn what type of intervention would appeal to other teens, instead of trying to guess what messages teens would

respond to. Next, the researchers interviewed 25 non-drinkers and moderate drinkers about their experiences with drinking or not drinking, the impact of drinking behavior on social situations, and strategies that they use to control their drinking behavior. The authors used **phenomenology**, a qualitative method that focuses on the subjective experience of a phenomenon, to analyze the results. Analysis involved "coding" the interviews, which refers to searching the transcripts for commonalities in the participants' descriptions of drinking or not drinking, and identifying the core features of the experience. They found that a common strategy that participants used to avoid binge drinking involved drinking until they hit the "sweet spot" where they could enjoy the positive aspects of alcohol consumption (like having fun with their friends), but avoid the negative aspects (like negative health effects or losing control). The idea of a "sweet spot" would have been difficult to identify using surveys or other quantitative methods, but by interviewing participants, the researchers were able to learn about a commonly used strategy to avoid the harmful effects of excessive alcohol consumption.

The next step was to use the information gathered both from the survey and interview to design the intervention materials. The researchers created videos promoting the idea of the sweet spot. Participants from the interview study were featured in the videos talking about their techniques for avoiding binge drinking. By using real people instead of actors, the researchers hoped to make the video more realistic and more appealing to young people. The videos were shown to students and teachers at five schools in England. Focus groups were conducted with students and teachers to evaluate the videos. The researchers chose to use focus groups to evaluate the videos rather than a quantitative method like a questionnaire to elicit more detailed feedback from participants. The focus group discussions were recorded and transcribed, and the researchers used **thematic analysis** to identify themes in participants' responses. The student participants felt that the "sweet spot" message was realistic and useful, and they felt that it would help young people resist the pressure to binge drink. Students discussed several improvements that could be made to the videos, including adding more personal stories of the negative impacts of heavy drinking. Teachers also agreed that the video could be a valuable tool for reducing harmful alcohol consumption, but some teachers noted that the sweet spot message may be difficult to implement in a high school setting because it may be seen to encourage drinking (note that the "sweet spot" suggests a certain norm). Based on the results from the focus groups, the next step will be to revise the videos and then evaluate their effectiveness in reducing harmful drinking behavior. Although more work still needs to be done to determine whether the sweet spot message can help reduce binge drinking, the results of de Visser and colleagues' (2015) study demonstrate that qualitative methods can play an integral role in designing and evaluating intervention programs.

Further Applications of Social Norm Theory

The social norm approach has been used to reduce high-risk drinking among students at many other colleges and universities across the United States (Berkowitz, 2004). In fact, a survey of 118 schools in 2002 indicated that nearly half had adopted some form of norms-based intervention to combat binge drinking (Wechsler et al., 2003). Social norm theory also has been applied to other social issues where individuals tend to misperceive the norm, including for example, cigarette smoking, driving while intoxicated, seatbelt use, gambling, tax compliance, risky sexual behavior, and energy conservation. In 2006 the National Social Norms Institute opened its offices on the campus of the University of Virginia with the mission of supporting research, evaluation, and the dissemination of information related to social norms programs with respect to a diversity of health issues and populations. The institute's website is an excellent

source of information concerning current and past work on social norms interventions (http://www.socialnorms.org).

The application of social norm theory in programmatic interventions that successfully reduce a variety of high-risk behaviors aptly demonstrates the potential for the development of beneficial interventions based on social psychological theory and research. The following section describes two other examples of applying social psychological theory to intervention design, and also underscores that many social problems can be very complex and call for complex solutions.

OTHER INTERVENTIONS

Examples of Other Interventions

Among the many excellent examples of how social psychological theory can be applied successfully to the amelioration of social problems is the work of Stice and colleagues on eating disorders. In the context of the severe functional impairment and health problems, including mortality, commonly associated with eating disorders and the reluctance of many people suffering from eating disorders to seek treatment, a large number of eating disorder *prevention* programs have been initiated. One of the most effective interventions, developed by Stice and his coresearchers, relies on the application of Festinger's (1957) cognitive dissonance theory (discussed in Chapter 2). In four published articles, Stice and colleagues report separate trial interventions that were based on the same program logic model and used essentially the same intervention strategy (e.g., Stice, Chase, Stormer, & Appel, 2001; Stice, Mazotti, Weibel, & Agras, 2000; Stice, Shaw, Burton, & Wade, 2006; Stice, Trost, & Chase, 2003). The thinking behind the intervention is that a woman's internalization of the thin ideal of beauty (resulting from sociocultural pressures) leads to body dissatisfaction, negative affect (e.g., sadness, anxiety), dieting, and eating disorder symptoms. Therefore, the interventions undermine a woman's internalization of the thin ideal, and improvements should follow in the other negative factors.

Young women (early teens into the 20s) with body image concerns who did not meet the criteria for having an eating disorder (e.g., anorexia nervosa) participated in a 3-hour dissonance intervention (spread over three occasions) in which they voluntarily argued against and critiqued the thin ideal (e.g., wrote essays, role-played). According to Festinger's (1957) theory, such counterattitudinal behavior would generate psychological discomfort (called dissonance) that would motivate the individual to internalize the thin ideal less, which in turn would cause decreases in body dissatisfaction, dieting, negative affect, and eating disorder symptoms. The key variables were measured by interviews and surveys for each study at pretest and posttest, and then depending on the study, at follow-ups of one, three, six, or twelve months. Across the four studies and all follow-up intervals, compared with control participants who had also reported eating disorder concerns, the women in the dissonance condition showed reductions in the three risk factors (i.e., thin-ideal internalization, body dissatisfaction, and negative affect) and also in the dieting and eating disorder symptoms. Stice, Marti, Spoor, Presnell, and Shaw (2008) conducted a 2- and 3-year follow-up of the intervention reported in Stice and colleagues (2006) and notably found that all of the reductions in the key factors had been sustained for either two or three years, as well as finding a lower risk of the onset of an eating disorder at three years. Extrapolating from the latter result, the researchers estimated that out of every 100 women who participated in the intervention, nine fewer would develop an eating pathology. Needless to say, these results are remarkably promising, perhaps especially for a relatively simple 3-hour intervention. Add to this that Stice and colleagues (2008) cite five other research teams who also have demonstrated the efficacy of the dissonance intervention. Clearly this is an excellent example of an evidence-based intervention.

There are also interventions that incorporate more than one theory into their designs. For instance,

Hansen, Meissler, and Ovens (2000) used aspects of social learning theory and the fundamental attribution error to create group play therapy programs for children with attention deficit/ hyperactivity disorder (ADHD). The major tenet of **social learning theory** is that we learn new behaviors by observing and imitating others (e.g., role models) as well as by observing consequences of behaviors (Bandura & Walters, 1963). The group play therapy program allows children to learn from others through the process of modeling and the enforcement of positive or negative consequences for actions. As reported in Chapter 1, the **fundamental attribution error** refers to the notion that people tend to underestimate the role of situational determinants of people's behavior and tend to overestimate the role of dispositional determinants (e.g., personality) (Ross, 1977). For children with ADHD, this means that the behaviors that they display (e.g., excitement) tend to be attributed (e.g., by significant others) to their condition, whereas situational influences (e.g., fun events) are ignored. The group play therapy intervention attempts to reduce this bias in judgment by conducting the therapy groups in a community-based setting away from stigmatizing mental health facilities, and by increasing awareness of the attribution error and its potential consequence for children with ADHD.

Complex Problems Require Complex Solutions

Although many of the problems that we have considered in this chapter for the purposes of explaining the design and evaluation of interventions/programs were presented as relatively unidimensional, it is important to recognize that many social and practical problems that occur in our incredibly multidimensional and complex physical and social world are anything but unidimensional. Without a doubt, many of the most serious social issues confronted by social scientists reflect very complex problems that are embedded in a highly interconnected cluster of causal variables, and thus are apt to be extremely challenging to solve. Diverse examples include environmental sustainability, raising a child, mental illness, and poverty. Highly complex problems tend to require resource-intensive, multifaceted holistic interventions that are able to take into consideration the interconnectedness of multiple key variables and address multiple causes. The following quotation from David Shipler (2004) centering on the issue of poverty aptly illustrates what we are suggesting:

> Every problem magnifies the impact of the others. And all are so tightly interlocked that one reversal can produce a chain reaction with results far distant from the original causes. A rundown apartment can exacerbate a child's asthma, which leads to a call for an ambulance, which generates a medical bill that cannot be paid, which ruins a credit record, which hikes the interest rate on an auto loan, which forces the purchase of an unreliable used car, which jeopardizes a mother's punctuality at work, which limits her promotions and earning capacity, which confines her to poor housing. . . . If problems are interlocking, then so must solutions be. A job alone is not enough. Medical insurance alone is not enough. Good housing alone is not enough. Reliable transportation, careful family budgeting, effective parenting, and effective schooling are not enough when each is achieved in isolation from the rest. (p. 11)

The following are two intervention efforts that have attempted to take a more holistic approach: (1) *comprehensive community initiatives*, which aim to transform distressed neighborhoods by engaging a variety of neighborhood stakeholders (e.g., residents, community agencies, businesses, government) around a common plan for change (Kubisch, Auspos, Brown, & Delwar, 2010); (2) *wraparound initiatives*, which target high-risk children and their families by assembling a diverse team of formal and informal support persons and agencies in their community (e.g., community leaders; representatives of natural or informal community support agencies/groups, such as recreation, faith, business, and service clubs; representatives of the formal child, family, and adult services) (Bruns & Walker, 2008).

For the Applied Social Psychologist, It Is Not Enough to Know Only That an Intervention Has Worked

Although this chapter has emphasized the importance of developing a program logic model to explain *why* an intervention will result in a particular outcome or set of outcomes, the applied social psychologist involved in designing and evaluating interventions may be the only stakeholder who is particularly concerned about understanding the intervening processes that link intervention to outcome. Generally speaking, other stakeholders care little, if at all, regarding how intervention outcomes come about as a result of program activities (cf. Mark & Bryant, 1984). For them, the bottom line is whether the intervention works. An overriding emphasis on results makes sense for most stakeholders because their investment in the intervention is predominantly practical. Program funders want visible, cost-effective returns on their dollars, program managers and staff members want to demonstrate their value to the organization through program accountability, and the only important thing for program recipients is that they experience the purported benefits of the intervention. Needless to say, it is of great importance to the applied social psychologist that the intervention proves to have its intended beneficial consequences. However, unlike other stakeholders, focusing on the practical aspects is not enough. As a scientist, it is necessary for the applied social psychologist to avoid giving insufficient attention to understanding why an intervention works and why it does not work. It is vital that the applied social psychologist does not compromise the scientific integrity of the intervention–evaluation process by dwelling only on the practical "does it work" question (i.e., the question of cause and effect) and giving insufficient attention to the "why it works" question (i.e., the question of explanation). For example, if we were to develop an intervention aimed at improving grade school students' academic performance by improving their self-concepts, it would not be sufficient from a social scientific perspective only to demonstrate that the students' grades improved after the intervention; it also would be important to confirm that their self-concepts improved significantly *and* that students whose grades increased the most tended to be those whose self-concepts improved the most, and those whose grades increased the least had self-concepts that improved the least. Evidence that addresses the program logic model as a whole is required for applied social psychology to move toward fulfilling its potential as a social science to contribute to a better world (Ross et al., 2010).

Further, Lodzinski (2012) points out that different people taking part in the same program often respond to that program in different ways; hence, no program is likely to work equally well for all participants. Given the fact that programs do not always benefit all clients equally, it is important for any program evaluation to shed light not only on "what happens?" and "why?," but "what happens to who?"; or put another way, "what works for who?" Thus an additional and important question to ask is whether anything sets those clients who benefit the most from the program apart from those who benefit the least; for example, with respect to age, sex, or marital status, or level of need. If one or more characteristics differentiate clients who benefit the most versus the least, then knowing that can help improve the ongoing development of the program, and also help refine not only the logic model, but also client selection and/or the matching of clients to various services or interventions either within the program or to other programs and services.

INFLUENCING SOCIAL POLICY

This chapter would be remiss if it did not recognize another avenue of application—influencing the development of social policy. The potential of psychology and other social sciences to contribute to public policy has long been recognized. Also long recognized is the existence of a considerable gap between the actual amount of social scientific knowledge about social issues and the impact of this knowledge on social policies (Hennigan, Flay, & Cook, 1980; Miller, 1969). Fifteen years ago, two recent American Psychological Association (APA) presidents, DeLeon (2002) and Zimbardo (2002b), challenged psychologists to become more involved in public policy development. Zimbardo noted that many of the most serious problems facing the United States (e.g., animosity of the Arab world against the United States, education failures,

addictions) have psychological causes and/or consequences and that "psychologists need to be heard and to be at the table of influential leaders and policy makers because psychologists have more to say about these issues than do members of any other discipline" (p. 432).

Probably the best-known example of social psychological research having a role in policy formation occurred in 1954 when the U.S. Supreme Court, in its *Brown v. Board of Education* ruling, struck down the 1892 *Plessy v. Ferguson* separate but equal doctrine, thereby making racial segregation in public schools unconstitutional (Benjamin & Crouse, 2002). In making its ruling, the court cited seven social science publications as having a role in its decision. The main thrust of the social science argument was that segregation negatively affected the self-esteem of African American children and also fostered interracial prejudice.

This event is particularly noteworthy because it marked the first time that the Supreme Court had recognized psychological research in a decision, and the ruling was perhaps the most socially significant one made during the 20th century. In recognizing the 50th anniversary of *Brown v. Board of Education* and the important influence of psychologist Kenneth B. Clark's studies on the court's decision, Tomes (2004) appropriately titled his article "The Case—and the Research—That Forever Connected Psychology and Policy."

Another example of social science research contributing to policy development comes from the criminal justice field in North America, which during the past 25 years has witnessed a shift in philosophy and operational strategy. The change has been from less emphasis on the traditional law enforcement model of policing (a reactive, response-driven approach) to more emphasis on the community-oriented model of policing (a proactive, police–community partnership approach). In embracing this transition, leaders in policing and relevant government agencies drew considerably on the research evidence that pointed to the limited effectiveness of the core operational procedures used in traditional policing, and to the need for more attention to quality-of-life issues and improving police–community relations (Schneider, Pilon, Horrobin, & Sideris, 2000).

Thus, social psychology can contribute to both the development of policy and the development of interventions. The difference between policy and intervention is that **policy** refers to a general course of action endorsed by an organization, whereas an *intervention* refers to the specific concrete action(s) (i.e., program activities) that the organization chooses to take to implement the policy. For instance, on the one hand, the leadership of a police agency may decide on the policy of implementing community policing on an organization-wide basis. On the other hand, interventions pertain to exactly how the agency chooses to implement the policy; that is, the actual steps taken to carry out the policy of community policing (e.g., involving

officers in courses on community policing principles, setting up a neighborhood mini-station, conducting foot patrols).

Without a doubt, influencing social policy is a very important applied function of the social science disciplines, including social psychology. However, instead of focusing on social policy influence, this chapter (and this book overall) concentrates on the role of social psychology in the design of interventions that are viewed as the *sine qua non* of applied social psychology. The path from social psychological knowledge to influencing social policy is seldom straightforward. Many factors that preclude the direct use of knowledge in policy decision making have been identified (e.g., Hennigan et al., 1980), including the failure of researchers to adequately communicate research findings to policy makers, time pressures on decision makers that undercut thorough assimilation of research evidence, resistance to change stemming from comfort with the status quo, pressures from stakeholders whose positions do not accord with the scientific evidence, and so forth. In the case of the development of interventions, the route from knowledge to practice is more direct in that there are likely to be fewer obstacles to application than is the case for social policy. In Chapter 12 further consideration is given to the topic of influencing social policy.

INTERVENTION ISSUES

Process Issues

The focus of this chapter has been on programmatic intervention. We have described the basic steps in the design of interventions, and although these steps are fundamental to the development of effective programs, it is important to recognize that they are not carried out in a vacuum. All interventions—and, by extension, intervention designs—have to operate within constraints, and it is sometimes very challenging to both work within these constraints and maintain the integrity and effectiveness of the intervention. The most prevalent constraint is budgetary. Other constraints are subtler. Following are three general constraints.

First, interventions must be paid for, and funding typically is rooted in policy directions that in turn are embedded in the funder's broader political philosophy or ideology (whether conservative or liberal). Thus, the view that interventions are driven exclusively by the emergence of empirically validated methodologies is naive (Mark & Bryant, 1984). To be sure, empirical validation is critical to the successful application of social psychological theory and knowledge, but interventions based on such insight must, to varying degrees, conform to funders' needs and wants. Ideas for interventions, no matter how well validated, will always have to be vetted for approval by those who have been approached to fund them.

Second, intervention design is a collaborative process in which the responsibility always is shared among stakeholders. For example, intervention design often involves professionals from different disciplines (sometimes together with program participants) working as a team. Hence, designing an intervention to assist in relapse prevention in a substance abuse clinic is likely to involve—in addition to the applied social psychologist—medical professionals and clinical psychologists as well as social workers and counselors. Each professional group will contribute a unique experience and perspective on the design of the intervention. To be effective, therefore, an intervention's designer(s) must be able to take into account a wide range of stakeholder ideas while at the same time ensuring that the key elements of the design remain linked with one another both logically and operationally to form a cohesive and integrated whole. Also note that the challenge is not only intellectual, but also interpersonal given that listening, relationship building, and negotiating become part of the toolbox of every applied social psychologist involved with intervention design. (You likely will find that your grounding in basic social psychology is extremely helpful in this regard. For an excellent chapter on the practice skills of the applied psychologist, see Fisher, 1982.)

Third, constraints that are specified by the law, and by various organizational policies and established procedures, also exist. Organizational constraints that must be accommodated include restrictions to access, availability of facilities, hours of operation, staffing availability, and scheduling restrictions.

None of these constraints can be ignored, so all must be addressed in the process of intervention design and eventual implementation. Sometimes it is possible to work around them, and sometimes it is not. For example, some constraints are nonnegotiable (e.g., maintaining confidentiality of client records, being required to accept nonvoluntary participants), whereas others may be negotiable to varying degrees. Typically, designers have to advocate for certain parameters, for example, getting more flexible intake or referral criteria to give access to more people and getting agreement from management to change the program delivery model in response to participant feedback.

Ethical Issues

As this chapter has illustrated, applied social psychologists contribute to improving the quality of life and the betterment of society as a whole through the application of social psychological theory and research. Recall from Chapter 3 that social psychological research undertaken to develop an understanding of social phenomena is guided by codes of ethics (American Psychological Association, 2010; Canadian Psychological Association, 2000). Just as ethical issues exist in the conduct of basic research, concerns also can arise around the ethical use of both research methodology and research findings in applied settings. In fact, the focus on effecting change in the functioning of individuals, groups, and organizations raises a host of ethical issues beyond those that typically emerge in understanding focused research. Ethical issues can arise in both the design and the evaluation of interventions, and they can challenge a practitioner's professionalism and integrity.

Although psychologists are guided by their national associations' codes of ethics, and often by specialty-specific codes of ethics, such as those for clinical and educational psychologists, some have pointed out (e.g., O'Neill, 1989, 1998) that ethical standards for much of applied psychology focus on issues that typically arise between a psychologist and an individual client. These writers point out that these ethical guidelines have been designed specifically to protect the *individual rights of clients* (e.g., maintenance of confidentiality, prohibition of sexual contact). As such, they are not wholly adequate for dealing with issues that arise with regard to programmatic interventions that by definition involve multiple stakeholders (e.g., program participants, program personnel, funders, members of the community at large). Two key questions that arise from this observation were voiced by O'Neill (1989). The first question is to whom (i.e., which stakeholder group) is the applied psychologist responsible? The second question is for what (i.e., which end product or deliverable) is the applied psychologist ultimately responsible?

As a practical matter, the *contract* that is drawn up between a practitioner (e.g., applied social psychologist) and his or her employing organization can be very helpful by providing some clarity with respect to both of these questions. For example, contracts typically specify the following: the individual or committee to whom the practitioner will report, the scope of the work expected, the end product of the work (e.g., a program evaluation report outlining conclusions and recommendations), timelines for the completion of the work, agreement on who owns the data collected or copyright to any materials produced, whether publication of the findings is permissible, and so forth. Typically, contracts do not spell out generally accepted norms of professional conduct (e.g., confidentiality of information, objectivity, prohibitions on profiting from privileged information) as adherence to these is assumed.

Contracts, however, cannot anticipate every dilemma that may occur. Ethical issues in program intervention can arise when the applied social psychologist is aware of or discovers information that, if divulged, will further the interests of one stakeholder group at the expense of another. As an example, consider an applied social psychologist who is hired to head the design of an intervention and finds that the employing organization (a government agency) only supports a politically popular intervention, which is revealed to have questionable support in evaluation research. The dilemma is that if the applied social psychologist does not reveal the lack of evidence for the program's hypothesis, it is likely that considerable resources will be wasted on an intervention that is ineffective, and so the intended program recipients will not be well served. On the other hand, if the lack of evidence is revealed, not only may the psychologist's job be at stake, but the program may well be implemented anyway.

To take a parallel example from intervention evaluation, consider the case of an applied social psychologist who has been hired to conduct an outcome evaluation of a major program offered by a social service agency. The evaluation determines that although the program benefits the program participants in incidental ways, it is largely ineffective. Such results may lead to the closure of the agency because this program represents the bulk of the funding that the agency receives. The practitioner is asked by the agency's management to focus more on the positive than on the negative in the evaluation report, in effect, distorting the overall findings of the evaluation. If the psychologist refuses to misrepresent the findings, his or her relationship with the agency (and possible future contracts) may be jeopardized along with the survival of the agency. On the other hand, if the psychologist does comply with the request, the people who need the services will not be served as well as they could be, and financial and other resources provided by the government will not be invested optimally.

It is important to note that these are just two examples and that dilemmas can stem from many factors, such as cross-cultural differences (e.g., among client groups, funders, and policy makers) and competing value systems. Some argue (e.g., Riger, 1989) that such ethical dilemmas are essentially political conflicts arising from the presence of many needs and scarce resources and the resulting necessity to compete for these resources. Kimmel (2004) suggested that applied social psychologists have frank and open discussions with the organization prior to embarking on any program design or evaluation project. The purpose of the initial discussion is to clarify the psychologist's role as well as to articulate the professional and ethical standards and any limits they may place on the extent to which the organization can be assisted. In an evaluation context like the second example above, it would be important to discuss up front the purpose of the evaluation and the implications of negative findings; for instance, are there serious funding implications, or can the findings be used as a developmental opportunity for the program?

Another approach to preventing or resolving ethical dilemmas is to involve various stakeholders (program recipients, front-line staff, managers, board members, funders, etc.) in making key decisions regarding the intervention design or evaluation project. A multistakeholder steering committee would help to address power imbalances, give recognition to different stakeholder needs, promote transparency, and ensure the sponsoring organization is held accountable for its decisions.

For more explicit guidelines to conducting evaluations in an ethical manner, you can refer to the Program Evaluation Standards developed by the Joint Committee on Standards for Educational Evaluation (Yarbrough, Shulha, Hopson, & Caruthers, 2011) which outlines five standards to which evaluators should adhere to make certain that the evaluation is useful, effective, fair, accurate, and appropriately documented to ensure accountability.

Kimmel (2004) pointed out that occasionally it is necessary for the applied social psychologist to refuse to participate in projects that have the potential to conflict with the ethical standards of the profession. For the applied social psychologist, there is rarely an "easy" way out of ethical dilemmas. It must be remembered that one's expertise carries with it the responsibility to always act in ways that place the interests of those who are in the greatest need of help above the self-interests of the professional. This is the essence of acting ethically.

SUMMARY

This chapter outlines some of the key components involved in the development of intervention strategies designed to address social and practical problems. Although we can design personal interventions, the focus is on programmatic interventions or programs—a collection of activities designed to address social or practical problems with the intention of preventing, reducing, or eliminating their negative consequences.

There are four steps involved in the development of programs: (a) identifying the problem, (b) developing a solution, (c) goal setting and designing the intervention, and (d) implementing the intervention. Evaluation of the effectiveness of interventions can be considered as a fifth step in the process of program development. There are two main types of program evaluation: process evaluations, which focus on whether programs have been implemented as planned, and outcome evaluations, which focus on whether programs meet their objectives. It is important to evaluate programs because they are not always effective and sometimes produce unintended undesirable consequences.

The chapter also presented a detailed example of an intervention aimed at reducing problem drinking at NIU. This intervention demonstrated the value of using theory in the design of programs. The chapter then explored how the results of interventions can be used to inform public policy, and, finally, noted a number of intervention issues, including program constraints and ethics.

PART II

APPLYING SOCIAL PSYCHOLOGY TO ARENAS OF LIFE

5

APPLYING SOCIAL PSYCHOLOGY TO CLINICAL AND COUNSELING PSYCHOLOGY

KENNETH E. HART

PHILLIP A. IANNI

CHAPTER OUTLINE

A few years ago, one of the chapter authors (K. H.) had a troubled student in a class he taught on personality and adjustment. Halfway through the semester, Deena (not her real name) began to pay visits to K. H. during his office hours. Deena was a single, attractive, 20-year-old woman who had moved out of her parents' home to attend college in another city two years earlier. She was anxious, lonely, and depressed, and her schoolwork was suffering because she had difficulty in motivating herself to study. When she did sit down to study, she could not keep her mind focused enough to concentrate.

As a result, her schoolwork had been piling up, and she said that she felt "snowed under" by a mountain of backlogged homework.

In terms of personality, Deena described herself as a loner. Her only hobby was playing online video games on her computer, and she said that she was losing interest in this. When she went to see the latest movies, she often went alone, and when she ate lunch at the school cafeteria, she usually sat in the corner at the table by herself while reading a newspaper. She commented with envy and sadness in her voice on the public use of cell phones by others, saying, "A cell phone for me would be a waste because I don't have anything to say and I don't have anyone to talk to." She added, "Who would want to talk to me anyway?" Her self-esteem was obviously very low. Deena also paid very close attention when she saw people who seemed to be enjoying life and having fun. Once she commented on how much other people smiled and showed their teeth. She said, "I could have rotten teeth, and no one would know because I never smile. There's nothing to smile about."

Deena was extremely concerned about how she appeared to other people. She worried obsessively that others might not like her. She dressed herself impeccably in the latest fashions and wore a lot of accessories. She also liked to wear perfume and makeup. Most of the money from her part-time job as a checkout clerk at the local supermarket went to pay for things that could help to make her look good in the eyes of others. Examples included her fitness club membership, clothing, and hair care and personal grooming.

During the spring semester of her sophomore year, Deena struck up an acquaintanceship with a man she had met in the library. Eventually, he asked her out for dinner and a movie. Before they went on their date, K. H. had the occasion to speak with Deena. She was an emotional wreck and was seriously considering canceling the date. In anticipating the dinner and movie, she exclaimed with muted enthusiasm, "He's so perfect. I've never liked anyone this much before!" But then a minute later, with a worried frown on her face, she also said, "I don't think I'll have much to say that's worthwhile. He'll think I'm boring." It was quite clear to K. H. that Deena was feeling overwrought with anxious anticipation. At the same time, she was also feeling pessimistic and discouraged enough to consider calling the fellow to cancel their date. She thought that she should be happy, and it bothered her that she was so anxious and sad.

As you read through this chapter, keep Deena's case in mind and try to answer the following questions:

- How might social psychological theory be useful in understanding Deena's emotional difficulties?
- Can social psychological theory and research be useful in helping to alleviate Deena's anxiety and depression?
- In trying to diagnose Deena's problems, what potential biases should one (e.g., K. H.) guard against?

Of what relevance is behavioral science to a distressed person like Deena? It is hoped that after reading this chapter, you will be able to apply social psychological theory and research

findings to understanding why people like Deena suffer from emotional distress. If you were a practicing psychotherapist who had Deena as a client, you could potentially use your understanding of social psychological theory and research to guide your choice of intervention strategies and avoid making mistakes during the process of diagnostic assessment.

So, why was Deena in so much emotional pain, and what could be done to help her? Biomedical scientists have identified a number of factors as important in the cause and cure of emotional and behavioral problems. Genetic factors and factors related to abnormal brain chemistry obviously play important roles, but these factors alone do not give the whole picture. Behavioral researchers have provided a more comprehensive view of human suffering by identifying psychosocial causes and psychosocial treatments. Social psychologists are among the mental health professionals who have taken a lead role in uncovering factors that may influence the onset and resolution of emotional and behavioral disorders.

The goal of this chapter is to demonstrate the relevance of social psychology to understanding, diagnosing, and helping people like Deena. In particular, the chapter describes some of the theoretical and practical breakthroughs that have elevated social psychology to a place of prominence in behavioral science efforts to improve our ability to understand psychological disorders. The chapter focuses in particular on two of these disorders: depression and anxiety. Because improved understanding of how and why people become depressed and anxious has implications for intervention and therapy, this chapter also demonstrates how social psychology has contributed to advances within the fields of clinical and counseling psychology.

It has been noted that there is a gap between basic social psychological research and clinical practice (Tashiro & Mortensen, 2006). However, some psychologists have attempted to bridge the gap between social psychology and clinical psychology. The abbreviated term given to this bridge is the **social–clinical interface** (Leary & Miller, 1986). Although this chapter focuses mainly on depression and anxiety, it should be noted that the social–clinical interface involves efforts to understand, diagnose, and modify a broad spectrum of other types of psychological problems, including those that involve jealousy, anger, shame, guilt, embarrassment, regret, and remorse. Moreover, a large number of social psychological principles have been applied to these problems. These include many of the better known theories of self (e.g., self-efficacy, self-esteem, self-presentation, self-awareness, self-concept, self-handicapping) as well as social psychological models based on attribution theory, expectancy theory, social comparison theory, cognitive dissonance theory, learned helplessness theory, and social support theory.

In this chapter, the issues of mutual concern to social and clinical/counseling psychology have been categorized as falling into one of three subdomains: the origins of psychological disorders, the treatment and prevention of psychological disorders, and the diagnosis of psychological disorders.

The origins of psychological disorders. This subdomain addresses the social and psychological factors that contribute to the onset or maintenance of emotional and behavioral problems. Several social psychological models have been developed to understand why psychological disorders arise. Indeed, a wide variety of disorders have been studied, with depression and anxiety being perhaps the best understood. In this chapter, each of these two disorders is examined from the point of view of a particular social psychological perspective.

The diagnosis of psychological disorders. This subdomain involves social and psychological processes that influence the treatment (and prevention) of psychological problems. Interface researchers who study within this domain attempt to answer questions about how and why people change as a result of counseling and psychotherapy. In addition to studying the processes of therapeutic change, social psychology can inform research that tests new interventions. This chapter examines the relevance of two different social psychological models in the treatment of anxiety and depression.

The treatment and prevention of psychological disorders. This final subdomain involves studying the social and psychological processes that might cause therapists to be less than 100% objective in how they assess and diagnose their clients' emotional and behavioral disorders. Social psychologists who work in this area study factors that might bias the process of identifying the nature of a client's difficulty. They also study the impact on the client's welfare of giving a diagnostic label to a client. This chapter presents examples of theory and research that have identified the stigmatizing impact of giving a client a psychiatric diagnosis. It also describes research that seeks to understand and prevent potential errors that mental health professionals some-times make based on faulty ways of thinking and of questioning clients.

After reading this chapter, you should be able to answer the following four questions:

- Why do people become so anxious and depressed?
- Of what value are social psychological theories in helping to better understand, diagnose, and treat people with problems, such as depression and social anxiety?
- What can we do to help alleviate or prevent this suffering?
- What errors and biases should clinical and counseling psychologists guard against when diagnosing clients as having a disorder worthy of treatment, and how are such errors and biases prevented?

THE ORIGINS OF PSYCHOLOGICAL DISORDERS

"I probably sound stupid." "What do they think of me?" "I feel so inadequate around these people." Have these or similar thoughts ever popped into your head in social situations with new acquaintances? If you are like most people, these types of thoughts will enter your mind from time to time. For people like Deena, they occur with a very high frequency and tend to be quite bothersome, causing extreme upset and intense feelings of distress. Technically, we call this type of distress **social anxiety** (also known as **social phobia**). Well-known signs of social anxiety include feeling tense and uptight or prone to embarrassment when interacting with acquaintances, blushing during conversations with strangers, feeling dread about having to speak to others whom one does not know well, feeling apprehensive about meeting new people, and avoiding social gatherings (see Figure 5.1).

Anxiety associated with interpersonal interaction can be so overwhelming as to cause some people to act in an unnaturally awkward, inhibited, and "stiff" fashion. This apparent aloofness

stimulates others to draw pejorative inferences about friendliness, self-confidence, and poise. For some people (e.g., Deena), anticipatory dread can also be so debilitating as to cause them to shy away from entering social situations in the first place. If socially avoidant behavior becomes habitual, it can gradually cause a person to become more and more detached and isolated from others. The resulting alienation, in turn, is experienced as loneliness and depressive-type symptoms.

Loneliness is defined as the sad yearning for intimacy that results from perceived deficiencies in the number and quality of friendships. There are two types of loneliness: social and emotional. The intensity of **social loneliness** is related to the degree of discrepancy between one's desired number of friends and one's actual number of friends. How much **emotional loneliness** one feels is determined by the discrepancy between one's desired level of intimacy and one's actual level of intimacy. Loneliness can sometimes be a stepping-stone to depression, which is a more serious emotional disorder. Well-known signs of depression include feeling tired and worn out, feeling overwhelmed by struggling with daily life, feeling unable to cope, experiencing thoughts about worthlessness and not playing a useful role in life, having a lack of interest in otherwise pleasurable activities (e.g., eating, sex), feeling sad and blue, and having so little energy that even the easiest task seems too difficult.

After reading this list of symptoms, you might have some sense of what it is like to experience depression. However, in order to really under-stand what it feels like to experience anxiety or depression, you probably need more detailed information. Recall from Chapter 3 that qualita-tive research can be used "for exploring and understanding the meaning individuals or groups ascribe to a social or human problem" (Creswell, 2009, p. 4), making it an ideal method to under-stand the experience of psychological illnesses.

A recent phenomenological analysis by Smith and Rhodes (2015) addressed the research question: What is the first experience of depres-sion like? The purpose of **phenomenology** is to

Figure 5.1 Speaking in Front of a Group of People, a Situation That Is Debilitating for Someone With High Social Anxiety

SOURCE: Photo Courtesy of Centre for Flexible Learning, University of Windsor.

generate a detailed description of a particular experience of a phenomenon (in this case, depression). In this study, Smith and Rhodes (2015) interviewed seven people who were seeking treatment for depression from a clinic in London, England. Participants were asked to describe what it was like being depressed, and the experiences they had on a daily basis. Interviews were transcribed and the researchers read the transcripts several times to identify themes (i.e., commonalities) within participants' descriptions of depression.

The authors found that the experience of depression was described in terms of loss and emptiness. For example, one participant described how she felt when she lost contact with her son after her divorce: "It's emptiness, it's nothing don't matter, it's being locked away, you just don't care about yourself. It's like part of you [is] gone, your heart, I don't know.

Perhaps half my heart has gone away." This type of vivid description is one of the major advantages of qualitative analysis. You probably have a much richer understanding of what it feels like to be depressed from reading that short quotation than from simply seeing the word "emptiness" on a list of symptoms. Researchers and clinicians can also benefit from learning about the lived experience of depression. By learning about the firsthand experiences of depression, researchers and clinicians can design more effective methods of treatment and prevention, and reassure clients that their experiences (such as feelings of emptiness) are shared by others.

Now, think back to Deena in the opening vignette. Try to identify how many of the telltale signs of depression she has. Also, try to assess whether or not she has most of the signs of social anxiety. Although Deena is certainly distressed and has several symptoms indicating possible depression and social anxiety, there is insufficient information to give a formal diagnosis of *clinical depression* or *social anxiety disorder* (you would have to be a trained psychotherapist and perform a formal diagnostic interview to give her these psychiatric labels). Despite an absence of an official diagnostic label, we think that it is safe to assume Deena is so distressed that she could benefit from counseling.

But, how did Deena come to feel so distressed? We encourage you to try to unravel the causal chain of determinants. As you read along, this section describes social psychological theories of symptom onset. You are invited to consider how they might apply to Deena's case. These theories seek to provide conceptual frameworks for understanding the role that psychological and social processes play in rendering people vulnerable to becoming depressed and anxious. In particular, this section discusses *cognitive–social risk factors*.

The Social Psychological Roots of Social Anxiety

Generally speaking, symptoms of social anxiety fall along a graded continuum of unpleasant emotions that are experienced by susceptible people when interacting with others. As such, social anxiety is a type of emotional distress that can vary in intensity. Feelings of nervousness tend to be especially pronounced in social settings where others are not well known. People at the highest end of the distress continuum are sometimes diagnosed as suffering from a debilitating impairment known as either social phobia or social anxiety disorder. The most extreme form of the condition is serious enough to merit professional intervention. People with full-blown social phobia have a pervasive, self-defeating, and debilitating fear of interpersonal situations. They feel an exaggerated sense of social inadequacy and dread severe embarrassment. According to the fifth edition of the American Psychiatric Association's (2013) *Diagnostic and Statistical Manual of Mental Disorders* (*DSM-5*),

social phobia (i.e., **social anxiety disorder**) is defined as "marked fear or anxiety about one or more social situations in which the individual is exposed to possible scrutiny by others" (section 300.23).

If you were a social psychologist and you were asked to offer an explanation to account for why some people are more prone to debilitating levels of social anxiety than are others, what would you say? Take a moment now to anticipate what social psychologists have suggested. Identifying specific cognitive–social culprits involved in the onset and perpetuation of symptoms of social anxiety is important because their identification improves our theoretical understanding of how symptoms develop. Furthermore, a good theoretical understanding has practical value because it provides practitioners with a blueprint for developing treatments that work to reduce anxiety in people who are already suffering. Having a blueprint can also lead to preventive interventions aimed at inoculating nonanxious people against developing the disorder.

Self-presentation theory. Leary and Kowalski (1995) developed a broad social psychological blueprint for social anxiety that sheds light on its origin, maintenance, and treatment. In other words, the theory is useful because it not only explains the psychological chain of events that makes people vulnerable to experiencing anxiety, but also describes how symptoms of social anxiety might be reduced (and prevented). Leary and Kowalski's **self-presentation theory** (SPT) emerged from a cognitive–social framework that was applied to understanding clinical samples of socially anxious people. This framework assumes that individuals attempt to manage or control the impressions that others form of them. According to SPT, other people's impressions of us are important because their impressions influence whether they behave in ways that reward us or punish us. Moreover to a certain extent, how we behave toward others influences how they behave toward us. SPT maintains that people can get others to treat them as they wish by paying close attention to the impressions they communicate to others and by intentionally altering these impressions for strategic impact.

Furthermore, according to Leary and Kowalski (1995), a person becomes prone to experience a fearful response in social circumstances when two conditions are present: high self-presentational motivation and low self-efficacy. This chain of events is shown diagrammatically in Figure 5.2. **Self-presentational motivation** refers to the degree to which people are concerned with how others perceive them. Obviously, some people are more concerned than others. When self-presentational motivation is high, people are very concerned with ensuring that others have a particular image of them. In contrast, people who have low self-presentational motivation do not care as much. But, why should people care what others think of them? In the opening vignette, why did Deena care? According to SPT, a person becomes motivated to communicate a particular impression to others in proportion to how much the person has at stake. If you are an employee, for example, you might be anxiously concerned about your supervisor's opinion of you because you know that your chances of promotion or for a pay raise depend, in part, on whether you are seen as competent and reliable. In Deena's case, she may have felt that the man she met in the library could turn out to be the "Mr. Right" she was yearning to find. Desperation often creates motivation.

Self-presentation theory maintains that people who are most vulnerable to developing social anxiety are those who are most strongly motivated to convey a particular impression to others. However, this is a "double-barreled" theory. For high self-presentational motivation to create high anxiety, a second process must also be in operation. Specifically, a person must also doubt his or her ability to successfully make the desired impression. Emotionally speaking, then, the "lethal combination" is wanting to impress others, on the one hand, but feeling unable to do so, on the other.

Social self-efficacy is defined as a person's level of *confidence* in his or her ability to convey a particular image to another person. Someone with low social self-efficacy has little confidence in his or her ability to influence the perceptions of others. A person with high social self-efficacy will possess a sense of certainty and confidence. If a person strongly doubts his or her ability to communicate a particular image (e.g., interesting, sexy, trustworthy, talented, reliable, loyal, competent), this person's social self-efficacy is said to be low. In this situation, if the doubting person's self-presentational

Figure 5.2 Diagram of Self-Presentation Theory

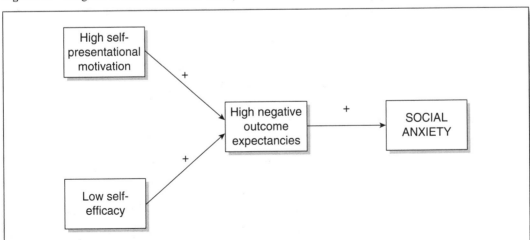

motivation also happens to be high, SPT predicts that the combination will produce high levels of social anxiety.

To summarize, according to SPT, a person experiences social anxiety only if two cognitive–social conditions are present simultaneously; namely, the person must (a) really want to make a particular impression, and (b) doubt his or her ability to succeed. These two conditions, however, do not produce social anxiety directly; they produce it only indirectly. What this means is that the first two conditions produce a third condition in the chain of causation. According to SPT, it is this third condition that directly causes symptoms of social anxiety. This third condition is called negative outcome expectancies. Negative outcome expectancies are said to mediate the association of motivation and self-efficacy to anxiety. In other words, expectancies explain how and why motivation and self-efficacy work to produce fear. People with high self-presentational motivation who also have low social self-efficacy are assumed to respond with fear because they have pessimistic (negative) expectancies about their future well-being. According to SPT, the fearful person's gut feeling of dread is directly caused by expectations that bad things are likely to happen because the person has failed to convey a certain impression. Thus, **negative outcome expectancies** are defined as anticipated aversive repercussions that are contingent on creating an undesirable impression. These repercussions or consequences can involve either not receiving a consequence that is desirable or receiving a consequence that is undesirable. People can fear the future for both reasons.

In the case of social anxiety disorder, the content (or focus) of the negative outcome expectancy often involves being convinced that one will be humiliated or embarrassed in public and that this will result in irrevocable social rejection or other types of horrific aversive consequences. **Anticipatory embarrassment** is the name of the emotion resulting from expecting short-term harm to one's social reputation. Social psychologist June Tangney and her colleagues found that anticipatory embarrassment is common among people who are socially anxious (Tangney, Miller, Flicker, & Barlow, 1996). Because embarrassment is defined contextually as an emotional reaction to a particular interpersonal situation, it is more of a *state* variable, meaning that it is a temporary condition caused by the situation.

Think back to Deena again. If you were a professional counselor who subscribed to SPT, how would you judge Deena's level of social self-efficacy? What about the strength of her self-presentational motivation? Try to determine whether the cognitive–social conditions would be conducive to the development of negative outcome expectancies and social anxiety. Do you think that knowing why Deena feels anxious might be useful in helping her to relax? As you continue to read on, see whether you can apply the cognitive–social concepts therapeutically to help ease Deena's emotional suffering.

CULTURE CAPSULE

East–West Differences in Social Anxiety

Cross-cultural differences in the prevalence of social anxiety disorders may be systematically related to variation along the sociocultural dimension known as **individualism–collectivism** (emphasized in several other chapters in this book, e.g., Chapters 10 and 14). In other words, vulnerability to social anxiety may be influenced by the degree to which a culture encourages its members to define their personal identities as independent of others (individualism) or as interdependent and connected to others (collectivism). Relative to countries in the West, such as the United States, Canada, and the United Kingdom, people's identities (i.e., how they define the self) in areas of the world such as East Asia, Africa, Central America, and South America tend to be interlinked with and dependent on relationships with others. For example, a typical Japanese woman might see her "self" as more connected and interwoven into the social fabric of her family and community than would a typical American woman, who might see herself as more self-sufficient and autonomous.

The East–West differentiation in the foundational underpinnings of the self-concept has implications for understanding social anxiety in a cross-cultural context. In the West, embarrassment and humiliation tend to occur in response to threats to a person's individual self. Also, negative outcome expectancies in the West tend to occur in response to threats to one's own self-interests. In more collectivistic cultures, however, a person may be more likely to feel embarrassed and humiliated for other people. Similarly, as a result of sharing a common identity with others, a person in a collectivistic society may experience more negative outcome expectancies when the welfare of others is in jeopardy. For these reasons, social anxiety may be experienced more often and more intensely in collectivistic countries like those in the Far East.

To test whether this cross-cultural difference in the social acceptability of social anxiety exists, Heinrichs and colleagues (2006) studied people from eight countries (Australia, Canada, Germany, Japan, Korea, the Netherlands, Spain, and the United States) to see whether their personal and perceived cultural norms were related to social anxiety and fear of blushing. While participants from collectivistic societies reported that their cultural norms were more accepting toward quiet and withdrawn behaviors, they experienced higher levels of social anxiety and a greater fear of blushing. These findings suggest that one's personal and cultural perception of social anxiety differs depending on one's culture. For mental health practitioners, the foregoing example illustrates the fact that cultural perceptions of social anxiety differ and that cultural differences need to be taken into account during therapy and counseling.

Tying the research to self-presentation theory. Research results support Leary and Kowalski's (1995) two-factor explanation for how symptoms of social anxiety develop. For example, the scientific literature has reported significant inverse relationships linking social self-efficacy to social anxiety. As expected, this research has found evidence that low self-efficacy is associated with high anxiety, whereas high self-efficacy is associated with low anxiety. This association seems to have *external validity* (i.e., generalizability) because it has been found in "normal" adults (Leary & Atherton, 1986), clinically distressed treatment seeking adults (Gaudiano & Herbert, 2003; Rosser, Issakidis, & Peters, 2003),

and adolescents with social anxiety disorder (Gaudiano & Herbert, 2007).

Other studies have also provided support for the *motivational* aspect of SPT. For example, research has found overreliance on others to be positively associated with social anxiety symptoms (Darcy, Davila, & Beck, 2005). Other support comes from negative expectancy research with clinical samples of persons classified as suffering from social anxiety disorder who overestimate the cost ("harmfulness") of negative interpersonal interactions (Smits, Rosenfield, McDonald, & Telch, 2006). These results, together with a host of similar findings reported by other authors suggest that anxiety-prone individuals tend to (unrealistically) anticipate that catastrophe will follow from minor social blunders. In the context of clinical models of psychotherapy, such as the Beck (1976) and Ellis (1962) approaches, this maladaptive style of thinking is termed *negative automatic thoughts* and *irrational beliefs,* respectively. From the perspective of Leary and Kowalski's (1995) two-factor model, overestimating negative repercussions simply connotes greater self-presentational motivation. Similarly, it is easy to reinterpret research linking social anxiety to greater need for social approval (e.g., Mallet & Rodriguez-Tome, 1999) as supporting SPT because desire for approval reflects the principle of self-presentational motivation. Thus, in addition to being a theory of causation and a model for guiding clinical intervention (by identifying targets for therapeutic change), SPT serves as a useful heuristic device for organizing and giving order to a wide range of seemingly unrelated research.

Despite the fact that SPT provides an elegant organizing theoretical framework, surprisingly few studies linking cognitive–social processes to social anxiety explicitly couch themselves within the framework offered by SPT. However, a recent series of studies by Catalino, Furr, and Bellis (2012) systematically tested the ideas behind SPT and found support for the theory. In three studies, Catalino and colleagues measured participants' self-presentation motivation and social self-efficacy. They found that both factors separately predicted self-reported social anxiety. Providing further support for SPT, they also found that self-presentation motivation and self-efficacy interacted to predict social anxiety.

FOCUS ON RESEARCH

Understanding Social Anxiety

Self-presentation theory (SPT) has proved to be useful in helping shed light on factors that might cause or contribute to social anxiety in young people. In particular, research has provided evidence to support the idea that symptoms of social anxiety in children and adolescents may have their roots in overinflated levels of self-presentational motivation coupled with underinflated levels of social self-efficacy.

Chansky and Kendall (1997) studied 9- to 15-year-olds. The research participants consisted of two subgroups known to differ on social anxiety. The *socially anxious group* consisted of a clinical sample of 47 participants enrolled in the Child and Adolescent Anxiety Disorders Clinic at Temple University. The *comparison group* consisted of a same age sample of 31 nonanxious counterparts.

In a laboratory setting, research participants were exposed to a situation in which they anticipated social interaction with an unknown peer of the same age. Participants in both groups were shown a videotape of another child playing a game and were told that the child was in an adjoining room. In anticipation of joining the other child to play, participants filled out a number of self-report assessments of their thoughts and emotions in response to the (anticipated) social situation. SPT would predict that the socially anxious children, as compared with the comparison group children, would report more negative outcome expectancies, lower social self-efficacy, and higher social anxiety when anticipating joining their playmate in the adjoining room.

Self-presentational motivation was assessed using a scale called the Social Expectancies Questionnaire, which taps the strength of both positive and negative outcome expectancies (i.e., anticipating acceptance or rejection). Anxiety and self-efficacy were assessed using the Social Anxiety Scale–Revised (La Greca & Stone, 1993) and the Perceived Competence Scale from the

Self-Perception Profile (Harter, 1982), respectively. The two groups of participants did respond differently to the situation involving anticipated social interaction. In accordance with SPT, the socially anxious group reacted with more social anxiety. When the two groups were compared in terms of self-presentational motivation, the socially anxious group responded with greater anticipation of rejection. There was a positive correlation between social anxiety and fear of rejection (i.e., negative outcome expectancies), suggesting (in line with SPT) that fear of rejection contributed to levels of social anxiety. Other results showed that the clinical group reported lower levels of social self-efficacy (i.e., confidence) than did the nonclinical group. As would be expected based on SPT, the treatment sample participants felt less confident in their social skills than did those in the nontreatment sample.

To summarize, Chansky and Kendall's (1997) study showed that young people receiving treatment for social anxiety disorder responded to an anticipated social situation just as SPT would predict. They felt less socially competent relative to control children and were presumably more concerned with the type of image they might portray. Thus, their self-efficacy was low, and their motivation was high. Furthermore, this combination of influences was uniquely related to heightened symptoms of social anxiety.

A Social Psychological Model of Depression

Have you ever received a lower-than-expected grade in a course, experienced a romantic breakup, or lost a job? Most students have experienced undesirable events or situations. This is because the human condition is inherently stressful. Social psychological theory and research look at how people think about stressful events and the way in which such thinking makes a difference to their mental health. It is not so much what happens to you that is important; rather it is how you perceive it. This section discusses how one's explanations for past events can affect vulnerability to symptoms of depression.

Let us start off with a brief exercise. Write down the numbers one to three in a notebook. Think back over the past 24 months and try to remember the three worst things that happened to you. Also think about why these situations occurred. Try to explain them briefly. Beside each number, write a sentence to indicate what happened and why. Do it now before reading further.

You likely offered a number of different explanations for your difficulties. These explanations

are called *causal attributions,* as noted in earlier chapters. Sometimes people will respond to the difficulties in their lives with explanations that are rather pessimistic. For example, in accounting for your own situations, you may have written something like this: "What made this happen is something that will never change and something that is undermining my whole life." Specific examples of pessimistic attributions for a job loss might include chronic illness, lack of intelligence, and discrimination.

This section reviews theory and research suggesting that people who habitually offer pessimistic explanations like this may be at risk for developing depressive symptoms. As you read on, you will come to understand the process by which a pessimistic attribution style works to make people vulnerable to symptoms of depression. You will see that this type of thinking is related to depression through feelings of helplessness and hopelessness. Later, the chapter discusses what counselors can do to help people resolve their bouts with depression and what can be done to prevent depression from happening in young people who are developmentally vulnerable.

Martin Seligman, a respected social psychologist, has spearheaded pioneering efforts to build bridges between social psychology and clinical psychology. Early in his career, in a series of experiments in which he exposed dogs to stressful events, Seligman (1975) administered painful electric shocks that could not be avoided or escaped. The dogs learned that the painful situations (the shocks) were uncontrollable. Later, these same dogs were placed in a similar "stressful situation," but this time the circumstances were slightly changed so that the dogs were given greater ability to cope. Specifically, during their second exposure to the stressful situation, the dogs could escape the electric shock.

The results of these experiments showed that dogs that had previously been exposed to uncontrollable shocks learned to passively accept new shocks. Even though the dogs could have escaped the new shocks if they wished, they did not even try. They seemed to have given up on the idea of coping by escaping. Instead of trying to do something to change their situation, they suffered passively when receiving the new series of painful jolts of shock.

Why would these dogs not try to do something to improve their situation? Seligman (1975) proposed that prior experience had taught the dogs that there was nothing they could do to change the situation. He suggested that the dogs, like humans who are depressed, had become psychologically helpless. Seligman's model became known as the **learned helplessness model of depression**. When applied to humans, the basic idea is that life experiences can sometimes teach people to give up in their attempts to cope.

In extending the animal model to humans, Seligman and his colleagues (Abramson, Seligman, & Teasdale, 1978) developed a cognitive–social model of human depression. This new model added some of the thinking components that were missing in the animal model. The 1978 human model was called the **attributional reformulation of the learned helplessness theory of depression**. The attributional model proposed that people are depressed because of the attributions they make for why

unfortunate things happen. According to the model, people who are prone to depression make pessimistic attributions that cause them to believe that there is nothing they can ever say or do to change their unfortunate circumstances. Technically, such a state of mind is called a *negative outcome expectancy* (discussed earlier) or simply *helplessness*. According to the 1978 model developed by Seligman and his colleagues, helpless thoughts about the future prompt symptoms of depression.

Recall the opening vignette about Deena, the student who came to K. H. for counseling. Although Deena appeared to be generally depressed in life, she was particularly depressed and dejected in anticipation of going out on a date with the fellow she met in the library. She even wanted to give up on the date before it happened. From the perspective of the attributional reformulation model, Deena had very strong negative outcome expectancies. She was convinced that the man would reject her, and she was probably also convinced that there was nothing she could do to change this eventuality. But, why was she so sure the situation would turn out poorly? Why did she have such a strong negative outcome expectancy? According to Seligman and colleagues' (1978) attributional model, Deena was probably making dysfunctional causal attributions for the imagined outcome. She was probably attributing her anticipated rejection to (a) something about herself (an *internal,* as opposed to *external,* causal attribution), (b) something that would not change (a *stable,* as opposed to *unstable,* causal attribution), and (c) something that would undermine her whole life (a *global,* as opposed to *specific,* causal attribution). In fact, she did tell K. H. that she had a boring personality and that she was unlovable. This would certainly classify as an internal, stable, and global attribution. If indeed Deena believed that this was the reason for her (anticipated) rejection, you can see how she might become depressed. After all, not being an interesting or lovable person is a hard thing to accept about oneself and is virtually impossible to change. These qualities would likely contribute to additional romantic failures in the future and lead to bleak expectancies.

The hopelessness theory of depression. The hopelessness theory of depression (HTD) developed by Abramson, Metalsky, and Alloy (1989) was based on the learned helplessness theory of depression. The **hopelessness theory of depression** suggests that depressive symptoms are most likely to occur when two factors are present at the same time: (a) a vulnerable person, and (b) negative environmental circumstances. Although either factor by itself may be only loosely connected to risk of depression, the co-occurrence of the factors is thought to be especially likely to make people susceptible to becoming depressed.

According to HTD, a *vulnerable person* is someone who has a characteristically negative style of interpreting the causes of aversive life events. This interpretative bias is sometimes called the **pessimistic explanatory style** or **depressogenic attribution style**. The term *style* connotes consistency of perceptual response across diverse types of stressful life events. A person who believes that "the root cause that made this bad thing happen is something that will never change and something that is undermining my whole life" is displaying the pessimistic attribution style. Such an explanation involves making stable and global causal attribution. **Stable attributions** represent a broad class of diverse causes that share one thing in common: The person thinks that the cause will endure over time and that it will be present in the future. A stable cause is one that is not likely to change over time (e.g., physical attractiveness). **Global attributions** also come in all shapes and sizes. However, each member of this class of causes has one thing in common: The person thinks that the cause has widespread influence on many aspects of his or her life; for example, physical attractiveness can serve as a global attribution because a person may think that being unattractive will affect many aspects of his or her life.

Let us look at some concrete examples of stable and global attributions. Imagine for a moment a situation in which you told someone that your lack of intelligence is what caused you to experience a stressful academic event (e.g., getting a poor grade on a psychology exam). Your lack of intelligence explanation is an example of an attribution that is both stable and global in nature. It is global because low intelligence could also give rise to many different stressful life events beyond just a poor psychology grade. In contrast, thinking that a low mark on an exam is due to insufficient effort spent studying is an example of a causal attribution that is *unstable* and *specific*. It is unstable because it can change in the future because you have control over it. You can always expend more effort studying in the future and thereby avoid suffering a similar fate again. It is also specific in that it is unlikely that lack of effort in studying for a psychology exam will have widespread adverse repercussions in other spheres of your life. There is likely a unique cause-and-effect relationship between the occurrence of this type of academic stressor (i.e., poor grade) and not studying enough. Thus, specific (vs. global) attributions for unpleasant events allow a person to have positive expectancies for the future. People who think this way feel more hopeful about their future chances of success, and their hope protects them against lapsing into depression. Conversely, attributing a poor grade on a psychology exam to lack of intelligence (a stable and global cause) has the opposite effect. It increases thoughts involving hopelessness, and this in turn causes emotions like depressed feelings to occur.

One chief advantage of HTD is that it offers useful and testable predictions that enable researchers to account for both the duration of depressive episodes over time and the severity of depression. Some depressed people have short-lasting episodes of depression, whereas others have longer episodes. Why is this? A useful theory should be able to account for differences among clients. According to HTD, the duration of an episode of depressive symptoms is influenced by the level of perceived stability of the root cause of the precipitating bad events. Take, for example, a person who is depressed and believes that his or her past academic failure is due to a lack of intelligence. By definition, a stable cause is unlikely to change in the future. According to HTD, a depressed student who accounts for academic failure in this manner will be depressed longer than will a student who believes that his or her academic failure is due to insufficient studying (an unstable/changeable cause).

Also, in terms of clinical observations, psychotherapists have noted that some clients suffer from a type of depression that is pervasive and all-encompassing. These clients experience symptoms of depression that are very widespread. They not only feel hopeless about their schoolwork, but also anticipate a bleak future in all of their life domains (e.g., romance, health, finances). Other depressed people, in contrast, have circumscribed "pockets" of depression. For instance, they might be hopeless with regard to their academic future, whereas their athletic futures and romantic futures seem bright. Why is this? According to HTD, the pervasiveness of symptoms of depression is related to whether a person offers specific or global explanations for past negative events. Accounts that are global lead to much more pessimism about the future than do accounts that are more specific in nature. Having more negative expectancies about the future, in turn, tends to breed a more all-encompassing type of depression.

As noted by Seligman and colleagues (Peterson, Maier, & Seligman, 1995) in their landmark book titled *Learned Helplessness: A Theory for the Age of Personal Control,* there is plenty of research to support the idea that explanatory style is a risk factor for the onset and maintenance of depressive symptoms. In terms of research evidence, these authors described several studies showing a link between the magnitude and presence of depressive symptoms and the tendency to make stable and global (and sometimes internal) explanations to account for why bad events happen. Although relatively fewer studies have examined the hypothesized role of negative outcome expectancies as a mediator between pessimistic attribution style and depressive symptoms, those that have tested this link have provided supportive evidence

(e.g., Buchanan & Seligman, 1995; Peterson & Vaidya, 2001).

It is important to emphasize that the attributions identified by HTD are thought to work in concert to generate depression through the mediating influence of generalized negative outcome expectancies. The theory itself calls these types of anticipatory cognitions *hopelessness expectancies.* Sometimes *hopelessness* is used as a shorter term. **Hopelessness** has been defined as "the expectation that highly desirable outcomes will not occur and that one is powerless to change the situation" (Needles & Abramson, 1990, p. 156). The flip side of this definition is that hopelessness also includes the expectation that highly undesirable outcomes will occur and that one is powerless to change the future outcomes. In either case, the heart of the cognitive problem for the person suffering from hopelessness is the belief that he or she is disempowered. This explains why depressed people seem to have given up on life. They "throw in the towel" because they believe that nothing they say or do will make a difference. Social psychologists would say that people who have given up or thrown in the towel do so because they believe (rightly or wrongly) that their future rewards and punishments in life are beyond their control.

The particular type of depression generated by generalized hopelessness expectancies is thought to be unique. This unique type of depression has a special name: **hopelessness depression**. Although many of the symptoms overlap with "regular" clinical depression as defined by the *DSM-IV-TR* (American Psychiatric Association, 2013), other symptoms are specific, including increased interpersonal dependency, and decreased self-esteem (Abela, Gagnon, & Auerbach, 2007), in addition to apathy and lethargy. In contrast, people who suffer from "regular" depression experience marked irritability, appetite disturbances, physical/medical complaints, and anhedonia (i.e., inability to enjoy or experience pleasure). There is considerable evidence from research to support the hypothesis that hopelessness depression exists and is distinguishable from traditional forms of (nonhopelessness) depression (e.g., Alloy & Clements, 1998; Joiner, Steer, Abramson, Metalsky, & Schmidt, 2001). Recent research shows that pessimistic attribution style predicts increases in hopelessness symptoms of depression (Abela et al., 2007).

Knowing why people develop emotional problems, such as depression and social anxiety can be very useful. For example, if attributions and expectancies explain how people get depressed or anxious, it should also be the case that therapies might help clients to reduce their suffering by modifying attributions and expectancies. Thus, mental health professionals who work with clients can use this information to help them be more effective in their therapeutic interventions. The next section describes how social psychological knowledge has been applied in clinical settings.

THE TREATMENT AND PREVENTION OF PSYCHOLOGICAL DISORDERS

To this point, you have learned how social psychology has contributed to an improved understanding of how people become vulnerable to experiencing depressive symptoms. The chapter has also discussed social–cognitive determinants of symptoms of social anxiety. As you have seen, both SPT and HTD suggest that social psychological processes that are cognitive in nature play a role in the onset and maintenance of these disorders. Thus, social psychology has helped to improve our understanding of the origins and maintenance of emotional problems.

In addition, social psychology has been instrumental in improving our understanding of the underlying processes by which therapeutic interventions help to ameliorate various psychological problems (see Figure 5.3). This section discusses the interface of social psychology with clinical and counseling psychology. This facet of the interface seeks to identify social psychological processes that may play a role in explaining how and why clients change as a function of therapy. This interface is also concerned with using social psychological insights to design new interventions and improve techniques for treating people

with mental illness. Although social psychology has been applied to understanding a wide range of therapeutic interventions (for a review, see Maddux & Tangney, 2010), for the purpose of consistency, this section focuses on treatments for anxiety and depression.

In this chapter, we focus primarily on examples from clinical psychology; however, much of the content is also relevant to counseling psychology. The distinction between clinical psychology and counseling psychology is subtle. Clinical psychologists usually have an area of specialty (e.g., substance abuse) and treat people with serious mental illness. In contrast, counseling psychologists have a more general approach to treatment and focus more on psychologically healthy individuals (Cobb et al., 2004). It should be noted that these are generalizations, and that the differences within the fields may be greater than the differences between them.

There has long been a gap between basic social psychological research and practice. As Tashiro and Mortensen (2006) point out in their review, this gap arises because of fundamental differences in the types of research carried out in the two disciplines. In general, basic research seeks to determine causality by conducting methodologically rigorous studies, often in laboratory settings. Basic research is said to possess high levels of **internal validity** (cause and effect can be reliably demonstrated), but lacks **external validity** (the degree to which one can generalize the findings to other situations and persons). The objective of applied research, on the other hand, is to find what interventions or treatments will be effective under real-world conditions. Applied research tends to have greater external validity, but weaker internal validity (Tashiro & Mortensen, 2006). Translational research seeks to bridge this gap by applying theory and causal relationships gleaned from basic scientific research to the treatment of mental illness. Similarly, another goal of translational research is to encourage researchers working in applied settings to revisit basic research when unexpected results occur. Thus, it is hoped that social psychology will inform clinicians in treating mental illness, and vice versa. The following

Figure 5.3   Using Social Psychologically Based Approaches to Therapy to Treat a Person With Psychological Problems

SOURCE: Photo Courtesy of Rebecca Purc-Stephenson.

examples illustrate how basic research can be "translated" into clinical application.

As you read further, consider each of the therapy approaches in terms of Deena's case presented in the opening vignette. She experienced significant feelings of hopelessness, depression, and social anxiety. How might social psychologically derived treatment models for anxiety and depression help Deena to become happier and more socially outgoing?

Self-Presentation Theory: An Approach to Treating Social Anxiety

Previously, we discussed SPT as a social psychological model of how social anxiety develops and persists. This model has several implications for the treatment of social anxiety disorder. First, by identifying the nature of cognitive–social targets for change, it helps to guide therapeutic interventions. (Do you remember Lewin's idea, from Chapter 1, concerning the practical usefulness of good theories?) The model suggests, for example, that interventions should seek to modify social self-efficacy and self-presentational motivation. Specifically, interventions should seek to increase the former and decrease the latter. Second, the model provides a useful theoretical blueprint for understanding how and why improvement occurs (or does not occur). For instance, if an existing treatment for social anxiety has been used and it does not reduce the client's anxiety, one might use SPT to infer the reason why it was ineffective. Specifically, this model could lead to the hypothesis that the treatment was ineffective because it failed to bolster a client's sense of confidence in communicating with others. In addition, the model suggests that an absence of therapeutic improvement might be attributable to a failure of therapy to diminish the client's motivation to project a desired image. Thus, SPT guides the change process by suggesting targets for therapeutic intervention. As you may recall, the theory hypothesizes that social anxiety is most likely to occur in people who lack social self-efficacy and who have high self-presentational motivation to impress others. Sometimes by design and sometimes by coincidence, existing cognitive–behavioral treatments for social anxiety disorder intervene in such a way as to reduce the excessive need for social approval. From the perspective of SPT, interventions that reduce the need for social approval benefit clients by decreasing their self-presentational motivation. In this regard, for socially anxious people it is likely that reduced motivation to impress others is one of the chief benefits of *rational–emotive therapy* (RET) (Ellis, 1962). RET is designed to help clients by reducing or eliminating their irrational and unrealistic concerns, in this case with respect to what others will think of them. The application of RET to social anxiety is a good example of how SPT helps to explain the change process in existing therapies.

Other interventions, such as *social skill therapies* may reduce symptoms of social anxiety by bolstering the client's sense of social self-efficacy (Gaudiano & Herbert, 2003). This is precisely what Bandura's (1977a) *theory of self-efficacy* would predict. Specifically, Bandura would suggest that the most effective way to increase self-efficacy among socially anxious clients is to provide them with "mastery" situations in which they can practice their interpersonal skills successfully. This probably explains why role-play enactments work to help socially anxious clients. The more people practice engaging in social situations with others, the less difficult and anxiety provoking they will be.

Gaudiano and Herbert (2003) conducted one of the first intervention studies to rigorously apply the concept of self-efficacy to clients suffering from social anxiety disorder. Consistent with SPT, self-efficacy was defined as the client's confidence in being able to convey a favorable impression to others. Research participants were a large sample of employed adults, most of whom suffered from avoidant personality disorder, a psychological problem that is characterized by debilitating levels of social anxiety. During the therapeutic intervention, the clients were engaged in a type of cognitive–behavior therapy that sought to reduce anxiety by teaching social skills. A key feature of the treatment included role-play enactments of social situations in which difficult social interactions were practiced and mastered. It was reasoned that learning social skills would naturally bolster clients' levels of social self-efficacy.

The research clients were assessed for levels of self-efficacy and anxiety prior to beginning the treatment program. Their levels of self-efficacy were also measured after it was finished. You may recall from Chapter 3 that this quasi-experimental method of investigation is called a pretest–posttest design.

The results provided support for the relevance of SPT in understanding how therapy produces change. From pretest to posttest, mean levels of social self-efficacy increased, and social anxiety decreased. Moreover, the magnitude of increases in self-efficacy ratings from pretreatment to posttreatment was associated with the magnitude of decreases in social anxiety. That is, the amount of reduction in anxiety paralleled the amount of increase in self-efficacy. This pattern is significant because it is precisely what one would expect to see if SPT offered a valid explanation for how and why therapy works to produce symptom reduction in clients.

Impressively, changes in self-efficacy associated with therapeutic involvement remained a significant predictor of reductions in social anxiety independent of other potential biasing extraneous influences. This latter finding suggests that the connection between self-efficacy and social anxiety is genuine and cannot be explained away as trivial or as secondary to other factors. A liberal interpretation of this study's main finding (remember that it was a quasi-experiment) is that changes in social self-efficacy mediated the effects of the treatment involvement on client improvement. In other words, there is evidence to suggest that the main reason why therapy worked as well as it did was because it bolstered levels of social self-efficacy.

As discussed in Chapter 2, when results from intervention studies are consistent with expectations based on a theoretical model, the results strengthen our confidence in the validity of the model. In this connection, the therapy study by Gaudiano and Herbert (2003) is significant because it provides empirical support for the validity of the SPT model of social anxiety. If we apply these findings to Deena's case, helping her to improve her own sense of social self-efficacy might give her the skills she needs to develop the close relationships for which she has been longing. In this treatment model, this skill building is done through role-playing and practice. Deena may be less worried about what others are going to think about her if she knows how to relate to them.

The findings reported by Gaudiano and Herbert (2003) also suggest that clinical psychologists may find this model of social anxiety as a practical blueprint for treating clients. In particular, the study is relevant to mental health professionals because it points to social skills training and role-play enactments as techniques for helping clients to decrease their interpersonal anxiety by increasing their social self-efficacy. It is hoped that future studies will further validate these techniques. Given that a multitude of social–cognitive factors (e.g., values, beliefs, expectancies, attributions) seem to be involved in the maintenance of symptoms of social anxiety, it is likely that future clinical research will show additional therapeutic techniques to be effective in remediation.

Hopelessness Theory Approach to Treating Depression

HTD also has implications for therapeutic intervention. With respect to the treatment of depression, hopelessness has always been a concept that is implicitly relevant to cognitive approaches, such as those developed by Beck (1976; see also Peterson et al., 1995). Technically speaking, HTD was a model developed to account for why people become depressed in the first place. Later, when the model started to be applied to understanding remediation of depression, the therapeutic goal shifted away from hopelessness and toward *hopefulness*. **Hopefulness** is defined as expecting good things to happen in the future. This principle of hopefulness was articulated by Needles and Abramson (1990), who extended the principles of HTD by suggesting that people recover from depression by becoming more hopeful. This section describes how knowledge of HTD has the potential to help clients overcome depression.

Theoretically, how can a psychological intervention help clients to develop increased levels of hopefulness? The hopefulness approach developed by Needles and Abramson (1990) suggests that counselors should attempt to do two things. First, they should engineer their clients' social environments in such a way as to increase the frequency of occurrence of positive life events. They might also consider recreational therapy or role-play enactments. Setting modest goals and achieving them on a daily basis may also result in pleasurable experiences. Second, counselors should encourage clients to think differently and to use an **enhancing attributional style**. This style is the opposite of the pessimistic attributional style. Thus, clients are encouraged to make global and stable attributions for positive events.

Recent research has tested the effectiveness of hope therapy for depression (Cheavens, Feldman, Gum, Michael, & Snyder, 2006). This therapy is not intended to treat pathology; instead, it is designed to help people set goals and find ways to achieve them. Levels of hope, meaning in life, self-esteem, depression, and anxiety were assessed before and after therapy. Participants in the treatment group showed greater improvements in hope, meaning in life, and self-esteem, as well as decreased levels of depression and anxiety. Vennig, Kettler, Eliot, and Wilson (2009) also found preliminary evidence for the effectiveness of increasing hopefulness to prevent the onset of depression.

They conducted a meta-analysis (i.e., a statistical method for combining results from different studies) of studies that tested the effectiveness of therapies to prevent the onset of depression. Therapies that included several hopeful elements were more effective at preventing depression than therapies that did not include hopeful elements. Given these findings, it seems that there is hope for the effectiveness of therapies promoting hopefulness for depression.

FOCUS ON INTERVENTION

Intervening Early to Prevent Depression

The Penn Resiliency Program (Gillham et al., 2007) is an excellent example of a psychotherapeutic intervention that was carefully crafted to target change in cognitive–social processes identified by the hopelessness model as being important mediators of depressive symptomatology.

The Penn Resiliency Program was tested with 697 middle school students who were considered to be at risk for developing depression. The main goal was to demonstrate that this theory-based intervention could prevent the onset of depression. Given that depressive symptoms have been shown to increase slightly over the middle school years and then rise with entry into high school, the researchers reasoned that they might be able to intervene during this developmental period. The means of preventing depression involved modifying explanatory style. In fact, the intervention consisted of two parts: cognitive restructuring and problem-solving skills acquisition.

Cognitive restructuring. The program sought to teach children about the nature and impact of pessimistic versus optimistic interpretations of life events. Because children in early adolescence are less able to engage in high-level mental abstraction normally associated with cognitive–behavioral therapy in adults, a number of creative techniques were employed to make cognitive restructuring procedures more accessible and engaging to the young "clients." Important cognitive–behavioral therapy concepts were introduced and elaborated on using novel delivery modalities, such as skits, stories, role-plays, and cartoons. Consistent with cognitive therapy models developed by Beck (1976) and Ellis (1962), these modalities were used to teach students attending the program to link how they feel and how they behave with the content of their thoughts. For example, in one set of worksheets involving cartoons (storyboards), students were asked to generate beliefs that would lead to a behavioral or an emotional consequence shown in the final frame of a cartoon story. Sometimes the children had to generate an explanation for an emotional outcome depicting a happy face with an upturned smile, and sometimes they had to do so for an outcome portraying a sad face with a downturned frown.

The consequences of optimistic and pessimistic explanatory styles were also communicated by skits involving two characters: Gloomy Greg and Hopeful Holly. In one particular set of skits, both Greg and Holly were described as attending a school dance. At the dance, when the music started

(Continued)

(Continued)

to play, both Greg and Holly asked peers to dance with them, only to be met with rejection. However, the skits diverged at this point, with Hopeful Holly's response significantly different than Gloomy Greg's response. Greg was depicted as attributing the rejection (negative social interaction) to stable and global causes (e.g., "I'm a loser, and no one likes me"). Greg also made pessimistic predictions representing negative outcome expectancies (e.g., "No one will dance with me—ever," "I'll never have fun at dances"). He gave up on dancing and sat down dejected on a wooden bench alongside the bleachers for the rest of the evening. Feeling hopeless about his future chances of dancing, he had a miserable and depressing time.

Hopeful Holly, in contrast, was depicted as attributing the negative interpersonal interaction to more unstable and specific causes (e.g., "Maybe I didn't smile enough," "Maybe he was too nervous to dance"). The skit also depicted Holly's predictions as more hopeful.

Skill acquisition. A vital second component of the Penn Resiliency Program is skill acquisition. It is true that shifting one's attributional style can provide hope that problems will dissipate and that some change is possible. However, modifying explanatory biases does not provide the behavioral skills required to enact or realize that hope of change. Thus, the second half of the program teaches problem-solving skills. These include emotion control techniques as well as strategies for relaxing, being assertive, negotiating with others, and avoiding procrastination. As with the cognitive component, skills were taught (illustrated) using skits, stories, and cartoon characters (e.g., Say-It-Straight Sally). These skills were enacted through participation in role-play scenarios.

The at-risk children who received the program were compared with a group of matched children who were also at risk, but did not receive the intervention. Results of this experimental intervention revealed that children involved in the program, as compared with control children, showed both improved explanatory style *and* reduced depressive symptoms. Importantly, these therapeutic benefits were maintained a full three years after the program ended. Thus, the Penn Resiliency Program was successful in reducing the expected upward trajectory of depression for an appreciable number of these young adolescents.

Positive life events and self-enhancing attributions (i.e., global and stable for positive events) are believed to combine to promote the growth of hopefulness. Hopefulness, in turn, is thought to offset depression, causing a person's mood to lift. Thus, to reduce symptoms of depression, one may alter how clients explain the good things that happen to them in life. Missing in the Needles and Abramson (1990) model is any mention of the importance of altering how clients explain the bad things that occur. As we will see, this omission is a limitation.

In addition to the research conducted under the Penn Resiliency Program (Gillham et al., 2007),

a number of other studies provide evidence supporting the validity of the hopefulness approach to alleviating depression (Johnson, Han, Douglas, Johannet, & Russell, 1998; Needles & Abramson, 1990). One study, for example, monitored changes in depression before and after treatment in a clinical sample of psychiatric patients (Johnson et al., 1998). These patients received cognitive–behavioral treatment for depression. Consistent with expectations based on the hopefulness approach to treatment, attributions for positive life events predicted decreases in depressive symptoms over time. These decreases in depression were directly linked to increases in hopefulness expectancies. Patients who made stable, global, and internal attributions for positive events had more hopefulness and less depression after treatment than did patients who did not attribute positive events in a manner consistent with this self-enhancing style.

Clinical research testing the Needles and Abramson (1990) model is contributing to its further empirical refinement. For example, we have seen that a *pessimistic attributional style for negative events* can lead to depression and that an *enhancing attributional style for positive events* can promote hopefulness. Is it reasonable to wonder whether these two styles interact in some way? Consider a study that examined the combined effect of both enhancing *and* pessimistic attribution styles (Voelz, Haeffel, Joiner, & Wagner, 2003). In this study, depressed inpatients were assessed at intake to a psychiatric hospital and again at discharge approximately nine days later. Patients received standard cognitive–behavioral treatment. Treatment efficacy was assessed by monitoring changes in hopelessness and depression from pretreatment to posttreatment. The results extended the Needles and Abramson (1990) model by suggesting that a pessimistic attribution style for negative events interacts with an enhancing attributional pattern for positive events to predict changes in hopelessness. Specifically, Voelz and colleagues' (2003) study showed that patients exhibiting a high degree of enhancing attributional style for positive events reported only moderate levels of hopelessness at the time of discharge regardless of whether they displayed a pessimistic attributional style for negative events. In comparison, patients showing a low degree of enhancing attributional style and a high degree of pessimistic style displayed high levels of hopelessness at the time of discharge.

Clearly, these data provide evidence that the Needles and Abramson (1990) hopefulness model is in need of modification. Specifically, a thorough model of the causes of hopefulness appears to require the integration of both an enhancing attributional style for positive events

and a pessimistic attributional style for negative events. If the results of Voelz and colleagues' (2003) study can be replicated, they suggest that mental health professionals working with depressed clients may wish to broaden the range of cognitive–social targets they attempt to modify. In particular, practitioners may wish to encourage clients to make stable and global attributions for positive life events and to make unstable and specific attributions for negative events. Thus, when good things happen, it might help to alleviate depression if clients can be made to believe that these things are due to (their own) personalities, attitudes, or intelligence. Conversely, when bad things happen, depression might be decreased in proportion to the extent to which clients can be persuaded to blame these things on fleeting extenuating circumstances.

By now, you should have a fairly good understanding of how social psychological theory can help us to explain why people develop certain emotional problems. You also should have an improved understanding of how social psychological theory and research can be applied in designing clinical interventions. Specifically, you have seen how social psychologically based therapeutic interventions are useful in helping clients to resolve symptoms of anxiety and depression.

THE DIAGNOSIS OF PSYCHOLOGICAL DISORDERS

The first two sections of this chapter considered why people become depressed and socially anxious and what can be done to overcome such problems. Those sections emphasized the social psychology of therapeutic clients. The focus of this section shifts from clients to mental health clinicians—the therapists. The study of mental health practitioners is the domain of this section of the chapter. Research in this domain focuses on understanding the processes by which clinicians assess and diagnose their clients.

Imagine for a moment that you are employed in a psychiatric setting as a clinical psychologist.

Your job is to diagnose and treat people suffering from a wide range of disorders. Some of the clients are depressed, whereas others have social anxiety disorder. Still others have drug or alcohol problems, schizophrenia, or other difficulties. Imagine that you have a new client coming for a first appointment with you. You have never met him, and you are not sure what his difficulties are. For all you know, he could have schizophrenia or be depressed or alcoholic. The client knocks on your office door, and you invite him in. How would you go about deciding which disorder (if any) this particular client has? Making such a decision is what *clinical diagnosis* is all about. Given that your goal is to be as accurate as possible, you should avoid pitfalls that might bias your judgment. Just as people who become depressed or anxious may be predisposed to think in certain ways, so too are clinicians (and people in general) predisposed to fall victim to certain patterns of thought. After reading this section, you will come to appreciate how important it is to remain as objective and unbiased as possible in judging others. You will also learn that this is not always an easy thing to do.

Clinicians, whether they are psychologists, psychiatrists, social workers, or others, are generally highly skilled professionals whose goal is to identify and alleviate people's emotional and behavioral problems. Research in clinical psychology has demonstrated that mental health practitioners are effective at treating mental illness. However, clinicians are also humans. As a result, they sometimes make the kinds of errors in judgment and thinking that afflict all people from time to time (Leary & Miller, 1986; Owen, 2008). In what follows, you will find a brief review of certain biases and errors in thinking that social psychologists believe practitioners should guard against when making clinical decisions. By **clinical decision making**, we mean the process of judging what is wrong with clients (assessment/diagnosis) and choosing among alternative approaches to treatment.

Imagine two scenarios. In the first, a person suffering from a serious anxiety disorder goes to a mental health professional for help, but the therapist fails to diagnose the problem accurately. In the second scenario, a client is inappropriately diagnosed with an anxiety disorder that he or she does not in fact have. With the first scenario, if a clinician mistakenly diagnoses a client's symptoms and fails to provide proper treatment, the client will continue to suffer from anxiety, and the client's level of emotional disability might even get worse over time. The first scenario describes a case where a **false-negative** judgment is made. This error involves not recognizing a bona fide problem that exists. In this case, an anxiety disorder diagnosis should have been made, but was not. Obviously, steps should be taken to avoid this type of mistake, and there is a need for more research on how to reduce false negatives.

Research on diagnosis and clinical judgment has given somewhat more attention to **false-positive** judgments, as in the second scenario above. A false positive exists when a diagnostic label is inappropriately given to a client. An example of a false-positive judgment is when a mental health professional incorrectly diagnoses a client with depression when in fact the client is mourning the death of a loved one and is actually suffering from a normal grief reaction. False positives and false negatives are further described in Table 5.1.

One of the most famous research demonstrations of the existence of a false positive came from an investigation by Rosenhan (1973). Rosenhan showed how context or setting can cause clinicians to distort their judgments of a client's problems. The lesson learned is that being in a therapeutic setting can influence clinicians to see apparent problems where none exists (i.e., to make false-positive judgments). As you read about Rosenhan's famous study, try to answer the following question: Why did the staff members make these errors in judgment? Following this research example is a discussion of how different types of influences can sometimes contribute to distorted perceptions among highly trained mental health professionals.

Table 5.1 Correct and Incorrect Diagnostic Decision Making and Outcomes

Clinician Conclusion	Actual Condition of Client	
	Client Has Depression	*Client Does Not Have Depression*
	True Positive	*False Positive*
Client is diagnosed with depression	• Client appropriately receives treatment for a condition that he or she actually has; potential to benefit from treatment exists	• Client receives treatment for a condition that he or she does not have; receives unnecessary treatment or fails to be treated for a condition that he or she actually has
	False Negative	*True Negative*
Client is not diagnosed with depression	• Client does not receive treatment for a condition that he or she actually has; condition might not improve and might actually get worse	• Client is appropriately not treated for a condition that he or she does not have; opportunity to consider other diagnoses exists

FOCUS ON RESEARCH

How Judgmental Errors Can Lead Us to See What We Expect to See

During the early 1970s, D. L. Rosenhan carried out a controversial study that raised many questions about the accuracy of psychiatric diagnoses. Rosenhan's research sparked a heated debate in clinical and social psychology that still goes on today. In his article, titled "On Being Sane in Insane Places," Rosenhan (1973) describes an experiment in which eight "normal" (mentally healthy) research confederates gained admission to 12 different inpatient psychiatric hospitals. These "pseudo-patients" came from a variety of backgrounds. Importantly, none was known to be suffering from psychiatric problems. The pseudo-patients approached different psychiatric hospitals faking psychiatric complaints. They told the staff members that they had been hearing voices. In each case, the pseudo-patient reported that the voices said "empty," "hollow," and "thud." All of them were admitted to hospitals. Once the pseudo-patients were hospitalized, they told the staff members that the auditory hallucinations had stopped. From the point of admission onward, the pseudo-patients acted normally.

The results of the study were astonishing. In all cases, false-positive judgments were made. Of the pseudo-patients, 11 were incorrectly diagnosed as having schizophrenia. The remaining pseudo-patient was given the diagnostic label of "manic depression." None of the pseudo-patients had his or her diagnosis reconsidered over the course of the hospital stay. On average, the pseudo-patients were hospitalized for 19 days, although one pseudo-patient was kept for 52 days before being discharged. This occurred in spite of the pseudo-patient acting normally during the stay. When the pseudo-patients took notes on what they were observing on the ward, the nursing staff members

(Continued)

(Continued)

pathologized this behavior, seeing it as an expression of assumed underlying psychopathology. When the pseudo-patients were discharged from the hospitals, they were released with essentially the same diagnoses they received when they entered the hospitals. The only difference was that their mental illness diagnosis was qualified with the term *in remission*.

Rosenhan's (1973) research provides evidence showing how false-positive errors are sometimes made in clinical decision making and how the consequences of such errors can harm the very people whom professionals are trying to help. The study also illustrates the biasing effects that labels derived from first impressions can have on subsequent assessments. Although "in remission" at their times of discharge, the pseudo-patients would continue to carry a stigmatizing label (e.g., "schizophrenic," "mental patient") with them after they left the hospitals. As you will see in the subsequent discussion, and in Chapter 12 on applying psychology to the community, other people often react in a negative manner to stigmatizing labels.

You might think that Rosenhan's (1973) findings reflect the era when he conducted his study, and you might believe that the same false-positive diagnoses likely would not be made today. Although there have been many improvements to the psychiatric system since the 1970s, some researchers and policy makers argue that more changes are needed. Murray Goddard, a psychology professor at the University of New Brunswick described a recent personal experience of institutionalization that was eerily similar to that of Rosenhan and the other pseudo-patients (Goddard, 2011). In 2010, Goddard travelled to the United States during a time of personal stress and upheaval. While there, he was admitted to a psychiatric institution and diagnosed with bipolar disorder. He felt that he was misdiagnosed, and yet he was not allowed to leave the institution for 21 days (two days longer than the average length of institutionalization in Rosenhan's study). He was not allowed to attend to personal matters like paying a bill, which resulted in a sense of powerlessness. Goddard also described how the psychiatric label that was applied to him dramatically impacted the way others (including friends and colleagues) interpreted his behavior, even after he was discharged. However, Goddard did note some differences between his experience and Rosenhan's (1973) observations of psychiatric institutions in the 1970s. In contrast to Rosenhan's (1973) reports of staff neglect and even violence toward patients, Goddard (2011) described the staff spending time with patients and working to accommodate patient requests, and he did not witness any violence toward patients. Goddard's (2011) account of a personal experience of being "sane in an insane place" suggests that while there have been many improvements in the psychiatric system in North America, more changes may still be needed.

Keep Rosenhan's (1973) research example, and Goddard's (2011) more recent personal experience, in mind while reading the following subsection on biases and errors in clinical decision making.

Biases in Clinical Decision Making

The effect of labeling on judgments of mental illness. Social psychologists have found that preexisting information (i.e., labels) may sometimes bias clinicians, resulting in false-positive or false-negative judgments. The **labeling effect** refers to a tendency to perceive clients in ways that are erroneous owing to the reactive effects of an existing psychiatric label (Corrigan, 2007). In the clinic, labeling refers to the possibility that a clinician may perceive a client's symptoms differently after the client has been given a diagnosis compared with before the client has been diagnosed.

For example, past medical records on new patients can result in labeling. Providing practitioners with clients' files is common practice when new clients have been referred. Although this practice seems innocent enough, information in client records may inadvertently "contaminate" a clinician's thinking, causing him or her to lose objectivity due to labeling bias. When a mental health professional gives a client a diagnostic label indicating the presence of a psychiatric disorder, the label quite often takes on a life of its own and has an influence beyond the therapeutic context. Members of society often react to the label, and sometimes a person labeled with a psychiatric diagnosis can be seen as "deviant" rather than in need of help. This *stigma* can even result in a loss of supportive services (Corrigan, 2007). Stigma is also associated with a reduction in life satisfaction (Corrigan, 2007), low self-esteem and self-efficacy (Drapaski et al., 2013), and increased depression (Ritscher & Phelan, 2004).

The negative effects of psychiatric labels have been illustrated in research by Link, Phelan, Bresnahan, Stueve, and Pescosolido (1999) that surveyed people's perceptions of clients with mental illness. One third (33%) of the people surveyed fell prey to the myth that a depressed person was "somewhat likely" to "very likely" to commit violence against someone else. Of course, this is an erroneous perception because it is not consistent with what mental health practitioners know about depression. In reality, depressed people tend not to be any more dangerous than nondepressed people. The myth of being dangerous was particularly prevalent for clients labeled as schizophrenic (66%), alcohol dependent (71%), or cocaine dependent (87%).

This same study (Link et al., 1999) also examined stereotypes of distressed people who have not been stigmatized by a diagnostic label. In particular, the researchers asked their research participants to rate a target person who was described as being distressed due to having

had "a rough time" in life. Participants were not told that the target person had a diagnosis of a mental illness. The effect of the absence of a psychiatric label was dramatic. Only 17% of the people surveyed believed that the distressed person was prone to violence. This is convincing evidence of the biasing effects of labels because the person being judged differed only on the basis of the existence of a psychiatric diagnosis.

Unlike members of the general public, mental health practitioners are much less likely to experience such biases toward people who have been labeled as having a psychiatric disorder. Although professionals who work with clients are less prone to obvious forms of prejudice, there is nevertheless some evidence that clinicians occasionally exhibit negative stereotypes. The existence of clinical prejudice is very subtle, but it is worth knowing about because it potentially can have an adverse impact on clinical diagnosis and treatment. If social psychologists can help their clinical counterparts to eradicate even subtle biases, client welfare should improve.

In a study that examined judgments of mental health service providers, Burk and Sher (1990) found that children of alcoholics were perceived by clinicians as having equally poor emotional health regardless of whether they were described as "class leaders" or as having "behavior problems." Normally, one would expect decisions about mental health to vary with these two descriptions. In fact, Burk and Sher did find that clinical ratings of emotional well-being of the children of nonalcoholics fluctuated (as one would expect) from being positive when the children were described as class leaders to being negative when the children were considered to have behavior problems. What can be concluded from the fact that the two sets of findings were so different? Although clinicians make every effort to remain impartial and generally succeed in so doing, they can sometimes fall prey to biased clinical decision making. As we will see, clinicians have begun to use this kind of research to improve the ways in which they make clinical decisions.

The effects of group stereotypes on clinical judgments. Perhaps you have noticed that clinical bias resulting from labeling can be induced by culturally provided labels and culturally acquired stereotypes. Mental health practitioners cannot help but notice the ethnicity or gender of their clients. For two decades, social psychologists have been studying whether culturally perpetuated labels and stereotypes can sometimes bias judgments made by mental health professionals (Solomon, 1992). Social–clinical research has focused on several categories of stereotypes, including those based on gender, race, ethnicity, religion, and sexual identity. Clinicians work hard to be objective and try not to let individual stereotypes and biases get in the way of providing clients with the best care. However, all people are susceptible to stereotyping other groups, and it is unfortunate that stereotypes may lead mental health professionals to misattribute or misdiagnose their clients' symptoms. As we will see, the sometimes unconscious nature of culture- and gender-based stereotypes can make it difficult for clinicians to take preventive or corrective steps aimed at guarding against racism or sexism (or other forms of bias).

What is the evidence to show that judgments of mental health professionals may sometimes be distorted by their clients' *social, racial,* and/or *economic* standing? Jenkins-Hall and Sacco (1991) conducted an experiment in which White male and female therapists were shown a videotape of a therapy client. The videotapes were made to differ based on the race of the client (Black or White), the presence of a disorder (depressed or nondepressed), and the gender of the client (male or female). Therapists were asked to rate each of the videotaped clients on a number of dimensions.

Some interesting biases were revealed. For example, White therapists were more likely to make false-positive diagnoses for Black clients. In particular, White therapists incorrectly rated nondepressed Black clients as having more depression than nondepressed White clients. Depressed Black clients were also rated more negatively than depressed White clients on an interpersonal rating scale that assesses assertiveness, attractiveness, social skills, and other factors. Thus, this research suggests that mental health professionals can sometimes hold culturally derived biases that result in false-positive diagnoses. Also, a therapist's race may have a subtle and mostly unconscious influence on his or her clinical decision making when it comes to treating and diagnosing people from other cultures. This type of bias in perceiving symptoms in clients of other races may help to account for the results of research showing that the diagnosis of mental illness in ethnic minorities is unusually high (Solomon, 1992).

The idea that mental health practitioners may sometimes display a type of "psychiatric racial bias" is also illustrated in other research showing that African Americans are more likely to be diagnosed with schizophrenia than are Caucasians (Bresnahan et al., 2007). Evidence showing differential rates of clinical diagnosis is especially interesting given that there is little objective evidence for actual differential prevalence of schizophrenia in the two groups. It is quite possible that the tendency to attribute schizophrenia to African Americans more often than to Caucasians is related to culturally based stereotypes. In terms of explaining this bias, it could be that race-related stereotypes bias the attentional focus of Caucasian clinicians in a way that causes them to pay excessive attention to client symptoms that are consistent with their own beliefs about the client's cultural reference group (Garb, 2005). Conversely, biased clinicians may ignore or discount client symptoms that are inconsistent with their (erroneous) stereotypes of people who are members of the client's race.

There has been a considerable amount of research that suggests clinicians' judgments are sometimes vulnerable to being influenced by *gender bias* as well. In a classic study conducted more than 40 years ago, Broverman, Broverman, Clarkson, Rosenkrantz, and Vogel (1970) found that clinician beliefs about mentally healthy adults were frequently closer to their concept of a psychologically healthy man than to that of a psychologically healthy woman. Despite the fact that our society has witnessed increased equality between the sexes, contemporary research is still finding gender biases among clinicians. Unfortunately, these biases provide conditions that discriminate against women. For example, a study by Danziger and Welfel (2000) showed that clinicians, on average, rated female clients as less competent (and hence more needful of therapy) than male clients. Furthermore, gender can influence clinicians' judgment when deciding on a diagnosis (Flanagan & Blashfield, 2005). Flanagan and Blashfield studied whether gender influenced the diagnosis of practicing psychologists and psychiatrists by giving them fictional case histories of people meeting the criteria for antisocial personality disorder, histrionic personality disorder, or a mix of symptoms. While the description given was the same regardless of the fictional client's gender, the clinicians provided a different diagnosis depending on whether the fictional client was identified as male or female when presented with the case with a mix of symptoms. Female clients were more likely to be diagnosed with histrionic personality disorder, and males were more likely to be diagnosed with antisocial personality disorder. These findings suggest that gender affects clinicians' judgment and could lead to misdiagnosis.

What can we conclude from the research on gender bias? First, just as there is a type of "psychiatric racial bias," there is also a type of "psychiatric gender bias." It is likely that mental health professionals are being influenced by this gender bias in a way that causes them to "overdiagnose" psychiatric disorders in women relative to those in men (Jane, Oltmanns, South, & Turkheimer, 2007).

Even a client's *age* can have a biasing effect on clinicians' judgments (Balsis, Woods, Gleason, & Oltmanns, 2007; Meeks, 1990). This idea has been borne out by research conducted by Suzanne Meeks, who examined clinicians' perceptions of client suitability for psychotherapy (Meeks, 1990). In this study, a sample of clinical psychologists (and trainees) read case histories of potential clients. Then they proceeded to rate the potential clients in terms of how responsive each client would be to a course of treatment. The cases differed in terms of how old the client was. There were three age groups: young, middle-age, and seniors. Can you anticipate which group received the worst prognoses?

If you guessed seniors, you are correct. Overall, clinicians assumed that elderly clients would be less likely to get well in therapy. This age bias was largely an unconscious one. When asked, clinicians could not give logical reasons to explain their prognostic decisions. What can we conclude from this study? First, subtle factors like a client's age can distort practitioners' judgments about treatment efficacy. If older clients are systematically being given poorer prognoses, it could be that treatment services are being erroneously withheld. Also, the study by Meeks (1990) suggests clinicians are sometimes vulnerable to making diagnostic and prognostic mistakes without realizing they are doing so. If this is true, it is difficult to imagine how we could develop educational programs designed to eradicate this type of bias.

Information about a client's *sexual orientation* can also distort clinicians' judgments and cause them to make decisions that are less appropriate than they otherwise could be. Wisch and Mahalik (1999), for example, examined pairs of male clients and male therapists. These researchers wanted to know whether male therapists who held more sexist views of gender roles were less comfortable with (and more likely to "pathologize") male clients who did not fit traditional gender role stereotypes. In this experiment, therapists were presented with a number of case vignettes of clients in which sexual orientation (heterosexual or homosexual) and emotional state (e.g., angry, sad) were manipulated. The authors suggested, based on their findings, that therapists with more rigid views of sexual identity would be more likely to overpathologize gay clients. In contrast, therapists who held less rigid views of sexual identity would be more likely to underpathologize. Thus, gender role traits of therapists and clients can interact to cause bias and distortion in diagnostic decisions. Other research shows that sexual orientation can influence clinicians' judgements of lesbian clients as well as gay men (Kerr, Walker, Warner, & McNeill, 2004).

The effect of anchoring and confirmation bias.
Labels and culturally based group stereotypes can act like psychological "anchors." Like anchors on ships, labels and stereotypes can have a constraining effect. Anchoring effects influence people's judgments and decisions in every sphere of life. In the context of clinical judgment, psychological anchors can make practitioners reluctant to deviate from their first impressions when they receive new information that might conflict with earlier information. In a clinical context, the **anchoring effect** is defined as a bias that occurs when a therapist's first impression about the nature of a client's problem artificially constricts the therapist's subsequent assessments (Meehl, 1960; Tversky & Kahneman, 1974).

Social psychological research examining clinical decision making shows that information presented early in the process of assessment and therapy can have a disproportionately strong impact on how subsequent information is attended to and interpreted (Friedlander & Stockman, 1983; Rosenhan, 1973; Temerlin, 1968). For example, mental health professionals who initially diagnose their clients as being clinically depressed may get stuck in their first impressions. Later, when new and perhaps different information becomes available, clinicians might find it tough to change their initial diagnoses. This is what happened in the case of the pseudo-patients in Rosenhan's (1973) study discussed earlier. As the therapeutic relationship with a client unfolds over time, new information that is inconsistent with old information will sometimes be uncovered. Ideally, when this occurs, the clinician should pause and consider revising the earlier assessment. Unfortunately, the anchoring effect suggests that revisions likely occur less often than they should. Instead, when the clinician is faced with new information that is discrepant with old information, the new information tends to be either ignored or misinterpreted.

The very existence of the anchoring effect is due mainly to a process called confirmation bias. Without confirmation bias, anchoring would not pose a problem because it would not exist. As you will see from the discussion that follows, **confirmation bias** is a process in which people (e.g., clinicians) tend to seek out information that confirms their initial hunches (e.g., diagnoses), and to ignore relevant information that disconfirms their initial hunches. So, it is a lopsided method of gathering evidence that is rife with problems.

Have you ever seen a television courtroom drama in which a lawyer asks "leading questions" of the witness in front of a jury? The lawyer's questioning strategy is obviously biased because it is directed in a way that increases the likelihood that the answers provided will confirm an initial premise. There is a problem with this method for gathering information. Even if the initial premise is wrong, asking leading questions might still produce apparent evidence to make the jury members think that the premise is correct.

Something similar may occasionally happen when a mental health professional becomes involved in the process of making a psychiatric diagnosis. The clinician starts off with an initial impression or hunch. Given the existence of a tentative hunch about the nature of a client's problem, confirmation bias is the tendency to be more likely to try to confirm the hunch rather than try to disconfirm it. Like blinders on a racehorse, this bias channels the clinician's attention and perception, causing the clinician to selectively focus on evidence that is likely to confirm the initial diagnosis. Confirmation bias not only points a clinician's attention in a certain direction, but also colors the interpretation of information that does not fit the first impression. In this way, irrelevant information and neutral information are perceptually distorted in a way that makes it conform to the preexisting premise (Garb, 2010).

In part, the process of confirmatory hypothesis testing accounts for why initial impressions (e.g., diagnostic labels provided by client records or others) are so difficult to disconfirm later in time. Imagine a mental health professional who has interviewed a client for the first time and has a feeling that the client suffers from social anxiety disorder because the client does not look her in the eye. Like the lawyer in our example, the clinician may be more likely to ask questions that "pull" from the client information that supports the diagnosis of social anxiety (Owen, 2008; Pfeiffer, Whelan, & Martin, 2000). The bias makes it more likely that the clinician would ask questions like "Have you ever felt shy and awkward when speaking with people?" Conversely, confirmation bias makes it unlikely that the clinician in this example will ask a question that seeks information that disconfirms the initial impression or diagnosis; that is, a question like "What would be an example of a time when you felt self-assured and confident when interacting with others?" At the same time, a clinician who is seeking to confirm that a client's problem is social anxiety will be unlikely to probe for information relevant to other possible problems, such as drug/alcohol abuse and depression.

The implication for improving clinical assessment and making it more accurate is that counselors should be taught to be more even-handed in their questioning; in fact, there is research evidence to suggest that therapists do pursue disconfirmatory strategies more than do laypeople (Pfeiffer et al., 2000). Although anecdotal evidence seems to support the process of confirmation bias, there is also evidence of this phenomenon from experimental research. In a classic experiment, Temerlin (1968) demonstrated that confirmation bias can compromise the accuracy of clinical diagnoses. In this study, mental health practitioners were asked to evaluate a case interview with a patient. Specifically, they were asked to analyze the evidence in the case and make a professional judgment concerning the nature and severity of the patient's problem. Using random assignment, half of the practitioners were initially told that the patient might be psychotic. This label (or anchor) was not given to the other professionals, who were

not given an initial hunch at the start. In fact, the client being interviewed was actually in good emotional health; however, this information was withheld from both groups. The professionals' responses in the two groups were significantly different. Professionals who were told that the patient might be psychotic were more likely to find evidence to confirm the patient was mentally ill and in need of therapy than were professionals who were not told about the diagnosis of psychosis. Thus, even though all of the professionals were presented with the same client history, the two groups came to interpret this information very differently.

As mentioned previously, clinicians try to remain objective, and they also go through intensive training to avoid the types of pitfalls identified in this chapter. Furthermore, Barak and Fisher (1989) argued that methodological problems in bias research make it impossible to draw sweeping conclusions about the prevalence or severity of clinician biases. Thus, we do not really know how widespread or problematic the biases are. About all we know for sure is that mental health practitioners will sometimes make mistakes in how they assess and treat their clients and that some of these mistakes are rooted in biases and constricted thinking that occurs in anchoring. Correcting for these confirmation biases may be difficult because clinicians (as well as laypeople) fall into this trap *unconsciously*. If you do not know that you are being affected in the first place, it is hard to catch yourself and make corrective changes. However, as we will see in the next subsection, there are some techniques to reduce this source of bias that clinicians can use, and do use.

Reducing errors and biases among professionals. Clinicians are at times susceptible to falling victim to the same decision-making biases as are laypeople. This is because these biases are rooted in cognitive–social processes that represent fundamental aspects of human information processing. However, clinicians are significantly less likely than laypeople to experience these biases in their work.

Just because laypeople fall into these traps more often than do professionals is no reason to be complacent. Improving the ability of practitioners to make accurate and unbiased decisions is important because the welfare of clients could be improved if the incidence of the biases were diminished.

How can these biases and errors be reduced or eliminated? As you have seen, clinical and social psychologists have taken steps to understand the biases, and this understanding has suggested solutions (Garb, 2010). For example, in terms of reducing racial/ethnic biases in treatment settings, clinical psychologists are paying more attention to cultural competency in both research and treatment (Sue, Zane, Nagayama-Hall, & Gerber, 2009). Furthermore, clinical and counseling psychology training programs that are accredited by the American Psychological Association are required to include education on cultural diversity. This includes attention to the influence of a client's age, gender, race, ethnicity, religion, sexual orientation, disability, socioeconomic status, language, and national origin (American Psychological Association Committee on Accreditation, 2007).

Less work has focused specifically on reducing errors involving cognitive distortions that do not involve biases toward particular groups of people. However, some research evidence suggests that education directed at reducing cognitive errors may produce improvements. For example, one experiment involved trainees in a professional program who were studying to be counselors (Chen, Froehle, & Morran, 1997). Trainees were divided into three groups. One group received specialized education on attribution processes. The second group received specialized education on how to be empathetic toward clients; that is, members of this group were taught how to adopt their clients' perspective so as to feel what the clients were feeling. The third group formed a control condition and did not receive any specialized education.

Trainees in the first two groups were less likely than those in the third group to commit the fundamental attribution error and make dispositional (internal) attributions for clients' symptoms. Chen and colleagues' (1997) study suggests that it is possible to counteract biases in thinking so as to help clinicians become more accurate in their judgments of their clients.

This hopeful viewpoint is supported by evidence from other social psychological studies (Garb, 2005; Pfeiffer et al., 2000). For example, with regard to confirmatory hypothesis testing, Pfeiffer and colleagues (2000) gave psychology doctoral candidates cases to analyze and judge. These mental health trainees were more likely to exhibit confirmation bias if they were initially given highly plausible diagnostic explanations of clients' difficulties rather than less plausible diagnoses. Trainees who were presented with unlikely hypotheses subsequently found evidence that disconfirmed the initial premises. What is remarkable about this study is that it demonstrated the possibility of shifting clinicians from a confirmatory strategy to a disconfirmatory strategy. This provides a reason to be optimistic because it suggests that a clinician's method of gathering information is amenable to being influenced.

Kim and Ahn (2002) examined how clinicians' theoretical views can bias their decision making. This is problematic as the *DSM* is intentionally atheoretical, and all symptoms of a disorder are weighted equally. In their study, clinicians were presented with a list of disorders described in the *DSM,* and were asked to list the symptoms and indicate their relative importance ("central" for major symptoms or "peripheral" for minor symptoms). Based on this information, the clinicians were given a description of a hypothetical client whose symptoms were consistent with either the central or peripheral symptoms of a disorder that the clinician had identified in the first phase of the study. They found that clinicians were more likely to give a diagnosis for a disorder if the client's symptoms were consistent with the perceived central symptoms of a disorder than if the client's symptoms were consistent with the perceived peripheral symptoms.

Another suggestion for improving the accuracy of clinical decision making involves training clinicians to assess current symptoms before asking clients about their history of mental health problems (including previous diagnoses and treatment). In this way, clinicians could avoid learning of labels applied by other mental health professionals that may inaccurately anchor their diagnosis of the client (Mumma, 2002). These findings highlight the importance of educating clinicians to scrutinize their own (and others') initial beliefs and entertain different possibilities to help reduce cognitive errors.

Final Thoughts

Obviously, understanding the nature of a problem is necessary to identify solutions to that problem. For this reason, clinical psychologists and other mental health service providers have a vital interest in understanding why their clients are distressed. Ideally, a professional's understanding should be accurate. After all, if it is accurate, it will direct a professional toward the best treatment. To the extent that solutions are properly matched to problems, clients are more likely to benefit and get better. Unfortunately, as this section has shown, a clinician's understanding is not always unbiased and accurate. Clinicians are sometimes prone to biases and cognitive distortions. Although practitioners are certainly accurate more often than not in their assessments, they do sometimes make poor decisions and faulty assessments. Efforts to reduce biases in treatment, research, and training are central in the work of clinical and social psychologists. Future studies at the interface between social psychology and clinical psychology will likely yield continued improvement in techniques to decrease biases and cognitive distortions in treatment settings.

SUMMARY

As noted at the outset of the chapter, scholars who have originated theory, research, and practice at the intersection of social psychology and abnormal/clinical psychology have constructed a special type of applied psychology. This broad interdisciplinary interface is known as the social–clinical interface. It involves the convergence of issues of mutual concern to social, abnormal, and clinical psychology. Social psychology can be applied to studying the origins of psychological disorders, the diagnosis of psychological disorders, and the treatment and prevention of psychological disorders.

This chapter provided a brief introduction to research that has been conducted within each of the three subdomains. It is hoped that you are now better able to understand how social psychological theories, concepts, and research can be applied in improving the understanding, diagnosis, and treatment of social anxiety disorder and depression. Although the scope of the interface encompasses far more than just anxiety and depression, and although the chapter discussed only a few of the theories and concepts that have been applied, it is hoped that the chapter provided you with enough of an overview to make the social–clinical interface understandable.

With regard to social anxiety, the chapter attempted to show how debilitating emotional and behavioral symptoms of social anxiety are consequences that result from the operation of negative outcome expectancies rooted in joint influence of (a) a very strong desire to make a favorable impression, and (b) doubts over one's ability to make a favorable impression. Literature was also described to show how self-presentation theory helps us to understand the theoretical processes through which professionally administered therapeutic interventions work to provide clients with relief from the debilitating symptoms of social anxiety.

The chapter reviewed theory and research suggesting that depressed mood may be caused by the expectation that highly undesirable outcomes will occur (and that desirable outcomes will not occur), and that one is powerless to change the situation. It suggested that the heart of the cognitive problem for people suffering from hopelessness is the subjective belief that events and circumstances in their lives are beyond their control. The chapter also reviewed literature showing how the hopelessness theory of depression can help to (a) identify targets for therapeutic change, and (b) understand the underlying cognitive–social dynamics that explain how treatments help to reduce depressive symptoms.

The chapter also described the social psychology of mental health professionals. The final section reviewed concepts relevant to understanding pitfalls and shortcomings associated with clinical judgment and decision making. It suggested that improved knowledge of the types of cognitive–social biases that professionals fall prey to should benefit clients. This benefit will occur in proportion to the extent to which mental health professionals become resistant to making errors in how they diagnose and treat clients.

If, after reading this chapter, you wish to learn more about the interface of social and clinical-counseling psychology, we have provided a brief reference list. There are three publications that deserve special mention. A more thorough treatment of the interface of social psychology and clinical psychology is given in a recently published book titled *Social Psychological Foundations of Clinical Psychology* (Maddux & Tangney, 2010). For a review of the interface of social psychology and counseling psychology, please consult the review article published by Strong, Welsh, Corcoran, and Hoyt (1992). We also recommend reading Tashiro and Mortensen's (2006) review article on "translating" social psychological research to clinical practice.

6

APPLYING SOCIAL PSYCHOLOGY TO SPORTS TEAMS

PHILIP SULLIVAN

DEBORAH L. FELTZ

LORI DITHURBIDE

Every year in Britain, the universities of Oxford and Cambridge compete in a boat race. The participants are true student athletes (with no scholarships), and the coaches are volunteers, but this is a significant sporting event that draws international attention. The race has been called one of "the most brutal, harsh, and uncompromising struggles in all of sport" (Topolski, 1989, p. 9).

After losing the race in 1986, the Oxford boat club faced a long year before meeting Cambridge again. Aside from the wounded pride and standard training, those 12 months included an inordinate amount of drama. One of the 1986 Oxford crew members, an American named Chris Clarke, returned the following year with several experienced American rowers who had enrolled in Oxford. Their plan was, simply, to put out as strong a team as they could, one that could not possibly lose to Cambridge again.

As often happens in sports, things did not go as planned. The team had little camaraderie, and members even showed outright hostility toward each other and the leaders of the club. The newer rowers did not agree with the established training routines; they felt that the training routines were not necessary to ensure success. Disagreements over training methods resulted in an attempt to oust the club president (who also rowed on the team). When this revolt failed, half of the team members, led by the American contingent, quit the club with just 6 weeks to go before the boat race.

A poorly trained, substandard crew was left to prepare for the race. The team showed no unity, had little confidence in its leaders, and was largely disinterested in the race. Training runs and exhibition competitions resulted in poor times, further decreasing team confidence. Team members admitted to each other that they had little chance of winning the race and provided a wide variety of reasons for this impending failure.

However, the team did not fail. Instead, it pulled off a historic upset victory against Cambridge. From a social psychological perspective, one key aspect of this triumph was that, during a final team retreat, the team voted on the lineup for the race with Cambridge, inserting the maligned club president into a key position in the boat. From that point onward, although time was running out, the crew's training performances were excellent.

This one story shows two separate examples of the importance of social dynamics within groups in sport. In the first case, a team that on paper easily should have won every race it entered typically underperformed and could not even remain intact for one full season. Later, a team that did not have the skills and abilities to match its opponent nonetheless won the race. In both cases, something more than the individual attributes of the players contributed significantly to team performance. These collective attributes and processes, and their impact on performance and other outcomes, are the focus of this chapter. Consider these questions:

- After the Americans joined, the Oxford rowing team members did not get along well, and members disagreed frequently. What might have been done to avoid such problems?
- Which one factor do you think was most responsible for the team's eventual success during the race? Why?
- Do you think that the team, after winning the race, would have become a more united group? Why or why not?

Chemistry is an often cited notion within sports. Although fans, athletes, coaches, and sport psychologists all seem to recognize it, chemistry is a vague concept. It appears as an all-encompassing component of team functioning as well as a panacea for all team ills. The layperson's term *chemistry* is implicitly understood to be the sum total of intangible attributes within a team. It can be perceived to include everything from respect between teammates, compatibility between players and coaches, and a lack of conflict within the team. It is dynamic, mysterious, and very valuable. It appears that at least part of the reason why teams are successful—or unsuccessful—lies in this notion of chemistry. It can mean the difference between winners and losers—"champs" and "chumps." However, it is important to note that team performance is not the only outcome of chemistry. Player and coach satisfaction, motivation, and a variety of other factors are also important consequences.

The performance of an English university rowing crew may be largely irrelevant to the typical psychology student. However, think for a minute about your own sporting experiences. Have you ever played a team sport at any level, recreationally or competitively? If you have, what lasting impressions has this experience left on you? Have you made some of your strongest friendships through sport? Have you ever dropped out from a sport or team just because of the "bad blood" within a group of athletes?

Have you ever played on a team that overachieved or grossly underachieved? If so, then the topics of this chapter, which are the essence of chemistry, will be relevant to you.

Go beyond your personal experiences as an athlete and think about the diversity of activity choices offered by your campus recreation program or the abundance of such programs for the youth and elderly in your community. Consider the place in our society of professional sports, the Olympics and Paralympics, and the X Games. When one stops to consider how significant sports (and particularly team sports) are in our everyday lives, one may find their presence to be overwhelming. Considering the relevance of these activities, it is not surprising that psychology has a specific field designated to the study of human behavior within a sporting context—sport psychology.

This chapter deals with the applied social psychology of sports teams. As a final part of this introduction, two points must be made. First, in accordance with the literature on the topic, the social psychology of sport is limited to the in-group social dynamics of sports teams. The vast majority of social psychological research in sport has focused on these attributes and interactions (i.e., this chemistry); thus, it is what is reviewed in this chapter. Second, the applied nature of social dynamics is seen in how these attributes and interactions have been conceptually and empirically linked to team performance and other valuable outcomes.

Figure 6.1 gives a schematic view of the application of social psychology to sports teams. Within any team situation in sport, there are certain "givens." A team will have a certain amount of ability, players will have certain personality characteristics, and coaches will have certain coaching styles. These may be considered the "input" into the team sport experience. The output would include variables, such as the satisfaction that individuals derive from their involvement with the team and team performance. In this model, social psychological factors (i.e., team chemistry) operate between these inputs and outputs. These factors occur at a collective level, are distinct from individual factors like personality, and have direct effects on

Figure 6.1 Framework for Understanding the Application of Social Psychology to Sports

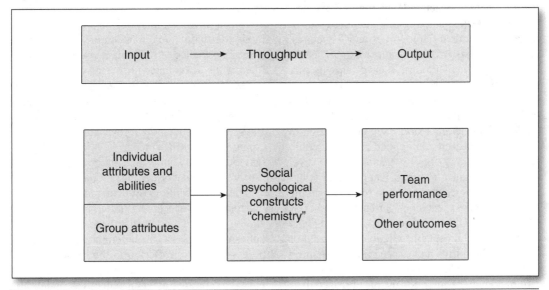

SOURCE: From Sullivan, P. A. (1993). Communication skills for interactive sports. *The Sport Psychologist, 7*, 79–91.

outcomes like team performance. The operation of the social psychological factors that make up chemistry represents the "throughput" of this model. By understanding what team chemistry is and how to influence it (i.e., through intervention strategies), one can maximize the positive outcomes of a team.

TEAM DYNAMICS

Scientists studying social behavior typically have to choose between using groups that exist naturally in the real world and artificially creating groups that possess certain desirable characteristics. Thus, studies can vary from a contrived "team" composed of five or so undergraduate psychology students who are asked to solve a puzzle to a natural team, such as doctors and nurses who actually perform open-heart surgery. For the purpose of conducting research, does it seem that one is too artificial and the other is too uncontrollable? One context that allows researchers to combine and balance both the need for reality and the need for controllability is sports.

According to Forsyth (1999), *groups* are best characterized by certain key features. These features include structured patterns of communication, interdependence among members, shared identity, and identifiable roles and structures. Although most of these features can be established in artificial groups, such groups usually lack a certain amount of generalizability to naturally occurring groups, and therefore offer less insight into the dynamics of sports teams.

As groups, sports teams have been a boon to both basic research and applied research within social psychology. Sports teams at any level typically contain a rich and recognizable structure. They have clear, agreed on roles that define the behavioral expectations for each member as well as norms that define and reinforce what behaviors are acceptable within the team. For example, the norms and expectations pertaining to coaches are clearly different from those pertaining to players. Individuals must balance their own motives and abilities with those of the team

members around them to achieve conjoint, mutually desirable outcomes. These groups operate within a larger social system that includes fans, parents, communities, and leagues. There is a wide variety of clear feedback; teams win and lose, player and team statistics are maintained, players are cut or quit, and so forth.

Given the characteristics of sports teams, it is understandable that most of the social psychological work has focused on their internal social dynamics. The most significant of the topics examined in sports teams are team cohesion, communication patterns, team confidence, and group goal setting. These topics are covered in this chapter. Consistent with the bulk of the research, primary consideration is given to team performance as an outcome of team processes while recognizing the importance of other outcome variables (e.g., satisfaction, morale). Finally, most of the research in this field has focused on interacting team sports (e.g., soccer, basketball) rather than on individual team sports (e.g., golf, wrestling) because performance outcomes in the former depend much more on the dynamics of group interaction.

Team Cohesion

If you have ever played a team sport, one of the issues that may be immediately recognizable is the importance of how much you liked or disliked your teammates. In fact, your attitudes toward teammates may be the main reason why you are or are not a member of that team today. Even professional athletes, such as the National Basketball Association's Tayshaun Prince, will comment how their team is "like a family." Obviously, team unity and interpersonal attraction are important issues in sport (see Figure 6.2).

The notion of unity (or camaraderie) has been the focus of much of the research in sport psychology. Typically, this has been referred to as **cohesion**, which has been defined as "a dynamic process which is reflected in the tendency for a group to stick together and remain united in the pursuit of its instrumental objectives and/or for the satisfaction of member affective needs"

Figure 6.2 The Important Dynamic of Cohesion in
Team Sports

SOURCE: Courtesy of Brock University Athletics.

(Carron, Brawley, & Widmeyer, 1997, p. 3).
Looking back at the story of the Oxford rowing
club in the opening vignette, it is clear that for a
large part of that season, the team showed very
little cohesion. Players feuded with one another
and rebelled against the coach. It was obvious
that they had little regard for instrumental objectives (e.g., how to win the race) or their
teammates' affective needs (e.g., accepting them
as friends). This lack of cohesion is most noticeable in the fact that the team that started the
season together did not stick together; half of the
team members quit.

Conceptual nature of team cohesion. The preceding definition of cohesion posed by Carron
and colleagues (1997) reflects four key characteristics of the construct, namely, that cohesion is
(a) multidimensional, (b) dynamic, (c) affective,
and (d) instrumental.

Being **multidimensional** simply means that
cohesion is not one simple factor, but rather the
sum of several interrelated factors. This reflects
one of the earliest notions of the concept of
cohesion. Festinger, Schachter, and Back (1950)
stated that cohesion is the sum total of all forces
that cause members to remain in the group. This
sum total can include a wide variety of factors.
For instance, players may stay on a team
because they like their teammates and/or the
coach, because staying on the team gives them
the best opportunity to be successful, because
they have no other teams to play for, or even
because they are being paid. The notion that
cohesion is **dynamic** means that although it is
relatively stable, cohesion does tend to fluctuate
over time. Team cohesion tends to wax and
wane over the course of a season. You may have
heard the sentiment that "winning cures everything." One thing that team success may "cure"
is a lack of cohesiveness. The relationship
between performance and cohesion is discussed
more fully later, but for now it is enough to
understand that players may (and often do) like
each other more when the team is performing
well. Thus, team performance is one factor that
contributes to the dynamic fluctuating nature of
cohesion. For example, despite all of the hostility displayed among members of the Oxford
rowing team, it would not be difficult to imagine
the team members hugging one another after
beating Cambridge.

Finally, it is important to note that cohesion is
both affective and instrumental in nature.
Affectivity refers to the emotional state of the
athletes. You cannot understand cohesion unless
you recognize that part of what keeps a team
united is how the players feel about one another.
Likewise, another big part of how cohesive a
team is has to do with its goals and objectives.
Goals and objectives are the most obvious features that help a team of players remain united;
this is the **instrumental** nature of cohesion. For
example, members of a team who do not socialize very much may still be very united over their
goal to win a championship. The affective and
instrumental aspects of cohesion suggest two

main dimensions of cohesion: *social cohesion* and *task cohesion*. There are teams that may be highly united as a social group, but are not organized or united with respect to accomplishing team goals. A senior adult softball team may be more concerned with team get-togethers and how members interact socially than with how the team performs on the field (i.e., high on social cohesion and low on task cohesion). Alternatively, there are teams that are highly cohesive with respect to their instrumental purpose, but not as social units. For example, Major League Baseball's (MLB's) Oakland Athletics team during the early 1970s won back-to-back World Series championships, but was notorious for clubhouse fighting and animosity among players. To say that either the senior adult softball team or the Oakland Athletics is not cohesive ignores the notion that there is both social cohesion and task cohesion. It is safe to say that most teams will display at least some amount of each aspect of cohesion.

Measurement of team cohesion. Cohesiveness in sports teams has been measured using a variety of instruments. Most studies have relied on standardized, quantitative self-report scales. The most commonly used measure is the Group Environment Questionnaire (GEQ) (Widmeyer, Brawley, & Carron, 1985).

The GEQ presents team cohesion as a four-factor structure reflecting two separate dimensions of cohesion. First, as we have seen, team cohesion can be social or task in nature; the group can be united as a social-oriented entity, a task-oriented entity, or both. Second, the notion of cohesion can mean different things from an individual perspective compared with looking at the group as a whole. The group may be a very united bunch (either socially or instrumentally), but that does not mean that every player identifies equally with the team. For instance, imagine a university varsity team in which one player is married and the rest are single. The married player might not socialize much with the team because of other commitments, but he or she can still recognize that the team is a tightly knit

social group. These two dimensions result in four factors of team cohesion: **group integration—social**, which refers to perceptions of the group as a whole regarding social issues (e.g., "Our team would like to spend time together in the off-season"); **group integration—task**, which refers to perceptions of the group as a whole regarding degree of task orientation (e.g., "Our team is united in trying to reach its performance goals"); **individual attraction to group—social**, which deals with individual perceptions of the group as a social unit (e.g., "Some of my best friends are on this team"); and **individual attraction to group—task**, which refers to individual perceptions of the group's task orientation (e.g., "I'm unhappy with my team's level of desire to win") (Widmeyer et al., 1985). Each factor of the GEQ is measured by the sum of its items, so that higher scores indicate a greater level of cohesion. The GEQ allows researchers to measure the multidimensional nature of cohesion and to examine the various antecedents and consequences of its multiple dimensions. Given its dynamic and multidimensional nature, there is a variety of antecedents and consequences of cohesion.

Antecedents of cohesion. Consistent with the overall theme of this chapter (see Figure 6.1), cohesion is a construct that cannot be understood independent of its inputs and outputs. This also can be seen in Figure 6.3, which shows cohesion as a central mediating process in team dynamics. Both individual antecedents (e.g., personality variables), and social antecedents (e.g., leadership style, role aspects) contribute to social unity and task unity, which in turn lead to individual and team outcomes. For example, individual consequences include member satisfaction and performance, and team consequences include overall team confidence and performance.

This section focuses on the inputs to cohesion, that is, those antecedent factors that shape and influence team unity. Both individual and social factors contribute to the cohesiveness of a group. Individual factors typically involve the personalities and demographic characteristics of

Figure 6.3   Conceptual Model of Team Cohesion

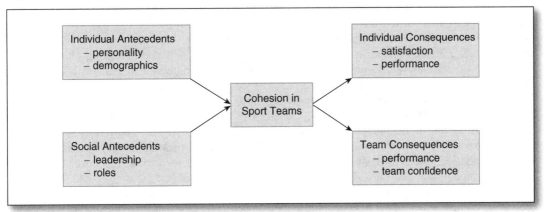

teammates. Although conventional wisdom may suggest that people feel closer to those who are similar to them on the most obvious characteristics, simple demographic similarity does not appear to be very important for cohesiveness in sports teams. Widmeyer, Silva, and Hardy (1992) found that team sport athletes rated social and racial similarities as minimally important for both task cohesion and social cohesion. Nondemographic individual attributes, such as personality and attitudes, may have a greater impact on cohesion. For example, the tendency of the individual to self-disclose (Stokes, Fuerher, & Childs, 1984) and the individual's perceptions of task-oriented motivational climate (Horn, Byrd, Martin, & Young, 2012) have been found to be positively related to all four factors of the GEQ. Thus, on one level, how cohesive a team is may depend on the individual attributes and perceptions of its members.

Although it may be important that teammates are alike in certain ways, they will not necessarily work well together. There is also reason to believe that it is important to have teammates who have *complementary attributes* as opposed to similar ones. For example, although leadership is important to team success, having a team full of leaders would most likely not be as functional as having a mix of leaders and nonleaders. Copeland and Straub (1995) discussed the importance of interpersonal

compatibility with respect to attributes, such as friendliness, dominance, and acceptance of authority. Having individuals who complement each other on these attributes appears to result in greater task cohesion (i.e., group integration—task) and more effective conflict management within the group.

Examples of social factors that influence cohesion are group size, leadership style, and member roles. With respect to *group size,* it appears that size affects task and social cohesion differently. A 1990 series of studies by Widmeyer and his colleagues using the GEQ showed that in laboratory-designed basketball and volleyball teams ranging in size from three to twelve members, individuals' attraction to the group's task was always greater in groups of three, whereas both aspects of social cohesion (i.e., group integration—social and individual attraction to group—social) were greater in larger teams and appeared to be optimal in groups of six (e.g., Widmeyer, Brawley, & Carron, 1990). The higher task cohesion in small teams likely is due to the fact that task coordination is easier, whereas larger groups are more likely to suffer from problems of coordination. On the other hand, a wider variety of sources for reliable social support contribute to higher social cohesion in larger groups.

Another group attribute related to team unity, at least task unity, is the coach's *leadership* style.

Correlational studies with samples of high school athletes in baseball, softball, and football have shown that **autocratic leadership** (i.e., the coach as leader makes all decisions and refrains from delegating any power) is associated with lower levels of task cohesion, as measured by the GEQ (Gardner, Light-Shields, Bredemeier, & Bostrom, 1996; Westre & Weiss, 1991). On the other hand, **democratic leadership** (i.e., the coach involves his or her athletes in making decisions that affect the team) is related to higher levels of task cohesion (this study combined both group integration and individual attraction to group factors of the GEQ into one task cohesion score). Thus, with respect to task cohesion, the most appropriate method of leadership would appear to be one that empowers the group and allows team members to have input into decisions and policies (Jowett & Chaundy, 2004).

Although the coach has an obvious role in sports teams, all team members are asked to fill certain roles. A **role** refers to a set of behaviors expected of a person in a particular social position or setting. On a sports team, roles may be formalized (e.g., the coach and team captain) or informal (e.g., the "practical joker"). There are several different aspects to how roles may affect cohesion. **Role clarity** refers to the extent to which one's role has been clearly defined. This is distinct from **role acceptance**, that is, the degree to which the person expected to fill a role agrees to comply with the requirements of the role. Finally, **role performance** refers to how well the individual actually completes the responsibilities of the role. To maximize cohesiveness, each of these aspects of one's role must be satisfied. For example, consider the plight of the Oxford rowing crew in the opening vignette. For many months, this elite and previously cohesive team experienced splintering into subgroups, poor performance, and intense personal dissatisfaction. It is likely that many of these negative outcomes would have been avoided if team members had accepted the roles that were best suited to them. It appears that the issues confronting the team originated with a small number of team members who did not like or accept the

roles they were expected to fulfill. They spent much energy in trying to take over the duties and responsibilities attached to the roles of other members (e.g., the club captain and coach). Their actions included protesting training methods and altering norms of team decision making. As a result, eventually half of the team members quit. Imagine that instead of having conflicts over the roles of the crew members, all of the rowers had clearly defined roles (e.g., concerning decision-making authority) and openly accepted their own roles. It seems obvious that the turmoil of the season would have been avoided and that a cohesive, satisfied, and successful team would have existed.

Research on how role clarity, acceptance, and performance affect both social cohesion and task cohesion has yielded two significant conclusions. First, the aspects, although interrelated, are also distinct. For example, just because a coach clarifies a nonstarting role for a player does not mean that the player will accept it. The player may fully believe that he or she should be a starter. The rejection of a clearly defined role could easily detract from both social cohesion and task cohesion in the team. The second major finding with respect to member roles and cohesion is that of the three aspects of member roles, role acceptance has the most influence on team cohesion (Dawe & Carron, 1990). Thus with respect to team cohesion, although it is important for roles to be clear and to be filled by competent people, the greatest benefit will accrue when team members accept the roles they are asked to fill.

Much like roles, intrateam norms have been found to be significantly related to team cohesion. Typically, intrateam norms in sport emphasize dynamics that should optimize team performance (e.g., practicing hard, minimizing conflict). Research has noted that both social and task cohesion are related to group productivity norms. Høigaard, Säfvenbom, and Tønnessen (2006) investigated these relationships with a sample of male teenage soccer players. They found that all four factors of the GEQ were positively correlated to three types of group norms (i.e., norms for productivity, role involvement, and supportive behavior). Furthermore, when collapsing across the four factors and just analyzing task and social cohesion, there was an interaction between cohesion, norms, and effort (i.e., social loafing). Specifically, when teams were characterized by high social cohesion, the effect of performance norms on effort depended on task cohesion. In cases of high social and high task cohesion, effort did not change between high and low performance norms. However, in cases of high social and low task cohesion, low performance norms resulted in dramatically less effort than did high performance norms. Therefore, it appears that regardless of how united teammates feel as a social unit, their bonding around a team task, and team norms of productivity, are instrumental in team effort.

Cohesion and performance. We now consider the possible consequences of cohesion, concentrating in particular on indexes of performance (see Figure 6.3). At the *individual level,* there is ample evidence that members of cohesive teams tend to work harder and experience more success. Bray and Whaley (2001) investigated the relationship between team cohesion (using the GEQ) and the individual efforts of male and female high school basketball players over the course of a season. An individual performance measure consisting of shooting percentage, rebounds, assists, steals, and total points was used. The researchers found that by the end of the season, cohesion predicted individual performance. These results supported earlier findings on collegiate baseball players (Apple, 1993). Specifically, Bray and Whaley (2001) found that individuals' perceptions of attraction to the group as a social unit offered the best prediction of individual performance, suggesting that improved individual success may be due to the greater effort invested by individuals in the context of a socially cohesive team. Elsewhere, Prapavessis and Carron (1997) found a positive relationship between individual attraction to the group's task and aerobic work rate in athletes from a variety of team sports.

Thus, the evidence suggests that cohesion is related to the performance of individual team members, although it cannot be stated with certainty whether social cohesion or task cohesion is more strongly related.

The preceding research links team cohesion with individual performance. We also can consider the connection between cohesion and *team* performance. In this regard, there is considerable anecdotal and research evidence that teams high in cohesion perform better than do teams low in cohesion. For instance, Mullen and Copper (1994) conducted a meta-analysis of the cohesion–performance relationship in many different groups, including sports teams. A **meta-analysis** is a statistical procedure for combining and integrating the results of separate studies to derive an overall assessment of the results, for example, the direction and magnitude of the relationship between variables (causal or otherwise). Mullen and Copper found that task cohesion significantly predicted team performance. Of particular relevance, this relationship was most significant with sports teams. Considering the multidimensional nature of cohesion, it is important to note that the Mullen and Copper analysis suggested that a team's task cohesion in particular is strongly related to performance. Teams that have clearly defined and mutually agreed on objectives tend to perform well. This reflects the often quoted sentiment heard in sports of "everyone rowing in the same direction," or "everyone being on the same page."

The evidence connecting cohesion with team performance may be viewed as suggesting that cohesion leads to better performance (as depicted in Figure 6.3). This is probably why many teams, from high school sports teams to professional sports teams, sometimes go on retreats and take part in team-building exercises. However, keeping in mind the discussion of correlation and causation in Chapter 3, it is also possible that the relationship is reversed, that is that better performance (individual or team) results in greater cohesion. That certainly is a reasonable possibility. Everyone likes winning, and when you contribute to and share such a positive event with teammates, it makes sense that everyone will like each other more.

The true causal nature of the cohesion–performance relationship has been difficult to ascertain. Just read the following quote from pitcher Damian Moss, formerly of MLB's Atlanta Braves: "I think this is the best team we've ever had . . . just the feeling of camaraderie. Everybody is happy to be here. They want to win. They're on the same page" (*Sports Illustrated,* 2002). Undoubtedly, Moss, a professional athlete on an elite team at the time, knew that cohesion and performance went hand in hand. However, it is much harder to determine whether he had any idea of which caused which. Was that the best team the Braves have ever had because everyone was on the same page, or was everyone on the same page because this was the best Braves team ever?

In an early study, Carron and Ball (1977) attempted to clarify the causal nature of the cohesion–performance relationship by assessing cohesion at different points in the season of intercollegiate hockey players. They administered the Sport Cohesiveness Questionnaire (Martens, Landers, & Loy, 1972) three times during the season: within the first two regular season games, at midseason, and after the regular season had been completed. Team performance was assessed by means of a win–loss ratio at midseason, and at the end of the season. Carron and Ball (1977) concluded that performance was a much better predictor of cohesion than cohesion was of performance. Causation was inferred because performance accounted for a greater amount of the variation in cohesion than cohesion did in performance.

Grieve, Whelan, and Meyes (2000) found similar results in an experiment where they created basketball teams with participants who were novice basketball players. Half of the teams were exposed to a cohesion-building intervention, and the remaining teams were subjected to a cohesion-reducing exercise. The cohesion-building intervention was designed to promote task-oriented self-disclosure by facilitating a discussion about role definitions (e.g., perceived roles on the team, communication styles). The

cohesion-reducing condition was designed, first to foster social cohesion by having players disclose information about themselves (e.g., major, year in school, social activities), and second and immediately prior to competition, to give individual players a change of team assignment so that teams were composed of members who had not communicated with each other previously. Grieve and colleagues found that cohesion (measured by the GEQ) had no effect on performance, but that successful teams subsequently reported higher levels of both group integration toward the task and individual attraction to the group's task. Recent evidence suggests that task cohesion may be more important than social cohesion with respect to team performance. In fact, it may be that social cohesion could have a negative effect. A recent study has speculated that high social cohesion may actually have a detrimental effect on team performance. Rovio, Eskola, Kozub, Duda, and Lintunen (2009) reported a season-long case study of a junior hockey team. It was found that although team performance deteriorated through the season, social cohesion remained high. Interestingly, team members reported overevaluations of the team's performance in training and games while the team's record declined. The authors speculated that "pressure to conform, groupthink, and group polarization increased because of the high social cohesion in the team. Finally, the players' unwillingness to evaluate the team's performance realistically led to further deterioration in performance" (Rovio et al., 2009, pp. 430–431).

Carron, Colman, Wheeler, and Stevens (2002) conducted a more complete examination of the cohesion–performance question: a meta-analysis of studies that related the cohesion of sports teams to performance, and teams that had used the GEQ to measure cohesion. They concluded that there are consistently strong relationships between performance and both social cohesion and task cohesion. More important, in contrast to the findings of Carron and Ball (1977) and Grieve and colleagues (2000), Carron and colleagues (2002) found that cohesion was as strong a predictor of performance as performance was of cohesion. With respect to the four factors of the GEQ, the authors concluded that "both of the group integration constructions (task and social) and both of the individual attractions to group constructs (task and social) showed a statistically similar small to moderate relationship to performance in sport" (Carron et al., 2002, p. 180).

It appears that the relationship between cohesion and performance is robust within sports teams as well as bidirectional. That is, teammates who experience success together probably will perceive more team cohesion, but the likelihood of team success can be increased by facilitating team cohesion, particularly with regard to team goals and objectives. The evidence of bidirectionality suggests that the arrows in Figure 6.3 connecting cohesion to consequences should point in both directions.

Cohesion and other outcomes. Although team performance is the most widely studied variable in relation to team cohesiveness, it is not the only one. In the opening vignette about the Oxford rowing team, low cohesion among team members seemed to be connected not only to poor performance, but also to low levels of satisfaction and confidence in the team. Research has shown that cohesion is related to a variety of nonperformance outcomes for both the individual athlete and the team. At the individual level, members of cohesive teams tend to be more satisfied and committed to the team. At the team level, cohesive teams tend to be more confident and interact with each other better (e.g., with respect to communication). These group attributes are further clarified in the following sections. It is worth noting that although cohesion and team confidence do tend to share a reciprocal relationship (as do other group factors), we cannot necessarily assume that the variables are causally related, much less specify the direction of causality.

Team Confidence

Although cohesion was the first group dynamic that attracted a lot of research in sport,

it is not the only important one. Level of self-confidence clearly is an important factor in sports teams. Some teams are composed of a collection of talented members who are confident as individuals, but lack confidence in their teams as a whole. Other teams might not have very many especially talented members, but have a common belief that as groups they can integrate their talents to perform successfully. Still other teams may collapse when the self-doubts of a few members become contagious. For example, Longman (2000) related the story of how the U.S. women's soccer team lost the semifinal match against Norway in the 1995 World Cup because the lack of confidence of a few players seemed to infect the entire team. A few years later, however, the 1999 World Cup had a very different ending, with the U.S. women beating China in a shootout for the championship. The U.S. team members said that they won because they believed in each other. Like cohesion, and consistent with the theme of this chapter, the concept of team confidence is best understood as an intermediate dynamic that both is influenced by certain factors and leads to certain outcomes.

Self-efficacy refers to the belief that one can act to successfully produce a given outcome under a given set of circumstances. It is essentially a situation-specific form of self-confidence. Self-efficacy has long been established as one of the primary psychological factors in human performance. Self-efficacy and self-confidence are used interchangeably in sport psychology and are used accordingly in this chapter (Feltz & Chase, 1998).

Bandura (1986), recognizing that much of human activity takes place in social contexts, proposed the notion of collective efficacy, also known as team confidence. Bandura (1997) defined **collective efficacy** as a group's shared belief in its ability to organize and execute the courses of action required to obtain a certain outcome. Bandura noted that one of the primary areas in which individuals work together to achieve a shared outcome is sports. Therefore, much of the research and theorizing about team confidence has focused on sports teams.

Team confidence and individual attributes. Because teams are composed of individuals, team confidence can be largely affected by the psychological characteristics of the members of the group. Perhaps the most obvious of these is the self-efficacy of each member. If all members of a team feel very confident about their abilities, it would seem to follow that confidence in the team as a whole would be quite high. Similarly, one would expect a team to display low team confidence if the members lacked confidence in their own abilities. In reality, however, most teams usually are somewhere between these two extremes. Some players feel quite confident in themselves, whereas other teammates might not.

Although the link between self-efficacy and collective efficacy has been noted several times (e.g., George & Feltz, 1995; Spink, 1990a), to date only two studies have researched the issue. Feltz and Lirgg (1998) examined the self-confidence and team confidence of male college hockey players on six different teams. Feltz and Lirgg measured how confident each player was in performing his role in an upcoming game as well as how confident the player was that the team as a whole would accomplish certain collective goals (e.g., outshoot the opposing team, "kill off" penalties). The measures of perceived self-efficacy and team efficacy were administered within a 24-hour period prior to each of 32 games. The researchers found that the aggregated self-efficacies of the players were significantly related to the collective efficacy of the team. In addition, Magyar, Feltz, and Simpson (2004) examined determinants of collective efficacy with junior rowers at a regional championship regatta. They found that the self-efficacy beliefs of rowers were related to their beliefs in the efficacy of their boat team (i.e., team efficacy). Magyar and colleagues also found that rowers' perceptions of the type of motivational climate that a coach creates were related to their team efficacy beliefs. Specifically, the more a coach emphasized a **mastery-oriented climate** (i.e., an emphasis on learning, improving, and working together), the higher the rowers' efficacy beliefs in the team.

Other individual-level factors that have been researched in conjunction with collective efficacy include precompetitive anxiety and affect; for example, by assessing the levels of individual anxiety and mood of a sample of male rugby players prior to competition, Greenlees, Nunn, Graydon, and Maynard (1999) found a relationship between individuals' perceptions of confidence in their team and how they felt prior to competition. For example, team members' concerns that the team would not perform well (i.e., low collective efficacy) were associated with higher levels of anxiety and negative affect.

Another way in which to consider the individual attributes that influence team efficacy judgments is to ask athletes what they think contributes to their confidence. Chase, Feltz, and Lirgg (2003) examined the sources of information that female collegiate basketball players provided in making self-efficacy and collective efficacy judgments prior to 12 basketball games. They found that the athletes rated past performance as a primary contributor to both self-efficacy and collective efficacy. However, some sources were noted particularly for self-efficacy and not for collective (or team) efficacy. Specifically, the athletes reported that outside sources (e.g., social distractions, school assignments) were influential with regard to their own confidence, but not with regard to that of the group.

Team confidence and cohesion. Given the aforementioned wealth of literature on cohesion, it is not surprising that cohesion has been linked to team confidence. Spink (1990b) found that collegiate female volleyball teams that were high in collective efficacy were also high in both social cohesion and task cohesion. Paskevich, Brawley, Dorsch, and Widmeyer (1999) also conducted an extensive study examining the relationship between collective efficacy and cohesion in a sample of collegiate volleyball players. They found that collective efficacy was significantly related to task cohesion, with both factors of task cohesion (group integration and individual attraction to the group) significantly discriminating between high- and low-efficacy groups. Using a different sport as a sample, Kozub and McDonnell (2000) found that team cohesion, particularly task cohesion, was highly related to collective efficacy for male rugby players. Thus, cohesion and collective efficacy are highly interrelated. Furthermore, Paskevich and colleagues' (1999) findings suggest that task cohesion might be more closely related to a team's confidence than is social cohesion. This makes sense: How confident a team is in its ability to achieve a specific goal is tied to the unity that the team has around the task of achieving the goal.

Team confidence and performance. According to Bandura (1986, 1997) and a wealth of research in sport psychology (cf. Feltz & Chase, 1998), the most powerful factor affecting confidence is previous experience. Simply put, individuals and teams are confident about doing things that they have done well in the past, and they lack confidence about doing the things that they have not done well in the past. Furthermore, research supports Bandura's contention that confidence beliefs are major determinants of athletic performance (Feltz & Lirgg, 1998; Kane, Marks, Zaccaro, & Blair, 1996; Myers, Feltz, & Short, 2004).

Thus, the relationship between confidence beliefs and performance is believed to be recursive: "Mastery expectations influence performance and are, in turn, altered by the cumulative effect of one's efforts" (Bandura, 1977a, p. 194). This relationship goes a long way toward explaining the phenomena of winning streaks and losing streaks. If a team wins, it is likely to be more confident that it can win again the next time. Conversely, if a team loses, it might lack the confidence needed to perform well in the next game. These two effects result in potential spirals that can be hard to escape. Success leads to confidence, which leads to success; conversely, failure detracts from confidence, which may result in further failures. Needless to say, the players on a team on a winning streak feel as though they can "beat the world," whereas players on a team that has not won lately often lack any faith in their team.

Research on winning and losing streaks helps explain the relationship between team performance and team confidence. But, what about the common experience of individual players "choking" during a team sport? How is choking related to confidence? "Choking" in sports refers to a brief, significant decline in athletic performance when the athlete is under pressure. Sports psychologists hold two competing theories for why successful athletes might choke. Self-focus theory suggests that choking occurs when athletes consciously pay attention to the technical information they need to perform a skill that would usually be automatic (e.g., taking a free-throw in basketball). This self-focus disrupts their performance of the skill, leading them to choke. In contrast, distraction theory suggests that choking happens when athletes process worry and self-doubt at the same time as they are trying to focus on the technical information needed to perform the skill. When a lack of confidence occurs, these feelings distract the athlete and can lead to choking. Because both of these theories focus on the athlete's thought process when choking, researchers need to "get into the heads" of the athletes to figure out what is going on. One of the best ways to gain access to the athlete's thought process is to use a qualitative research method like an interview.

Hill and Shaw (2013) conducted a qualitative study to test the competing theories of choking in team sports. They interviewed eight men who played on competitive sports teams, including rugby, football, and hockey teams. The goal of the study was to learn more about choking from people who had firsthand experience in order to better understand the cause of choking behavior. Participants were asked to describe, evaluate, and explain their experiences of choking, and Hill and Shaw (2013) analyzed the results using phenomenology. As you might recall from Chapter 3, phenomenology is a qualitative research method that allows researchers to explore a phenomenon (such as choking in team sports) in detail as it appears to the person experiencing it. By studying the transcripts of the interviews and identifying commonalities in the interviews, Hill and Shaw (2013) found support for the distraction theory of choking. They found that most participants perceived choking to be caused by anxiety about the outcome of the game, about meeting others' expectations (such as teammates, coaches, or spectators), and about their performance. The participants felt that this anxiety caused them to be distracted, which led them to choke. Based on these results, it seems clear that a lack of confidence can lead to the experience of choking. Interestingly, some participants also described choking when they felt overconfident. By using a qualitative research method, the researchers were able to gain a deep understanding of athletes' personal experiences of choking. Future research using experimental methods could be used to help determine the circumstances under which overconfidence versus low self-confidence may lead to choking.

FOCUS ON RESEARCH

Team Confidence and Performance

Several laboratory experiments have addressed the relationship between team confidence and performance, and their results have consistently pointed to a strong association between these two variables. For example, Hodges and Carron (1992) had three-person groups engage in a competitive task against another group. Unbeknownst to the participants, the group they were competing against was made up of experimental confederates who were familiar with the purpose of the study and enacted a predetermined script. The two groups were told that they would be competing in two tasks: a hand dynamometer task (a measure of hand strength), and a medicine ball task (a muscular endurance exercise). Each participant was told to squeeze the dynamometer as hard as possible. Strength scores for each group member were then summed to produce a total strength score for his or her group. The hand dynamometer task was used to manipulate the collective efficacy of the groups. After the strength scores had been calculated, each experimental group was given bogus feedback about its combined strength relative to the confederate group. In the *high–collective efficacy condition,* the experimental groups were informed that their group strength scores were substantially higher than that of the confederate group. Experimental groups in the *low–collective efficacy condition* were told that their combined strength scores were substantially lower than that of the confederate group. Each experimental group then participated in a series of four performance trials on the medicine ball task in which the group had to hold up the ball for a longer time period than the confederate group. Before doing so, the experimental group was asked to indicate, on scales ranging from 0% to 100%, how likely it was that their group would win and how confident the group was in its assessment of its chances. The product of these two scores served as a measure of collective efficacy. Had they known the truth about the materials used in the experiment, the experimental groups likely would have indicated that their chances were 0% because the medicine ball used by the confederate group was actually filled with foam, even though it looked identical to the one used by the experimental groups. Not surprisingly, the experimental groups lost every time.

The results revealed that the bogus feedback on the dynamometer task was effective in influencing collective efficacy. Groups in the high–collective efficacy condition had higher expectations of success in the subsequent medicine ball task than did those in the low–collective efficacy condition.

The results concerning performance were more interesting. Following the inevitable initial loss to the confederate group, groups in the low–collective efficacy condition demonstrated decrements in their performance on the medicine ball task over subsequent trials. However, following their initial failure, groups in the high–collective efficacy condition actually demonstrated improvements in their performance. These results clearly demonstrate the value of positive feedback in producing collective efficacy and affirm the application of Bandura's self-efficacy theory to groups.

Two other studies employed similar designs to assess collective self-efficacy. In one experiment (Lichacz & Partington, 1996), team participants engaged in a tug-of-war against a device that measured the strength of their collective pull. In another experiment (Greenlees, Graydon, & Maynard, 2000), the amount of time the team spent on a biking machine was measured. In each of these studies, after the group had performed, team members were given misleading feedback about their performance. In both studies, teams that were told they had performed well were more confident than those that were told they had performed poorly. Subsequently, the high-confidence teams performed better during a second performance trial.

To date, only two published studies have examined the relationship between team performance and confidence with actual sporting groups over the course of a season. These studies corroborate the laboratory evidence. As noted earlier, Feltz and Lirgg (1998) followed six collegiate male hockey teams over the course of a season and measured individual and collective efficacy before each game as well as subsequent team performance. Team confidence was measured by asking each player how confident he was that his team could accomplish certain goals (e.g., beat the opposing teams, force more turnovers than the opposing teams). Feltz and Lirgg found that team confidence positively predicted team performance. They also found that although collective efficacy increased after wins and decreased after losses, individual self-efficacy was not affected by team performance. This finding supports the notion that collective efficacy is indeed a group attribute rather than an individual attribute. The researchers suggested that a team's accomplishments are more apparent and less ambiguous to a team member than are his or her own accomplishments in the team context. Therefore, the visible team wins and losses may have a greater effect on players' team efficacy judgments than on efficacy judgments about themselves.

In a subsequent study, Myers and colleagues (2004) examined the influence of efficacy beliefs on the offensive performance of American football teams and the reciprocal relationship between collective efficacy and offensive performance over a season of competition. The reciprocal relationship between collective efficacy and performance had not been measured previously in a field setting. The Feltz and Lirgg (1998) study had not examined the week-to-week influence of aggregated collective efficacy on team performance, nor had it examined the week-to-week influence of previous performance on subsequent collective efficacy. Myers and colleagues (2004) surveyed 10 football teams within a 24-hour period prior to each of eight games over eight consecutive weekends. Their results were consistent with those of Feltz and Lirgg (1998): Team performance by the offense (i.e., points scored, total yardage, average yardage gained per play, number of punts, and game outcome) significantly predicted collective efficacy, and collective efficacy significantly predicted the next game's offensive performance. Together, both laboratory and field studies suggest that to affect team performance and alleviate anxiety and negative affect, coaches and athletes should focus on confidence in the collective capabilities of a team rather than emphasizing individual confidence.

It is also possible that teams may become overconfident as a result of past success, and this in turn may lead to complacency, lack of focus, and less willingness to try new strategies (Vancouver, Thompson, Tischner, & Putka, 2002). Such complacent behaviors may lead to future failures. Anyone who watches sports on television has seen teams lose to weaker opponents because the stronger teams did not take their opponents seriously enough. Although this possibility has not been studied empirically in sport, Marks (1999) found with work teams that high–collective efficacy teams performed worse than low–collective efficacy teams in terms of coordination processes in situations that were novel or nonroutine. Thus, it might be that in sport situations that demand flexibility (e.g., a change in offensive or defensive strategy), high-efficacy teams may be reluctant to give up the strategies that have led to their previous successes.

Effective Communication

If a team is a group of people acting together to achieve a shared goal, it goes without saying that team members must communicate with one another to achieve the goal. How could players who cannot talk or signal to one another decide how to play together? If you try to imagine such a situation, you begin to realize just how many interpersonal behaviors communicate meaning and information—not just words and hand signals, but also eye contact, body language, and physical touch.

As essential as communication is to groups, team communication still has not been widely studied. Perhaps this is not that surprising. Communication may be difficult to study because it is so ubiquitous. If **communication** can be defined as interpersonal acts that exchange meaning and information, then what is no communication? One player can ignore a teammate, and that would still be considered communication. No wonder so little research has been done.

Nature of team communication. Recently, a relatively precise conceptualization of communication

emerged in the work of Sullivan and Feltz (2003) who defined communication in a very specific sense. They used the phrase *effective communication in sports* to refer to those interactions that enhance the operation of the team and its members. For instance, messages between teammates that result in improved team performance or more satisfied players would be considered effective communication because they contribute to a better functioning team. This notion is based on the definition of communication as "a symbolic process by which two people, bound together in a relationship, provide each other with resources or negotiate the exchange of resources" (Roloff, 1981, p. 30) and is couched within the theoretical framework of social exchange theory (e.g., Foa & Foa, 1974). A **resource** is any commodity, whether material or symbolic, that can be exchanged through interpersonal behavior (Foa & Foa, 1974).

Social exchange theory refers to a school of theories of interpersonal interaction that have been used to explain nearly everything from marriage to traffic jams. These theories assume that all interactions are a form of negotiation and an exchange of resources that are valued by the actors. The various social exchange theories tend to offer different classifications of these resources, but they may be said to include both tangible (e.g., money) and intangible (e.g., love) resources. Basically, anything that may be given by one person to another and is valued can be a resource.

There are several key characteristics in a social exchange interaction. First, the people are assumed to be interdependent; that is, their actions and decisions rely in part on the actions and reactions of the other people in the situation. Second, these relationships work best, if in the long run they are reciprocal and mutually beneficial. Thus, in any one discrete interaction, people may actually give more than they receive so long as they can expect to derive some long-term benefit from that relationship.

Social exchange theories also tend to assume that people are rational actors. People not only evaluate the costs and benefits of their current relationships, but also evaluate the ratio of costs and benefits in other possible relationships. For example, a player on a team will have some sense of all the benefits he or she derives from being a member of the team (i.e., in terms of resources, such as respect and information). He or she also will have evaluated the costs of this membership (i.e., in terms of resources, such as money and time). Based on the balance between these costs and benefits, as well as on the expected costs-and-benefits ratio of being a member of another team, the player may decide to stay with the current team, switch teams, or quit playing altogether.

The main benefit of social exchange theory is that it offers concrete boundaries for what can be seen as "communication." Any interaction that rewards (or punishes) another through the exchange of resources is an act of communication (Kelly & Thibault, 1978). Thus, the interactions between teammates or partners are characterized by what one individual "provides" to the other (e.g., information, emotional support), and what the other person has to "pay" for these resources (e.g., respect, reciprocated emotional support). Obviously there are many types of this kind of communication within sports teams; for example, coaches giving players tips, and athletes patting each other on the back.

Communication resources in sport. Despite the limited research on communication in sport, there is a consistent theme of identifying types of communication that involve valued resources. Typically, researchers have focused on the task-oriented messages between teammates, even though sports teams are also important as social groups. For example, based on an analysis of communication patterns in elite volleyball teams, Hanin (1992) identified four main styles of communication: Messages that dealt with planning strategy or technique were labeled **orientation messages**, whereas those between teammates that served to motivate or energize team members were labeled **stimulation messages**. Discussions that focused on assessments of play, ability, or effort were labeled **evaluation messages**.

All other communications were termed **task-irrelevant messages**. Not surprisingly, a distinct performance-based pattern of communication was observed. Teams tended to display orientation messages before performance, stimulation messages during performance, and evaluation messages after performance. Overall, stimulation messages were the most frequent type of communication, and the amount of task-irrelevant communication was negligible. Although these results are based only on a sample of teams from one sport, it is not unreasonable to suggest that the general communication pattern reflects the functioning of most elite sports teams. Such teams will be extremely task conscious, and interactions within the team will reflect this focus, whether they occur before, during, or after games.

Other task-oriented resources reported in the literature include giving tips to teammates about their play (Williams & Widmeyer, 1991). Other social resources that have been investigated include displaying understanding and acceptance (Sullivan, 1993), and displaying both trust and expressions of warmth (DiBerardinis, Barwind, Flanningam, & Jenkins, 1983).

An important, but little studied, aspect of communication in sports teams is nonverbal communication, particularly given the physicality of the context of sport. Kneidinger, Maple, and Tross (2001) investigated the role of gestures and touch among baseball and softball players. Teams were observed for a total of 20 games. The researchers found that females displayed touching behaviors more frequently than did males and that females tended to show different touching behaviors, particularly those that involved multiple actors, for example, team hugs and hand piles (Figure 6.4). In contrast, males were more likely to engage in one-on-one interactions (e.g., high fives). Furthermore, females tended to engage in more touching behaviors (e.g., back slaps, butt pats) after negative game events than did males. The incidence of more touching among the female ball players is consistent with gender role norms that support the display of physical expressiveness in females more than in males.

Communication and performance. Like much of the work applying social psychology to sport, research on communication shows a dual nature involving social and task issues. Actually, with communication, this dichotomy goes beyond sport and dates back to the distinction Bales made in 1950 between social communication and task communication in groups. For instance, consider the following two quotations from the tale of the Oxford rowing crew's 1987 race against Cambridge described in the opening vignette (Topolski, 1989). Before the race, the coach addressed the team in a motivational speech

> This is your weather, I told the crew, and out there it's your water—no one can cope with those waves like you guys can, least of all Cambridge. You have the weight and technique for rough water—and better still, you have the nerve for it. And, I don't think Cambridge has that nerve. If it stays like this, I really think you could pull it off tomorrow. (pp. 274–275)

After winning the race, the captain of the team had these words for the coach: "We could have been disqualified out there, Dan . . . because we had ten men in our boat [including you] and they only had nine" (p. 300).

Whether discussions within the team are "fire 'em up" speeches (as the rowing coach made) or sincere statements of recognition (as the captain of the rowing team subsequently made), there are undoubtedly many important effects of such messages.

The research that has focused on task communications (e.g., motivating, strategizing, teaching technique) has indicated that these messages are positively related to a team's performance (Dale & Wrisberg, 1996). Research on golf and tennis teams has found that winning teams are characterized by significantly more conversations between and during plays than losing teams (Lausic, Tennebaum, Eccles, Jeong, & Johnson, 2009; Widmeyer & Williams, 1991). Interestingly, social communication, which is more concerned with expressions of emotion and how members are treated and accepted, also has

been shown to be related to performance (DiBerardinis et al., 1983) and team cohesion (Sullivan, 1995; Sullivan & Feltz, 2003). The relationship between social communication (e.g., expressions of acceptance of teammates) and role clarity was explored by Cunningham and Eys (2007); they found that frequent expression of social communication among teammates was positively correlated to athletes' perception of role clarity.

An alternative way of conceptualizing intrateam communication in sport is as a social cognitive exchange (Eccles & Tenenbaum, 2007). In this framework, messages between teammates are part of a larger process that contributes to the development and functioning of a team mental model—the sharing and manipulation of information among team members to achieve a shared goal (Hinsz, Tindale, & Vollrath, 1997). As suggested by Hinsz et al., (1997), a shared mental model is a collective cognitive representation of group processes. The messages team members share in forming a shared mental model need not be verbal or intentional. Consider a softball team practicing a double play. The key individuals (i.e., first base, second base, and shortstop) would all share key information about the rules, skills, and tactics to complete this performance. In addition, as they repeatedly practiced the drill, they would also communicate certain tendencies that would allow them to anticipate each other, such as how quickly the shortstop can transfer the ball from glove hand to throwing hand, or how well the first baseman can extend in any given direction. As these teammates repeatedly interact, this information (which might not ever be explicitly articulated) is learned and shared so that the three players perform better together. Eccles and Tenenbaum provide several suggestions for optimizing this communication. For example, teammates could work to develop a shared language (terms or gestures that are short and concise and known (perhaps exclusively) to all team members. Cross training, in which individuals train for some time in the roles of their

Figure 6.4   Gender Differences in Physical Communication: Females Hugging

SOURCE: Courtesy of Brock University Athletics.

teammates so as to gain an appreciation of their demands, could also allow for more effective cognitive exchange.

Team Goal Setting

In the sport psychology literature on individual performance, goal setting is a major topic. Research with individual athletes showing the importance of goal setting suggests the potential value of goal setting with groups. However, research examining team goal setting has been less common. We speculate that this is the case because team goal setting is not as common in the practical sense. That is, goal setting is most often an individual behavior. In addition, conducting research on this topic has presented some analytical issues. Due to the nested nature of sport teams, and only the recent emergence of advanced statistical software, group goal setting has yet to become a popular research topic in the sporting arena.

Nature of goals and goal setting. Athletes can have different types of goal orientation (Burton, 1989). **Outcome goals** focus strictly on the competitive result of an event. These goals are based on social comparison, that is, how one does relative to others. With outcome goals, individuals focus on winning, and if they do win—regardless of how it comes about—their goal has been achieved. Correspondingly, if an athlete plays the best game of his or her life and loses, it would be considered a failure. **Performance goals** focus on achieving success based on self-comparison. The objective is to improve one's own performance; the actual outcome of the competitive event might not be considered important at all. **Process goals** are focused on the skills to be performed during competition, such as trying to complete all passes during a hockey game (Kingston & Hardy, 1997).

Regardless of which goals are endorsed, there is little doubt that setting goals improves performance (Kyllo & Landers, 1995). Although there is a variety of conceptual explanations of why goal setting might be so effective, most researchers in sport psychology endorse Locke and Latham's (1985) direct mechanistic view of how goals work. According to Locke and Latham, setting goals can have four direct effects on performance, namely that (a) goal setting may increase someone's effort toward the requisite behavior, (b) goal setting may prolong persistence once the behavior is initiated, (c) goals may direct the performer's attention to important elements of the performance, and (d) goals may foster development of new learning strategies.

Research has revealed several important aspects of effective goal setting. Goals should be specific, realistic, and challenging. The time frame should not be ignored when setting goals, and both short-term and long-term goals should be used. Evaluation and feedback based on these goals should be carried out in a consistent and timely fashion in both competitive and training situations (Weinberg & Gould, 1999).

Group goal setting. Brawley, Carron, and Widmeyer (1992) conducted an exploratory investigation of the nature of group goals with team sport athletes. They found that most team goals, as opposed to individual goals, were vague and imprecise. This was true with respect to both the exact nature of the goals (e.g., the goals were not stated in terms of an objective standard like time of possession), and the time frames for their accomplishment (e.g., no deadlines were set). With respect to types of team goals, Brawley and colleagues found that the majority of team goals endorsed during practice were performance goals (e.g., give maximum effort in each drill), whereas goals during a competition comprised a balance among outcome goals (e.g., win the game), process goals (e.g., perform each skill as it should be done), and performance goals.

Eys, Patterson, Loughead, and Carron (2006) developed a three-stage protocol for implementing a team goal-setting program. Their protocol outlines four principles of team goal setting: (a) selecting the team goals, (b) establishing the target for the team goals, (c) coaches reminding players of the team's goals, and (d) evaluating, providing feedback, and reevaluating the team

goals for effectiveness. In the first stage of the protocol, the rationale for the goal-setting program and the setting of team goals are discussed and carried out with the team. The coaches then remind their players of the team's goals in the second stage. This can be done verbally, or by posting the team goals in a visible location in the locker room. The third stage is when the goal evaluation and feedback occurs.

Although fairly recent, the protocol established by Eys and colleagues (2006) for implementing a team goal-setting program has been used in intervention research. Senécal, Loughead, and Bloom (2008) implemented a season-long team goal setting intervention with female high school basketball players where teams were randomly assigned to either an experimental (i.e., team goal setting) or a control condition. Previous research had indicated that team goal setting had been identified by athletes as being the most effective in their team-building programs (Stevens & Bloom, 2003). Results of the season-long intervention indicated that the teams in the experimental condition had higher perception of team cohesion at the end of the season than the teams in the control condition (see the "Focus on Intervention" section for a more detailed description of this intervention and its results).

FOCUS ON INTERVENTION

Goal Setting and Team Cohesion

In their season-long team-building intervention program, Senécal and colleagues (2008) used team goal setting to increase perceptions of team cohesion among female high school senior basketball players. The authors of this study aimed to add to earlier team-building research by addressing previous issues in the body of literature identified by Brawley and Paskevich (1997). For example, previous studies often used the coach as the team-building facilitator; however, these coaches may not have the skills, knowledge, or attributes required to successfully facilitate a team-building intervention. Furthermore, previous research rarely used a control group and was not season-long in duration. Lastly, because past studies often used multiple intervention topics and strategies, it was therefore difficult to determine which strategies failed or succeeded in increasing perceptions of team cohesion or other outcome variables. This intervention sought to address these issues by conducting a season-long intervention facilitated by a Sport Psychology Consultant (SPC) using team goal setting, which has been identified by athletes as the most effective technique in team building (Stevens & Bloom, 2003).

Senécal and colleagues (2008) followed Eys and colleagues' (2006) protocol for implementing a team goal-setting program. Teams that were randomly assigned to the experimental group were informed that working together to find common objectives for their team could help them work better as a team. The athletes generated both long- and short-term outcome goals as a team and were then asked by the SPC what they believed they must do to accomplish these goals. Athletes first worked individually, then in small groups, and then as a whole team to identify and prioritize performance indices (or goals) that were most important to the team (e.g., rebounds, turnovers). Prior to each game, the coach would remind his or her team of these performance indices, and in turn the teams were informed of their performance with regard to these indices following each game. Lastly, the SPC met with the team to review and discuss the goals, and after a block of three games any modifications, if necessary, were made to these goals. The teams in the control condition did not receive such intervention and were only informed that they would have to complete measures of cohesion twice in their season—once at the beginning and the other at the end of the season (as did the teams in the experimental condition).

Results indicated that there were no significant differences in perceptions of cohesion between each condition at the beginning of the season prior to the start of the intervention. However, at the end of the season, there was a significant difference in these perceptions. Teams in the intervention condition held significantly higher perceptions of cohesion than did the control group. It should be noted, however, that the teams in the experimental condition did not increase their perceptions of cohesion, but the teams in the control condition had a significant decrease in their perceptions of cohesion. That is, the teams in the experimental group receiving the intervention maintained their perceptions of cohesion throughout the season whereas those in the control condition did not. The authors cite a potential ceiling effect as an explanation for the lack of increase in cohesion perceptions.

TEAM BUILDING

Team building refers to the active planned process of optimizing the abilities of teammates toward maximizing individual performance, team performance, or social outcomes. To a considerable extent, team-building interventions typically are directed toward improving a team's internal social dynamics (i.e., chemistry). In other words, interventions are aimed at one or more of the very social psychological factors that have been reviewed in this chapter: cohesion, confidence, communication, and goal setting. There is some research on the explicit practice of team building within sports.

Family Psychology Intervention

A unique approach to team building is the use of family therapy for sports teams. As Schindler-Zimmerman (1993) observed,

> Athletic teams look like and function much like families. . . . The coaching staff, especially at the university level, assumes a surrogate parental role. . . . The more experienced or older players take on older sibling roles teaching the new recruits "the ropes" and generally taking on more team responsibility. (p. 29)

It has been noted that many of the issues dealt with by sport psychologists (e.g., conflict resolution, role clarification, group unity) also are issues for which family psychologists have well-designed group-based interventions (Grau, Möller, & Gunnarsson, 1988; Schindler-Zimmerman, 1993; Schindler-Zimmerman & Protinsky, 1993; Schindler-Zimmerman, Washle, & Protinsky, 1990).

Schindler-Zimmerman and colleagues (1990) developed one such intervention dealing with a college female volleyball team over the course of a season. The consultants focused on developing in team members the perception that the team, like a family, is a social system. As a social system, teammates and coaches have a great impact on each other; therefore, treating any one person individually is not very beneficial. With this goal in mind, one intervention strategy involved having the team members discuss issues, such as labeling and rituals, including the meanings they convey (e.g., how meaningful it can be to simply say someone has "bad hands"), and how to change the boundaries of the system.

Schindler-Zimmerman and colleagues (1990) designed a program based on repeated short meetings that addressed four specific problems: (a) one player receiving special attention from the coaching staff, (b) the team's propensity to complain during practice, (c) the coaches' polarized roles on the team, and (d) the need for a sense of team confidence. Each of these issues was approached with a specific objective and an individualized consultation plan. Let us consider one example. The issue of one player receiving special attention had to do with one of the team's star players, who was perceived as unmotivated. To motivate her, the coaches treated her differently from the other players and encouraged her teammates to do the same. This was interpreted as a coalition between different levels of the team (i.e., coaching staff and players) that was resulting in a poorly functioning team. The consultants designed an intervention consisting of the coaches and teammates of the star player first recognizing the harmful consequences of these behaviors (e.g., decline in cohesiveness), and then actively "backing off" when they initiated or witnessed such interactions. This intervention was deemed a success based not just on the subjective evaluations of all the players (including the star) and coaches, but also on the subsequent performance of the star player and the team as a whole.

Communication Training Intervention

Sullivan (1993) developed an extensive communication training program for sports teams designed to optimize the interpersonal communication skills of the athletes. Although Sullivan did not present a theoretical rationale for why communication would affect team performance, she did base her intervention on an empirical link between the two concepts. Summarizing the applied literature in the field, she argued that team communication appeared to influence performance indirectly through team cohesion. As a team communicates more openly, the sense of cohesiveness in the team is enhanced. And as we have seen, team cohesion is positively related to performance.

Sullivan's (1993) communication training program was applied to seven teams, including their coaches. In total, more than 80 male and female team sport athletes participated. The intervention lasted for the entire season and consisted of seven stages. Each stage entailed a specific objective with corresponding activities that were designed to enhance different interpersonal communication skills of the teammates.

Table 6.1 summarizes the seven stages of the communication program. Sullivan (1993) concluded that the program successfully enhanced "team members' awareness of their own communication skills and/or competence" (p. 90). This conclusion was supported by numerous comments made by the athletes, including "we have increased awareness of our team communication issues" (Sullivan, 1993, p. 88); "we are following through on the court with what we're discussing in these activities" (p. 89); and "I will give my opinion more to people with whom I feel intimidated" (p. 89).

Table 6.1 Seven Stages of Sullivan's (1993) Communication Training Program

Stage	Objective	Activity
1	Effective listening	Teammates generate a list of good listening skills and guidelines for implementing them.
2	Self-assessment	Teammates share and comment on self-completed personality assessments.
3	Identification of problems	Pairs of teammates generate a list of problems facing the team; team consensus is reached on the total list of problems.
4	Self-disclosure	Each athlete participates in an exercise involving completing a sentence (e.g., "On the team, I need to improve my ability to . . . ") in front of the team.
5	Concerns about the current season	Team members write down one fear and one hope for the season; these comments are reported (anonymously) to the team.
6	Norm of acceptance	Small groups within the team share personal stories about mistakes made and lessons learned.
7	Self-evaluation	Each player evaluates the team's progress on team members' being genuine with one another, communicating in an understanding fashion, valuing each other as individuals, and accepting one another.

CULTURE CAPSULE

Team Dynamics Across Cultures

Physical activity has been a significant aspect of every recorded culture, and sport has no national or social boundaries. Theoretically, one would expect that teams in different societies and cultures would operate similarly in terms of psychological constructs. Most of the theories and theoretical constructs touched on in this chapter do not recognize cultural boundaries. Conceptually, the importance of role clarity for an Indian cricket player is equivalent to that of a linebacker in the National Football League. Likewise, team confidence, as a social cognition, would be expected to be as influential a construct in a wide variety of sports.

However, much of the published research in the field has been based in North America and Western Europe. Given the importance of social dynamics for group processes, such as leadership, cohesion, and communication, one cannot assume that the concepts and research discussed in this chapter are equally applicable to different cultures. It is encouraging to note that the researchers currently working in the field appreciate this issue. For instance, Carron and colleagues (1997), in summarizing the research on team cohesion in sport and the use of the GEQ, noted that the most serious challenge to the measurement is the validity of the GEQ across cultures. Cohesion and its behavioral indicators may have very different meanings in different cultures. Carron and colleagues

(Continued)

(Continued)

suggested using great care in applying a particular conceptual model to other cultures. Heuze and Fontayne (2002) followed these suggestions in applying the GEQ to a French sporting sample. Like the English version, their adapted scale measures both social cohesion and task cohesion in four interrelated factors. However, Heuze and Fontayne had to rewrite some items, drop other ones, and add new ones that were culturally relevant.

Cultural differences in the interaction between leadership and cohesion was examined by Ryska, Yin, Cooley, and Ginn (1999). They found that Australian and American coaches differed in their coaching strategies to increase team cohesion. American coaches focused their coaching strategies on task-related cohesion whereas Australian coaches focused their coaching strategies on social cohesion. Considering the material throughout the chapter on the differential effects of task and social cohesion, this coaching difference could have profound implications in terms of team dynamics.

We can look with excitement to increased research on the meaning of team chemistry—including its antecedents and consequences—in various cultures around the world, and to discovering the extent to which the kinds of findings about sports teams in North America reviewed here surface elsewhere. For instance, is cohesion, which appears to be a vital component of successful teams in North America, even more important to teams in collectivistic cultures with their greater valuation of groups over individuals? Furthermore, is the relative importance of social cohesion greater than that of task cohesion in collectivistic cultures?

SUMMARY

This chapter has presented some of the relevant theory and research on the application of social psychology to sports teams. Sports teams provide a valid and realistic venue for conducting applied social psychological research. Sport has been a valuable context within which to increase our understanding of issues, such as team cohesion and confidence, styles of communication, and team goal setting. The application of this understanding can be seen in the development of team-building interventions in sport.

Based on the material presented in the chapter, we can now elaborate the initial framework for understanding the application of social psychology to sports that was presented in Figure 6.1. This more extensive framework is shown in Figure 6.5. This is a causal model whereby "input" influences "throughput," which in turn influences "output"; moreover, "output" is conceived as in many cases

influencing "input" and/or "throughput." The "input" in this framework is still the individual attributes of the team members that include players' abilities and characteristics (e.g., self-confidence, the tendency of individuals to self-disclose, goal orientation). The "throughput" of the model still represents the notion of team chemistry, but now we can be more specific concerning the meaning of this term—dynamic interpersonal factors, such as team cohesion, collective efficacy, effective communication, and team goal setting. Given that these group dynamics represent the central part of the model, the framework can now include applied strategies specifically designed to affect team chemistry. This is noted by the inclusion of team-building strategies as a separate part of the model. Note that these are interventions designed to affect team chemistry (e.g., task cohesion), and thus have an indirect effect on team performance and other outcomes. Finally, as with the input component of the model, it is possible to

Figure 6.5 Detailed Framework for Understanding the Application of Social Psychology to Sports

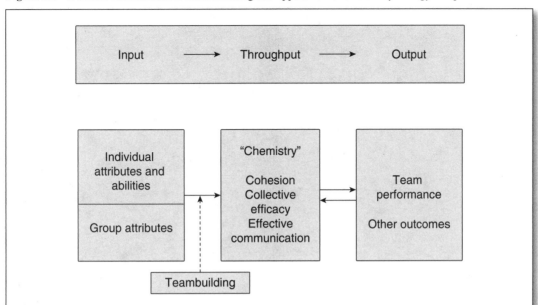

be more specific concerning the output component. Although output refers primarily to team performance, other outcomes can include, for example, individual performance and satisfaction.

Thus, it can now be seen that well-studied psychological constructs, such as cohesiveness and collective efficacy are what social psychologists intuit when they hear the word *chemistry*.

Such notions are indeed characteristic of how teams function; they have a definite impact on performance, and can be influenced to optimize team performance. The team-building process may occur somewhat coincidentally, as with the Oxford rowing crew described in the opening vignette, or more likely through explicit team-building programs.

7

APPLYING SOCIAL PSYCHOLOGY TO THE MEDIA

DAVID R. EWOLDSEN

BEVERLY ROSKOS

On October 30, 1938, the Mercury Theatre broadcast Howard Koch's radio adaptation of H. G. Wells's The War of the Worlds. *The production was directed by, and starred, Orson Welles. After the opening credits for the Mercury Theatre, the radio play began with the announcement that the audience was listening to the music of Ramon Raquello's orchestra from the Meridian Room of the Park Plaza (a fictional hotel) in New York. During the next 45 minutes, the music was frequently interrupted, and then completely stopped, by news reports. The reports told of flashes of light from Mars and a metallic cylinder landing in a farm in Grover's Mill, New Jersey. A later news flash declared that Martians were emerging from the cylinder and using a heat ray to attack spectators. At one point, the radio broadcast was apparently taken over by the military to coordinate efforts against the Martian invaders. Civilians were advised to flee from towns in central and northern New Jersey, and a list of the best escape routes was provided (Koch, 1970). Unfortunately, many people missed the opening announcement that this was a production of the Mercury Theatre. An estimated 6 million people heard the* War of the Worlds *broadcast. Of those, approximately 28% thought that the news reports were real. People fled from their homes by car, bus, and train. Other people tried desperately to seal their homes against the Martians' poison gas. Still other people called their families and friends to warn them of the attack by the Martians and to talk with their loved ones for perhaps a final time (Cantril, Gaudet, & Herzog, 1940). The Mercury Theatre's production of* The War of the Worlds *has gone down in history as a prime example of how powerful media can shape people's social reality.*

At the other extreme, Republican Senator William Knowland held a 20-hour telethon on October 31 and November 1, 1958, in an attempt to salvage his campaign for governor of California. By all accounts, the telethon was run professionally and competently. Schramm and Carter (1959) conducted a phone survey of 563 persons living in San Francisco to study the effects of this extraordinary effort by Knowland. The results of the survey are interesting in terms of what they tell us about the limitations of the media. The survey found that the majority of people who watched the telethon were already committed supporters of Knowland—not the audience that Knowland wanted to reach if he hoped to convince more people to vote for him. Did the telethon have any effect on how people voted? Of the 563 people surveyed, 2 reported that it did. Of these 2 people, 1 reported that the telethon convinced him to vote for Knowland and the other reported that it convinced him to vote against Knowland. Knowland's telethon demonstrates one of the limitations of the media: People often watch programs that reflect what they already believe. If that is the case, can the media change people's minds? It might be the case that the media may reinforce what people think, but will not change what they think.

The media have become an integral part of our lives. By 1971, more than 95% of all households in the United States and Canada had televisions (Centerwall, 1989). Do you know anyone who does not own at least one TV? In 2009, the average adolescent lived in a household with 3.8 television sets, and 2.8 DVD or VCR players (Rideout, Foehr, & Roberts, 2010)—in other words, there are more television sets in an average household than there are people living in that average household! Can you think of anyone who does not listen to the radio, read newspapers or magazines, or go to movies? Indeed, you can now watch TV on your cell phone, while pumping gas for your car, or while riding an elevator.

The last decade has witnessed profound changes in how adolescents use the media (Rideout et al., 2010). The average time spent with various media by adolescents (ages 8 to 18) in 2009 was 7 hours and 38 minutes per day. This represents an increase of over an hour from 1999 (6 hours and 19 minutes). But, even more dramatic is the increase in the total amount of media these adolescents are exposed to each day—an astounding 10 hours and 45 minutes! This represents a 44% increase from the amount of media adolescents were exposed to in 1999 (7 hours and 29 minutes). Of course, you may be wondering how it is possible to be exposed to close to 11 hours of media while only spending about 7 hours and 30 minutes using the media each day. But, how many times do you search on the Internet while watching a TV program, or text a friend while listening to your iPod? Using multiple media simultaneously—or multitasking—is becoming more prevalent. In 2009, adolescents spent 29% of their time with the media using at least two different types of media—up from just 16% of the time in 1999 (Rideout et al., 2010). Multitasking is made easier by how easily teens can access myriad different media technologies. In 2015, approximately 99% of teenagers in the United States had access to one or more of the following media technologies: game console, smart or cell phone, desktop or laptop computer, or tablet (Lenhart, 2015).

Another change is how people access the media. Historically, when talking about using the "media," it meant watching TV programs when they were broadcast, going to movies, and reading newspapers (Rideout et al., 2010). Of course, the media include so much more than that today, and people's ways of accessing the media have expanded dramatically. For example, the amount of time adolescents spend watching a TV program when it is broadcast actually declined by 26 minutes from 3 hours and 5 minutes per day in 1999 to 2 hours and 39 minutes per day in 2009. Yet, total time watching TV increased from 3 hours and 47 minutes per day in 1999 to 4 hours and 29 minutes per day in 2009 (Rideout et al., 2010). This shift from watching live TV to watching time-shifted TV has continued (Nielson, 2014). Today's adolescents can watch a TV program whenever they want using DVRs, Video or Television on Demand, and DVDs. And, they can watch a TV program on the Internet, their cell phones, or MP3 players.

Clearly, there are profound changes occurring in people's media use. But, these changes have been occurring over the last century. One hundred years ago, newspapers were the primary media outlet, and movies were just beginning to become popular. Radio did not really take off until the 1920s, and while television stations first appeared in the United States in the 1940s, it was the 1950s when television became popular (Pavlik & McIntosh, 2011). Given these profound changes in our media outlets, it is important to consider the effects of the media on our lives.

- Do the media create a violent society?
- Can the media increase our level of general fearfulness?
- What happens when people watch pornography?

- Do the media influence what we think are important issues?
- Can the media have an effect on elections?

The *War of the Worlds* broadcast suggests that the media can have profound effects on our lives. Yet, Senator Knowland's telethon indicates that the media have little or no impact on what we think. What does the research say? Research on the psychological effects of the media has covered many areas. This chapter explores the effects of media violence, pornography, and political coverage because these three issues have been studied extensively by social psychologists and have important social implications. There are many other areas not covered in this chapter, including the effects of the media on racism, education, body image, and diffusion of information. The overwhelming majority of the research focuses on U.S. media because most of the research has been done in the United States, and because the U.S. media quickly dominated the world's major media systems (McChesney, 1999).

HOW DOES MEDIA VIOLENCE AFFECT US?

How difficult is it to turn on a TV for an entire evening and not watch some type of physical violence? Based on studies of media violence on TV programming in the United States, it is extremely difficult. Focusing only on intentional physical violence, 58% of all TV programs during the 1994–1995 season contained some type of physical violence or a credible threat of physical violence (Wilson et al., 1997). If you are watching premium channels, such as HBO and Showtime, an astonishing 85% of the shows contain violence. If that is not bad enough, of those shows that contain violence, two thirds contain four or more violent interactions (Smith et al., 1998; Wilson et al., 1997, 1998). Of course, just because a TV program contains violence does not mean that it is promoting violence. Perhaps the message of the program is actually one of antiviolence. Maybe some of these TV shows include violence to focus on the harmful effects of the violence for the victim and the victim's family and friends. Although such shows do exist, they are rare. Only 4% of the shows during the three seasons from 1994 to 1997 had antiviolence themes (Smith et al., 1998). This means that TV shows are 15 times more likely to either contain proviolence messages, or *at best* be neutral toward violence, than to contain antiviolence themes. Unfortunately, the level of violence found on television programming has remained fairly steady for decades (Morgan, Shanahan, & Signorielli, 2009).

Figure 7.1 illustrates the percentages of programs within different types of TV programming that included violence from 1994 to 1997 (with violence defined as intentional physical violence). Clearly, dramas (75%) and movies (90%) contained a lot of violence. In addition, notice the increase in violence in both comedies and music videos over the 3-year period. However, the most disturbing aspect in the figure is the percentage of children's TV shows that contain violence. The fact that approximately two thirds of all children's shows contain violence, and that most of these shows contain multiple acts of violence (just think of the number of acts of violence in one episode of *The Simpsons* or *South Park*), is distressing. The recent proliferation of video games increases the amount of media violence that children are exposed to on a daily basis. The typical child will witness more than 8,000 murders and 100,000 acts of violence on network TV alone before reaching 18 years of age (Bushman & Anderson, 2001). Imagine how high these numbers would be if movies, video games, massively multiplayer online games (MMOGs), and comic books were included in that count.

Figure 7.1 Percentages of TV Shows Containing Violence for Different Types of Shows for the 1994–1995, 1995–1996, and 1996–1997 Seasons

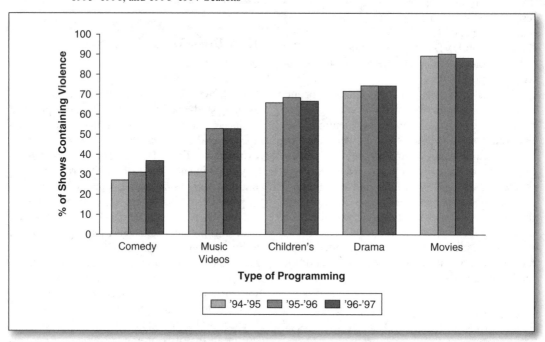

SOURCE: Adapted from Wilson and colleagues (1997, 1998) and Smith and colleagues (1998).

The Consequences of Viewing Media Violence

When you were growing up, your parents may have forbidden you from watching a certain TV show because it was too violent. Particularly violent or gory movies are rated PG-13 or R so that younger children will not be exposed to this kind of media violence. Why all the fuss about it? One common belief you might have heard is that only violent people, or people with certain characteristics, watch violent TV programs. However, a longitudinal survey in which children were studied when they were just beginning elementary school and then when they were in their early 20s found that violent people are no more likely to watch violent TV programs than are nonviolent people (Huesmann, Moise-Titus, Podolski, & Eron, 2003). Another common belief about violent TV programs and movies is that they may help people to relieve their stress and aggressive impulses, so violent TV shows and movies may actually *decrease* violence (Feshbach, 1961). This is commonly called the **cathartic effect** of watching violent media. Unfortunately, the vast majority of research studies do not support the idea that TV violence has a cathartic effect (Bandura, 2009).

The social scientific literature on media violence is overwhelming. Hundreds of studies, including quasi-experiments, longitudinal studies, and experiments have examined the effect of TV violence on violent behavior (Bushman, Huesmann, & Whitaker, 2009). Across all of these studies, the results consistently demonstrate that TV violence increases aggressive behavior. In fact, Potter (2003) identified more than 30 different effects of watching TV violence, including increased imitation of violence, short- and long-term increases in aggressive behaviors, increased fear, desensitization to violence, and greater acceptance of violence.

One type of research on TV violence is *quasi-experiments*. Quasi-experiments on TV violence use naturally occurring manipulations of exposure to TV to explore the impact of TV on aggression. When considering the results of the quasi-experimental studies, it is important to realize that the studies consider only exposure to TV *in general* and not exposure to TV violence in particular. For example, the Federal Trade Commission (FTC) stopped granting TV broadcasting licenses from 1949 to 1952 to study how best to regulate this then-new communication technology. The FTC's actions created a quasi-experiment with two conditions: cities with TV stations prior to 1950 and cities with TV stations starting in 1952 or later. Hennigan and colleagues (1982) took advantage of this natural manipulation to look at violent crime rates in these two city types. If TV increases violence, then violent crime rates should have increased in the cities that had been granted broadcast licenses prior to 1950 before they increased in the cities that did not receive licenses until 1952 or later. Crime rates did increase sooner in those cities where TV was introduced earlier (Hennigan et al., 1982). However, during the early years of TV, it was not violent crimes that increased; instead, the presence of a TV station in a community increased rates of nonviolent theft (excluding auto theft). Apparently, TV with all of its commercials may have made salient to people what they did not have, thereby increasing people's motivations to steal. Although this quasi-experiment did not find evidence that general exposure to TV influenced violence, other quasi-experiments have found such evidence.

Another quasi-experiment occurred in Canada when in 1973 a small town nicknamed "Notel" (i.e., no television) received TV broadcasts for the first time. There were three conditions in this quasi-experiment: a city with no TV stations (Notel), a city with one TV station (nicknamed "Unitel"), and a city with multiple TV stations (nicknamed "Multitel"). Rates of physical violence in Notel were compared with those in Unitel and Multitel both before and two years after the introduction of TV to Notel (Joy, Kimball, & Zabrack, 1986). Unitel and Multitel were similar to Notel in terms of violence prior to 1973. The rates of aggression in Unitel and Multitel children did not change during the 2-year period after 1973. However, rates of both physical aggression and verbal aggression increased dramatically in Notel children after the introduction of TV.

Perhaps the most damning quasi-experiment on the effects of TV violence is Centerwall's (1989) analysis of homicide rates after the introduction of TV in the United States, Canada, and South Africa. Whereas TV was introduced in the United States and Canada at approximately the same time during the early 1950s, the South African government banned TV broadcasts until 1975. Interestingly, following the introduction of TV in each of these three countries, the homicide rates remained fairly constant for roughly 10 to 12 years, but then *doubled* by the 15th year. The fact that the homicide rate doubled after the introduction of TV in each of these countries led Centerwall to conclude that TV violence is responsible for approximately half of the violent homicides in each of these countries. However, if TV is the culprit, why was there a 15-year lag between the introduction of TV and the increase in homicide rates? The most likely answer is that children are most vulnerable to the effects of violence on TV (Wilson et al., 2002). But, how often do you hear about young children committing murder? Rather, the effect of the introduction of TV on violent homicides may have been delayed until children who were 3 or 4 years old when TV was introduced were old enough to begin committing acts of violence—typically in their late adolescent years—approximately 15 years after the introduction of TV. Clearly, Centerwall's estimate that TV violence is responsible for half of the homicides in the United States, Canada, and South Africa is an overestimate (Perry, 2007). As tends to be the case with quasi-experimental designs, there were many factors that Centerwall did not (and could not) control for in his analysis, including violent social upheavals in two of these countries at the same time that violent homicides increased (the civil rights and antiwar movements in the United States, and the antiapartheid movement in South Africa). However, the data do indict TV.

Longitudinal studies have also found evidence that TV violence increases violent behavior

(Huesmann et al., 2003). For example, in 1977 approximately 600 first- and third-grade children from the Chicago area were interviewed concerning their TV viewing habits. Roughly two thirds of the children were reinterviewed between 1992 and 1995 when they were between 21 and 23 years of age. The levels of violent TV that these children watched in 1977 were a stronger predictor of their levels of violence 15 years later than were their levels of aggression when they were children (Huesmann et al., 2003). This relationship held even when other factors that influence adult aggression were controlled, including parents' level of aggression, socioeconomic status, and intelligence.

Of course, *experimental studies* are the best technique for establishing causal relationships between two variables. Numerous experimental studies have demonstrated such a relationship between TV violence and aggressive behavior. A meta-analysis (i.e., a statistical procedure for assessing the overall results of numerous studies) of 230 experimental studies of media violence with more than 100,000 research participants in total found that exposure to media violence consistently resulted in higher levels of a variety of aggressive behaviors (Hearold, 1986; see also Paik & Comstock, 1994). However, it is important to remember that most of the experimental studies were conducted in a laboratory setting, and so the aggressive behaviors were "milder" than the aggression found outside the laboratory (Giles, 2003). For example, many studies involved giving a person an electric shock or a loud blast of an aversive sound to the victim's ear. Although these behaviors obviously are not "nice," they are certainly not as violent as an aggressive assault or a homicide.

One limitation of the research on media violence is that it has focused nearly exclusively on TV and movie violence. However, when you play a typical video game as is the man in Figure 7.2, how many acts of violence do you view? Of course, the issue of video games is much more complex because you not only are watching the violence, but in many ways are committing it. Many early commentators were

Figure 7.2 Playing Violent Computer or Video Games, Which Can Have Similar Effects as Watching TV Violence

particularly worried about video games for this very reason—people were in some way actually engaging in the violence when playing a video game rather than simply viewing the violence (Bowman, 2016). Research has shown that playing—or even just watching—violent video games can have the same effects as watching TV violence (Anderson, 2004; Anderson, Gentile, & Buckley, 2007). This area of research has become extremely controversial with some researchers arguing that video games do not have any effect on aggressive behavior (Ferguson, 2015; Markey, 2015). However, much of the research on video games has been somewhat simplistic in its assumptions about gaming (Okdie et al., 2014).

One of the limitations of the research on video game aggression is that the research has focused on solo game play (Ewoldsen et al., 2012). This bias toward studying solo game play may reflect the technological limits of early violent video games which typically only allowed solo game play. However, today the overwhelming majority of video games—and violent games in particular—have multiplayer options, and more importantly, allow cooperative game play. Surveys find that most video game players want to play games cooperatively against either the game or other players (Velez & Ewoldsen, 2013).

An obvious question is whether playing a video game cooperatively has the same effects as playing a game violently and research suggests that it does not (Velez, Mahood, Ewoldsen, & Moyer-Guse, 2014). Cooperative game play has been found to mitigate the effects of the violent content of a game on subsequent behavior so that players who play either solo or competitively are more aggressive than players who played cooperatively. Indeed, several studies have found that cooperative game play results in no increase in aggressive behavior compared to people who did not play any video games (Velez, Whitaker, Greitemeyer, Ewoldsen, & Bushman, in press). Further, cooperative game play appears to increase cooperative behavior after game play (Ewoldsen et al., 2012; Velez, 2015). Research has also found that playing video games that involve prosocial behaviors, such as helping other players or cleaning up the environment have been found to increase prosocial behaviors in adolescents (Gentile et al., 2009; Greitemeyer & Osswald, 2010; also recall that this research was described in Chapter 3).

Players often have the choice to behave aggressively or prosocially when playing video games. Therefore, some video game researchers have argued that research that focuses exclusively on the video game content as opposed to the video game player is missing an important element. In line with this reasoning, Oswald, Prorock, and Murphy (2014) suggest that in order to understand the link between violent behavior and video games, it is important to study not only the characteristics of the video games, but also the experience of gameplay from the player's perspective. To determine how gamers perceive meaning in video game play, Oswald and colleagues conducted a qualitative analysis of video game players' descriptions of the experience of playing video games (recall from Chapter 3 that qualitative research is useful for providing in-depth information about the subjective meaning of experiences). The purpose of the study was to add to the quantitative research on video game playing, and to determine whether there is more to the experience of playing violent video games than previously identified. In this study, people who played video games were recruited from a university and from online message boards. Participants were asked to write about their most recent experience of playing a video game. Oswald, Prorock, and Murphy (2014) then conducted a **content analysis** of participants' descriptions of the video game experience. Content analysis involves classifying descriptions into categories (often called "themes") that share the same broad meaning in order to gain new insights about a phenomenon. By identifying themes, researchers are able to organize a large amount of data (in this case, written descriptions of the experience of playing video games) into easily understandable groupings that help communicate the meaning of an experience. The researchers identified six major themes describing the video game experience. The most commonly occurring theme was "emotional responses." Participants described experiencing positive emotions when playing video games, including excitement and humor. Some participants described experiencing negative emotions like frustration, but these experiences were much less common. Participants also described the video game experience as very social. They played with friends (both online and face-to-face) and also interacted with strangers online. Even violent video games often involved cooperation and sociability. Another important aspect of video game play was goal attainment. Participants described working toward specific goals within the game, either individually or with others. Oswald and colleagues found that participants who wrote about violent video games did not simply describe negative emotions and aggressive behavior, but instead wrote about video game play as a positive experience involving positive emotions, sociality, and goal attainment. The results of this qualitative analysis of the meaning of videogame play suggest that the standard approach to studying video games may miss many important aspects of video game play. Specifically, the results suggested that people play video games, even violent ones, for reasons that are often overlooked by

more quantitative research. Therefore, one explanation for the inconsistency of research attempting to link aggressive behavior to video game violence is its focus on the video game content instead of the player.

A final point to remember about violence and the causes of aggression is that aggressive behavior is *overdetermined*. A behavior is said to be **overdetermined** when it has multiple causes. Many different factors can cause a person to be aggressive. For example, males tend to be more aggressive than females. Likewise, some people seem to have aggressive personalities, and this increases their likelihood of acting aggressively. Other factors that have been identified as influencing aggression include frustration and anger, stress, general arousal, the temperature, loud noises, and having been abused as a child (Geen, 2001). Likewise, culture obviously plays a major role in aggressive behavior. The incidence of aggression and violence is higher in the United States than in Canada, even though the TV programming is very similar in the two countries. This is because the United States has a more aggressive culture (Geen, 2001; Nisbett & Cohen, 1996).

Imitation of Violence

On March 9, 2001, Lionel Tate was convicted of murdering Tiffany Eunick. She was 6 years old at the time of her death. In causing Tiffany's death, Lionel used wrestling moves he had seen performed by one of his favorite TV wrestling stars. Tiffany's injuries from the wrestling moves were equivalent to a fall from a three-story building. Lionel was 14 years old when he was convicted of murder and sentenced to life in prison.

You may have heard about some of the early studies focusing on imitating TV violence where children watched a short film of a child beating up a bobo doll. A bobo doll is a large inflatable doll that often looks like a clown and is used as a punching bag. Later, when the children were given an opportunity to play, they imitated the child they watched in the film and also beat up the bobo doll (Bandura, Ross, & Ross, 1963).

In one experiment exploring imitative violence (Hicks, 1965), children watched an 8-minute film of a person beating up a bobo doll. The person was either an adult male, an adult female, a boy their age, or a girl their age. The person hit the bobo doll with a bat, hit the doll with a mallet, threw balls at the doll, and sat on the doll and punched it. A final control group of children did not watch any film. The children then were placed in a room with toys that included a bobo doll, a bat, a mallet, and balls. The experimenter observed how much the children imitated the violence they had watched in the film. After a period of six months, the children returned to the laboratory to play in the same room with the same toys. Again, the experimenter observed how much the children imitated the violence they had watched in the film six months earlier. The design of this experiment was a 2 (age: adult or child model) X 2 (sex: male or female model) X 2 (time of imitation: immediately or six months later) with a control group.

As you can see in Figure 7.3, children who watched either children or adults act aggressively toward a bobo doll imitated that violence when given a chance to play immediately after viewing the violence as well as six months later when they were brought back into the setting (Hicks, 1965). You will remember that a control group of children did not watch anyone beat up the bobo doll. These children's data are not included in the figure because they did not act aggressively *at all* either the first time they were allowed to play with the toys or six months later (Hicks, 1965).

People often criticize these studies, arguing that the children naturally hit the bobo doll because that is what one does with a bobo doll (although, of course, the control children did not hit the bobo doll). The research is much more complex than this simple criticism would suggest. When children see another child perform aggressive behaviors in a movie and the aggressive child is either rewarded or punished, the children are more likely to act aggressively later when the child performing the aggressive behaviors is rewarded than when the child is punished (Bandura, 1965; Bandura et al., 1963; Steuer, Applefield, & Smith, 1971).

Figure 7.3   Numbers of Imitative Acts of Aggression That Boys and Girls Engaged in Either Immediately After Seeing a Rewarded Actor Perform the Actions or 6 Months Later

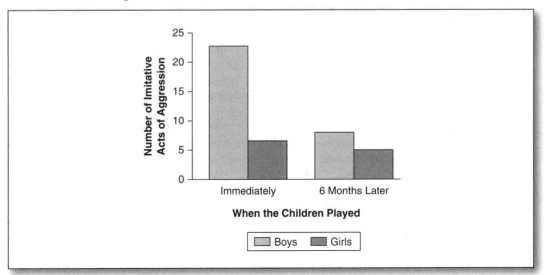

Numerous studies have demonstrated that people are more likely to perform behaviors that they are rewarded for performing. However, Bandura (1965; see also Bandura et al., 1963) demonstrated in the bobo doll experiments that even *watching* other people perform a behavior that is rewarded increases the likelihood that the viewer will perform the rewarded behavior. The performing of a behavior because one observes it being rewarded is called **vicarious learning**. Vicarious learning is the foundation of Bandura's (1986, 2009) social cognitive theory of mass communication.

How we learn to imitate violence. Bandura (1986, 2009) argued that much of what you learn is learned vicariously through the media. According to his **social cognitive theory**, there are four processes that must occur for vicarious learning to occur. The first is *attention*. To learn vicariously, people must attend to what is being modeled. Factors influencing whether one attends to the modeled behavior include how salient and attractive the behavior is to the individual. Clearly, media violence is very prevalent, exciting, and salient, and so it attracts attention. The second process is the *representational process,* which entails remembering the modeled behavior. Obviously, people cannot model a behavior that they cannot remember. The representational process also involves mentally rehearsing the behavior, thereby increasing the likelihood that it will be recalled at a later time. How many times have you seen young children playacting about committing an act of violence they viewed on TV? Through their fantasy, they are rehearsing that behavior. The third process is the *behavioral production process,* which focuses on how people learn to perform the behavior they have observed. Part of this process involves learning how to generalize the observed behavior into other types of related, but novel behaviors. For example, a child may observe the bobo doll being hit with a mallet, but may generalize this violent behavior to hitting his or her little brother with a mallet, or to hitting the bobo

doll with a baseball bat. The final element in Bandura's model focuses on the *motivational process*. People do not perform every behavior they observe; rather they perform those behaviors that they are motivated to perform. This explains why children imitate rewarded behavior, but not punished behavior. The reward provides a vicarious motivation for performing the behavior. In sum, according to social cognition theory, viewers are more likely to act aggressively if they watch media violence, remember the violence they watched, figure out how to perform the violent behaviors and practice those behaviors, and are somehow motivated to perform the violent behaviors.

Much of the research on Bandura's social cognitive theory of mass media has focused on the final element of Bandura's model, that is, motivational processes. As already discussed, one factor that increases motivation and the likelihood of performing violent behavior is the rewarding of violent behavior (Bandura, 1965; Bandura et al., 1963). A second motivation increasing factor is the viewer perceiving the violent behavior as justified (Berkowitz & Powers, 1979; Hoyt, 1970). Examples of justified violence that have been studied include violent behavior that is in self-defense, that results in getting even with someone, and that is aimed at a particularly nasty person. A third factor is the viewer perceiving the violence as realistic (Huesmann et al., 2003). A final factor that influences motivation is the viewer identifying with or liking the perpetrator of the violence (Huesmann et al., 2003). If a child identifies with mixed martial arts fighters like Anderson Silva, then that child will be more likely to imitate the fighting moves seen on the *Ultimate Fighting Championship* series or other mixed martial art events.

Another factor that appears to play an important role in people's motivation to perform violent behavior is *desensitization*. People may learn aggressive behaviors vicariously, but moral concerns and normative pressure will keep most of them from acting violently. However, if people are desensitized to violence, they will be less likely to view violence as morally wrong. Unfortunately, TV and video game violence desensitizes people to violence (Drabman & Thomas, 1974; Funk, Baldacci, Pasold, & Baumgardner, 2004). People who watch a lot of TV violence or have just been exposed to a violent program show less physiological response to media or real violence. Furthermore, an experiment by Drabman and Thomas (1974) demonstrated that children who are desensitized to violence by viewing TV violence are less likely to help other children who are being hurt. In their study, 22 boys and 22 girls were brought into the laboratory and either watched an excerpt from a violent cowboy film or watched no film. Then the children were asked by the experimenter to help him watch two younger children through a video monitor while he ran a quick errand. The boys and girls in the study were actually watching a film clip of two children who became progressively more aggressive toward each other. This experiment had a 2 (exposure: violent film or no film) X 2 (sex: boys or girls) design. Consistent with the desensitization hypothesis, boys and girls who had watched the violent film took a significantly longer amount of time to tell an adult about the two children fighting than did boys and girls who watched no film. Research also suggests that playing violent video games can lead to desensitization (Engelhardt, Bartholow, Kerr, & Bushman, 2011).

In sum, people might want to act violently, but do not do so because they know that it is wrong. Desensitization to violence increases people's tolerance of violence and decreases their motivation *not* to act aggressively, thereby increasing the likelihood that they will act violently.

Countering the effects of violence in the media. A concern about children and society demands that some action be taken to counter the effects of watching violent TV. Currently, rating systems are used to indicate whether a TV program or movie contains violence and is suitable for children to watch. But, what is the effect of rating systems? Social psychological theory suggests that rating scales may backfire and actually

increase children's and adolescents' desire to watch programs rated as violent. Think about it. When someone tries to limit what you can do, how do you react? Often, people react to restrictions on their behavior by wanting to perform the restricted behavior even more. In Chapter 4, this idea was referred to as psychological *reactance* and was identified as a reason why some people resist interventions. "Forbidden fruit" is often the most desirable kind of fruit. Therefore, it is not surprising that research has found that the rating systems used to identify programs that children and adolescents should not watch actually increase the desire of adolescents—particularly boys—to want to watch the programs (Bushman & Stack, 1996; Cantor, Harrison, & Nathanson, 1998).

However, other research based on Bandura's (1986, 2009) social cognitive theory does suggest a way in which to counter the effects of violent TV on children. Recall that watching rewarded violence increases people's tendency to act violently. However, what happens if children see the violence as not rewarding? In that case, children should be vicariously conditioned to not act violently. What can be done so that the violence is not rewarding? What if you thought about the violence from the perspective of the victim? Do you think that the victim of the violence finds the violence rewarding?

To test the idea that decreasing the reward value of violence might decrease its effects, Nathanson and Cantor (2000) conducted an experiment in which they had two groups of boys and two groups of girls watch a *Woody Woodpecker* cartoon that contained violence (see also Nathanson, 2004). One group of boys and girls simply watched the cartoon. The boys and girls in a second group were instructed to think about the feelings of the person who was the victim of Woody Woodpecker's assaults. A third group of boys and girls did not watch any TV. This experiment had a 2 (empathy: simply watch or watch and think about victim) X 2 (sex: girls or boys) design with a separate control group (no TV). Nathanson and Cantor found that when children were told to identify with the victim of the aggression by thinking about how the victim felt, they did not enjoy viewing the violence as much as did children who simply watched the cartoon. The effect of the intervention on aggression was measured by asking the children to indicate their attitudes toward a series of aggressive behaviors, such as "If another kid tried to take something that was mine, I might push or hit that kid" (Nathanson & Cantor, 2004, p. 131). As can be seen in Figure 7.4, boys who thought about how the victim felt expressed less aggressive attitudes than boys who simply watched the violent cartoon. The empathy manipulation had no effect on the aggression of the girls. However, females are generally less influenced by media violence than are boys (Geen, 2001), as is clearly demonstrated in the figure. This finding indicates that parents and educators should talk with children about the feelings of victims of violence as well as about the feelings of the victims'

families. In other words, we need to increase children's sensitization to violence.

Media Violence and Aggressive Thoughts

Imagine that you are sitting at a stoplight, and it turns green. The driver of the pickup in front of you is not paying attention and continues to sit there instead of going. Would you be more likely to honk your horn if there were a gun in a gun rack in the back of the pickup than if the gun rack were empty? Regardless of whether you actually honk the horn, according to Berkowitz's (1984) **neoassociationistic model of media priming**, the presence of the gun would increase the likelihood that you would have aggressive thoughts. Of course, the increase in aggressive thoughts heightens the likelihood that you will behave in

Figure 7.4   Propensities for Children to Act Violently After Watching a Violent Cartoon (normal viewing), Being Instructed to Empathize With the Victim (empathy toward victim), and Not Watching the Cartoon (no TV)

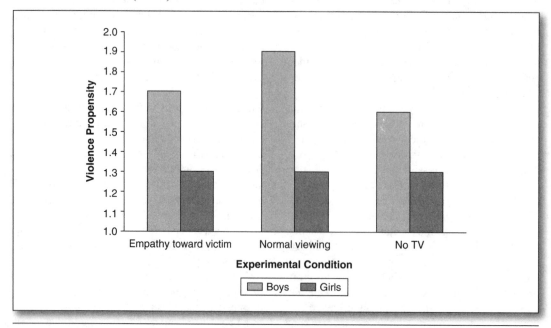

SOURCE: Adapted from Nathanson and Cantor (2000).

an aggressive manner and honk your horn—and that might be dangerous given that the person in the pickup has a gun.

The neoassociationistic model of priming is based on research in cognitive psychology and social psychology. **Priming** refers to the effect of a preceding stimulus or event on how we react to a subsequent stimulus. Priming procedures were first used in cognitive psychology to explore the structure and representation of information within network models of memory. **Network models of memory** assume that information is stored in memory in the form of *nodes* and that each node represents a concept (e.g., there is a "gun" node in memory). Furthermore, these nodes are connected to related nodes in memory by *associative pathways* (e.g., "gun" is linked to "crime," but not to "cornflakes"). An additional assumption of network models of memory is that each node has an *activation* threshold. If the node's level of activation exceeds its threshold, the node fires. When a node fires, it can influence the activation levels of other related nodes. For example, if the gun node fires, activation spreads from the gun node to related nodes like the crime node. Consequently, the related node now requires less additional activation for it to fire. A typical behavioral outcome of spreading activation is that a judgment (e.g., the judgment that a crime is occurring) is faster when it has been primed by a related concept (gun) than when it has been primed by an unrelated concept (cornflakes). In a slight twist on the earlier example, you would be more likely to interpret an ambiguous behavior (e.g., being bumped) as a hostile act if you had just seen a pickup with a gun in the gun rack than a pickup with an empty gun rack. A final assumption of network models of memory is that the activation level of a node will go away over time, making it a short-term effect. Priming of aggressive thoughts is a short-term effect of TV violence. You are not going to think about crime for the rest of the day after seeing the gun in the gun rack in the back of the pickup (Roskos-Ewoldsen, Klinger, & Roskos-Ewoldsen, 2007). However, it is important to remember that other effects of TV violence, such as increased likelihood of imitation and increased fear may last for years (Harrison & Cantor, 1999; Hoekstra, Harris, & Helmick, 1999).

FOCUS ON RESEARCH

Priming Aggressive Behavior

Many studies have demonstrated that people who are exposed to a violent TV clip are more likely to think aggressive thoughts (Roskos-Ewoldsen et al., 2007). However, does priming aggressive thoughts translate into aggressive behavior? Certainly, we do not want people running around thinking aggressive thoughts because of violent TV programs, but the important issue from a societal standpoint is whether violent TV programs prime violent behavior. In a classic study, Josephson (1987) investigated the priming effects of violent media on children's behavior. In that experiment, Josephson gathered measures of young boys' trait aggression by asking the boys' teachers to indicate how aggressive the boys were both in class and on the playground. Later, the boys saw either a violent TV program or a nonviolent one. To test priming, the violent TV segment contained recurring images of violent characters using walkie-talkies, whereas the nonviolent program contained no walkie-talkies. As a result, the walkie-talkies served as a prime for the violent television program, but not for the nonviolent program. Josephson was also interested in whether frustration influenced

(Continued)

(Continued)

the level of violent priming. When people become frustrated, they are more likely to act violently. Either before or after watching the TV program, half of the boys saw a 30-second nonviolent cartoon segment that had been edited to become increasingly static riddled, eventually worsening to "snow." At that point, the experimenter stopped the cartoon and apologized to the boys for "technical difficulties" with the TV. Stopping the cartoon segment frustrated the young boys because they could not watch a TV cartoon they liked.

After viewing their assigned programs, the boys were mock interviewed and then sent to the school gymnasium to play floor hockey. For the mock interview, either a walkie-talkie or a microphone was used. In this way, half of the boys were exposed to the violence-related cue (the walkie-talkie) and half were not (the microphone). This rather complicated experimental study involved a 2 (TV show: aggressive or nonaggressive) X 2 (trait aggression: high or low) X 2 (frustration: high or low) X 2 (interview method: walkie-talkie or microphone) design.

The boys took turns playing floor hockey and were observed both on and off the floor for signs of aggressive behavior, including pushing down other boys, hitting other players with their hockey sticks, and calling other boys abusive names. After three 3-minute periods of hockey, the boys were returned to their teachers.

The results indicated that the violent TV viewing primed boys who were high in trait aggressiveness to act more violently during initial sports activity (i.e., during the first period of play). This effect on aggressive boys was heightened both when violent programming was coupled with the violence-related cue and when violent programming was followed by frustration. However, as predicted by Berkowitz's (1984) neoassociationistic model, the priming effect lessened with time. The boys were most violent during the first period of play and were about equally violent in the second and third periods. There was no effect of the TV program, presence of the violence-related cue, or frustration on the boys who were low in trait aggressiveness.

Numerous studies have supported Berkowitz's (1984) neoassociationistic model. As noted earlier, the model leads to the prediction that the mere presence of weapons will prime violent thoughts and behavior. This *weapons effect* has been demonstrated in numerous studies (Carlson, Marcus-Newhall, & Miller, 1990). For example, Berkowitz and LePage (1967) conducted an experiment involving research participants evaluating each other's performance on a task by giving mild electric shocks for poor performance. For some of the research participants, a shotgun and a pistol were visible when they entered the room. Other research participants saw a pair of badminton racquets when they entered the room. Control group participants saw no such stimuli when they entered the room. The participants were told that a previous experimenter had left the guns or badminton racquets. Consistent with the weapons effect, participants shocked their partners more when the guns were present than when the badminton racquets were present or when nothing was present. Likewise, recall the earlier example concerning the gun in the gun rack in the back of a pickup that did not move when the light turned green. Turner, Layton, and Simons (1975) actually studied this situation. Despite the fact that the person in the pickup had a gun, people were more likely to honk, and to honk more times, when the gun was present than when it was not present. Think about the number of weapons you see during an average night of TV viewing. What effect do all of these weapons you see on TV or at the movies have on your thoughts, on your interpretations of others' behavior, and on your own behavior?

Media Violence and Fear

How often has a movie made you afraid? Clearly, the Mercury Theatre's broadcast of *The War of the Worlds* terrified many people. However, the fear that resulted from that broadcast was short-lived. Has watching a movie or TV show made you afraid for a long time? During the 1970s, the movie *Jaws* had such an effect on many people. The movie involved a great white shark that attacked swimmers and boaters off a small New England town. Many people (including one of the chapter authors) reported that they would not go swimming in the ocean for years after seeing *Jaws*. In a questionnaire study, Harrison and Cantor (1999) found that more than a quarter of the college students they studied had watched a movie or TV show prior to turning 11 years of age that was still affecting them eight or more years later (see also Hoekstra et al., 1999). Students reported still having nightmares related to their frightening viewing experiences or still refusing to go to certain places like a beach because of their experiences. Imagine still having fright reactions from a TV program you watched eight years ago. But, think about it this way: If one program can have such a profound effect, what is the effect of watching thousands of hours of TV programs and movies that contain violence and other frightening events like tornadoes, on people's level of fear?

Most research on fright reactions to the media has focused on children. More than 90% of all children are seriously frightened by the media at some point in their young lives (Cantor, 2009). Furthermore, the fright reactions can be very powerful. Children who are frightened by the media may experience nightmares and sleeplessness, high degrees of stress, and even depression (Cantor, 2009). The things that frighten children change as they grow older. Up to six years of age, scary looking things frighten children, even if these things are not dangerous (Cantor & Sparks, 1984). For example, children at this age are scared of the Incredible Hulk because he looks scary even though he helps good people. However, after nine or ten years of age, things

that could realistically happen are scarier than things that just look scary. More abstract threats are scarier to adolescents. The movie *The Day After* depicted the effects of a nuclear war in the United States. A survey study found that younger children were not as scared by the movie as were children over 12 years of age (Cantor, Wilson, & Hoffner, 1986).

The way that children respond to scary media also changes as they grow older. Younger children are more likely to use behavioral coping strategies, such as holding onto a favorite toy and covering their eyes. Older children use more cognitive coping strategies, such as reminding themselves that the fear inducing stimuli are not real and minimizing the threat of the threatening stimuli (Cantor, 2009). Do you remember watching a scary movie and repeating to yourself that it was not true?

Cultivation theory focuses on the effects of heavy exposure to TV (i.e., more than four hours a day). Cultivation theory maintains that TV operates as the primary socializing agent in today's world; that is, TV is where people learn about their world and their culture (Morgan et al., 2009). In particular, TV cultivates heavy viewers' social reality. Research has consistently found that TV influences heavy viewers' perceptions of the world (Shrum, 1999, 2009). For example, men are characters on TV shows at roughly a 2:1 ratio to women (Gerbner, Gross, Morgan, Signorielli, & Shanahan, 2002). In addition, women on TV are portrayed in a more stereotypical manner. As a result, questionnaire studies have found that people who are heavy viewers of TV tend to have more sexist views of women (Gerbner et al., 2002; Morgan, 1990). Likewise, commercials for different products promote materialism. Surveys have found that people who watch more TV and more commercials in both the United States and Korea are more materialistic (Kwak, Zinkhan, & Dominick, 2002).

According to cultivation theory, one of the consequences of media violence is that people begin to see the world as more dangerous and "mean" (Morgan et al., 2009). Considering the amount of violence on TV, what kind of world do people learn about from TV? Cultivation theory suggests that heavy viewers of TV should see the world as a more violent and hostile place than do light viewers. In fact, heavy viewers of TV *do* perceive the world as a more dangerous and hostile place than do light viewers (Roskos-Ewoldsen, Davies, & Roskos-Eowldsen, 2004; Signorielli, 1990). Much of the research on cultivation theory has relied on correlations between how much TV a person watches and how hostile he or she perceives the world. However, you now know from reading this book that a correlation between two variables does not tell us which event is causing the other or whether a causal relationship exists between the two events at all. One could argue that people who perceive the world as a dangerous and hostile place may be less likely to engage in activities outside the home and, as a consequence, are more likely to watch TV. But, experimental research has demonstrated that watching shows that contain a lot of violence, and where the perpetrators are not brought to justice, causes increases in people's anxiety (Bryant, Carveth, & Brown, 1981). In this research, participants watched five hours of pre-recorded TV shows once a week for six weeks. After the 6-week period was complete, the participants' anxiety levels were measured. For some of the research participants, the TV shows were violent, and the perpetrators of the violence were not caught. For the other participants, the shows were violent, but the perpetrators of the violence were brought to justice. In this way, Bryant and his colleagues were able to show that watching violent TV programs in which the perpetrators are not brought to justice increases anxiety. Just as TV shows can scare children, viewing a lot of TV can scare adults.

Cultivation theory focuses on overall viewing of TV rather than on watching particular types of shows. However, given the various types of shows on TV, which shows depict the most excessive amounts of realistic violence? The evening news probably has the heaviest concentration of realistic violence of any TV programming. In particular, the local news should be particularly

frightening because the violence is occurring where viewers live. In questionnaire studies, parents reported that their children are scared by the local news (Cantor & Nathanson, 1996). Likewise, roughly 25% of children who were in the fourth to sixth grades spontaneously reported during interviews that the local news was scary, and more than half of the children who were interviewed in one study could identify news stories that had scared them (Smith & Wilson, 2002). Interestingly, younger children (first to third grades) reported being scared by news stories covering natural disasters, whereas older children were more likely to be scared by stories dealing with violence and crimes. In fact, children who watch more evening news gave higher estimates of the number of murders that occur in a nearby city (Smith & Wilson, 2002). The local news creates a scary world for these children. Survey research with adults also finds that heavier viewers of the local news are more likely to experience fear and be concerned about crime rates in their community than are lighter viewers (Romer, Jamieson, & Aday, 2003).

In sum, violence is a staple of contemporary TV and movies. Unfortunately, this violence may be literally helping to kill off its audience. As this section of the chapter has demonstrated, the influences of TV violence are subtler than people often realize. TV violence can lead children to model the violence, particularly if the violence is perceived as real and rewarded and if the children identify with the person carrying out the violence. TV violence can also increase people's aggressive thoughts and temporarily increase the likelihood that people will react violently. Finally, TV violence increases viewers' levels of fear.

The next section introduces research on the effects of viewing pornography on people's attitudes, beliefs, and perceptions of the world. Like the research on TV violence, the research on pornography focuses on the negative effects of a specific genre of media programming. Some of the questions concern the effects of pornography on people's attitudes toward women, the family, and rape. As you will see, research on pornography has also focused on ways in which to counter the negative effects of pornography on people's attitudes and beliefs.

WHAT HAPPENS WHEN WE WATCH PORNOGRAPHY?

The first question to ask is what is meant by pornography. **Pornography** is any *sexually explicit material* that you can find offline (magazines, DVDs, peep shows) or online on the Internet (text, audio, or visual). Sexually explicit material (pornography) "depicts sexual activities in unconcealed ways, often with close-ups of (aroused) genitals and of oral, anal, and vaginal penetration" (Peter & Valkenburg, 2008, p. 580), and its primary purpose is to arouse the user sexually. You can see immediately the difference between pornography and the simulated sex on TV or in movies like *Sex and the City*. Real though the simulated sex may seem, we know that it is only simulated. These simulated sexual activities are called *embedded sexual material* (Kingston, Malamuth, Fedoroff, & Marshall, 2009). **Embedded sexual material** involves content that is intensely sexual in nature, but is embedded within a story and is not the emphasis of the story. Embedded sexual material is often found in movies rated R or NC-17 (Classification and Rating Administration, 2011) and in TV programs rated TV-14 or TV-MA (TV Parental Guidelines, 2011). Sometimes the embedded material is nonviolent (embedded nonviolent sexual material), and sometimes it involves violence (embedded violent sexual material).

Scholars of pornography generally study three kinds of pornography: erotica, nonviolent pornography, and violent pornography (Kingston et al., 2009). **Erotica** shows nonaggressive sexual activity between willing, sensitive, and caring partners. In erotica, the partners share in the initiation and choice of activities. In contrast, **nonviolent pornography** is nonaggressive explicit sexual activity typically among casual acquaintances. Neither men nor women are portrayed as having feelings of compassion and

empathy, as seen in erotica, let alone self-respect. Instead, participants are portrayed as having one primary interest—satisfying their sexual desires and fantasies, especially those of the men involved. **Violent pornography**, as the phrase suggests, portrays violence or coercion that is juxtaposed with, or an integral part of, explicit sexual activities with an underlying theme of dominance. Violent pornography is usually centered on an extreme stereotype of male dominance and female subservence where the more powerful coerce the less powerful. Women in particular are degraded and demeaned. They are sexual playthings for men to use and discard. Violent pornography includes sadomasochism and the infamous snuff films in which the female victims are tortured sexually and then killed. **Embedded violent sexual material**, on the other hand, is found in any R-rated film that includes a sensual scene followed immediately by, or juxtaposed with, graphic violence. These films are sometimes called slasher films or women-in-danger films. You can probably recall a few films where scantily clad young women are shown terrified and running from crazed murderers. The distinction between violent pornography and embedded violent sexual material is important because if you or your friends have brothers or sisters who are young teenagers, they can probably view embedded violent sexual material fairly easily. Because of the ease of viewing embedded violent sexual material even by young teenagers, many experiments in this area have used embedded violent sexual material in addition to pornography. It is hoped that these same teenagers will have a much more difficult time viewing violent pornography, although that is changing as access to pornography on the Internet increases.

Research in this area has focused on whether watching these kinds of pornography (or embedded violent sexual material) has any harmful effects. If exposure to any type of pornography or embedded violent sexual material causes a harmful effect, such as greater callousness toward women, then society at large may want to consider ways of limiting these effects, either by restricting access to the material, or by educating the public about their effects. It is probably safe to say that most researchers in this area prefer education to restriction.

One way in which to study the harmful effects of pornography is to look at the association between the availability of pornography of any kind in various countries and the corresponding levels of sex-related crimes, such as rape, exhibitionism, and voyeurism. Of course, studies of this kind can only examine the effect of general exposure to pornography; they cannot examine the effect of exposure to different types of pornography, such as erotica, violent pornography, and nonviolent pornography. Examples of some of this research include examinations of the effect of loosening pornography restrictions on sex crimes in Denmark, and of relations between the number of sex shops, number of adult theaters, and circulation of sexually explicit magazines and sex crime rates in the United States and other countries (for a review, see Gunter, 2002). Unfortunately, the results of this line of research are unclear (Gunter, 2002). Some *correlational* studies find relationships between the amount of sexually explicit materials available and sex crimes, whereas other studies do not. In addition, there are other extraneous variables that may explain any relationships that exist. For example, the availability of sexually explicit materials may correspond with more lenient attitudes toward sexuality, which may also translate into less reporting of sex crimes (Gunter, 2002).

Experimental research designs are much more informative regarding *causality*. Let us consider some common features of experiments on pornography and embedded violent sexual material. They involve showing participants, typically males, a film, video, or video clip that depicts sexuality (erotica, nonviolent pornography, or embedded violent sexual material) and then asking them to fill out various questionnaires. For example, Linz, Donnerstein, and Penrod (1988) had male participants watch either two or five films with embedded violent sexual material (R-rated slasher films) or nonviolent pornography. Some studies also included

a control condition in which the film or video was nonsexual and nonviolent. In the experiment by Linz and colleagues, participants in a control condition watched either two or five nonsexual, nonviolent films aimed at teenagers. Most often, watching the films and filling out the questionnaires are portrayed as two separate studies so that participants will not see a link between watching the films and answering the questionnaires. The particular effects that researchers look for vary widely. For example, Linz and colleagues looked at the influence of these films on desensitization to the female victims in the films or victims of rape. Other typical examples of the effects that are studied include (a) acceptance of rape myths, such as "In the majority of rapes, the victim is promiscuous or has a bad reputation," and "Any healthy woman can successfully resist a rapist if she really wants to" (Allen, D'Alessio, & Brezgel, 1995); (b) callousness of attitudes toward women, such as "A man should find them, fool them, fuck them, and forget them," and "A woman doesn't mean 'no' until she slaps you" (Zillmann & Bryant, 1982); and (c) judgments about a victim and perpetrator in a rape trial, such as innocence or guilt of the alleged perpetrator, and if guilty, how many years the perpetrator should serve in prison (Linz et al., 1988). Sometimes men's aggressive behavior is measured. In one case, men were given the opportunity to shock a female participant electrically (Donnerstein & Berkowitz, 1981). Of course, in reality there was no shock given because the shock situation is a setup. The female participant was actually a confederate who pretended that she was being shocked.

There are two cases in which potentially harmful effects have been noted: long-term exposure to nonviolent pornography, and any exposure to embedded violent sexual material, that is, those R-rated films. These effects are discussed in the following subsections. Absent from this discussion are the effects of erotica, short-term exposure to nonviolent pornography, and violent pornography. These effects are not discussed for several reasons. First, there is very little research on the effects of erotica on people's thoughts and beliefs other than that it arouses both men and women (Gunter, 2002). Although some authors have suggested that erotica may be useful for sex therapy, there is scant research on the utility of erotica in sex therapy and the results are inconsistent (Gunter, 2002). Indeed, the one consistent effect found for erotica is that exposure to erotica increases viewers' tendency to masturbate. Second, research on short-term exposure—less than an hour—to nonviolent pornography has produced inconsistent results, sometimes revealing more callousness toward women, and sometimes not (Linz, 1989). However, more recent research suggests that the effects may be subtler than this; men who watched nonviolent pornography briefly were more dominant and less anxious when put in a situation where they had to solve a problem with a female partner (Mulac, Jansma, & Linz, 2002). The men might not have been more callous, but they still attempted to dominate the female partner—albeit in a more subtle manner. Finally, although there is little research on the effects of violent pornography (probably for ethical reasons), what is true of embedded violent sexual material will also likely be true for violent pornography. After all, they are in the same category in that they both portray sexual violence.

Effects of Long-Term Exposure to Nonviolent Pornography

During the 1980s, the U.S. government convened a commission to evaluate the available evidence on the effects of erotica and nonviolent pornography. The U.S. Department of Justice (1986) then produced the report titled the Attorney General's Commission on Pornography final report that concluded that substantial exposure to nonviolent pornography is causally related to increases in sexual violence and sexual coercion. Long-term or substantial exposure actually involves less exposure than one might think. Typically, long-term means watching approximately five hours of material spread over

a 6-week period. In comparison with its conclusion regarding nonviolent pornography, the commission was unable to agree on the harmfulness of erotica, but concluded that there is not a causal relation between exposure to erotica and acts of sexual violence.

At that time, the actual research on long-term exposure to nonviolent pornography provided more of a mixed bag of results than was suggested by the commission's report (Linz, 1989). The experimental research on exposure to nonviolent pornography was focused on its effects on people's attitudes and beliefs rather than on actual physical violence because of ethical concerns and because attitudes and beliefs influence behavior (Roskos-Ewoldsen, 1997). Some of the earlier studies had found more leniency toward assailants in rape cases, as well as increased sexual callousness, following exposure to nonviolent pornography (Mullin & Linz, 1995; Zillmann & Bryant, 1982, 1984), whereas others had not (Linz et al., 1988; Padgett, Brislin-Slütz, & Neal, 1989). Linz (1989) reviewed a number of studies that pointed to a variety of reasons for these discrepancies. Recall that research participants often are told that watching the films and completing the questionnaires are two distinct studies. Linz found that if participants in these studies believe that watching the films is in fact related to the questionnaires, a link between viewing the nonviolent pornography and participants' beliefs is less likely to surface. Perhaps participants are "faking good" when they complete the questionnaires under this circumstance so as not to appear to be influenced by the pornography. Likewise, as the realism of a rape trial increases, films are less likely to have an effect.

Newer research appears to be more definitive at least in terms of attitudes and beliefs (for a review see Malamuth & Huppin, 2007). This newer research involves meta-analysis, which is a statistical method of combining the results from many different studies. Conclusions from two different meta-analyses of studies (male participants only) reveal a small, but consistent relation between exposure to nonviolent pornography and negative attitudes toward women. In one meta-analysis focusing on correlational studies (Hald, Malamuth, & Yuen, 2010), the researchers measured the amount of nonviolent pornography consumed by adult male participants and the extent to which they held negative attitudes toward women. The correlations were small, but statistically significant, and they were positive: The more pornography a person consumed, the more likely he was to have negative attitudes toward women. Of course, this does not mean that consuming pornography causes more negative attitudes. It could be the other way around: Men who have more negative attitudes tend to consume more pornography. Very recent correlational research indicates that this idea that attitudes precede consumption may be the case for adult men (Baer, Kohut, & Fisher, 2015) and adolescent boys (Doornwaard, Bickham, Rich, ter Bogt, & van den Eijnden, 2015; Livingstone & Smith, 2014). To tell whether consumption causes negative attitudes, however, an experiment needs to be conducted. As discussed earlier, an experiment involves a condition in which people are exposed to pornography—nonviolent, in this case—and a control condition in which they are not. Attitudes toward women are measured after exposure. If attitudes toward women are more negative in the pornography condition than in the control condition, then one can conclude that exposure to pornography causes negative attitudes toward women. This is exactly what was found in the meta-analysis of experimental studies (Allen, Emmers, Gebhardt, & Giery, 1995). Negative attitudes toward women were higher in the nonviolent pornography group than in the control group. However, the differences were much larger for men who already had anger issues or were already hostile toward women. In other words, men who already have a tendency of hostility toward women should not be watching nonviolent pornography (or violent pornography for that matter) because it will cause them to be even more hostile toward women, at least in their attitudes and beliefs.

There are other effects of viewing substantial amounts of nonviolent pornography that are not necessarily directly related to callousness toward women. In particular, some researchers have looked at changes in *attitudes* regarding family *values* (for a summary, see Manning, 2006). Family values include, at their core, a parental commitment to the family and to the nurturance of children. Of course, nonviolent pornography portrays just the opposite; it shows a world of transitory relationships that provide the greatest sexual pleasures that can be experienced without emotional involvement (Zillmann, 1994). You can probably see the problem here: One set of values conflicts with the other. Does this conflict matter? Definitely, according to both correlational research (Albright, 2008; Manning, 2006) and experimental research (Zillmann & Bryant, 1982, 1988a, 1988b). In one of Zillmann and Bryant's experiments, 70 men and 70 women from the local community either watched nonviolent pornography that could be rented at an adult video store, or watched nonsexual, nonviolent videotapes. They watched six 1-hour videotapes over six weeks. Roughly a week after the final viewing, they were asked to participate in an ostensibly unrelated study on the American family and aspects of personal happiness. The effects that Zillmann and Bryant found were eye-opening and occurred for both sexes. Figure 7.5 shows that participants who viewed the nonviolent pornography, as compared with participants who viewed nonsexual videos were (a) less sexually satisfied, (b) more accepting of myths related to health risks of sexual repression, (c) more accepting of nonexclusive sexual intimacy, and (d) more accepting of premarital and extramarital sex, and they also (e) judged the importance of being faithful as less important. In addition, the people who watched the nonviolent pornography even wanted fewer children.

Furthermore, Zillmann and Bryant (1986) showed that substantial exposure to nonviolent pornography enhances people's interest in other kinds of pornography. In their experiment, 80 men and 80 women were randomly assigned to one of two conditions. In one condition, participants watched one hour of comedies one day a week for six weeks. In the second condition,

Figure 7.5   The Influence of Long-Term Exposure to Nonviolent Pornography on People's Judgments

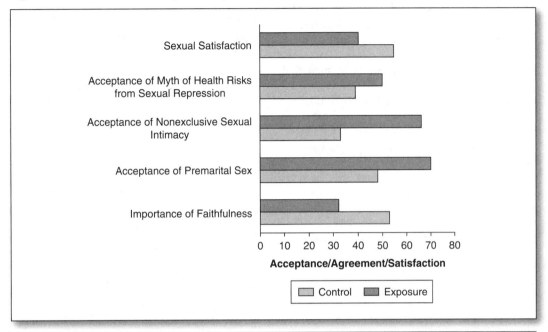

SOURCE: Adapted from Zillmann (1994).

participants watched one hour of commonly available pornography one day a week for six weeks. Then, two weeks after their final session, participants were brought back to the laboratory. When they arrived, the experimenter apologized for an approximately 15-minute delay in the study and invited the participants to watch any of six videotapes while they waited. They were assured that no one would interrupt them during this delay. The six videotapes were a G-rated movie, an R-rated movie, a nonviolent pornography movie, and three violent pornography movies (the violent pornography movies consisted of one on bondage, one on sadomasochism, and one on bestiality). Participants who had been exposed to six hours of nonviolent pornography movies were more likely to show an interest in videos depicting less common sexual practices— the bondage, sadomasochism, and bestiality tapes—than were participants who had seen nonsexual videos. Together, these studies suggest

that viewing nonviolent pornography has effects beyond callousness toward women—effects that may change how we view our relationships with other people and ourselves. The findings of this research are consistent with cultivation theory. As discussed earlier, cultivation theory hypothesizes that the social reality of heavy viewers of TV and movies is shaped by what they watch. As this research demonstrates, more exposure to nonviolent pornography changes viewers' social reality, especially their social reality related to sex and sexual relations.

Effects of Exposure to Embedded Violent Sexual Material

The combination of sex and violence has particularly disturbing effects on our thoughts, intentions, and behaviors. A review of research on embedded violent sexual material suggests that in contrast to the effects of nonviolent pornography, even a few minutes' exposure to embedded violent sexual material has many adverse effects (Intons-Peterson & Roskos-Ewoldsen, 1989). Because most of the participants in this body of research are men, the conclusions are mainly about men. The effects on men include (a) increases in sexual arousal, (b) increases in rape fantasies, (c) decreases in sensitivity to the embedded violent sexual acts, (d) increases in acceptance of rape myths and of violence toward women, and (e) increases in tolerance toward rapists. In other words, normal males (i.e., showing no propensity for rape) who view embedded portrayals of sexual violence have lowered opinions of women and increased tolerance of violence toward women. Furthermore, after watching embedded violent sexual acts, men who report a high likelihood of raping if they could get away with it show more aggression against women in a laboratory setting, are more likely to hold callous attitudes about rape and to believe in rape myths, and show higher levels of sexual arousal to rape depictions than do men who report a lower likelihood of raping (Malamuth, 1981).

As you can see, the effects of exposure to embedded violent sexual material in the laboratory have been studied extensively. However, no evidence indicates that viewing embedded violent sexual material (or violent sexual pornography) actually leads to rape or other assaults against women (Intons-Peterson & Roskos-Ewoldsen, 1989). Clearly, there are strong ethical constraints against experimentally studying the causes of rape because this research would require that experimenters show men (perhaps men who are prone to violence against women) violent pornography and then wait to see whether they actually rape or otherwise harm women. This is not what researchers want to do; in fact, they want to do just the opposite. Researchers want to prevent such occurrences as much as possible, and this is why they have devoted a great deal of effort trying to figure out how to lessen the effects of portrayals of violent sexuality, both embedded and explicit.

Reducing the Harmful Effects of Exposure to Violent Sexual Material

There are four general ways in which to reduce or eliminate the harmful effects of exposure to violent sexual material (both embedded and explicit). One way is to *legally ban the distribution and sale of these materials.* If you think about this seriously, you can see that this is not feasible except for extreme forms of these materials, such as snuff films. To ban all violent sexual materials would mean that many R-rated films—the slasher kind—would be banned. In the United States, any law to ban these materials would likely violate the First Amendment, which includes the right to free exercise of speech. Many other countries have similar rights.

A second way in which to mitigate the harmful effects is to *teach critical viewing skills.* These skills would help people to become more discriminating and discerning consumers of information. Although there are no studies directly related to viewing violent pornography, other studies have shown impressive reductions in violent behaviors in children after critical viewing training (e.g., Huesmann, Eron, Klein, Brice, & Fischer, 1983). Huesmann and colleagues' (1983) study involved children who watched violent TV shows regularly. Half of the children received critical viewing training that focused on violent TV shows (training group), and the other half discussed nonviolent TV shows (control group). The training emphasized that the behaviors seen in violent TV shows do not represent the behaviors of most people (i.e., that these behaviors are not the norm), that the aggressive feats were illusions produced by camera angles and special effects, and that the average person uses other methods to solve problems similar to those encountered in the shows. In other words, the children were taught to perceive the violence as unrealistic. When tested two full years after training, these children were less aggressive than children in the control group. The training had affected these children's lives in a positive way, and the effect was long-lasting. It would be of great interest to see if the benefits of developing critical viewing skills generalize to the embedded sexualized violence seen in R-rated slasher films.

A third way in which to mitigate the effects is to *debrief people after viewing violent sexuality.* The debriefing is similar to the training described in Huesmann and colleagues' (1983) study, but it is much shorter in duration. The debriefing typically involves telling the participants about the likely negative effects of exposure to violent sexual material, including information to counter rape myths. All of the studies using embedded violent sexual material include a debriefing of some sort. It would be unethical to do otherwise. Researchers strive to undo any potential harm that may have been caused by their experiments. To address the question of whether the debriefings actually work, a meta-analysis was conducted examining all studies that measured the efficacy of debriefings by comparing the postdebriefing rape myth scores of participants exposed to embedded sexual material with either predebriefing scores or the scores of a control group (Allen, D'Alessio, Emmers, & Gebhardt, 1996). The researchers found that debriefing was effective in undoing the negative effects of exposure to this material. In all of the studies considered, educational debriefings negated the impact of exposure to embedded violent sexual material. One obvious difficulty with debriefings, however, is that it is probably unfeasible to append a debriefing to all, or even most, commercially available media. Many producers would probably not add

debriefings unless they were legally forced to do so. Even if producers were to add them, would viewers wait around after a movie to watch one? Probably not.

A fourth (and better) way in which to mitigate the harmful effects of exposure is to *inform people about the effects ahead of time.* This would inoculate them against the effect before they were exposed to the material. These prebriefings are basically educational in nature. One variant is to explicitly warn people of the possible effects of exposure to violent embedded or explicit sexual material, dealing specifically with the desensitization and callousness that are likely to occur. Another variant includes sex education programs focusing on the similarities and differences of female and male sexual responses, with the differences including what the two sexes consider to be sexual signals, communication skills, and consideration for one's partner. This type of education is intended to make people less susceptible to myths encountered in the media. Yet another variant includes movies, DVDs, or YouTube videos aimed at larger audiences that are designed to raise awareness and understanding about rape (e.g., *A Scream from Silence; Behind Closed Doors*) and violent pornography (*The Price of Pleasure*). As with the debriefings, the question is whether these prebriefings reduce the negative effects of exposure to violent sexual material. The answer is yes. In the meta-analysis by Allen and colleagues (1996), the prebriefings were found to be even more effective than the debriefings.

FOCUS ON INTERVENTION

Mitigating the Effects of Exposure to Violent Sexual Materials

A study by Intons-Peterson, Roskos-Ewoldsen, Thomas, Shirley, and Blut (1989) illustrates how prebriefings can serve as effective interventions for the effects of exposure to violent sexual material. In this experiment, 90 adult participants from the local community and university were recruited through local advertisements and were paid for their participation. Only participants

(Continued)

(Continued)

who were low to moderate on a set of aggression scales participated in the experiment. Participants high in aggressiveness were precluded from the study for ethical reasons because these people show the strongest long-term effects of exposure to violence. Participants were told that the major purpose of the project was to evaluate the appropriateness of various kinds of information about sex for use with high school audiences, and that because two projects needed to have films evaluated, the participants would take part in two sessions spaced two weeks apart. They were also advised that they might be exposed to violent pornography (in reality it was embedded violent sexual material).

This, however, was simply a cover story. The study actually investigated the influence of two types of prebriefing film on participants' acceptance of violent sexuality. The first film, called the *rape prebriefing* presented participants with current information about rape and general rape myths, and also included a discussion of rape's traumatic effects on victims. The second film, called the *sex education prebriefing* had as its theme the desirability of respecting and being considerate of one's sexual partner. Participants were randomly assigned to view either the rape prebriefing, the sex education prebriefing, or no prebriefing film (the control group). On arriving at the laboratory, participants completed demographic questionnaires and a rape myth acceptance scale, watched one of the prebriefing films (except for control group participants), and then watched a 15-minute segment of one of three types of commercially available videos. One had embedded violent sexual material (*Toolbox Murders,* R-rated), another portrayed nonviolent pornography (*Pretty Girls,* X-rated—in today's rating system this would be NC-17), and a third was nonviolent and nonsexual (*The Great American Wilderness,* G-rated).

Afterward, participants responded to a number of questionnaires. Included in this questionnaire package was a rape myth acceptance scale. At the end of the first testing day, all participants watched a *debriefing* video (as opposed to a *prebriefing* video) that explained the effects commonly associated with the viewing of pornographic films and the likely consequences. It also discussed and debunked rape myths (recall from Chapter 3 that debriefing participants is an important component of ethical research). All participants returned two weeks later to complete the second session, ostensibly to evaluate more materials. In fact, the session consisted simply of completing the rape myth acceptance scale and many other questions about the films.

Note that participants were tested about their acceptance of rape myths three times: once before the prebriefing, a second time after watching the commercial films, and a third time two weeks later. Thus, the experiment involved a 3 (prebriefing type) X 3 (commercial video type) X 3 (time of testing) design with 10 participants in each condition. The dependent variable was the measure of rape myth acceptance.

The results for the rape myth acceptance scale are shown in Figure 7.6. Higher scores indicate more rape myth acceptance, whereas lower scores indicate less rape myth acceptance. As you can see, the two prebriefing films were equally effective at mitigating the negative effects of exposure to embedded violent sexual material. There are three findings of note. First, at the first test, rape myth acceptance was similar for all groups. Second, rape myth acceptance increased among control participants immediately after watching the R-rated commercial film (the one that had embedded violent sexual acts). This is the typical research finding in the literature. In contrast, for both of the prebriefing groups, rape myth acceptance declined immediately after watching the embedded violent sexual material. This decline indicates that prebriefings lessened the negative effects of exposure to violent sexuality. Finally, at the third testing that occurred two weeks after the debriefing, everyone's rape myth acceptance was either back at its normal level (control condition), or at a decreased level (prebriefing conditions) suggesting that both the prebriefings and the debriefings were effective. The only exception was the group that saw no prebriefing and saw the nonviolent, nonsexual commercial film. (There was reason to believe that some members of this group were angered that they did not see any pornography!) These results show clearly that prebriefings emphasizing concern for one's sexual partner or about rape education lessen the effects of exposure to violent sexual material, at least to embedded violent sexual material. In addition, both kinds of prebriefings appear to be equally effective in mitigating the negative effects of exposure to embedded violent sexual material. These results are encouraging because the kinds of information incorporated into the prebriefings can easily be presented to groups within an educational setting.

Figure 7.6   Effects of Educational Prebriefing and Content of Video on Rape Myth Acceptance

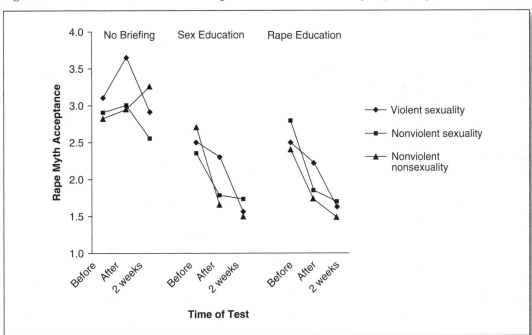

SOURCE: Intons-Peterson, M.J., Roskos-Ewoldsen, B., Thomas, L., Shirley, M., & Blut, D. "Will educational materials reduce negative effects of exposure to sexual violence?" *Journal of Social and Clinical Psychology, 8,* 266(1989).

In sum, there are three kinds of pornography: erotica, nonviolent pornography, and violent pornography; they differ from embedded sexual material in their explicit portrayal of sex and its primary intent of arousing the user sexually. There is little research on erotica other than that it arouses both men and women. Substantial exposure to nonviolent pornography has its effects mostly on attitudes about family values and happiness, and on attitudes toward women. On the other hand, even minimal exposure to violent sexual material, including R-rated slasher films, leads to greater callousness and acceptance of violence toward women. Fortunately, educational programs that emphasize respect for other people, and especially toward one's partner, lessen these negative effects.

The final section of this chapter explores the interaction between the media and political systems. The previous two sections focused on the social psychological study of the influences of two specific types of media content: TV violence and pornography. The research on the media and politics focuses much more on the influence of political news coverage and political advertising on beliefs and behavior. For example, what effect does the media's coverage of an issue have on people's beliefs about that issue? Like the research on TV violence and pornography, the research on the media and politics again suggests that the media do influence our beliefs, thoughts, and attitudes.

DOES POLITICAL NEWS COVERAGE AFFECT US?

During the early part of the last century, people thought that the media could have profound effects on how people perceived the world. The *War of the Worlds* radio broadcast suggested that the media could shape people's thoughts. A classic example of "powerful" media comes from Walter Lippmann's 1922 book, *Public Opinion*. In 1914, there was a small island where people from France, England, and Germany lived together. A steamer that stopped every 60 days

was the only connection this small island had with the outside world. On a particular day in September, the steamer arrived and delivered newspapers announcing the outbreak of hostilities in Europe that turned out to be the beginning of World War I. All of a sudden, the French and British citizens on the island were also at war with the German citizens on the island. Nothing had changed on the island, yet people who had been friends were now enemies simply because they had learned of the start of World War I. The residents' reality changed because of the delivery of a newspaper.

How the Media Influence Our Thoughts

The view that the media could have such powerful effects on what people think began to change as more research was conducted using newspapers, radio, and TV. During the 1950s and 1960s, social scientists began to argue that the media have little or no influence on how people perceive the world (Rogers, 1994). Recall Senator Knowland's telethon where the telethon had minimal impact on whether people voted for him. Studies like this one led to the conclusion that the media do not determine what we think. But, does that mean that the media have no influence?

Influencing people's thoughts. During the late 1980s, the U.S. public's concern about the problem of illegal drug use steadily increased. In November 1985, no respondents to a national political survey listed drugs as the number one problem facing the United States. However, by November 1989—just four years later—more than 50% of the respondents listed drugs as the number one problem in the country (Dearing & Rogers, 1996). This increase occurred even though objective measures of the drug problem suggested that, if anything, it was decreasing. For example, drug-related deaths decreased during this time period. What was going on? Why were people becoming more concerned about the "drug problem" when the drug problem appeared to be under control? Obviously, no single factor can explain why the U.S. public became more concerned about the problem. One factor that certainly played a role was the media's focus on drugs. Several studies have documented that the news media's extensive coverage of drugs during the mid- to late 1980s certainly raised public concerns about the drug issue (Dearing & Rogers, 1996; Gozenbach, 1996). Figure 7.7 shows how media coverage of the drug issue—in this case *The Washington Post*—predated the country's concern about the drug issue. As you can see, shortly after the number of articles on the drug problem increased, the number of people rating drugs as the most important problem facing the United States increased. Also of interest, the figure shows that later, as people began to judge the problem as less important, the press decreased the number of articles devoted to the drug problem.

The idea that the media can shape what issues we think about or what issues we think are important is referred to as **agenda setting** (Iyengar & Kinder, 1987; McCombs, 2014). When the media set the agenda, the media are not influencing what people think; rather, the media coverage is influencing what people think about. The media did not influence whether people thought that the use of drugs was wrong or whether the real problem was unfair sentencing of drug offenders. Media coverage of the drug issue resulted in people thinking that the drug issue was an important one. Several hundred studies in the United States and in Europe have demonstrated that the media do set the public's agenda (Dearing & Rogers, 1996; McCombs, 2014; Shehata, 2010). Furthermore, media coverage of an issue can result in the public becoming more concerned about the issue even when real-world indicators of the problem may

Figure 7.7   The Relationship Between Newspaper Coverage of the War on Drugs and the Public's Judgment That Drugs Were the Number One Problem in the United States

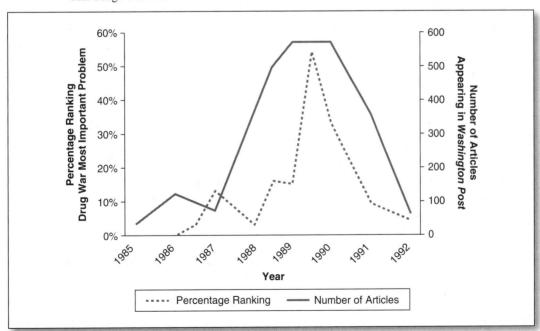

SOURCE: Dearing, J. W., & Rogers, E. M. (1996). *Agenda setting*. Thousand Oaks, CA: Sage.

suggest that the problem is declining (Gozenbach, 1996).

When discussing agenda setting, it is important to keep in mind that there are really three kinds of agenda that are important. The **public agenda** involves the issues that the public thinks are important. The **policy agenda** involves the issues that government officials and policy makers think are important. The **media agenda** involves the issues that the media are covering extensively. Research suggests that the media often set the public's agenda and that the public sets the policy agenda (Dearing & Rogers, 1996). But, the policy agenda can influence the media agenda as well. Research on the 2005 Virginia gubernatorial campaign demonstrated that what the two candidates—Tim Kaine and Jerry Kilgore—discussed during the election was influenced by the media's agenda, but the candidates were also able to shape what the media covered (Dunn, 2009). Specifically, each of the candidate's press releases influenced what issues the four major newspapers in Virginia covered.

The reason why the media can influence the public's agenda is that extensive media coverage of an issue makes that issue *salient* (Iyengar & Ottati, 1994). The **availability heuristic** suggests that people make judgments based on how easy it is to recall instances of something from memory (Tversky & Kahneman, 1974). For example, if someone calls you as part of a survey and asks what is the major problem facing the country, the availability heuristic predicts that you will answer with the issue that first comes to mind. Consequently, anything that makes an issue more salient to you increases the likelihood that you will recall it and report it as an important issue. When you read the newspaper and the front-page headlines report a drought in a distant country, they will make the issue more salient. If the media include graphic pictures of starving children, they will also increase the salience of the issue. Likewise, if all of the media are covering the issue, that will increase the likelihood that you will see multiple stories about the issue and will increase its salience. Also, if the media continue to cover the issue over weeks or even months, that will further increase the salience of the issue. So, there are a lot of different ways in which the media can increase the salience of an issue. All of these different elements of how the media cover the issue work to make you think that the issue is important.

Although there are many impressive examples of how the media set the public's agenda, it is important to understand that the media do not always set the agenda. For example, survey research has demonstrated that the media are not likely to set the agenda for local issues (Behr & Iyengar, 1985). Of course, if you think about it, this makes sense. If the issue is a local issue or it affects your life directly, do you need the media to tell you that this is an important issue? For example, think about a person who has been laid off during a recession. Do you think that media coverage of the economy is necessary for that person to think that the economy is a major issue?

A final issue to consider is how the Internet may be undermining the agenda setting function of the media. People can customize news portals on the Internet so that they receive news stories on topics that they are already interested in instead of the media outlets determining what stories are given the most prominence. Surveys today indicate that a growing number of people rely on the Internet for their political news (McCombs & Stroud, 2014; Tran, 2014). A critical question concerns whether people's ability to personalize news websites undermines the ability of the media to set the agenda (Tran, 2014). Likewise, many Internet news outlets let the public determine the prominence of stories by how frequently a story is clicked on. Stories that have the greatest number of clicks are moved to more prominent locations on the website so the media's agenda more directly reflects the public agenda. A new research tradition is emerging on agenda melding, which focuses on the dynamic relationship between traditional media and nontraditional media like the Internet (McCombs & Stroud, 2014). However, research continues to find that traditional media has a stronger influence on agenda setting than do nontraditional media (Martin, 2014; Shehata & Stromback, 2013). Partly, this reflects the fact that many online news outlets are simply news aggregation websites that publish stories from the traditional news outlets. Undermining the agenda setting function of traditional media likely requires Internet news sites which publish original news.

What information do we use to judge the president? One area that has been studied extensively is political priming. **Political priming** is the idea that the issues that the media are covering influence the information that people use to judge the president and other politicians (Carpentier, Roskos-Ewoldsen, & Roskos-Ewoldsen, 2008; Iyengar & Kinder, 1987; Roskos-Ewoldsen et al., 2007; Roskos-Ewoldsen, Roskos-Ewoldsen, & Carpentier, 2009). In 1991, President George H. W. Bush enjoyed very high approval ratings. Indeed, many political pundits did not think the Democratic Party would be able to field a candidate that could beat Bush in the 1992 presidential election given how popular he was in early 1991. However, if you are familiar with recent U.S. history, you know that Bush did not win reelection in 1992. Instead, he was defeated by a young Democrat from Arkansas named Bill Clinton. How did Bush go from such a high level of public approval to losing the election to Clinton?

There are a number of factors that influenced the outcome of the 1992 election. Research on media coverage of events suggests that the media's preoccupation with domestic issues during late 1991 and 1992 certainly played a role in the declining popularity of President Bush. When you judge how well the president is doing his or her job, you have a lot of different pieces of information that you could use to make the judgment. You could use the president's performance on the economy, civil rights, or international affairs, or you could use how well the president dresses. Political priming is concerned with the role that the media play in what information you use to judge the president. Thus, the idea behind political priming is that the media do not influence what you think specifically; rather, they

influence *what information you use* to make your judgment of the president. Calling this political priming is unfortunate because it is easy to think that political priming is like Berkowitz's (1984) model of media priming of violence that was discussed earlier. However, the two are very different. For example, when the media prime violence, the effect goes away relatively quickly, but political priming effects from the media can last for weeks (Carpentier et al., 2008; Roskos-Ewoldsen et al., 2007).

Arguments about calling this phenomenon priming aside, according to the research on political priming, if the media are focusing primarily on international affairs, then people will use their impressions of how well the president is doing in international affairs to judge how well the president is doing overall. However, if the media are focusing primarily on domestic affairs, then people will use their impressions of how well the president is doing on domestic issues to judge how well the president is doing overall. People tended to have very positive impressions of how well President Bush handled international affairs, but tended to have negative impressions of how well he handled domestic affairs. A combination of survey research and content analysis of the major stories on the evening news and in major newspapers demonstrated that when the media were covering the first war in Iraq, people who had positive evaluations of Bush's handling of international affairs formed a positive impression of his overall performance despite the fact that people generally did not think he was doing a good job of handling the U.S. economy. In late 1991 and 1992, when the media turned their attention away from the Middle East and focused on domestic issues, people used their negative evaluations of Bush's handling of domestic affairs to judge his overall performance. Consequently, the ratings of Bush's job performance plummeted, despite the fact that the people thought that he did a good job of handling international affairs (Iyengar & Simon, 1993; Krosnick & Brannon, 1993). In other words, the media agenda seemed to be implicated in the outcome of the 1992 election because the media primed the criteria that people used to judge Bush's job performance.

Effects of Negative Media Coverage of the Government

People's confidence in political institutions has dropped precipitously in the United States over the past 40 years. In 1964, roughly 75% of the U.S. population trusted the nation's government. By the mid-1990s, the number of people in the United States who trusted the government had fallen to approximately 25% (Moy & Pfau, 2000). The declining trust of the government has gone hand in hand with declining rates of voter turnout at national and local elections. The declining confidence in the government may undermine the effectiveness of the president, Congress, the courts, and law enforcement agencies. Furthermore, if people do not trust the president and Congress, the mistrust can undermine efforts at reforming the political system. For example, recent attempts at campaign finance reform in the United States have been met with growing cynicism as to whether the reforms will have any real influence. Others have gone so far as to argue that if confidence sinks too low, the country might not be able to respond to a crisis as effectively (Moy & Pfau, 2000).

Many people argue that there is good reason for the declining trust in the U.S. government (Cappella & Jamieson, 1997; Moy & Pfau, 2000). During the 1960s, both the civil rights movement and the war in Vietnam undermined confidence in the government. During the 1970s, President Richard Nixon resigned because of the Watergate scandal. During the late 1970s, the Iran hostage crisis, where a handful of students in Iran held U.S. embassy personnel hostage for more than a year, further undermined people's confidence in the presidency. During the 1980s, the United States elected an *actor* as president, and the Iran–Contra scandal and numerous other scandals rocked Ronald Reagan's presidency. President Clinton was nearly impeached because of his sexual involvement with White House intern Monica Lewinsky. And, of course, there are charges that the evidence about the existence of weapons of mass destruction that were used to justify the U.S. war in Iraq was doctored by the George W. Bush administration. However, there are good reasons to believe that the various scandals that have occurred are not the only reason why people's confidence in the U.S. government is so low. Many people charge that the media have played a key role in the declining image of the government (Moy & Pfau, 2000).

Do the media undermine confidence in the government? You have probably heard people complain that the news media focus only on the negative. People often lament the fact that the news media cannot seem to show anything positive or uplifting about the country or the government. In particular, the media are often accused of presenting overly negative portrayals of politicians. Surprisingly, a recent content analysis of the media found that although most media (e.g., newspapers, news magazines, and the local news) are somewhat negative in their treatment of the government, they are not the worst. Radio talk shows (e.g., *The Rush Limbaugh Show*), and TV entertainment talk shows (e.g., *Late Show with David Letterman, The Tonight Show with Jay Leno*) are particularly negative in their portrayals of the government (Moy & Pfau, 2000).

But, does this negative coverage of the government and politicians influence the public's knowledge of, and confidence in, the government? Numerous surveys and studies have found that people who are exposed to negative coverage of the government trust the government less. The most extensive study, involving a survey of more than 1,200 adults on this issue, revealed some interesting things about the media and perceptions of political institutions in the United States (Moy & Pfau, 2000). Consistent with most people's folk wisdom, this research suggested that reading newspapers and watching TV news programs (e.g., *60 Minutes*) increased people's understanding of the political system. However, other types of TV programming, such as entertainment talk shows actually decreased people's understanding of the government. People who read newspapers and news magazines or watched their local TV news had higher confidence in the government. Conversely, people who watched the national news on TV or listened to politically oriented radio talk shows were more cynical of the government—especially of the president. Of course, it is important to remember that although Moy and Pfau's (2000) study is by far the most extensive one on this issue, only surveys were used. As a consequence, it is difficult to know the direction of causation. Listening to radio talk shows may increase people's cynicism of the government. However, it also may be the case that those people who are particularly cynical of the government are more likely to listen to radio talk shows. Probably, both occur; radio talk shows probably attract people who are already cynical of the government, but radio talk shows certainly reinforce cynical views of the government.

How is the story told? The framing of stories.
There are many different slants or angles that a reporter can take for a story. **Framing** refers to how the story is presented or its angle (Iyengar, 1991). Assume that a reporter is going to write a story about the latest war in Iraq. The reporter could focus on the issues that led up to the war, such as the United Nations' inspectors and disagreements between the United States and Britain, on the one hand, and France, Germany, and Russia, on the other, over the war itself and the charges that Iraq had weapons of mass destruction. The reporter might instead focus on President George W. Bush's motivations for wanting to go to war with Iraq, including Iraq's oil reserves and the attempt by Iraqis to assassinate the president's father. The reporter might choose to use a human interest angle and focus on one of the U.S. soldiers who fought in Iraq, or on an Iraqi family's experiences during the war. These are just a few of the different ways in which the reporter could frame the story.

How a story is framed is important because the story's frame will make certain aspects of the story salient while other elements are deemphasized or ignored (Iyengar, 1991). For example,

if the story focused on the experiences of a U.S. soldier fighting in Iraq, then the story might highlight the dangers of the war in Iraq and the fanatical zeal of certain paramilitary groups within Iraq. This kind of frame would likely fuel negative Western stereotypes of people from the Middle East.

How a story is framed can have important influences on the judgments people make related to the story (Iyengar, 1991; Kahneman & Tversky, 1982). For example, Iyengar (1991) found that when stories about poverty took a human interest angle and focused on a particular poor person, people were more likely to blame the individual as responsible for being poor. However, when the stories provided thematic coverage of poverty and focused on the history of poverty in this country and government programs to aid the poor, people were less likely to blame individuals for being poor and focused more on poverty as a problem that society is responsible for causing.

How political stories are framed contributes to the growing mistrust of the government (Cappella & Jamieson, 1997). In covering a political campaign, a reporter could use what is called an **issue frame** and focus on the issues that are important, the background of the issues, and the pros and cons involved with the issues. For example, an issue in the 2000 U.S. presidential campaign concerned the role of the United States as a peacekeeper in various countries. A story that took an issue frame might focus on the history of the United States acting as a peacekeeper in Somalia and Eastern Europe during President Clinton's administration and the impact of these activities on how other countries perceived the United States. On the other hand, a story could use what is termed a **strategy frame**. A strategy frame focuses on the motivations behind the different positions that politicians are taking. For example, a story with a strategy frame might argue that Bush was opposed to the United States acting as an international peacekeeper because polls have shown that most Republican voters are opposed to it. Because of a strategy frame's focus on the motivations for why a politician supports a policy, the strategy frame tends to make the politician look self-interested and not particularly concerned about the greater good for the country.

In a series of experiments, Cappella and Jamieson (1997) demonstrated that reading articles with a strategy frame increased participants' cynicism toward politics to a greater extent than did reading articles with an issue frame. This increase in cynicism occurred whether the strategy frame focused on a politician's motivations for a stance on an issue (health care reform), or on the motivations of a candidate while running for office (mayor's race in Philadelphia). The public generally wants politicians who are concerned about people's well-being. However, by focusing on the motivations behind a politician's stance on an issue, the strategy frame tends to make the politician look as though his or her primary concerns are with how he or she looks to the general public and with getting elected or reelected. Because most strategy frames focus on the negative motivations of politicians, these frames reinforce the public's perceptions that politicians are only out for their own good. In our everyday lives, we tend not to trust people who look out only for themselves, and the same holds true for politicians who we perceive as looking out only for themselves. Clearly, journalists can play an important role in the political process because what they choose to focus on—the frame for the story—can influence the readers' interpretation of the story.

Political advertising gone bad. The elements of a political campaign that make it "negative" involve an emphasis on the undesirable characteristics of the opponent. Unfortunately, in the United States, most negative campaigns do not focus on the disadvantages of the opponents' positions on the issues. Rather, the typical negative campaign focuses on what a despicable individual the opponent is. Negative political campaigning has been around for a long time. For example, in the presidential election of 1800, the Republicans attacked the Federalist candidate,

John Adams, by arguing that he was a hypocrite and a fool, had no virtues, and was a wretch (Johnson-Cartee & Copeland, 1991). However, as many commentators have noted, political campaigns began getting much more negative during the last 30 years of the 20th century (Johnson-Cartee & Copeland, 1991). At the same time that negative political campaigning has been increasing in the United States, voter turnout has been dropping (Ansolabehere & Iyengar, 1996). The question is whether negative campaigning turns off the electorate (Bradley, Angelini, & Lee, 2007).

Several experimental studies demonstrate very clearly that negative campaigns decrease voter turnout. In an experiment using actual advertisements from a California senate campaign and the Los Angeles mayoral campaign, it was found that negative advertisements decreased people's intentions to vote (Ansolabehere & Iyengar, 1996). In addition, several experimental studies have demonstrated that when *both* candidates run negative advertisements, as opposed to just one or neither candidate running negative advertisements, this seems to create a synergy that results in *both* candidates being evaluated as less desirable. Furthermore, research participants reported that they would be much less likely to vote when they witnessed campaigns where both candidates were negative (Houston & Doan, 1999; Houston, Doan, & Roskos-Ewoldsen, 1999; Houston & Roskos-Ewoldsen, 1998). Specifically, it appears that negative campaigns create the perception that voting is a lose–lose situation (Bradley et al., 2007). Lose–lose situations are those that people try to avoid. How do you feel when you are placed in a situation where you have to choose between two undesirable options, for example, continuing to have a painful tooth or going to the dentist? These are situations that people find to be aversive. It is no wonder that negative campaigns have turned off the voting public and increased people's cynicism.

In sum, the research on agenda setting and political priming clearly shows that the media can and do effect what political issues people think about and what information people use to make political judgments. However, the influence of the media is more subtle than people tend to think. The media clearly do not *dictate* what people think. If the media influenced what people thought, there would not be so much disagreement about various issues. The media do not influence whether people think a particular proposal for welfare reform is a good idea or a bad idea. However, the media can influence whether

people think that welfare reform is an important issue. Likewise, the media can influence whether people's judgment of how well the president handles welfare reform influences their evaluation of the president. These effects of the media are subtle, but they can be important. The media also play a role in people's increased cynicism of the government. The media's focus on negative events, how they frame stories, and the negative campaigns that politicians run in the media all create a deepening distrust of government.

CULTURE CAPSULE

Media Influence Across Cultures

One area where much more research is needed concerns the influence of the media in different cultures. As was noted in the beginning of this chapter, the majority of research on the psychology of the media has been conducted in the United States. However, there has also been research conducted on the media in other countries. For example, most of the interesting research on agenda setting has been conducted in Europe. Likewise, research on cultivation theory has been conducted in Europe, Asia, South America, and the Middle East. Heavy viewers of TV in all of these areas show cultivation effects in that TV influences their perceptions of their social reality.

However, there is research suggesting that culture can play an important role in the psychological influences of the media. St. Helena is a remote island in the South Atlantic Ocean. Indeed, Napoleon's second exile was to St. Helena, and he died on the island. St. Helena is so remote that the first TV broadcast occurred there on March 31, 1995. Obviously, this event provided researchers with another opportunity to conduct a quasi-experiment on the influence of TV, and that is what researchers did (Charlton, Gunter, & Hannan, 2002). In particular, research focused on the effects of the introduction of TV on children's aggression, much like the research that was conducted in the town of "Notel" in Canada during the 1970s (Joy et al., 1986). However, unlike Notel, there have been no increases in violence since the introduction of TV on St. Helena (Charlton et al., 2002). Why? Of course, one possibility is that there has not been enough time for TV to influence the aggressiveness of the children. Recall that Centerwall (1989) argued that it took 15 years for the effects of TV to influence homicide rates. However, the research on Notel found increases in both verbal aggression and physical aggression just two years after the introduction of TV to that town. TV had been in St. Helena for more than five years with no increase in children's physical or verbal aggression. Why the difference? The best explanation is that St. Helena is a unique culture. In particular, people on St. Helena are much more prone to watch out for each other than are people in other Western cultures (Charlton et al., 2002). The greater sense of responsibility for others that characterizes this culture may serve as a buffer that protects children from the negative consequences of exposure to TV.

SUMMARY

As the topics covered in this chapter have demonstrated, the psychological effects of the media are varied. When a particular type of content, such as violence is prevalent in the media, the effects can be quite pronounced. Media violence can lead to long-term imitation of violent behavior. Quasi-experiments suggest that the media can play a large role in the number of homicides in a country. Conversely, TV violence can temporarily increase one's aggressive thoughts. Likewise, TV and movies can result in fright reactions that can be short term or last for years, or they can increase heavy viewers' perceptions of the world as a dangerous and hostile place in which to live.

Pornography, another popular genre of media, can also have serious consequences. Although little research has been done on erotica, research on nonviolent pornography demonstrates that both men and women have more negative views of family life, and men have more negative attitudes toward women, after watching a substantial amount (six videos) of nonviolent pornography. Violent sexual material—in the form of violent pornography or embedded violent sexual acts—has the most serious psychological effects. Even short-term exposure to violent sexual material can increase men's acceptance of rape myths and result in more negative views of women.

The research on political news coverage suggests that the media can have very subtle psychological effects. The media can influence what people think are the important issues facing the country. How a story is framed can influence people's interpretation of an issue. Heavy coverage of an issue will influence how people judge the job that the president is doing. In addition, the media can create cynicism toward political leaders and institutions.

It is hoped that this chapter has demonstrated why social psychologists and other social scientists are interested in studying the media. There are many more areas where media psychology has been studied, including prosocial benefits of the media, the effects of the media on racism, the factors that influence how enjoyable a movie is, and why people watch the shows they watch. In other words, a lot of research has been conducted. However, there are still many issues that need to be addressed. How do the changes in the technology of the media influence the effects of watching TV? Will people experience stronger effects of exposure to TV violence when watching HDTV than standard TV? Do people show the same effects when watching a small screen on their cell phone as they do when watching a 60-inch TV? Current research suggests that physiological effects of TV viewing (arousal, desensitization) may be more pronounced with large-screen TVs or better-quality TVs, but screen quality or size seems to have no impact on the cognitive effects of TV viewing, such as priming effects (Bracken, 2005; Bracken & Botta, 2010; Ivory & Kalyanaraman, 2007). Given the rapid changes that are taking place in the media, especially the Internet and now smartphones, there will always be a need for social psychologists to study the psychological consequences of the media.

8

APPLYING SOCIAL PSYCHOLOGY TO HEALTH

KATHRYN D. LAFRENIERE

KENNETH M. CRAMER

CHAPTER OUTLINE

Health Psychology Defined
The Biopsychosocial Model
Social Variables and Health
Promoting Health and Preventing Illness
Persuasion and Social Influence in Media
Health Coverage
Health Literacy: Evaluating Health-
Related Information on the Internet
Family, Peer, and School Influences

Changing Health Behavior
Health Belief Model
Theory of Planned Behavior
Transtheoretical Model
Stress, Coping, and Social Support
Stress and Coping
Social Support
Summary

During the summer of 2002, the story of a New York man's lawsuit against the fast-food industry for contributing to his obesity made newspaper headlines and was widely discussed on television news. The man, who was 5 feet 10 inches tall and weighed roughly 270 pounds, had filed a lawsuit claiming that many of the major fast-food chains were guilty of false advertising because they were misleading about the nutritional value of their food. The man had been eating fast food several times a week for most of his life, and at 56 years of age he had a number of health problems that tend to be linked to obesity, including diabetes, high blood pressure, and a series of heart attacks. During the same summer, a similar lawsuit was filed in New York by the parents of two teenage girls who were also obese and suffered from high cholesterol, high blood pressure, heart disease, and diabetes. This lawsuit was directed at McDonald's and two of its branches, claiming that they had failed to clearly disclose the ingredients and effects of their food, which tends to be high in fat, sodium, and cholesterol. The parents claimed that in the absence of information to the contrary, they believed that fast food was healthy for their children. Samuel Hirsch, the lawyer who filed both of these cases, suggested that McDonald's food was "addictive" and that the corporation's billion-dollar advertising campaigns tend to unduly target and influence children to make unhealthy choices.

These lawsuits came on the heels of several well-publicized lawsuits against the tobacco industry in which extremely high punitive damages awards were made to plaintiffs who argued that the tobacco companies failed to adequately warn consumers about the risks of smoking. In one tobacco lawsuit case, the original amount awarded was as high as $28 billion, but was later reduced to $28 million. To date, the fast-food lawsuits have not met with the same success as tobacco industry lawsuits. In October 2010, a judge dismissed an attempt by Samuel Hirsch to file a class action suit against McDonald's, and individual cases that have blamed the fast-food industry for causing obesity have not been successful in North America.

When you read about these kinds of lawsuits, what is your initial reaction? Are these just frivolous lawsuits in which opportunistic lawyers are trying to profit from multibillion-dollar industries by using current knowledge about the health risks associated with obesity and smoking? Are decisions about what kind of food to eat and whether or not to smoke simply individual choices whereby people need to take personal responsibility and not shift the blame onto others? Or, do industries that spend billions of dollars on advertising campaigns also bear some responsibility to guide individuals toward making positive health choices?

Most of you will probably come out on the side of individual responsibility and dismiss these lawsuits as frivolous. Although there has been an alarming increase in the prevalence of obesity in recent decades (see Figure 8.1), the majority of people who responded to a WNBC online poll said that restaurants are not responsible for the health of their customers (Center for Consumer Freedom, 2002). Most adults in our society clearly understand that smoking is a dangerous habit and that a steady diet of fast food does not constitute a nutritious balanced diet. However, a group called the Physicians Committee for Responsible Medicine, which promotes preventive medicine, published a commentary that discusses why fast-food lawsuits are good (Barnard & Kursban, 2002). In the article, they pointed out that the fast-food industry manipulates American perceptions about food and influences people's choices through billion-dollar advertising campaigns as well as through more direct means, such as contracts with school food service departments and sponsorship of educational events. In other words, the power and political clout of a multibillion-dollar industry means that we are not necessarily on a level playing field when it comes to nutritional choices.

In fact, although it is easy to suggest that an obese person should simply make better nutritional choices and lose weight, or that a smoker should safeguard his or her health by quitting smoking, the reality of the situation is much more complicated. One thing that we know about health is that the better off people are financially and educationally, the healthier they tend to be. As we go down the socioeconomic ladder, health outcomes become poorer as well (Adler et al., 1994; Adler & Snibbe, 2003). Again, this suggests that we are dealing with an uneven playing field where adopting healthier behaviors is harder for some people (those who are financially disadvantaged) than it is for others. Smoking habits lead to smoking addiction, and many current smokers have made very strenuous attempts to quit that have failed repeatedly. So, although we might want people to

Figure 8.1   Prevalence of Obese (BMI ³ 30) and Extremely Obese (BMI ³ 40) U.S. Adults Aged 20 to 74 Years Old From 1960 to 2006

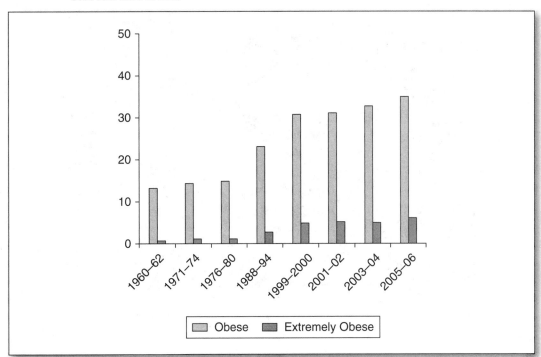

SOURCE: National Center for Health Statistics (2008).

assume greater personal responsibility for their health choices, we also need to recognize that there are substantial barriers to doing so. If there were no such barriers, we all would be fit, trim, and healthy nonsmokers (see Figure 8.2).

An area of applied social psychology that addresses such concerns is *health psychology.* Although health psychologists can also be trained in clinical psychology, many of the principles of health promotion, health behavior change, and adjustments to illness are based on social psychology theories and concepts, and these are the focus of this chapter.

As you read through the chapter, keep the following questions in mind:

- Who is responsible for my health? Is it entirely up to me, or are there social and societal influences that operate as well?

- How can psychology be used to promote healthy choices?
- How do we go about changing our unhealthy behaviors and adopting healthier ones?
- Can psychological factors contribute to our likelihood of getting particular illnesses?
- Does psychology have anything to offer to people who already suffer from physical illnesses or symptoms?

HEALTH PSYCHOLOGY DEFINED

Health psychology is the branch of applied psychology that is concerned with examining psychological influences on physical health. There are a number of aspects to this relationship between psychological considerations and physical health. The classic definition of

Figure 8.2 Eating Habits: A Major Contributor to Physical Ailments

SOURCE: Photo courtesy of Kathryn Lafreniere.

health psychology that is most often cited includes all of these aspects:

> Health psychology is the aggregate of the specific educational, scientific, and professional contributions of the discipline of psychology to the promotion and maintenance of health, the prevention and treatment of illness, the identification of etiologic and diagnostic correlates of health, illness, and related dysfunction, and the analysis and improvement of the health care system and health policy formation. (Matarazzo, 1980, p. 815)

In other words, health psychology is concerned about how we can promote better health habits and help to prevent illness, how psychological factors might influence our likelihood of becoming ill, and how knowledge from psychology can be used to help those who already suffer from particular illnesses. In addition, it also enables us to examine how health care can be provided to patients in the best possible way.

Health psychology is a relatively new area of concentration within psychology. It first appeared during the 1970s and really took hold during the early 1980s, when a select group of universities began to offer undergraduate and graduate health psychology courses and the journal *Health Psychology* was first published. Now, health psychology courses are widely available at most universities, and there are a number of journals devoted to psychological and social influences on health.

A number of factors contributed to the rise in popularity of health psychology through the end of the 20th and into the 21st century (Brannon, Feist, & Updegraff, 2014; Taylor & Sirois, 2012). For one thing, medical and technological advancements have meant that people are living longer, yet few elderly people are completely free of disease or dysfunction. Many people live with chronic illnesses, such as hypertension (high blood pressure), diabetes, and heart disease.

Although medical science is concerned with developing medications and technologies to help control these diseases, psychology can help to manage psychological aspects of living with chronic illnesses so that patients can enjoy a better quality of life throughout their life spans. In addition, the chronic illnesses that are most predominant today (e.g., heart disease, diabetes, cancer) are different from the acute infectious diseases that people died from a century ago (e.g., tuberculosis, influenza, pneumonia). Chronic illnesses are influenced by lifestyle factors, such as whether or not people smoke, their diets and levels of physical activity, and even their stress levels. Thus, psychological factors can play a much stronger role in helping to prevent and manage chronic illness than is the case for infectious diseases. Another factor that helped to set the stage for health psychology's rise in popularity is the high cost of health care. Although an extraordinary number of high-tech diagnostic and treatment options exist today (e.g., CT [computed tomography] scans, MRIs [magnetic resonance images], radiation treatments), they are extremely costly, and the idea of allocating resources toward promoting healthy habits to prevent illness seems to be a cost-effective choice. Again, psychology makes an important contribution in helping people to alter their bad habits and make healthier lifestyle choices.

In addition to these other factors, toward the end of the 20th century there was growing dissatisfaction with the traditional **biomedical model** of health and illness (Brannon et al., 2014; Taylor & Sirois, 2012). The biomedical model is the theoretical framework that guided medical advances leading to the ability to conquer a number of life-threatening diseases. The biomedical model is based on the idea that illness can be completely explained by examining problems in an organism's biological functioning. This approach leads us to focus on lower-level biological processes (e.g., cell functioning, biochemical imbalances) rather than to examine health in a broader context that also includes psychological functioning and social influences (Brannon et al., 2014; Taylor & Sirois,

2012). The biomedical model also tends to focus on disease more than on health, and it conceptualizes health quite simply as the absence of disease. The biomedical model was important in leading to the discovery of a number of specific disease-causing agents, such as bacteria and viruses, and these discoveries in turn led to advances in medical technology to cure a number of life-threatening infectious diseases. Despite the importance of the biomedical model, it is limited in that it failed to account completely for the fact that not everyone who is exposed to the same virus will acquire a particular disease; furthermore, even when people do get sick, there are large differences among individuals in terms of the severity of symptoms they experience and how they respond to treatment. It seemed clear that a broader model was needed to conceptualize health and illness, and this led to the emergence of the biopsychosocial model, which is the primary model of health and illness underlying health psychology.

The Biopsychosocial Model

In contrast to the biomedical model, the **biopsychosocial model** (as its name implies) sees health as being determined by biological, psychological, and social factors (Engel, 1977). Use of the biopsychosocial model does not mean that we completely reject the biomedical model; instead, it suggests that we recognize that the biomedical model does not lead to a complete understanding of health and illness. Although it is clear that the role of biology will always be important in explaining illness, the biopsychosocial model demands that we also pay attention to psychological and social influences. Consequently, issues such as the particular meanings that patients attach to their illnesses, patients' motivation to recover (or not), patients' response styles (whether they stoically minimize symptoms rather than tending to exaggerate symptom reporting), and to what extent patients benefit from support from other people when they are ill are seen as important determinants of how people experience illness (DiMatteo & Martin, 2002).

Social Variables and Health

The focus of this book is on applications of social psychology, so the emphasis in the remainder of this chapter is on social variables within the biopsychosocial model. Although at first glance it might be easier to understand the relevance of biological variables (e.g., genetic factors, exposure to viruses), and psychological variables (e.g., individual differences in experience of pain or other symptoms, personal coping styles), there are a number of ways in which social factors can have an impact on health. As we have already seen, socioeconomic factors, such as income and educational level, influence our probability of becoming ill. In addition, sometimes we try to adopt good health habits (e.g., exercising) because we are influenced by friends or family members who also engage in these behaviors; or we try to give up bad habits (e.g., smoking) because we know that important people in our lives are concerned about or disapprove of these behaviors. Although it might not always seem to be the case, our interactions with our physicians and other health care providers constitute social relationships, and the nature of these social interactions can affect our health outcomes. Social factors also have a lot to do with how we cope with illness or stress. In general, the presence of others has beneficial effects on our health in that the support we receive from our loved ones can help us to feel better, adopt healthier behaviors, and generally decrease our experience of stress. However, it is sometimes the case that the social influence of other people can have negative effects rather than positive ones. For example, if you work or attend school in a very competitive cutthroat environment, the social presence of others is more likely to add to your stress than to relieve it. Recently, there has been a great deal of research interest in the issue of "caregiver stress," that is, the idea that looking after elderly or disabled family members can place stressful demands on an individual, often leading to negative health consequences (e.g., Schulz & Beach, 1999; Talley & Crews, 2007).

Health psychology is a very broad area, encompassing virtually all of the ways in which we can consider psychological and social factors in relation to health. It would be easy to teach a full-year university course in health psychology and never run out of relevant and exciting material to discuss. Consequently, any brief treatment of health psychology involves a very limited selection of specific topics within this area of study and is meant to whet the appetite for further study rather than to cover the entire field exhaustively. Following from the definition of health psychology, this chapter focuses on three major areas in which social psychology has been applied to health: (a) promoting health and preventing illness, (b) changing health behavior, and (c) studying stress, coping, and social support.

PROMOTING HEALTH AND PREVENTING ILLNESS

One of the major areas in which psychology has a great deal to contribute to people's health concerns health promotion and prevention of illness. **Health promotion** refers simply to efforts that are made to encourage people to engage in healthy behaviors, such as eating a healthy and balanced diet, exercising regularly, getting enough rest, and refraining from smoking and abusing alcohol. Health promotion is a philosophy that guides action to achieve good health. The actions undertaken to achieve optimal health and well-being occur at multiple levels, including the efforts of individuals, medical practitioners, psychologists, community and government health policy makers, and the mass media (Taylor, 2006).

Prevention typically refers to more targeted efforts to reduce the probability of getting an illness in the first place or to reduce the severity of an illness or disorder once it does occur. Prevention can also take place at multiple levels in terms of who is responsible for undertaking the preventive efforts (e.g., the individual, medical practitioners, the government), and also in terms of the timing of the preventive actions in relation to the illness outcomes. Prevention efforts that are aimed toward healthy individuals so as to keep them healthy and avoid their risk of contracting diseases are called **primary prevention**. For example, a school-based program that educates elementary school students about the health risks of smoking would be considered primary prevention. If this sounds a lot like health promotion, it is because primary prevention and health promotion do overlap to a large extent in that they share the goal of keeping a well population disease free. **Secondary prevention** occurs at a later point, when people are already affected by a medical condition or disorder, and the goal is to prevent the condition from leading to more severe health consequences. For example, getting a mammogram is a secondary prevention strategy for women. If a woman has a malignant tumor in her breast, conducting the breast screening will not prevent the occurrence of cancer altogether, but it might mean that the malignancy will be detected early enough for her to be successfully treated before the disease has spread, greatly improving her chances of complete recovery. Finally, **tertiary prevention** refers to situations in which the disease or disorder has not been prevented, but efforts are made to reduce the extent of the disorder's impact on patients (Bishop, 1994). An example of tertiary prevention would be a patient undergoing rehabilitation to attempt to recover some of the skills and abilities that he or she lost as a result of a stroke.

Let us return to a question that was posed near the beginning of this chapter. Who is ultimately responsible for our health? Most of us would probably say that we have to assume responsibility for our own health, and yet many people consistently make unhealthy choices, leading to prevalence rates of illnesses that are strongly influenced by lifestyles. Statistics show that the leading causes of death in Canada and the United States are heart disease, cancer, and stroke (Brannon et al., 2014; Taylor, 2006; Taylor & Sirois, 2012), and that the majority of deaths today are related to preventable causes, such as

smoking, poor diet, alcohol abuse, and physical inactivity (Brannon et al., 2014). Clearly, individual efforts at adopting healthier behaviors are not entirely successful. Other initiatives aimed at promoting good health and preventing illness are necessary. These health promotion and primary prevention activities can come from a number of sources, but this section focuses on just a few of these. First, it considers health messages that are delivered through the mass media, how individuals are persuaded by this content, and how they can become more savvy consumers of the overwhelming amount of health information that is out there. Second, it looks at the influence of family members and peers on our attitudes and intentions regarding our health.

Persuasion and Social Influence in Media Health Coverage

Social psychologists have studied the issue of social influence since the 1950s, when Carl Hovland and his colleagues (e.g., Hovland, Janis, & Kelley, 1953) studied attitude change in a series of experiments at Yale University. **Social influence** refers to the idea that interactions with other people can lead to changes in our attitudes, beliefs, values, and behavior. Interventions of any type can be considered a form of social influence. **Persuasion** refers to a specific kind of social influence in which a particular message or appeal is used to try to change someone's attitudes or beliefs (DiMatteo & Martin, 2002). In Chapter 7, you learned about how media messages influence us in a variety of ways. Of particular interest in health psychology is the use of messages to persuade people to adopt healthy lifestyle habits. For example, how do we convince others to exercise more, get vaccinated, quit smoking, or refrain from drinking and driving?

Many social psychologists have examined features of persuasive communications to see which factors make a difference in whether the messages will be noticed, remembered, and acted on. In general, these researchers have studied two different kinds of persuasive messages:

informational appeals and fear appeals. **Infor-mational appeals** provide people with facts and arguments about why it is important to engage in particular health behaviors. Although this sounds like a simple enough task, it is critical that the informational message is constructed in a way that makes it likely that the target audience actually "gets it." To be effective, an informational appeal must first grab people's attention, and it must be clear and easily understood. It must also be able to truly persuade the audience, and it must be memorable enough for people to retain it. Finally, and most importantly, it should stimulate the audience to take appropriate action. For an informational message to persuade people to take action, it generally needs to come from a source that is seen as credible (e.g., a physician, a nutritionist), attractive to the target audience, and perceived as similar to the audience members (Bishop, 1994). A message to an African American community about the importance of nutrition and exercise in preventing diabetes will probably be more convincing if it comes from an African American physician than if it comes from a Caucasian physician.

For a message to be effective, it has to be noticed in the first place. On a daily basis, we are exposed to all kinds of health messages—in newspapers and magazines, in television public service announcements, on billboards and posters in subways and buses—yet we probably retain information from few of these sources, and act on fewer still. It is easy to turn the page in a magazine or flip to another channel on the television when we encounter a health message, particularly if its content strikes a nerve about bad habits that already bother us. Media health campaigns that are sponsored by governments or charitable organizations pay advertising companies a great deal of money to develop health campaigns that are noticeable, memorable, and persuasive. One way of grabbing people's attention is through the use of fear. **Fear appeals** are based on the idea that people will be more likely to pay attention to a message, and to subsequently act to change their health behavior, if their related fears are activated. Because diseases,

accidents, and death all are intrinsically fear inducing, it is not all that difficult to appeal to people's fears about these consequences resulting from making poor health choices (Bishop, 1994). Most of us are probably familiar with fear appeals in the media, such as depictions of the aftermath of fatal car accidents as a result of drinking and driving and pictures of how smoking can damage a person's lungs.

Do these kinds of scare tactics work? Evidence from research studies has shown mixed results. Early studies by Hovland and others suggested that the greater the fear produced by the appeal, the more effective it was in persuading a person to change his or her behavior. Other persuasion researchers, such as Irving Janis and his colleagues (e.g., Janis & Feshbach, 1953), hypothesized that very high levels of fear were probably counterproductive in that people might be so upset that they would simply tune out very threatening messages and that inducing moderate levels of fear would be more likely to persuade people to follow health recommendations. More recent meta-analyses, in which a number of research studies of fear appeals were examined simultaneously tended to support the first position; that is, that increases in fear seem to lead to greater persuasion. However, they also found that fear appeals seem to have their greatest impact on people's *intentions* to change their behavior rather than necessarily leading to actual changes in behavior (cited in Devos-Comby & Salovey, 2002). Another concern is that messages that aim to arouse fear might actually elicit other negative emotions like sadness. Devos-Comby and Salovey (2002) discussed this possibility in relation to fear appeals about HIV prevention. Although fear is seen to be persuasive in motivating people to take action, sadness and thoughts of death and suffering might have an opposite effect, leading to a sense of hopelessness and lack of confidence in one's ability to adopt healthier behaviors.

Other approaches have focused on specifying the *conditions that seem to increase the effectiveness of fear appeals*. For a fear message to have its greatest impact, it should clearly convey that engaging in unhealthy behaviors or not engaging in healthy ones will lead to negative health consequences. The message should also emphasize to people that these negative consequences are real and can happen to them. A fear message should also contain a very specific behavioral recommendation, making it totally clear what actions people should take to avoid the negative health outcomes (e.g., use a condom, wear sunscreen). The message should also emphasize that people can do it, that is, that they will be able to make this change in behavior to safeguard their health (Bishop, 1994; DiMatteo & Martin, 2002). Another issue concerns the timing of the message: When the negative health outcomes are due to happen very soon and immediate action can be taken to prevent them, fear messages are likely to be more effective. Fear appeals that depict middle-age people having heart attacks, with recommendations to reduce dietary cholesterol and increase exercise, are unlikely to be perceived as requiring immediate action on the part of college students in their early 20s. On the other hand, fear appeals depicting the terrible consequences of drinking and driving accidents that are televised just prior to New Year's Eve are likely to be perceived as more relevant by young people. Even if they are attended to only long enough to persuade young people to take cabs home from New Year's Eve parties, they will have had a very beneficial effect.

Another way in which the mass media exert social influence about health concerns is through reporting dramatic incidents in the news that relate to health issues. During the spring of 2003, media headlines were dominated by stories of the outbreak of SARS (sudden acute respiratory syndrome) in China and in Toronto. In addition, stories about "mad cow disease" (also known by the technical name of bovine spongiform encephalopathy) grabbed the attention of the North American public after a single cow in Alberta was found to test positive for this disease. Although the probability of North Americans getting either SARS or the human form of mad cow disease remained incredibly low, and certainly far lower than the probability of getting

injured or killed in the course of everyday activities like driving a car, there were massive reactions of fear and panic to these perceived health threats. The U.S. government banned imports of Canadian beef, and polls by Canadian newspapers suggested that a number of Canadians intended to stop eating beef. Toronto and China were the subjects of World Health Organization travel advisories in which people were officially warned not to visit these locations. Consequently, the economic impact of behavioral reactions to these health scares was substantial, with severe effects on the Canadian beef industry and on tourism in Toronto and China.

Why do people panic in the face of health risks that are so statistically improbable? If we were truly concerned about all kinds of things that might lead to our premature deaths, wouldn't we also consistently avoid activities that are even riskier, such as smoking, engaging in unsafe sex, and even driving a car? Clearly, people's perceptions of risk are often at odds with reality. Many people who fear traveling by airplane, for example, are completely unconcerned about highway driving, where their risk of a fatal accident is actually much greater. Concerning fear of crime, psychologists have sometimes referred to a phenomenon called the **fear–victimization paradox**, that is, the finding that sometimes the people who are most fearful are actually the least likely to be victimized. Elderly women tend to fear crime the most, and yet they are least likely to be victimized. Young men, on the other hand, are the least likely group to fear violent crime, and yet they are the most likely to fall victim to it (Duffy & Wong, 2003). One possible explanation for this paradox concerns media influences (recall media cultivation effects covered in Chapter 7). For example, the experiences of young men being assaulted in bar fights rarely attract much media attention, whereas an elderly lady who is the victim of a violent home invasion robbery is likely to be front-page news. That is, the media are selective in their coverage of events, and more unusual (i.e., statistically improbable) occurrences tend to garner a lot of attention. In the minds of media consumers, however, these events appear to be more prevalent than is actually the case.

Experts in risk perception have also identified a number of other factors that explain overblown reactions to rare health risks, such as SARS and mad cow disease (Gatehouse, 2003). One factor is *novelty*; new diseases are perceived to be scarier than diseases which we already know (e.g., influenza). In April 2009, a new influenza strain that came to be known as H1N1 (or "swine flu") emerged, and there was widespread concern that this would lead to a worldwide pandemic. The World Health Organization (WHO) issued its highest-level alert about an H1N1 pandemic, and in North America, public health officials urged all citizens to get vaccinated against the disease (Gilmour & Hofmann, 2010). By the flu season in the fall of 2009, there were widespread public health campaigns telling people to stay home when they had a fever, demonstrating proper handwashing technique, and suggesting that

people refrain from casual hugs and handshakes with acquaintances (see Figure 8.3). Although many people followed the health recommendations designed to prevent the transmission of the disease, the majority of American and Canadian adults did not get the H1N1 vaccine. While H1N1 was estimated to cause more than 18,000 deaths worldwide, this represents a lower rate of deaths than is typically caused by regular seasonal influenza. Although the feared H1N1 pandemic never materialized, there were good reasons for public health officials to be concerned about this new strain of influenza. For example, compared with normal seasonal flu, the H1N1 virus tended to attack a much younger age group, leading to concerns about a high rate of premature deaths. The presentation of a novel disease whose course is uncertain leads to fear on the part of both health officials and the general public.

The degree to which we believe we can *control* something is also a factor that affects our

Figure 8.3 The Dramatic Effect of H1N1 ("Swine Flu") on Hospital Procedures in the Detroit Area

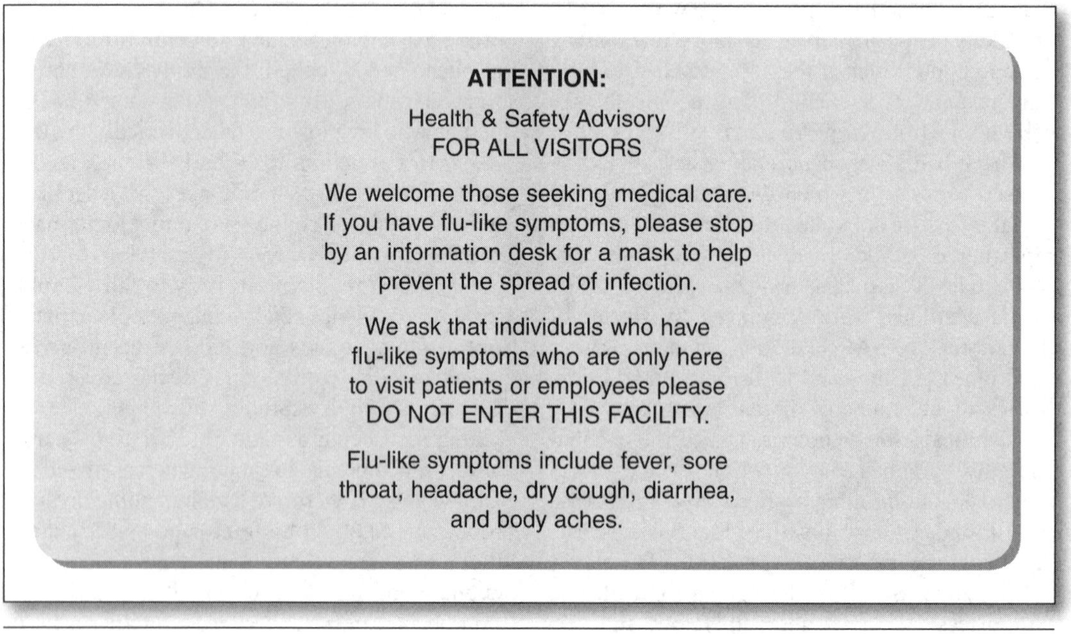

ATTENTION:

Health & Safety Advisory
FOR ALL VISITORS

We welcome those seeking medical care.
If you have flu-like symptoms, please stop
by an information desk for a mask to help
prevent the spread of infection.

We ask that individuals who have
flu-like symptoms who are only here
to visit patients or employees please
DO NOT ENTER THIS FACILITY.

Flu-like symptoms include fever, sore
throat, headache, dry cough, diarrhea,
and body aches.

SOURCE: Courtesy of Frank Schneider.

risk perceptions. Thus, we may still be smoking and not exercising, but believe that we are in control and can change these habits any time we choose. At the same time, it seems like a mere accident of fate that we could contract a deadly disease by being in the wrong place at the wrong time, or by eating a contaminated hamburger. Another factor that elevates our risk perception relates to the *severity of the outcome.* A disease like the human form of mad cow disease, which attacks the brain and leads to dementia, paralysis, and death, is seen as particularly dreadful, and therefore of greater risk. Our overall perception of risk can also be altered by well-publicized *dramatic world events.* Halpern-Felsher and Millstein (2002) found that after the terrorist attacks of September 11, 2001, adolescents perceived their risk of dying as being significantly higher than did adolescents surveyed about risk during the years preceding the terrorist attacks. Interestingly, this heightened perception of risk extended well beyond the risk of a terrorist attack, generalizing to unrelated risks, including dying in an earthquake or a tornado. Dramatic media coverage of tragic events appears to increase our sense of vulnerability to all sorts of risks to our health.

HEALTH LITERACY: EVALUATING HEALTH-RELATED INFORMATION ON THE INTERNET

The proliferation of both Internet users and Internet sites that post health-related information has created new ways to influence people about potential health risks and health-enhancing behaviors (Cline & Haynes, 2001). Even when people engage in recreational use of the Internet on social media, they are likely to be bombarded by the latest health claims, trends, and sometimes alarming health warnings that are posted by their friends and acquaintances. Recent health-related hot topics have included warnings that the consumption of bacon and other processed meats is a risk factor for colorectal cancer, discussions of

the health benefits versus risks of consuming red wine, gluten-free foods, and chocolate, and mounting evidence that insufficient sleep leads to many more negative health consequences than was previously known. While some of these issues represent legitimate areas of health concern, others seem to represent fluctuating health trends, where the same substance (e.g., red wine, gluten) is alternatively viewed as unhealthy, neutral, or having beneficial effects on health. Even more concerning is when outright misinformation is perpetuated on the Internet and through popular media. One of the most notorious examples of this kind of misinformation was a study published in the prestigious medical journal *The Lancet* in 1998 by Dr. Andrew Wakefield that suggested a possible association between the measles, mumps, rubella (MMR) vaccine and the development of autism in children (cited from Holton, Weberling, Clarke, & Smith, 2012). Wakefield's study was the subject of considerable criticism in the scientific community, but was widely disseminated in the popular media. Many parents became concerned that their children would be at serious risk of developing autism and chose not to vaccinate their infants, resulting in detectable decreases in immunization rates in both the United Kingdom and the United States. In 2008, both countries experienced their largest measles outbreaks in more than a decade. Wakefield's study was officially retracted from *The Lancet* in 2010, based on allegations of his professional misconduct and the suggestion that his data had been falsified to provide greater support for the link between the MMR vaccine and autism (Holton et al., 2012). Unfortunately, initial dramatic claims, such as the MMR vaccine-autism link tend to garner much greater attention in the popular media and wield more influence among health consumers than a subsequent retraction of an article by a scientific journal.

In the face of changing "evidence" and competing claims, how are individuals able to sift through the barrage of information to determine which health recommendations are worth following? One factor that influences people's ability to understand and evaluate health information is their degree of **health literacy**. This concept refers to the knowledge and competencies that individuals possess to help them comprehend and apply the health information that they encounter in today's complex world. It encompasses abilities, such as reading and understanding health information, communicating effectively with health care professionals, and being able to follow medical instructions (Sørensen et al., 2012). One dimension of health literacy is **critical health literacy**, which involves the use of advanced skills to critically analyze and apply health information to one's own life (Nutbeam, 2000). Individuals vary in their reading and comprehension skills that contribute to their degree of critical health literacy, and people with low general literacy will tend to be poorer at engaging in critical analysis of health information on the Internet. Nonetheless, research in communication and information literacy suggests that people can be taught to evaluate online information more critically, by looking for a number of specific criteria that enhance its authority (Cline & Haynes, 2001; Metzger, 2007). For example, consumers of health information should seek evidence of expertise by looking for websites in which authorship or sources are clearly identified, and references and links to other authoritative sources are provided. Trustworthiness of website information is enhanced by clear statements that disclose the purpose in posting the information, declare any potential conflicts of interest with the sponsors of the site, and include disclaimers that suggest that information provided on the site is not a valid substitute for advice from a licensed health practitioner. Credibility of messages is heightened when information on the website shows current or recent dates, the site is well organized, and the site provides multiple sources of data, such as graphs and diagrams that logically support the material that is presented in text (Cline & Haynes, 2001). In addition, individuals who visit websites should look for certifications or seals that reflect approval by reputable organizations (e.g., government health agencies)

as well as information about the authors' qualifications. Elements that detract from the credibility of a health information website include typographical errors, broken links, poor navigation, presence of commercial advertisements, and enticements to pay for access to further information (Metzger, 2007). By paying close attention to the website features listed above, individuals can increase their critical health literacy and become more astute consumers of health information on the Internet.

Family, Peer, and School Influences

Clearly, the media are not solely responsible for shaping our attitudes and intentions about our health. There are a number of other sources of social influence for health promotion and prevention, including schools, family, and friends. This subsection considers some of these other sources of influence. Although these sources can affect people of all ages, the primary focus here is on social influences that affect young people, from the teen years through young adulthood. During these years, critical choices are made about the kinds of behaviors one will adopt, and habits are formed that may be very resistant to change later in life.

Who has the greatest influence on young people's health behavior—parents or peers? A large number of investigations have examined family influences, peer influences, or both on the health beliefs and behaviors of young people, and different results have emerged for different populations studied. For example, one study of urban minority middle school students found that more than 50% of the sixth to eighth graders in the sample had used alcohol, 20% had smoked tobacco, 13% were sexually active, and 12% had used marijuana. Parent influences were greatest when it came to alcohol use, but overall, peer influences were found to be most consistently associated with engaging in risky health behaviors (Beal, Ausiello, & Perrin, 2001).

One study of students at an elite university showed a different pattern of results, with a much stronger role of parental influence on young adults' health beliefs and behaviors (Lau, Jacobs Quadrel, & Hartman, 1990). Although health behaviors, such as alcohol consumption and eating habits, became worse when the students left home to attend the university, overall, parental influence did not disappear when the students were no longer living at home. The authors suggested a **model of windows of vulnerability**, where the influence of parents on health beliefs and behaviors will be important throughout life, but where during certain critical periods, young people will be vulnerable to the effects of other important social influences that may expose them to different health beliefs and behaviors. Lau and colleagues (1990) speculated that these critical periods occur during adolescence (when the normal developmental process of seeking independence from parents occurs), on leaving home to live on their own, and again later when they set up more permanent homes of their own with significant others. In addition, parental influence was found to be strongest for behaviors in which the parents themselves showed a great deal of consistency among their health beliefs, their behaviors, and how they trained their children. For example, parents who believed in the importance of seat belt use, trained their children to always wear seat belts, and also routinely used seat belts themselves had stronger "training effects" of this behavior. If parents want their children to adopt healthy habits, it is very important that parents practice what they preach.

A study by Nathanson and Becker (1986) examined the influence of parents, peers, and partners on teenage women's contraceptive-seeking behavior. They found that the majority of nearly 3,000 young women at a family planning clinic reported that their parents or peers had been involved in their actions to obtain contraception. Although the majority of young women who brought others with them to the clinic were accompanied by their girlfriends (54.1%), more young women came with their mothers (16.1%) than with their boyfriends (13.5%). More than half of the young women reported that their mothers knew about their visits to the clinic, and more than two thirds of this group stated that their mothers approved of their decision to obtain contraception. Approximately one quarter said that their fathers knew, and 42.1% of this group reported having their fathers' approval as well. Having their mothers' approval was rated as very important by a majority of these young women and was seen as more important than having their peers' approval (apart from their boyfriends). Interestingly, Black teens reported significantly higher approval from their mothers than did White teens. The authors speculated that a combination of more powerful extended family networks and greater concern for the consequences of unprotected sex among Blacks might account for this difference. Overall, the results of this investigation demonstrate that parents are probably a much more powerful source of social influence over teens' decisions to obtain contraception than one would expect, and so they have great potential to encourage their children to safeguard their sexual health. More recent research by Frisco (2005) also supported the importance of parental influence on young women's contraceptive use. Data from 3,828 young women who participated in a national longitudinal educational study indicated that parents' involvement in their children's education more than doubled their adolescent daughters' odds of using contraceptives, and that parents' educational involvement was specifically associated with an increased likelihood that their daughters would use oral contraceptives, condoms, and multiple methods of birth control.

Substance abuse in adolescents seems to be influenced by both family and peers. Because adolescents are especially vulnerable to peer pressure, many adolescents begin smoking by experimenting with their friends and then gradually become addicted. When teens try their first cigarette, it is usually in the presence of their peers, but parental smoking is also a source of influence (Sarafino, 2002). Adolescence is a critical period of intervention for substance abuse behaviors. If young people reach 21 years of age without developing a smoking habit, it is extremely unlikely that they will be smokers as adults (Friedman, 2002). Early alcohol use is predictive of higher rates of alcohol dependence during adulthood. Some surveys have shown that those who started using alcohol at 14 years of age had rates of alcohol dependence that were four times greater than those who started drinking at 20 years of age. Those who started drinking by 14 years of age also showed significantly higher rates of injuries while under the influence of alcohol (Spoth, Redmond, Trudeau, & Shin, 2002).

The best way to prevent teens from having later substance abuse problems is to try to prevent their initiation into these behaviors in the first place. In other words, primary prevention efforts that target as many young people as possible, before the children develop problems with alcohol, smoking, and/or drugs, are critical. What makes a substance abuse prevention program effective? Various intervention efforts have been attempted, with some based in schools and with a focus on families.

FOCUS ON INTERVENTION

Reducing Substance Abuse

To see which type of intervention would be most effective in preventing initiation into substance abuse, Spoth and colleagues (2002) compared a school classroom-based program alone, the same classroom-based program combined with another program that involved family influences, and a control group whose members did not receive either program.

Their study used a very large sample made up of 1,664 seventh graders from 36 different schools who were randomly selected from 22 counties in a Midwestern state. This intervention study had three conditions. The first condition involved a group that received two programs. One program was a classroom-based Life Skills Training Program, which aimed at providing knowledge about substance abuse and how to avoid it as well as skills to help teens manage their lives and resist substances in a social situation. The second program was the Strengthening Families Program (for parents and children 10 to 14 years of age), which had the goal of reducing substance abuse through strengthening parenting skills, parent–child communication skills, and youth skills in resisting peer pressure. In the second condition, a different group of students received the Life Skills Training Program only. A third group, serving as a control condition, received no interventions. The 36 schools were randomly assigned to one of these three conditions so that children within the same school all received the same program (or were in the control condition). The Life Skills Training Program took place over 15 sessions during regular classroom periods and involved interactive teaching techniques plus out-of-class homework assignments. The Strengthening Families Program involved weekly evening sessions for 7 consecutive weeks. In each session, there were separate parent and youth curriculum sessions for the first hour, and then the parents and children were together for a family session for the second hour. Spoth and colleagues predicted that children who were in the combined program (Life Skills Training Program + Strengthening Families Program) would show the lowest levels of initiation of substance use, followed by those in the Life Skills Training Program alone, and that the children in the control group would be most likely to initiate substance use. This was almost, but not quite, the pattern of findings that they observed. Scores on an overall measure of initiating substance use (rates of starting to use alcohol, cigarettes, and marijuana) were indeed lowest for those in the combined program and highest for those in the control condition. However, scores for children in the combined program did not differ significantly from those for children who received only the Life Skills Training Program. When the rates for the different substances were examined separately, only alcohol showed the predicted pattern, with rates of initiation for the group receiving the Life Skills Training Program alone being significantly higher than those for the combined group, and the control group showing initiation rates significantly higher than those for both of the intervention groups.

What do Spoth and colleagues' (2002) results tell us about the effectiveness of these interventions? First, they strongly support the need for some kind of intervention in that the children in the control group showed significantly higher rates of starting to use substances than did those in the groups that received the intervention programs. Second, they suggest that, although the Life Skills Training Program was effective in reducing the rate of new use of marijuana, cigarettes, and alcohol, the addition of the Strengthening Families Program produced even stronger results when it came to alcohol use. Given that alcohol is widely available and associated with a number of problem behaviors, such as impaired driving, fighting, and sexual assaults, programs that prevent early alcohol use would seem to be especially valuable. Involvement of parents, in addition to programs that can be delivered through regular school classrooms, would seem to be particularly important in trying to prevent later alcohol-related problems in children.

CHANGING HEALTH BEHAVIOR

The previous section dealt with sources of social influence for promoting healthy behavior and attempting to prevent problems or illnesses from occurring in the first place. In this section, the focus is more specifically on how we can get people to change unhealthy behaviors in favor of healthier ones. A number of theories have been developed to help explain the dynamics of health behavior change and to guide intervention efforts in this area. This section deals with three of the most influential theories: the health belief model, the theory of planned behavior, and the transtheoretical model.

Health Belief Model

A number of factors influence whether people will practice healthy behaviors, including demographic factors (i.e., socioeconomic status), early socialization of health habits, emotional factors, access to the health care system, and cognitive factors (Taylor, 2006). Cognitive factors include our beliefs about how likely it is that we may

become ill and our perceptions of how likely it is that particular health practices will prevent illness. The **health belief model** (Janz & Becker, 1984; Rosenstock, 1974) concerns these cognitions and how they predict people's health-protective behaviors.

The health belief model suggests that the actions we take to safeguard our health are influenced by a number of factors, including general health values, perceived susceptibility to illness, perceptions of illness severity, expectation of treatment success, self-efficacy, perceived barriers and benefits, and cues to action. Each of these components is examined briefly in the following subsections.

General health values. The health belief model assumes that we have some interest in our health and concern about maintaining good health in the first place.

Perceived susceptibility to illness. Here we ask ourselves the question, "How likely is it that we will develop this particular problem?" Our perception of a health threat depends on our general knowledge about a particular disease or disorder and the specific knowledge that this condition might be connected with us personally. If you know that smoking, hypertension, and high cholesterol are risk factors for coronary heart disease, and you also know that you are a smoker with high blood pressure and high cholesterol, it should make you feel more personally vulnerable to the threat of heart disease. Media health campaigns attempt to influence our sense of personal vulnerability to health threats by directly stating that a negative health outcome, such as a fatality related to drinking and driving, *can happen to us.*

Perceived severity of illness. Knowing that we may be vulnerable to a particular disease or disorder might not be enough to make us change our behavior. We might also ask ourselves, "How serious are the consequences of this problem?" The way in which we answer this question indicates whether we think the health threat is serious enough to warrant our taking action. If we have seen a family member suffer from breast cancer, for example, we are probably very aware of the toll that this disease can take, will appraise it as being very serious, and will be convinced of the need to engage in regular breast screening. On the other hand, we might not bother to get a flu shot because we do not see getting the flu as a severe health threat.

Expectation of treatment success. Here we ask ourselves, "If we change this particular behavior, how likely is it that doing so will reduce this particular health threat?" Sometimes we underestimate the degree to which our health habits might be related to our chances of becoming ill. If we think that our probability of getting a disease is going to be related mainly to family history and genetic predisposition, we might be unconvinced about, for example, developing healthier patterns of eating and physical activity. If we do not think that our actions will make a difference, we probably will not be motivated to change our health behavior.

Self-efficacy. This concept, originated by Bandura (1977a), is one with which you are already familiar. **Self-efficacy** refers to our perception of whether or not we actually have what it takes (e.g., skills, confidence) to carry out a behavior. Most people who smoke know that doing so is a major risk factor for lung cancer and other serious diseases. They also know that quitting smoking is an extremely effective way in which to substantially lower their risk of contracting these diseases. The problem is that knowing these things is not enough if people are convinced that they cannot quit smoking. Unless we have some confidence that we can change our health habits, the health belief model is unlikely to predict our taking healthy actions.

Perceived barriers and benefits. Another component of the health belief model suggests that we do a kind of cost–benefit analysis, weighing the costs of changing health behaviors against any perceived benefits that making such changes might bring. For example, a person who undertakes an exercise program might have to overcome perceived barriers, such as not having enough time, not having a good place to exercise, and finding exercise boring, but may decide that the health benefits of physical activity outweigh these costs. In some versions of the health belief model, self-efficacy (or, rather, the lack of it) is considered as a perceived barrier to making health changes rather than as a separate part of the model. The idea of a cost–benefit analysis represents another point of intervention: Media health campaigns often focus on the low cost of making a behavior change relative to the high cost of suffering illness consequences.

Cues to action. Some versions of the health belief model have also incorporated the idea of cues to action. **Cues to action** are events or messages that act as triggers to get people to adopt healthy behaviors. Hearing that someone we know was in a serious traffic accident might serve as a cue to action in that we might be more careful about speeding, using seat belts, and not drinking and driving as a result. Some health interventions have deliberately incorporated such cues to action, for example, mailing people reminder postcards when they are due for a dental checkup and giving women waterproof cards (for their showers) instructing them how to perform a breast self-examination.

Research on the health belief model has generally found support for the model or at least for some of its component parts (Jones, Smith, & Llewellyn, 2014; Ragin, 2015; Taylor & Sirois, 2012). For example, Out and Lafreniere (2001) conducted a study that employed "Baby Think It Over,"® a lifelike doll that simulates the functions of a real infant, to see whether exposure to the infant simulator would modify adolescents' attitudes toward teen pregnancy and the consequences of teen pregnancy. After two to three days of constant exposure to the infant simulator (i.e., caring for the doll 24 hours a day), teens in the intervention group were more likely to accurately assess their personal risk for an unplanned pregnancy, and more likely to produce concrete examples of consequences related to child rearing than were teens in the comparison group (who were not exposed to the simulated infants). In other words, role-playing parenting tended to increase the teens' *perceived susceptibility* and their awareness of the *severity* of consequences of a teen pregnancy. Other studies have found at least partial support for the health belief model with respect to diverse health behaviors, including the use of sunscreen (Jackson & Aiken, 2000), preventive dental care, breast self-examination, dieting for weight loss, AIDS risk-related behaviors, participation in health screening programs (cited in Taylor & Sirois, 2012), and healthy eating in college students (Deshpande, Basil, & Basil, 2009).

A number of studies have evaluated interventions based on the health belief model. For example, Fitzpatrick and colleagues (2008) evaluated a community-based physical activity program that took place in Georgia senior citizen centers. This 4-month intervention program was based on the health belief model, and emphasized health conditions common to the elderly that are associated with decreased physical activity (increasing perceived susceptibility and severity), the benefits and barriers to physical activity in the elderly, cues to action, such as providing "how to" instructions for the exercises, and specific training to boost self-efficacy. Fitzpatrick and colleagues found that the program resulted in significant improvement in objective measures of physical functioning, self-reported increases in minutes of daily physical activity and step counts, and the perception of fewer barriers to physical activity. Most notably, the percentage of participants who reported engaging in a minimum of 30 minutes of moderate exercise on at least 5 days per week rose from 55% to 66% following the intervention, and this level of exercise is associated with numerous physical and mental health benefits.

Although the health belief model makes intuitive sense and has been supported by a number of research investigations, it is not without limitations. Not all studies that have tested the model have found supportive results, and most investigations have found only partial support rather than evidence for all components of the model. Some critics have argued that although the health belief model provides a list of relevant variables that influence health behavior, it does not explain precisely the expected relationships among these variables. Furthermore, each study that tests the health belief model tends to use different ways in which to operationalize and measure the variables, and this makes it difficult to compare results across different investigations meaningfully (Bishop, 1994; Brannon et al., 2014; Jones et al., 2014).

Theory of Planned Behavior

Clearly, the goal of any health promotion effort is to get people to change their actual behavior, for example to get them to exercise more, quit smoking, or use sunscreen. As you learned in Chapter 2, according to the **theory of planned behavior** (Ajzen, 1991), the way to change people's behavior is to alter their **behavioral intentions**. Behavioral intentions are decided on in advance of most behaviors and are the best predictors of what people will do. For people to adopt healthier behaviors, they have to change their behavioral intentions.

You'll recall that according to the theory of planned behavior, behavioral intentions in turn are influenced by three things: attitudes toward the behavior, subjective norms regarding the behavior, and perceived behavioral control (see Figure 8.4 so you don't need to flip back to Chapter 2). To illustrate these components with a health example, suppose that Maya, a 21-year-old university student, is a smoker. Obviously, quitting smoking is a target behavior that could result in more positive health outcomes for Maya. Her behavioral intention to attempt to quit smoking will be influenced by the components of the theory of planned behavior. Maya's *attitudes* toward quitting smoking are basically positive. She knows about the health risks of smoking and believes that quitting will ultimately be important for her health. Maya's decision to quit smoking

will also be influenced by *subjective norms,* which are her perceptions of what other important people in her life think about smoking and her motivation to comply with what others think. Maya knows that her parents disapprove of her smoking, as do a lot of her close friends as well. On the other hand, most of her coworkers at the bar where she waitresses are also smokers, and they do not think that quitting smoking is all that important. So, when it comes to this part of the model, it is a bit less clear-cut in that Maya has people in her life who support her smoking behavior and others who really want her to quit. Because the people closest to her are the ones who disapprove of her smoking, Maya's motivation to comply with their wishes is likely to be greater, and so they will act as a positive influence on her behavioral intention to quit.

The last predictor of behavioral intention is *perceived behavioral control,* that is, the degree to which people believe that they have control over a specific behavior. Perceived behavioral control is influenced largely by a person's sense of self-efficacy (Ajzen, 1998). In Maya's case,

Figure 8.4 Theory of Planned Behavior

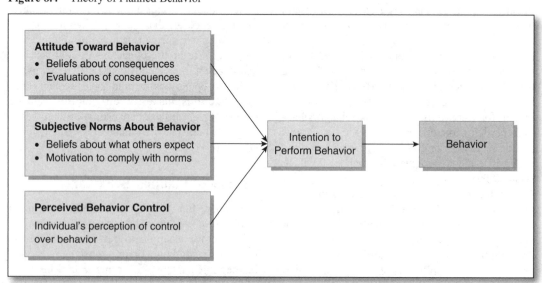

SOURCE: Adapted from Ajzen (1991).

she is fairly confident about her ability to quit smoking. Although she has made quit attempts that did not take previously, she believes that she is under less stress now and in a better position to quit smoking at this point. Maya is also determined not to let her previous relapses into smoking discourage her from trying to quit again. In the theory of planned behavior, this component of perceived behavioral control is particularly important. Even if a person has a positive attitude about making the targeted behavior change and subjective norms that favor the change, if perceived behavioral control is low, it is unlikely that the behavioral change will be made. With respect to smoking cessation, for example, a number of previous studies have found perceived behavioral control to emerge as the strongest predictor of both intention to quit and actual smoking cessation (Norman, Conner, & Bell, 1999). Does the same hold true for other health-related behaviors?

The theory of planned behavior has been applied to a number of different health behaviors and safety practices, including using condoms, taking oral contraceptives, using sunscreen while sunbathing, engaging in breast screening practices, performing testicular self-examinations, and participating in exercise (Taylor & Sirois, 2012). In a test of the theory of planned behavior, Nemme and White (2010) examined university students' intentions to text while driving, as well as their actual texting behavior. Texting while driving is a highly dangerous practice that is illegal in the majority of U.S. states and Canadian provinces, as well as in Australia, where the research was conducted. In this investigation, Nemme and White measured the usual theory of planned behavior components of attitudes, subjective norms, and perceived behavioral control in predicting both intentions to text and actual behavior (i.e., number of texts sent and read while driving). They expanded the "subjective norm" component of the model by also including a measure of group norm (assessing whether participants believed that members of their specific reference group of peers would be likely to engage in the behavior) and moral norm, or the

tendency for texting while driving to go against one's principles. Nemme and White found considerable support for this expanded version of the theory of planned behavior. Holding positive attitudes toward this dangerous behavior predicted intentions to send and read texts while driving. Subjective norms and perceived behavioral control influenced intentions to send, but not read, texts while driving. That is, students who believed that others would not disapprove of them sending texts while driving, and who felt that they had control over their ability to send texts while driving, reported a greater intention to do so. In addition, both group norm and moral norm predicted intention to send and read texts while driving. Students who believed that members of their peer group approved of texting while driving and engaged in these behaviors themselves were more likely to report intentions to send and read texts while driving. Conversely, students who saw these behaviors as morally wrong were less likely to report intentions to text and read text messages while driving. Intentions were predictive of actual texting while driving behavior in this study. Overall, the findings of this study suggest that programs aimed at reducing students' tendencies to engage in this dangerous practice need to adopt a multifaceted approach that addresses all components of the theory of planned behavior.

Transtheoretical Model

You are probably pretty familiar with the kinds of healthy habits that are currently recommended, such as engaging in regular vigorous exercise, quitting smoking, limiting alcohol intake, eating healthy foods (e.g., fruits, vegetables, whole grains), and getting enough sleep. Even though you are aware of what you *should* be doing to safeguard your health, you likely have some health habits that could stand to be improved. Perhaps you are having trouble fitting exercise into a busy schedule of studies and part-time work or are finding that you are frequently studying late into the night and not getting enough sleep. Stop for a moment and try to think of a health habit for which there is some room for improvement on your part. Once you have identified the health habit that could use some improvement, ask yourself whether you are thinking about changing this situation. Perhaps you are not even thinking about trying to make a change; you've got so much else "on the go" right now that trying to change one of your health habits is the least of your concerns. Or, perhaps you are thinking about changing this habit not right now, but rather way down the road when you have more time to devote to it. Maybe you have plans to change this habit fairly soon, but have not actively started yet. Or, maybe you have already started to change this health habit, and so you are actively working on it.

Health psychologists now recognize that people tend to be in different stages of readiness to make a particular health behavior change. Prochaska and DiClemente (1983, 1986) developed the **transtheoretical model** (also known as the "stages of change" model) to account for these individual differences in the course of changing health behaviors. According to this model, people can be classified as being in one of five stages with respect to making a particular health behavior change: precontemplation, contemplation, preparation, action, or maintenance. Each of these stages of change is listed in Figure 8.5 and is discussed in the following subsections.

Precontemplation. During the precontemplation stage, people express no intention to change their health behavior. People may be in the precontemplation stage with respect to a specific health behavior because they do not see that behavior as problematic or because they have considered changing and decided against it.

Contemplation. During the contemplation stage, people are aware that they should undertake a change in a health behavior and are seriously considering doing so. People are classified

Figure 8.5   The Five Stages of Change in Prochaska and DiClemente's (1983) Transtheoretical Model of Health Behavior Change

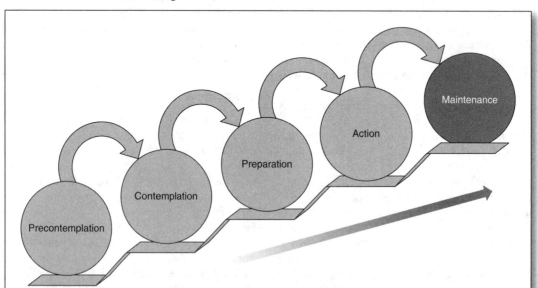

SOURCE: Adapted from Prochaska and DiClemente (1983).

into this stage if they indicate that they are thinking of making a change within the next six months, but in reality people often stay in this stage for years when they do not follow through on more specific actions toward changing their health behavior.

Preparation. People in the preparation stage are ready to make a health change and intend to do so within the next month. Sometimes people who have made an unsuccessful change (e.g., quitting smoking and then relapsing to take up the habit again) are in this stage, preparing for their next quit attempt. During the preparation stage, people usually start to take some action that will lead to their ultimate behavior change. For example, they might sign up for an exercise class that has not begun yet, or they might cut down on the number of cigarettes they smoke per day in advance of quitting altogether.

Action. During the action stage, people are successfully modifying their health behavior. For example, smokers will have quit and are completely abstaining from smoking during this stage.

Maintenance. After six months of successful behavior change during the action stage, people are considered to enter the maintenance stage. At this point, they continue to work to maintain the health behavior change they have made. During this stage, for example, ex-smokers try to maintain their self-abstinence, or exercisers try to stick with their regular programs of physical activity. There are some differences of opinion with respect to how long the maintenance stage lasts. Some formulations of the transtheoretical model include a sixth stage, *termination*, that occurs after people have spent a sufficiently long time in the maintenance stage and have no temptation at all to return to the problem behavior. But, with many problematic behaviors, such as addictions, relapse—returning to the negative behavior, even if only temporarily—occurs more often than not. For this reason, the realistic goal for most people is to remain in the maintenance stage (Prochaska, DiClemente, & Norcross, 1992).

What are the advantages of conceptualizing health behavior change according to these stages? For one thing, this conceptualization captures the actual processes that people go through in leading up to a health behavior change, actually making the change, and then struggling to maintain it. It also helps to explain why so many health interventions are unsuccessful. If the goal of a health program is to try to get all youth smokers to quit smoking, for example, the program is doomed to fail. Most smoking cessation programs are aimed at individuals who are at least in the preparation stage in that they are ready to change their behavior. Yet, many smokers are not at all prepared to make such a change. Prochaska and colleagues (1992) reported that only some 10% to 15% of smokers are in the preparation stage at any given time, whereas some 30% to 40% are in the contemplation stage, and 50% to 60% are still in the precontemplation stage. Given that smoking programs are geared toward people in the preparation stage, is it any wonder why their success rates tend to be so low? Thus, another advantage of the model is that it prompts us to consider individual differences in the design and execution of interventions.

Another advantage of the transtheoretical model is that it offers a more optimistic picture of the outcome of relapse situations, where people revert to the negative health behavior they tried to change. Rather than conceiving of relapse as an "all or nothing" situation, the stages of change model sees relapse as simply spiraling back to a previous stage and allows for the fact that this happens quite often. People who attempt to quit smoking and then slip up after three weeks and smoke a few cigarettes have clearly left the action stage in that they are no longer abstinent from smoking. But, what stage describes them now? An "all or nothing" approach to relapse would say that they have to start over at the very beginning. In fact, it is quite unlikely that they really have reverted back to the beginning, according to the model. This would mean a return to precontemplation for most smokers, and yet those who were successfully abstinent from smoking for a few weeks are probably at least at the contemplation stage (i.e., aware of the need to quit again and planning to do so in the future) and perhaps even at the preparation stage (i.e., ready to make another attempt at quitting fairly soon). Interventions that are guided by this model will help those who are struggling to make difficult health changes to see that all is not lost and that quitting for good might mean that they go through the preparation stage several times.

Perhaps the biggest benefit of the transtheoretical model is that it provides a framework for tailoring health interventions to suit the current stage of each individual who needs to make a health behavior change rather than assuming that a single intervention will work for everyone (Prochaska et al., 1992). Measures have been developed to classify people into the five stages; once a person's stage of readiness to change is known, the approach used to help that person facilitate change can be applied. Although it might seem that people in the precontemplation stage are completely unlikely to respond to intervention efforts, this is not always the case. The costs of their health behavior and the benefits of altering it can be pointed out, for example, with the goal of moving these people to the contemplation stage, where they should be more responsive to appropriate intervention efforts. For each stage, there are different strategies that can be effective in guiding people to the next stage of ultimately making the behavioral change.

Interventions that are based on the transtheoretical model enable health programs to tailor the messages and materials to a person's current stage of readiness to change. Prochaska, DiClemente, Velicer, and Rossi (1993) conducted research to determine whether programs matched to stage of change were more effective than other smoking cessation programs. They randomly assigned 756 smokers to four different conditions: (a) a *standard condition* in which participants received smoking cessation manuals and booklets; (b) an *individualized condition* in which participants received a series of manuals that were matched to their current stage of change and all of the stages that followed (e.g., someone in the contemplation

stage would receive manuals for contemplation, preparation, action, and maintenance); (c) an *interactive computer report condition* in which participants received the manuals appropriate for their stage (and all subsequent stages, as in the individualized condition), as well as computer reports that included a full description of their stage of change, individualized feedback on how they were doing on the processes of change, and information on how to cope with tempting situations they might encounter during that stage; and (d) a *personalized counselor condition* in which participants received all of the materials in the interactive computer report condition, along with a series of short telephone calls from trained counselors to provide personalized feedback in which participants' signs of progress were reinforced, as counselors tried to help them progress to the next stage.

Prochaska and colleagues (1993) found that all of the stage-matched conditions were significantly more effective than the standard condition in getting people to quit smoking and remain abstinent. The interactive computer report intervention showed the best success rates. Individuals in this condition showed more than double the rates of quitting (when quitting was measured six months after the intervention) than did individuals in the standard condition. When they examined long-term abstinence from smoking (i.e., at 18 months), they found that participants in the computer condition showed substantially higher rates (nearly three times as high) than those of people in the standard condition. While the personalized counselor condition was also found to be more effective in leading people to quit and to maintain their abstinence than the standard condition, it was still less effective than the interactive computer condition. Therefore, the overall pattern of results supports the transtheoretical model in that interventions that were tailored to the characteristics of individuals during each stage of change were found to be more effective than a standard "one size fits all" approach. Interestingly, the interactive computer version of the stage-matched intervention worked best of all—even better than the personalized counselor condition. It appears that people do well with individualized feedback, but this feedback might be better received when it comes from an impersonal source like a computer-generated report rather than an actual counselor. This finding suggests that individualized feedback can be delivered through computer reports in a fairly cost-effective and widespread manner compared with the resources required to deliver feedback through individual counselors.

The transtheoretical model was initially developed to address addictive behaviors, and the majority of research using this model has been on smoking. However, predictions made by the model have been supported in relation to a number of other health behavior changes, including predicting binge-drinking behavior in college freshmen (Ward & Schielke, 2011), reducing dietary fat, controlling one's weight, getting mammograms, adopting exercise programs, and using safer sex practices (Salovey, Rothman, & Rodin, 1998). Some studies have failed to find support for the predictions made by the transtheoretical model, however, and there have been criticisms of the measures used to classify people into stages as well as questions regarding whether the stages themselves are identified accurately (e.g., Herzog, 2008; Littell & Girvin, 2002; Weinstein, Rothman, & Sutton, 1998). Nevertheless, the transtheoretical model is extremely useful in describing the complexity of the processes that people go through to change their health behaviors, and it is likely to remain influential in guiding further research and intervention efforts.

STRESS, COPING, AND SOCIAL SUPPORT

Until this point, the focus of this chapter has been primarily on applying knowledge from psychology to guide health promotion and primary prevention efforts and to determine how people can change their health behaviors. Although it is clear that psychology has a great deal to offer that might enhance the effectiveness of programs to get people to adopt healthier lifestyles, the role

of social psychology with respect to people who are already in distress is somewhat less clear. As you saw in Chapter 5, social psychology certainly has much to offer with respect to helping people to deal with psychological disorders. We now address whether social psychology has anything to offer people who suffer from physical illnesses or symptoms of stress.

A great deal of current research, guided by the biopsychosocial model, addresses the psychosocial aspects of various illnesses and disorders. There is growing recognition that treating the body is only one aspect of treating the patient's condition. The course of a number of serious illnesses that people live with today (e.g., heart disease, diabetes, cancer) is affected by psychological and social factors. This section considers two areas in which health psychology has made contributions to the ways in which people experience illness and distress: the study of stress and coping and the influence of social support on health.

Stress and Coping

What sorts of things have stressed you out over the past couple of days? Maybe you are worried about upcoming exams and assignments that are due, and you do not know when you will have time to prepare for them. You might be concerned about ongoing issues like how you are going to afford next semester's tuition and whether the status of your long-distance relationship has changed. Or, perhaps you are just experiencing some little annoyances that drive you crazy, such as discovering that your car's gas gauge is right on empty when you are already running late for class, or finding out that your work schedule has been changed so that you cannot go out with your friends on Friday night. How would these events make you feel, and what would you do to reduce the stress they cause?

It is easy to identify the feeling of being stressed, but it is not always clear why certain events bother us so much or what we should do to manage our stress. Stress experts have examined the processes of stress and coping so as to help people understand the sources of stress in their lives and learn how to manage stress effectively. Lazarus and Folkman (1984) defined **stress** as "a particular relationship between the person and the environment that is appraised by the person as taxing or exceeding his or her resources and endangering his or her well-being" (p. 19). Lazarus and Folkman's definition reflects their approach, which is referred to as a **transactional model of stress**. The basic idea of their model is that the experience of stress results from ongoing transactions between people and the environment. During the course of these transactions, people will encounter particular situations, events, or other people that may or may not induce the feeling of stress. These are referred to as **stressors** in Lazarus and Folkman's transactional model (illustrated in Figure 8.6). Based on their encounters with these potentially stressful events, people make an **appraisal**, that is, a judgment as to how to respond to the stressors. Do they perceive the stressors as threats (e.g., something potentially harmful) or as challenges (e.g., an obstacle to be overcome)? Do they feel stress as a result of their encounter with the stressors? The model suggests that if people make a stressful appraisal—seeing the stressors as threatening or harmful—then they will feel stress as a result. According to this model, the experience of stress is an individual phenomenon, and no two people will experience it in exactly the same way. What may be stressful to one person (e.g., driving on a very busy highway) might be quite relaxing to

someone else. What is critical here is not the stressor itself, but rather how people appraise it.

Once people have appraised a situation as being stressful, they go on to the third stage of the model, where they evaluate their coping options or resources to deal with the problem. **Coping** refers to thoughts, feelings, and behaviors that people engage in when trying to reduce stress. Consistent with the idea that the experience of stress is an individual phenomenon, so too is the way in which people cope with particular stressors. People differ in the coping strategies that they use, and even the same individual will often use different coping strategies in different situations. Coping strategies can be classified into two general types: problem-focused coping and emotion-focused coping (Lazarus & Folkman, 1984; Lazarus & Launier, 1978). With **problem-focused coping**, people deal directly with the problem that has caused them to be stressed. This might involve standing up to others who have wronged them or taking a problem and breaking it down into smaller component parts that people can manage. **Emotion-focused coping** involves people trying to regulate their emotions so that they can minimize the distress caused by the situation. Emotion-focused coping is sometimes the only recourse in situations where people are dealing with an outcome that cannot be altered. For example, if a loved one dies, people cannot change that fact, but they can try to manage their emotions, perhaps by reappraising the situation to try to see something positive in it (e.g., thinking about how grandmother lived a full and

Figure 8.6 Components of Lazarus and Folkman's (1984) Transactional Model of Stress

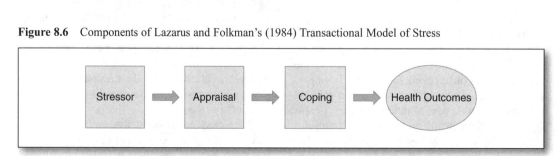

SOURCE: Adapted from Lazarus and Folkman (1984).

happy life and touched so many people's lives before she died). However, some emotion-focused coping strategies can be maladaptive in that they involve things, such as people trying to pretend that the problem does not exist and trying to comfort themselves by using drugs, alcohol, or other medications. Effective coping tends to reduce the negative effects of stress, whereas ineffective coping does not reduce the stress and might even make things worse.

Negative effects of stress can affect people's health, so the final stage of the transactional model is the predicted *health outcomes*. People who experience a great deal of stress, and particularly those who show poor coping responses, tend to show higher rates of illness. For example, research has shown that people who report higher levels of stress show a higher incidence of respiratory illnesses and other infectious diseases, suggesting that stress has a suppressive effect on the immune system (Sarafino, 2002). In addition, associations between stress and other illnesses, including headaches, hypertension, diabetes, asthma, and rheumatoid arthritis, have been noted (Brannon et al., 2014).

Many researchers have focused on the stressor component of this model to determine what kinds of situations or events are potentially stressful. Although the transactional model of stress suggests that we appraise events in unique and individual ways, there are still some general approaches to identifying stressors. One approach to measuring stress suggests that *major life events* that happen in our lives cause us to undergo significant readjustment in our lives. Holmes and Rahe (1967) drew up a list of major life events called the *Social Readjustment Rating Scale*. The events on the list were the ones most commonly suggested by clinical experts as requiring people to make a lot of changes in their lives. Included on the list are events that are both negative (e.g., death of a spouse, divorce, being fired) and positive (e.g., getting married, outstanding personal achievement, vacation), but in all cases they require people to adjust and make changes. According to this approach, people who have experienced a high number of major life events over the course of a year will be more likely to develop health problems.

Although debate exists about the merits of the life event stress perspective, including criticism of its assumption that even events that are usually experienced as positive can still be experienced as stressful (e.g., Thoits, 1982), research studies continue to find that even positive life events can create a considerable amount of stress in people's lives. For example, Cramer and Lafreniere (2003) conducted a study of the stress involved in wedding preparation. In the study, 69 grooms-to-be and 188 brides-to-be were surveyed at a wedding exposition about their wedding plans as well as their wedding-related difficulties, their degree of perceived stress, and the sources of support available to them. Brides identified family problems, financial constraints, and having an older groom as sources of stress, whereas grooms were stressed by financial constraints, larger weddings, a fast approaching wedding date, and having a young bride. Interestingly, religious or cultural differences between brides and grooms were not related to increased stress, and neither was geographical separation. Data for 58 couples were available, allowing the researchers to compare the brides' and grooms' perceptions of stress for the same wedding rather than examining women's and men's perspectives on weddings in general. Both brides and grooms in these couples showed levels of perceived stress that were significantly higher than stress levels seen in typical community samples. Comparisons of brides and grooms revealed that brides were significantly higher in perceived stress, wanted more control, had more control, and anticipated more family disagreements than did grooms.

Other approaches to stress suggest that it is not necessarily the big events that cause us to feel stressed; instead, it can be the *minor annoyances* that we are subjected to on a daily basis. Lazarus and his colleagues proposed that relatively minor stressors that characterize everyday life can lead to negative health outcomes. They devised a measure of the cumulative impact of these, called the *Hassles Scale* (Kanner, Coyne,

Schaeffer, & Lazarus, 1981), which included items about minor annoyances, such as misplacing things, having concerns about money, and experiencing problems with neighbors. Kanner and colleagues (1981) found that Hassles Scale scores proved to be a better predictor of symptoms than did major life events. Some researchers (e.g., Pillow, Zautra, & Sandler, 1996) have suggested that major life events tend to result in an increase in the number of daily hassles, thereby increasing our overall amount of distress.

Although appraising events as stressful is an individual process, and not everyone will agree on what is stressful and what is not, there are certain *characteristics of events that make them more likely to be perceived as stressors* (Taylor & Sirois, 2012). First, negative events are more likely to elicit stress than are positive ones. Even though positive events (e.g., planning a wedding) involve change and require considerable energy, there is clear evidence of rewards for our efforts. This is not the case with negative events, which involve problems, difficulties, or losses, but are not associated with any apparent immediate payoffs. Second, events that are unpredictable or uncontrollable are more likely to be seen as stressful rather than events that are predictable and controllable. Third, being overloaded with tasks and having too much to do at the same time increases the likelihood that we will report being stressed out. So, it is not just the characteristics of the individual events, but also the overall quantity of tasks that we have to manage that contributes to the feeling of being stressed.

Finally, events that are vague and undefined tend to be perceived as more stressful than straightforward clear-cut events. With ambiguous events, we must initially devote time and energy to figuring out what the problems are before we can begin to deal with them effectively.

The transition from high school to university—a major life event—can be a stressful time for many students. Whether students leave home to attend school or live with their parents and commute, embarking on a university career presents significant challenges that can lead to stress and adjustment problems. Although entering university is usually seen as a positive event, it represents a transition that is likely to involve several of the characteristics of stressful events discussed previously. Students have little control over which university accepts them, and many students are forced to leave home to attend university because they are not accepted into a nearby university, or because there is no university within close proximity. Compared with the more structured environment of high school, attending university is likely to involve more ambiguous expectations and demands on students. The total picture that emerges is one in which students have to make a great number of changes in their lives that collectively may appear to be overwhelming. Consequently, some students experience loneliness and learning burnout that negatively impacts their academic experiences (Stoliker & Lafreniere, 2015). Leaving home to live away for the first time is likely to intensify this perception of stressful overload.

FOCUS ON RESEARCH

Adjusting to University

In a study that examined factors thought to influence the transition to university, Lafreniere, Ledgerwood, and Docherty (1997) compared 50 students (25 males and 25 females) who moved away from their parents' homes to attend university with 50 students (25 males and 25 females) who continued to live at home on measures of family support, perceived stress, and adjustment to university. The researchers hypothesized that students who left home for the first time to attend university would experience more stress and poorer adjustment than would students who continued to live at home with their parents. Students who perceived high levels of family support were also expected to fare better, in terms of showing lower stress and better adjustment, than students who perceived their families to be less supportive.

The findings of this study did not support the hypotheses that students who left home, and those who perceived lower parental support, would experience more stress and poorer adjustment to university. When participant gender was examined in relation to these variables, however, a much more interesting pattern of results emerged. Male students who continued to live at home with their parents while making the transition to university reported the least amount of stress. For female students, the opposite pattern was shown, with continuing to live at home while beginning university being associated with an elevated risk of stress. This finding is illustrated in Figure 8.7. In addition, both male and female students who perceived a high level of support from their families tended to report similarly high levels of adjustment to university, irrespective of whether or not they left home for the first time to go away to school. For students who reported low levels of family support, however, the pattern of results mirrored those seen for perceived stress. That is, females reported significantly better adjustment to university when they lived away from home, whereas males appeared to be better adjusted when they continued to live at home. Lack of support from family, then, appeared to exert differential influences on young women and young men in facilitating adjustment to university.

Lafreniere and colleagues (1997) speculated as to a number of reasons for the differential results by gender. One possibility is that families who are insensitive to the needs of their children might not appreciate the difficulty of the new academic challenges that these children face as they begin university. For example, parents might expect their adolescent children who still live at home to contribute very heavily to housework, cooking, and the care of younger siblings and fail to realize that these responsibilities might be in conflict with the intense demands of attending university. Given that the majority of household responsibilities tend to be shouldered by women in our society (e.g., Hochschild, 1989), it may be that female students who live at home might experience more stress that comes from overload and role conflict than do their male counterparts. In addition, male and female students are likely to differ in terms of how they seek and use social support to ease the stress of the transition to university life. Previous studies have shown that adolescent women are more likely than adolescent men to discuss their problems with peers and that adolescent male students are less likely than adolescent female students to express anxiety about academic demands or to ask their teachers or counselors for help. Consequently, young men who are having difficulty in adjusting to the life changes associated with going away to university might keep their feelings to themselves and not benefit from the support they might be able to receive through building new social networks.

Social Support

As Lafreniere and colleagues' (1997) study illustrates, the effects of social support are important in helping to alleviate the negative effects of stressful circumstances. **Social support** refers to the resources that we get from other people. One way of conceptualizing social support examines the size of our social network and the number of links that we have to other people—family members, friends, acquaintances, and others. Social network measures help us to identify who

Figure 8.7 Perceived Stress as a Function of Place of Residence and Gender

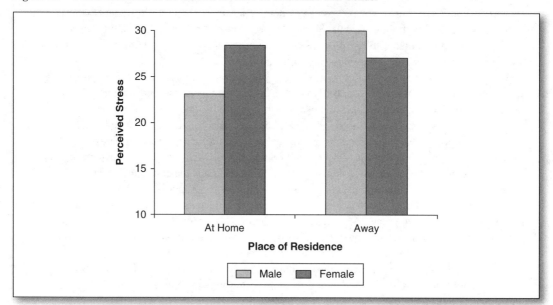

might be socially isolated, for example, with few friends and family members nearby (Brannon et al., 2014). Simply having a lot of social contacts does not necessarily mean that we are benefiting from social support. The other aspect of social support refers to the quality of our relationships and to whom we can turn when we have problems or are under stress. The use of social support, or whether we feel comfortable asking others for help when we need it, is also a critical element.

Social support can fulfill many different functions in our lives. We get **emotional support** from others, who provide us with love, empathy, and security. When others let us know that we are valued for our personal qualities and ideas and are accepted despite our faults, we receive **esteem support**. Practical help that we receive from others, such as having them lend us money, give us rides, and help out with our chores is referred to as **tangible** or **instrumental support**. **Informational support** refers to getting advice, suggestions, or feedback from others and is especially helpful when we are in a situation, or are encountering a problem that is new to us. Finally, we get **network support** when we feel a

sense of membership in a group that shares our interests or provides us with social companionship (Sarafino, 1998).

There are a number of ways in which social support has been found to contribute to health. One way is through influencing people to practice healthy behaviors. Individuals who are socially isolated have fewer people to encourage them to stick with their diet or exercise program, to distract them from a temptation to relapse to smoking, or to insist that they see a doctor about a health concern (Brannon et al., 2014). One study involving women over 50 years of age found that even coworkers in a factory setting can be a significant source of encouragement to practice breast self-examination and other breast screening practices (Stamler, Thomas, & Lafreniere, 2000).

Social support can also influence the components of the transactional model of stress and coping (Lazarus & Folkman, 1984). If people are socially integrated and able to use effective social support from others, it is likely that they will encounter fewer stressors in the first place given that loneliness and lack of social contact are stressors in and of themselves. Even if a person encounters a number of potentially stressful events, the presence of others who provide effective support can reduce the probability that the person will make stressful appraisals about these events. For example, if you suddenly find out that you have to move to a new apartment, but you know that you have a number of friends who will help you to move and allow you to stay with them during the transition, you will be less likely to perceive the forced move as a particularly stressful occurrence. In addition, knowing that you have support from others can enhance your coping abilities in stressful situations. Friends and loved ones can provide emotional support and esteem support and can remind you that you have the strength to get through some tough times (Brannon et al., 2014).

A number of researchers have examined the role of social support in relation to particular chronic and life-threatening illnesses. For example, studies have shown that emotional, informational, and tangible support are all important in reducing depression in AIDS patients (Taylor & Sirois, 2012). Literature reviewed by Hegelson and Cohen (1996) identified helpful and unhelpful aspects of social support for cancer patients. Across a large number of studies, emotional support emerged as being most important to cancer patients, particularly when it came from spouses, family members, and friends. The absence of emotional support from these sources was experienced as harmful to patients' adjustment. Informational support was seen as helpful, but only when it came from health care professionals. Hegelson and Cohen's review also revealed some interesting misconceptions that many people have about providing support to cancer patients. For example, people without cancer believed that they should try to "cheer up" cancer patients, whereas cancer patients themselves said that this kind of unrelenting optimism was more disturbing than helpful. People without cancer also believed that cancer patients would be better off not discussing their illness, whereas cancer patients reported wanting to discuss worries and concerns about their illness. Healthy people perceived cosmetic effects of cancer (e.g., losing a breast) as being a more central concern of cancer patients than it

actually was. From the perspective of cancer patients, minimization of the problem, empty reassurances, and forced cheerfulness were unhelpful behaviors, as was misplaced empathy, that is, having people without cancer tell them, "I know how you feel." Probably the most hurtful behavior reported by cancer patients was having friends avoid seeing them because the friends were uncomfortable with their illness. To provide effective support to someone with a life-threatening disease, it is important not to make assumptions about what will be helpful, but rather to find out what will be most beneficial from the patient's own perspective.

Research also shows that social support is a key aspect of recovery for people experiencing chronic pain. Zheng and colleagues (2013) conducted a qualitative study of the experience of people taking opioid medications for chronic (noncancer-related) pain. The researchers interviewed 20 people with chronic pain about their experiences with pain and with taking opioid medications to manage it. The researchers used a **narrative** approach to analyze participants' descriptions of their experiences of chronic pain and opioid use. As described in Chapter 3, narrative research involves gathering detailed stories about a particular life experience. Researchers then look for patterns across and within the stories and attempt to organize the stories into a coherent framework, taking into account context. Researchers who use a narrative approach often identify certain types of narratives within participants' stories. For example, in this study, Zheng and colleagues (2013) identified three overarching narratives within participants' descriptions of their experiences with chronic pain. Just under half of the participants told stories of feeling like they would never recover from the pain they were experiencing. Their stories involved several setbacks, including worsening pain, severe side effects from the medication, and an overall sense of hopelessness. The researchers labeled this type of story a **chaos narrative**. In contrast, one quarter of participants told stories that involved hope and an expectation that they would become well again.

These stories were labeled **restitution narratives**. The remaining participants focused on self-transformation when describing their experience of chronic pain and opioid use. These participants told a **quest narrative** in which they offered help to themselves or others throughout their illness, and were able to slowly reduce their use of pain medication.

After identifying these three narratives within participants' interviews, the researchers looked for factors that influenced the type of narrative. In other words, the researchers wondered why certain people experienced chaotic and hopeless narratives when going through chronic pain, whereas other people were more hopeful, and experienced restitution or quest narratives. The researchers identified several factors that seemed to differentiate between negative and positive

narratives, and two important factors involved social support. Participants who experienced hopeful, positive narratives despite chronic pain and opioid use felt supported by health care professionals, and the health care system, and they also described high levels of social support from friends and family members. In contrast, people who remained stuck in chaos narratives reported unsupportive interactions with health care professionals, such as feeling like they were bounced from one doctor to another. Participants who felt a lack of social support and social isolation typically described their experience of chronic pain and opioid use in terms of chaos and hopelessness. By identifying the stories that people tell about their lives with chronic pain, researchers were able to learn about how to help people live in hope.

CULTURE CAPSULE

Patient–Practitioner Interactions

The way in which doctors and nurses interact with their patients undoubtedly affects patient care. Research has shown that there are a number of factors that negatively influence patient–practitioner communication and that poor patient–practitioner communication can lead to negative consequences for the patient, including not following treatment recommendations (Taylor & Sirois, 2012). When the doctor and patient come from very different cultures, these problems in communication pose an even greater challenge (Gurung, 2014). Many cultures have conceptions of the causes of illness and the appropriate treatments and ways of supporting patients that differ greatly from the typical Western medical approach. For example, in some cultures, illnesses and medical conditions might be believed to result from witchcraft, evil spirits, or the "evil eye" (Turner, 1996). Although no single practitioner can be expected to know all cultural beliefs that relate to illness and healing, awareness of different cultural practices leads to more sensitive patient care (Gurung, 2014; Yox, 2003), which in turn can increase patient compliance with medical treatments.

This issue was brought home by one of the chapter authors' students, who related the following anecdote after hearing a lecture on patient–practitioner interactions and culture. The student's grandmother had recently immigrated to the United States from Africa. Shortly after her arrival, she developed joint pain in her knees and was prescribed anti-arthritic medication. She refused to take the medication, insisting that the pain was a result of a *tokoloshi,* a small mischievous creature that is believed by members of a number of cultures in Southern Africa to be responsible for all kinds of ailments and difficulties. The grandmother believed that the *tokoloshi* had sneaked into her suitcase and followed her to North America, and that on its release it had caused the pain in her knees. Her family members were unable to convince her that her pain was the result of a medical condition that could be treated by her medicine, and they eventually took her to see a South African doctor. The doctor understood the grandmother's concern and mentioned that once toko-loshis are released, they detest crossing water. He suggested that by crossing a bridge over the river that ran through their city and taking her medicine, the tokoloshi and the pain it caused would disappear. Sure enough, this proved to be the case!

This anecdote may lead you to believe that the South African doctor was merely humoring his patient as a means of cajoling her into taking the medication that would cure her medical condition. This interpretation misses the point. As we have seen throughout this chapter, psychological factors influence the prevalence and course of physical ailments. The doctor in this story understood that biology, psychology, and social factors interact to produce health. Knowing this, he was able to successfully manage a situation that might have left a patient feeling ill.

SUMMARY

Social psychology has a great deal to contribute to the study of health and interventions to improve people's well-being and quality of life. The field of health psychology is concerned with promoting health and preventing illness, identifying psychological factors that might influence illness, and improving the ways in which health care is delivered. The biopsychosocial model, or the idea that health is determined by biological, psychological, and social factors, underlies health psychology and guides research and interventions that arise from it.

The best way to improve the health of the population is to promote healthy choices and prevent people from becoming ill in the first place. Psychologists have applied their knowledge of persuasion to improve the ways that health promotion efforts can influence their target audiences. Fear appeals, for example, must be carefully designed so that they can arouse fear about negative health consequences in a way that encourages people to pay attention to messages, and subsequently to act to change their health behaviors. Family, peer, and school influences have also been shown to affect the health-related behaviors of young people.

School-based programs can help to prevent young adolescents from initiating substance abuse, and including parents in these programs seems to help prevent early initiation into alcohol use. Parents are also a powerful source of influence over teens' decisions to obtain contraception and have great potential to encourage children to safeguard their sexual health.

Three influential theoretical models of health behavior change were described. The health belief model suggests that our decisions to engage in healthy behaviors are influenced by a number of factors, including our perceived susceptibility to illness, perceived severity of illness, expectations for treatment success, costs and benefits of health behaviors, and cues to action. According to the theory of planned behavior, the way in which to change people's behavior is to alter their behavioral intentions. Behavioral intentions are influenced by people's attitudes toward the behavior, by subjective norms (i.e., perceptions about what important others think about the behavior), and especially by perceived behavioral control, that is, the degree to which people believe that they have control over the behavior. The transtheoretical or "stages of change" model describes the stages of readiness to change a particular health behavior: precontemplation, contemplation, preparation, action, and maintenance. Tailoring health programs to make messages and materials appropriate to each individual's stage of readiness to change seems to hold particular promise.

A major focus in health psychology concerns stress and coping. The transactional model of stress, appraisal, and coping is based on the idea that we experience stress from ongoing transactions with the environment and that the way that we appraise or evaluate events can trigger stressful reactions. Coping strategies to reduce stress include problem-focused efforts, where we try to change the stressor itself, and emotion-focused efforts where we try to regulate our emotions to minimize the distress. Social support can help to mitigate the effects of stress and can also provide emotional comfort to people who are ill. Not all social input from others is necessarily helpful, however, and social support is most effective when it is tailored to meet the needs of the patient.

Although this chapter presented theory and research in several of the major areas of health psychology, it actually represents a very limited selection of topics in this subdiscipline of psychology. Health psychology also considers issues, such as the use of health services and the experience of hospitalization, adherence to medical treatments, pain and its management, psychological aspects of each of the major chronic and life-threatening illnesses, and experiences associated with dying and bereavement. If you enjoyed reading this chapter, we encourage you to pursue your interests further by reading a book or taking a course in health psychology.

9

APPLYING SOCIAL PSYCHOLOGY TO EDUCATION

LOUISE R. ALEXITCH

"One of the best experiences of my life."

   " . . . .was a way of bringing dreams and aspirations into reality."

   " . . . .the [program] showed me a lot of opportunity . . . .of what I want for my future. I know that I belong somewhere in the healthcare field."

   These are just a few of the comments of students who completed the University of Toronto Summer Mentorship Program (SMP; University of Toronto, n.d.). Launched in 1994, the SMP was established to address concerns over the lack of African Canadian and Indigenous students pursuing professions in the health sciences. The 4-week program is designed to expose high school students from minority backgrounds to the university environment, and by job shadowing and providing some hands-on experience, to encourage these students to consider careers in professions such as nursing, medicine, dentistry, pharmacy, and social work (Ogilvie, 2010). To be eligible for the SMP, students must be from one of the targeted underrepresented groups, must be enrolled in one of the participating Toronto area high schools, and have good academic standing. Because students from minority backgrounds often believe that they are not smart enough or do not have the means to be successful at the university level, then exposing these students to role models who are encouraging and supportive may change the way they see themselves. Indeed, mentoring is a key component of the SMP's success by helping students to see people like themselves as health care professionals (Ogilvie, 2010). *To date, more than 600 students have completed the program, with about one third having pursued medical careers* (Ogilvie, 2010; University of Toronto, n.d.). *In the words of one SMP graduate: ". . . I was just this little boy from the Reserve. . . . I was meeting all these kinds of doctors and I was blown away by what they could do. I would not have thought of that without this program."* (Ogilvie, 2010).

- What factors may have affected the students' motivational levels and aspirations?
- Why did these students, who previously viewed themselves as marginal students, come to view their academic abilities more positively?
- How do interactions with mentors, teachers, and role models affect students' academic achievement and aspirations?

We can all remember instances from our school pasts that we cherish—good friends, inspirational teachers, and moments of accomplishment. We also can recall instances that we would much rather forget—schoolyard bullies, a teacher who made us feel foolish, or feelings of isolation. Social psychology has helped to uncover the intrapersonal and interpersonal processes that operate in the educational environment. For example, there are social psychological theories to explain how students' learning experiences may have led the minority students in the opening vignette to view their academic abilities in a more positive light. In the first section of the chapter, *intrapersonal processes,* such as attitudes, achievement motivation, and beliefs about one's academic skills are discussed.

Also, we must not forget that acquiring an education is very much a social process in that teachers interact with students and students interact with each other. In the vignette, it seems that the minority students' interactions with health care professionals led the students to alter their academic aspirations. The second section of the chapter, *interpersonal processes* considers how teachers and students interacting together can

affect students' beliefs about their abilities and their levels of academic achievement.

Of course, many educators and researchers also have applied social psychology in schools to address more general social issues, such as violence, prejudice and discrimination, and health-related behaviors. Interventions based on social psychological concepts are aimed not only at improving the academic achievement of students, but also at creating learning environments that foster the development of broad-based emotional, social, and cognitive skills in students. The final section of the chapter focuses on the problem of school aggression in the form of bullying and school shootings. It shows how the school environment reflects broader societal norms regarding aggression, and how schools can be used as vehicles for addressing this pressing social issue.

INTRAPERSONAL PROCESSES: INCREASING SUCCESS, REDUCING FAILURE

Susan, a psychology major, is worried about her performance in a statistics course. She worries that she "can't do math." To deal with her feelings, she engages in activities that help to distract her from the requirements of the course like going out with friends the night before her statistics exam. She finds reasons like "computer problems" for not submitting her assignments on time (or at all). As a result, Susan fails the exam. How does she feel about statistics now? How would you feel if you were Susan? Because she failed, Susan believes that her original conception of her ability is correct: She is lousy at math. Can students' beliefs about their academic ability be changed? Can these changes result in better academic achievement and motivation to learn? Social psychology and decades of research have shown that these changes can occur.

What Factors Affect Student Performance?

What is it about Susan that may have led to her poor performance in statistics? Is it her negative attitude toward math or her previous negative experiences with math courses? Susan attributes her performance to a lack of ability in math. Will this attribution lead her to engage in some nonadaptive behavior like procrastination? This subsection reviews some of the factors (and related social psychological theories) that may positively or negatively affect academic performance.

Attitudes and academic behavior. In a classic review of research examining the link between attitudes and behavior, Wicker (1969) indicated that attitudes and behavior might not always be consistent. Susan may value statistics as part of her training in psychology, but her behavior (i.e., going out with friends instead of studying) seems inconsistent with her positive attitude. In an effort to address such inconsistencies, Ajzen (1991, 2002) formulated the **theory of planned behavior** (see Figures in Chapters 2 and 8). The theory takes into account multiple determinants of behavior (attitudes, subjective norms, and perceived behavioral control) that predict a person's intention to behave in a particular fashion, and such behavioral intentions predict eventual behavior. Both behavioral beliefs (i.e., beliefs that an action will lead to a certain outcome) and the evaluation of the outcome comprise an *attitude toward the behavior.* For example, you may believe that working hard in college will lead to academic success, and that academic success is important; these two beliefs form your positive attitude toward doing course work. But, many behaviors are performed in a social context—we are aware of what others expect of us, and we may (or may not) be motivated to comply with these expectations. Therefore, in addition to our attitudes, *subjective norms* may also affect behavioral intention and behavior. You may be aware that your parents expect you to be a serious student and to work hard in college. Because you do not want to disappoint them, you are motivated to meet their expectations.

But, we do not always have control over whether we can, in fact, carry out the intended behavior that will lead to our desired outcome. *Perceived behavioral control* refers to the level of capability (how difficult the behavior is perceived to be) and controllability that we have over any intended behavior (Ajzen, 2002). For example, you would like to get good grades in college, and you know that good grades are looked on favorably by your family, friends, and professors. You know that to accomplish this, you must work hard by engaging in behaviors, such as keeping up with your readings, studying on a regular basis, and getting all assignments done. You may, however, still end up with a *C* average simply because you do not have good study skills, believe that you lack the ability to comprehend the material, or live in a noisy "party" dorm. If you lack the study skills needed to get good grades in college (or believe that you cannot develop such skills), you might not work very hard. That is, your intention to work hard and the degree to which you work hard will be diminished by your perceived lack of control. Recent research (e.g., Lipnevich, McCann, Krumm, Burrus, & Roberts, 2011; Singh, Granville, & Dika, 2002) has shown that attitudes, beliefs, and expectations about mathematics and science—*independent from actual ability*—can significantly affect students' achievement in these areas.

Using the theory of planned behavior as a framework, Sideridis and Padeliadu (2001) compared the importance of achieving good grades in elementary school children who were high-performing readers with that in elementary school children who were low-performing readers. Specifically, the researchers wanted to examine how the children's motivation to achieve good grades was related to the key components of the theory of planned behavior: (a) attitudes toward high academic achievement (beliefs about the consequences of studying and evaluation of the importance of doing well in school); (b) subjective norms about high academic performance (beliefs about the importance that others place on the children's academic performance and how motivated the children are to comply with others' expectations); (c) perceived behavioral control (how easy or difficult the children view studying to be); (d) behavioral intention (how determined the children are to study hard to achieve high grades); and (e) actual academic performance in language and mathematics.

Sideridis and Padeliadu (2001) found that high- and low-performing readers had very different profiles based on the theory of planned behavior. Compared with high-performing readers, low-performing readers undervalued the importance of being a good student, expressed weaker intentions to work hard to achieve, perceived weaker subjective norms about the importance of academic achievement, and demonstrated poorer academic performance. It seemed that the perceived importance of doing well in school predicted attitudes about studying, and beliefs about the consequences of working hard that was linked to perceived control over the ability to achieve good grades, could also be related to the perception of subjective norms. What does this mean for teachers, students, and their parents? It means that if one can increase the importance of learning in students, and also increase students' beliefs about their abilities and the amount of control they have over their academic outcomes, students will want to work harder (behavioral intention) to achieve better grades.

Academic self-concept and performance. At first glance, the students whom we read about in the opening vignette and Susan, our hapless statistics student, may have little in common—one is a success story, and the other is not. In both cases,

however, students' experiences in school changed the way that they saw themselves. Due to their positive interactions with researchers, professionals, and other students in the mentorship program, the minority students could now picture themselves in health or science professions and believed that they could be successful in university. The way in which they saw themselves changed, and their grades and aspirations shifted accordingly. In contrast, Susan believes that she just "can't do math." She attributes her poor performance to a lack of mathematical aptitude, expects to fail any upcoming tests in statistics, and will feel embarrassed by her performance (especially if other students do well). Will Susan be motivated to study harder? Probably not—as she sees little point to it. She might even be tempted to drop the course or change her area of study altogether.

The feelings, attitudes, and perceptions that students hold about their academic ability—especially when compared with those of other students—is called **academic self-concept** (Cokley, 2000; Cokley & Patel, 2007). Academic self-concept has been found to affect motivation and performance in school settings (*self-enhancement effect*), and similarly, good performance in school leads to a more positive academic self-concept (*skill development effect*). Therefore, academic self-concept and academic achievement have a reciprocal relationship, with academic self-concept both the cause and the effect of academic achievement (Cokley & Patel, 2007; Guay, Marsh, & Boivin, 2003; Marsh, Trautwein, Lüdtke, Köller, & Baumert, 2005). Moreover, there is evidence that academic self-concept can differ on the basis of a student's age, gender, or ethnicity. For example, in a sample of elementary school children, Guay and colleagues (2003) found that as children grow older, their academic self-concept becomes more stable and is more strongly tied with academic achievement. This implies that it is important for teachers to create a classroom environment that not only enhances students' positive beliefs about their scholastic skills, but also gives them constructive feedback concerning their performance.

Although it is extremely important to help elementary and high school students develop a positive academic self-concept so that they do well in school, put more effort into tasks, and set higher goals, it does not mean that we should forget about academic self-concept when students enter college. Susan certainly has been affected by her beliefs and expectations concerning her math ability (very likely developed from previous negative experiences in similar circumstances). These beliefs subsequently influenced the amount of effort she put into the requirements of her statistics course, and quite possibly will influence decisions about her major. Her academic self-concept (especially with respect to math ability) will be further affected if she learns that others in her class are having less difficulty with statistics. Rodriguez (2009) examined not only the extent to which academic self-concept and outcome expectations predicted academic attitudes (perceived usefulness and importance of course material) and academic performance in undergraduate business students, but also how academic self-concept

predicted the learning strategies that these students elected to use. He found that students who had high academic self-concepts were more likely to use learning strategies that promoted more in-depth understanding of the material, integration of concepts, and a more critical approach to the course content. Not surprisingly, these strategies predicted significantly better academic attitudes and performance. Therefore, college instructors should design courses and learning tasks that promote more positive beliefs and a sense of competency early in a student's program of study. These in turn will motivate students to employ more effective learning strategies, set higher academic goals, and place greater importance on the value of their education—all of which lead to greater academic success. Students who do not develop a positive academic self-concept (like Susan) become disinterested in their education, use more ineffective learning strategies, and show poorer academic performance—all of which fuel an even more negative academic self-concept (Marsh et al., 2005; Rodriguez, 2009).

CULTURE CAPSULE

The Role of Culture in Academic Self-Concept and Achievement

Academic self-concept and achievement is an especially critical issue for minority students. Recall that the minority students in the opening vignette changed the way they saw themselves due to their experiences in the mentorship program. We can guess that their academic self-concept became consistent with being a university student; that is, they came to "identify" with being in an academic environment. As we saw earlier, this change in their academic self-concept should bring with it higher motivation to succeed, more involvement in learning tasks, and greater importance placed on academic success.

Unfortunately, this does not happen for students in all cultural groups. Kevin Cokley and his colleagues (Cokley, 2000, 2002; Cokley, McClain, Jones, & Johnson, 2012; Cokley & Moore, 2007) have studied how academic self-concept is related to a variety of factors, such as racial and ethnic identity, psychological disengagement, and academic outcomes in African American students. In particular, there is concern over the achievement gap between African American men and women: not only are African American women more likely to enroll in college than their male counterparts, they outperform African American men and earn two-thirds of the Bachelor's degrees awarded to African Americans (Cokley & Moore, 2007; U.S. Department of Education, 2013).

(Continued)

(Continued)

According to Cokley (2002) and others (e.g., Steele & Aronson, 1995), African American students begin school with a positive outlook and are motivated to succeed; however, as these students move through the education system, their identification with academics, their motivation to do well, and their enjoyment of school all decrease significantly. Why? And why are African American *males* particularly vulnerable? As it turns out, teachers tend to hold lower expectations for them, and are more likely to take punitive action against them for their conduct. The students, themselves, may be struggling to remain engaged in an educational system that they perceive to be hostile toward them, as well as lacking in cultural relevancy and high-achieving Black male role models (Cokley, 2002; Cokley et al., 2012; Cokley & Moore, 2007; Steele & Aronson, 1995). We will get into how the expectations of others may affect a student's academic success later in the chapter, but for now we can view this "disconnect" between one's academic self-concept and success in school as *academic disidentification* (Cokley, 2002; Cokley & Moore, 2007; Steele & Aronson, 1995).

To explore the phenomenon of academic disidentification, Cokley (2002) compared the relationship between academic self-concept and academic performance (GPA) in two groups of college students—359 African American students and 229 European American students—representing different years of enrollment and a variety of undergraduate programs. Consistent with our earlier discussion, there was a positive correlation between academic self-concept and GPA for both groups of students. When scores for academic self-concept by ethnicity were examined, however, African American students had significantly less positive academic self-concept scores when compared to European Americans. Furthermore, when Cokley (2002) examined the correlation of academic self-concept and performance by year of enrollment and by gender, he found that the correlation sharply *decreased* for African American males, stayed the *same* for African American females and European American males, and *increased* for European American females. This implies that the educational environment can have a profound effect on how students see themselves—whether positive or negative. If faced with an unwelcoming cultural climate, the lower expectations of others about one's ethnic group, and the occasional failure at a task, a student may come to believe that school (or a specific domain within school like mathematics) does not define him or her and is not important. Their self-concept shifts away from the academic realm to a nonacademic sphere, and hence academic disidentification (Cokley, 2002; Steele, 1997).

Procrastination and self-handicapping in school. The development of negative attitudes toward school and downplaying the importance of academic success may lead students to engage in a variety of behaviors that protect their self-concept or enhance their self-image. These ***self-serving strategies*** (see also Chapter 5) may seem harmless, positive, and even adaptive at first, but many social psychologists believe that in the long run self-serving strategies may be self-defeating (Baumeister & Scher, 1988). Two examples of self-defeating strategies commonly used by students are procrastination and self-handicapping (a variable that was considered in Chapter 5 in the context of personal uses of social psychology).

Procrastination, defined as delaying the completion of a task or intended course of action, can be either an adaptive or a maladaptive coping strategy depending on one's reasons for engaging in it and the type of student that you are

(Ferrari, 2001; Steel, 2007). If you have ever put off working on a term paper or preparing for an upcoming test, you are not alone: Estimates show that a large majority of college students procrastinate in their academic work at least some of the time (Steel, 2007). We all know students who state that they like working under the pressure of an approaching deadline and feel that they produce far better work by "pulling an all-nighter"—and it might be true for those students. We do, however, know many more students who procrastinate because they are afraid of failing (and the impact that failure would have on their academic self-concept), feel that they do not have the skills to complete the task, or just find the assigned tasks to be unpleasant.

Recent researchers (e.g., Burnam, Komarraju, Hamel, & Nadler, 2014; Howell & Watson, 2007; Klassen, Krawchuk, & Rajani, 2008) have found that procrastination is primarily a motivational issue, related to the self-regulation of behavior. Being able to self-regulate behavior and being intrinsically motivated is important to how tasks are managed, planned, and completed. Students who tend to be more intrinsically motivated are able to organize their time more effectively, and are better able to devote their cognitive efforts and attention toward learning (Burnam et al., 2014; Howell & Watson, 2007). Burnam et al. (2014) found that students who scored higher on self-determined motivation were less likely to procrastinate and more likely to achieve higher grades than their less motivated counterparts due to being more organized, having higher personal standards, and not experiencing procrastination as a problem behavior. This means that intrinsically motivated students are not only unlikely to procrastinate, but if they do, they do not suffer the ill effects that we usually associate with procrastination, such as poor quality of work, incomplete/late assignments, and lower grades. It seems that less competent or less intrinsically motivated students are unable to self-regulate their behavior, and therefore are more likely to engage in procrastination as a way of avoiding expected negative outcomes, such as academic failure and the loss of self-esteem

(Burnam et al., 2014; Ferrari, 2001; Howell & Watson, 2007; Kim & Seo, 2015).

In their review of 33 studies, Kim and Seo (2015) confirmed that procrastination was negatively associated with academic performance, but that the reasons for the poor performance found in students who procrastinate could be explained by the association of procrastination with a number of academic-related variables, such as specific context, test anxiety, low self-efficacy, and self-handicapping (Beck, Koons, & Milgrim, 2000; Burnam et al., 2014; Klassen et al., 2008). For example, our statistics student, Susan, may procrastinate due to negative feelings toward mathematics, and so she may devote more of her energies instead toward courses that she enjoys and in which she feels that she can perform better (self-efficacy). Susan may also devote more time to nonacademic (but seemingly more attractive) pursuits, such as going out with friends or catching up on episodes of a favorite TV show instead of studying for her upcoming statistics test. The latter strategy is called **self-handicapping**, and it is one strategy that maladaptive procrastinators (like Susan) often use. Indeed, procrastination and self-handicapping are very much linked together in producing poor academic outcomes (Beck et al., 2000; Ferrari, 2001).

Self-handicapping refers to creating barriers to successful performance prior to (or simultaneous with) an achievement task (Berglas & Jones, 1978; Urdan, 2004; Urdan & Midgley, 2001). In essence, people handicap their own performance on a task so that they have a ready excuse for failure. In this way, self-handicapping not only reduces the cost of failure by shifting blame away from individuals, but also enhances the value of success because success occurred despite the handicap. Susan has a statistics test coming up and is afraid that no matter how hard she studies, she will do poorly on the test. By choosing to go out with friends the night before the test, she has not only put off studying until the last possible moment (procrastination), but she now has time to study for only a few hours. Handicapping her own performance has two advantages for Susan: If she fails the test, she can attribute her poor performance to not studying enough and being out with friends the night before. If she happens to do well on the test, she can feel especially pleased about her good performance because she attained it under handicapped conditions. Either way, Susan protects her self-esteem from yet another confirmation of her inability to do math (this relates to attributional styles that you can read more about in Chapter 17).

Martin, Marsh, Williamson, and Debus (2003) conducted a qualitative study to gain a better understanding of the experiences of students who engage in self-handicapping behavior. They interviewed twenty-four first year university students who scored very high or very low on a questionnaire measure of self-handicapping. The high self-handicappers (i.e., students who scored very high on self-handicapping behavior) described engaging in a range of "pointless time wasting" activities before a test or assignment, such as cleaning the fish tank, organizing their wardrobe, and even alphabetizing their books! The high self-handicappers also described feeling like this behavior was beyond their control. Students who often engaged in self-handicapping behaviors tended to talk about school as a competitive environment, whereas the low self-handicappers didn't describe school in this way. Instead, low self-handicappers described the purpose of school as mastering the material, not beating the other students. Understanding more about self-handicapping through a qualitative study can help researchers and educators design learning environments where self-handicapping behavior is not as likely. For example, collaborative as opposed to competitive environments could be created to decrease students' perceptions of their need to protect their self-esteem by outperforming the other students. Collaborative learning environments focus on helping students master a task through working together with other students. If students aren't afraid of having to compete with others, they may be less likely to go to extreme lengths to protect themselves from the fear of failure through self-handicapping.

Although self-handicapping might sound like a good strategy, a number of researchers (e.g.,

Thompson, 1994; Urdan & Midgley, 2001; Zuckerman, Kieffer, & Knee, 1998) noted that repeated use of self-handicapping can have negative effects on academic self-concept, academic performance, and other measures of achievement over the long term. Murray and Warden (1992) warned that reliance on self-handicapping as a strategy in academic settings may interfere with being able to take responsibility for one's performance even when it is a successful outcome. Zuckerman and colleagues (1998) examined the relationship between self-handicapping and several measures of academic adjustment, such as academic performance, coping strategies, and self-esteem in a large sample of undergraduate students over a period of one year. High self-handicappers were found to employ more negative coping strategies (e.g., psychological and behavioral disengagement, negative self-focus) and performed less well academically than students who were low self-handicappers. Not only did high self-handicappers do less well academically than their low self-handicapping counterparts, they also employed less effective study habits. Finally, high self-handicappers showed poorer adjustment to college over time, which led them to rely even further on self-handicapping as a method for coping. Thus, a cycle was created in which self-handicapping and poor adjustment in an academic setting reinforced one another.

Given that self-handicapping may have detrimental long-term effects, what can educators do to encourage students to put effort into their academic work even if the students may fail at some tasks? How can teachers help students to avoid attributing poor performance to a lack of ability, and instead to view it as a normal part of the learning process? Surprisingly, some classroom environments actually may promote the use of self-handicapping (Turner et al., 2002; Urdan, Midgley, & Anderman, 1998). Urdan and colleagues (1998) found that students in classrooms where ability and competition were emphasized were more likely to report using self-handicapping strategies than were students in classrooms where individual mastery, effort, and learning were emphasized. When the classroom structure is designed to emphasize the idea that performance is linked to ability, students who believe that they are not very good will be more likely to engage in strategies (e.g., self-handicapping) that protect their academic self-concepts.

To create a classroom environment that emphasizes individual mastery and effort rather than ability and performance, teachers have used instructional strategies, such as providing students with choices among learning tasks, creating multiple ways in which students can demonstrate their knowledge about a topic, and helping students to set short-term achievable (but still challenging) learning goals. For example, Turner and colleagues (2002) found that sixth-grade students in mathematics classes were less likely to engage in self-handicapping

and other avoidant behaviors when they were in classrooms where teachers emphasized learning, motivated students to demonstrate new skills, and accentuated enjoyment of the material. Teachers in these classrooms told students not to feel ashamed when they could not understand some of the math and that it was OK to make mistakes (see Figure 9.1).

How Can Student Performance Be Improved?

The research on self-handicapping, procrastination, and academic self-concept suggests that improving students' performance may be accomplished by changing the reward contingencies

Figure 9.1   A Teacher Helping to Make Learning Fun

SOURCE: Photo courtesy of Cassandra Lee Davis.

and teaching strategies in the classroom. In other words, if a teacher wants to change a student's behavior, he/she might want to change the way that learning requirements are communicated to students or change the amount of control given to students over their learning. Of course, the focus on the interactions between the individual and the situation reflects the social psychological perspective. The following sections describe how the emphasis on grades and competition in a classroom can adversely affect students' motivation to learn and what educators can do to prevent this from happening.

Intrinsic motivation and external rewards. It is generally believed that in an *intrinsically oriented* system, people will be inherently motivated to engage in an activity, whether it is a hobby, an exercise, or something new to be learned. That is, individuals will engage in this behavior not for external rewards (e.g., grades, recognition, fame), but rather because they simply enjoy engaging in the activity. It is also known that providing large tangible rewards for an activity may backfire and undermine people's intrinsic motivation for the activity (Deci & Ryan, 1985; Freedman,

Cunnigham, & Krismer, 1992; Lepper & Henderlong, 2000).

Why does such undermining occur? Why would people draw less intrinsic enjoyment from an activity when they receive external rewards for engaging in it? And what does this have to do with school and with the way in which we educate children? Deci and Ryan (1985, 2012) and others (e.g., Lepper & Henderlong, 2000; Tang & Hall, 1995) have argued that schools are very extrinsically oriented. You may remember a teacher giving you a "gold star" when you did well on a school project, or you may recall being embarrassed in front of others when you did poorly. Gold stars, grades, ranks in class, and competition all serve to focus children on the extrinsic aspects of learning. The unintended message conveyed to students is that working on academic tasks is not interesting or is of little value, and that rewards are needed to get people to learn (Deci & Ryan, 1985; Freedman et al., 1992; Lepper & Henderlong, 2000). Moreover, this message is more pronounced as children progress through the school system, leading to a maladaptive shift in students' approach to learning—from an intrinsic to an extrinsic orientation.

FOCUS ON RESEARCH

Intrinsic Motivation, Learning, and Autonomy Support in the Classroom

Previous research has found that students will be more intrinsically motivated, exhibit more autonomy and self-regulation, and be more engaged in learning when their classroom environment minimizes external incentives (e.g., grades), is not too controlling or restrictive (e.g., deadline oriented), and is one in which students' learning is more self-directed rather than teacher-directed (Deci & Ryan, 2012; Reeve, 2004; Vansteenkiste, Simons, Lens, Sheldon, & Deci, 2004). Sungur and Tekkaya (2006) investigated the effectiveness of a teaching strategy called *problem-based learning (PBL)* on the development of intrinsic goals and self-regulated learning of 10th-grade students. PBL places the responsibility on students to access necessary information, to structure and achieve learning goals, and to monitor their understanding of the material. The effectiveness of PBL was compared to traditional instruction which involves the teacher delivering lectures, providing textbook readings, and shaping classroom discussions through questions and explanations.

In a quasi-experimental design, Sungur and Tekkaya (2006) used two preexisting biology classes (both led by the same teacher) and assigned one class to the PBL condition while the other class received the traditional instruction method. Students in each of the classes met for four 45-minute sessions per week for six weeks, and were given almost identical course syllabi outlining the course content that was to be covered in the class. Students were measured, both pre- and posttest, on intrinsic and extrinsic goal orientation, how they perceived the value of the course content, self-efficacy, and on their use of various learning strategies (e.g., cognitive elaboration, critical thinking, self-regulation, managing time, peer-assisted learning, and help seeking behavior).

Results from the pretest showed that there were no preexisting differences on any of the dependent measures between the two classes. Posttest measures, however, indicated a number of differences between the two groups. PBL students reported engaging in tasks for intrinsic reasons, such as curiosity and mastery, and were more likely to perceive biology as interesting, important, and useful than students in the traditional group. Furthermore, students in the PBL condition reported greater use of cognitive strategies, such as critical thinking, integration of new material to help answer questions, problem-solving, and generative note-taking than students in the traditional learning group. In helping to learn the material, students in the PBL group also tended to collaborate with their peers to a greater extent—and were more appreciative of working with their classmates than those in the traditional group.

One current theory that helps to explain the connection between students' motivation and academic behavior is Deci and Ryan's (1985) **self-determination theory**. Self-determination is the degree to which an individual sees him or herself as being autonomous, being able to make choices and act on those choices, having a feeling of belonging to others in the social environment, and being able to self-regulate their behaviors without feeling pressured to behave in a particular manner (Deci & Ryan, 1985). In other words, does a student's desire to learn a task come from within, or is it imposed and controlled from the outside by teachers, parents, or society? Self-determination is clearly seen in intrinsically motivated behavior. For example, a student may spontaneously choose to do some extra reading on a topic without thought of a better grade in the course in order to understand more about a concept. Intrinsic motivation, however, occupies only one end of the self-determination continuum. As we move away from pure intrinsic motivation, we encounter behaviors that are more extrinsically motivated (see Table 9.1). **External regulation**, at the other end of the continuum, is normally what we would think of as pure extrinsic motivation. In

this case, the student would work on an assignment to simply obtain a good grade and avoid punishment, and would take no pleasure from engaging in the work.

Between intrinsic motivation and external regulation, Deci and Ryan (1985; Ryan & Deci, 2004) have identified three intermediary levels of extrinsic motivation: **integrated regulation**, **identified regulation**, and **introjected regulation**. Integrated regulation occurs when individuals integrate both internal and external information into a coherent set of values, goals, and priorities, and these become a part of the self. In this case, being a "good student" becomes part of the person's self-concept, and he or she has internalized external priorities (Ryan & Deci, 2004). In identified regulation, individuals engage in activities to help them achieve goals that have become important to them. This is a more utilitarian view of education. A student may choose to complete assignments and study hard for tests, because this helps move the individual toward achieving a goal (e.g., obtaining a degree), and not because he or she has an intrinsic interest in learning. In introjected regulation, the individual is ruled by feelings of "should" and "ought" (Ryan & Deci, 2004). In this case, an individual's

Table 9.1   Self-Determination Theory: Examples of Intrinsic and Extrinsic Motivation

Regulatory Styles	Amotivation	Extrinsic Motivation				Intrinsic Motivation
		External Regulation	Introjected Regulation	Identified Regulation	Integrated Regulation	
Associated Processes	Low perceived competence; low self-efficacy	Salience of extrinsic rewards or punishments; compliance	Focus on approval from self and others	Valuing of activities and goals	Congruence of goals within self-schema	Pure interest in activity; inherent satisfaction
Response to Question: *Why do I go to university?*	I really don't know why I'm in university and I don't care.	I need a university degree to get a high-paying job.	My family expects me to attend, and I don't want to let them down.	A university education will help prepare me for my desired career.	It is important to have a university education to participate fully in our society.	*I love to learn new things.*

SOURCE: Adapted from Ryan and Deci (2000).

choices are not integrated into the self, and the choices are still very much controlled from outside the individual. So, a student may study for an exam to avoid a bad grade, but also because he or she would feel bad about disappointing their parents. Finally, there is **amotivation**, which falls somewhat outside the self-determination continuum. Here the student will be plagued by feelings of low self-efficacy, incompetence, and a sense that there is little connection between her actions and her outcomes.

The degree to which students feel self-determined, the messages that they receive from others about what is important, and how they end up defining successful performance will influence the academic goals that they adopt. This is the basis of **achievement goal theory** which focuses on the reasons students have for trying to succeed in school (Elliot & McGregor, 2001; Harackiewicz, Barron, & Elliot, 1998; Urdan & Schoenfelder, 2006). Basically, a student may pursue two types of goals: **mastery** and **performance**. When students adopt mastery goals, they focus on learning and developing competence in a particular area. This often includes pursuing

school tasks that are challenging, not giving up easily when faced with difficulties, and periodically asking themselves, "Have I learned?" When students adopt performance goals, they also want to develop competence in a particular area, but they do it to demonstrate their ability relative to others. These students are also more likely to avoid difficult tasks because there is a potential for failure to occur. A student who is performance-oriented may ask him or herself, "How am I doing compared to others in the class?" (Harackiewicz et al., 1998; Urdan & Schoenfelder, 2006).

Mastery goals are typically associated with better study habits, use of more elaborative learning strategies, and greater interest in school when compared to performance goals (Harackiewicz et al., 1998; Harackiewicz, Barron, Pintrich, Elliot, & Thrash, 2002a). Therefore, we would assume that mastery goals are better for students than performance goals. That is not entirely true. The finding that performance goals do not always result in poor academic performance (as one would have expected) has led to the incorporation of the **approach** and **avoidance** dimension to the mastery and performance goal distinction (Elliot & McGregor, 2001; Harackiewicz et al., 2002a; Senko, Hulleman, & Harackiewicz, 2011). Mastery goals are now divided up into two categories: mastery-approach (e.g., striving to learn or improve skills) and mastery-avoidance (e.g., trying to avoid losing one's competence or fear of declining skills). Similarly, performance goals are divided into performance-approach (e.g., trying to appear/do better than others) and performance-avoidance (e.g., wanting to avoid failure or appearing worse than others). The avoidance aspect, whether mastery or performance oriented, is linked to poorer academic outcomes, whereas the approach dimension is tied to better academic outcomes. For example, both mastery-avoidance and performance-avoidance goals are linked to high anxiety and low achievement; and performance-avoidance goals, in particular, are associated with self-handicapping (see Senko et al., 2011, for a review). On the other hand, performance-approach goals are associated with good academic performance and positive academic self-concept, whereas only mastery-approach goals are linked to the use of in-depth learning strategies and intrinsic motivation (Harackiewicz et al., 2002a).

As you have probably already figured out, both self-determination theory and achievement goal theory have significant implications for the way in which we structure the classroom environment, for how we encourage students to become interested in learning, and for getting students to stay in school. Using self-determination theory as a basis, Vallerand, Fortier, and Guay (1997) examined how different types of motivation were related to dropout rates in high school students. Those who exhibited lower levels of self-determined motivation (i.e., intrinsic motivation, integrated regulation, or identified regulation) were not only more likely to express an intention to drop out of high school, but were also more likely to follow through with that intention. One critical element in Vallerand and colleagues' (1997) study was how students' motivation to be engaged in school was affected by their perceptions of others in the school environment

(teachers, parents, and school administrators). If students felt that their teachers (for example) encouraged them to make their own decisions concerning academic activities and believed that they had some degree of control over their schoolwork, then students felt more competent and exhibited a higher level of self-determination and, consequently, a lower intention to leave school.

In a longitudinal study, Harackiewicz, Barron, Tauer, and Elliot (2002b) investigated the contribution of achievement goals to academic outcomes over the course of students' college careers. Specifically, the researchers examined how mastery goals, performance-approach, and performance-avoidance goals were related to interest in psychology, enjoyment of classes, and grades in 471 students who had been enrolled in Introductory Psychology at the beginning of the study. Harackiewicz et al. (2002b) found that in both the short-term (one semester) and long-term (four to seven years), performance-approach goals positively predicted grades whereas performance-avoidance goals had a negative effect on grades. Overall, mastery goals were not related to grades; however, they were positively related to enjoyment of courses and continued interest in taking psychology courses. The researchers concluded that students may stick to a discipline when they have both an intrinsic interest in the program (mastery) and can demonstrate competence in the area (performance). Furthermore, as Harackiewicz et al. (2002b) argue, it may be an adaptive motivational strategy for students to adopt both types of goals. When you think about all the courses that you have to take as part of your degree program, would you really do all this if you did not want to learn more about the topics? You must, however, also be practical: grades are emphasized throughout your college career and they are an important factor in allowing you to graduate or apply to a professional school for further education.

So, what all of this tells us is that both mastering concepts (i.e., in-depth learning) and a perception of competence (i.e., grades, how one compares to others) are important for students' academic development. We also know that too much of an emphasis on grades, rewards, and competition has been known to undermine intrinsic motivation, mastery goal orientation, and self-determination (Deci & Ryan, 1985, 2012; Harackiewicz et al., 1998). *How, then, do we design the classroom environment so that there is a focus on learning rather than predominately on extrinsic factors?*

If we want to use self-determination theory as a basis for structuring rewards in a classroom setting, Johnmarshall Reeve and his colleagues (Reeve, 2004; Reeve, Ryan, Deci, & Jang, 2008) suggest strategies that teachers can use to promote autonomy and self-regulated learning in students—and thereby maintain intrinsic motivation among students. For example, rather than behaving in ways that may be perceived to be controlling by students, teachers need to give students more time to engage in independent work, praise the quality of the work being produced (rather than its completion and meeting deadlines), spend more time listening to students' questions, provide more rationales for engaging in particular tasks, and give feedback that focuses on improving mastery of a task. Even the physical environment of the classroom can have an impact on students' motivation to learn. For example in autonomy-oriented classrooms, students rather than the teacher are positioned closer to the learning materials so that they may freely access these materials (Reeve, 2004; Reeve et al., 2008). All of these actions help students to maintain a sense of control over their learning, believe that their actions (and outcomes) come from them and are not imposed on them by others, and develop a sense of competence in academic tasks. In essence, the classroom environment and learning itself become rewarding for students.

FOCUS ON INTERVENTION

Increasing Mastery Goal Orientation in Physical Education

Receiving feedback is part of the learning process. As students, we can remember times when a teacher gave us encouragement and positive feedback on a test, project, or other school-related task. And yes, sometimes, we received negative feedback when our attempts did not turn out so well. Do you recall how the positive and negative feedback made you feel? Did it increase or decrease your motivation on subsequent school tasks? Did it change how you perceived or valued those activities?

Erturan-İlker (2014) investigated the differential effects of positive and negative feedback on students' achievement goals and perceived motivational climate in a physical education class. Forty-seven students from the 9th grade who were taking a physical education course as a required part of their curriculum served as participants. The intervention took place over six weeks (90 minutes per week) in which students were to learn volleyball skills through practices, drills, and exercises. Feedback was provided by the teacher to each student individually, and was delivered either during or immediately after a student completed a task. Students were given an average of eight feedback comments per lesson. Comments focused on students' performance, ability and effort, with half of the participants receiving positive feedback (e.g., "You performed very well"), and the other half of the participants receiving negative feedback (e.g., "Your effort was poor"). Students were given pre- and post-intervention measures relating to goal orientation (i.e., mastery approach, performance-approach, performance-avoidance), and how students perceived the motivation of the classroom and teacher (i.e., whether a mastery, performance-approach, or performance-avoidance orientation was emphasized/valued).

Results showed that students who received the positive feedback from their teacher showed a significant increase in their mastery and performance-approach goals and a decrease in their performance-avoidance goals. Performance-avoidance goals, however, increased in the negative feedback group. That is, students in the negative feedback group were more concerned about being worse (instead of being better) than other students rather than focusing on learning volleyball skills. Moreover, students in the positive feedback group perceived the classroom climate to be more mastery (learning) oriented than students in the negative feedback group. The latter group perceived the classroom climate to be more oriented toward performance rather than learning. Erturan-İlker also noted that feedback in general, regardless of whether it was positive or negative, tended to make students feel that the classroom was more performance-approach oriented.

The results of this program have two implications for teachers in physical education: (1) giving positive feedback to students not only increases the likelihood that they will adopt mastery goals, but that they will see the classroom environment as one in which learning (rather than only performance) is valued; and (2) providing students with feedback of any sort helps them to gauge their learning and performance, and to perceive tasks as positive challenges rather than threats.

Students comparing themselves to other students. The previous section highlighted the fact that the classroom is an environment in which students are almost constantly evaluating themselves in comparison to others. As students, we are regularly given information not only about our own performance, but also about the performance of others in class. Even in classrooms which are designed to de-emphasize competition, students still compare their efforts, abilities, and outcomes to those of their peers (Dijkstra, Kuyper, van der Werf, Buunk, & van der Zee, 2008). In assessing our performance and abilities according to Festinger's (1954) **social comparison theory**, we may use two types of standards: objective and social. According to this theory, in the absence of an objective standard (e.g., the proportion of correct responses on a test), we are likely to judge our performance and abilities (as well as our personality characteristics) in comparison with those of other people in our environment (e.g., "Am I smart?" "Do I have many friends?"). Usually, comparisons are made with others who are similar or close to us in terms of the relevant characteristics (called *lateral comparisons*). Comparisons also may be made with people who are slightly better than we are on

particular abilities and traits (called *upward social comparisons*), or with people who are worse off than we are (called *downward social comparisons*). The comparisons that we choose serve not only different purposes, but also have different effects on us. If our goal is to make ourselves feel better (*self-enhancement*), then we will engage in downward social comparisons. Downward social comparisons will occur when we feel threatened, and serve a self-protective purpose by making us feel better about our current abilities, achievements, and personal attributes (Gibbons et al., 2002). Upward social comparisons, on the other hand, occur when we are motivated to better our performance *(self-improvement)* and help us set higher goals by providing information to us about what we are capable of achieving (Blanton, Buunk, Gibbons, & Kuyper, 1999; Dijkstra et al., 2008; Wehrens, Kuyper, Dijkstra, Buunk, & van der Werf, 2010).

Let us say that you received a 75% on a math test, whereas a classmate of yours received a 93% on the test. Comparing your performance with that of your classmate, you may end up feeling bad even though the grade you received was a fairly good one. Perhaps you are disappointed with yourself because you had expected to do better than a 75%. As a result, you may simply choose to compare yourself to another class-mate—one who got an 82%. Or, you could discuss the test results with your higher-performing classmates and get useful information on how to improve your grade on the next test. The 75% you received may motivate you to try harder the next time by giving you a sense of what you are capable of achieving and by raising your self-confidence and feelings of self-efficacy. Or, finally, you may simply decide not to worry about your math performance anymore by devaluing the importance of mathematical competence, and choosing instead to focus on how you compare to your classmates in terms of writing ability. Indeed, researchers have noted that making social comparisons can have emotional, cognitive, and behavioral consequences (Dijkstra et al., 2008; Wehrens et al., 2010). For example, although making upward social comparisons can help a student improve his/her future performance, it can also increase a student's anxiety levels and be detrimental to his/her academic self-concept, especially when that student is placed in a high-achieving class.

What all this means is that there are a number of possible outcomes when students engage in social comparisons that go beyond simply making upward or downward social comparisons. Recent studies (e.g., Blanton et al., 1999; Boissicat, Pansu, Bouffard, & Cottin, 2012; Dijkstra, 2008; Gibbons et al., 2002; Lane & Gibbons, 2007) have revealed that students' choice of comparison changes as children get older, and may change depending on the specific circumstances (i.e., positive or negative feedback about academic performance), the classroom context (range of abilities present in the classroom), or the degree to which a student identifies with others in the class. Boissicat et al. (2012), for instance, noted that the more a student identifies with lower-performing classmates and the more they see themselves as different from their more successful classmates, the less academically competent they will feel. The type and level of comparison that a student makes is very often associated not only with available comparison targets, but also with a student's need to maintain his or her self-esteem and self-concept.

Although classrooms at first glance may seem to be homogeneous entities with all children close in abilities and with similar chances to achieve, the reality is that classrooms are often made up of children of very different backgrounds, abilities to learn, and opportunities to succeed. What happens, for example, when a classroom is made up of children from different ethnic and socioeconomic backgrounds? An important factor to consider is the degree to which students feel that they have control over their performance and ability. The theory of planned behavior, achievement goal theory, and self-determination theory all emphasize the need for students to view their academic achievement as under their own control in order for optimal motivation and learning to occur. Being exposed to higher performing peers may provide information to students on how to improve, may increase motivation to improve, and may even help a student set higher goals for the future (Blanton et al., 1999; Dijkstra et al., 2008; Wehrens et al., 2010). However, it is critical that students perceive that it is not only important to improve, but also *possible* to improve (Huguet, Dumas, Monteil, & Genestoux, 2001; Wehrens et al., 2010). Keil, McClintock, Kramer, and Platow (1990) argued that the emphasis on social comparison standards and procedures in educational settings may be detrimental to children who consistently perform more poorly than their peers. After repeated lack of improvement in their academic performance, these students may experience less confidence in their abilities, may lose their motivation on academic tasks, and may experience lowered feelings of self-worth, consequently leading to lower academic achievement.

Children with learning disabilities are one group of students faced with constant challenges in school. Renick and Harter (1989) found that social comparison processes played an important role in how elementary school students with learning disabilities perceived their academic competence when they compared themselves to their peers with normal achievement in a regular classroom and when they compared themselves to their peers with learning disabilities in their special needs classroom. The researchers also were interested in which group (the peers with normal achievement or the peers with learning disabilities) the students with learning disabilities spontaneously used as a comparison group. Students with learning disabilities reported that they perceived themselves to be more academically competent in the special needs classroom than in the regular classroom and that they spontaneously compared themselves with their regular classroom peers. A disturbing finding was that the students with learning disabilities' perceptions of their own academic competence decreased across the grades tested in the study (third through eighth grades), suggesting that as these students progress through school they become increasingly aware that there is a gap between their own academic performance and that of their peers with normal achievement, a gap that they may never be able to close. According to Renick and Harter, it is this knowledge that may have a detrimental effect on the self-perceptions and feelings of self-worth of children with learning disabilities.

In view of the fact that social comparison processes can have both positive and negative effects in the classroom, what can educators do to capitalize on the ego-boosting aspects of making comparisons, and thereby increase student achievement? The next section may offer some answers by exploring the interpersonal dynamics of the classroom.

INTERPERSONAL PROCESSES: TEACHERS AND STUDENTS INTERACTING

People spend many of their formative years in a school environment. Prior to college or university, they are in school approximately six hours a day, five days a week, and ten months a year, for about twelve consecutive years. Although many school administrators, educators, and researchers focus their attention on how the school environment influences the development of basic

academic skills, the capacity to acquire knowledge, and overall scholastic achievement, school also provides a medium for social and emotional development. Asp and Garbarino (1988) called school "the most pervasive socializing institution (outside of the family) in the lives of children" (p. 170). It should come as no surprise, then, that social psychologists have long been interested in how teachers and students interact in the school environment and how these interactions affect the development of individuals.

Teacher Expectations and Student Achievement

In 1968, Robert Rosenthal and Lenore Jacobson published *Pygmalion in the Classroom*, a study which generated not only excitement and criticism, but decades of research into the effects of teachers' expectations on students. In their classic experiment, Rosenthal and Jacobson told teachers early in the school year that based on the results of an IQ test, some of their students had above average academic potential, and would likely perform very well during the school year. In actuality, this group of students, labeled "bloomers," had been randomly selected and were on average no smarter than the other students in their classes. The teachers were unaware that the feedback they had been given was false and the students themselves were not told about the label given to them. By the end of the school year, the bloomers showed significant increases in their IQ scores when compared to students in the control condition. Remarkably, the teachers' expectations had come true. How did the improvement come about? Rosenthal and Jacobson suggested that because the teachers believed the bloomers to be above average students, they began to treat these students differently. In-class observations revealed that teachers provided the bloomers with the following:

- A warmer climate by giving them more attention, support, and encouragement
- More challenging material to learn

- More feedback, both positive and negative, on their schoolwork
- More opportunity to respond in class and a longer time to respond

It is important to note that the teachers did not deliberately set out to treat these students differently from others in their classrooms, and they felt that they had treated all students equally and fairly. On closer examination, Rosenthal and Jacobson's study was actually an illustration of Robert Merton's (1948) concept of self-fulfilling prophecy. **Self-fulfilling prophecy** refers to having expectations about another person that influences how you perceive and behave toward that person. Your expectations, and the behavior based on these expectations, in turn, affects the way in which that person behaves when interacting with you. In essence, the other person will behave in ways that confirm your expectations, leading to a strengthening of your beliefs and preconceived notions about that individual. Let's take an example. You are at a social gathering and are introduced to Joe, who you learn is a major in physical education. You might hold a number of ideas about the type of person who is a "phys ed" major: focused on bodybuilding, interested in sports, less academically inclined, and so on. These ideas will influence how you interact with Joe—you may discuss the success of the college football team, you may ask him about effective physical training strategies, or you may want to know what he thinks about the use of steroids in sports. Joe will have no other option but to respond to your questions and choice of topics, and you are unlikely to give Joe an opportunity to discuss his interest in classical music. As a result, your expectations and beliefs about people in physical education are confirmed, and become a self-fulfilling prophecy. What about Joe? Eventually, his self-concept may also be affected so that it is consistent with others' expectations of him.

Now, let's see how this works in a classroom setting. A student may respond to a teacher's high expectations by becoming more interested in schoolwork and working harder, all of which

lead to better academic performance. The teacher observes the student's behavior and is likely to conclude that his or her expectations regarding the student are correct and accurate. Thus, the cycle is complete and reinforced. Essentially, the teacher is changing the student's academic self-concept to conform to the teacher's own expectations and beliefs about the student. This, of course, has serious implications not only for the student's academic self-concept and achievement, but also for choices and decisions the student might make later in life (e.g., choice of occupation). It also may help to explain the changes in self-perception, performance, and future goals observed in the minority students in the opening vignette. The mentors held positive expectations for the students and provided them with a variety of learning opportunities and feedback that reflected these expectations. The result was the successful completion of research projects, a change in the way in which the students viewed their academic abilities, improved performance in high school courses, and higher academic aspirations.

Since Rosenthal and Jacobson's (1968) initial study, decades of research have further clarified the connection between teachers' expectations and the academic outcomes of students. For instance, recent reviews of research into this topic have consistently found only a small (albeit significant) effect of teachers' expectations on the academic achievement of students (Brophy, 1983; Jussim & Harber, 2005). Moreover, positive and negative expectations do not affect students to the same degree, and certain groups of students may be more affected by what teachers expect from them than others (Jussim & Harber, 2005; Rubie-Davies, Hattie, & Hamilton, 2006; Wood, Kaplan, & McLoyd, 2007). In their study of 98 teachers and about 1,500 students enrolled in 6th-grade math classes, Madon, Jussim, and Eccles (1997) examined the relationship between teachers' expectations (whether positive or negative) and the development of self-fulfilling prophecies in certain types of students. For instance, are students who have negative self-concepts or who perform poorly in school (low achievers) more susceptible to the expectations of teachers than are students who have positive self-concepts or who perform well in school (high achievers)? To address this question, teachers' perceptions of their students' self-concepts and their ability, effort, and performance concerning math were surveyed and examined in relation to their students' math achievement.

The results indicated that teachers' perceptions and expectations (whether positive or negative) predicted achievement more strongly for low achievers than for high achievers. That is, low achievers were more susceptible to what teachers thought of them than were high achievers. Why might this happen? Madon and colleagues (1997) suggested that the history of past school experiences (mostly negative) may make low-achieving students more sensitive to the expectations of teachers, thereby affecting their motivation and self-concepts more keenly. In particular, low-achieving students who for years have been deprived of rewarding school experiences may be inspired by teachers' positive expectations. On the other hand, students who are academically more successful may have many more psychological resources to draw on even when faced with teachers' negative expectations, and therefore are not as greatly affected by teachers' perceptions.

What happens to students' academic performance when teachers' expectations fall along racial or gender lines? Performance in a specific academic domain (e.g., math, science, sports) may be affected if that domain carries some special significance tied to a student's social identity. For example, teachers frequently hold negative expectations about the achievement of girls in mathematics and science. Similarly, teachers may expect that students from minority groups (e.g., African American, Latino, Indigenous) will perform more poorly in a number of academic areas when compared to White students (Madon et al., 1997; Rubie-Davies et al., 2006; Wood et al., 2007). For example, Wood et al. (2007) found that teachers held lower expectations for the academic achievement of African American

males than for their female counterparts across elementary and high school levels. Rubie-Davies et al. (2006) noted that teachers had lower expectations related to reading ability for Maori students than they did for all other ethnic groups in their classrooms, and thereby negatively affected the performance of these students by the end of the academic year. Very often, students in stigmatized groups also believe that they are less capable than their nonstigmatized peers and that the expectations of others may be an accurate reflection of their academic abilities (Wood et al., 2007). The anxiety that students feel when they are faced with expectations consistent with stereotypes about their group is called **stereotype threat** (Steele, 1997; Steele & Aronson, 1995). The fear that they will confirm a stereotype in the eyes of others has been shown to adversely affect students' academic motivation, self-concept, and academic performance (Lawrence, Crocker, & Dweck, 2005).

Using children from three elementary school grades (Grades 1, 3, and 5), McKown and Weinstein (2002) wanted to determine how different types of teacher expectations (under- or overestimates of students' academic abilities) were related to achievement in mathematics and reading for students in academically stigmatized groups (e.g., girls in math, African Americans in all subjects), and nonstigmatized groups (Caucasian children and boys). Specifically, they examined how teachers' expectations for children at the beginning of the school year were related to children's academic performance at the end of the school year. They found that the academic performance of children in the stigmatized groups was affected negatively by teachers' underestimates of their abilities, but was not affected positively by teachers' overestimates of their abilities. For example, in the third grade, African American children were 2.5 times as likely to confirm teacher underestimates of their reading ability compared to teacher overestimates of their reading ability. Caucasian children in the third grade, on the other hand, were only 0.5 times as likely to confirm teacher underestimates (compared to overestimates) of their reading ability.

It seemed, then, that children in the nonstigma-tized groups benefited from teachers' overestimates of their abilities and were not affected by teachers' underestimates of their abilities. An even more interesting (and disturbing) finding was that the expectancy effects on students' achievement either were consistent across elementary school grade (in the area of reading) or became greater over time (in the area of math). McKown and Weinstein suggest that as children become older, and familiar with the school setting, they are bet-ter able to perceive the expectations held by others about them and to be able to judge the accuracy of those beliefs. Unfortunately, this means that they also become aware of prejudice and general expectations concerning their social group.

FOCUS ON INTERVENTION

Reducing the Effects of Negative Teacher Expectations

Given what we know about the effects of teachers' expectations on students' academic achievement, what do we do about it? Is there a way in which we can counteract the negative effects that teacher expectations can have on academic performance, especially for students in marginalized groups?

One approach is to provide teachers with training to help them recognize the differential expec-tations that they may hold for high- and low-achieving students and to instruct them on how to engage in behaviors that reduce the disparity in students' achievement. The goal of the training is to improve the academic achievement of *all* students (Gottfredson, Marciniak, Birdseye, & Gottfredson, 1991). The Teacher Expectations and Student Achievement (TESA) program provides teachers with such training (Kerman, Kimball, & Martin, 1980). Recall that Rosenthal and Jacobson (1968) identified a number of teacher behaviors that reflected their expectations of students' abili-ties (e.g., giving "bloomers" more opportunity to respond in class). The TESA program focuses on 15 classroom behaviors that teachers commonly display when interacting with students of different achievement levels. The behaviors are similar to those observed by Rosenthal and Jacobson as being indicative of teachers' expectations of students. The behaviors are divided into three categories: (a) response opportunities (e.g., amount of time waiting for students to answer, complexity of questions directed at students), (b) feedback to students (e.g., amount of praise given for success, feedback given on tests and assignments), and (c) personal regard (e.g., number of positive interactions, amount of eye contact with students). Teacher training is provided in five 3-hour sessions, with each session focusing on one behavior from each category. Between sessions, each teacher observes and gives feedback on the classroom behavior of at least three other teachers, and that teacher is also observed teaching and giving feedback. The main goal of this training is to make teachers more aware of their expectations concerning students and to make them more sensitive to the way in which they respond to students.

Evaluations of the TESA program reveal that teachers and school personnel find the training to be very helpful, and teachers report making use of the strategies outlined in the program (Cantor, Kester, & Miller, 2000). In addition, the program has been shown to increase teachers' positive interactions with low-achieving students (Gottfredson et al., 1991). Finally, although the effects of this training do not always lead to increases in the achievement of minority students or poorly per-forming students (as theory and research would suggest), teachers report that students still develop more positive attitudes toward learning (Fenton & O'Leary, 1990).

Students Interacting With Other Students

Forming and maintaining friendships, acquiring leadership skills, learning how to resolve conflicts and cooperate with others, and developing a positive self-concept are all by-products of attending school. In the classroom, a child learns how to be not only a student, but also a member or leader of a group, and is exposed to the norms, language, and values of the community (Asp & Garbarino, 1988). From the standpoint of researchers and educators, these social, cognitive, and emotional skills prepare an individual for life outside of school, as well as enhancing academic achievement.

Academic effects of peer interaction. Children who experience social, behavioral, and emotional difficulties in school are at a disadvantage for reaching their academic potential. In particular, children who have poor peer relationships, where they are either actively rejected or ignored by their peers, fail to develop competency in many areas of their lives, including academic achievement (Bullock, 1992; Coolahan, Fantuzzo, Mendez, & McDermott, 2000; Véronneau & Vitaro, 2007). Simply playing with others helps a child to become socially competent, be more self-confident, and do better in school. Indeed, as early as elementary school developing positive peer relationships has been found to enhance students' academic self-concepts, achievement motivation, engagement in school, as well as overall performance (Ladd, Price, & Hart, 1988; Molloy, Gest, & Rulison, 2011; Véronneau, Vitaro, Brendgen, Dishion, & Tremblay, 2010). In particular, Molloy et al. (2011) found that peers have a significant effect on academic effort, motivation, and the development of skills as students proceed through middle school (i.e., Grades 5 to 7).

But, what happens when no one wants to be a child's friend? Children and adolescents in disadvantaged groups, such as ethnic minorities, the poor, and the mentally or physically disabled, are especially at risk for "not fitting in,"

and consequently for experiencing difficulties in school. For example, adolescents who continually experience rejection by their peers are at greater risk for dropping out of school, even though many are at least average in intelligence and have the ability to graduate (Bullock, 1992; Véronneau & Vitaro, 2007). Although the effects seem to be stronger for boys than for girls, the pattern is the same for both genders: Early poor social adjustment leads to future academic difficulties, a perception that the school environment is aversive, and eventual failure in school (Bullock, 1992; Ladd et al., 1988; Véronneau et al., 2010).

Coolahan and her colleagues (2000) investigated how peer interactions may be connected to learning readiness in children who are from poor families. Using more than 500 children enrolled in a Head Start program, they looked at multiple dimensions of peer play and how these factors related to achievement-orientated variables (e.g., interest in learning, persistence on tasks, cooperative attitude), and problem behaviors (e.g., aggressive outbursts, disruptive play). Three general relationships emerged: (a) Children who demonstrated positive play behaviors also engaged in classroom learning activities, (b) children who hovered around play activities, but did not interact with others very much, were inattentive in class and less motivated to learn, and (c) children who were disruptive in their peer play also displayed conduct problems during classroom activities.

Researchers have also noted the importance of establishing positive peer relationships in developing academic competence for children and adolescents with disabilities and behavioral difficulties. Children with attention deficit/ hyperactivity disorder (ADHD) are often at risk for academic underachievement because their behavior disrupts their abilities to attend to teachers and take part in group discussions (DuPaul, Ervin, Hook, & McGoey, 1998). In an effort to increase ADHD students' attention to their school tasks (and thereby improve their academic performance), DuPaul and colleagues (1998) had a small group of elementary school children diagnosed with ADHD tutored by their peers without ADHD on a variety of school subjects (e.g., math, spelling). The results showed that the disruptive off-task behavior of the children with ADHD decreased and that their attention to academic material increased.

The findings presented here suggest that successful interactions with others can lead to stronger academic motivation and performance in later grades (Coolahan et al., 2000; Véronneau et al., 2010). Moreover, as was seen in DuPaul and colleagues' (1998) study, encouraging students to help one another learn may be effective in not only boosting academic achievement, but in promoting social and personal development. The classroom intervention strategies outlined in the next section describe how structured peer interactions can help children achieve social and developmental goals in addition to learning goals.

Peer-assisted learning. Nowhere has the relationship between peer interactions and academic achievement been more clearly demonstrated than in **peer-assisted learning**. *Peer-assisted learning* (PAL) is a general term which encompasses a broad variety of strategies where students are acquiring knowledge and skills through interactions with other students (Calhoon, 2005; Evans & Moore, 2013; Topping, 2005). These interactions may occur on a one-on-one basis as in peer tutoring (like DuPaul et al., 1998) or in a small group format, as in cooperative or collaborative learning. Even within these two categories of PAL, there are various approaches. For example, peer tutoring can be unidirectional, with one student in the dyad always taking on the role of the teacher, or it can be reciprocal, wherein the two students teach one another during the tutoring sessions (Evans & Moore, 2013; Topping, 2005). Peer tutoring can also be organized so that only some students in the classroom may be engaged in tutoring others or where all class members are organized into tutor-tutee pairs (called classwide peer tutoring) (Calhoon, 2005; Topping, 2005).

Whichever PAL approach one takes, both peer-tutoring and cooperative learning have been shown to have a significant impact on students' outcomes, such as gains in academic achievement, enhanced academic self-concept, motivation to learn, and social behaviors (Ginsburg-Block, Rohrbeck, & Fantuzzo, 2006; Topping, 2005). In particular, peer tutoring results in gains for both tutors and tutees: tutors report improved communication skills and a greater understanding of academic content, and the tutees report higher satisfaction with school, better academic skills, and less anxiety (Evans & Moore, 2013; Okilwa & Shelby, 2010). Receiving tutoring from one's peers is especially beneficial for students from marginalized or underprivileged backgrounds and for students with disabilities (DuPaul et al., 1998; Ginsburg-Block et al., 2006; Okilwa & Shelby, 2010).

Calhoon (2005) examined the effectiveness of a linguistic training program delivered through classwide peer tutoring to middle school special education students who had been diagnosed with a reading disability. Students who were assigned to the linguistic training program received help from their tutor with essential reading activities, such as phonetics (e.g., letter-sound correspondence) and summarizing read material (e.g., reading comprehension). Because it was reciprocal peer-tutoring, each student got the chance to act as a tutor for the other student in the pair. Results of the linguistic training program/peer-tutoring group were compared to a matched group of students who were receiving traditional remedial reading exercises. Students who were in the peer-tutoring group outperformed the control group in word identification and reading comprehension. Calhoun (2005) felt that the immediate feedback, the opportunity for student practice, as well as the interaction with other students may have led to the positive results.

Another effective PAL method, and an example of collaborative learning, is the jigsaw classroom technique (Aronson, Stephan, Sikes, Blaney, & Snapp, 1978; Slavin, 1990). With this procedure, the students in the class are divided into small groups of five or six members. Groups are typically heterogeneous, composed of students from different performance levels

Figure 9.2   Peer-Assisted Learning: Students
Helping Each Other to Learn

SOURCE: Photo courtesy of Cassandra Lee Davis.

and ethnic backgrounds. Each group is assigned the task of learning about a particular topic, and each student within the group is responsible for learning a small portion of the topic. Each student from the group meets with the members of other classroom groups who have been assigned the same subtopic; these children work together to learn the subtopic. Then the students take the information that they have learned back to their groups and teach the material to other members of their groups. Because each student is evaluated individually, it is important that all group members pay attention to what their fellow group members present. In other words, members of the group rely on one another to learn all

parts of the assigned material, and no student is considered to be more or less important than another student. What the jigsaw classroom technique does in the long term is improve the overall atmosphere of the classroom by having students interact with each other in a positive and constructive manner so that they may achieve their learning goals (Aronson, 2002). In addition, students are given opportunities to interact with classmates with whom they usually might not interact (e.g., peers of different ethnic backgrounds, socially ostracized peers).

But, how is it that an individual personal process like learning can be improved by a group activity? What can social psychology tell us about why PAL methods are effective in promoting learning? The jigsaw classroom technique works in several ways. First, competition among individual students, which can be detrimental to an individual's self-esteem and performance, is reduced. Second, a sense of belonging in the classroom is increased, and this especially can have a positive effect on students who for whatever reason may be initially excluded. Third, teamwork also adds an element of fun and helps to emphasize that learning is important and valuable, creating an overall positive climate in which peers can provide encouragement to each other (Aronson, 2002; Hanze & Berger, 2007; Slavin, 1990). If you recall the discussion of achievement motivation earlier in the chapter, you might see the jigsaw classroom technique as a strategy which enhances the pursuit of mastery goals (i.e., acquiring knowledge and skills) and approach performance goals (i.e., demonstrating competence to others). In addition, the jigsaw classroom technique might increase students' intrinsic motivation by allowing students to take a more active role in their learning.

Using 137 physics students in the 12th grade, Hanze and Berger (2007) explored how the jigsaw classroom technique can impact students' learning goals, self-determination and self-concept. Students learned about one topic (e.g., scanning electron microscope) through traditional instruction and learned about a second topic using the jigsaw classroom method.

Students were measured on a number of psychological variables, such as goal orientation, academic self-concept, intrinsic motivation and the use of cognitive processing strategies, as well as academic performance. Interestingly, Hanze and Berger found that the jigsaw technique was not more advantageous than traditional instruction in terms of academic performance. But, when compared to traditional instruction, students reported more use of in-depth cognitive strategies, more involvement in their learning, and stronger intrinsic motivation when they were undergoing the jigsaw technique. Students simply enjoyed the cooperative learning environment more than the traditional instruction. Moreover, the positive effects of the jigsaw technique on self-concept, motivation, competence, and feelings of belonging were more dramatic for the weaker, less confident students in the class.

So far, we have discussed how student–teacher and student–student interactions can affect students' academic performance and overall development, both positively and negatively. PAL methods can certainly lead to better academic performance and better social interactions among students. Because individuals spend so much time in the social environment of school, some of the negative social behaviors that plague our society, such as prejudice and violence, may find their way into the school setting. As a result, social psychologists view the school system as providing a handy medium to study and address broader social issues like aggression.

When Interactions Turn Ugly: Aggression in School

In April 1999, two heavily armed male adolescents, wearing masks and black trench coats, walked into their Colorado high school and opened fire on students, teachers, and staff members. By the time the shooting was over, dozens of people were dead or injured, and the two young gunmen were also dead from self-inflicted gunshot wounds. Tyler Clementi, an 18-year-old student at Rutgers University, jumped to his death from the George Washington Bridge in September 2010. Clementi had been filmed by his roommate kissing another man. The roommate allegedly urged other students and Twitter followers to watch Clementi and his partner via a webcam. In April 2012, Kenneth Weishuhn, age 14, hung himself in the family's garage. He had told his mother that because he was gay, he was being subjected to relentless bullying both in-person and online from peers, which included death threats and a Facebook hate group. Unfortunately, as Table 9.2 shows, these are only a few incidents of school aggression and its terrible consequences that have taken place in recent years.

Understandably, we are shocked when we learn of such occurrences. We may wonder what is going on in our schools. Are students, particularly adolescents, more aggressive than ever before? What might motivate a young person (either alone or in a group) to torment a peer so mercilessly? In the aftermath of school shootings, classmates describe many of the young perpetrators of school violence as outcasts or outsiders. Shooters, themselves, often report incidents of rejection or bullying by others—meaning that in some cases, individuals may be both perpetrators and victims of aggression. While school shootings may not be as widespread as the media would have us believe, reports show that school bullying (and its latest incarnation, cyberbullying) is quite common. Can social psychology help to explain what causes some young people to take such harmful actions against others? If we can identify the factors that lead someone to take their own life or the lives of others, perhaps we can develop policies and interventions to prevent such incidents from occurring in the first place (see Figure 9.3).

Causes of youth aggression. School-related aggression is a heavily researched topic. Here are some general findings from the literature in this area:

- Males are more likely than females to be involved in instances of school violence, either as perpetrators or as victims (Furlong & Morrison, 2001).

Table 9.2   Sample of School Shootings Around the World

Date	Location	Perpetrators and Victims
March 11, 2009	Winnenden, Germany	A secondary school shooting spree by a 17-year-old, who had been attending the same school, resulted in the death of 16 people.
April 16, 2007	Blacksburg, VA	A 23-year-old student with a history of mental illness killed 32 people in two separate attacks on a college campus—and then killed himself.
September 13, 2006	Montreal, QC, Canada	A student at a college campus opened fire with a semiautomatic weapon, killing 1 person and injuring 19 others. After being shot in the arm by police, he committed suicide.
April 29, 1999	Taber, AB, Canada	A 14-year-old boy walked into his secondary school and opened fire with a .22-caliber rifle, killing 1 teen and wounding another.
March 24, 1998	Jonesboro, AR	Two boys, 11 and 13 years of age, opened fire on students, teachers, and staff members from the woods near their middle school after luring people out with a false fire alarm. After the shootings, 4 students and 1 teacher were dead, and 10 others were wounded.
December 1, 1997	West Paducah, KY	A 14-year-old boy opened fire at a high school prayer meeting, killing 3 students and wounding 5 others.

SOURCE: Adapted from news reports in *The Globe and Mail, The National Post,* and *Newsweek.*

- Bullying is at its highest rate during middle school and then decreases starting around the 10th grade (Wang, Iannotti, & Nansel, 2009).
- The use of weapons is more common among high school students than among elementary school children (Furlong & Morrison, 2001).
- About one third of students (ages 12 to 18) report being bullied at school (Wang et al., 2009).
- Among middle school children, 22% reported involvement in cyberbullying: 4% as perpetrators, 11% as victims, and 7% as both (Kowalski & Limber, 2007).
- Students who bring guns to school tend to be male, report frequent use of alcohol and drugs, designate themselves as gang members, and are more likely to be involved in aggressive behavior (e.g., assaults at school, juvenile crimes) (Furlong & Morrison, 2001).

So, what makes some young people behave so horribly to each other? Are they suffering from some neurochemical imbalances? Can mental illness or a personality disorder be the culprit? These are, of course, possible answers, and the causes of aggression are as varied as the types of aggression expressed. Recent explanations for school aggression (Benbenishty & Astor, 2005;

Figure 9.3   The Need for Anti-Bullying Programs to Be Implemented in Schools

SOURCE: Photo Courtesy of Centre for Flexible Learning, University of Windsor.

Henry, 2009; Kowalski, Giumetti, Schroder, & Lattanner, 2014; Yoon & Barton, 2008) have taken a multilevel approach to examining this problem. That is, individual students will bring particular traits, skills, and abilities to school, along with norms and experiences from their home, culture, neighborhood, and larger society. These elements will interact with the school environment, which includes fellow students, teachers, administrators, institutional polices, and the physical environment, and will ulti- mately affect a student's behavior and achieve- ment. Therefore, to study the problem of school aggression at any particular school, whether it is bullying, verbal abuse, social rejection, or shoot- ings, one must look at the interaction of many different variables—intrapersonal and interper- sonal—in order to adequately address the issue (Benbenishty & Astor, 2005; Henry, 2009; Kowalski et al., 2014). For example, students with psychological problems may be at greater risk for being rejected by peers and for academic failure, leading to alienation and anger toward the school, its teachers, and fellow students. These students may come to believe that aggres- sion is the only effective way of dealing with feelings of isolation and that their violent actions are justified. They may not see any alternative means of coping effectively with the harmful antisocial behavior that is directed at them. Unfortunately, their aggressive behavior also may serve to further alienate them from their peers and teachers—in this way making them both the perpetrators *and* the victims of school- related aggression (Benbenishty & Astor, 2005; Henry, 2009).

Like school shootings, another form of aggression—bullying—has also been getting lots of media attention. Bullying involves a disparity of power between the bully and victim(s), occurs repeatedly, can take a direct form, such as hitting, kicking, or name-calling, or can be more indirect, such as spreading rumors about another person or ostracizing someone (Kowalski & Limber, 2007; Wang et al., 2009). Kowalski and collea- gues (2014) performed an extensive review of the literature on a relatively new form of indirect bullying: **cyberbullying.** Cyberbullying is car- ried out in an electronic context through e-mail, text messaging, or social media venues like Facebook. It is distinctive from traditional bully- ing in that victims can be subjected to an attack almost anywhere and anytime, and without knowing the identity of the perpetrator—making it a particularly insidious type of bullying (Kowalski et al., 2014). Moreover, unlike tradi- tional bullying, cyberbullies need not be physically stronger or particularly popular them- selves to victimize a peer, thereby changing the power dynamics usually seen in old-fashioned bullying (Kowalski & Limber, 2007). Moreover, victims of cyberbullying often have to face tra- ditional bullying as well (Lapidot-Lefler & Dolev-Cohen, 2015). Regardless of its form, bullying can have enormously damaging effects on their targets: depression, anxiety, poor perfor- mance at school, stress, lowered self-esteem, and thoughts of suicide (Kowalski et al., 2014).

Incidents of aggression resulting in physical and psychological harm have repercussions not only for the students involved in the incidents, but also for all students, teachers, and staff mem- bers. The overall school climate can be deeply affected. School is no longer seen as a safe envi- ronment in which the emphasis is on academic achievement and on building interpersonal skills and relationships. Students can no longer focus solely on their learning because they also must be very vigilant about who they interact with, where they walk, and who is saying what about them on social media. Moreover, if students notice that teachers, staff members, and others in positions of authority ignore the harmful behav- ior, then students are likely to feel that they are alone (Benbenishty & Astor, 2005; Furlong & Morrison, 2001; Henry, 2009). This is very likely how both Clementi and Weishuhn, the two youths who took their own lives, might have felt: alone, harassed, and rejected.

Since aggression is a type of social inter- action (albeit a negative one), then we can use social psychology not only to understand why it occurs, but to help prevent it. As outlined in Bandura's **social cognitive learning theory** (Bandura, 1983; see also Chapter 7), a child may learn by observing others that certain behaviors can result in desirable (or undesirable) outcomes. For example, a child may learn that aggressive behavior is not always punished, and is in fact sometimes rewarded. A bully's behavior, for instance, allows him or her to gain power over a target, and bullies often enjoy a certain degree of social status among their peers (Wang et al., 2009). Engaging in cyberbullying, in particular, removes any negative consequences that one might experience when harming someone face-to-face: the bully does not have to contend with observing up close the harm inflicted on the target, thereby taking away any undesirable outcomes or inhibitions (such as feelings of empathy) to aggressive behavior (Bandura, 1983; Kowalski et al., 2014; Lapidot-Lefler & Dolev-Cohen, 2015).

In essence, then, a child's behavior in school may be influenced by what he or she perceives to be not only rewarding, but typical, expected, and "normal." A number of researchers (e.g., Cialdini, Kallgren, & Reno, 1991; Deutsch & Gerard, 1955) have identified three normative social processes that may operate within a social setting: (a) **descriptive norms** (i.e., what an individual perceives to be *typical* behavior in a setting), (b) **injunctive norms** (i.e., what people are *expected* to do or *ought* to do in a setting), and (c) **norm salience** (i.e., to what extent the norms are clearly *conveyed* in the setting). Descriptive norms help the individual to define a situation and process the information from the situation efficiently; it may be easier just to follow what others are doing in a setting, especially if the individual is in an unfamiliar environment. Injunctive norms dictate what ought to be done in a situation and inform the individual of the rewards or punishments associated with following (or not following) the norms. Descriptive and injunctive norms are said to affect the individual's behavior if he or she is made aware of them; if the norms in a

situation are made salient, the individual knows how to behave in norm-consistent ways. We can think about how these processes relate back to Bandura's social cognitive learning theory: That is, the observation of other people's behavior and the consequences attached to that behavior are important influences on the individual.

Henry (2001) studied how normative social processes in the classroom environment may influence aggressive behavior in children. Using a large sample of elementary school children, he had children report on their perceptions of classmates (i.e., aggressive behavior of peers, popularity and rejection of aggressive peers) and on their beliefs about the appropriateness of physical aggression and verbal aggression. In addition to the children's reports, Henry used observational methods to assess teacher and student behaviors in the classroom. He employed these measures to examine the descriptive norms in the classroom (perception of average aggression level of the child's classmates), injunctive norms (the child's expectations concerning aggression in the classroom), and norm salience (the child's views about the popularity of aggressive classmates and the teacher's reactions to aggressive behavior).

The findings showed that children's perceptions of the level of aggression in the classroom (descriptive norms) had no relation to their actual aggressive behavior, but that children's *expectations* about how they ought to behave in the classroom regarding aggressive behavior (injunctive norms) were significantly associated with their aggressive behavior. That is, students' beliefs about what was appropriate in the classroom influenced their aggressive behavior more than did their observations of actual aggressive behavior in the classroom. Furthermore, just as theory regarding normative social processes would suggest, children believed that aggressive behavior was unacceptable if they saw that classmates who engaged in it were reprimanded or unpopular among their peers. However, if children believed that aggression was approved of and tolerated in the classroom, they regarded it as acceptable, and, thus, aggressive behavior was more prevalent.

Reducing aggression in the school environment.

What can be done to minimize those aspects of school environments that promote aggression? Are there strategies or programs that could have prevented the tragedies described earlier in this section? In their review of school violence and bullying prevention programs, Yoon and Barton (2008) have noted that such efforts have been employed at multiple levels (consistent with the approach discussed earlier). Prevention programs may be designed to address the overall school environment and practices (e.g., amount of adult supervision in playgrounds, hallways, and cafeterias), academic performance (e.g., students who have learning difficulties are at greater risk for engaging in aggressive behavior and for being victims), behavior management techniques (e.g., teachers' awareness and response to bullying), and academic climate and expectations (e.g., emphasizing competition rather than cooperation among students). Basically, effective strategies need to focus on the social context in which aggressive behavior occurs (Benbenishty & Astor, 2005; Yoon & Barton, 2008).

Developed in Finland, the **KiVa Anti-Bullying Program** (Salmivalli & Poskiparta, 2012; Williford, Elledge, Boulton, DePaolis, Little, & Salmivalli, 2013) works on the principle that bullying is a group phenomenon where the attitudes and behaviors of peers (who are neither bullies nor victims, but who operate as bystanders) reinforce the bully through social rewards (e.g., laughing along, ostracizing/ignoring the victim). The goal of the program is to change this normative behavior by reducing the rewards gained by bullies (and consequently, their motivation to bully), and by teaching children how to provide support to victims (Salmivalli & Poskiparta, 2012). The program consists of two primary components: (1) *universal actions* (lessons that raise awareness of how group dynamics may be maintaining bullying, increase empathy toward victims, and teach strategies to help bullying victims); and (2) *indicated actions*

(strategies on dealing with specific incidents of bullying that defend and support victims). In both components, school staff and teachers not only provide classroom activities to counteract bullying behavior, but explicitly encourage students to support bullied classmates. Salmivalli and Poskiparta (2012) investigated the effectiveness of KiVa with 234 schools (approximately 28,000 students) across Finland; half of the schools were assigned to the intervention program and the other half of the schools operated as the controls. KiVa was found to reduce bullying and victimization significantly with children in Grades 1 to 6. Moreover, students in the KiVa program showed increased enjoyment of school, academic motivation, and performance when compared to students in the control schools. Similarly, in another large-scale study of KiVa focused primarily on cyberbullying, Williford et al. (2013) found that elementary school students in the KiVa program reported a lower frequency of cybervictimization and cyberbullying over time when compared to students in the control condition.

Other strategies, such as the jigsaw classroom technique, are also effective in improving interpersonal and intergroup relationships in a classroom, thereby reducing conflict and other antisocial behaviors among students (Aronson et al., 1978; Slavin, 1990). Having students representing different cultural backgrounds, social strata, and abilities working together on a common assignment not only enhances learning (as discussed earlier), but also results in the classroom norm becoming one of cooperation and interdependence rather than competition and conflict. Indeed, among students, the jigsaw classroom technique has been shown to promote greater tolerance for diversity, greater empathy and compassion for others, and increased self-esteem (Aronson, 2002; Aronson et al., 1978). Consequently, no matter what approach you take, creating a positive and supportive social environment at school not only reduces incidences of aggression among students, but also leads to greater motivation to learn, better academic performance, and improved psychological health for all students.

FOCUS ON INTERVENTION

A Program to Reduce Violence in Schools

The jigsaw classroom technique represents an intervention that occurs in the school itself and is directed toward developing a school climate that does not condone and support violence. Other intervention strategies address factors occurring outside of the school environment that may be contributing to school-related violence (see Benbenishty & Astor, 2005, for a review). Eddy, Reid, and Fetrow (2001) describe an elementary school program aimed at children who are at risk for developing delinquent and violent behaviors during adolescence. The program, called Linking the Interests of Families and Teachers (LIFT), incorporated elements of Bandura's social cognitive learning theory by teaching children and their parents nonaggressive methods of dealing with anger, frustration, and conflict. The LIFT program contained three components: (a) a classroom-based social and problem skills training component for the children, (b) a playground-based behavior modification component for the children, and (c) a group-delivered training component for the parents.

For the classroom component, LIFT classroom instructors met with all students in a classroom for one hour twice a week for 10 weeks. Each session included listening to lectures and role-playing on social and problem-solving skills, practicing skills for interacting with peers, and engaging in unstructured free play on the playground. Students were taught relationship skills, such as identifying feelings, dealing with anger, responding appropriately to others, and cooperating and problem solving within peer groups.

For the playground component, students were divided into small groups. The groups engaged in various activities together, allowing them to demonstrate (and receive social approval for) prosocial behaviors and the inhibition of negative interactions with peers while playing.

For the third component, sessions were held with parents during the same 10-week period that their children were undergoing their program components. Each parent session involved information and role-playing activities aimed at fundamentals of discipline (e.g., using small positive and negative consequences, paying attention to early signs of problem behaviors), and family management skills (e.g., giving encouragement, making behavior change contracts with children). These activities were based on social learning and behavior modification principles that state that modeling and rewarding prosocial behavior will lead to an increase in the desired behavior.

The LIFT program was implemented in an urban area in Oregon using schools from three school districts (Eddy et al., 2001). During the three years that the program was in effect, schools randomly chosen for the program were compared with control schools in the same district. What did the researchers find? Between the fall and spring of the first year, children in the LIFT program were less aggressive on the playground and were perceived as more positive by their teachers than were children in the control group. In addition, parents of LIFT children behaved less negatively with their children in parent–child problem-solving sessions. What about the long-term impact of the program? These results were also positive. Three years following the program, LIFT students were less likely to associate with delinquent peers and were less likely to engage in alcohol and drug use than were students in the control group.

(Continued)

(Continued)

Interventions, such as LIFT, highlight the importance of principals, teachers, and school administrators in providing a cooperative (rather than competitive) learning environment, one that rewards prosocial behavior, such as sharing and compassion, and teaches students how to engage in effective (and nonaggressive) problem solving and communication (Yoon & Barton, 2008). In short, we need to "change the process of the typical classroom so that our schools can transform themselves into more humane social environments for all students" (Aronson, 2002, p. 214).

SUMMARY

Intrapersonal (or individual) factors associated with academic achievement can affect students' perceptions of their abilities and can affect their academic performance. Attitudes (beliefs about one's ability to achieve a desired outcome and perceived importance of that outcome), subjective norms (others' expectations and how motivated one is to comply with those expectations), and perceived behavioral control (perceived control over the behavior and its outcome) may contribute to students' academic performance. Attitudes toward school, beliefs about one's academic abilities, and perceptions about being a student all form part of a student's academic self-concept. A positive academic self-concept is related to greater motivation, higher academic aspirations, and better academic performance. The program described in the opening vignette is a good example of how mentoring and a supportive environment can have a positive impact on the academic self-concepts of minority students.

In contrast, negative attitudes toward school, fear of failing, and poorly developed academic skills are associated with a variety of self-serving strategies, such as procrastination and self-handicapping. Unfortunately, reliance on these self-serving strategies may have negative effects on academic self-concept, academic performance, and other measures of achievement (such as being able to effectively regulate one's learning behavior) over the long term. Moreover, students may come to believe that they cannot take credit for their academic performance even when success does occur, thereby further undermining their motivation to perform well in school.

The emphasis on external rewards (e.g., grades, praise, awards) and competition—so common in the school environment—also may adversely affect students' motivation to learn and the quality of academic work that they produce. Furthermore, when students compare themselves to others, especially higher performing peers, they may start to see themselves as less academically competent and lose interest in school. A classroom that is structured in this way may lead students to believe that they have little control over their academic work, that they are simply engaging in tasks to please others, that comparing oneself to others is the norm (social comparison), and that getting a reward is more important than developing a sense of accomplishment. Such an environment serves to undermine a student's self-determination (i.e., intrinsic motivation). In contrast, when students are in an environment that emphasizes autonomy, choice and control over tasks, and both mastery- and performance-approach goals, then students become more intrinsically motivated to learn, grades improve, and engagement in school increases.

Because the school setting is a social environment, social psychologists also have looked extensively at the interpersonal processes that occur in the classroom. Teachers' expectations can become self-fulfilling prophecies; that is, teachers' expectations about their students can affect how they behave toward those students, and in turn can change the way students see themselves. Expectations also can be detrimental to academic performance and students' self-concepts when they differ on the basis of students' race, gender, or disability. Operating as mentors and teachers, the university researchers who interacted with the minority students in the opening vignette held positive expectations for these students and offered them a variety of learning experiences. As a result, the students became more confident in their academic abilities, completed their research projects successfully, showed improved performance in their subsequent high school courses, and expressed higher academic aspirations.

Interactions with peers, in addition to teachers, can affect students' academic achievement and the development of a variety of social and cognitive skills. Peer-assisted learning (PAL) has students working with other students, either in dyads or in groups, and has been used to enhance both academic and social competence in students. These methods reduce conflict, increase a sense of belonging for the students, enhance academic self-concept, and increase students'

motivation toward schoolwork. One PAL method, the jigsaw classroom technique, has been applied effectively to address the problem of aggression in schools.

Social psychologists examine the various forms that school aggression may take, such as physical and verbal abuse, social rejection, and bullying. Of particular interest is how school-related aggression may be reinforced and maintained through the observation of others' behavior, the social rewards related to behaving aggressively, and the normative processes and expectations present in the school environment. Recently, bullying, especially cyberbullying, has been found to be especially damaging not only to the victim, but to the overall school climate. Successful programs address multiple levels of factors that are aimed at the individual (e.g., a student's cognitive and psychological functioning), family (e.g., abuse in the home environment), school (e.g., teacher and peer reactions to bullying), and the larger society (e.g., glorification of violence in the media).

10

APPLYING SOCIAL PSYCHOLOGY TO ORGANIZATIONS

Larry M. Coutts

Jamie A. Gruman

CHAPTER OUTLINE

The Individual in an Organizational Context
    Making Sense of Others in the Work
        Environment
    Job Satisfaction: Antecedents and
        Consequences

Interpersonal Processes in
    Organizations
    Communication
    Group Decision Making
Summary

"That's it!" Tim said into his videoconference microphone. "I can't talk to you. And I'm tired of you constantly criticizing my ideas. I'm going to lunch. Don't ask me when I'll be back!"

For the past two years, employees at Computen Inc. had been experiencing high levels of job dissatisfaction at many of their international subsidiaries, and many of Computen's brightest employees had left the organization to work for competitors. In response, senior managers at Computen had assembled a five-person international task force to examine the job satisfaction issue and to develop recommendations to increase employees' enjoyment of their work and reduce turnover. The task force was instructed to produce a report outlining its recommendations to the regional managers within six months. Tim, an American production supervisor, was one of the members of that task force and was frustrated with the behavior of some of his fellow team members.

"I can't talk to these people," he was overheard complaining to a coworker. "They don't seem to understand any of the important issues causing our problems."

The rest of the team members were Subir, a marketing manager from India; Chris, a production supervisor from Britain; and Audrey and Veneeta, who together ran the Computen operation in Singapore.

During the first few videoconferences following the formation of the task force, it had become increasingly clear that there were significant differences of opinion among some of the team members regarding how best to examine and address the problem, but in the interest of being collegial, no major conflicts had emerged. Since then, however, nearly every meeting had resulted in disagreements and open confrontations among the team members. Audrey and Veneeta, the only two members who seemed to be getting along, joked that members of the task force were probably experiencing less job satisfaction than were any other employees in the company.

The task force was scheduled to submit its recommendations in less than a month. However, it had made little progress during the five months it had been meeting and had virtually nothing to report to the regional managers.

- How might the task force members' perceptions of each other influence their behavior toward each other?
- Why did the task force members seem to have trouble communicating?
- Might a better decision regarding how to deal with the job satisfaction problem have been made if only one person had been assigned to make recommendations to the regional managers?

Attempts to understand the dynamics inherent in organizations by drawing on social psychological concepts are not new. The first major treatise on the topic is titled *The Social Psychology of Organizations* and was published in 1966 by Katz and Kahn. In 1979, Karl Weick published the second edition, *The Social Psychology of Organizing*. These two volumes represent the classic works in this area (Katz & Kahn, 1966; Weick, 1979).

It is difficult to imagine how one could navigate successfully through the whitewater of organizational life without appreciating how and why people interact as they do. Similarly, how would it be possible to effectively manage a group of people if one were ignorant of the interpersonal dynamics that can either lead to fruitless conflicts or produce remarkable achievements?

This chapter discusses some of the social psychological phenomena that influence behavior in organizations. Unfortunately, because of space limitations, it addresses in some depth only four of the many topics in the social psychology of

organizations: social perception, job satisfaction, communication, and group decision making. The goal is that after reading this chapter you will have developed an appreciation of how social psychology can be applied in organizations, and how understanding social psychology can make you a more effective member of an organization.

Before beginning the first major section, however, the next few paragraphs briefly describe two other interesting organizational topics that have captivated the research efforts of social and organizational psychologists: leadership and work motivation.

Leadership. The extant leadership literature is huge, encompassing well over 10,000 research studies. Researchers have made vast strides toward understanding the essential nature of leadership as a real and powerful influence in organizations. Simply defined, **leadership** "occurs when particular individuals exert influence on the goal achievement of others in an organizational context" (Johns & Saks, 2001, p. 272). In this sense, leadership is inherently social and is a special case of interpersonal influence in which individuals or groups follow the wishes of the leader. The approach to understanding the elusive concept of leadership has taken many roads, including trying to identify leadership traits, explore how leaders emerge in groups, and understand the consequences of various leadership behaviors. In addition, several theories of leadership have been proposed.

In *path–goal theory,* for example, House (1971) proposed that the leader's responsibility is to show subordinates the path to valued goals. Moreover, the particular style of the leader (e.g., supportive, directive, participative, achievement oriented) will positively or negatively affect subordinates' satisfaction, motivation, and (ultimately) performance depending on both the subordinates' personal characteristics (e.g., needs, skills) and the work environment (e.g., nature of the task, nature of the work group).

As noted by Avolio, Walumbwa, and Weber (2009), current research and theories of leadership focus on a myriad of different aspects of the leadership dynamic, including for example, the leader, followers, peers, supervisors, work setting, and culture. Contemporary leadership research also includes individuals representing the entire spectrum of diversity, including public, private, and not-for-profit organizations, as well as samples of populations from nations around the globe. Importantly, leadership is no longer viewed simply as an individual characteristic or difference, but rather is depicted in various models as dyadic, shared, relational, strategic, global, and a complex social dynamic (Avolio, 2007; Yukl, 2006). (For an extensive overview of current theories, research, and future directions in leadership, see Avolio et al., 2009.)

Work motivation. With respect to human factors that managers can influence, employee performance is often described as a joint function of ability and motivation, and one of the primary tasks facing managers is to motivate employees to perform to the best of their abilities (Pinder, 1998). As implied in the preceding statement, motivation and job performance are not synonymous. You may be very skilled in performing a certain task, but that does not necessarily mean that you are highly motivated to perform well. Conversely, you may be highly motivated to perform a particular task well, but your lack of ability to perform that task may prevent you from succeeding.

Motivation is a broad and complex topic, but is generally defined as the set of processes that

account for the direction, level, and persistence of a person's effort toward attaining some goal (Schermerhorn, Hunt, & Osborn, 2005).

There are several theories of work motivation, all of which are concerned with the reasons, other than ability, that some people perform their jobs better than others. For example, **need theories**, such as Maslow's (1943) *need hierarchy theory* are concerned with *what* motivates people, that is, the categories of needs that people are motivated to satisfy (e.g., safety needs, esteem needs). **Process theories** of work motivation focus on *how* motivation occurs. One such process theory is *equity theory* (Adams, 1965), which postulates that employees are motivated to achieve a condition of equity or fairness in their dealings with other people and with their organizations. Specifically, employees compare the inputs they invest in their jobs (e.g., work accomplishments, talents, experience) and the outcomes that they receive (e.g., pay, good treatment, enjoyment, status) against the inputs and outcomes of some other relevant person or group. When these ratios or comparisons are equal, employees should feel that fair and equitable exchanges exist with their organizations. However, inequitable comparisons result in a state of dissonance or tension that motivates employees to engage in behavior designed to relieve the tension. Such behavior may involve raising or lowering work efforts to reestablish equity or withdrawing from the situation that is causing inequity. Alternatively, because people may be unwilling to undertake some of the actions necessary to respond behaviorally to inequities, they may opt instead to simply change their perceptions (cognitions) of the situation. Thus, for example, the employee who feels that he or she is underpaid relative to their colleague may simply rationalize that the colleague "really is more productive than I am," thereby convincing himself or herself that the other's higher pay is justified. Although there is a great deal of evidence to suggest that people are motivated to redress perceived inequities at work through the various behavioral and cognitive approaches posited by equity theory, it appears that in recent years equity theory has been subsumed under a much broader conceptualization of organizational justice (Latham & Pinder, 2005). (For a concise review of work motivation theory and research at the dawn of the 21st century, see Latham & Pinder, 2005.)

As you undoubtedly have begun to appreciate after reading much of this textbook, understanding social behavior necessarily involves understanding both the person and the situation. Behavior in organizations is no different. For example, knowing why a manager acted toward a subordinate in a particular manner requires that you understand something about the manager and something about the particular situation (e.g., pressure the manager was under, history between the manager and the subordinate). Accordingly, this chapter is divided into two main sections. The first section deals with the individual in an organizational context and focuses largely on what individuals bring to the organization, that is, aspects of themselves that affect their perceptions, attitudes, and behavior in the work environment. The second section deals with interpersonal processes in organizations and focuses on how social factors influence individual and group work behaviors. Clearly, however, the two areas are not completely distinct; there is much overlap. As you will see, for example, the amount of satisfaction that an individual derives from a job is a function of his or her personal characteristics and the nature of both the work itself and the work environment.

THE INDIVIDUAL IN AN ORGANIZATIONAL CONTEXT

Making Sense of Others in the Work Environment

In the workplace, as in any other social setting, employees may encounter a wide range of people, from friendly to unfriendly coworkers, pleasant to unpleasant customers, and supportive to unsupportive supervisors. How do people make sense out of all this information about the ways in which others act? Social psychologists have devoted a considerable amount of research effort to addressing this question. Social perception (also called social cognition) is the process of understanding or making sense of people. More formally, **social perception** is the process of selecting and interpreting information about how we view others and ourselves. Because information about people is often subjective and open to interpretation (Fiske, 1993), our behavior is often based on our perceptions of what reality is rather than on reality itself. People often have very different views about the environment around them. For example, different employees are likely to have more or less positive perceptions of their company's employee recognition and reward program depending on whether or not they like their jobs, their coworkers, and their boss. Thus, the social perception process serves as a screen or filter through which information passes before it has an effect on people. The quality or accuracy of people's perceptions, therefore, has a major impact on their responses to a given situation.

This section of the chapter considers two key components of social perception and how they relate to the work environment: (a) the perceptual biases that occur in people's attempts to build an overall impression of others based on what they know (or think they know) about them as individuals and as members of groups, and (b) how people make attributions about why others behave as they do. Although perceptual biases have been discussed in previous chapters, they are considered here as well to underscore their importance in the social work environment.

Perceptual Biases

Considerable effort is required to perceive and interpret what others do. As a result, we develop cognitive shortcuts to make this task less burdensome. These shortcuts are valuable. Not infrequently, they allow us to reduce ambiguity in social situations and to make accurate perceptions rapidly. In this way, our cognitive shortcuts provide us with valid information for making predictions. For example, if a stranger approaches you on a dark street and demands to see your wallet, you are unlikely to interpret this event as a harmless request to view pictures of your family. However, our cognitive shortcuts are not infallible. The shortcuts we use to efficiently interpret and make sense out of our social world can cause **perceptual biases**—errors that distort the perception process—that in turn lead to faulty judgments. When these biases operate, we short-circuit our search for information and instead rely on our assumptions to fill in the missing information. The following two subsections explore two perceptual biases that affect organizational behavior: selective perception and the halo effect. Later, in discussing the ways in which we attempt to determine *why* others behave as they do (causal attribution), two other types of perceptual distortion—the fundamental attribution error and the actor–observer effect—are considered.

Selective perception. Because it is impossible for us to assimilate everything we are exposed to, any characteristic that makes a person, an object, or an event stand out increases the probability that it will be perceived. This tendency toward **selective perception** explains why a manager may reprimand or reward one employee for doing something that goes unnoticed when other employees do it. Because the manager cannot observe everything going on around him or her, the manager engages in selective perception. Several studies have shown that people's experiences and interests can significantly influence what they notice. For example, Waller, Huber, and Glick (1995) asked the question, "Do executives' functional backgrounds influence what they perceive?" Through the use of questionnaires and interviews, the researchers asked 63 top executives from manufacturing, health care, and other service organizations to identify what important changes had occurred in their organizations during an 18-month period. Waller and colleagues predicted that the changes executives perceived to be important (e.g., productivity,

acquisition of resources, development of human resources) would be directly related to the proportions of time they had spent in various business functions, such as finance, marketing, personnel, production, and sales. This is indeed what they found.

But, how does selectivity work as a shortcut in judging other people? Because we cannot assimilate all that we observe, it is important to reduce the amount of information we have to process. So, we take in bits and pieces selectively chosen and organized around our **schemas**, that is, the mental structures that people use to organize their knowledge about the social world around themes or subjects (Kunda, 1999). For example, if you are led to believe that a new coworker is highly capable and industrious, you will tend to notice each of his or her accomplishments. However, if you expect that the new employee is somewhat lacking in ability and motivation, you will more likely take note of his or her failures. Thus, although selective perception may allow us to get a "quick fix" on others, there is the attendant risk of seeing only what we want or expect to see, thereby drawing unwarranted conclusions from an ambiguous situation (DePaulo, Kenny, Hoover, Webb, & Oliver, 1987).

Halo effect. A **halo effect** operates when we draw a general impression of an individual on the basis of a single characteristic, such as intelligence, sociability, or appearance (Nisbett & Wilson, 1977). Solomon Asch conducted an early demonstration of the halo effect. Asch (1946) gave participants a list of traits and asked them to evaluate the person to whom those traits applied. When a list of traits, such as *intelligent, skillful, practical, industrious, determined,* and *warm* was used, the person was judged to be wise, humorous, popular, and imaginative. When *cold* was substituted for *warm,* a completely different set of perceptions was obtained. Clearly, the participants allowed a single trait to influence their overall impressions of the person being judged.

In the work setting, the halo effect is most likely to appear in a supervisor's appraisal of a subordinate's job performance. In fact, the halo effect is probably the most common bias in performance appraisal (Lowenberg & Conrad, 1998). Think about what happens when a supervisor evaluates the performance of a subordinate. The supervisor may give prominence to a single characteristic of the employee like enthusiasm, and allow the entire evaluation to be colored by how he or she judges the employee on that one characteristic. Even though the employee may lack the requisite knowledge or ability to perform the job successfully, if the employee's work shows enthusiasm, the supervisor may very well give him or her a higher performance rating than is justified by knowledge and ability. Murphy and Anhalt (1992) suggested that the halo bias is not necessarily a general characteristic of supervisor ratings. Instead, they showed that the halo effect is dependent on specific features of the rating situation, such as the amount of contact the supervisor has had with the employee, and the occurrence of some significant performance problem.

A powerful factor that can create a halo is the **similar-to-me** effect. This effect occurs when people perceive others who are like themselves more favorably than they do others who are dissimilar. This potential source of bias was demonstrated by Pulakos and Wexley (1983), who found that when supervisors evaluate employees, the more similar the parties are, the higher the ratings the supervisors give. However, Turban and Jones (1988) provided evidence of an alternative explanation for this effect in the work environment. They suggested that perceived similarity may result in more confidence and trust between the supervisor and the employee. This could lead to a more positive and informed working relationship, which in turn would lead to deeper insights (rather than bias). Such insights could contribute to more accurate, and sometimes more favorable, performance appraisals. Nevertheless, it should be obvious that the similar-to-me effect could potentially have significant negative implications in an increasingly culturally diverse workplace where other employees are bound to be different.

The Attribution Process

In our interactions with others, we often want to know *why* they behave or perform in the ways that they do. For example, you might notice that a new employee has been putting in extra hours at work. You wonder whether the new employee is simply behaving in a way that most people would in starting a new job, or whether he or she is a particularly conscientious and hardworking person. In other words, you want to know what *causes* the new employee's behavior. The process of assigning a cause to a behavior is called the **attribution process**.

Harold Kelley, a social psychologist, developed a theory of attribution that focused on how people decide whether the cause of a behavior is external or internal. According to Kelley's (1973) **covariation model**, when we observe the behavior or performance of another person, we consider whether the individual is responsible for the behavior (internal cause) or whether something outside the individual caused the behavior (external cause). When we believe that behavior is *internally* caused, we view it as under the personal control of the individual—the result of his or her personality, values, ability, and so forth. *Externally* caused behavior is viewed as resulting from factors beyond the control of the person—situational factors, such as the physical setting, task difficulty, and the presence and behavior of other people. As depicted in Figure 10.1, the covariation model suggests that, in trying to explain the reason(s) why a person engages in a particular behavior or performs at a certain level, people rely on three types of information:

- *Distinctiveness.* Does the person engage in the behavior in many types of situations, or is it distinctive to one type of situation? If the person behaves the same way in other situations, distinctiveness is low; if he or she behaves differently in many situations, distinctiveness is high.
- *Consensus.* Do most people engage in this behavior in this situation, or is it unique to this person? If others behave similarly, consensus is high; if they do not, consensus is low.

- *Consistency.* Does the person engage in the behavior regularly and consistently in this situation? If the person acts the same way at other times, consistency is high; if he or she does not, consistency is low.

Notice in Figure 10.1 that, depending on how we perceive these three types of information, we are likely to make either an external attribution or an internal attribution. We are likely to conclude that this person's behavior stemmed from *external* causes if we know that (a) this person does not act in the same manner in different types of situations (high distinctiveness), (b) other people also act like this person in this situation (high consensus), and (c) this person does not behave in the same manner at other times (low consistency). In contrast, we will probably conclude that this person's behavior stemmed from *internal* causes if we know that (a) this person acts in the same manner in other situations (low distinctiveness), (b) other people do not act like this person (low consensus), and (c) this person behaves in the same manner in similar situations at other times (high consistency).

To illustrate, suppose that you are the supervisor of an employee who performs well across a variety of tasks (i.e., different situations); in other words, the employee's success on a particular task is not unusual (low distinctiveness). Furthermore, you notice that he or she is the only employee who performs this task well; other employees do not succeed on this task (low consensus). Finally, you observe that the employee performs this task well at different times (high consistency). As Figure 10.1 indicates, given

Figure 10.1   Model of the Attribution Process

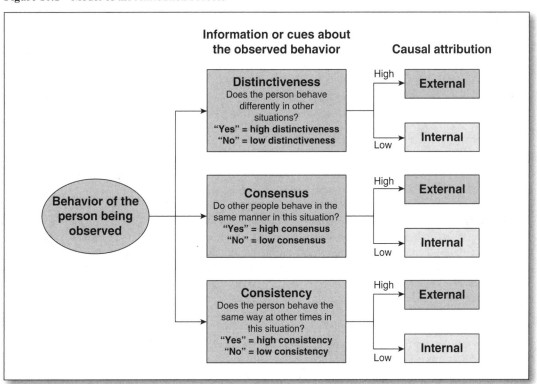

SOURCE: Adapted from Robbins and Langton (2001). Reprinted with permission by Pearson Education Canada, Inc.

these observations—low distinctiveness, low consensus, high consistency—you are likely to attribute the employee's successful performance to internal factors, such as ability and effort. Now imagine another employee who is successful on one particular task, but not on others (high distinctiveness), where other employees also succeed on this task (high consensus), and the employee is not always successful on this type of task (low consistency). Under these circumstances, you are likely to attribute the employee's success on the task to external factors, such as the (easy) nature of the task and luck.

Biases in Attribution

One of the more interesting findings from attribution research is that there are perceptual biases that distort our attributions. Although the covariation model suggests that determining causal attribution is a completely rational process, you probably suspect that people do not always appear to draw conclusions about internal or external causality through a careful and systematic analysis of distinctiveness, consensus, and consistency cues. And you would be correct! In fact, there is substantial evidence that when we judge the behavior of other people, we tend to underestimate the influence of external or situational factors and to overestimate the influence of internal or personal factors (Miller & Lawson, 1989; Ross, 1977). You will recall from some earlier chapters that this is called the **fundamental attribution error**. This phenomenon stems from the fact that it is usually far easier to explain others' actions in terms of their personal dispositions than to be aware of and recognize the complex pattern of situational factors that may have affected their actions (Gilbert & Malone, 1995).

As you might imagine from your own work experience, this tendency can have a significant impact in organizations to the extent that supervisors assign employees too much blame for their failures and too much credit for their successes. Needless to say, this bias can also apply to how employees view their supervisors. For example, Mitchell and colleagues (e.g., Mitchell & Kalb,

1981; Mitchell & Wood, 1980) investigated factors that influence a supervisor's causal attribution of poor work performance on the part of an employee. Consistent with the fundamental attribution error, they found that supervisors were more likely to attribute an employee's poor performance (e.g., high rate of errors) to internal factors than to external ones regardless of the extent to which other employees performed as poorly. (Note that this finding is inconsistent with the high consensus prediction of the covariation model.) Moreover, the supervisors' reactions to the poor performance were directly related, in a predictable manner, to their attributions such that the more internal the attribution, the more likely they were to recommend disciplinary action. Interestingly, Struthers, Weiner, and Allred (1998) reported that supervisors are likely to put more weight on effort than on ability in appraising employee performance. That is, if a supervisor believes that a particularly high level of performance is the result of great effort on the part of a worker, that worker will receive a more positive performance appraisal than if his or her high level of performance is perceived as resulting from ability or talent. Similarly, a performance failure attributed to a lack of sufficient effort will be judged more harshly than will a failure attributed to lack of ability.

Finally, an interesting twist on the fundamental attribution error is that we judge the causes of our own behavior differently than we judge the causes of others' behavior. This bias in causal attribution is called the **actor–observer difference** (Jones & Nisbett, 1972). It refers to the fact that whereas we tend to see others' behavior as being caused by (internal) dispositional factors, we are more likely to see our own behavior as resulting from (external) situational factors. Thus, the same behavior can trigger internal attributions in the observer of the action and external attributions in the actor, that is, the person performing the action. For example, in the case of a supervisor (observer) evaluating the performance of an employee (actor), the supervisor has a tendency to attribute the level of performance to personal characteristics of the employee, such as ability, effort, and personality. That is, the supervisor tends to believe that the employee's performance is due primarily to his or her personal qualities and tends to deemphasize the role that situational factors might have played in the performance outcome. Thus, in some situations, the supervisor may blame the employee for poor performance when the failure was actually due to circumstances beyond the employee's control. On the other hand, the employee (actor) is likely to overemphasize situational factors, and in cases of failure will try to lay the blame elsewhere, for example, by faulting the working conditions, coworkers, or even

the supervisor. The actor–observer bias not only leads to inaccurate perceptions of work performance, but also is likely one of the main reasons why supervisors and employees frequently disagree when it comes to performance appraisals. There is some evidence to indicate that this situation may be more frustrating for employees than for supervisors. Krueger, Ham, and Linford (1996) found that employees (actors), but not supervisors (observers), were aware of the actor–observer bias in specific rating situations, suggesting that employees may realize that supervisors are being biased, but might not be able to make their supervisors aware of it.

FOCUS ON RESEARCH

One Reason Managers May Be Reluctant to Delegate Work

In a laboratory experiment, Pfeffer, Cialdini, Hanna, and Knopoff (1998) investigated the extent to which the amount of supervision provided by a manager would influence his or her subsequent evaluation of both the quality of a subordinate's work and the subordinate's ability. MBA students were invited to participate in a study of "how differing management styles and levels of information affect the quality of a finished work product." Participants arrived at the laboratory in pairs and were separated into individual rooms, where they were told that they would be chosen randomly to assume the role of either a manager or a worker in an advertising agency. Supposedly, the agency had been asked by a wristwatch manufacturing company to design a print ad for a new watch that the company was marketing. Through a bogus draw, each participant was assigned the role of manager and informed that the participant in the other room would take the role of a worker who had been assigned by the agency to design the ad. Participants were told that their role was to supervise the worker's creation of the advertisement, and to subsequently evaluate its quality and the ability of the worker. However, "because of other demands on their time," the opportunity to interact with the worker would be limited. This allowed the researchers to set the stage for the manipulation of the amount of supervision provided.

In the *low-supervision* condition, participants were told that they would have no opportunity to interact with or provide feedback to the worker until the ad was completed. In this condition, after the worker supposedly had completed the ad, participants evaluated both the quality of the ad and the ability of the worker. In the *high-supervision* condition, participants were told that they could review the first draft of the ad and give written feedback to the worker (delivered by the experimenter) prior to completion of the final product using a standardized checklist of suggestions (e.g., provide pricing information). Similar to the low-supervision condition, after the worker completed the ad, the participants evaluated both the ad and the worker. The ad was exactly the same for all participants

(Continued)

(Continued)

in both supervision conditions. Participants' evaluations of the final ad were based on four 7-point scales ranging from 1 (*poor*) to 7 (*outstanding*) on which they rated its (a) creativity and originality, (b) interest level, (c) demonstrated "business sense," and (d) overall quality. The ratings on these four items were combined to form an overall evaluation index. The worker's ability to develop marketing concepts was rated by participants on a 7-point scale ranging from 1 (*very low*) to 7 (*very high*).

Did the amount of supervision provided affect participants' evaluations of the ad and the worker? Yes. In fact, the results were quite dramatic. On average, participants gave the ad a rating of 5.0 in the high-supervision condition and only 3.5 in the low-supervision condition. (Remember, it was the same ad in both conditions.) In addition, participants rated the worker's ability higher in the high-supervision condition (mean approximately 5.5) than in the low-supervision condition (mean approximately 4.2). Thus, when participants played a more active role in supervising the work, they evaluated the quality of the exact same product *and* the ability of the worker substantially higher than when they played a more passive role—a striking instance of perceptual bias.

Pfeffer and colleagues (1998) concluded that as managers become more involved in the supervision of a subordinate's work, their evaluation of that work is likely to become much more favorable. As the researchers noted, "Self-aggrandizing perceptions of this sort are perhaps not surprising given extensive evidence of self-enhancement tendencies in much of human functioning" (p. 319). They suggested that the tendency for supervisors to evaluate the quality of work they were involved in overseeing more positively helps to explain why they may be reluctant to empower employees with greater autonomy and decision-making authority. On the positive side (at least for employees), managers who supervise in a more controlling fashion might not assume all of the credit for themselves. It appears that managers also assign greater credit to subordinates' abilities as their estimates of work product quality rise.

Job Satisfaction: Antecedents and Consequences

People in organizations form attitudes about many different things, including their amounts of pay, their opportunities for promotion, their coworkers, their bosses, and (of course) *their jobs*. These feelings about one's job are known as job satisfaction. **Job satisfaction** can be defined as a person's attitude toward his or her overall job as well as toward various aspects of the job; it is a predisposition to respond to one's work environment in a favorable or unfavorable manner (Steers & Porter, 1991).

Whether or not you are aware of it now, job satisfaction will be important to you. In fact, it may very well underlie the reason you are in college, that is, to maximize the likelihood that you will have the knowledge, skills, and abilities to obtain the kind of job you want when you graduate. If it seems that you have been in school forever, think about how long you are likely to work over the course of your life—eight hours a day, five days a week until approximately 65 years of age. Needless to say, you will be much happier if you are satisfied with the job(s) you have during that time.

The two most widely used approaches in measuring job satisfaction are the global approach and the facet approach. The **global approach** considers overall job satisfaction and simply asks an employee to respond to one general question like the following: "All things considered, how satisfied are you with your job?" Answers usually are provided on a 5-point rating scale ranging from *highly satisfied* to *highly dissatisfied.* The **facet approach** is more sophisticated. In this approach, job satisfaction is considered to be composed of feelings and attitudes about a number of different key aspects or facets of the job. Typical facets within this approach are the nature of the work itself, quality of supervision, pay, fringe benefits, promotion opportunities, job conditions, and relations with other people, such as supervisors and coworkers. These facets are rated on a standardized scale and then summed to create an overall job satisfaction score (e.g., Price & Mueller, 1986). Much of the research on job satisfaction uses the facet approach in its measurement.

This section discusses two areas of job satisfaction that have captured the attention of researchers during the past several decades: (a) the factors that determine job satisfaction, and (b) the effects of job satisfaction on both individual and organizational outcomes. Unfortunately, the section is only able to scratch the surface of this fascinating and important topic because research studies on job satisfaction number in the thousands (Hulin & Judge, 2003), and given recent theoretical and empirical developments in the area, these studies are likely to continue for some time to come.

Determinants of Job Satisfaction

Now that we know a little about what job satisfaction is and how it is measured, let us consider the determinants of job satisfaction. In other words, what "causes" people to like their jobs, and perhaps more interesting, why do some people have different attitudes toward the same job in the same organization? These questions have been addressed in hundreds of empirical studies and several theoretical models, such as Thibaut and Kelley's (1959) *comparison level model of satisfaction,* Hackman and Oldham's (1976) *job characteristics model,* and Salancik and Pfeffer's (1978) *social information processing model.*

With regard to empirical work, one early review of the literature indicated that the most important factors contributing to job satisfaction reflect characteristics of the job and work environment—mentally challenging work, equitable rewards, supportive working conditions, and supportive colleagues (Locke, 1976). More recent research has revealed that personal dispositions also play a major role in determining how satisfied people are likely to be with their jobs (Ilies & Judge, 2003). A summary of some of these factors is shown in Figure 10.2. The left side of the figure shows those factors considered to be related to the extent to which a person will be satisfied with his or her job: the perceived characteristics of the job, the social and organizational aspects of the work environment, and the individual's personal characteristics. The right side of the figure shows the consequences or outcomes of job satisfaction (discussed later). Because of space limitations, only a few of the antecedents of job satisfaction are considered: (a) the core characteristics of a job as proposed by Hackman and Oldham's (1976) job characteristics model, (b) the role of the social context as proposed by Salancik and Pfeffer's (1978) social information processing model, and (c) personal dispositions.

Job characteristics. **Job characteristics** refer to the content and nature of job tasks themselves. Five such core characteristics, listed in Figure 10.2, are central to Hackman and Oldham's (1976) influential job characteristics model, which is based on the premise that workers can be motivated by the intrinsic nature of job tasks. Considerable empirical support exists for the relationship between the five job characteristics and job satisfaction. Using meta-analysis, which, you will recall, is a statistical technique that combines the results of a number of studies that address a set of related research hypotheses, Fried and Ferris (1987) estimated that the mean correlations between the five job characteristics and global job satisfaction are as follows:

Figure 10.2 Antecedents and Consequences of Job Satisfaction

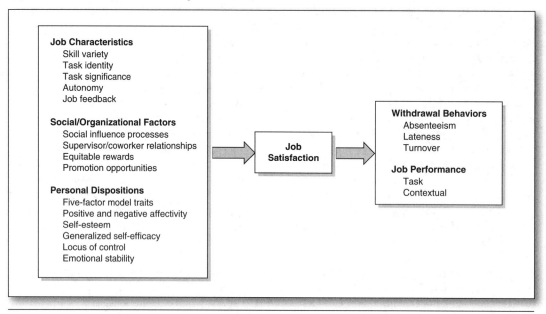

SOURCE: Adapted from Levy (2003) with permission from Houghton Mifflin Company.

- *Skill variety* (degree to which the job allows employees to perform different tasks): +.29
- *Task identity* (degree to which one can see one's work from beginning to end): +.20
- *Task significance* (degree to which one's work is seen as important and significant): +.26
- *Autonomy* (degree to which one has control over how to conduct one's job): +.34
- *Job feedback* (degree to which the work itself provides feedback concerning one's effectiveness): +.29

The preceding relationships between job characteristics and job satisfaction are consistent with the more general finding that among the major job satisfaction facets (pay, promotion opportunities, coworkers, supervision, and the work itself), *satisfaction with the work itself typically emerges as the most important facet for overall job satisfaction* (e.g., Rentsch & Steel, 1992). Not surprisingly, for most of us our work must be personally interesting and meaningful for it to be satisfying. Moreover, according to Hackman and Oldham (1976), the

relationship between job characteristics and job satisfaction should be even stronger for those employees with high **growth need strength** (GNS), which is defined as employees' receptiveness to challenging job characteristics; in other words, the extent to which they want their jobs to contribute to their personal growth and development. There is some evidence for this; Frye (1996) reported average correlations between job characteristics and job satisfaction of .68 for high-GNS employees and .38 for low-GNS employees. However, in general, research has shown that the relationship between job characteristics and job satisfaction is not reliably moderated by GNS (Oldham, 2012).

Before leaving our discussion of job characteristics as potential determinants of job satisfaction, a few cautionary notes are appropriate. One limitation of most studies that have investigated the role of job characteristics in job satisfaction is that job characteristics were assessed by means of self-report questionnaires. That is, the employees complete a job satisfaction measure as well as a measure describing the characteristics of their job, rating it on skill variety, autonomy, and so forth. As discussed in Chapter 3, merely demonstrating that variables are correlated does not mean that one variable necessarily causes the other variable. Although it might be intuitively appealing to conclude that more interesting and meaningful jobs are likely to result in higher job satisfaction, it could also be the case that people who like their jobs are inclined to describe them more favorably than are people who are dissatisfied with their jobs. Thus, job satisfaction might be the cause, rather than the consequence, of job characteristics as rated by workers on questionnaires. Or, the relationship between perceptions of job characteristics and job satisfaction might be bidirectional in that each influences the other (James & Tetrick, 1986).

Social/organizational factors. As shown in Figure 10.2, a variety of social and organizational factors play an important role in determining the extent to which employees are satisfied with their jobs. For example, the nature of an employee's relationships with supervisors and coworkers and the extent to which one perceives his or her work rewards (e.g., pay, promotions, working hours) to be equitable in comparison with the rewards obtained by other employees have a significant impact on the employee's feelings of job satisfaction.

Social influence processes also affect one's level of job satisfaction. For example, the social information processing model of job satisfaction (Salancik & Pfeffer, 1978) is based on the premise that people "adapt attitudes, behavior, and beliefs to their social context and to the reality of their own past and present behavior and situation" (p. 226). In other words, employees develop their levels of job satisfaction based on the information available to them, including the immediate social environment. According to Salancik and Pfeffer, the social environment provides cues that individuals use to construct and interpret the nature of their jobs. One such process involves employees observing the levels

of motivation and satisfaction of other employees and then modeling those levels. This modeling occurs because jobs are often complex incorporating ambiguous stimuli, and employees might be uncertain about how to react to the multidimensional components of their jobs (e.g., job characteristics, supervisors, pay). Knowledge of how an employee's coworkers evaluate their jobs gives the employee some idea as to how to react. For example, if you are continually exposed to negative statements from your coworkers about their lack of decision-making authority, you too may come to perceive your job as lacking in such autonomy, and therefore, as less satisfying. Conversely, if your coworkers talk positively, you are likely to be influenced by these positive evaluations, and, thus to be more satisfied with your job.

In sum, the job characteristics model holds that job satisfaction is determined largely by objective features of the job, such as the variety of skills required to perform the work and the importance of the work performed. On the other hand, the social information processing model posits that job satisfaction is based on the effects of social influence in the work environment. As noted previously, there is considerable empirical (albeit correlational) support for the job characteristics model. In general, research also has supported the social information processing model. For example, in a laboratory experiment, Mirolli, Henderson, and Hills (1998) found that participants rated a task as more enjoyable when they were exposed to a confederate's positive comments about the task than when they were exposed to a confederate's negative comments about the task. In a field study of 66 civilian employees at a U.S. military base, Pollock, Whitbred, and Contractor (2000) reported that information from the social environment (i.e., communication and friendship networks among coworkers) had a significant effect on individuals' job satisfaction. Thus, both the social environment and job characteristics seem to be important factors in the extent to which people are satisfied with their jobs. So too are personal dispositions, which are discussed next.

Personal dispositions. Few studies prior to the mid-1980s focused on individual differences, much less personality as sources of job satisfaction (Hulin & Judge, 2003). Since that time, however, two seminal studies by Staw, Bell, and Clausen (1986) and Arvey, Bouchard, Segal, and Abraham (1989) have provided considerable impetus to investigations of the role of dispositional factors as determinants of job satisfaction. Staw and colleagues made use of data from the intergenerational studies initiated at the University of California, Berkeley, during the 1920s. Beginning in adolescence, participants were assessed on a number of characteristics using interviews and questionnaires several times during their lives. Scores on 17 of the characteristics were combined into a measure of affective disposition (e.g., *cheerful, warm, negative*). Staw and colleagues reported striking results showing that positive affective disposition assessed as young as early adolescence was significantly correlated (.34) with overall job satisfaction assessed at 54 to 62 years of age.

In an even more provocative study, Arvey and colleagues (1989) found significant similarity in job satisfaction levels of 34 pairs of identical twins reared apart from early childhood (i.e., each pair was identical in genetic makeup, but lived in different environments). The intraclass correlation between the twins' ratings of job satisfaction was .31, meaning that if one person tended to be satisfied with his or her job, so did the person's identical twin. It appears that individuals are born with characteristics that predispose them to be more or less satisfied with their work. In the words of Hulin and Judge (2003), "Heritability of job satisfaction is very likely indirect, operating through heritability in personality or other dispositions" (p. 263). However, as noted by Ilies and Judge (2003), neither Staw and colleagues' (1986) study nor Arvey and colleagues' (1989) study documented any direct evidence for the relationship between specific personality traits and job satisfaction.

Subsequent research has attempted to address this issue, focusing on a variety of personality traits, including those that are central to the *five-factor model* of personality (e.g., neuroticism), *core self-evaluation traits* (e.g., self-esteem), *positive affectivity* (the tendency to experience enthusiasm, confidence, cheerfulness, etc.), and *negative affectivity* (the tendency to experience anxiety, hostility, anger, etc.). Various meta-analyses of the findings of these studies have been conducted and the results (summarized in Hulin and Judge, 2003) are shown in Table 10.1. The overwhelming majority of correlations shown in Table 10.1 are significant, which clearly supports the relevance of personality to job satisfaction. Generalized self-efficacy and positive and negative affectivity appear to be the most highly correlated with job satisfaction. Thus, the more people believe in their own competence and effectiveness, and the more they are disposed toward positive emotions rather than negative emotions, the more likely they are to be satisfied with their jobs.

Although research investigating the extent to which individual differences in personality influence job satisfaction is likely to continue with fervor, it is important not to minimize the impact of environmental and social factors (e.g., job characteristics, social influence processes) on job satisfaction.

In this regard, **person–job fit** models posit that job satisfaction results from complex interactions between personal dispositions and environmental (job) characteristics (Hulin & Judge, 2003). Researchers pursuing this approach argue that a person's job satisfaction will be higher to the extent that there is a good match between his or her personal characteristics and the nature of the job (Kristoff, 1996). For example, the empirical evidence is fairly consistent in showing that the closer the correspondence between what people say they *want* in their jobs (e.g., autonomy) and what they say they *have* in their jobs, the greater their job satisfaction (Edwards, 1991).

Consequences of Job Satisfaction

What consequences may be expected from workers who are satisfied or dissatisfied with

Table 10.1 Mean Estimates of the Relationship Between Personality and Job Satisfaction

Personality Trait (and meta-analysis source)	Mean Corrected Correlation
Five-factor model traits (Judge, Heller, & Mount, 2002)	
Neuroticism	−.29
Extroversion	.25
Openness to experience	.02
Agreeableness	.17
Conscientiousness	.26
Core self-evaluation traits (Judge & Bono, 2001)	
Self-esteem	.26
Generalized self-efficacy	.45
Locus of control	.32
Emotional stability	.24
Positive and negative affectivity (Connolly & Viswesvaran, 2000)	
Positive affectivity	.49
Negative affectivity	−.33

SOURCE: Adapted from Hulin and Judge (2003). This material is used by permission of Wiley.

their jobs? This question has generated a vast amount of research during the past several decades, with particular attention given to how job satisfaction affects job performance. In addition, the effects of job satisfaction on many other important organizational and personal outcomes have been well documented. Such outcomes include employee withdrawal behaviors (e.g., absenteeism, turnover), counterproductive behaviors (e.g., theft, sabotage, interpersonal violence), and employee well-being (e.g., physical and mental health, general life satisfaction). This subsection briefly reviews the research on employee withdrawal behaviors and then turns its attention to the relationship between job satisfaction and job performance. It concludes with a discussion of the possible causal nature of this relationship.

Employee withdrawal behaviors. As you might expect, people who dislike their jobs are more likely to avoid or *withdraw* from them, either in

the form of absenteeism (i.e., missing work) or in the form of voluntary turnover (i.e., quitting). Absenteeism is an expensive behavior in North America. For example, over a decade ago, Lu (1999) estimated that sick pay, lost productivity, and overstaffing to compensate for absentee workers annually cost American and Canadian organizations up to $46 billion and $10 billion, respectively. Obviously, not all absenteeism can be attributed to job dissatisfaction. People miss work for many unavoidable reasons, including illness, family problems, and weather conditions. Nevertheless, several researchers have investigated the relationship between absenteeism and job satisfaction. In an early review of the literature, Porter and Steers (1973) concluded that both voluntary turnover and absenteeism increase as job satisfaction decreases. But, these relationships are not especially strong. For example, in a meta-analytic review of research findings pertaining to absenteeism, Hackett and Guion

(1985) reported an average correlation of only −.09 between absenteeism and job satisfaction. They also found that absenteeism was more closely related to some facets of job satisfaction than to others, particularly satisfaction with the nature of the work itself.

Voluntary turnover is also costly to organizations. By the time an employee is recruited, hired, trained, and evaluated, an organization has invested a considerable amount of time and money in that individual. As noted by Levy (2003), when an employee quits, not only is the initial investment in the person lost, but the organization also must spend additional money in a new cycle of recruitment, selection, and training. There are many factors that contribute to turnover, such as age, level of education, marital status, and number of dependent children (Cotton & Tuttle, 1986). Employees who are young, are well educated, and do not have families to support are more mobile, and therefore more likely to seek out alternative employment opportunities. In addition to perceived ease of movement, researchers also have looked at the role that job satisfaction plays in decisions to leave an organization. In general, research indicates a moderately strong relationship between job satisfaction and turnover, with less satisfied workers more likely to quit (e.g., Steel & Ovalle, 1984).

In sum, the empirical evidence suggests that although job satisfaction is related to various types of employee withdrawal behavior, it is more predictive of turnover propensity than of absence propensity. Needless to say, not all employees who dislike their jobs quit, so this begs the question: Do those employees who are dissatisfied and stay on the job perform more poorly? The next subsection tries to answer this question.

Performance. As noted by Judge, Thoresen, Bono, and Patton (2001), the investigation of the relationship between job performance and job satisfaction is one of the most venerable research traditions in applied psychology. Since the Hawthorne studies of the 1920s and 1930s

(Roethlisberger & Dickson, 1939), researchers and managers alike have been captivated by the intuitively appealing notion that "a happy worker is a productive worker." Until recently, however, this notion received little empirical support. For example, in an influential meta-analytic review of the research literature, Iaffaldano and Muchinsky (1985) concluded that job performance is at best only weakly related to job satisfaction. Their estimated correlation of .17 between satisfaction and performance was based on the average of the correlations between specific job satisfaction facets (e.g., pay, coworkers, and promotion opportunities) and job performance.

Recently, the Iaffaldano and Muchinsky (1985) meta-analysis has been criticized on both statistical and conceptual grounds (Judge et al., 2001). The statistical flaws are beyond the scope of our current purpose, so only the latter is addressed here. Judge and colleagues (2001) argued that averaging the correlations between job performance and specific *facets of job satisfaction* is conceptually different from the relationship between performance and *overall job satisfaction*. Accordingly, they suggested that one must create a composite of the job satisfaction facets as opposed to averaging the individual correlations between each facet and job performance. Using this approach in their own meta-analysis, Judge and colleagues estimated the corrected correlation between job satisfaction and job performance to be .30, nearly twice as high as the earlier estimate reported by Iaffaldano and Muchinsky (1985).

Another aspect of performance is organizational citizenship behavior. As initially defined by Organ (1988), **organizational citizenship behavior** refers to employee behavior that is "discretionary, not directly or explicitly recognized by the formal reward system, and that in the aggregate promotes the effective functioning of the organization" (p. 4). Organizational citizenship behavior can be distinguished from specified job requirements, that is, what an employee must do according to his or her job description. For example, organizational citizenship behavior involves performance behaviors, such as voluntarily assisting coworkers; alerting others to work-related problems; conscientiously performing one's own work (e.g., not wasting organizational resources; involving oneself in the life of the organization, such as going to meetings and keeping abreast of the larger issues affecting the organization); and tolerating the inevitable inconveniences and impositions of work without complaint. It may have occurred to you that job satisfaction must surely have some impact on the extent to which an employee will "go above and beyond the call of duty" to get the job done. If so, you are right.

In fact, research has shown that the more people are satisfied with their jobs, the more good citizenship contributions they tend to make (Konovsky & Organ, 1996). However, the relationship appears to be moderated by perceptions of fairness. When fairness is controlled, job satisfaction is unrelated to organizational citizenship behavior (e.g., Moorman, 1991). In other words, when employees perceive organizational processes and outcomes to be fair, they are more likely to trust their employers. And when employees trust their employers, they are more willing to engage in behaviors that go beyond their formal job requirements (Organ, 1990).

The question of whether satisfaction "causes" performance. Although you know by now that correlation does not imply a causal relationship between two related variables, some people might assume that job satisfaction "causes" job performance. After all, as mentioned previously, for many years both managers and social scientists assumed that a happy worker was a productive worker, reflecting the belief that satisfaction causes performance. On the surface, the notion that people who are satisfied with their jobs are subsequently likely to expend greater effort on their jobs seems logical. But, a simple "satisfaction produces performance" relationship might not necessarily be the case. There are other possibilities. Judge and colleagues (2001) reviewed seven different theoretical models that have been used to describe the satisfaction–performance relationship. A simplified description of five of the models is shown in Table 10.2. Because of space limitations, only the first two models are described in detail. This will give you at least a taste of the theoretical complexity surrounding this area of inquiry.

Model 1, often attributed to the human relations movement, represents the traditional perspective that people who like their jobs work harder, and therefore perform better. As noted by Judge and colleagues (2001), this model is grounded in the broader stream of social psychology attitude research in which researchers have assumed that attitudes (e.g., job satisfaction) have direct implications for behavior. For example, Eagly and Chaiken (1993) stated that depending on whether

Table 10.2 Models of the Relationship Between Job Satisfaction and Job Performance

Model	Description
1	Job satisfaction causes performance (i.e., attitudes lead to behavior).
2	Job performance causes job satisfaction (i.e., attitudes follow behavior).
3	Job satisfaction and job performance are reciprocally related (i.e., attitudes lead to behavior, and in turn are changed by behavior).
4	Job satisfaction and job performance are only spuriously related (i.e., the satisfaction–performance relationship is due to the relationship of each of these variables to one or more unmeasured variables).
5	The job satisfaction–job performance relationship is moderated by other variables (i.e., the relationship exists only to the extent that other factors are present; e.g., job performance affects job satisfaction if it leads to important job rewards like pay).

we evaluate an object favorably or unfavorably, we will tend to engage in behaviors that foster/support it or hinder/oppose it, respectively. Within this attitude–behavior perspective, it follows that if a person evaluates his or her job favorably (i.e., has high job satisfaction), the person will put in greater effort to perform well. Obviously, the converse also is true. Few studies have actually hypothesized a unidirectional "satisfaction causes performance" relationship, and of those that have, the results are inconclusive (Judge et al., 2001).

In Model 2, the implied causal relationship between satisfaction and performance is reversed. Performance is deemed to cause satisfaction in the sense that people who perform well are likely to benefit from that performance, and those benefits could enhance satisfaction. In this regard, Lawler and Porter (1967) suggested that performance leads to job satisfaction through the provision of intrinsic and extrinsic rewards. For example, if effective job performance leads to extrinsic rewards (e.g., an increase in pay, a promotion) or intrinsic rewards (e.g., a sense of accomplishment), and these rewards are perceived as fair, receiving these rewards leads to job satisfaction. Although several studies have tested this model, the results are mixed with some claiming a significant "performance causes satisfaction" relationship (e.g., Brown, Cron, & Leigh, 1993), and others showing no causal relationship (e.g., Brown & Peterson, 1994).

Before leaving this section, it is worthwhile to mention the results of a more recent, but somewhat limited, meta-analysis of the relation between job attitudes and performance. Based on meta-analytic regression analyses of 16 studies that had repeatedly measured performance and job satisfaction and/or organizational commitment, Riketta (2008) found some support for the common assumption that job attitudes influence performance.

In concluding this section, we should note that Judge and colleagues (2001), following their extensive review of the literature, proposed an integrative model of the relationship between job satisfaction and job performance because they believed that several of the models are best considered in a unified framework. In their integrative model, Judge and colleagues suggested that there likely is a bidirectional causal relationship between satisfaction and performance (i.e., Model 3 in Table 10.2). However, the relationship could be moderated by other variables like personality (i.e., Model 5). For example, Mount, Harter, Barrick, and Colbert (2000) found that job satisfaction was more strongly related to job performance for less conscientious employees than for conscientious employees. Presumably, conscientious employees who are dissatisfied are less willing to reduce their levels of performance (i.e., because they are still conscientious even though they are not happy with their jobs). In addition, Judge and colleagues (2001) suggested that the causal effects between satisfaction and performance may be mediated by other variables like positive affect. Thus, job satisfaction might lead to better job performance because employees who like their jobs are more likely to be in good moods at work, and this in turn facilitates job performance through higher levels of motivation (Isen & Baron, 1991).

CULTURE CAPSULE

Job Satisfaction Across Cultures

Many studies conducted in North America have shown that job characteristics are related to job satisfaction. As with research in all areas of psychology, we cannot be certain that the results of studies done with workers in Western societies will generalize to countries with very different cultures. Pearson and

Chong (1997) investigated the differential effects of various predictors of job satisfaction in a sample of 286 nurses working in a Malaysian public health organization. Because of the Chinese values and collectivistic culture of Malaysia, the researchers hypothesized that Malaysians would be more sensitive to collectivist-related *interpersonal aspects* of work like feedback from others and dealing with others than to individualist-related *job characteristics*, such as skill variety, task identity, task significance, autonomy, and job feedback. In turn, Pearson and Chong predicted that the collectivist-related aspects of work would be more highly correlated with job satisfaction than would the individualist-related factors.

As expected, there were no significant correlations between any of the five job characteristics and job satisfaction (the correlations ranged from −.09 to +.07). Thus, job content was not related to the extent to which the Malaysian nurses were satisfied with their jobs, a finding that is considerably different from findings typically reported in North American studies. However, the informational attributes of feedback from others (measured by the appropriate section of Hackman & Oldham's 1980 Job Diagnostic Survey) was substantially related to the nurses' job satisfaction; the correlation was .40. Pearson and Chong (1997) explained these results as reflecting the collectivistic culture of the Malaysians, whereby individuals place great value on the relationship-oriented components of their work environment, enabling the development of harmonious relations with supervisors and coworkers. This study clearly indicates that we must be cautious in assuming that research findings in Western organizations can be replicated in the organizations of other cultures.

INTERPERSONAL PROCESSES IN ORGANIZATIONS

Communication

Organizations can range in size from small two-person "mom and pop" corner stores to large transnational companies with tens of thousands of employees. Regardless of their size, to carry out work within and across these organizations, employees, managers, and executives need to communicate with each other. In fact, managers spend approximately 80% of their time communicating (Trevino, Daft, & Lengel, 1990). By definition, **communication** involves social behavior that is two or more people interacting with each other and transmitting information. In fact, Semin (2007) suggests that communication is the most fundamental topic social psychologists can address because it represents the foundation of social life. As elaborated below, the precise nature of communication behavior is not as simple as it may appear. There are a number of subtle activities involved in the act of communicating. Some of them might not be immediately apparent, but are nonetheless essential for conveying information effectively. To better understand the significance of each of these activities, let us consider a simple model of the communication process.

A Model of Communication

As depicted in Figure 10.3, when communication occurs, a **message** is conveyed. A message refers to the verbal and nonverbal information that is imparted from one party to another. This message must be conveyed by way of a **channel**, which refers to the medium through which the message is transmitted (e.g., computer cables, telephone wires, air molecules in the case of face-to-face communication). During this process, the **sender** refers to the individual who conveys the message. Note that before the sender can transmit a message, that message must be **encoded**, constructed from the sender's thoughts, and transformed into a communicable form. After being transmitted, the message is then **decoded** (perceived and interpreted) by a **receiver**. Of course, communication is not a one-way process. The receiver may decide to respond to the sender. When this occurs, the receiver becomes the sender, and the entire process is reversed.

You probably can imagine ways in which the communication process can break down at any point along this chain. In fact, you may remember the delight you experienced noticing these breakdowns occurring when playing the "broken telephone" game as a child. As you may recall, this game involves seating children in a line and having the first child whisper a short made-up story into his or her neighbor's ear. Each successive child whispers the "same" story to his or her neighbor farther down the line until the end of the line is reached. The last child then tells his or her version of the story, and the child who first made it up notes whether it remained intact by repeating the original story to the group. Invariably, the children find that the story has mutated as it progressed down the line. How should we account for this phenomenon, and what might be some of the implications for communication in small and large organizations?

Perspectives on Communication

With our model of communication in mind, let us consider a few different ways in which organizational communication can be viewed. Krone, Jablin, and Putnam (1987) distinguished among the mechanistic, psychological, and interpretive–symbolic perspectives of communication. (They also discussed a systems interaction perspective that is not elaborated here.) Each of these perspectives involves a different **locus of communication**, that is, the point in the communication process that is the focus of the particular perspective (Fisher, 1978). For example, in the **mechanistic perspective**, the locus of communication is the channel (see Figure 10.3), and communication is viewed primarily as a transmission process with a primary focus on the mechanics of sending a message. Because effective transmission is considered central in this perspective, research in this tradition might focus on factors like the communication skills of managers, including their choice of medium, and on the overall effectiveness of their transmission of information. These skills should be important given the necessity for coordinated activity in organizations of all types.

Research within the mechanistic perspective has provided evidence that communication skills can in fact have a number of practical consequences in organizations. For example, Sypher and Zorn (1986) measured the communication skills of employees at a large U.S. insurance company and found that those possessing stronger communication skills tended to occupy higher levels in the corporate hierarchy and tended to be promoted more often. Similarly, Penley, Alexander, Jernigan, and Henwood (1991) found that managers with better developed communication skills outperformed those

Figure 10.3 Communication Process

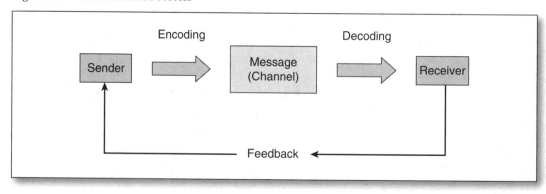

with less developed skills. Finally, it has been shown that managers who choose to use communication media that match the complexity and ambiguity of the messages they send are rated as higher performers (Trevino et al., 1990). Given the need to clarify objectives, sell ideas, coordinate activities efficiently and effectively, and provide accurate feedback to people in organizations, the results of the preceding studies should not be surprising. Fortunately, it's possible to design interventions to enhance employees' communication skills and produce positive organizational outcomes. For example, Beranek and Martz (2005) demonstrated that virtual teams that received communication skills training reported higher cohesiveness and satisfaction.

If you'd like to improve your own communication skills, you can draw on a number of different strategies. Let's focus on the specific skill of being persuasive and how to effectively sell your ideas to others. Research shows that leaders who use more image-based rhetoric are regarded as more charismatic (Emrich, Brower, Feldman, & Garland, 2001). Image-based rhetoric involves using words that help your listeners easily paint a picture in their minds of what it is you're talking about. So, for example, when trying to sell people on the idea of pursuing a course of action that will involve some difficulties, instead of saying "we have a challenge ahead of us," you can say "we have a big mountain to climb." Such visual imagery will result in you being perceived as more charismatic and you're likely to be more persuasive.

Conger (1991) suggests a number of techniques that leaders use to be persuasive. For example, they amplify values. This means they present their ideas in terms of how they help to promote outcomes that are consistent with the values of the audience. So, to be persuasive don't just focus on what's important to you; focus on what's important to your audience and how your ideas are consistent with their values. This is a variation of the WIIFM principle—"what's in it for me?" Your audience needs to know what's in it for *them* if they follow your lead, and how your ideas are aligned with their values.

Leaders also strategically use rhetorical devices, which are stylistic ways of communicating intended to produce effects in listeners. Metaphors are an example of a rhetorical device that can be used intentionally to be more persuasive. Indeed, Conger (1991) suggests leaders use metaphors, analogies, and stories to produce vividness, clarity, or to convey particular emotions to their audiences so that what they say has more impact. Leaders also use other speech techniques, such as repetition, rhythm, and alliteration for greater impact. Alliteration involves repeated use of a consonant. For example, if you say "we must manage this monstrous mess" you've just used alliteration by repeating the consonant 'm'. Strategically injecting these sorts of speech tactics into what you say can turn an average communication into a mesmerizing one.

Cialdini (2001) suggests that leaders can enhance their persuasiveness by drawing on a number of principles. One of the principles involves liking; because people like those who are like them, in order to increase how much people like you in your role as a leader you should make an effort to discover and discuss similarities between yourself and the people or person(s) you are trying to persuade. Another principle involves social proof. People tend to rely on the opinions of others when forming their own opinions. So, if you want to be persuasive try to enlist the endorsement of others who support your ideas and share these endorsements with the people you're trying to convince of the merits of your position. A third principle involves authority. People tend to listen to those they consider experts. So, before you start trying to convince someone of something, make it clear to them why you're an authority on the subject. Your credibility can come from experience, training, or having done some homework on the topic. Regardless, wherever your authority comes from, don't keep it a secret. Advertise it. Make sure people know why they should listen to you. A final principle we'll mention involves scarcity. People tend to be attracted to things that are rare. So, it may sometimes be useful to highlight the exclusivity of information you have, or use loss language when presenting your idea. Loss language highlights the things people will miss out on if they don't pursue the rare, temporary opportunity you're presenting. Of course, as noted by Cialdini (1991), you should only use loss language if the limited window of opportunity is genuine. Intentionally deceiving people is not only ethically deplorable, in the long term it can undermine your entire career because people will learn to not trust you.

The second perspective of communication is the **psychological perspective**. In this perspective, the locus of communication is people's conceptual filters (Krone et al., 1987). **Conceptual filters** consist of attitudes, cognitions, and perceptions (Fisher, 1978) that may distort information exchange. The basic idea within this tradition is that, as discussed earlier in the chapter, there is too much information in the environment for people to attend to all of it. As a result, people learn to automatically filter out what they consider to be unnecessary information. This is a form of *selective perception*. A potential problem with filtering information is that what is considered unimportant by one person may be considered important, or even vital, by another person. As a consequence of incongruent conceptual filters among communication partners, breakdowns in communication may occur. The psychological perspective focuses on the way in which conceptual filters affect encoding by the sender and decoding by the receiver.

It is important to recognize not only that conceptual filters limit the information to which people attend, but also that psychological processes will tend to make people confident that the particular pieces of information they focus on are important and that the ignored pieces are less important. Consider the breakdowns in communication that could occur between a marketing manager, whose primary focus is sales, and an operations manager whose primary focus is efficient production. Because these managers focus on different objectives, the conceptual filters they use in thinking about their work will likely be different, and this may produce communication difficulties that lead to conflict.

An example of research within the psychological perspective is a study conducted by Dunkerley and Robinson (2002). These investigators explored the communication styles of American and British managers working in the United Kingdom. Dunkerley and Robinson found that the style of communication of American managers tended to be direct and task focused, whereas the British managers' style tended to be more circuitous, cautious, and focused on maintaining the work relationship. This may appear to be a simple example of cultural differences, and in fact it is. However, more fundamental than the overt differences in behavior are the underlying differences in conceptual filters that lead these groups to focus on different aspects of their shared interactions. Of particular relevance to our discussion is that managers from each country believed that their own communication style was superior and tended to denigrate the communication style of the managers from the other country. For example, one American manager commented that "the British approach is inefficient" (Dunkerley & Robinson, 2002, p. 399), whereas one British manager stated that "the American approach is simplistic" (p. 402). Both parties' conceptual filters influenced the information they attended to and deemed important.

Given these findings, we might expect that an American manager would be susceptible to filtering out a British colleague's comments about their relationship because the comments are deemed irrelevant. Similarly, we might expect that a British manager might get offended when an American manager curtly makes direct requests. Note that in Dunkerley and Robinson's (2002) study, managers were explicitly asked about their thoughts regarding the communication style of their "foreign" colleagues. However, when people are at work, they typically are not asked to think about these types of issues. Evaluations of other people and other people's ideas occur automatically, and we generally do not notice the effects that our filters may have on our judgments.

The third approach to understanding organizational communication is called the **interpretive**

symbolic perspective (Krone et al., 1987). In this perspective, the locus of communication is the shared meaning that develops between or among the parties involved in the act of communicating. Referring back to Figure 10.3, we would say that just like the psychological perspective, the focus of this perspective is on encoding and decoding. However, this time we are not concerned about the biasing effect of filters; instead, we are concerned about the development of categories of thought (i.e., the filters themselves) that allow communication to occur. Consider the following example. If a friend speaks to you about one of your professors, you and your friend need to have a shared understanding of the word *professor* before any effective communication can take place. In fact, you need to have a shared understanding of every word in every sentence. The interpretive symbolic perspective suggests that categories of thought or word definitions (e.g., *professor*) are not objective features of our environment, but rather are created by people through a process that is sometimes called **consensual validation**. This is defined by Weick (1979) as the development of a "common sense" that people agree on because their collective experiences make it seem correct. Consensual validation reduces the level of uncertainty we experience by allowing us to share meaning, and by imposing order on a potentially confusing and chaotic environment.

The interpretive symbolic perspective has its roots in the theory of **social constructionism** (Gergen, 1985), which posits that reality is constructed by means of the consensual validation achieved through social interaction. As Edley (2001) noted, we should not make the mistake of believing that there is no reality apart from that which we create socially. We should, nonetheless, recognize that our interpretations of much of our experiences are influenced by our socially constructed categories. The terms we use to label people (e.g., secretaries vs. executive assistants), situations, and events influence the ways in which we think about them, how we react to them, what we expect from them, and what we consider to be normal and appropriate.

The example of research within the interpretive symbolic tradition considered here involves an observational field study. Bennington, Shetler, and Shaw (2003) analyzed the communication of representatives from three organizations—a waste disposal company, a state regulatory agency, and a community activist organization—who were participating in a public meeting to discuss changes in the waste disposal company's operations. Bennington and colleagues noted that some of the words that the company representatives and community activists used were identical, but had different connotations; that is, the representatives did not create shared meaning among the three groups. As a result, the representatives of the three organizations found it difficult to effectively explain their respective points of view to each other, and the meeting ended with no resolution to the main issue under consideration. In this case, the parties did not agree on the categories of thought that shaped their understanding of reality, and this precluded their negotiating an agreement.

As another example, consider the communication difficulties that might arise during performance management meetings if a manager and his or her subordinate have different mental representations of what is meant by effective performance. The employee might think that performing the job well simply means completing the assigned tasks properly and on time, whereas the manager might view effective performance as also including the taking of initiative and adapting well to changes (Griffin, Neal, & Parker, 2007). Such different mental representations could certainly lead to misunderstandings and other difficulties. As such, managers and subordinates need to have a shared meaning of effective performance in order for the performance management process to succeed (Gordon & Stewart, 2009). Intervening in an organization to create a common language and shared meaning about performance can improve the performance management process (Beer, Ruh, Dawson, McCaa, & Kavanagh, 1978).

Do you think that the broken telephone effect and the problems encountered by the task force in the opening vignette might best be explained by the mechanistic, psychological, or interpretive symbolic perspective? You should be able to imagine how each perspective could play a role.

Nonverbal Aspects of Communication

No discussion of communication would be complete without addressing its nonverbal aspects. **Nonverbal communication** refers to all information conveyed by a sender, apart from the words themselves, that plays a role in the transmission of meaning. The tone of your voice, the way in which you are dressed, the mannerisms you use, the features of your smile, and whether you make eye contact when speaking all are examples of nonverbal aspects of communication. It is important to know that in certain situations, people's nonverbal signals can sometimes convey more accurate information than the actual words they use (Burgoon, 1994; Mehrabian & Ferris, 1967).

In a survey of applications of nonverbal behavior in marketing and management, DePaulo (1992) noted that researchers and consultants have addressed issues of nonverbal behavior in areas such as advertising, sales, public relations, service delivery, leadership, supervision, and security. DePaulo concluded that nonverbal behaviors play a significant role in many areas of organizational functioning. Consider a few examples. In an experiment in which a variety of nonverbal behaviors were manipulated, Leigh and Summers (2002) found that salespeople who made more eye contact were perceived by buyers to be more believable and that those who were less hesitant in their speech were perceived as more interesting and persuasive. The importance of nonverbal behavior also has been demonstrated in studies of the employment interview, which happens to be the work-related topic area in which the most nonverbal communication research has been conducted (DePaulo, 1992). For instance, in an experiment using videotaped interviews, Howard and Ferris (1996) found that interviewers rated job candidates as more suitable for employment when the candidates

displayed high levels of certain nonverbal behaviors (i.e., direct eye contact, smiling, and head nodding) than when they displayed low levels of these behaviors.

It may surprise you to learn that it also has been shown that the nonverbal behavior of interviewers can influence the behavior and perceived suitability of job applicants. Liden, Martin, and Parsons (1993) conducted an experiment in which job applicants were interviewed by an interviewer who displayed either warm or cold nonverbal behaviors. In the warm condition, the interviewer maintained eye contact most of the time, leaned forward in his chair, smiled occasionally, and faced the applicant. In the cold condition, the interviewer made no eye contact, leaned back in his chair, did not smile, and sat sideways relative to the applicant. The results revealed that the verbal and nonverbal behaviors of applicants interviewed by the cold interviewer were rated more negatively by independent judges than were the verbal and nonverbal behaviors of those interviewed by the warm interviewer. It seems not only that an applicant's nonverbal behavior matters in job interviews, but also that the interviewer might actually be able to influence the verbal and nonverbal behaviors that the applicant exhibits.

As suggested by the preceding study, interviewers may use nonverbal behaviors to infer characteristics of job applicants and determine their suitability for a position. If accurately decoding an applicant's nonverbal behavior is necessary to determine his or her suitability for a position, might the effectiveness of a job interview be compromised if it were conducted in such a way that some nonverbal behavior was missing? This was precisely the question posed by Blackman (2002). Blackman had pairs of university students conduct mock job interviews. In each pair, one student was randomly selected to play the role of interviewer and the other to play the role of job applicant. The interviews were conducted either face-to-face or over the telephone. Subsequent to each interview, both participants completed personality questionnaires assessing the personality of the job applicant. The purpose of the study was to determine whether there would be a difference in the degree of agreement between the interviewer's and applicant's assessments of the applicant's personality as a result of the interview method. As it turned out, there was. Blackman found that the difference was greater in the telephone interview condition than in the face-to-face interview condition. She concluded that the lack of nonverbal information available to the interviewer in the telephone condition might have reduced the accuracy of the interviewer's assessment of the job applicant's personality.

Nonverbal communication may also be lacking among employees who work together despite being physically distant from each other, as occurs in virtual teams. Research on the communication style of virtual work groups interacting through asynchronous media, such as chat rooms or e-mail has shown that in contrast to groups in face-to-face communication, virtual work groups display the following characteristics: Volume of information increases, efficiency decreases, establishing common ground takes longer, quality of feedback is reduced, and message comprehension is lower (DeSanctis & Monge, 1999; Driskell, Radtke, & Salas, 2003). Those who communicate exclusively using electronic media like e-mail may have a more difficult time in achieving consensual validation (Weick, 1979) because decoding social cues that are helpful in establishing meaning is more difficult.

We should also note that communication problems can occur within groups that communicate using more modern video-based technology. Providing, observing, and decoding the nonverbal behavior of team members may be more difficult when interacting remotely through computer screens than when interacting face-to-face (Driskell et al., 2003). To date very little research has been conducted on how communication is affected by video-based technologies (c.f., Anderson, McEwan, & Carletta, 2007; Gonzalez-Navarro, Orengo, Zornoza, Ripoll, & Peiro, 2010). However, the available research suggests that video-based communication may differ from face-to-face communication. Groups interacting

through videoconferencing have more difficulty regulating their conversations. For example, such groups take fewer turns in discussing how to complete a task, require more time for turn-taking, and interrupt each other less often (which sounds like a good thing, but doesn't reflect the style of face-to-face conversations); however, these differences wane over time (Van der Kleij, Schraagen, Werkhoven, & De Dreu, 2009). So, it seems that although video-based communication isn't comparable to face-to-face interaction, over time employees may be able to adjust to this form of communication. However, it's still too early to have a solid appreciation of the effects of video-based communication in organizations, or the specific capacity for this medium to process nonverbal communication cues.

Group Decision Making

Small groups have always been a major focus of social psychological inquiry. Levine and Moreland (1998) note that an understanding of groups is necessary for the analysis of social behavior because groups provide the social context in which much social behavior occurs. Because of this, researchers have long been interested in better understanding the effects of group-level phenomena, such as cohesion (e.g., Casey-Campbell & Martens, 2009), culture (e.g., Schein, 2006), composition (e.g., Joshi, 2006), and conflict (e.g., Levine & Thompson, 1996). Although these topics are interesting in and of themselves, they also are important because of their practical implications for group decision making.

Traditionally, how groups make decisions and what factors promote high-quality versus low-quality decisions have been important concerns for organizations because most important decisions in organizations are made by groups (Donaldson & Lorsch, 1983). Today, however, these concerns are even more significant due to the growing prevalence of semiautonomous and self-managed work teams. In the United States, 80% of Fortune 500 companies have at least half of their employees working in teams (Joinson, 1999). In contemporary organizations, teams are often responsible for making group decisions that previously have been under the purview of individual managers. As more team-based organizations develop, group decision making becomes much more prevalent, and the consequences of group decision making become more significant. Under these conditions, understanding the social psychology of group decision making becomes more important than ever before.

You might think that the trend toward group decision making is a good idea and that it is obvious that groups should make better decisions than individuals. However, our intuitions about the results of group decision making often are inaccurate (Davis, 1992). Groups do not always make better decisions than individuals. For example, this is because groups can exert pressure on people to conform to bad ideas and exacerbate individual decision-making biases.

Groupthink

Janis (1983, 2007) proposed that a number of tragic decisions in history (e.g., the Kennedy administration's Bay of Pigs invasion) could be explained by his theory of groupthink. **Groupthink** essentially refers to a process of flawed decision making that occurs as a result of strong pressures among group members to reach agreement. That is, one or more of several antecedent conditions induce concurrence seeking tendencies that override effective decision making by preventing a group from engaging in careful and thorough consideration of all relevant information.

Among the antecedent conditions that Janis proposed were high group cohesiveness, directive leadership, high stress, and insulation of the group from outsiders (Janis, 1983; Janis & Mann, 1977). In addition, Whyte (1998) suggested that groupthink might arise from an exaggerated sense of collective efficacy, for example, when overconfidence among group members leads them to falsely assume that it is unnecessary to fully examine possible advantages of alternative decisions. In fact, the evidence concerning which

antecedent conditions do promote the development of groupthink is actually rather equivocal. Baron (2005) has noted that research examining the factors that lead to groupthink are often inconsistent and contradictory. Whether or not some of the proposed antecedent conditions lead to groupthink may be moderated by the presence or absence of other conditions (Brehm, Kassin, & Fein, 1999). For instance, there is some experimental evidence that high stress (e.g., necessity of reaching a fast decision) promotes groupthink especially under conditions of high cohesiveness (Turner, Pratkanis, Probasco, & Leve, 1992).

Notwithstanding the importance of understanding the determinants of groupthink, of particular relevance to the focus of this chapter is that problems connected to groupthink can victimize groups in a wide variety of organizational contexts. For example, groupthink tendencies have been observed in groups as diverse as a university board of trustees (Hensley & Griffin, 1986), and battery assembly work teams (Manz & Sims, 1982). Scharff (2005) suggests that groupthink may even help us understand the disastrous events at WorldCom, which committed the largest accounting fraud in the history of the United States.

Although there isn't strong evidence that the processes identified by Janis lead to groupthink, the processes themselves are actually fairly common and affect decision making in many different kinds of "ordinary" groups (Baron, 2005). Because such processes can adversely affect the quality of decisions made in organizations, it is important to understand how organizations can take steps to ensure that groups engage in effective decision-making processes. Janis (1983) proposed a set of prescriptions for preventing groupthink. The prescriptions generally focus on helping a group to carefully examine all relevant information and courses of action to ensure that it does not rush into making a poorly informed and reasoned decision. Clearly, the leader has a critical part in initiating steps to prevent groupthink. For example, the leader should ensure that each member of the group assumes the role of "critical evaluator." In addition, the leader should as much as possible remain impartial and not voice his or her preferences and expectations until all other group members' views have been heard. Research supports the importance of intervention strategies to reduce the possibility of the flawed decision-making processes connected with groupthink (Brehm et al., 1999).

If, in the case of groupthink, concurrence-seeking tendencies can propel groups into making bad decisions, another group phenomenon that may serve to enhance a group's tendency to reach agreement on (bad) decisions is group polarization.

Group Polarization

More than 50 years ago, Stoner (1961) demonstrated that when people made decisions after engaging in a group discussion, the decision made by the group as a whole tended to be riskier than the average of the decisions the people had made individually prior to the discussion. Initially, this effect was called the **risky shift**. However, the label changed when researchers later noted that sometimes group decisions were actually more conservative than decisions initially made by the group's individual members. This phenomenon eventually was relabeled **group polarization** because it was determined that the group tended to polarize (make more extreme) the initial position of the majority of its members. That is, if group members' views on average are mildly supportive of a position, then as a result of group discussion the group's final decision tends to be more strongly supportive. Conversely, if before entering the group discussion individual members on average moderately oppose an issue, the group's decision tends to be more strongly opposed.

Group discussions polarize other kinds of decisions as well as those involving risk. In fact, group polarization can influence the deliberations of any kind of group, including most certainly those in the world of organizations. One example comes from a study by Whyte (1993). Business students were asked to imagine having to decide whether they would sink additional money into

various business projects that were doing badly. Evidence of polarization occurred when the students were more likely to invest more money when deciding as a group than when deciding as individuals. The results have serious practical implications because group polarization exacerbated the notion of "too much money to quit," a phenomenon that has been financially damaging to many companies. In a real-world example of polarization in the business world, Zhu (2013) found evidence of polarization in the price that boards of directors were willing to pay to acquire companies. When individual board members of acquiring companies had experience with paying relatively high (or relatively low) premiums to acquire companies in the past, the board as a whole chose to pay even more (or even less) of a premium to acquire a real target company.

We should return to the likely connection between groupthink and group polarization. For one thing, the polarization process may underlie a group's tendency to rush into a premature decision in the case of groupthink. Also, perhaps the overconfidence hypothesized to be an antecedent of groupthink may result from the polarization of confidence among individual group members. Let us consider what social psychological mechanisms help to account for group polarization.

The most likely explanation for group polarization involves the concepts of normative influence and informational influence (Deutsch & Gerard, 1955), both of which are present to varying degrees in every social situation. **Normative influence** refers to pressure to conform to the expectations of others so as to gain social approval or avoid negative social consequences like being ostracized. For example, in a group meeting, if an employee has reservations about the majority view, but goes along with it because he or she does not want to annoy the other members of the group, the employee is experiencing normative influence. **Informational influence** refers to changes in behavior or attitudes as a result of information obtained from other people that provides evidence about the nature of the social situation. In ambiguous situations that are not readily amenable to objective verification, we often turn to others to provide us with information about what is correct and to guide our behavior. For example, if an employee in a group meeting changes his or her position on an issue based on the convincing nature of the arguments presented by the other group members, the employee is experiencing informational influence. Essentially, the distinction between normative influence and informational influence involves the difference between conforming in order to be accepted and conforming in order to be right, respectively.

So, which is it? If you were taking part in a group discussion, do you think your views might become more extreme because you felt pressure to conform so as to be accepted by the group (normative influence), or because your definition of the situation was guided by information provided by other members of the group (informational influence)? It turns out that there is evidence to support both forms of influence in producing polarization. Support for normative influence has centered on demonstrations that mere knowledge of the positions or opinions of other people (without exposure to discussion) can produce polarization and that whether or not polarization occurs depends on whether or not individuals believe that the positions or opinions derive from members of their in-group (Eagly & Chaiken, 1993). These demonstrations suggest that pressure to conform to the expectations of important reference groups serves as one ingredient in producing group shifts toward more polarized positions.

Evidence of informational influence rests on studies that support what is termed **persuasive arguments theory** (Burnstein & Vinokur, 1977). According to this theory, polarization occurs when most of the arguments that group members hear favor one position over another. In a group where most or all members favor a particular position, most of the arguments raised during the group deliberation will reflect that position. Because the preponderance of information supports the position, the members become even more persuaded, and thus polarization occurs. Eagly and Chaiken (1993) pointed out that the degree of polarization toward a position correlates directly with (a) the number of pro-position arguments available to group members, and (b) the extent to which the arguments are valid. However, recent research also demonstrates that simply repeating information can polarize decisions (Schultz-Hardt, Giersiepen, & Mojzisch, 2016). So, it seems that polarization can occur as a result of the desire to be accepted by the members of one's group, and also as a consequence of being exposed to many strong or repeated arguments favoring a particular position. As organizations implement more team-based structures, group members and managers should be aware of these types of social processes, be vigilant about the effects that these processes may have on group decisions, and recognize that designing groups to have a diversity of viewpoints will make them less susceptible to polarization (Yaniv, 2011).

Normative influence and informational influence serve as useful constructs in helping us to understand the decisions made by groups and how they may differ from those made by individuals. In addition to shedding light on why decisions become polarized, these constructs may help us to understand why groups fail to reduce, and sometimes actually intensify, certain decision-making biases that we observe in individuals.

Decision-Making Biases in Groups

Human beings have a limited capacity to hold information in memory and have great difficulty in evaluating numerous pieces of information simultaneously or in quick succession. As discussed earlier in the chapter, to help in the processing of information, people regularly and automatically use cognitive shortcuts, or **heuristics**, when making judgments. These heuristics allow people to make efficient decisions without taxing their mental resources. We saw earlier that cognitive shortcuts can result in perceptual biases. Another consequence of using heuristics is that they sometimes lead people to make decisions that are inferior in quality to objective standards. For example, in Chapter 7, you read about the *availability heuristic* (Tversky & Kahneman, 1973). The availability heuristic can have the effect of making people think that issues are more common and/or more likely than they actually are.

There are a number of decision-making biases to which people fall victim, and it has been demonstrated that groups do not always diminish—and sometimes even exacerbate—these biases. This might sound surprising. Should it not be the case that individual group members can serve as *error checkers* and that groups will produce more accurate solutions to problems? Not always. Group members do tend to serve an error-checking function when the demonstrability of a solution is high; for example, when someone in the group has access to data that clearly indicate the correct answer. This is sometimes referred to as a *truth wins* process of decision making. However, when the demonstrability of a solution is low (i.e., the solution is very hard to discover), a *majority wins* process, where the group accentuates the dominant tendencies of its members, seems to characterize group decision making (Tindale, 1993). When the demonstrability of a solution is low, the group may fall victim to the same biases that affect individuals.

One well-known bias to which people regularly succumb is called the hindsight bias (Fischoff, 1975). The **hindsight bias** refers to people's tendency to believe, in retrospect, that an event was more predictable than it actually was. For example, before the launch of a new product, employees in a company may have conflicting views as to whether the product will succeed in the marketplace. However, if the product eventually does succeed, people retrospectively considering their prior confidence levels will often claim that they knew all along that the product would be well received. Simply put, people believe that they are better at predicting outcomes than they actually are, and once an outcome is known, they tend to believe that they would have predicted it. This bias can jeopardize effective decision making because it can produce overconfidence and prevent learning from experience (Fessel, Epstude, & Roese, 2009). Despite the reasonable conjecture that error-checking group members could serve to eliminate or at least reduce the hindsight bias, research has demonstrated that groups have no appreciable effect on its magnitude. Studies by Stahlberg, Eller, Maass, and Frey (1995) and Bukszar and Connolly (1988) indicate that the hindsight bias is present to the same extent in group judgments as it is in individual judgments.

A second bias to which individuals regularly fall victim is the **confirmation bias** (Wason, 1960) that is discussed in Chapter 5. This bias refers to people's tendency to seek out and pay attention to information that supports their favored positions and to ignore disconfirming information. Schulz-Hardt, Frey, Lüthgens, and Moscovici (2000) explored the magnitude of the confirmation bias in groups and individuals. They had 200 participants read a case study involving a chemical company that had to make the decision of whether or not to invest in a developing country. Some participants were placed in groups and informed that after a 10-minute discussion, they would be asked to make a preliminary group decision, and then after more group discussion, a final group decision. The remaining participants were not placed into groups and were simply asked to make an initial individual decision, and, later a final individual decision. After they had made their initial decisions, and before they were asked to make their final decisions, the groups and individuals were provided with the opportunity to receive additional separate pieces of information that either favored or opposed investment in the developing country. Schulz-Hardt and colleagues' results (2000) revealed that confirmation bias occurred in each condition in that both groups and individuals demonstrated a clear preference for additional information that supported the initial decisions they had made. Interestingly, the researchers also found that groups chose significantly more supporting information than did individuals. Thus, confirmation bias was significantly stronger in groups, a convincing illustration of groups failing to serve the error-checking function. Based on the preceding discussion of normative influence and informational influence, what do you think might have caused the intensification of this bias in groups? What consequences do you think group confirmation bias might have on the effectiveness of organizations?

A third bias we consider is based on the **representativeness heuristic** (Kahneman & Tversky, 1972), which leads people to make categorical judgments based on the extent to which an object, event, or individual is perceived to fit or represent a particular category. This heuristic can produce a bias in which base-rate information (i.e., statistical probability) is insufficiently weighted. For example, imagine being at a party where you know that 30 doctors and one jockey are in attendance. Imagine next that you are introduced to a very short man. How likely would you be to guess that this man is the jockey? According to Kahneman and Tversky (1972), you are likely to allow the fact that the short man is representative of jockeys to bias your judgment and conclude that the person races horses for a living. Notice that in this case you are ignoring base-rate information, which would suggest that the person is most likely a short doctor. This bias has been demonstrated repeatedly in individuals, but only a few studies have explored the extent to which the representativeness heuristic is present in groups.

One such study was conducted by Argote, Seabright, and Dyer (1986) who presented participants working alone or in five-person groups with base-rate information that there were nine engineers and 21 physicians in a group of 30 people. Participants were then provided with descriptions of three members of the group and were informed that each description had been randomly drawn from a set of file cards containing descriptions of all the group members. One description, Ben's, was made to sound like an engineer. Another description, Jonathan's, was made to sound neutral. The final description, Roger's, was intended to sound like a physician. Participants were simply asked to indicate the probability that the individual in each description was one of the engineers in the group. Note that the statistical probability of randomly drawing an

engineer from the group is .30. The results of the study revealed a clear bias based on the representativeness heuristic. Individuals' probability estimates that Ben, Jonathan, and Roger were engineers were .63, .36, and .21, respectively. The corresponding group estimates were .74, .36, and .20. Both individuals and groups were greatly influenced by the description of Ben and allowed it to substantially bias their estimates. However, the groups tended to amplify this bias; when judging the likelihood that Ben was an engineer, the groups were significantly more influenced by the description than were the individuals and produced an estimate further from the base rate. Argote and colleagues explained these results in terms of persuasive arguments theory, suggesting that group discussion tended to expose members to additional arguments in favor of relying on the individuating information.

More recently, Hinsz, Tindale, and Nagao (2008) similarly demonstrated that groups can exaggerate individuals' tendencies to ignore base-rate information when making decisions, and explained their results in terms of how groups are attracted to decisions that "fit" with the way most group members perceive the task on which they are working. The better a decision alternative fits the group (i.e., when most group members are processing information in a similar way), the more likely it is that the group will accentuate the prevailing cognitive processes of its members and further bias decisions.

These results are only a sample of the research on biases in group decision making. However, the conclusion is clear: Groups do not always produce higher-quality decisions than individuals. As discussed, social psychological processes help to explain why this is the case. Today, as more and more employees work in teams, it is important that they and others pay attention to how social dynamics may influence their group decisions.

*Decision Making and
Information Technology*

Earlier in this chapter we discussed virtual teams and how communication can be affected when employees who are physically separated work together through the use of information technology. As you might expect, collaborating through technology can also affect group decision making. For example, instant messaging allows group members to engage in "invisible whispering," which can alter group processes and influence decisions (Dennis, Rennecker, & Hansen, 2010).

In 1987, McGuire, Kiesler, and Siegel demonstrated that groups interacting face-to-face (FTF) displayed greater bias in their decision making than did groups engaging in text-based computer-mediated communication (CMC). McGuire and colleagues' results suggest that there may be less social influence exerted on group members when they interact by way of computers. But, which form of influence is reduced—informational or normative? The traditional view has been that with the use of information technology, normative influence decreases relative to informational influence (Reid, Ball, Morley, & Evans, 1997). In his review of the literature, Bordia (1997) concluded that there is greater equality of participation in CMC groups and that CMC groups perform better than FTF groups on idea generation tasks. Bordia's conclusions imply that there is less normative pressure in CMC groups and suggest that McGuire and colleagues' (1987) results—less-biased decision making in CMC groups—also can be attributed to a reduction in normative influence.

In a direct test of the relative impact of normative influence and informational influence in computer-mediated decision making, Reid and colleagues (1997) examined the discussion patterns of FTF and text-based CMC groups as they tried to reach a decision about how to handle an alleged case of child abuse. In examining the comments made by participants in both conditions, the researchers found that CMC members made fewer comments that demonstrated informational influence and made more comments that demonstrated normative influence. These results counter the prevailing view that CMC reduces normative influence relative to informational influence.

However, the story is probably a little more complicated. The degree to which the different forms of influence affect the decisions of virtual groups is likely impacted by the degree of anonymity of the participants (Valacich, Sarker, Pratt, & Groomer, 2009), and the level of "virtuality" of the medium (Gonzalez-Navarro et al., 2010). Technologies that are more similar to FTF conversations (i.e., teleconferencing) are likely to invoke different forms of influence than those that are less like FTF conversations (i.e., text-based communication). Also, recent research suggests that the impact of these two forms of influence in computer-mediated work environments may depend on the nature of the task (Huang & Li, 2007). Further research is required to sort out these questions.

Group decision making is affected not only by social influence processes, but also by the communication processes discussed earlier. Effective decision making may be negatively affected during CMC because social cues necessary for accurately decoding messages are reduced. Baltes, Marcus, Sherman, Bauer, and LaGanke (2002) concluded that nonanonymous CMC groups are less effective in their decision making, particularly when they are under time pressure, and take longer to reach decisions than do FTF groups. Why does this occur? Strauss and McGrath (1994) suggested that CMC is most likely to adversely affect group decision making when there is a need to perceive the emotions of others, when persuasion is required, or when value-based consensus building is needed (i.e., when social cues greatly facilitate interaction). In this regard, Baltes and colleagues (2002) suggested that the more lifelike the medium (e.g., real-time exchange of information and presence of nonverbal information), the better the computer-mediated decision making. Along these lines, it has been suggested that in order to improve the functioning of teams that will work together via computer it's advisable to have the members of such teams meet in person first so they can get to know each other at least a little bit better (Kennedy, Vozdolska, & McComb, 2010).

In a recent review of the literature on research on virtual teams, Gilson, Maynard, Jones Young, Vartiainen, and Hakonen (2014) suggested that virtual teams create delays in information exchange, more misunderstandings, and less information seeking. They also suggested that there are ways to enhance the success of virtual teams, such as making sure members feel equal and connected, establishing goals, fostering regular communication patterns and structured processes, and properly designing rewards.

So, it appears that computer-mediated decision making is affected not only by changes in social influence processes that occur when people interact through computers, but also by difficulties inherent in communicating using information technology. Organizations are well advised to take these issues into account and to carefully consider task requirements when considering processes and procedures that can enhance the effectiveness of decision making by groups interacting by way of computers.

FOCUS ON INTERVENTION

Reducing Confirmation Bias in Work Groups

Recall that Schulz-Hardt and colleagues (2000) found that one of the biases that affect groups (more than individuals) is that they engage in biased information seeking and tend to gather data that confirm their original positions. This is clearly not a recipe for effective organizational decision making based on a thorough consideration of available data. In a follow-up investigation designed to test the effectiveness of interventions aimed at reducing this bias, Schulz-Hardt, Jochims, and Frey (2002) examined the effect of intentionally producing conflict during a group decision-making task. In a manner slightly different from that in the study conducted by Schulz-Hardt and colleagues (2000), an experiment was conducted in which 201 employees and managers read an economics case involving a company that had to make a decision regarding whether to transfer some of its operations to "Country A" or "Country B." After evaluating the case individually, participants were asked to choose which country represented the best alternative and then were provided with the opportunity to receive new information (i.e., brief articles) regarding the choices they had made. Participants were told that each article was written on a separate sheet of paper and was either in favor of or opposed to an investment in Country A or Country B. Participants made their choices, but were informed that the articles would not be distributed prior to a subsequent group discussion. Based on participants' choices regarding the countries in which they chose to invest, homogeneous and heterogeneous three-person groups were then formed and instructed to make group decisions about which country should receive the investment. Homogeneous groups consisted of participants who had chosen the same country, whereas heterogeneous groups consisted of a two-person majority and a one-person minority. At the same time, one member in half of the groups in both conditions was assigned a "devil's advocacy" role in which he or she was required to identify all disadvantages, mistakes, and false assumptions underlying the investment choice that his or her particular group was considering. Both of these manipulations—group composition and devil's advocacy role—were designed to stimulate conflict in the groups. After discussing the case, groups made their final decisions and were again provided with the opportunity to receive new information regarding the countries in question (the same articles provided to individuals previously). The articles that the groups chose served as an indication of the extent of confirmation bias.

The results revealed that, as expected, homogeneous groups displayed the confirmation bias; however, heterogeneous groups showed no confirmation bias. Also, groups with a member playing the devil's advocacy role facilitated the search for information conflicting with the groups' tendencies and reduced the confirmation bias. It should be noted, however, that genuine dissent (present in heterogeneous groups) was more effective in eliminating the confirmation bias than was contrived dissent (i.e., devil's advocacy).

These results clearly underscore the potential for designing interventions to reduce bias in group decision making. It appears that training group members to consciously explore alternative ideas and carefully choosing members of groups such that a diversity of opinions is available are successful interventions for reducing the bias inherent in some group decisions. In fact, the devil's advocacy procedure in particular is often employed as an intervention to reduce groupthink.

Summary

This chapter has attempted to convey to you the breadth of application of the theories, principles, and research findings of social psychology to understand social behavior in organizations. The first main section of the chapter focused on individual psychological processes in an organizational context. It began by exploring social perception and noted how certain perceptual biases, such as selective perception and the halo effect, influence the ways in which we view and interpret the behavior of others in the work environment. It then discussed the attribution process and noted how our perceptions of the distinctiveness, consensus, and consistency cues of another person's behavior influence whether we conclude that the person is responsible for the behavior (internal cause), or that something outside the person caused the behavior (external cause). It also discussed how the fundamental attribution error and the actor–observer effect distort the accuracy of our attributions.

Next, the first section focused on job satisfaction, a topic that is likely to be of interest to most of you throughout your working careers. It first touched briefly on how job satisfaction is measured by social scientists, and then explored some of the factors thought to be related to job satisfaction, including the characteristics of the job itself, the social and organizational environments in which the job is situated, and the personal dispositions of the job incumbent. It also looked at some of the potential consequences of job satisfaction, including the relationship of job satisfaction to employee withdrawal behaviors and job performance. The section concluded with a discussion of the complex question of the nature of the causal relationship between job satisfaction and job performance.

The second main section of the chapter addressed the role of interpersonal processes in organizations. It examined three ways in which to conceptualize organizational communication by considering the mechanistic, psychological, and interpretive symbolic perspectives. It noted that all three perspectives contribute to a fuller understanding of effective communication in organizations. It also discussed the importance of nonverbal behavior in the communication process, particularly how it can affect judgments made during an employment interview.

Finally, the second section explored decision making in groups. It showed how certain phenomena, such as groupthink and group polarization can victimize groups in a wide variety of organizational contexts. It also discussed how certain biases, such as hindsight bias, confirmation bias, and the representativeness heuristic are not necessarily diminished through group input, and in fact may be exacerbated in group discussions and decision making. The section ended with a brief discussion of the effects of information technology on group decision making. In general, it appears that computer-mediated decision making may be adversely affected not only by changes in social influence processes, but also by difficulties inherent in communicating using information technology.

11

APPLYING SOCIAL PSYCHOLOGY TO THE CRIMINAL JUSTICE SYSTEM

DAVID M. DAY

STÉPHANIE B. MARION

CHAPTER OUTLINE

On the evening of November 14, 1999, Dmitri "Matti" Baranovski, a 15-year-old high school student from Toronto, sat with about six friends in the Harryetta Gardens playground in a park near their school and not far from where Matti lived with his mother. They often would come to the park to talk, socialize, and just hang out.

At approximately 8:45 p.m., they were approached by a group of 10 to 12 older teens and were asked whether they had any cigarettes and money. The intruders were wearing balaclavas over their faces so that their identities were not readily apparent. When Matti and his friends told them they had no cigarettes or money, the young men persisted in their demands. At this point, Matti stood up against the group and told the older teens to stop bothering him and his friends.

The details of what happened next are not entirely clear. According to newspaper reports, three of the young men began to punch and kick Matti about his face and body. Matti's friends ran away, leaving him alone with his assailants. As a result of the attack, Matti fell to the ground as he continued to be brutally hit and kicked. One kick caused Matti's head to simultaneously rotate and snap back, tearing the vertebral artery in his neck and killing him. The attack lasted only a few minutes, after which the assailants fled.

One of Matti's friends had run across the street to a residence to summon help. The first 911 call came in at 9:02 p.m. (Wong, 1999). By the time the paramedics arrived on the scene, Matti's body was lifeless. Although he was revived later at the hospital, Matti died during the early morning hours of the next day.

It was later revealed that the young men had apparently come to the park looking for a fight with another group whose members failed to show up. They then turned their attention to Matti and his friends and decided to rob them. It also was revealed that at least two cars had passed by the scene that evening on the busy street that runs by the park. The drivers, on hearing Matti's screams, had slowed down or even stopped. In all cases, no one came to assist Matti or called for help. According to one newspaper report (Wong, 1999), a woman driving by stopped her car when she and her two sons, who were passengers in the car, heard the noises from the attack. They reported hearing a loud cry for help and a lot of Russian words, followed by someone yelling "Get to the ground!" At that point, the woman, fearing that there might be weapons involved, became scared and drove off.

This vicious attack raises many questions about the nature of criminal behavior and about people's responses to criminal acts that may be examined from a social psychological perspective. Moreover, beyond the particular criminal incident, social psychological theory and research can be applied to understand and address other aspects of the criminal justice system, including the police investigation, the criminal trial, and the incarceration and rehabilitation of criminal offenders. Some of the questions that social psychologists could address include the following:

- What situational factors of that evening might have influenced the behavior of Matti's assailants?
- What factors might account for the responses of the bystanders who, on hearing the commotion, slowed down, but did not stop to assist?
- Once the police become involved in a crime, what elements make for an effective investigative interview with witnesses, victims, and suspects?
- In a court case, how might the personal characteristics of a defendant or the situational characteristics of the courtroom influence decisions made by the judge or jury members?
- Can we increase the effectiveness of prisons by altering their social climates and creating more "humane" environments behind bars?

With regard to the potential role of social psychology in answering these questions, consider the following statement made by Schuller and Ogloff (2001), "Given that public policies, laws, and court decisions are based on assumptions about human behavior, the very subject matter of psychology, psychologists can play a vital and important role in this area" (p. 6). Consider also that criminal behavior is a social act, involving violations of socially defined laws. Some crimes are committed against people directly, including both violent offenses (e.g., murder, robbery, uttering a death threat), and nonviolent offenses (e.g., fraud, voyeurism, exhibitionism). In many cases, particularly among youths, crimes are committed by groups of individuals acting together. What social psychologists bring to these issues are theories and methodologies that take into account the role of both the person and the situation to account for behavior. This approach provides a more integrative and multilevel framework for addressing the issue of crime than does focusing only on the person or only on the environment.

To illustrate, criminal acts may be viewed from a **social ecological perspective**, that is, as the result of an interaction between the person and the environment. This notion derives from Kurt Lewin's famous theorem:

B = f(P, E), which states that *behavior* (*B*) is a function (*f*) of the *person,* (*P*), the *environment* (*E*), and the *interaction* between the two (Lewin, 1951). With regard to criminal behavior, an individual may be compelled to offend only in the presence of an environmental stimulus that acts as a sort of "trigger." For example, a person might shoplift only after walking into a large department store; indeed, some offenders can be quite picky regarding the stores from which they will steal. In the absence of the large department store, the crime would not take place. As another example, a drug addict might start "jonesing" or craving a "hit" on seeing drug paraphernalia sitting on a table.

In practice, social psychology has been of value to the police in developing techniques for interviewing suspects, to defense attorneys in demonstrating how a person can come to be wrongfully accused of a crime, to lawyers in selecting possible jurors for a trial, and to forensic psychologists in conducting risk assessments of offenders to predict the probability of future criminal behavior. Whereas many such topics may be explored, a full discussion of the contributions of social psychology is beyond the scope of this chapter. The topics examined here relate to four aspects of the criminal justice system where the application of social psychology has been particularly fruitful: (a) explaining criminal behavior, (b) conducting the criminal investigation, (c) conducting the trial, and (d) incarcerating offenders. The chapter first examines criminal incidents from a social psychological perspective, focusing in particular on the attack on Matti.

THE CRIME AND THE CRIMINAL

The Social Psychology of a Crime

In some respects, the tragedy of the beating death of Matti Baranovski described in the opening vignette is reminiscent of the story of Catherine "Kitty" Genovese, who in 1964 also was killed by her attacker in Queens, New York. This incident has received considerable attention in both the social science literature and the public media because of the original reports that a number of the victim's neighbors were witnesses to the attack, but had failed to intervene, although the number of such witnesses does remain in question (Manning, Levine, & Collins, 2007).

Research on bystander intervention (Darley & Latané, 1968; Latané & Nida, 1981) has shown that various factors influence a person's decision to assist in an emergency situation, including the ambiguity of the situation and the perceived similarity of the victim to the potential helper. Another factor is the number of bystanders who witness the emergency. There is considerable research evidence of a phenomenon known as the **bystander effect**, which states that people are less likely to help in an emergency when other bystanders are present. One explanation for the bystander effect is that the presence of others lowers the individual bystander's sense of responsibility. The drivers who passed by the Toronto park and heard Matti's cries that evening might not have intervened because they thought that given the busy road nearby, others would intervene. Moreover, this **diffusion of responsibility** (i.e., the diminished sense of responsibility a person feels when he or she believes that others would or should intervene) is more likely to occur when a bystander can remain anonymous (the driver may remain in his or her car and continue driving without much notice), when there are relatively few victims (only Matti's voice was heard screaming), and when the victim is perceived to be dissimilar to the potential helper (Russian words were heard). What would you have done if you had been a passerby that evening? Unfortunately, it seems that many of us would not have offered help. In Toronto on April 24, 2010, Yusuf Hizel, a 79-year-old male, was doing what many of us do on a regular basis, riding public transit home for the evening. At about 8:30 p.m. while taking the subway, Mr. Hizel was robbed by two men who asked for then demanded money. When Mr. Hizel stood up to press the passenger assistance alarm, the two men pulled him down and held him while one grabbed his wallet. They fled the subway at the next station. The attack took place in full view of perhaps two dozen other passengers. As Mr. Hizel cried out for help, no one came to his assistance, or even called for help (White, 2010). Fortunately, the two men, both in their late 20s, were later arrested for the crime.

Let us consider the behavior of Matti's assailants. What situational factors might have accounted for their violent actions? We could begin by asking questions like the following: Would these young men have attacked Matti if they had not been wearing masks over their faces? Would they have engaged in the violent behavior if they had not been in a group, that is, if they had been on their own with Matti and his friends? To what extent did such factors contribute to Matti's beating? Although we cannot know for sure, we can speculate based on sound principles derived from well-controlled social psychological research.

Wearing balaclavas over their faces provided the young men with a sense of anonymity and loss of personal identity, much like members of the Ku Klux Klan wearing hooded robes. Research on **deindividuation** (i.e., a diminished sense of self-awareness) suggests that people, under the cover of anonymity in which their identities are concealed, may deliberately choose to engage in behavior about which they might otherwise be inhibited, including aggression. For example, Zimbardo (1969) demonstrated in a laboratory experiment that female research participants wearing Ku Klux Klan–type hoods and outfits delivered shocks for twice as long to an experimental confederate as did other research participants whose identities were revealed by large name tags.

The young attackers also were not acting alone. Moreover, they had come to the park prepared to fight. The notion of **social facilitation** (Zajonc, 1965) informs us that a person's performance on a well-learned task will be enhanced by the heightened arousal caused by the presence of others. Perhaps the aggressive behavior of these young men was well learned—something they were accustomed to doing, and indeed something they were primed to do that

evening. Within their antisocial peer group, such behavior might even be considered "normative." As a result, the presence of the group might have heightened the young men's levels of arousal, which in turn enhanced their tendencies to engage in aggression, resulting in the vicious unprovoked attack.

Furthermore, it was alleged that Matti's assailants had come to the park intending to fight with another group whose members failed to show up. This aborted confrontation may have led to a heightened sense of frustration and anger among the young men. According to the **frustration–aggression hypothesis** (Berkowitz, 1989), frustration—defined as anything that blocks a person from attaining a goal—may have been a trigger for their aggressive behavior in the presence of a new set of potential victims.

A fourth factor that may influence antisocial behavior and aggression in particular is the presence of *situational cues* that incite the behavior. Recall the laboratory experiment by Berkowitz and LePage (1967), discussed in Chapter 7, in which the presence of a gun rather than a badminton racquet, was shown to increase the aggressive behavior of research participants. Moreover, according to Anderson and Bushman (2002), some social contexts restrict opportunities to act aggressively, whereas others provide ample opportunities:

> Church services contain many impediments to aggression—witnesses, strong social norms against aggression, and specific nonaggressive behavioral roles for everyone in attendance. Country/Western bars on Saturday nights present better opportunities for aggression. Many aggression facilitators are present: alcohol, aggressive cues, aggression-prone individuals, males competing for the attention of females, and relative anonymity. (p. 43)

Perhaps, under the cool cover of night in a secluded area of a park, the stage was set for violence to erupt as a group of deindividuated, frustrated, and aggressive young men turned their sights on Matti and his friends.

But, these factors do not explain all of the events of that evening, nor do they explain the events leading up to or subsequent to the attack on Matti. In fact, although deindividuation and social facilitation are good examples of some of the **proximal variables** (i.e., those occurring close in time to the event) that can influence criminal behavior, there is another set of factors that also is important, referred to as **distal variables** (i.e., those occurring in the distant past relative to the event). As we will see, a comprehensive social psychological theory of criminal behavior should include both sets of determinants.

It should be noted that recognition of the situational determinants of criminal behavior is not meant to imply that an individual's *personal responsibility* for engaging in antisocial acts should be reduced or diminished in any way. Rather, it is meant to acknowledge that many factors—both situational and individual differences—are needed to fully explain crime.

The Origins of Criminal Behavior

Existing theories of criminal behavior implicate a wide range of variables that reside within the person, the person's immediate environment, and the broader sociological context. Presented in what follows are some of the major theoretical paradigms from biology, sociology, and social psychology that have been put forth to explain criminal behavior. Although this chapter emphasizes the social psychological perspective, it is important to always remember that the perspectives of other disciplines contribute to a more complete understanding of psychological phenomena, including the etiology of criminal behavior. A general discussion of biological and sociological theories is presented first, followed by a consideration of several social psychological approaches.

Biological Theories

Biologically based theories view criminal behavior as the result of genetics, psychophysiology, neurological functioning, and biochemistry. Studies of genetic influences, for instance, have noted a greater preponderance of criminals among sons whose biological parents also were criminals (Lytton, 1990). The well-documented finding that males have a greater propensity for physical aggression than do females has been attributed to higher levels of testosterone (Dabbs, Carr, Frady, & Riad, 1995) and the presence of an extra Y chromosome (XYY) (Crowell, 1987), although the latter observation has been disputed (Mednick, Moffitt, Gabrielli, & Hutchings, 1986). In addition to these inherited biological characteristics, acquired biological deficits may influence criminal behavior. Even before birth, factors may conspire against the developing fetus, predisposing it to impulsive, hyperactive, or aggressive behavior. For example, a lack of proper nutrients during critical periods of prenatal development, or pre- or postnatal exposure to toxic agents (e.g., alcohol, cigarettes, lead, drugs) may result in mild or severe deficits in cognition (e.g., learning disabilities, social information-processing deficits, low verbal IQ) and behavior (e.g., poor motor coordination, poor self-control) (Hodgins, Kratzer, & McNeil, 2002)—factors that are known to place a child at risk for aggression. There is growing recognition that theories of crime need to be more biologically informed. The role of two indicators of autonomic arousal, for example, low resting heart rate and low skin conductance, has received considerable attention recently (Choy, Farrington, & Raine, 2014), and both have been shown to be important biological markers of criminal and antisocial behavior.

Sociological Theories

Some of the most enduring theories of crime are those that are based on sociological principles. These traditional theories (e.g., anomie, strain, control, subculture), although widely diverse attempt to explain crime in relation to various factors in society, such as social class, poverty, and social inequity. Thus, a person's socioeconomic status, determined by education, occupation, income, and neighborhood characteristics, explains substantial variability in criminal behavior. Lower socioeconomic status is associated with a higher rate of crime. However, the causal mechanisms purported to connect these variables will differ depending on the particular theory. For example, according to strain theory (Cohen, 1960), criminal behavior is caused by undue strain (frustration) experienced as a result of pathological social structures (e.g., social inequality, poverty) that prevent a person from achieving the middle-class expectations for material success. The strain leads the person to engage in socially deviant behavior like crime to attain goods and social prestige. Subculture theory (Wolfgang & Ferracuti, 1981) states that individuals who engage in criminal activity are merely conforming to the hedonistic, hostile, and destructive values of lower-class culture. Indeed, in the deviant subculture, the nonconformists who do not engage in theft, drug use, and gang affiliation are said to be the true deviants (Andrews & Bonta, 2016).

Social Psychological Theories

Theories of criminal behavior from a social psychological perspective tend to consider the influence of both dispositional and situational factors. For example, as Hoge (2001) noted, social ecological models explain crime as a function of the interaction among multiple "forces operating at the level of the individual, their immediate social environment, and more distal factors within the larger social environment" (p. 58).

Recall that according to Bandura's (1977) **social learning theory** (discussed also in Chapter 4), criminal activity represents learned behaviors that develop through a person's interactions and experiences with the social environment. This learning takes place as a result of various processes, including observing and imitating the criminal behavior of others, receiving positive consequences for engaging in criminal behavior (e.g., peer approval), realizing that such behavior can effectively lead to desired outcomes (i.e., have instrumental value), and developing a high sense of self-efficacy in using antisocial means to achieve one's aims. As we will see, these notions have greatly influenced the development of current social psychological theories of crime.

This subsection focuses on the **general personality and social psychological model** of **criminal behavior** developed by Andrews and Bonta (2016). According to Andrews and Bonta, the likelihood that a person will engage in criminal behavior is increased by the presence of risk factors in his or her life. Eight categories of risk factors—some personal and some environmental—are proposed:

1. An early age of onset for antisocial behavior

2. Temperamental and personal characteristics that are conducive to criminal activity (e.g., impulsivity, aggressive energy, weak problem-solving abilities)

3. Antisocial attitudes, values, and beliefs

4. Association with procriminal peers and isolation from noncriminal associates

5. Negative parenting and family experiences (e.g., harsh and abusive discipline, poor parental monitoring and supervision, low family cohesion)

6. Low levels of school or vocational achievement

7. Poor use of leisure time and low levels of involvement in prosocial leisure pursuits and recreational activities

8. Abuse of drugs and/or alcohol

In addition, characteristics of the immediate situation are considered to interact with characteristics of the individual to increase the likelihood of criminal activity.

The factors in Andrews and Bonta's (2016) model are viewed from a developmental perspective, either appearing early in a person's life (e.g., temperamental factors, family factors) or emerging over time through middle childhood and into adolescence (e.g., antisocial attitudes, negative peer influences). In addition, the amount of influence of each set of factors on the propensity to engage in antisocial acts will vary depending on the stage of a person's life. For instance, the influence of family factors will be greater during childhood, and the influence of peer factors will be greater during adolescence (Wiesner & Capaldi, 2003). Clearly, Andrews and Bonta's model recognizes that the factors that influence the development of individuals who are predisposed to criminal activity are numerous and their inter-relationships are complex.

Drawing on both Andrews and Bonta's (2016) model and a social learning perspective, one can see how the factors that the person brings to the situation, such as antisocial attitudes and per-ceived self-efficacy, in interaction with factors in the immediate situation, such as peer support for antisocial acts, are related to criminal behavior. For example, a person who values the use of anti-social behavior (e.g., violence, theft) as a means of achieving certain ends (e.g., settling a personal score, obtaining money), who feels competent to carry out the behavior (i.e., has high perceived self-efficacy), and who does not feel constrained in any way to behave in an antisocial manner has a relatively high likelihood of committing an offense, particularly in the presence of an oppor-tunity and antisocial peers. Add the influence of other social psychological factors discussed ear-lier, such as deindividuation and frustration, and there may be a recipe for disaster. Two elements of Andrews and Bonta's model—antisocial atti-tudes and antisocial peers—are examined in more detail in the following paragraphs.

Antisocial attitudes and criminal behavior. The study of attitudes, including antisocial attitudes, and their relation to behavior is an important endeavor in social psychology. Attitudes are gen-erally thought of as evaluative judgments that a person makes about an issue, an object, an event, or a person. Thus, a person's attitudes toward crime may be relevant to his or her tendency to commit a crime.

Andrews and Bonta (2002) identified five elements that comprise an antisocial pattern of attitudes (including values and beliefs): (a) high tolerance for deviance in general, (b) rejection of the validity of legal authority and institutions, (c) use of cognitive distortions (e.g., rationaliza-tion, denial) to make one's antisocial behavior acceptable, (d) interpretation of a wide range of environmental stimuli as a reason for anger, and (e) a style of thinking that is generally antisocial. Sample items from the *Measures of Criminal Attitudes and Associates* (Mills, Kroner, & Forth, 2002), a 46-item, self-report inventory of anti-social attitudes, are presented in Table 11.1. Taken together, antisocial attitudes, values, and beliefs once stabilized have been shown to be among the strongest predictors of criminal behavior, more so than social class, personal distress variables (e.g., low self-esteem, anxiety), and family–parenting characteristics (Gendreau, Little, & Goggin, 1996). Correlations between antisocial attitudes and criminal behavior have been found to be in the range of .35 to .40 (Andrews, Leschied, & Hoge, 1992).

Antisocial peer group and criminal behavior. Studies have shown that offending behavior,

Table 11.1 Sample Items From the *Measures of Criminal Attitudes and Associates*

	Response	*Alternatives*
It's understandable to hit someone who insults you.	Agree	Disagree
I have a lot in common with people who break the law.	Agree	Disagree
I could see myself lying to the police.	Agree	Disagree
Rules will not stop me from doing what I want.	Agree	Disagree
I would run a scam if I could get away with it.	Agree	Disagree

SOURCE: Mills, Kroner, and Forth (2002).

NOTE: Individuals who agree with these and similar types of items score high on antisocial attitudes.

particularly among adolescents, is apt to be deeply embedded within an antisocial peer group, the second element (i.e., risk factor) of Andrews and Bonta's (2016) model that is our focus. The influence of the peer group can come about in one of two ways: (1) through a relatively casual and time-limited association with delinquent peers, or (2) through a clearly indoctrinated, long-term affiliation with other antisocial youths—like membership in a street gang. Adolescents who follow the first path are identified as the adolescence-limited group, and those who follow the second path are identified as the life-course-persistent group (Moffitt, 1993).

For **adolescence-limited individuals**, antisocial behavior is limited, as the name implies, to the teen years. The onset of their problem behaviors is largely explained as resulting from an association with delinquent peers. These individuals experience few developmental risk factors (e.g., harsh and punitive parenting, academic problems), and include as many females as males. Their criminal behavior is typically mild in nature, involving primarily nonviolent offenses (e.g., property damage, drug use, and shoplifting) rather than violent offenses. The criminal activity tends to end within a few years of onset.

Indeed, the adolescence-limited group comprises the vast majority of adolescents given that rule-breaking behavior becomes common during this period of life. For example, Moffitt, Caspi, Dickson, Silva, and Stanton (1996) found that only 6% of male adolescents in their survey reported *not* engaging in some form of delinquent activity (e.g., drug use, underage drinking, and smoking).

The process by which an association with a delinquent peer group and the subsequent criminality of the adolescence-limited group comes about is related to a perceived "maturity gap" experienced by these young people. This is the discrepancy between what they would like to do as they strive for greater autonomy and self-reliance, and what they are allowed to do given the social and legal constraints on their behavior. It becomes increasingly apparent to the adolescence-limited group that the small numbers of youths

who already display antisocial characteristics, including a flagrant disregard for rules, do not experience the maturity gap to the same extent that they do. Consequently, this antisocial precocity "becomes a coveted social asset" (Moffitt, 1993, p. 687) leading some youths to mimic the antisocial behaviors and attitudes of the antisocial group. During this period of development, participation in delinquent activities becomes normative social behavior. As Moffitt (1993) explained, for those youths who become adolescence-limited delinquents, their antisocial activity "is an effective means of knifing-off childhood apron strings and of proving they can act independently to conquer new challenges" (p. 688). For healthy adolescents, the antisocial behavior is discontinued within a few years of its onset with the impending social and emotional maturity and responsibilities of early adulthood.

For the **life-course-persistent group**, the influence of the delinquent peer group follows a more lengthy and complex developmental pathway (Moffitt, 1993). This precocious antisocial group comprising fewer than 10% of adolescents is more likely to consist of males than females, experience many developmental risk factors, and show an early age of onset for problem behaviors (i.e., before 12 years). These individuals tend to engage in a wide variety of antisocial acts (e.g., violence, drug use, vandalism) referred to as "versatility." They are also at particular risk for becoming chronic and serious offenders with lengthy criminal careers (Piquero, Farrington, & Blumstein, 2003). Their trajectory often begins with exposure to harsh and punitive discipline practices during childhood, lack of effective parental monitoring, parental criminality or psychopathology, failure at school, and rejection by nondeviant peers. Such factors lead them into the company of similarly fated individuals (Patterson, DeBaryshe, & Ramsey, 1989). The antisocial behavior of life-course-persistent adolescents is further reinforced within their delinquent peer group where it becomes more serious and diverse in nature, often including violence. The process by which this peer reinforcement takes place is referred to as deviancy training (Dishion & Piehler, 2007).

FOCUS ON RESEARCH

Exploring the Deviancy Training That Occurs Among Delinquent Peers

Dishion, Spracklen, Andrews, and Patterson (1996) conducted an observational study in which they examined the notion of **deviancy training**, that is, how the socialization process in a deviant peer group takes place. Given the considerable evidence of the causal role of the antisocial peer group in the commission of serious delinquent behavior, studying how this influence is exerted is important to the development of effective early intervention and prevention programs.

The major goal of Dishion and colleagues' (1996) research was to *examine the relationship between the social interactions of pairs of 13- and 14-year-old males and their rates of antisocial behavior two years later.* The researchers analyzed the conversations of 186 boys, each with one of his friends, as they engaged in a 25-minute problem-solving task in a clinic-based laboratory setting. The sample of 186 boys was part of a longitudinal study of antisocial behavior in high-crime neighborhoods. The problem-solving task for each pair of boys involved five segments: (a) planning an activity together, (b) solving a problem that occurred recently for the target boy (from the sample of 186) about not getting along with his parents, (c) solving a problem that occurred recently for the target boy about not getting along with his peers, (d) solving a problem that occurred recently for the friend about not getting along with his parents, and (e) solving a problem that occurred recently for the friend about not getting along with his peers.

The videotaped interactions were coded to assess normative and rule-breaking talk during the task. The boys' reactions during the interactions and the discussions also were coded as either positive (i.e., characterized by laughter), or negative (i.e., characterized by pauses in the conversation). Long-term data also were gathered. At the end of a 2-year follow-up, based on police records, the pairs were classified as either not arrested, mixed arrested (one boy arrested), or both arrested. In addition, at the end of two years, the boys' self-reported delinquent behavior was measured.

The analyses of the boys' interactions that had occurred two years prior to being classified into one of the three arrest groups revealed that the most common *normative topics* had included recreation, school, family, money, social, and peer relations. The most common *deviant topics* had included mooning the camera, using drugs, stealing, vandalizing, victimizing women or minorities, making obscene gestures, and getting into trouble at school. As shown in Table 11.2, boys in all three groups had discussed both topic types. However, there was an important difference. The *no-delinquent group* (neither boy arrested at the end of the 2-year follow-up) and *mixed group* (one boy arrested) had spent much more time discussing normative topics than rule-breaking topics. On the other hand, and importantly, the *delinquent group* (both boys arrested) had spent more time discussing rule-breaking (deviant) topics than normative topics. In addition, the conversations of the *no-delinquent* and *mixed* groups had been characterized by approval through laughter for talk about prosocial topics whereas the *delinquent* group had showed approval through laughter for talk about antisocial activities. Thus, only the delinquent group had demonstrated a pattern of social interaction that encouraged the display of deviant behavior. It was further revealed, at the end of the 2-year follow-up, that the tendency to discuss rule-breaking topics (but not normative topics) at 13 and 14 years of age was associated with increases in self-reported delinquency at 15 and 16 years of age, even after controlling for prior levels of delinquency. Dishion and colleagues (1996) concluded that the

(Continued)

(Continued)

types of social interaction that reinforce rule-breaking discussions that they observed in their study (i.e., providing approval and acceptance for antisocial values and attitudes) are indications of the deviancy training that takes place within delinquent peer groups on the streets. They further suggested that such interactions contribute to an escalation in criminal behavior over time. At the same time, caution must be exercised in generalizing the findings of this study given the questionable *ecological validity* (see Chapter 3) of the investigation's problem-solving task. Interactions between boys who are observed in a contrived setting of a clinic may not be reflective of the interactions that take place away from the prying eyes of social scientists.

Table 11.2   Mean Number of Topics Discussed per Minute by Arrest Status of the Dyads

	Neither Boy Arrested	*One Boy Arrested*	*Both Boys Arrested*
Rule-breaking topic	1.90	3.01	8.59
Normative topic	14.61	12.49	6.27

SOURCE: Dishion, Spracklen, Andrews, and Patterson (1996).

Treatment Implications

In keeping with the general personality and social psychological approach, the effective treatment of antisocial behavior involves targeting the factors that support or maintain the criminal behavior. As outlined in the model, this includes targeting factors, such as antisocial attitudes, beliefs, and peer associations as well as family factors. For example, treatment programs that target antisocial thinking as one component of a rehabilitation strategy have been shown to yield positive effects in reducing the risk of reoffending or recidivism (Coates, Miller, & Ohlin, 1978).

One successful intervention strategy, the Multi-systemic Therapy (MST) program for seriously violent youths (Henggeler, Schoenwald, Borduin, Rowland, & Cunningham, 2009) attempts to influence the multiple social systems in which young people are embedded (e.g., family, school, peer, neighborhood, justice system) to bring about a decrease in criminal behavior. Thus, program staff members intervene in several ways and areas, including working with the families to modify parenting practices and dysfunctional dynamics within the youths' homes, linking the families to community supports, diverting the youths from negative peer associations, providing individual counseling, and providing supports at school.

Outcome evaluations of MST programs, using experimental and quasi-experimental designs have found the intervention to be promising. Pointing to its clinical utility, the program has been shown to be superior to usual services for offenders, such as psychiatric hospitalizations and individual counseling. Positive gains in reducing the rates of recidivism have been observed for up to five years after treatment (Edwards, Schoenwald, Henggeler, & Strother, 2001). For example, Borduin and colleagues (1995) reported that the rate of recidivism four years after discharge from a treatment program was only 22% for program youths, compared with 72% for youths who received individual counseling, and 87% for youths who refused either type of treatment. This is a sizable difference in program effectiveness. Last, according to Aos, Phipps, Barnoski, and Lieb (2001), MST yields $13.36 in benefits to public safety for every $1 spent. These findings speak clearly to the value of an approach that addresses both personal and social factors that influence criminal behavior.

The general personality and social psychological approach also suggests that efforts to *prevent* the onset of antisocial and delinquent behavior may begin during early childhood. Appropriate targets for prevention and early intervention strategies include (a) young children who show signs of aggression, impulsivity, and poor social skills; (b) the home environment to provide parent training in the use of inductive discipline techniques (e.g., instructing, explaining) rather than punitive discipline techniques (e.g., hitting, yelling); and (c) the school environment to support children who display academic or behavior problems (Welsh & Farrington, 2007). One can only wonder whether Matti would be alive today if his assailants had been involved in an early intervention program, or an intervention like the MST program.

THE RESPONSE OF THE CRIMINAL JUSTICE SYSTEM

The previous section suggested that myriad factors, both proximal and distal, likely led the young men to pick on Matti and his friends and then brutally beat Matti to death. Once a crime has been committed, various areas of the criminal justice system become involved. For instance, in an effort to bring a case to its proper resolution, the police must identify and interview witnesses and possible suspects and must gather evidence to build a strong case for the prosecution to present in a court of law. This section examines several ways in which social psychology has been applied in three areas of the criminal justice system: (a) the criminal investigation, (b) the events in the courtroom, and (c) the prison setting (which is where Matti's attackers are likely to end up if they are convicted).

The Police Investigation

Once the police determine that a crime has occurred, they begin their investigation. This means that evidence about the crime should be carefully and systematically gathered in an effort toward substantiating an allegation against one or more suspects who may be tried in court, given sufficient evidence. The process of conducting an investigation can be extremely complex. Eyewitnesses, victims, and suspects must be properly interviewed and evidence must be gathered in ways that are in keeping with the law (e.g., no entrapment, no beating a confession out of a suspect, no improper searches, no contamination of "trace evidence," such as hair, fingerprints, and bodily fluids).

In following proper police procedure, the required maximum attention to detail places considerable demands on the investigating officers. In this regard, social psychological research guided by social psychological theory has played a significant role in identifying possible sources of bias and error that occur during police investigations, and in developing procedures to increase the accuracy and integrity of the work of police officers. The practical utility of this research has been to assist police in guarding against systemic biases that may invalidate their investigations and in applying empirically valid procedures, for example, for conducting investigative interviews and constructing police lineups (Wells et al., 2000). Some of this research literature contributed considerably to the development of a document called *Eyewitness Evidence: A Guide for Law Enforcement* (Technical Working Group for Eyewitness Evidence, 1999), which was put together by a panel of experts convened by the U.S. Attorney General. The panel included social scientists, prosecutors, defense lawyers, and law enforcement officers. The guide provides a set of national guidelines for "the collection and preservation of eyewitness evidence for criminal cases" (Wells et al., 2000, p. 581) and has been distributed to more than 17,000 police services across the United States and Canada. However, despite the fact that psychological research has continued to produce findings that support the validity of these guidelines, a recent survey reports that only 56% of police agencies in the United States have changed one or more of its policies since the Guide was published (Police Executive Research Forum, 2013). This pace of change is an example of how long it sometimes takes for research to influence practice.

Let us consider some social psychological contributions to improving the effectiveness of police interview procedures.

The Investigative Interview

Interviewing witnesses, victims, and suspects constitutes a significant part of a criminal investigation. Sometimes a distinction is made between *interviewing* a witness or victim, and *interrogating* a suspect (Bennett & Hess, 2001). Although an objective of both types of interviews is to elicit information about a crime, a unique goal of the interrogation is to obtain a confession from the suspect (Leo, 2008). In fact, police in North America are trained to conduct interrogations only with individuals who they believe are guilty (Kassin et al., 2010). This can be problematic because sometimes a suspect is "determined" by police to be guilty based on reliable evidence, but at other times such a determination is based on little more than a hunch. Because good interviewing skills should be used in both types of interviews, the broader term *investigative interview* will be used in this section when discussing interviews with either witnesses or suspects.

How should the investigative interview be conducted to elicit the most accurate, complete, and detailed information? How might the social dynamics of the interview context influence the effectiveness of the interview? It is clear that the way in which an interviewer behaves can alter the behavior of the interviewee. For instance, Akehurst and Vrij (1999) demonstrated that fidgety behavior (e.g., continuous fiddling with a pen) by an investigating officer can elicit fidgety body movements in an interviewee. Such parallel behavior is in keeping with the notion of **interactional synchrony**, which is the tendency of people to coordinate their body movements during conversations. Of course, in this instance the danger is that the fidgetiness of an interviewee might be interpreted by the investigating officer as suspicious and possibly as a sign of lying and deception. This is in spite of the evidence that suggests that people who are lying (i.e., engaged in a cognitively complex task) usually make fewer body movements than do people who are being truthful (Sporer & Schwandt, 2007). In fact, using an investigative interview training called the Reid technique, most of the behavioral cues to deception that police officers are taught and lay people believe are exhibited by liars, are actually *not* good indicators of whether someone is lying or telling the truth, including, for example, gaze aversions and posture shifts (DePaulo et al., 2003; Masip, Barba, & Herrero, 2012). Most good indicators of whether someone is lying or telling the truth are actually related to *what* they say and not *how* they say it. For example, truth-tellers tend to include more details and more spontaneous corrections in their narrative (see DePaulo et al., 2003, for a comprehensive review of deception cues).

The expectations of an interviewer can also influence the behavior of an interviewee in such a way that the behavior confirms the interviewer's expectations. For example, in a study by Hill, Memon, and McGeorge (2008), participant-interviewers of suspects of a mock crime were told either that the suspect was probably guilty or that the suspect was probably innocent. The interviews were audio-recorded, and naive participant-observers then listened to the recordings and made judgments of the guilt or innocence of the suspects. The observers were more likely to believe that a suspect was guilty when the interviewer had the preconceived idea that the suspect was guilty than when the interviewer had the preconceived idea that the suspect was innocent. What is especially noteworthy about the results was the fact that while the observers listened to the recordings, they could not hear the voice of the interviewer; they could hear only the suspect. Therefore, the observers had been influenced by the interviewer's expectations, but only in an indirect way; that is, the expectations influenced the responses of the suspects, which in turn influenced the judgments of the observers. This research nicely demonstrates within the context of criminal investigations the pitfalls of **self-fulfilling prophecies**, that is, the way in which a person's expectations can influence his or her own and others' behaviors in a way that will confirm the person's beliefs.

False and possibly incriminating information may be elicited from a suspect in an improperly conducted interview, particularly if the suspect is vulnerable in some way (e.g., due to young age, low intelligence, or anxious mental state), or if the interviewing officer already has made up his or her mind about the guilt or innocence of the person (Kassin et al., 2010; Narchet, Meissner, & Russano, 2011).

FOCUS ON RESEARCH

The Ease of Eliciting False Confessions From College Students

A fascinating laboratory experiment by Kassin and Kiechel (1996) demonstrated how easily people can be led to confess to crimes they did not commit and to not only confess, but also internalize the false confessions and confabulate details of the events to make them consistent with their false confessions. A total of 75 university students participated, one at a time, in the experiment. They were led to believe that they were participating in a study on reaction time in which they had to type letters on a computer keyboard as quickly as possible as the letters were read to them by another person. The other person was actually an experimental confederate. At the start of the experiment, participants were warned by the experimenter against pressing the "ALT" key because doing so would cause the computer to crash, and all of their data would be lost. Shortly after the task began, the computer ceased functioning, and a very distressed experimenter accused the participant of pressing the forbidden ALT key. Initially, each participant denied hitting the key. The experimenter then tinkered with the computer, confirmed that the data had been lost, and asked whether the participant had hit the ALT key. The experimenter also asked the confederate what had happened and handwrote a confession for the participant to sign. The experimenter explained that as a consequence for signing the confession, the participant would receive a telephone call from the principal investigator.

How the participants responded to the accusation of hitting the ALT key depended on the experimental condition to which they had been randomly assigned. Two independent variables were manipulated: low versus high vulnerability, and absence versus presence of a falsely incriminating witness. In the low-vulnerability condition, the pace of the task was slow, so a participant might be reasonably certain that the ALT key had not been pressed. In the high-vulnerability condition, the pace of the task was very fast, decreasing a participant's certainty about not having pressed the key. In the absence of a falsely incriminating witness condition, the confederate told the experimenter that he or she had not seen what happened. In the presence of a falsely incriminating witness condition, the confederate said that he or she had seen the participant press the ALT key. Thus, there were four conditions: low-vulnerability/no-incriminating witness, low-vulnerability/incriminating witness, high-vulnerability/no-incriminating witness, and high-vulnerability/incriminating witness.

(Continued)

(Continued)

Overall, a full 69% of the participants signed the confession admitting that they had hit the ALT key when, of course, they had not. In the condition that was most biased toward yielding a confession—high-vulnerability/incriminating witness—100% of the participants signed the confession. Moreover, most of the participants in this condition internalized the belief that they were guilty: 65% later admitted to a waiting research participant (another confederate) that they had ruined the experiment, and 35% confabulated additional information about how and when they hit the ALT key when asked by the experimenter to reconstruct the event (e.g., "I hit it with my right hand when I typed the letter G").

Since the publication of Kassin and Kiechel's (1996) study, several researchers have replicated and extended these findings. A study by Klaver, Lee, and Rose (2008) demonstrated additional ways in which the likelihood of eliciting a false confession can be increased or decreased. In their study, the rate of false confessions was significantly reduced (but not eliminated) when the plausibility of participants' "crime" was decreased (for example, by accusing them of having pressed the ESC key rather than the ALT key), and the rate was significantly increased when the experimenter used an interrogation technique called *minimization* (i.e., an implicit promise of leniency, for example, by stating that the participant "didn't mean to press the key" (Klaver et al., 2008). In yet another study, the rate of false confessions increased when interrogators used the *bluff* technique (i.e., pretending that evidence exists that could incriminate or exonerate the suspect (Perillo & Kassin, 2011). Whereas this technique might be useful with guilty suspects who fear that this evidence will invariably prove their guilt, innocent suspects tend to believe this evidence will prove their innocence and eventually render any incriminating statement they make invalid. Similar studies also have found that false confessions can be obtained even when participants are told there will be a financial loss or cost associated with confessing (Horselenberg et al., 2006), and even when participants' purported crime involves more deliberate actions, such as cheating on a test (Russano, Meissner, Narchet, & Kassin, 2005).

This research represents another example of the power of the situation. It highlights the powerful effect of the social context on eliciting false confessions. Kassin and Kiechel's (1996) original study and the research on false confessions that followed was motivated by a popular investigative interviewing training program called the Reid Technique, which consists of a set of highly confrontational and aggressive suspect interrogation tactics (Inbau, Reid, Buckley, & Jayne, 2013). These tactics include repeated accusations and statements of the certainty of the suspect's guilt; not letting the suspect speak and repeatedly shutting down his or her denials; telling the suspect that there is irrefutable evidence against him or her (even if that evidence does not exist); minimization and justifications for the commission of the crime; and providing the suspect with a theme describing why and how he committed the crime. Despite wide criticism from social scientists that these techniques are coercive and often lead innocent suspects to falsely confess (Kassin, 2015), the Reid technique has become standard practice in North America. In California, 19-year-old Bradley Page confessed to the murder of his girlfriend after detectives interrogated him using the aggressive tactics proscribed by the Reid technique (Leo, 2014). During a 16-hour interrogation, the detectives told him that he had flunked a lie detector test; that he was seen near the scene of the crime; and that officers had found his fingerprints nearby. None of those details was true. His confession came in spite of the fact that there was no evidence whatsoever against him. He seemed to have a solid alibi and no motive. Nonetheless, he was sentenced to nine years in prison as a result of his statement, but was released after serving two years and eight months. Despite his questionable confession, the lack of evidence against him, and new evidence pointing to another suspect (a convicted serial murderer!), Bradley Page's case was never reopened, and his probable innocence was never acknowledged.

Because the idea of a false confession is so counterintuitive (i.e., it is difficult for most of us to imagine why any innocent person would admit to committing a serious and violent crime), confession evidence is very persuasive to investigators, jurors, and judges. This phenomenon can be viewed as a demonstration of the **fundamental attribution error (FAE)**, which occurs when we overestimate the influence of internal factors and underestimate the influence of external factors when we evaluate others' behaviors. In addition to the influence that confession evidence has on police officers and courtroom decision-makers, the damaging effect of a false confession is compounded by the corruptive effect it can have on other pieces of evidence. For example, recent research has demonstrated that eyewitnesses are more likely to misidentify an innocent suspect from a lineup when they are told that this suspect has confessed to the crime (Hasel & Kassin, 2009), that handwriting analysts are more likely to conclude that a handwriting sample from an innocent suspect matches the writing of the perpetrator when they believe that the suspect has confessed (Kukucka & Kassin, 2014), and that alibi witnesses are less likely to support a suspect's true alibi when they believe the suspect has confessed to the crime than when they believe the suspect has denied involvement (Marion, Kukucka, Collins, Kassin, & Burke, 2015). Thus, the presence of a confession can 'encourage' other evidence that suggests the guilt of a suspect and 'discourage' evidence that suggests his or her innocence. These phenomena have been attributed to **forensic confirmation biases** (Kassin,

Dror, & Kukucka, 2013), which occur when a prior expectation about the guilt (or innocence) of a suspect influences a witness' judgments and perceptions toward new evidence in a confirmatory manner. Therefore, it is no wonder that false confessions are a common contributing factor of wrongful convictions, occurring in 13% to 24% of such cases (Kassin, Bogart, & Kerner, 2012; www.exonerationregistry.org).

When it comes to interviewing witnesses, applied social psychological research has led to the identification of some of the key variables that distinguish a productive interview from an unproductive one. In numerous studies conducted over the past four decades, Elizabeth Loftus, Gary Wells, and their colleagues (e.g., Loftus & Palmer, 1974; Wells et al., 2000) have identified some of the more *common errors* that police make in conducting interviews, all of which can limit the amount and quality of information obtained from witnesses. Nearly three decades ago, a content analysis of 11 police interviews selected at random from the Miami–Dade Police Department in Florida revealed that police often made mistakes, such as asking too many closed-ended questions (e.g., "Was the offender tall or short?"), asking too few open-ended questions (e.g., "Tell me everything you saw"), interrupting witnesses in the middle of their narratives, asking leading questions (e.g., "Did you see the knife?"), and asking questions in a fixed and inflexible order (Fisher, Geiselman, & Raymond, 1987). Such questioning techniques may have the effect of both drawing out brief and concise answers that contain few details and leading an interviewee to selectively attend to certain aspects of the incident to the exclusion of other—perhaps more important—aspects (Fisher, 2010). Closed questions and leading questions can also encourage a witness to guess and provide incorrect information.

Fortunately, research has determined a number of techniques of a good interview. Among psychologists one of the most widely accepted interviewing techniques is the **cognitive interview** (CI) (Fisher & Geiselman, 1992). The CI involves asking open-ended and nonleading questions, and using strategic silence. Interviewers are encouraged to use follow-up questions (e.g., "You said before that the person who stabbed the student looked angry. Can you tell me more about what that means for you?"), and the interviewees' own words to phrase questions in order to convey good listening skills, facilitate rapport, increase trust, and provide opportunities for the interviewer to elicit additional and more accurate information. A procedure involving explicitly encouraging witnesses to describe events in as many details as possible without guessing and allowing interviewees to tell their stories with minimal interruption or redirection elicits better information than does a procedure that involves asking a barrage of questions. The use of mnemonic instructions or situational cues may facilitate recall of events. Bringing interviewees back to the scene of a crime, either physically or psychologically, is a valuable technique that may trigger important memories. In addition to using techniques from the CI, investigators should also continue to reevaluate working hypotheses in light of new information.

Overall, compared with the typical police interview, studies done both in the laboratory and in the field have shown that addressing the social dynamics and patterns of communication between the interviewer and the interviewee (i.e., by applying the interviewing principles of the CI) can increase the amount of information a witness recalls by 20% to 50% without sacrificing accuracy (Fisher, 2010). The CI has also proved useful with people of different ages, cognitive abilities, and socioeconomic and educational backgrounds. In one study, for example, Stein and Memon (2006) compared the amount of information that was gathered from witnesses of a mock crime by university students who were trained as interviewers in two different ways. Two interviewers were trained in CI techniques, whereas two others were trained in the interview method that was used by the local police service. The contents of 61 audio-recorded interviews conducted by the four interviewers were analyzed for the amount of relevant information that was elicited. The results indicated that the interviewers who had received the CI training elicited

47% more correct information than did the interviewers who had not received CI training, and without an increase in the proportion of inaccurate information provided by the witnesses.

Despite decades of empirical research demonstrating the superiority of the CI, analyses of investigative interviews from 23 experienced detectives from Florida (Fisher & Schreiber, 2007), and another from 19 Canadian investigative supervisors (Wright & Alison, 2004) provided little evidence that the actual interview techniques used by police have improved. Although these samples are small, the results were reminiscent of the study by Fisher and colleagues (1987) described earlier in this section; rapport building with the witness was minimal, open-ended questions were rare, suggestive questioning was common, and interviewers frequently interrupted their witnesses. On a more promising note, police services in other countries, such as the United Kingdom, New Zealand, and Norway have more vigorously and successfully incorporated CI techniques into their training programs for both suspect and witness interviewing.

Special steps must be taken when interviewing child witnesses or victims, particularly young children like preschoolers, because they may be especially susceptible to the demand characteristics of the interview context. For example, repeating a question to a child may signal to the child that his or her first answer was not acceptable. The child might then change his or her answer even though the first response was correct (Köhnken, 1996). As a result, the reliability of children's testimony can easily become contaminated through the use of improper procedures, thus possibly leading to miscarriages of justice. At the same time, there is widespread agreement in the literature (Lamb, Orbach, Hershkowitz, Esplin, & Horowitz, 2007) that children are capable of providing accurate and reliable testimony "provided they are questioned in a neutral, non-suggestive manner" (Köhnken, 1996, p. 269). The use of a structured forensic interview, such as the National Institute of Child Health and Development (NICHD) Investigative Interview Protocol, has been shown to improve the effectiveness of investigative interviews with children, provided interviewers are well trained to use the instrument (Lamb et al., 2007).

Witness Identification of Suspects

Imagine that you are sitting in class. Your professor is writing notes on the board about the upcoming exam. Suddenly you detect, out of the corner of your left eye several students getting into what appears to be a heated, although muffled, argument. Although you try to ignore the ruckus and pay attention to your instructor, you notice, again to your left the flash of something shiny and metallic. In an instant, you realize that one of the students has just been stabbed with a knife. In the moments that follow, through all the commotion that has transpired, as your professor and classmates become aware of the situation, you glance back to see three students running out of the room through the rear exit, with one of these students appearing to be leaving behind a trail of blood.

You have just witnessed a crime. As an eyewitness, you are asked to be interviewed by the police. How much information are you able to provide about what you saw? How accurate is your perception of the events that transpired? Can you recall what the person who stabbed the student was wearing? Was the victim a male or a female? Will you be able to identify the perpetrator in a police lineup?

As an eyewitness, you may at some time be asked to identify a perpetrator from a variety of formats, including a collection of photographs (i.e., "mug book"), a photo lineup, a "live" lineup, or a "showup" (i.e., a single suspect brought to you for possible identification). The identification of a suspect by an eyewitness represents one of the most important pieces of evidence in building a case for the prosecution. Given the importance of this kind of information, there is an essential need to develop lineup identification procedures that reduce eyewitness errors, including the very serious error of *false identifications.*

The consequences of wrongly accusing an innocent person of a criminal offense can be dire. In 2016, the Innocence Project, an organization working toward freeing the wrongly convicted, reported that mistaken eyewitness identification was a contributing cause in 72% of the 325 criminal cases in which a convicted person was subsequently exonerated through DNA testing (Innocence Project, 2016). You are encouraged to gain a deeper awareness of these terrible miscarriages of justice by visiting the Innocence Project website to review the profiles of the individuals who were exonerated. One such individual is Ronald Cotton, who in 1984 was convicted of raping Jennifer Thompson who was 22 years old at the time. Jennifer positively identified Ronald from both a photo lineup and a live lineup as the man who attacked her. As a result, he was sentenced to prison for life. In 1987, the case was retried because another man, Bobby Poole, who was in prison at the time for another crime had bragged that he was the actual perpetrator. In court, however, Poole denied committing the offense, and again Cotton was found guilty. This time he received two life sentences. In 1995, the victim was asked to provide a blood sample so that DNA tests could be done on evidence from the case. She gladly complied because she was certain this evidence would confirm what she had known all along. However, the DNA results indicated that Poole was, in fact, the man who had attacked her. As a result, Poole was sentenced for the crime, and Cotton was released from prison after serving 11 years for a crime he had not committed (Dowling, 2000). Remarkably, Jennifer Thompson and Ronald Cotton have since become friends, and their journey of reconciliation and forgiveness has been told in their compelling and uplifting book, *Picking Cotton: Our Memoir of Injustice and Redemption* (Thompson-Cannino, Cotton, & Torneo, 2009).

Based on a prodigious body of social psychological research, it is now well established that eyewitnesses are prone to making errors in judgment under certain circumstances (Wells et al., 2000). Experimental studies on eyewitness identification typically involve staging a mock crime (e.g., robbery) in front of a group of research participants, or having participants view a video of a mock crime and then identify the perpetrator from an array of suspects. The conditions of a crime scene that are thought to affect a witness's ability to accurately identify the culprit are manipulated by the researcher to identify factors that may facilitate or undermine eyewitness accuracy. For example, studies have shown that witnesses tend to make fewer errors when they are under low stress at the time of the witnessed crime, when the perpetrators do not have a weapon, when witnesses can make an identification shortly after the crime, and when witnesses can attend to perpetrators' entire faces rather than to select features (e.g., due to a disguise, Wells, Memon, & Penrod, 2006). One other factor affecting the accuracy of an eyewitness is his or her race vis-à-vis the race of the perpetrator of the crime. The **cross-race effect** is a well-established phenomenon that refers to the tendency for individuals to be better at recognizing and identifying faces of their own race than faces of a different race (Young, Hugenberg, Bernstein, & Sacco, 2012).

The conditions under which participants are asked to identify the culprit from a police lineup also have been manipulated in studies to identify the optimal procedures for reducing errors. Lineups can vary in terms of composition, using either all suspects or one suspect and several **foils** (i.e., people who are known to be innocent). In a review of the literature, Wells and Turtle (1986) reported that when a lineup consists entirely of suspects rather than a suspect and foils, witnesses are more likely to identify an innocent person as the perpetrator, resulting in charges being brought against the innocent person. Wells and Turtle explained that the use of foils allows for the possibility of the eyewitness making a *known error*. Without foils, there can be no known errors, and thus less opportunity to detect witness fallibility.

To further reduce errors, the foils must be carefully selected to ensure that they share certain physical characteristics with the suspect. Wells and colleagues (2000) reported that, in the absence of clear guidelines, a common procedure is for lineups to be constructed so that only the suspect fits the description of the eyewitness. This would bias the witness toward selecting the

person whom the police believe committed the offense. The photograph in Figure 11.1 shows the police lineup used in the trial of Ivan Henry in 1983. Mr. Henry is the person in the lineup who is being held by the three police officers and who has the number 12 around his neck. At the time of Mr. Henry's arrest, he was charged with 17 counts involving sexual offenses of women. He was brought in for a physical lineup, but refused to participate in part because he believed the lineup would be biased as he was the only redheaded person among those who were to be members of the lineup. Despite his protests, Mr. Henry was forced to participate by the police officers as shown in the photo. In spite of the fact there was no evidence linking him to any of the complainants or crime scenes and no reliable precourt identification of him by any of the complainants, Mr. Henry was found guilty on all counts and sentenced to an indefinite period of incarceration as a dangerous offender. On October 27, 2010, after serving 26 years of his sentence, he successfully appealed his case to the British Columbia Court of Appeal at which time he was acquitted of all charges. The appeal court judgment stated that

the physical line-up should not have been conducted at all because it became a farce. There was no telling what influence the prominent display of Henry by the police officers during that event ultimately had on the six complainants when they were asked in court if they could identify the assailant. . . . The process of identification was polluted so as to render in-court identification of Henry on each count highly questionable and unreliable. (*R. v. Henry*, 2010)

Furthermore, research has shown that foils must not be *too* similar to the suspect because that would make it unnecessarily difficult for the witness to discriminate among the lineup members (Tredoux, 2002). As a middle ground, the foils should generally fit the description of the perpetrator given by the witness prior to the lineup, for example, a tall man with a medium build, dark hair, and a mustache. Witnesses also should be told prior to the lineup procedure that

Figure 11.1   Police Lineup Used in the Appeal Case of Ivan Henry

SOURCE: Photo courtesy of the British Columbia Court of Appeal.

the suspect *might or might not* be in the lineup. This serves to guard against a witness feeling pressured to identify one of the lineup members as the perpetrator, for example, the one who matches the description most closely, as happened when Jennifer Thompson selected Ronald Cotton's lineup picture. The confidence level of a witness's identification decision also should be recorded immediately, before any feedback is received from investigators or other witnesses. Studies have shown that confidence tends to increase dramatically after positive feedback is received and tends to decrease, albeit to a lesser degree, after negative feedback is received (Steblay, Wells, & Douglass, 2014). This can then influence jurors' perceptions of the accuracy of the eyewitness identification. Thus, the lineup should be conducted by an officer who is unaware

of the identity of the suspect so as not to consciously or unconsciously guide the witness (Smith & Cutler, 2013). Presenting the lineup individuals one at a time (**sequential lineup**) rather than all at once (**simultaneous lineup**), and asking the witness to state whether the person is the perpetrator may serve to reduce the rate of misidentifications. The reduction occurs because in a sequential lineup witnesses must compare each lineup member with the representation of the perpetrator in their minds rather than adopting a strategy of choosing the lineup member who most closely matches this representation (Steblay, Dysart, & Wells, 2011). Recommended procedures for composing and administering an effective mug book or lineup are presented in the aforementioned document, *Eyewitness Evidence: A Guide for Law Enforcement* (Technical Working

Table 11.3   Some Recommended Procedures for Preparing a Photo Lineup

The officer should ensure that:

1. Each lineup should include the photo of only one suspect.

2. Photos of foils should resemble the general description of the perpetrator provided by the witness, such that the suspect's photo does not stand out from the rest of the photos. At the same time, foils should not resemble the suspect to such an extent that it is difficult to distinguish them.

3. A minimum of five foils should be in a lineup.

4. All photos should have the same format (e.g., color or black-and-white, Polaroid, 35 mm, digital) so that none unduly stands out.

5. Do not reuse foil photos for different lineups shown to the same witness.

6. No identifying information or information regarding previous arrests should appear on the photos.

SOURCE: Technical Working Group for Eyewitness Evidence (1999, p. 29).

Group for Eyewitness Evidence, 1999). Sample recommendations for a photo lineup are presented in Table 11.3.

The Courtroom

A lengthy police investigation led three men to be charged with second-degree murder in the beating death of Matti Baranovski. Their criminal trial was conducted according to the adversarial model of the legal system that is adopted in North America, Britain, and a few other countries. Under the **adversarial model**, two sets of lawyers, one for the defense and one for the prosecution, present their arguments, question witnesses, and make their case before an impartial judge, and perhaps a jury, who will determine the guilt or innocence of the defendant(s). (This is in contrast to the inquisitorial model that is adopted in some European countries like France, where the court takes an active role in the investigation of the facts of the crime.)

Since the publication in 1908 of Hugo Münsterberg's book, *On the Witness Stand: Essays on Psychology and Crime,* applied psychologists have been actively involved in conducting research on the courtroom, including the behavior of jurors. Social psychologists have been particularly interested in understanding the social processes (e.g., attributions, social influence, group decision

making) that take place within the courtroom among the lawyers, judges, witnesses, defendants, and jurors.

This subsection examines three issues that are relevant to understanding how jurors think and behave as individuals and as members of a group: jury size, juror impartiality, and inadmissible evidence.

Jury Size

A jury of "one's peers" is composed of individuals from the community-at-large who are selected at random from voter registration and enumeration lists and are summoned to appear for jury duty. In the United States, a jury may be composed of either six or twelve members. The smaller number is meant to be a time- and cost-saving measure. In keeping with the British tradition, Canadian criminal law only allows for a 12-person jury. The jury that rendered the verdict in Matti's case was highly unusual in that it was made up of 11 jurors (six men and five women) after one juror was dismissed from the jury because she failed to disclose that she worked in a bank that had been robbed and was subpoenaed midway through the trial to testify as a witness. (Note that in Canada a trial will go on with a minimum of ten jurors, allowing up to two jurors to leave for unforeseen circumstances.)

Is there a functional difference between 6- and 12-member juries? An abundance of social science research concerning social perception, minority opinion, and normative and informational social influence (see Chapter 10) has had a bearing on answering this question. However, applying knowledge gleaned from research has sometimes been challenging because the courts have not always interpreted the findings correctly. For example, in *Williams v. Florida* (1970), the U.S. Supreme Court ruled that no adverse effects would result from reducing the size of the jury to six members from twelve members, in other words stating that the 6- and 12-person juries are "functionally" equivalent. Drawing on social science research at the time, including Asch's (1951) classic studies of conformity in groups, the Supreme Court erroneously concluded that a juror in a 5-to-1 split faces the same pressure to conform as does a juror in a 10-to-2 split. However, Asch actually had demonstrated the opposite— that having at least one ally in a group increases an individual's ability to resist pressure to conform (see also Saks & Marti, 1997).

What else does the research show about the effects of jury size? The results of a meta-analysis conducted by Saks and Marti (1997) indicated that jury size tends to have a greater impact on the deliberation process than on the jury's verdict. Although the overall distribution of verdicts (i.e., guilty vs. not guilty) from small and large juries tends not to differ, smaller juries tend to spend less time deliberating and tend to recall fewer details of the case. Moreover, consistent with what Asch (1951) found, studies confirm that it is easier to be a minority member in a 10-to-2 split than it is to be a minority member in a 5-to-1 split. Indeed, a 12-person jury is twice as likely to arrive at a hung verdict as a 6-person jury (Ellsworth & Mauro, 1998). Finally, statistically, larger juries are thought to be more representative of the diverse community from which they are drawn (Diamond, Peery, Dolan, & Dolan, 2009).

Juror Impartiality

Rather than a single judge, the strength of the jury is that consideration of the facts of the trial

evidence are based on the combined perspectives of 12 ordinary individuals who are brought together to function as a group to reach a unanimous decision. As Vidmar and Schuller (2001) explained,

> Because jury verdicts are rendered by members of the community, their legal decisions about guilt or innocence are assumed to have greater legitimacy and public acceptance than decisions by a single judge. The jury also serves as the conscience of the community because it is drawn precisely from the community in which the crime was committed. (p. 130)

Therefore, for a jury to function as intended, the members not only must be representative of the community, but also must be free of any preconceived biases that might prevent them from rendering a fair decision. In other words, jury members must be impartial. But, what does this mean, and how is it achieved? In *R. v. Parks* (1993), the Court of Appeal for Ontario defined **partiality** in much the same way as a social psychologist; that is, as having an attitudinal (i.e., prejudicial) and a behavioral (i.e., discriminatory) component that could potentially affect a juror's verdict on a case. What has the research found about the relationship between juror attitudes and verdict decisions?

Considerable research on the attitude–behavior link has shown that attitudes and behavior are strongly correlated, but only under certain conditions. Ajzen and Fishbein (1977) reported that attitudes correlate with behavior when the attitudes are *specific* to the behavior, for example, when predicting whether a person will start jogging based on his or her attitude toward jogging rather than on his or her attitude toward exercising in general. Similarly, Schuller and Yarmey (2001) reported that within the courtroom, attitudes that are specifically relevant to a particular case will predict a juror's verdict (e.g., a juror's attitude toward sexual abuse will predict his or her verdict in a sexual assault case). Likewise, Ellsworth (1991) found that favorable attitudes toward the death penalty are predictive of guilty verdicts in capital murder trials (in which the defendants can be sentenced to death).

What are the possible sources of bias in a juror? Vidmar and Schuller (2001) identified four types of juror prejudice: interest, specific, generic, and normative prejudice. First, **interest prejudice** refers to a juror having a particular interest or stake in the outcome of a trial. For example, a juror might be related to someone who is called to testify or might know someone who has been charged with the same offense. Second, **specific prejudice** occurs when the juror holds attitudes or beliefs that might interfere with his or her ability to be impartial in a particular case. Specific prejudice might arise from exposure to pretrial publicity presented in the media that biases the juror's judgment of the case. Third, **generic prejudice** refers to possessing general attitudes (e.g., racist views) that would interfere with an unbiased evaluation of the evidence. Finally, **normative prejudice** refers to a juror believing that there is such strong community sentiment supporting a particular outcome of the case that his or her ability to decide the case impartially based on the evidence becomes compromised in favor of the perceived normative attitude.

There are several remedies that may be invoked to deal with biased jurors. First, as stated, if a potential juror is deemed to be biased, he or she can be removed during the *voir dire* (i.e., the preliminary examination to determine the competency of a juror). Second, with a high-profile crime, extensive pretrial publicity sometimes can make it difficult to select impartial jurors from the community in which the crime took place. In such an instance, the location of the trial can be moved to another city. Third, if during a trial there is a risk that members of a jury might become aware of information that could bias their judgment (e.g., hearing a rumor, seeing information in the media), the trial can be adjourned until sufficient time passes to allow the prejudicial information to become less salient. Vidmar and Schuller (2001) noted that the latter is the most rarely used solution.

We have considered possible sources of bias in individual jurors, but can a jury as a whole be biased? One area of research that has attracted much attention is how the racial composition of a jury can influence the outcome of a trial. For example, do juries composed entirely of members of a racial majority perform differently than juries composed of at least a few members of a racial minority? A review by Sommers (2007) suggests that they do. Most empirical and archival research has focused on the difference between all-White juries and either mixed White and Black juries or mixed White and Latino juries. The most consistent finding is that the greater the proportion of White members on a jury, the greater the likelihood of a conviction, especially when the defendant is a member of a racial minority (i.e., Black or Latino), or when the victim is White. There is also evidence that suggests that compared with all-White juries, mixed-race juries deliberate for longer periods of time, discuss more facts, and recall more accurate details from the trial (Sommers, 2006). Interestingly, this difference is not solely due to the added contributions of minority jurors, as White jurors in mixed juries also report greater and more accurate details and are generally more thorough in their discussions than White jurors in homogeneous juries. Therefore, the presence of jurors of different races may serve to benefit both the performance of the group and the performance of individual jurors, although the underlying mechanism responsible for such effects is not yet well understood (Sommers, 2007).

Inadmissible Evidence

The function of the jury is to reach a decision about the guilt or innocence of the defendant beyond a reasonable doubt based solely on the admissible trial evidence. The jury sometimes may be exposed to evidence that is determined to be unreliable or deemed by the judge to be legally inadmissible, in which case the jury members may be instructed to "disregard" what they have just seen or heard. In the Matti Baranovski case, for example, the jury heard that the prosecution's star witness, a 16-year-old male, had told the police that he saw the whole thing and reported in considerable detail what had happened, describing how each of the three suspects had "soccer kicked" Matti "like a lifeless bag . . . like a rag doll" (Gadd, 2003, p. A11). Under cross-examination, however, the witness admitted that he had fabricated the whole story three days after the killing to protect himself from prosecution. He was repeatedly caught in lies under oath, and it also was revealed that he had his own criminal history for robbery, theft, and drug offenses, leading the judge to refer to him as an "unsavory witness." Moreover, the defense attorney claimed that the police, acting under intense pressure from the public to make an arrest, adopted this witness's version of the crime and failed to consider disconfirming evidence. All this negative information about the witness and the actions of the police led the judge to instruct the jury to disregard the witness's testimony in arriving at the verdict. How do the members of a jury deal with evidence that they have been exposed to, but that turns out to be inadmissible, fabricated, or otherwise false?

Research suggests that it is difficult for jurors to simply erase such information from their minds. In a meta-analysis of 48 studies investigating the effect of judicial instructions on the ability of jurors to ignore inadmissible evidence that was pro-prosecution, Steblay, Hosch, Culhane, and McWethy (2006) found that compared with mock jurors who did not receive inadmissible evidence, mock jurors who received inadmissible evidence and were then instructed by the judge to disregard it were more likely to give guilty verdicts (37% vs. 46%, respectively). Moreover, of mock jurors who were exposed to inadmissible evidence, those who were instructed to disregard it convicted more often than those

who were not given such instructions! This suggests that not only do jurors have difficulty following instructions to disregard evidence, but the instructions themselves may make the evidence more salient to jurors as well. However, Steblay and colleagues (2006) did find that the impact of inadmissible evidence was diminished when an explanation of *why* the inadmissible evidence is not reliable accompanied the instructions to disregard, and when the jurors were again reminded of the instructions at the end of the trial. Although the findings in the literature are by no means unequivocal, Lieberman and Arndt (2000) noted that various social psychological theories, including belief perseverance, the hindsight bias, and reactance help to account for the above findings concerning juror responses to situations involving inadmissible evidence.

On July 23, 2003, after a four-and-a-half-month trial and seven days of deliberation, the jury found two of the three young men accused in the death of Matti Baranovski guilty of manslaughter. The third was acquitted due to a lack of evidence. In the end, did the three defendants receive a fair trial given the complexities of the case? Based on the admissible evidence, did the jurors construct a valid narrative or "story" of what happened that November evening (Pennington & Hastie, 1986), or—as the defense claimed—was justice denied? Although the trial has ended, the court's decision was subsequently appealed to the Ontario Court of Appeal. It was heard by the court on March 6, 2007, and dismissed on May 3, 2007 (*R. v. Mariani,* 2007). The time, it seems, had come for the two men to be handed over to the prison system to serve out their sentence.

CULTURE CAPSULE

Sentencing Circles—An Aboriginal Approach to Sanctioning

Sentencing circles represent a unique, community-based approach to criminal sanctioning that draws on traditional healing practices of North American aboriginal cultures. The underlying

(Continued)

(Continued)

philosophy of the sentencing circle is *restorative justice*, or repairing harm. There is a focus on heal-ing (the victim, the offender, and the community), engaging in respectful dialogue, taking respon-sibility, achieving consensus, condemning the behavior and not the person, and rebuilding community relations. The sentencing circle involves a process in which people sit together in a circle and face each other. The people typically include victims, offenders, friends, family mem-bers, and various members of the community, including elders and representatives of the tradi-tional criminal justice system (e.g., judges, lawyers, and police). Indeed, a fundamental principle of the sentencing circle is that the process is seen as more important than the sentence (Griffiths & Cunningham, 2000). In deciding to use a sentencing circle, all relevant stakeholders, including the victim and the offender must agree to the process. Ensuring that the sentencing circle is seen as a safe place for open dialogue is of paramount importance. Sentencing circles are coordinated by community members in collaboration with representatives from the criminal justice system. They may be used for a variety of offenses, and for both adult and juvenile offenders.

Within the sentencing circle, each member has a chance to speak while holding a *talking piece*, which can be anything that has a connection to, and meaning for, the community (e.g., feather, stone, stick, piece of sculpture). At the end of the process, the participants as a group formulate a sanction that addresses the needs of all stakeholders. The agreement that is reached is signed by the offender, the victim, and the police with the understanding that the agreement will be implemented by the community. As a result, the community rather than the justice system alone has control over the disposition of the case and ensuring that the sanction is carried out. The agreement may include conditions, such as an apology to the victim and the community, compensation payment to the victim, community work, house arrest, banishment to a wilderness location, surrendering weapons or ownership of a vehicle, and entering a counseling program for substance abuse, anger manage-ment, or domestic violence (Griffiths & Cunningham, 2000). Although there is very little formal evaluation of sentencing circles (Wilson, Huculak, & McWhinnie, 2002), the available evidence suggests that they are a promising alternative to the traditional criminal justice system's response to crime that far too often excludes the community and the victim from the justice process (Braithwaite, 2000; McAlinden, 2011; Souza & Dhami, 2008). Indeed, there has been a slow, but steady move-ment across North America and elsewhere toward restorative community justice practices as a viable and effective response to crime (McAlinden, 2011).

The Prison Setting

For their crime of killing Matti Baranovski, the guilty men were sentenced to ten years in prison and joined the many thousands of other people, both in Canada and in the United States, who already were confined to prison. According to the U.S. Department of Justice (n.d.), in the United States, as of year-end 2013, there were 1,574,700 inmates serving time in state and federal prisons (Carson, 2014) at a cost of roughly $8.5 billion (for correctional facilities only), which is just a fraction of the $27.3 bil-lion of the total Department of Justice budget (Office of Management and Budget, 2015). In addition, these individuals represented only a small proportion of people serving time in the two countries given that the vast majority of convicted criminals—about 70% in the United States in 2013—serve their sentences in the community, such as through probation or parole (Glaze & Kaebel, 2014).

If asked to reflect on what it is like inside a prison, you might draw on images you have seen in the media, for instance on television shows, such as *Orange is the New Black, Prison Break,* and *Oz,* or in movies, such as *The Shawshank Redemption, The Green Mile,* and *Dead Man Walking.* Your sense might be that prisons are hard, cold, and brutal places where inmates keep their mouths shut and mind their own business; where the sound of slamming heavy steel doors pervades the place as access from one corridor to the next is carefully monitored and controlled; where there is a clear hierarchy among the prison population that is controlled by the toughest "solid" inmates and the sex offenders are on the bottom rung; and where the correctional officers, also known as guards or "screws," look askew from this coercive environment or even contribute to it.

On the other hand, your impression might be that prisons are quite the opposite, that is, that they are places where inmates enjoy many rights and privileges; where they receive a bed and "three squares" a day and can engage in recreational activities; and where they can upgrade their educations, acquire valuable trade skills, and participate in treatment programs (and all at no financial cost to them). To an extent, these depictions might characterize some maximum (the former) or minimum (the latter) security facilities. However, the reality is more complex than this given that there is a wide range of social environments—from very repressive to more humane—found within prison walls across North America. This subsection examines the social climate of correctional facilities, including the impact of a "therapeutic" prison environment on offenders' chances for rehabilitation and subsequent reintegration into society.

Goals of Prison

What purpose is served by a prison sentence? Prisons serve different (sometimes conflicting) functions, one of which is to protect society by removing a criminal from the streets, and this also serves as a form of punishment for the criminal's antisocial behavior. This function represents the goal of incapacitation. Other goals include general deterrence (for society); specific deterrence (for the individual); rehabilitation (i.e., to correct or modify the criminal behavior and prepare the offender for reintegration into society); denunciation (i.e., to send a message that this type of behavior will not be tolerated); and retribution (i.e., to serve a sentence as "repayment" for the crime). Each goal reflects a different conceptualization of justice, equity, and fairness dating back to the ancient philosopher Aristotle. Since the 1970s, we have seen a shift away from a philosophy that endorses the goal of rehabilitation to one that places greater emphasis on punishment and a "get tough on crime" perspective (Benson, 2003).

Although governments and policy makers may hold certain goals for prison, one of the best ways to determine whether prisons actually meet the goals that they are intended to meet is to study the experience of being incarcerated from the perspective of the offenders. In fact, qualitative research with inmates serving long sentences shows that offenders themselves see prisons as serving each of these goals. In a study of inmates' experiences of long-term incarceration, Yang, Kadouri, Revah-Levy, Mulvey, and Falissard (2009) interviewed 59 male inmates of three large prisons in France. All inmates had been in prison for at least ten years at the time of the interview. The researchers were interested in understanding prisoners' perceptions and interpretations of the prison environment, and their interpretations on how the prison environment affects their views of themselves. The researchers asked the prisoners three open-ended questions about their thoughts on the prison experience (remember from Chapter 3 that open-ended questions allow participants to respond in their own words to a survey or interview question). The researchers then analyzed participants' responses to these questions using two qualitative methods: **grounded theory** and computer-assisted linguistic analysis. Computer-assisted linguistic analysis involves using a computer program to identify patterns in the text. The computer program searches the text of the interviews for strings of words that often appear together. This form of analysis can help researchers identify patterns in the data that they might have missed, but it is simply used as a tool and the results must be interpreted by a person. The researchers identified seven themes in participants' descriptions of the experience of long-term incarceration. One of the themes involved the participants' understanding of the goals of prison. Participants' descriptions of the goals of prison could be mapped onto the theoretical functions of prison mentioned in the preceding paragraph. For example, one participant spoke about seeing the purpose of prison as a way of making positive changes in his life. He said "Today I am working on myself, I regret, I am conscious of the crime, of the wrong I have done." This response reflects a view of prison as furthering the goal of rehabilitation. Another participant's description of the experience of prison reflected the goal of incapacitation. This prisoner said, "Prison has prevented me from doing more foolishness outside." Other participants spoke of their experience in prison in ways that reflected the goals of retribution and deterrence. By interviewing participants about their experiences of prison life, researchers can gain in-depth information about whether prisons are meeting their goals, through the eyes of the prisoners.

How effective is the practice of incarceration in preventing future crime? Despite the results of the study just described, research suggests that it is of limited value, and may in fact contribute to an increase in the risk of recidivism. Furthermore, longer sentences have been found to be unrelated to the risk of recidivism (Griffiths & Cunningham, 2000). Although there are many possible reasons to explain the limited effectiveness, one possible explanation is that the prison environment is not conducive to the offender making the kinds of personal changes that lead to a reduced risk of reoffending. In other words, there is a poor *fit* between the environment and the needs of the inmate. If we change the prison environment to match the needs of the offender, would the result be a better outcome? The answer is a resounding yes, although matching the individual to the appropriate environment is by no means an exact science.

Social Climate of Prisons

One way in which to think about the social dynamics of a prison environment, or its *social climate*, is in terms of the notion of the keeper and the kept. At the most basic level, the role of the prison staff members is to enforce the rules, and the role of the inmates is to toe the line. Moving beyond this simplistic paradigm, as you extend the concepts of roles and relationships, there exists a vast array of social climates.

The notion of social climate derives from various streams of psychology, including the work of Barker (1968) on the impact of environments (i.e., "behavior settings") on human behavior, and Murray's (1938) theory of personality. Murray proposed that behavior is determined by the degree of fit between the needs of the individual (e.g., need to affiliate, need to achieve) and environmental *press* (demands), which entail aspects of the environment that either facilitate or impede the likelihood of the individual meeting these needs. For example, a designated study area in a student residence building that is furnished with sofas, a television, and a fully stocked bar fridge might impede satisfaction of achievement needs, but promote satisfaction of affiliation needs.

Measuring the social climates of prisons. Moos (1973) seized on the notion of the person–environment relationship and suggested that environments like individuals have "personalities" similar to the needs put forth in 1938 by Murray (e.g., achievement-oriented environments, interpersonally supportive environments, controlling environments). Furthermore, Moos believed that these environmental personalities could be assessed, at least as they are perceived by the setting members. As a result, he developed a number of scales to assess the environments of various settings, including psychiatric wards, university residence halls, and sheltered care settings for the elderly. One scale, the Correctional Institutions Environment Scale (CIES), measures correctional environments (Moos, 1987).

According to Moos (1987), the social climate of a correctional setting, such as a prison, jail, detention center, or group home for offenders, comprises three broad dimensions, each of which can be assessed by three subscales. The dimensions and their subscales are as follows:

- Relationship-Oriented (involvement, support, and expressiveness);
- Personal Development (autonomy, practical orientation, and personal problem orientation); and
- System Maintenance and System Change (order and organization, program clarity, and staff control).

To measure a correctional environment, the 90-item CIES (or 36-item short form) may be completed by both residents and staff members. The result is a comparison of the profiles of their unique perceptions across the nine subscales. In a study of residents' and staff members' perceptions of the social climate of a medium-security facility for adolescents, Langdon, Cosgrave, and Tranah (2004) found that the two groups perceived their shared social climate quite differently, with youth having a more negative perception than staff. In comparison to staff, youth rated the facility's social climate lower on promoting their personal development and higher on staff control. At the same time, youth in the less restrictive, open custody units of the facility rated the social climate more positively on the autonomy and support subscales than youth in the more restrictive, secure custody units. Finding the right balance between maintaining social control and fostering positive growth and development in the residents is a challenging task for staff working in a correctional facility. The CIES may provide useful data to help achieve this balance.

As well, each informant group (staff members and residents) may complete the CIES twice—once in terms of the "real" environment, and once in terms of the "ideal" environment. The difference between the residents' and staff members' averaged profiles and between their averaged real and ideal profiles reflects the different perceptions of the social climate and may identify areas for program development. For example, if staff members rate their ideal version of a group home for adolescent sex offenders as being high on the three Personal Development dimension subscales, but rate the home in which they work as low on the subscales, the discrepancy might suggest areas for improvement to bring the facility in line with the staff members' vision of an effective group home that will meet the needs of the client population.

Moos (1987) further suggested that the profile of scores across the nine subscales of the three primary dimensions may be regarded as reflecting a setting's particular orientation. Some facilities may place particular emphasis on supporting residents and fostering their involvement in helping each other (Relationship-Oriented). Other settings may encourage residents to take responsibility for their personal growth and development and to develop practical life skills (Personal Development). Moreover, some residences may emphasize the value of maintaining order and structure and ensuring that residents follow the rules (System Maintenance and System Change). Although no study has directly tested the notion of a person–environment fit with criminals, in theory offenders should be matched with the type of facility that best suits their needs. For instance, offenders who have strong needs to work toward self-improvement may be better served by a setting that is oriented toward Personal Development, whereas residents who require a great deal of structure and staff control may be best suited to a facility that is oriented toward System Maintenance and System Change.

The Stanford prison simulation. As stated previously, the social climate of a prison comprises various dimensions that define the "personality" of the setting. These dimensions reflect the nature of the roles and relationships between staff members and inmates, including the ways in which the inherent power imbalance is negotiated, the role of static (e.g., electronic surveillance) versus dynamic (e.g., relationships among staff members and residents) security barriers between staff members and inmates, and the ways in which rules are enforced and order is maintained.

If the social climate of a prison were placed on a single continuum of the staff–inmate relationships, we might place the Stanford prison simulation (Haney, Banks, & Zimbardo, 1973) and its demonstrated potential for the cruel treatment of prisoners near one end and a "therapeutic community" (see next subsection) and its humane approach to the treatment of prison inmates (Lipton, 1998) near the other end.

The Stanford prison simulation was a powerful demonstration of how social roles influence behavior. In this investigation, 21 healthy male volunteers were screened on various personality measures, and then randomly assigned to one of two roles: a mock prisoner or a mock guard. After being "arrested" at their homes, the prisoners were taken to a mock prison constructed in the basement of the psychology department building at Stanford University and were placed in cells, to be watched over by the prison guards. The results, as they unfolded over the next few days, were startling and unexpected. While playing out their assigned roles, some of the guards became increasingly abusive and cruel, using degrading forms of punishment, including locking prisoners in a closet and withholding food. The prisoners experienced various negative psychological effects, including disorganized thinking, fits of rage, and acute depression. As a result of these deleterious outcomes, the simulation was halted after only six days, although the original plan called for it to last for 14 days (see Figure 11.2).

Figure 11.2 Stanford Prison Simulation

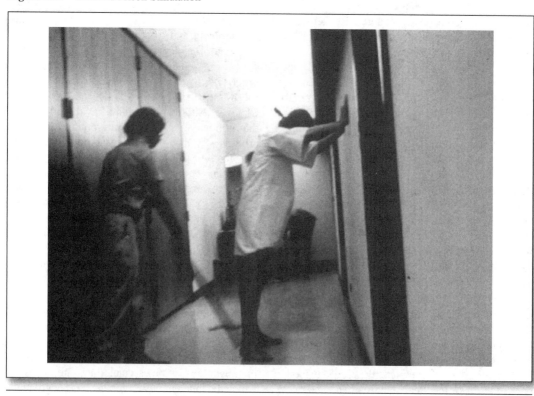

Although only a simulation, the Stanford prison simulation reminds us of the inherent power imbalance that exists within a correctional setting and its potential for abuse. The oppressive conditions in prisons for women have been particularly well documented, although reforms over the past few decades have brought about some improvements (Van Voorhis, 2012). The harsh and degrading conditions of prisons come in many forms and degrees of severity, including poor sanitary or health conditions, overcrowding, limited opportunities to exercise, assaults on staff members and inmates, hunger strikes, and prison riots. We were reminded by the shocking story of abuse at the Abu Ghraib prison in Iraq of how social roles and power imbalances in prison settings can escalate and compel otherwise responsible and commendable individuals to commit atrocious acts. Several U.S. soldiers and officers have since been charged and convicted of serious crimes after it was reported that they had taken part in the assault, rape, torture, and even murder of civilian Iraqi detainees. There is also some evidence that prison staff members are complicit in peer-on-peer violence. In a survey of 100 incarcerated juvenile offenders, 47% stated that they were aware of prison staff members who had either said or done something to put an inmate at risk for harm, for example, starting a rumor or letting an inmate into another inmate's cell (Peterson-Badali & Koegl, 2002).

A riot on February 29, 1996, at Bluewater Youth Centre, a 90-bed secure-custody facility for juvenile offenders in Goderich, Ontario, stands as a stark reminder of the potential for abuse of prison inmates. Correctional officers were on strike at the time, and substantial changes were made to inmates' routines and schedules, including a reduction in supervision, activities, and treatment programming. During the angry rampage, inmates set fires, broke windows, and plundered bathrooms, causing $250,000 in damage. Staff members may have "planted" matches and barbecue fluid and may have encouraged the dissent that triggered the riot. As a result of the incident, 52 male youths were transferred to other facilities, including a detention center designed primarily for adult offenders. During the course of being either transported to a facility or held at the detention center, some youths were punched, kicked, hit with batons, and/or yelled at by managers acting in the place of correctional officers. Several youths had hair yanked out of their heads as they were escorted into a building, and some were kicked so hard that they had boot marks across their faces. Staff members said that they needed to intimidate the youths to maintain order. At a second detention center, a 16-year-old boy with serious behavior problems who had become identified as a "rat" was placed in a "segregation" cell with another youth, contrary to institutional policy. Two days later, the cell mate beat the 16-year-old to death in spite of the victim's repeated calls for assistance. In the end, 30 charges were laid against seven managers and two bailiffs, and 12 youths received $1 million in total compensation from the province of Ontario. A public inquest into the death of the one youth resulted in 119 recommendations, many of which dealt with the transportation and treatment of young people in custody.

Prison Approaches to Rehabilitation

Therapeutic communities. At the other end of the social climate continuum, we find a more humane prison environment known as a therapeutic community. Maxwell Jones is the person most closely associated with therapeutic communities. Jones (1953) developed a number of principles on which the traditional therapeutic communities were based, including democratization, communalism, reality confrontation, and peer group influence.

Drawing on various perspectives within social psychology and clinical psychology, including social ecological, social learning, and humanistic theories (Vandevelde, Broekaert, Yates, & Kooyman, 2004), a **therapeutic community** is a holistic residential environment that is designed to promote the personal growth and development of the residents. The primary aim is to bring about changes in attitudes, beliefs, and behaviors that lead to a healthier and more adaptive lifestyle on return to the community than the lifestyle that led the person to be admitted into the facility in the first place (e.g., substance abuse, criminality). The core concept is *living learning* as the therapeutic community adheres to the principles of honesty, openness, self-governance, and learning from individuals' efforts to live together (Grant, 1980). In contrast to other therapeutic approaches, the distinguishing feature of the therapeutic community is the role of the community, which is the primary vehicle for promoting social and psychological change.

Extending the therapeutic community concept to correctional settings, additional principles include building relationships with one another, authority figures, and women and children; attending to antisocial attitudes, values, and beliefs as well as victim awareness, contrition, and consequences for the victim; and developing strategies for avoiding reoffending (Lipton, 1998). A prison-based therapeutic community builds on the notion that prisons are microcosms of the larger coercive and maladaptive environments that inmates often inhabit on the streets. As such, therapeutic communities provide opportunities for offenders to experience a highly structured setting that models a cooperative prosocial environment. However, residents must be carefully screened before being admitted to a therapeutic community because the approach is only for those prisoners who are motivated to participate in the unique environment. Furthermore, as Wexler (1995) noted, a prison-based therapeutic community must recognize that it "is a 'guest' of corrections and that while treatment is highly important, it is secondary to security" (p. 62; Kubiak, 2009). At the same time, for the therapeutic community to succeed, it must be seen as separate, and in other ways reasonably autonomous, from the custodial prison environment. Prison-based therapeutic communities have been implemented in many states, including New York, California, Oregon, and Texas, as well as in Canada and elsewhere in the world.

FOCUS ON INTERVENTION

Stay'n Out Program—A Prison-Based Therapeutic Community

The Stay'n Out program is an example of a well-defined prison-based therapeutic community. Developed in 1977 in New York, Stay'n Out is a 12-month program for male and female prisoners with substance abuse problems (Lipton, 1998). Program participants are phased into the program over three stages: (a) induction, (b) treatment, and (c) consolidation of treatment gains and reentry into the community.

The *first stage* (*induction*) involves orientation, assessment, and assimilation into the therapeutic community model. The *second stage* (*treatment*) is aimed at personal growth. The treatment program is highly structured with daily schedules for group, work, and community activities. This orderly and regimented schedule is meant to counter the disorder that many offenders experience on the streets and that may be suffused with boredom, negative thinking, and drug use. On a day-to-day basis, residents involve themselves in group seminars, often led by other residents, where they discuss a wide range of issues focusing on positive and prosocial behaviors, such as self-reliance and personal responsibility rather than dwelling on negative issues, such as criminality and addictions. Residents are expected to participate in group counseling that focuses on self-discipline, self-worth, respect for authority, and acceptance of guidance for problem areas. Although there is little formal written curriculum, the programming is communicated orally and derived from the day-to-day experiences of the residents.

During this phase, residents are able to earn positions of increased responsibility through hard emotional work (e.g., engage in appropriate sharing and expressing of feelings within a therapeutic context). The *final stage* (*reentry*) involves strengthening and reinforcing the treatment gains that have been made and developing a discharge plan. At each stage, there are clearly defined goals, activities, and expectations with both positive and negative consequences when deserved.

Conceptually, in terms of the Moos (1987) dimensions described earlier, Stay'n Out would be characterized as high on both the Relationship-Oriented and Personal Development scales, and as moderate to high on the System Maintenance and System Change scale. From a theoretical standpoint, drawing on self-help traditions (Levy, 2000), social learning theory (Bandura, 1977b), and theories of intergroup relations (Yalom, 1995), the focus of each Stay'n Out program component is on learning to respect oneself and others through positive interpersonal relations within the shared environment. The more seasoned residents model appropriate behavior, share their insights with new members, and directly and immediately confront and neutralize any negative or "jailhouse" attitudes and behaviors that are displayed by the residents. Moreover, some of the staff members are "ex-addicts/felons who serve as credible role models" (Wexler, 1995, p. 63).

Is the Stay'n Out program effective? Evaluation research has consistently demonstrated its effectiveness with drug-using offenders. For instance, using a quasi-experimental design, Wexler, Falkin, and Lipton (1990) followed up with several hundred men who had participated in either Stay'n Out, a nontherapeutic community-milieu drug-treatment program, or a drug counseling treatment program, as well as a "no treatment" comparison group (i.e., offenders who volunteered for Stay'n Out, but never entered). The results indicated that three years after release from prison, only 26.9% of the Stay'n Out group had recidivated, compared with 34.6%, 39.8%, and 40.9% of the community-milieu, counseling, and no treatment groups, respectively. The Stay'n Out group also had fewer parole violations than the other groups. Moreover, the longer the individuals participated in the Stay'n Out program (up to 12 months), the more positive the postrelease outcomes. Similar positive treatment gains have been observed with male and female offenders in other prison-based therapeutic communities implemented around the world (Lipton, 1998; Wexler, 1995). Today, in contrast to a political climate that increasingly favors punitive measures for criminal offenders, prison-based therapeutic communities like Stay'n Out stand out in embracing the philosophy of rehabilitation over punishment and favoring the humane treatment of prisoners. As a result, the practice of therapeutic communities remains controversial and is not widespread, although their effectiveness with certain populations of offenders, particularly those with substance abuse problems, has clearly been demonstrated (Inciardi, Martin, & Butzin, 2004).

Boot camps. Over the past three decades, the correctional boot camp (also known as shock or intensive incarceration) has become an increasingly popular alternative to traditional prison for juvenile offenders. MacKenzie, Wilson, and Kidder (2001) reported that by the year 2000, there were at least 70 boot camps for juveniles in the United States. Although the specific elements of boot camps vary considerably from one boot camp to another, they are generally designed as highly structured residential programs that last between six and thirty weeks. Boot camps use military-type components, including uniforms, drills, physical training, chain of command, manual labor, and a focus on strict discipline. There is an emphasis on immediate punishment for misconduct, usually involving a form of physical activity (e.g., push-ups). These programs are rigorous and highly regimented with activities that keep the youths occupied from dawn to dusk. Additional components may include life

(Continued)

(Continued)

skills training, academic education, and drug and alcohol treatment. Aftercare community-based programming, which lasts from six to nine months, also may be included. The aim of boot camps is to teach life skills and instill a sense of self-discipline and personal responsibility, factors that are believed to be causally related to a reduction in criminal behavior.

Evaluations of boot camp programs suggest that despite their many advocates, they are of limited value in reducing the risk of recidivating after discharge. A 5-year quasi-experimental evaluation conducted by the California Youth Authority (1997) indicated that youths who participated in a boot camp program did not differ from youths in a control group on a variety of important indicators—rates of criminal activity and rearrest, severity of subsequent offenses, school attendance, number of days worked, and number of positive drug tests. These null findings were corroborated by a meta-analysis of 43 experimental or quasi-experimental evaluation reports by Wilson, MacKenzie, and Mitchell (2008). With an overall odds ratio of 1.02, Wilson and his colleagues found no differences in the rate of recidivism between the youths who participated in a boot camp and the youths who participated in comparison programs.

As you may have noticed, the social climate of boot camps differs greatly from that of therapeutic communities. In terms of Moos's (1987) framework, boot camps are especially high on the dimension of System Maintenance and System Change. The apparent ineffectiveness of this kind of programmatic intervention contrasts sharply with the promise shown by the more Relationship-Oriented type of intervention like Stay'n Out. As MacKenzie and colleagues (2001) stated, "Critics argue that many of the components of the camps are in direct opposition to the type of relationships and supportive conditions that are needed for quality therapeutic programming" (p. 128). Certainly, one lesson that has been learned from the boot camp experience is that positive treatment gains will be limited when programs place a greater emphasis on surveillance and control (which support the principles of incapacitation and punishment) than when programs address the youths' psychological and social needs by providing treatment and aftercare services (which are in keeping with the principles of rehabilitation) (Kurlychek, 2010). Some modifications to services and programs for youth have led to the current "third generation" of boot camps, which place greater emphasis on the development of educational and vocational skills (National Institute of Justice, 2003).

Summary

Social psychologists have pursued many avenues in the application of theories and well-controlled research methodologies to explain and investigate matters concerning crime and the justice system. With regard to the criminal event, this chapter described that rather than focusing exclusively on the personal characteristics of the individual offender, other environmental factors, such as the presence of others and situational cues that incite aggressive behavior, also may be implicated as determinants of criminal activity.

The notion of a person–environment interaction has been incorporated into the general personality and social psychological model of the etiology of criminal behavior. Moreover, given the influential role of the peer group in the criminal activity of youths, the chapter described a study that identified a pattern of social interaction displayed by pairs of 13- and 14-year-olds that facilitates antisocial thinking and behavior.

Social psychological research has contributed to the development of more effective police interviewing techniques that have led to appreciable increases in the amount of information recalled by witnesses without sacrificing accuracy. Research-based procedures for conducting police lineups and constructing mug books have been developed to reduce the incidence of eyewitness error in the identification of witnesses. The chapter reviewed evidence regarding three factors—jury size, juror impartiality, and inadmissible evidence—that influence interpersonal dynamics and decision making involving the key players in court cases (i.e., lawyers, judges, witnesses, defendants, jurors).

The work of Moos in assessing the social climates of social settings (e.g., prison settings) was discussed. Therapeutic communities, representing prison environments that have relationship/personal growth orientations have been shown to be effective in reducing the risk of recidivism among certain offender types (e.g., those with substance abuse problems). On the other hand, there is little evidence that the more control- and discipline-oriented boot camps have rehabilitative value.

12

APPLYING SOCIAL PSYCHOLOGY TO THE COMMUNITY

KATHRYN D. LAFRENIERE

STEWART PAGE

CHARLENE Y. SENN

CHAPTER OUTLINE

In July 2010, 15-year-old Justin Aaberg took his own life. An openly gay teen living in Anoka, Minnesota, Justin was dealing with the breakup of a relationship and other adolescent struggles, but also had to endure harassment and a lack of support at his high school based on the fact that he was gay. In September of that same year, Billy Lucas, a 15-year-old from Greensburg, Indiana, hanged himself. His friends said that he was constantly picked on at school, victimized by name-calling and threats because he was perceived to be gay. That same month, five other suicides by bullied gay youth and youth perceived to be part of the LGBT (lesbian, gay, bisexual, and transgender) community were reported in the press, prompting the Human Rights Campaign (an organization that advocates for LGBT civil rights) to issue a nationwide action alert to ask schools to implement anti-bullying campaigns that included content on sexual orientation and gender identity. While it has long been known that LGBT youth are at high risk for suicide and self-harm (with an estimated risk of suicide that is four times greater than that for heterosexual teens), the rapid succession of highly publicized stories about teens who committed suicide in response to anti-gay bullying and harassment captured the attention of the public that fall.

In response to the tragic deaths of Justin Aaberg, Billy Lucas, and the other youth suicides, Dan Savage, an openly gay columnist, sought to find a method to speak to the alienated and inaccessible at-risk LGBT youth population. Realizing that some individuals would not want to allow him the chance to reach out to these young people, Savage turned to a method that would enable him to share his simple message: He created a YouTube channel. The message was that while it can be hard for LGBT youth to envision a bright future when they are feeling so alienated and harassed in the high school environment and their community, it gets better. The It Gets Better Project sought to show LGBT teens that they had great potential and a positive future, and that they needed to stick around to see how much better things could be for them later in life. Starting with a single hopeful video by Savage and his partner, Terry Miller, the It Gets Better Project soon took off, and in a few months their website had showcased nearly 10,000 videos and had over 30 million views. Videos were initially posted by gay adults who recounted their own difficulties as LGBT teens, but described how much their lives had improved after high school, and how glad they were that they had not ended their lives prematurely. Their messages were soon joined by those of prominent figures around the world of all sexual orientations, including President Barack Obama and Secretary of State Hillary Clinton, as well as many celebrities, activists, universities and colleges, businesses, and organizations. Eventually, the number of video submissions surpassed the limit on the YouTube channel, and an additional website was created to host the personal narratives of how life gets better. In addition to the optimism they conveyed, the videos sent out the message that there is support available to LGBT teens, and the website provided specific information about where teens could seek help in the form of crisis intervention and distress lines (Savage & Miller, 2011).

Dan Savage is not a community psychologist, but the unique approach that he took to the problem of LGBTQ youth suicide is very consistent with a community psychology perspective. In the words of Julian Rappaport (2000), community psychology involves "turning tales of terror into tales of joy" (p. 1). The *It Gets Better Project* is an excellent example of taking a tragic situation and trying to bring about a different ending by creating support, hope, and optimism about the positive lives that lie ahead for LGBT youth.

As you read through this chapter and learn more about the field of community psychology, think about the following questions:

- How does creating a positive sense of community lead to better outcomes for people who are at risk?

- How can we influence people to see diversity in a positive light rather than labeling and stigmatizing those who are different?

- How can the work of community psychologists lead to social action that brings about beneficial changes in society?

WHAT IS COMMUNITY PSYCHOLOGY?

Defining Community Psychology

There is no single definition of community psychology that all community psychologists would adopt. Dalton, Elias, and Wandersman (2007) offered one definition that is consistent with the way we approach community psychology in this chapter:

Community psychology concerns the relationships of individuals with communities and society. By integrating research with action, it seeks to understand and enhance quality of life for individuals, communities, and societies. Community psychology is guided by its core values of individual and family wellness, sense of community, respect for human diversity, social justice, citizen participation, collaboration and community strengths, and empirical grounding. (p. 15)

There are a few aspects to this definition that are worth noting. For one thing, it suggests that it is critically important to consider the influences of community and society on the well-being of individuals. This represents a shift in perspective from psychological traditions that focus on individual psychopathology and deviation from the societal norm, in which the goal is to treat people at the individual level to help them better adjust to societal demands. In community psychology, there is true recognition that many people have problems in living that arise from their disadvantaged or aversive circumstances rather than from any individual deficits on their part, and that real change must occur at the community and societal level, as well as in bolstering the individual's ability to cope. A second part of the definition concerns the integration of research and action to achieve these aims of effecting positive change in society. In community psychology, research and action go hand in hand. Research in community psychology is directly aimed at solving societal problems and enhancing the well-being of community members, and it involves collaboration with members of the affected groups or communities. Findings from community psychology research go beyond the academic literature, and feed into new programs and interventions aimed at improving people's lives.

Another unique feature of this definition is that it explicitly states some of the core values of community psychology. This approach is in stark contrast to research traditions within psychology that are based on the idea of **positivism**, in which it is presumed that researchers have to maintain a position that is "objective" and value-free. This does not mean that community psychology

researchers do not take a "scientific" approach; rather, it means that they are explicitly stating that their research is influenced by the values of community psychology, and that these values do affect the way they approach research and community intervention. In Chapter 1 you read about the relevance of personal values in applied social psychology. As you read through this chapter and learn more about community psychology, we invite you to consider whether the values and aims of community psychology are consistent with your own values and approaches. If so, community psychology might be the field for you.

Origins of Community Psychology

Much of community psychology in North America developed during the 1960s out of the general area of mental health. Several problems with institutional (i.e., hospital-based) mental health services came to light during these years. One problem was the high cost associated with in-hospital treatment of people with mental disorders. Many institutionalized patients, often persons of modest or low financial means were experiencing long hospital admissions, and there were few other means available for their care. But, the social environments of mental health institutions themselves became a source of concern among mental health professionals and observers of mental health practices (e.g., Goffman, 1961; Rosenhan, 1973). Institutions were criticized as being dehumanizing and ineffective in terms of helping patients to develop skills needed to function adequately in the community after hospitalization. Little was done about prevention of mental disorders or exploring means of assistance other than through hospitalization. Another problem was that the labeling of persons as "mental patients" bore negative effects; that is, having received mental health treatment in an institution too often became a stigmatizing and negative characteristic (as discussed in Chapter 5). Personal and employment difficulties often resulted—and still do—when authorities, such as potential employers, discovered that individuals had received such treatment.

Around the same time, a number of social and political forces, including the civil rights movement and social reforms introduced by President John F. Kennedy and later supported by President Lyndon B. Johnson's administration, signaled the beginning of a new, socially progressive era. One of these reforms involved the establishment of Community Mental Health Centers as an alternative to hospitalizing mental health patients. This led some psychologists and others in the mental health field to consider what kinds of community resources are needed to assist formerly hospitalized (or deinstitutionalized) mental health patients to reenter and live successfully in the community, and thus to avoid rehospitalization—or to avoid hospitalization in the first place. More detailed accounts of the influence of social and political forces on the development of community psychology can be found in the works of M. Levine and A. Levine (1970; M. Levine, 1981), who advanced the hypothesis that during more socially conservative times, models of mental illness tend to emphasize individual causes (biological factors, personality traits, personal failures to resist substance abuse, etc.), while in more socially progressive times, the contribution of unhealthy environments to mental health tends to be more fully considered. Thus, in the socially activist climate of the 1960s, North American psychology was ready for an alternative to the previously oppressive treatment of people with mental illnesses, and a shift to a model that considered the role of environmental stresses in influencing the health of individuals and communities.

In response to changes brought about by the new Community Mental Health Center system, in May 1965 a group of 39 psychologists met in Swampscott, Massachusetts, to discuss new training directions in the field of clinical psychology. Although there was very little demographic diversity present in the group, which included one woman and was primarily composed of men of European American descent, the conference attendees shared a perspective that they were operating outside of mainstream psychology, to some extent, given their interests in applying their skills in the community. These psychologists shared a view that many mental health problems were influenced by social conditions outside the individual, and they believed that efforts at treatment needed to target change at the community level. Moving beyond their initial goal of reforming community mental health training, they proposed the new and distinctive field of community psychology, which would be broader than the field of community mental health. They determined that the roles of community psychologists would include conducting action research to assess the effectiveness of their community change efforts, developing prevention programs, collaborating with community members and groups, and advocating for social change (Dalton et al., 2007). Thus, the Swampscott conference is usually regarded as the "birthplace" of community psychology in the United States.

Community psychology in Canada arose from somewhat different origins, and Walsh-Bowers (1998) argued that community psychology has an even longer history in Canada than it does in the United States. He noted that applied mental health research was already under way at the University of Toronto and McGill University in Montreal between World War I and World War II, and that a focus on prevention and early intervention was clearly evident at that time. In the 1940s and 1950s, William Line and colleagues at the University of Toronto were actively engaged in community research and action, and as early as 1951, Line is reported to have referred to their work in primary prevention as "community psychology" (Walsh-Bowers, 1998). While the activities of applied psychologists like William Line would undoubtedly be regarded as consistent with community psychology today, they were supplanted in Canadian universities by an academic focus on experimental research on basic processes and a professional focus on clinical psychology that dominated in Canada for many years.

Community Psychology Values and Approaches

As was mentioned previously, a defining feature of community psychology is that it makes explicit reference to its underlying core values, and activity in community psychology tends to be organized around these values and philosophical goals. Different community psychologists have identified different specific values and approaches, and the ones that we list here are primarily drawn from those identified and defined by Dalton and colleagues (2007) and by Duffy and Wong (2003).

The values and approaches that we consider to be important in community psychology are listed and briefly defined below:

Sense of community. This refers to the degree to which community members feel a sense of belonging or membership in their community and is characterized by interdependence and attachment to other community members.

Ecological perspective. In adopting an ecological perspective, community psychology is concerned with the fit between people and their environments, as well as the consequences of not achieving an optimal person–environment fit. In addition, an ecological perspective suggests that we need to consider problems at multiple levels of analysis. Thus, an individual is simultaneously influenced by microsystems (e.g., families, teams, classes), organizations (e.g., one's university or workplace), and macrosystems, which represent larger societal structures (e.g., one's cultural group or the political structure of the nation).

Wellness and prevention. Here, wellness refers to both physical and mental well-being. Community psychology approaches to wellness focus on preventing problems, promoting the development of competencies and resilience, using social support effectively, and providing intervention programs.

Respect for diversity. Community psychology respects diversity, valuing differences among people rather than assigning negative and stigmatizing labels to those who are not members of the dominant group or culture.

Social justice. This value refers to the fair and equitable distribution of resources and opportunities within society, and advocating for the rights of the least privileged members of society.

Collaboration and community strengths. Community psychologists have a less hierarchical relationship with the community members that they serve than is the case with psychologists from many other areas of psychological practice. They attempt to develop collaborative relationships where the expertise and experience of community members are valued and in which real input is sought from community members to develop research questions, plan programs, and so forth.

Citizen participation and empowerment. This value refers to helping people to gain control over their own lives and to take active roles in participating in issues that affect their communities. Examples of citizen participation include attending "town hall meetings" to voice opinions about issues that affect one's community, becoming members of community boards, and forming grassroots organizations centered on community concerns.

Social action and activism. Other goals of community psychology are to analyze social change and guide social action toward resolving social problems. Thus, community psychologists plan and implement research that leads to change in public policies, and that attempts to change structural and social barriers.

Empirical grounding. This value is based on the idea that research plays a large and important role in the activities of a community psychologist. Research and action are seen as interconnected: Community action is informed by research, and research in the community is designed to lead to concrete action.

In addition to defining each of these community psychology values, we have identified a list (shown in Table 12.1) of some of the most prominent researchers and authors whose major works have centered on one or more of these values. Whereas not all of the individuals listed in Table 12.1 are primarily identified as community psychologists, their contributions have formed the foundation of much of the influential literature in the field. This list is by no means exhaustive, but represents a good starting point for students who are interested in reading in selected areas of community psychology in greater depth.

Although it is impossible to provide in-depth coverage of all of community psychology's values and goals in the space of a single chapter,

Table 12.1 Core Values and Influential Authors in Community Psychology

Value	Influential Authors	
Sense of community	• David Chavis • David McMillan • Seymour Sarason	
Ecological perspective	• Kurt Lewin • Roger Barker • Urie Bronfenbrenner • James Kelly	• Edison Trickett • Rudolf Moos • Tracey Revenson • Kenneth Miller
Wellness and prevention	• Emory Cowen • Seymour Sarason • Gerald Caplan • Abraham Wandersman • Kenneth Heller	• Geoffrey Nelson • Maurice Elias • Marybeth Shinn • Stephanie Riger • Victoria Banyard
Respect for diversity	• Edison Trickett • Kenneth Maton • Hazel Markus • Shinobu Kitayama	• Meg Bond • Anne Mulvey • Anthony D'Augelli
Social justice	• Julian Rappaport • Isaac Prilleltensky • Geoffrey Nelson • Irma Serrano-Garcia	• Bernice Lott
Collaboration and community strengths	• Julian Rappaport • Leonard Jason • Kenneth Maton • Yolanda Suarez-Balcazar • Paul Toro	• Meredith Minkler • Stephen Fawcett • Patrick Tolan • G. Anne Bogat
Citizen participation and empowerment	• Julian Rappaport • Stephanie Riger • Kenneth Maton • Abraham Wandersman	• Paul Florin • Irma Serrano-Garcia • Carolyn Swift • Barry Checkoway
Social action and activism	• Saul Alinsky • Paulo Freire • Mary Brydon-Miller • Isaac Prilleltensky	• Leonard Jason • Patrick O'Neill
Empirical grounding	• Kurt Lewin • Mary Brydon-Miller • Marybeth Shinn • Leonard Jason	• Patrick Tolan • Victoria Banyard

they should be kept in mind as important themes that underlie a community psychology approach. In the remainder of the chapter, we will focus on three specific values from those listed above. We will examine how different environments and situations can influence whether either a positive or a negative *sense of community* is experienced by its members. Community psychology's value of *respect for diversity* will be considered, as well as what happens when people are labeled and stigmatized based on being different. Finally, examples of research that have aimed to create meaningful social change through informing *social action* will be reviewed.

SENSE OF COMMUNITY

What are some of the factors that determine whether people experience a particular community in a positive or in a negative way? How can the work of community psychologists influence how community members perceive their communities? McMillan and Chavis (1986) extensively studied the concept of **sense of community.** According to their model, positive sense of community comprises four elements:

1. *Membership*. This is the idea that a community has geographical or social boundaries, and we can determine who belongs in the community and who does not. Membership in a community can bring about a sense of emotional safety, belonging, and the desire to invest in one's community.

2. *Influence*. This refers to the power an individual has within a community and the power the community has over the individual. Individuals who feel as though their presence in the community doesn't make a difference are unlikely to feel a strong sense of community.

3. *Integration and fulfillment of needs*. Community members are interdependent. This refers to the idea of shared values among community members, satisfying each other's needs, and sharing goods and resources.

4. *Shared emotional connection*. Community members in a cohesive community will feel a shared bond with others within their community. This can be a result of a spiritual bond, or cultivated through shared experiences, celebrations, or rituals.

In the following sections, we discuss research that has examined real cities, neighborhoods, and virtual communities, and examine some conse-quences of both a positive and a negative sense of community.

Life in the City

Consistent with the ecological concept of **person–environment fit**, people differ individually in terms of their preference for living in urban, suburban, or rural environments. Some people will tend to thrive in a busy city, while others would vastly prefer to live in a quieter setting found in a smaller town or suburb. Despite the fact that many people experience a number of benefits from living in large urban centers, the preponderance of research on cities tends to identify problems and stresses related to city life and is primarily focused on poor and working-class neighborhoods (Wandersman & Nation, 1998). Some of the earliest research on the character of city environments was conducted by Philip Zimbardo and his colleagues at Stanford University during the late 1960s and early 1970s. For example, Zimbardo's researchers deliberately abandoned vehicles on city streets, and then observed how over time the cars were stripped down and then finally deserted. Zimbardo (1969) suggested that the overwhelming amount of stimulation and crowding experienced by people living in cities, coupled with their sense of relative anonymity, led to them becoming *deindividuated*, losing a sense of their individual personhood. According to the notion of deindividuation (see Chapter 11), this loss of a sense of themselves as individuals leads people to become less concerned with self-evaluation, reduces their self-restraint, and increases their probability of engaging in antisocial behavior.

Stanley Milgram, known by most psychology students for his classic studies on obedience to authority, which were discussed in Chapter 1, also wrote about the consequences of urban life. Milgram (1970) believed that it was not just the demographic characteristics (high population density, crowding, etc.) that determined our psychological experience of living in cities, and he focused on the concept of stimulus overload to provide a psychological explanation for how people react to urban life. **Stimulus overload** is a concept that describes a condition in which our nervous systems are overwhelmed to the point that we cannot simultaneously respond to everything in the environment (e.g., traffic, crowds), so we adapt by setting priorities and selecting where we focus our attention. Much of this adaptation involves psychologically retreating so that we cut down (perhaps unconsciously) on responding to all the things that demand our attention. Milgram indicated six ways in which this retreat occurs. First, we try to rush through social situations, devoting as little time as possible to each perceived obstacle as we hurry on our way. Second, we prioritize what we pay attention to so that some things that we deem to be low priority will be avoided; for example, we might avoid looking at the homeless person on the street who asks us for money. Third, we set up structures that take the personal element out of our transactions. Milgram cited the example of bus drivers requiring exact change to eliminate the need for a social transaction. This trend has become even stronger in 21st-century life. Instead of dealing with a bank teller, we now withdraw cash from the ATM, and a number of our purchases can be made online without ever encountering a store clerk. Fourth, we erect barriers to social interaction as we go about our daily life. For example, we screen phone calls so that we don't have to talk to others, and many people shut out the surrounding social environment by listening to music through earphones, or finding reasons to check their cell phones while ignoring the people around them. Fifth, we use *filters*; for example, communications or complaints as in a business or government office often have to go through complex automated phone menus or layers of people before they reach their intended targets. Sixth, we create specialized agencies to deal with particular issues, so people with problems are quickly referred elsewhere. For example, we might believe that there are social service agencies in our city to deal with homeless people, and that this absolves us of any responsibility for assisting them. Collectively, these adaptations to the overload that characterizes life in the city contribute to the distinctive nature of the behavior of city dwellers, which is often regarded as hurried and somewhat callous toward others.

One powerful example of the influence of the social environment that might be found in big cities involves a phenomenon known as the **bystander effect** (e.g., Darley & Latané, 1970), which occurs when multiple people who witness an emergency situation fail to intervene (see Chapter 11). It is believed that this occurs partly as a result of what is called **diffusion of responsibility**, where observers do not help because they believe that *other* observers will help. In a series of studies in which they arranged for fake, but realistic emergency situations to occur in public places, Darley and Latané (1970) found results that seemingly contradicted common sense. If an emergency (e.g., someone apparently experiencing a fall or being robbed) occurred in the midst of several observers, the person in need of help was less likely to receive it than if the incident occurred in the presence of one observer alone. One explanation offered by Darley and Latané was that a diffusion, or spreading out, of responsibility occurs when there are others around, and that process leads to a much reduced likelihood that any individual person will feel personally and individually responsible for taking action. People can easily "hide" psychologically by attributing responsibility to others without feeling undue guilt or bringing attention to themselves. An individual in a group perceives that he or she will not be individually blamed for failing to act. Since large cities are densely populated, there are almost always other people nearby who might be (erroneously) expected to take responsibility in an emergency situation. Perhaps the most notorious example of this phenomenon was the 1964 case of Kitty Genovese, a young woman who was murdered as she walked toward her apartment in Queens, New York, late at night. A number of neighbors witnessed, heard, or became aware of the attack, which lasted approximately 30 minutes, yet no one intervened in time to prevent her death.

Is life in the city inevitably characterized by stress, crime victimization, and callous disregard for the plight of others? Fortunately, community psychologists can point to a number of successful interventions that have been effective in helping urban residents with issues, such as neighborhood relations, gang activity, disease prevention, health promotion, stress reduction, and child-rearing issues. Black and Krishnakumar (1998), for example, described programs based in schools and shopping malls where videotaped or computerized presentations have assisted low-income and urban adolescent mothers in dealing with parenting and health issues. The effectiveness of many such programs may be credited to the community application of **social learning theory** (Bandura, 1986), in which participants are exposed to role models who provide examples of positive outcomes for people from the neighborhood who have "made it."

In addition, Wandersman and Nation (1998) described a number of features that can negatively impact the mental health of city dwellers. These included structural characteristics of the urban neighborhood (such as the percentage of families living in poverty and the number of single-parent-led families), the presence of neighborhood decline (e.g., a high number of abandoned buildings, signs of vandalism), and environmental stressors, such as noise and crowding. Despite the presence of such negative influences, Wandersman and Nation suggested that community psychologists can promote resilience in urban residents by promoting a social support system in which neighbors are in partnership with each other, developing and bolstering the efforts of block organizations that prevent crime and neighborhood decline, and studying and trying to reduce the impact of environmental stressors, such as noise and traffic. In particular, building a strong social network among adults in the neighborhood is instrumental in promoting healthy outcomes, preventing negative outcomes, such as child abuse and delinquency, and empowering residents to improve their surroundings.

The Internet as a Community and Source of Help

The Internet as a community. Here we depart from the typical view that communities mean the physical presence of others and that ideas from psychology apply only to "real life." With the development of the Internet, we now have a new type of community, that is, an electronic or virtual one (Rheingold, 1993; Turkle, 1984; Wallace, 1999). The Internet has provided social psychologists with a new source of research data; for example, a large number of recent studies have examined chat rooms, discussion groups, and the impact of social networking sites like Facebook (e.g., Lee, 2000; Reich, 2010). We now can examine and study the things that people do and say within a virtual community, where their actions and real identities are often kept anonymous.

Internet use has become a very common feature of most people's daily lives in North America. In 2009, approximately 69% of Americans had Internet access in their homes (U.S. Census Bureau, 2011) while the percentage was even higher for Canadians, with 77% reporting home Internet access that year (Statistics Canada, 2010). Most people do not give much thought to the possible negative consequences of virtual life, because the numerous advantages of the Internet are so clearly evident. All the same, social scientists have considered how our increasing preference for online activities might affect behavior in the non-virtual world. A study by Putnam (1995, cited in Kraut et al., 1998) found that in the United States, there has been an increasingly steep decline in what Putnam described as "civic engagement and social participation" (Kraut et al., 1998, p. 1017). That is, people seem to belong to organizations less, are generally less "social," and are seemingly less able to form significant connections with others. Putnam noted that if this is true, there are consequences for the community. As the amount of time devoted to virtual living increases, schools do not run as well, politicians care less, and the streets may be less safe.

There is also evidence that virtual living and social disengagement have personal consequences, if we assume that face-to-face social contact generally means better health and a greater sense of well-being (Cohen & Wills, 1985). Thus, we are beginning to see much more social psychological research exploring the social and personal effects of the Internet on its users. In one study, Kraut and colleagues (1998) gathered data on 169 Internet users in 73 households over a 2-year period. They found that although the Internet was used frequently for communication purposes, it was associated with declines in communication among family members and in the size of family members' social subgroups. There were also increases in loneliness and depression associated with Internet usage. Kraut and colleagues referred to the Internet's effects as causing a "disengagement from real life." We are in need of more research on these and other personal and social consequences of Internet use and of living virtual lives—and accepting them as "real"—within virtual communities. An excellent discussion of the social and psychological side effects of new technology and Internet use can be found in Kipnis (1997). In fact, we would add the Internet, with its positive and negative effects, to the growing list of global issues of relevance for social and community psychologists (Marsella, 1998).

Do people experience a sense of community on the Internet? In a recent U.S. study, Reich (2010) synthesized findings from two focus group studies and two surveys (an example of using the mixed-method approach, described in Chapter 3) that examined adolescents' use of social networking sites (such as Myspace and Facebook), and the connection between their online and offline interactions with peers. In total, the combined sample was composed of 394 participants, most of whom were Latino adolescents. Reich examined the focus group transcripts and survey data in relation to the four elements of sense of community that were identified by McMillan and Chavis (1986) and noted earlier in this chapter.

When Reich (2010) examined the adolescents' responses in relation to the concept of *membership*, she found mixed results. Whereas members of social networking sites tended to have large friend networks, their networks contained a number of people they didn't know, or knew on a very limited basis, and many of their "friends" did not know others in their network. Thus, it was hard to define the boundaries of a community given the difficulties in identifying a cohesive group to which all members belonged. In terms of emotional safety, which is another feature of *membership*, the evidence was also mixed, with some participants reporting that their social networking friends helped them with problems, but many reporting that being on Facebook or Myspace actually led to more drama, misunderstandings, and aggravation of problems among friends. While participants reported that they invested a lot of time in their social networking activities, their emotional investment tended to be low, and they did not report that they felt a strong sense of identity as a Facebook or Myspace user. The sense of community concept of *influence*, which refers to the power that you have within your community and the power that the community has over you, was not strongly supported in this study. While users of social networking sites have power as individuals to add, delete, or block "friends," the participants did not report that the online social networking community had a large amount of power or influence over them.

In terms of the *integration and fulfillment of needs*, there was somewhat stronger support that social networking contributes to this element of sense of community. Participants reported some degree of shared norms concerning social networking activities, and there were some examples of collaboration among "friends" toward a common purpose. Facebook and Myspace were reported to fulfill needs for interaction with others, and members used the sites as a way to exchange information about events, and to share interests and media resources, such as video clips and links to bands. Reich also found some limited support for the idea of a *shared emotional connection* among members of the social networking sites. While some expressed the idea that the connections were superficial and not always sincere, there was an overall sense that participation on the sites led to beneficial contact with others, and that members often honored and supported each other (e.g., by posting positive comments to acknowledge or congratulate each other). Overall, the findings of Reich's study seemed to suggest that participation on social networking sites promotes a sense of "networked individualism" (Reich, 2010, p. 703) rather than a true sense of community.

Other recent studies have also examined and tested the construct of "virtual sense of community" (e.g., Blanchard, 2008), and refined ways to measure this construct (Abfalter, Zaglia, & Mueller, 2012). A number of studies have found that establishing a sense of community online can be particularly advantageous for particular subgroups of people who may experience specific barriers to participation in communities of interest offline. For example, Obst and Stafurik (2010) studied adults who participated in online support groups, newsgroups, and discussion forums specific to people with physical disabilities. Their results indicated that the amount of time that participants spent on these disability-related online forums was positively related to their online sense of community and perception of online social support. Overall, they found evidence that a virtual sense of community did exist for these participants, and that it was related to their individual well-being. Johnston, Worrell, Di Gangi, and Wasko (2013) surveyed individuals who participated in a number of different online health communities, including forums on diabetes, depression, rheumatoid arthritis, and chronic obstructive pulmonary disease (COPD). Their findings showed that participation in these online communities provided benefits to participants in that they were able to acquire useful information and social support from these forums. In addition, participation in these communities led to greater patient empowerment outcomes for these individuals, which was associated with being able to effectively extract useful information from these online sources. Finally, in a study of 222 Internet users who were older adults (aged 55 and up, with more than 28% over age 69), Sum, Mathews, Pourghasem, and Hughes (2009) reported positive benefits from belonging to an online community, including a greater sense of

community and more positive well-being. Those who were more frequent Internet users were highest in online sense of community, and Internet use was associated with a number of benefits for these older adults, including greater satisfaction with health, more extensive contact with family and friends, and higher overall well-being. Taken together, these findings suggest that a virtual sense of community can provide substantial benefits to individuals, and that people who may face geographic or mobility barriers to participation in offline communities may find such online communities to be particularly beneficial.

The Internet as a source of help. The general movement toward receiving counseling help or treatment in the community (rather than through hospitalization) is mirrored in the increasing use of online help for both medical and psychiatric problems, often in the form of online community self-help groups. These can provide both factual information and social/emotional support for people dealing with a common problem. In many ways, this development reflects the virtual equivalent of well-known nonvirtual face-to-face community groups, such as Alcoholics Anonymous and those associated with community crisis centers. As was discussed above in the case of virtual health communities, some people cannot easily access traditional in-person helping resources for their personal, social, or medical problems. Of course, the development of online help groups also creates many questions. For example, concerns are sometimes raised about anonymity and confidentiality of both users and help givers and about how the effectiveness and integrity of these groups might be evaluated. Other questions arise as to which individuals are best qualified and most skilled to be involved as virtual community helpers or counselors. These same questions may, of course, also be asked about face-to-face groups.

Winzelberg (1997) summarized the results of several studies showing that online support groups can be helpful as supportive communities in terms of providing information as well as social and emotional support for women (and some men) suffering from various types of eating disorders. Winzelberg also noted another positive factor unique to online community groups, namely, that users are able to participate during late night or early morning hours. Obviously, this is an advantage over conventional support services in nonvirtual communities.

Virtual community support groups can provide a beneficial and usually low-cost alternative to traditional or professional forms of assistance. Davison, Pennebaker, and Dickerson (2000) studied live support groups in Dallas, New York, Chicago, and Los Angeles as well as two online domains (America Online and Internet newsgroups). The nonvirtual groups met in all kinds of places—churches, empty offices, shopping malls, and so forth. Support group activity generally was highest for medical conditions usually seen or experienced as stigmatizing or embarrassing, such as AIDS, alcoholism, breast cancer, and prostate cancer, and was lowest for serious, but less embarrassing conditions like heart disease. Online support group activity was greatest for people with conditions limiting their mobility, such as multiple sclerosis and chronic fatigue syndrome. Davison and colleagues concluded that virtual support groups appear to be well suited for "those whose disability impairs mobility, and more striking, the online community allows for anonymity. Potent social factors like physical attractiveness, vocal characteristics, ethnicity, and social skills are neutralized" (p. 211). Davison and colleagues noted that both virtual and nonvirtual support groups are attractive to people attempting to cope with embarrassing, stigmatizing, or disfiguring conditions. The authors suggested that sufferers can, through the use of both virtual and nonvirtual community support groups, escape their usual social networks (e.g., friends, relatives, fellow workers) and that this lessens the anxiety they normally experience in having to deal with the social consequences (e.g., looks, glances, perceived evaluations of others) of their illnesses. It appears that the effectiveness of traditional health services can be enhanced by including health professionals, as well as other helpers or facilitators as participants in both virtual and nonvirtual support group activities.

FOCUS ON INTERVENTION

Helping to Support Young Mothers

Being a young single mother who lacks a social support network can be very challenging. Young mothers face tremendous stressors that can result in increased physical and mental health problems, isolation, and alienation. In their efforts to help such mothers deal with the stresses associated with their difficult circumstances, Dunham and colleagues (1998) evaluated a trial pretest–posttest intervention designed to provide social support and a sense of community to young single mothers. The researchers recruited 42 mothers from Canadian community agencies that specialize in providing social and medical services. All of the mothers were between 15 and 20 years of age, and their children averaged 5.2 months of age. None of the mothers was employed full-time outside of the home, and all but three were receiving some form of government assistance. Dunham and colleagues provided all participants with computers and six months of access to an electronic bulletin board system on which they could discuss their lives, discuss the situations they faced, and share information with other young single mothers. Electronic bulletin boards were early precursors of today's discussion boards and online interest groups. The bulletin board was accessible 24 hours a day, 7 days a week, and served as a computer-mediated social support network by allowing for multiuser, text-based conferencing; public exchanges of messages; and private e-mail interactions for up to eight online participants at a time. At the time that Dunham conducted this intervention study, neither ownership of home computers nor Internet use were nearly as widespread as is the case today. In the mid-1990s, only about 18% of Canadians were using the Internet (Dryburgh, 2001). Providing the technology and means for these young mothers to communicate around the clock with others in similar circumstances was an innovative use of what was considered to be cutting-edge technology at the time this research was conducted.

To determine whether the social support provided by accessing the bulletin board affected participants' stress levels, a measure of parenting stress was administered to all mothers before the intervention began and again six months later during a postintervention interview. On completion of the intervention, participants also completed a scale assessing the sense of community they felt toward the computer-mediated social support group.

The high frequency of system use revealed how valuable some of the mothers found the electronic support group. Over the six-month period, the system was accessed 16,670 times, that is, an average of 397 times per participant, although there was great disparity in the amount of use among participants. Some accessed the bulletin board regularly (high participation rate), others were more sporadic (moderate participation rate), and some stopped using the board altogether (low participation rate). The analysis of the pre- and postintervention measures revealed the value of accessing the bulletin board. For example, Dunham and colleagues (1998) found a significant relationship between consistency of participation in the bulletin board and decreases in parenting stress. They also found that the young mothers who accessed the bulletin board frequently were more likely to develop a stronger sense of belonging to a community. Given that young mothers often report high levels of stress and a sense of isolation, these results are encouraging. They suggest that access to online peer support networks can serve as an effective intervention in helping to mitigate the stressors associated with being a young single mother.

It should be noted, however, that because there was no control group, this study was a quasi-experiment (see Chapter 3). This pretest–posttest research design does not allow us to conclude that the positive outcomes were necessarily due to the online social support intervention. It is possible that an uncontrolled extraneous variable accounted for the relationship between accessing the online support group and the outcome measures employed in this intervention (see Chapter 3). However, as noted in this chapter, there is other evidence suggesting the benefits of online social support.

DIVERSITY VERSUS PREJUDICE AND STIGMATIZATION

April 8, 1974, surely began as a normal enough day in North America's cities. Undoubtedly, the usual quota of crimes was committed, both major and minor. Statistical chances are that rapes, assaults, and burglaries were committed, probably in a city environment and perhaps in the midst of observers, witnesses, or others who did little or nothing to intervene. In New York City,

pedestrians crossed the street (green light or not) after checking to see whether others were about to cross. In Los Angeles, still others were affected by pollution and smog. Some citizens wondered about the formation of community groups to protest industrial pollution, toxic wastes, and numerous assaults on the environment.

But, that evening in Atlanta, Georgia, a major and historic event occurred in Major League Baseball. Henry "Hank" Aaron, a member of the Atlanta Braves, hit career home run number 715, thereby eclipsing the former record of 714 career home runs held for many years by Babe Ruth. Home run number 715 was a historic and fitting reward for a renowned athlete. But, throughout the previous 1973 baseball season as Aaron was approaching the home run record, his life was made difficult by many people and groups. They issued death threats against him and threatened the safety of his children. He was forced to hire security guards for himself and his family. Although many were happy and excited about what was happening, some baseball fans accepted Aaron's accomplishments rather passively and without much enthusiasm or admiration. Still others verbally abused him, hurled gross and insulting racial comments, and even threw objects at him during games while the other fans nearby typically did nothing to object or intervene. Many citizens could not tolerate the fact that a Black player was threatening to break a White player's home run record—untouched for 39 years.

As Hank Aaron was threatening to break Babe Ruth's record, what factors might have accounted for the positive reactions of some, the passive reactions of others, and the negative reactions of still others? Although some fans were apparently less than thrilled, why did others run onto the field and try to run the bases with Aaron after the historic home run number 715? Such questions lie at the heart of a consideration of the value of diversity, versus a perspective that leads to prejudice and discrimination.

The Importance of Diversity

As noted earlier, *respect for diversity* is one of the core values of community psychology. Community psychology values the strengths and contributions made by all groups and recognizes that people differ in their styles of living, their worldviews, and their social arrangements (Duffy & Wong, 2003). Respecting diversity also means that we refrain from adopting a standard of "normal" behavior that is based on the mainstream culture, which would suggest that those

who deviate from the norm are automatically seen as being deficient in some way (Duffy & Wong, 2003). Instead, community psychologists take a *strengths perspective*, seeing cultural differences as valuable assets and resources rather than as deficits. Community psychology also adopts a perspective that recognizes diversity along a number of dimensions, including a consideration of differences in ethnicity, gender, sexual orientation, age, social class, and disability status. Many community psychologists now consider these characteristics through an intersectional lens, recognizing that a person's gender, ethnicity, sexuality, disability status, and social class all operate simultaneously to influence the individual's experiences and opportunities, and that it is difficult to separate out the sources of oppression in individuals who occupy multiple disenfranchised categories. The concept of **intersectionality** originated in feminist activism and legal studies (Crenshaw, 1989) and is now used productively in feminist and community psychology. Intersectionality recognizes that people occupy multiple identity categories, that there is diversity within these categories, and that inequality, privilege, and power all play a role in influencing life experiences of individuals in different categories (Cole, 2009). Community psychology's value for social justice relates to the importance of respect for diversity (Rudkin, 2003). *Social justice* is based on the idea that we are not always "playing on a level playing field," in that certain groups have historically been subjected to discrimination and unfair treatment, and have been denied the privileges accorded to members of dominant groups. In order to promote fair and equitable allocation of resources and opportunities for all members of society, community psychologists conduct research and engage in action to promote the rights of the most vulnerable and least privileged members of society.

Various approaches to the topic of diversity are more fully developed in Chapter 14. In the sections that follow, we consider the flip side of respect for diversity by examining the consequences of being labeled as "different" or "deviant" in some way, and the conditions under which such stigmatization occurs.

Research on Stigmatization

Stigmatization refers to labeling someone as being deviant, different, or flawed in some way. Sociologist Erving Goffman wrote landmark books on stigmatization—*Asylums* (1961) and *Stigma* (1963)—which led to several community-based studies on the issue of stigmatization in North America. It was Goffman's view that a stigmatizing characteristic would often function as a **master status**, that is, a dominant prism through which other people judge the individual, discarding or ignoring other statuses or roles the individual might have. Many of the pioneering studies of stigma during the late 1960s and the 1970s were undertaken by Amerigo Farina and his colleagues at the University of Connecticut (e.g., Farina & Felner, 1973; Farina & Ring, 1965).

More recent studies of stigmatization of individuals with mental illnesses (see Page, 2000; Page & Day, 1990) have assessed the level of community acceptance in several cities of persons believed to be, or to have formerly been, psychiatric patients. The level of verbal acceptance (i.e., what people *say*) of these individuals is typically found to be high, for example, when interviews, surveys, or questionnaires are used to assess acceptance. However, many studies (e.g., using unobtrusive research methods in which people don't know they're being studied) have found that the actual level of behavioral acceptance (what people *do*) is usually much lower. At the University of Windsor, for example, we examined a critical problem faced by many stigmatized persons, namely, that of finding accommodations in the community (e.g., Page, 1981). In these studies, we frequently employed a research method used in the U.S. civil rights movement. Although many variations are possible, the basic method used telephone inquiries placed to landlords who were publicly advertising rooms or apartments for rent in the community. After we confirmed that a room or an apartment was actually unrented, calls

inquiring about the room or apartment were made by, or on behalf of, a person described as a current or former psychiatric patient who portrayed himself or herself as in need of accommodations. In approximately 90% of such situations the phone call elicited deliberately falsified information concerning the rental status of the advertised room. Again, the basic results followed a single theme: *public acceptance, but private rejection.* In other words, the findings of this research demonstrated acceptance of people with mental illnesses when their responses were obtained with measures (e.g., surveys, interviews) that are subject to the influence of *social desirability* (which give rise to an "I don't want to look bad" approach to responding), but other data showed rejection of psychiatric patients when responses were obtained with measures in which participants' responses were believed by them to be private and unobserved by others.

The series of "room for rent" studies also found something intriguing and paradoxical about stigma and how we react to others. Specifically, although landlords in the community often gave false information when confronted by someone (usually a male researcher) with a stigmatizing characteristic, they also frequently did the same thing when the characteristic was *neutral or even positive,* for example, when the person inquiring was a stutterer, spoke with a strange voice, was elderly, or said he was very active in politics, was a police officer, or was a professor. Apparently, individuals will seek to avoid situations in which they must somehow face or deal with a person bearing a negative characteristic, especially where they believe that their means of avoidance is undetectable. But, if individuals also do this when the characteristic is not negative, it appears that they are rejecting not only the person who is "negatively different," but also those who are just *different.* Simply put, having to deal with *difference* involves the expectation of having to expend extra effort or to undergo some kind of hassle—experiences that most people would prefer to avoid. Of note here is the early, although still highly relevant, theory of Thibaut and Kelley

(1959) called **social exchange theory**. Thibaut and Kelley pointed out that in real or anticipated social situations, such as the potential rental situations in our examples, people will usually (instantly and internally) calculate the anticipated psychological "rewards" and "costs" of various actions (e.g., renting vs. "getting out of" renting a room), and then behave according to these personal calculations. That is, they will ultimately carry out the action perceived as likely to bring lower psychological costs and/or higher rewards—in effect, leading to the least amount of hassle.

Bernard Weiner, a social psychologist at the University of California, Los Angeles, put forward a complicated, but commonsense explanation of stigmatization. Weiner's (1995) view is that people tend to be more negative and rejecting toward someone if they judge that the person is "blameworthy" in some way. That is, more blame is assigned if it is believed that someone was personally able to control an action or stigmatizing condition (e.g., getting lung cancer from smoking, getting AIDS from unprotected sexual contact), but failed to do so. In other words, people tend to be more rejecting if they believe that the person truly had the moral responsibility to avoid the action or situation that led to the impaired condition, but did not exercise it. A number of investigations have examined predictions based on Weiner's ideas in relation to illnesses, such as lung cancer and AIDS (e.g., Mantler, Schellenberg, & Page, 2003; Schellenberg & Bem, 1998), and have found some support.

Acceptance of research findings based on research methods that are likely to be influenced by social desirability biases and the desire to express socially popular opinions can lead to erroneous conclusions about community acceptance of people with stigmatizing conditions. For example, Crocetti, Spiro, and Siassi (1973) on the basis of questionnaire and interview research concluded that the stigma of mental illness had disappeared and that people with mental illness need not fear community rejection. Other studies that have drawn similar conclusions, mainly in a Canadian context, are described in Page and Day (1990) and Page (2000). These studies found as a

result of educational efforts and programs initiated by mental health authorities that many individuals within the general public have learned to become more accepting in terms of their overt verbal and written reactions toward the concept of "mental patient." We have found, however, that when the community's *actual behavior* toward stigmatized groups is studied in situations where rejection is believed to be hidden and undetectable, such rejection (e.g., as demonstrated by a landlord's unwillingness to rent an available room) can and does occur. Such discriminatory actions contravene the Canadian Human Rights Act and the Canadian Charter of Rights and Freedoms, as well as the U.S. Fair Housing Act, the U.S. Human Rights Act, and the U.S. Civil Rights Act.

Given that stigmatization of those who are "different" is still a pervasive feature of modern life, how do we change the picture for stigmatized individuals? Drawing on a review of social psychological research about stereotyping and attitude change, Corrigan and Penn (1999) suggested a number of strategies to change people's stigmatized perceptions of people with severe mental illness. They indicated that *protest*, which occurs when stereotyped depictions of severe mental illness are brought to the attention of the public and decried, can actually lead to negative "rebound effects." This idea is based on the finding that when people are asked to suppress their thoughts about a particular image, the image paradoxically intrudes into the person's consciousness with even greater force. Thus, asking people to *not* think in negative and stereotypic terms about people with mental illness might prime them to do exactly the opposite. A better strategy, according to Corrigan and Penn, is to provide individuals with active types of education that involve a combination of formal presentation of information with discussion and simulations, and that present the situation for individuals with mental illness in a more positive and hopeful light. Programs that involve personal contact with stigmatized individuals in real community situations, especially where the contact is cooperative and egalitarian in tone, can also help to reduce psychiatric stigma. This kind of positive contact can enhance and make more positive the community norms concerning reactions to stigmatized individuals.

The Media and Stigmatization

A major concern regarding the problem of stigmatization in the community concerns the media's role, particularly with regard to newspaper, television, and movie portrayals. As discussed in Chapter 7, many social psychologists believe that the mass media greatly influence their consumers through social learning mechanisms, such as imitation and modeling. This view is clearly associated with the research and theory of Bandura (1986) discussed earlier. For example, with regard to mental illness, we find that television and movie portrayals frequently tend to be negative and unflattering toward people associated with psychiatric labels. This tends to be particularly true in portrayals of aggression and violent acts, in which reference is frequently made to mental illness on the part of the perpetrator (Diefenbach, 1997). These portrayals are generally inaccurate in the implication that people with mental illness are typically violent or aggressive toward others. Moreover,

news broadcasts seldom report positive or outstanding accomplishments by those bearing the mental illness label, so there is little to counteract the frequent negative portrayals of those with serious mental illness. Similarly unbalanced media portrayals can also partly explain the stigmatization of other groups too.

Wahl and Lefkowits (1989) found that presenting counterinformation (i.e., reminding viewers that individuals with mental illness are seldom perpetrators of violence) did not positively affect attitudes toward mental illness among viewers who saw a film portraying violent acts committed by an individual who was supposedly mentally ill. One cannot conclude for certain, therefore, that giving counterinformation will always help in affecting attitudes elicited by media portrayals. One factor that might affect the influence of counterinformation on attitudes toward people with mental illness concerns the timing of the intervention. What if counterinformation that presented people with serious mental illness in a more positive light was given *before* people were exposed to stigmatizing portrayals of people with mental illness? In a subsequent study, Thornton and Wahl (1996) tested this hypothesis. This study is described in detail in the "Focus on Research" feature below.

FOCUS ON RESEARCH

Media and Perceptions of Mental Illness

Thornton and Wahl (1996) conducted an experimental intervention designed to ameliorate the negative effects on attitudes of the stereotypic portrayal of people with mental illness in newspaper articles. The researchers had 120 university students participate in what was described simply as a study of newspaper articles. The study had three experimental conditions and a control condition. In the three experimental conditions, participants read an article that was representative of the kind of media portrayal that stigmatizes mental illness. The article graphically described a murder committed by a person with mental illness who was characterized as different, without social identity, unpredictable, and dangerous. However, before reading the stigmatizing article, participants in the three experimental conditions read either (a) a factual article on mental illness (*stigma condition*),

(Continued)

(Continued)

(b) an article that addressed misconceptions and the truth about mental illness (*prophylactic information condition*), or (c) an article that described media distortion of mental illness (*prophylactic media condition*). The first articles that participants read in the two prophylactic conditions were designed to inoculate, or protect, participants from the biasing effects that the stigmatizing article was anticipated to have on their attitudes toward individuals with mental illness. The factual article in the stigma condition was expected not to have a beneficial effect. Participants in the control condition did not read the stigmatizing article. Instead, they read two health-related articles that were not related to violence or mental illness. The control condition served as a baseline against which the three experimental conditions could be compared.

Subsequent to reading the stigmatizing article, participants completed two questionnaires. The first had four subscales that assessed participants' attitudes toward mental illness. Each subscale tapped a different dimension of this attitude. The second questionnaire measured two variables: participants' expected reactions of fear/anxiety and participants' perceived danger of people with mental illness.

The results of Thornton and Wahl's (1996) investigation revealed that after reading the stigmatizing article, participants in the stigma condition *were less accepting* of people with mental illness. They also reported greater fear, anxiety, and perception of danger with respect to people with mental illness. Thus, exposure to a stigmatizing newspaper article clearly made the participants' attitudes toward people with mental illness more negative.

On the other hand, the results also revealed that both prophylactic manipulations succeeded in inoculating participants against the biasing effect of the stigmatizing article. Participants in both the prophylactic information condition and the prophylactic media condition reported attitudes toward people with mental illness that were very similar to those of the control participants who had not been exposed to the stigmatizing article. Especially noteworthy is the fact that participants in the prophylactic information condition revealed attitudes that demonstrated even *less* desired avoidance of people with mental illness than did participants in the control condition. The intervention was clearly effective in countering the negative effects of the stigmatizing article.

BRINGING ABOUT SOCIAL CHANGE

One of the goals of community psychology is to analyze social change and to guide social action toward resolving social problems. This is an area where the approach taken by community psychology differs greatly from that in most other areas of psychology. Rather than just focusing on efforts to change or support individuals so that they can better adapt to the problems they are confronted with, community psychologists seek to create positive change at the community and societal level in order to create a better world and prevent problems in the future. Checkoway

(1995) proposed six different strategies for achieving such change:

1. *Mass mobilization.* This describes temporary movements in which large numbers of people are amassed to bring attention to particular societal issues or problems. Dramatic examples of this strategy occurred in Egypt and Tunisia in 2011, where the populace protested and ousted its leaders. Other examples include rallies like the "Million Mom March" in 2000, which brought attention to the need for tighter restrictions on handguns.

2. *Social action.* Social action strives to create powerful organizations at the community level,

often through the development and activities of "grassroots organizations." Examples would include students forming coalitions to protest tuition increases or community residents organizing to improve the conditions in their neighborhood. Tactics used in social action efforts are often referred to as "activism."

3. *Citizen participation.* This strategy aims to get citizens involved in their communities, for example, by serving as representatives on community panels and boards of government agencies so that they have political influence and can participate in changing public policy.

4. *Public advocacy.* This usually involves lobbying or applying pressure on public officials to pass laws or influence social policies.

5. *Popular education.* Educating and disseminating information to community members can be an important strategy for changing attitudes and beliefs and possibly even behaviors. Educational interventions need to be culturally appropriate and delivered in a format that will be understood and accepted by community members.

6. *Local services development.* This refers to a process whereby people provide services to their own local community, which serves the dual function of empowering community members and providing needed services. Sometimes agencies provide assistance or "startup" funds for these efforts. For example, *Women for Women International* provides assistance to women in war-torn countries in the form of microloans and job-skills training.

In the sections that follow, we go into greater depth about some of these strategies, with particular emphasis on social action and activism, and on how community psychologists use findings from research to achieve social change.

Social Action and Activism

The idea behind **social action** is that by organizing you can stimulate collective action in the community that generates power to create change. One of the classic works in the area of social activism is Saul Alinsky's 1971 book *Rules for Radicals.* Alinsky was an *organizer*,

that is, a community-based strategist who helped to organize and mobilize poor neighborhoods and communities when they needed help to increase responsible behavior in landlords and improve living conditions. He believed that there was power in organizing people for social action, and that the power of organized people could be used to counter the power that comes from the most influential (usually the wealthiest) segment of society. His goals were those of empowerment and social justice, which involved finding and implementing community strategies that would redistribute power away from the "haves" and toward the "have-nots." Alinsky recognized that powerful and wealthy community groups or city governments, like people in general, have psychological needs. For example, they need to be liked and to "look good." Moreover, they can easily refuse, delay, or turn down polite and reasonable requests (or complaints) from citizens' organizations or spokespersons so long as their need to look good is not threatened by the potential for unflattering publicity, and as long as they are sure to remain in charge. Thus, Alinsky knew that bringing about community change depended on protesters being able to use tactics that went "outside the experience" of those in charge (see Figure 12.1). He organized communities by helping them to adopt protest tactics that carried the potential to embarrass the powerful and that were not the kinds of tactics with which the "haves" were already prepared to deal.

In one scenario, as a means of protesting unfair municipal employment practices, Alinsky and fellow protesters threatened to use teams of jobless individuals to simultaneously occupy all of the restrooms at Chicago's O'Hare airport, just when these facilities would be needed by passengers exiting from incoming flights. Fearing the reactions of business travelers and other passengers who might be inconvenienced by this tactic, the municipal politicians swiftly agreed to meet to discuss concessions regarding the employment conditions. In another scenario, Alinsky and his associates threatened to organize a "shop in" of a Chicago department store at which Black employees were hired only for the

Figure 12.1   A Women's Studies Student Protesting the Sexist Publication Policies of a Student Newspaper

SOURCE: Photo courtesy of Mike Ngo.

most menial staff positions. In this tactic, 3,000 Black shoppers would be bussed downtown to descend on the department store on a busy Saturday where their presence would be perceived to be disruptive in the store. At this point in time (the 1960s), race relations were uneasy, and such a large influx of Black shoppers would "end the [W]hite trade for the day" (Alinsky, 1971, p. 147). Also, the Black shoppers intended to slowly browse through the merchandise for the better part of the day without buying anything until near closing time. When Alinsky's intended tactic was "discovered" (or, more to the point, leaked), the store owners hastily arranged a meeting with the protesters to discuss making changes in their hiring practices. The tactics worked. Overnight, 186 new jobs opened up. For the first time, Blacks were given opportunities for jobs on the sales floor and in executive training. Like the municipal politicians, the store owners realized that Alinsky's tactics could not be opposed gracefully or effectively. They saw that further publicity would only bring more attention to Chicago's community problems and the poverty that created them.

Alinsky's (1971) "rules" consisted of a number of nonviolent tactics that used creativity and the strengths of community organization to counter the influence of the rich and powerful establishment. Many of his rules, such as "The threat is usually more terrifying than the thing itself" (p. 129), and "Power is not only what you have, but what the enemy thinks you have" (p. 127), are still used creatively by community activists today. In the fall of 2011, the Occupy Wall Street movement began when a group of activists camped out in Zuccotti Park in the Wall Street financial district of New York City. The Canadian nonprofit magazine AdBusters initiated the suggestion for a peaceful occupation of Wall Street to protest growing income inequality, and started the Twitter hashtag #OccupyWallStreet. A loosely organized group of activists had already begun to protest financial austerity measures on the sidewalks of New York, and the #OccupyWallStreet hashtag was taken up as a call to action (Sledge, 2011). Fueled by social media, thousands of protesters congregated in Zuccotti Park and their encampments remained there until they were forced out in late November of that year. Despite little initial coverage in mainstream media, the Occupy Movement took hold in New York and also spread to other major cities. The movement made extensive use of social media to create and share content quickly, but its supporters were criticized for engaging in "clicktivism" or "slacktivism", terms meaning to perform simple online actions, such as signing petitions or sharing content as a substitute for real-life activism (Gamson & Sifry, 2013). Many conservative media outlets suggested (or perhaps, feared) that the Occupy Wall Street movement was based on Alinsky's radical tactics, while progressive activist sources suggested a need to extend and update Alinsky's rules. For example, Sara Robinson of activist news outlet AlterNet suggested that the post-Occupy world requires new rules for radicals, including "Find and nurture innovators," and "Replicate success" (Robinson, 2012).

Using Research to Influence Social Change

Returning to the core values of community psychology that were described at the beginning of this chapter, you will recall that community psychologists place importance on **empirical grounding**. This refers to the idea that research is an important component in community psychology and that research and action are seen as strongly interconnected. Community psychologists use various research methods to investigate issues relevant to the community, including both quantitative and qualitative research strategies. Some specific applied social

psychology research traditions have been especially influential in community psychology; two are described briefly below.

Action research was developed and advocated for use in psychology by Kurt Lewin (1946). Lewin argued that when psychologists seek to facilitate social change, they must conduct "comparative research on the conditions and effects of various forms of social action and research leading to social action" (p. 35). In Lewin's view, change can occur only if an iterative process of research is followed. As Figure 12.2 indicates, this process begins with an idea (for social change); then involves planning that includes appropriate "fact finding," execution of the plan (i.e., action), and evaluation of the effectiveness of the action taken (usually involving more fact finding), followed by another cycle of planning, action, and evaluation; and so forth.

The process that Lewin (1946) suggested is different in emphasis and content from the standard research process that we all learn in research methods courses. In that model, the process for a single research project is much more like a straight line. The planning takes

Figure 12.2 The Action Research Process

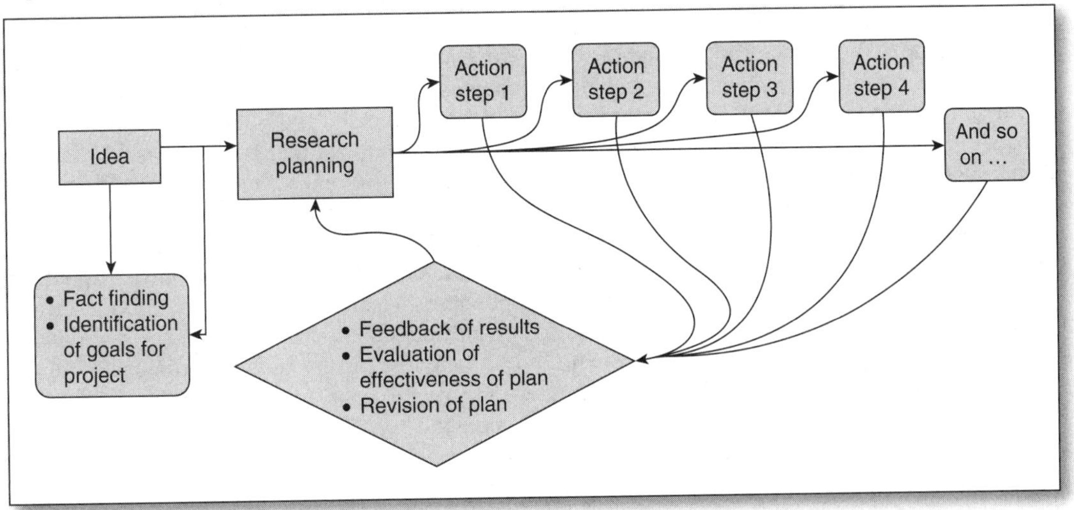

SOURCE: Lewin (1946).

place, the study is carried out, and the project is considered to be complete when the original plan has been executed and the data have been analyzed and interpreted. The data from that study may then be used to evaluate the theory driving the research. Future studies to continue the process may be planned by that researcher or other researchers. But, the essence of a good research study, according to the principles underlying mainstream psychological research design is that a study is planned well and then carried out exactly as specified. Lewin was not discarding all aspects of the standard research process, but he placed more emphasis on the effectiveness of the particular intervention to solve the social problem. He believed that for any research plan to accomplish this, it must be flexible and revised constantly on the basis of new information. This requires multiple cycles of planning, data gathering, and plan revising by the same researcher(s) and within the same project. Lewin also thought that for any social change to be long lasting, the action plan must be developed based on diagnosis of the problem within the specific social context (e.g., the local community or factory) and must involve the cooperation of the people from that setting.

Participatory research evolved in Latin America and other parts of the "Two-Thirds World"—Asia, Africa, and Central and South America—from roots quite separate from action research traditions (Park, 1999). (The term *Two-Thirds World* is used by activists to illustrate that the so-called First World is only a small proportion of the world's countries and peoples.) Paulo Freire (1970) is often given credit for beginning this research tradition through his popular education process. Freire dedicated his book *Pedagogy of the Oppressed* (translated from the original Spanish) "to the oppressed, and to those who suffer with them and fight at their side" (p. 7). It was Freire's view that "authentic education" was truly working *with* an oppressed group rather than providing information *for* or *about* the group. Freire put this perspective into action with peasants in Brazil who learned to read as they

also learned about their own culture, heritage, and status within Brazilian society. He facilitated social action based on people's own discovery of their social position and their solutions for change. He suggested that many social and political change efforts had been unsuccessful because they were designed based on the perspectives of the educators and politicians rather than on the perspectives of the people for whom the plans had been developed.

If you have ever participated in a psychological study, how much did you contribute to the direction of the research, to what was studied, and to how the conclusions were used? If you are like most undergraduate students, you probably have been asked to fill out a survey or take part in an experiment. Although your beliefs, behaviors, attitudes, and perceptions were no doubt of great value to the researchers in completing their study, your role as a participant was quite limited. **Participatory research** involves a very different level of involvement. A study can be said to be participatory when it requires the involvement of people from the group or community of interest in some or all of the stages of research. Maguire (1987) suggested that "participatory research combines three activities: investigation, education, and action" (p. 29). The *investigation* part of the process is a "social" investigation "involving participation of oppressed and ordinary people in problem posing and solving" (p. 29), and is not an academic library exercise (although no one says that you should not also make yourself aware of any previous research or theory about the problem). Both the participants in the study and the researchers are *educated* in the process about the possible causes of the problem "through collective discussion and interaction" (p. 29). Finally, both the researchers and the participants "join in solidarity to take collective *action,* both short and long term" (p. 29, emphasis added). The reasoning is clear. The people who are going to be affected by change efforts should be involved in directing that change, and mutual education will be necessary for that to occur.

CULTURE CAPSULE

Methods That Give Meaning to Cultural Experience

Conducting meaningful research in the community requires genuine mutual collaboration with community members. As discussed elsewhere in this chapter, this usually entails conducting participatory research, in which the people who will be affected by the research are involved at all stages of the research process. **Community-based participatory research** involves an equitable partnership between the researchers and members of the community that is being researched, and is aimed at creating positive community change (Minkler & Wallerstein, 2003). While the goals of community-based participatory research are certainly laudable, there are significant challenges involved in eliciting active and meaningful participation from community members. As you can imagine, the community members who might be best able to participate in all aspects of research that address relevant community goals are likely to be most similar to the academic researchers who partner with them; that is, they are likely to be higher in education, fluent in the language of the researchers, and able to assertively express their perceptions of their community's struggles and needs. The challenge for community-based researchers, then, is to incorporate methods into their research that allow for people who are truly different from the researchers to contribute meaningfully to the research.

One technique that has been used successfully in some community-based participatory projects is called **Photovoice** (Wang & Burris, 1994). This technique is based on Freire's (1970) concept of empowerment education and involves having community members take photographs to document their experiences. By sharing their photographs with others and explaining why they chose the particular images that they display and what these pictures represent to them, even individuals who were traditionally "unheard" in previous research are able to communicate important aspects of their experience (Foster-Fishman, Nowell, Deacon, Nievar, & McCann, 2005). The use of Photovoice in research has been gaining popularity in recent years. Catalani and Minkler (2010) critically reviewed 37 Photovoice projects published between 2000 and 2008, and concluded that the technique is a promising tool to engage community members in the process of community-based participatory research, and suggested that it can be particularly effective in eliciting participation in hard-to-reach communities.

Photovoice is particularly well suited to document the experiences of ethnic minority groups, since it allows community members from these groups to overcome language and cultural barriers in communicating with the researchers and others engaged in the research process. A number of studies have used Photovoice in this way. Wang and Burris (1994) pioneered the use of the technique to assess the needs of rural Chinese women. Others have used it to establish intergenerational communication among young African American women who were homeless, and elderly low-income African American women (Killion & Wang, 2000); to evaluate a public housing revitalization project in a neighborhood that included Cambodian, Vietnamese, and Russian immigrants (Stevens, 2010); to describe the challenges experienced by Bosnian refugee youth living in Canada (Berman, Ford-Bilboe, Moutrey, & Cekic, 2001); to explore relationships between experiences of intimate partner violence and sexual health among Latina immigrants in the Southwestern United States (Moya,

(Continued)

(Continued)

Chávez-Baray, & Martinez, 2014); and to document children's experiences with food security in a Canadian Indigenous community (Genuis, Willows, Alexander First Nation, & Jardine, 2015).

One group of community-based researchers (Streng et al., 2004) conducted a qualitative exploratory study called *Realidad Latina* (i.e., "Latino Reality") that used Photovoice to examine the immigration experiences of ten Latino youth who had recently settled in North Carolina. Participants were recruited from a Latino student-run club in their high school. They completed photo assignments in which they were asked to take photos that illustrated what it was like to be a Latino adolescent living within their community, and what their life was like as Latino students within their high school. This was followed by group discussions (conducted in Spanish) that focused on both problems and solutions raised by their photographs, as well as an art exhibition in which their photographs were displayed to parents, local community leaders, and school personnel. Several themes emerged from the discussions of their photographs, including a sense of a limited future, feelings of rejection, limited use of English, institutional racism, value for their Latino identity, the desire for community support, and the importance of Latino role models. Whereas the participatory project was empowering to the Latino students, it met with some resistance from school personnel who had not attended the photographic exhibition and had reacted negatively and defensively to the themes that were identified. This kind of "friction" is not necessarily regarded as a bad thing in that it could serve as a catalyst for further dialogue that could stimulate meaningful community change. On the whole, the use of the Photovoice technique proved to be an excellent vehicle for the Latino adolescents to use their creativity in a way that was empowering and provided an insider perspective that was geared toward both identifying problems and finding relevant community-based solutions.

Activism in Research

Most participatory research is also activist research. That is, the researchers are taking a position and action on a controversial issue or social problem (activist, Merriam–Webster, 2016). Usually, the researcher is working for the benefit of the oppressed group. For example, Cancian (1993), a self-described participatory researcher described the process as "a radical type of activist social research in which the people being studied, or the intended beneficiaries of the research have substantial control over and participation in the research" (pp. 93–94). You may recall from Chapter 1 that this represents the engaged research approach to applied social psychology.

However, not all activist research is participatory. It is possible to conduct research using a variety of methods and processes where direct participation of the people involved the most with

the issue is not included. Nancy Russo's empirical work debunking "post-abortion trauma syndrome," a condition fabricated by the anti-abortion lobby is one such example (Russo & Denious, 2001; Russo & Zierk, 1992). Russo worked as part of a task force of the American Psychological Association's Division 35 (Society for the Psychology of Women) to investigate this issue.

Russo and her colleagues conducted a secondary statistical analysis of survey data gathered for the U.S. Bureau of the Census. It was a very well-conducted national probability sample of male and female youth ages 14 to 21 years. This study was originally designed to examine youths' experiences in the labor market, but included many questions on health and fertility, including follow-up surveys eight years later of 5,295 women. This follow-up included measurement of women's self-esteem and adjustment, that is, variables that the anti-abortion lobby had claimed were irreparably harmed by abortion. Russo found that women who had abortions had higher overall levels of well-being on follow-up than did women who had not had abortions, even though the stresses of unwanted pregnancies were experienced. Delaying childbirth and having fewer children spaced further apart were also related to higher levels of self-esteem and well-being. Russo found no evidence that abortion is harmful to women. She did not claim that abortion is directly related to a sense of empowerment and well-being, but rather argued that it has an indirect relationship through reducing the number of children birthed by a woman. The task force then collaborated with a pro-choice group, Pro-Choice Forum, that had a large international online audience to disseminate the information from Russo's and others' studies. Russo stated, "This is our attempt to let people know the facts" (quoted in Crawford, 2003). You should note that there is no participation of a group of women who have had abortions in the design, conduct, or interpretation of the results from this study. The researcher is the sole force driving the research. Therefore, this is an example of activist research that takes a stand on an issue (pro-choice on abortion), and action (conducting a study and disseminating the results in a politicized forum), but not of participatory research.

In the sections that follow, we describe additional research, which used different methods and strategies to bring about social change through influencing policy and attempting to change structural or social barriers.

Influencing Policy

Policies are plans and procedures that bodies (such as governments) have for specific issues to ensure that certain overall goals can be met (Policy, Merriam-Webster, 2016). It is not unusual for researchers to want to influence social policy. Many researchers have press conferences or send reports of their findings to government offices in the hope that decision makers will take them into account. Some government officials peruse the scholarly literature for assistance with policy problems. During times of openness to the social sciences (this fluctuates quite dramatically over time), researchers are even hired by the government to study problems or test possible solutions. But, there are many times when social scientists watch in horror as governments and government officials make policy decisions that fly in the face of the empirical literature. For example, Jeremy Travis, former director of the National Institute of Justice within the U.S. Department of Justice summarized the social science research on crime deterrence. In a speech to the United Nations, he pointed out that decision makers, in attempting to deter crime, have consistently moved to increase the "severity of punishment," when in fact research shows that changing the "certainty of punishment" is more effective (Travis, 1995, p. 1). Another good example of policies that were not based on empirical evidence is found in the Canadian laws surrounding pornography. Until the early 1990s, Canadian law focused on the sexual explicitness of images. Decisions about what materials to prohibit or restrict were made on this basis even though there was no scientific evidence that explicitness was harmful. It was not until a Canadian Supreme Court decision, *R. v. Butler* (1992), that lawmakers took the views of social scientists into account and began to focus on content that had been empirically demonstrated to be harmful (e.g., representations of violence, degradation, and/or dehumanization of persons). Representations of adult sexuality without these qualities, no matter how explicit, are now protected under Canadian law.

Although they may want to influence social policy, it is unusual for researchers to directly attempt to do so. A study by Jason and Rose (1984) is an example of this rare approach. First, you need some background. Strict seat belt laws in Canada have resulted in 90% compliance by citizens. Legislators across states in the United States have been much less consistent in their application of regulations, resulting in only 70% compliance (American College of Emergency Physicians, 2001). Child restraint legislation (i.e., mandatory use of car seats) came much later, with both countries having abysmal records of correct car seat use. Yet, there is incontrovertible evidence that many children's lives would be saved by the correct use of car seats.

Many states did not have child restraint legislation when Jason and Rose (1984) began their investigation. Illinois had already defeated a law once, and the issue was coming up again. Jason and Rose planned an experiment to test whether provision of scientific information about the issue would influence the state senators who would be voting on the new Illinois legislation on child restraints. The experimental study used personally addressed letters containing empirical and technical information about child restraints. The information in the letters came from two studies that the authors had conducted: an observational study set up at intersections in several states to examine the use of car seats with children under five years of age (very low levels of correct restraints were observed), and a survey of attitudes toward the bill being put forward (indicating that nearly 80% of citizens would support the law). Half of the state senators were selected at random to receive the letter. The vote in the Illinois Senate was recorded. Significantly more of the senators who had received the letter voted in favor of the bill (79%) than did senators who had not received it (53%). The bill, which had been narrowly defeated during the previous round, was supported and became law. The experiment by Jason and Rose provides a clear indication of the potential of researchers to influence important public policy decisions.

Researchers who do their work in the world outside of a university setting have to be especially careful about the ethical implications of their research. Among many other ethical issues, they must push themselves harder to consider the ramifications of doing the research versus not doing it. They must decide between carrying out their studies in the best way possible from a research standpoint (and thereby increasing the validity of the findings, but perhaps risking some adverse consequences), and doing studies in less controlled ways (and thereby losing the ability to be sure about the causes of the results). These

decisions are always important to researchers, but decisions made by applied social psychologists and community psychologists may have more impact on society. Jason and Rose (1984), the authors of the child restraint study, pointed out that they took a risk by carrying out an experiment in this situation because many children's lives were at stake. If the support for car seats had not been so high to begin with, sending the letters to only half of the senators was a risk that probably should not have been taken. The random assignment of senators to conditions was a necessary feature of an experimental design that could test the effect of the letters on subsequent voting behavior. Now that we know that letters of this type can make a difference, would you insist on random assignment on the next issue? Why or why not? You may want to bring up this issue in class to get the views of your classmates and professor. Ethical decisions are always about balancing risks and benefits. There are no easy answers.

Another researcher who has attempted to change policy is David Riley with his 1997 work on "latchkey" children (i.e., children who are left at home unsupervised for some part of the day), but in this case the affected policy was on a community level rather than on a governmental level. Although there is some evidence in the research literature that having more responsibility can provide children with opportunities to grow in positive ways, other research suggests that young children left unsupervised are more likely to be plagued by fears, or develop dependence on drugs, alcohol, and/or cigarettes during their teenage years. When Riley first began thinking about this, he used public lectures, radio shows, and press releases to raise public awareness about the prevalence of latchkey situations, and the risks of this lack of supervision for the children. He described all of these efforts as having had "zero effect" (Riley, 1997, p. 425). People in the communities where the reports were publicized dismissed Riley's work because they felt that it did not apply to them in their own towns or cities. Riley doubted that this was the case, but he took some time to understand that these people from the general public might have a point. He stated, "At the time, I did not realize that they were voicing a cogent methodological critique: They were questioning the external validity of the research I cited" (p. 425). When Riley finally listened, he suggested that they—he, the researcher, and the people from the actual community—conduct the research in the specific communities to see whether the issue of latchkey children was or was not a problem. As a result, he embarked on ten years of mainly successful studies and interventions.

The work of Riley (1997) is an example of research that affects local nongovernmental policy. This type of policy development occurs when communities and organizations choose a plan of action to help them make future decisions. With Riley's approach, in each community a planning committee made up of teachers, parents, and men and women from the business community was created. With Riley's assistance, the planning committee developed and administered a mail survey of parents of schoolchildren up to the sixth grade. The survey asked the parents about situations in which the children were left without adult supervision, and about the safety knowledge possessed by their children (e.g., whether they know about fire safety). A report was written describing the results, including direct quotes from these local surveys. This report was then presented to the broader community in a variety of ways, and the community planning committee almost always took action.

An immediate outcome of the pilot survey in the first community studied was the large number of parents who called their local schools to ask about the types of safety and self-care information that their children were receiving. From this, the researchers (Riley and the community planning committee) realized that the survey itself was an intervention that produced change. As a result, the research projects in all subsequent communities were changed to survey *all* parents of children of a particular age rather than a sample of parents. Riley agreed to help other communities set up similar projects in the state. His own involvement became less and less as the

number of communities involved increased. Riley described his reduced role as an accidental (it began due to his being overwhelmed by the workload), but empowering component of the research. The expert status of the researcher was undermined, and the communities themselves "owned" their research, and the research process.

Riley (1997) evaluated the effectiveness of the actions taken within the project. He found that the local planning committees felt obliged to act on their own reports and that many changes resulted. Long- and short-term changes in the communities over a 7-year period included new jobs (e.g., businesses related to child care needs) and new school-age children's programs, with thousands of children being served. As of 1997, the project had been replicated in many communities spanning 12 states. Projects were carried out by other researchers and community planning committee members who obtained the needs assessment materials from Riley. The success of Riley's efforts shows us how a simple participatory approach can support major community and social policy changes around an issue. Without the community planning groups, whose members tailored their projects to their own communities, would people have listened to the results? Riley maintained that they would not have listened.

Changing Structural or Social Barriers

Researchers have tried to change society by going into the communities where injustices exist and developing research projects that aim to overcome structural or social barriers. Sometimes change is accomplished by empowering the social group or facilitating its members' social action in some way. This is not to imply that the groups "need" research to take action. Many groups are already active before they meet the researchers. In all cases, however, the research projects provide something additional, usually expertise or skills training to gather data required to strengthen community positions or demands. In other situations, researchers must try to influence society at a more basic level by giving voice to people, a point of view, or a perspective that has not been heard. Other times, researchers try to change long-standing attitudes in communities. The following subsections discuss two very different examples to show how the research process can work for larger-scale social change.

Overcoming physical barriers. Mary Brydon-Miller has been involved in a number of participatory projects on diverse issues. The example focused on here is her work in the community of people with physical disabilities in western Massachusetts (Brydon-Miller, 1993). The members of this community had long been involved in the independent living movement (active all over North America), working for autonomy and control for persons with disabilities. In this instance, the group, which was based in the Independent Living Center, asked for Brydon-Miller's help in identifying the accessibility needs of people with physical disabilities, and in assessing the best routes for their advocacy to take. Brydon-Miller (1993) had a number of objectives for the project that built on the group's existing strengths. She wanted to ensure that the members of the group had sufficient skill and information to engage in productive self-advocacy, that people in the community understood the specific problems related to accessibility, and that the design and implementation of advocacy actions matched the consensus understanding of the disabled community in that area. Brydon-Miller also had "more process-oriented objectives," including a desire to ensure that members of the disabled community saw themselves as "experts in the field of disability" (p. 127), and that they had ownership of the research and advocacy that resulted. She also wanted to demonstrate that advocacy, and particularly self-advocacy, was an effective tool for social change.

Brydon-Miller (1993) used face-to-face interviews as a first step, not only to identify information about "accessibility-related concerns," and "strategies for dealing with inaccessible environments"

(p. 128), but also to encourage participants to reflect on their own experiences in more detail. She then presented a summary of the interviews at a workshop at the center. Prior to this meeting, Brydon-Miller believed that the most useful action to take would be to organize a large-scale conference involving policy makers and politicians. The participants at the workshop were not at all interested in her idea. Many new issues and possible solutions were identified, and a different advocacy project was chosen: to work toward greater accessibility of a local shopping mall. A committee was created and named the Community Accessibility Committee.

The first research action taken was to investigate (through observation) the current state of accessibility of the mall. Then discussions were held about possible strategies and tactics to overcome the many barriers to accessibility that had been identified. Suggestions ranged from a protest outside the mall during the Christmas shopping season to writing to the mall executives. Letter writing had been attempted in the past by the center staff members and had been unsuccessful. However, it was eventually decided that writing a detailed letter with all of the relevant details from the mall survey would be more appropriate. Not much happened as a result of that first letter, but the group did not give up. The group followed up with a complaint submitted to the Architectural Barriers Board. Five years later, after extensive negotiation and a number of court battles, all requested changes to the mall were made, including an elevator to the second floor, providing full accessibility to those in wheelchairs. The committee has continued its work on other sites of inaccessibility in the community since that achievement.

Brydon-Miller (1993) initiated the research based on her knowledge of the community, carried out the early phases of the research, and did all the report writing. All other aspects of the research process and advocacy were shared between Brydon-Miller and the committee. There was a strong activist focus to the entire project. In this example, action research cycles of planning, implementation, and evaluation were carried out by the researcher and the committee within a fully participatory process that culminated in social action and social change.

Overcoming social barriers: *Changing prejudicial attitudes and stereotypes.* A Canadian example of a 40-year project that has addressed the need for change in prejudice and stereotypes is the work of Wallace E. Lambert at McGill University (Lambert, 1992). Lambert and his colleagues attempted to influence attitudes and stereotypes toward French Canadians and bilingualism in an increasingly multicultural Canada. Their early work entailed conducting experimental studies involving audiotapes of bilingual Canadians who spoke in either French or English. This research documented much less favorable impressions of persons speaking French than of persons speaking English. The most surprising finding was that this bias existed in samples of French Canadian participants as well, demonstrating an in-group prejudice. The authors of the study were dismayed when the media and other colleagues interpreted the results in ways that supported the status quo rather than challenging it (e.g., as proof of French inferiority, as proof that English dominance had created "losers"). Three decades later, a replication by Genesee and Holobow (1989) demonstrated no change in the phenomena. Lambert (1992) concluded that focusing research on a social question does not ensure social change.

Lambert continued doing research to dissect the workings of prejudice in this context and to identify possible solutions. Lambert reported that his work with English Canadian parents in developing and initiating "immersion education" in the schools had the most impact (on social change) of all his work. English-speaking students were taught in French by French teachers nearly exclusively for the first three years of their schooling. Parents were actively involved in pushing for these program developments. The researchers helped to design the program and then evaluated its effects over time. They were able to demonstrate the efficacy of this model of education to facilitate bilingualism without damaging children's skills in other areas. Also of considerable significance is that the students not only became fluently bilingual, but also resisted prejudice and became open to the benefits of other languages and cultures.

Lambert's (1992) ideas about immersion education spread, and many other schools across Canada, as well as in the United States and Europe, have adopted similar educational programs. One part of the research program just outlined had participatory components. The study that launched immersion programs in the schools could not have been successful without the intense involvement of English-speaking Canadian parents who wanted a bilingual future for their children. Most of Lambert's other studies use laboratory or survey methods where students or other citizens provide data in the more standard way. So, this research project as a whole is not participatory research. The research program does provide an interesting example of something that did not *start out* being action research, but that in retrospect over 40 years of work *is* action research. After each study, the researcher, his colleagues, and students adjusted their views and perspectives, thought about the problem in a different way, and implemented another phase of the research to address the new concerns.

SUMMARY

Now that you have read this entire chapter, we ask you to recall the opening example of the *It Gets Better Project*, in which adults communicated directly with LGBT youth in an attempt to present a more hopeful vision of their future, one that might prevent the tragic outcomes of prejudice and harassment that had already taken too many young lives. Although Dan Savage, who initiated the project, is not a community psychologist, it should be apparent that his project is very much in keeping with a community psychology approach. By adopting an approach that respects and celebrates diversity, he showed that it is possible to counter some of the harmful and stigmatizing effects of prejudice and discrimination. The creation of a

YouTube channel and a website designed to allow LGBT role models and other supportive adults to speak directly to LGBT youth surely creates a strong and positive sense of community for young people who may feel isolated and marginalized. The fact that the YouTube channel was immediately inundated with such a surge of positive videos that it crashed the site is an indicator that there is a powerful context and desire for social change in the direction of greater understanding and support of LGBT youth.

In this chapter, we wanted to give you a sense of what the field of community psychology entails. Community psychology was defined, and some of the historical influences on its development were described. A unique feature of community psychology is the explicit acknowledgment of the values that drive the priorities and activities of those engaged in its practice. We specifically focused on three particular community psychology values: *sense of community*, or the degree to which particular communities serve people's needs for membership and belonging; *respect for diversity* versus the consequences of labeling and stigmatizing those who are different; and *activist and research strategies* to bring about social change. This chapter by no means represents an exhaustive or complete treatment of the field of community psychology, and we hope that it stimulates in readers a desire to pursue further reading or take courses in this exciting area of psychology. Just as importantly, we hope that this chapter has instilled in you a desire to consider ways in which involvement in your own community can help to "turn tales of terror into tales of joy" (Rappaport, 2000, p. 1).

13

APPLYING SOCIAL PSYCHOLOGY TO THE ENVIRONMENT

ROBERT GIFFORD

"A California student linked to a radical environmentalist group is being held without bail as he faces charges for allegedly firebombing 125 sport utility vehicles [SUVs] last August [2003]. . . . Human life is risked by the nature of these offences," U.S. Magistrate Carolyn Turchin said during a hearing as she decided not to release 23-year-old Billy Cottrell.

    The Pasadena, California, man was arrested on March 9, 2004, and accused of damaging or destroying vehicles at car dealerships and homes in the Los Angeles area. The bill for the property damage was an estimated $2.3 million. At the time, Cottrell was a second-year graduate student in physics at the California Institute of Technology, and e-mails from computers at that school had claimed responsibility for the SUV mayhem on behalf of the extremist group Earth Liberation Front. On its website, the Earth Liberation Front called Cottrell "an environmental campaigner."

    Federal Bureau of Investigation (FBI) officials said in an affidavit that Cottrell was also involved in a plot to plaster SUVs with 5,000 bumper stickers that read "My SUV Supports Terrorism." Many environmentalists disapprove of SUVs because of their high gas consumption. If convicted, Cottrell could have spent 40 years behind bars. One charge that he faced, using a destructive device during a violent crime, carries a minimum sentence of 30 years in federal prison ("Suspected SUV Bomber Held Without Bail," 2004). In April 2005, Billy Cottrell was convicted of conspiracy and arson charges and sentenced to eight years in federal prison. In September 2009, his convictions for arson were overturned, but his conspiracy conviction was affirmed. Billy Cottrell was released in August 2011.

One might ask the following questions:

- Why is gas consumption such a contentious issue?
- If SUVs consume so much gas, what interventions can be implemented to discourage people from buying them?
- As more people drive SUVs, does that encourage still more people to purchase them?

"Wherever you go, there you are." This old saying is another way of conveying the idea that no matter what you do—whether you are interacting with others or are alone—and no matter what behavior or thought you are engaged in, you do it *somewhere*. This somewhere is the physical environment, and it is often a crucial influence on our actions, thoughts, and well-being. But our actions, both individually and collectively, also have an enormous impact on the physical environment—sometimes beneficial, but sometimes harmful.

The task of psychologists interested in the environment is to examine a great variety of topics besides the issues involved in extreme actions aimed at defending the natural environment. Environmental psychologists study not only how the physical environment (e.g., buildings, weather, nature, noise, pollution, street arrangements) affects our behavior, thinking, and well-being, but also how our behavior (e.g., energy conservation, vandalism, activism, automobile use, recycling, water use) affects the environment (e.g., climate change, water shortages, pollution, reduced biodiversity).

Many topics examined by environmental psychologists have social aspects, including the following: violence in jails; weather and altruism; the design of the built environment in relation to crime, privacy, crowding, and territoriality; the effects of noise and lighting on interpersonal relations; spatial arrangements in offices and schools; social aspects of managing natural resources; and our role in climate change (Gifford, 2008).

One chapter cannot possibly describe fully the range, activities, and actions of environmental psychologists. A recent textbook (Gifford, 2014) describes more than 3,000 published studies in environmental psychology, and even that represents only a fraction of the field's research literature. However, to give you a taste of environmental psychology, including the contributions of social psychology, this chapter focuses on two major topics that should give you a good sample of the field as a whole.

The first topic is **resource dilemmas**, which are sometimes called *commons dilemmas*. These are situations in which individuals must choose between self-interest (taking or using unsustainable amounts of a natural resource, such as water or fish) and the interests of the community or environment (taking a sustainable share, or less, of the resource). Which social factors do you think might come into play as individuals make these decisions? Given that no one person is likely to be given control of an entire water supply, fishing grounds, or the climate, how might you conduct some research to understand what causes greed or cooperation in these situations?

Second, environmental psychologists work to improve the physical environment. Two ways in which they do so are called social design and defensible space. **Social design** is a process by which any building (e.g., office, school, residence, factory, retail store, prison) may be designed in collaboration with those who will actually use that building so that it is more user-friendly, as opposed to being designed solely by an architect who will never use the building. Outdoor spaces, such as streets and plazas can also be designed either to support human interaction or to ignore it. What social factors might be important in a process like this? Have you ever worked, gone to school, or visited a building that did not facilitate your work, your purpose for using the building, or your social life? Social design could have helped.

Defensible space represents a way of fighting crime through careful arrangement of the physical aspects of communities, retail buildings, and residences. The way in which a building or community is designed can encourage or discourage burglars, robbers, and vandals. What could those design factors be? How could social psychology be a part of this kind of research?

Like the efforts of other psychologists, the work of those who study environmental issues may be grouped into two complementary branches: experimental and applied. Nearly all of environmental psychology is applied in the broad sense that its efforts are stimulated by the recognition of problems in involving interactions between individuals, on the one hand, and their built or natural settings, on the other hand. Virtually all environmental psychologists hope to contribute in some way to the eventual solution of such problems. Even the most experimental of environmental psychologists hope that the results from their studies will be considered in the design of offices, factories, homes, streetscapes, or parks, or in programs designed to increase how much people engage in such efforts as recycling, energy conservation, and reductions in car use.

Environmental psychologists have learned an enormous amount about person–environment relations during the 50 years the field has formally existed. They know much about social environmental dynamics, such as how typical interpersonal distances change with different situations; which social factors are likely to improve or inhibit pro-environmental attitudes; how interpersonal relations lead to water conservation; how crowding affects social interaction; how noise influences helping behavior; how temperature is related to interpersonal violence; and which messages are more likely to encourage climate positive behaviors. Many environmental psychologists

have designed behavioral interventions to change and improve behavior toward the goal of more sustainable, climate-friendly practices.

As discussed in Chapter 1, however, good social scientists also want to understand *why* people act the way they do. Therefore, psychologists who focus on the physical environment have developed interesting theories to help explain things, such as who will cooperate and who will not when resources are scarce, how cultures vary in seeking privacy, the cultural meanings conveyed by building facades, the strategies residents use for dealing with spatial conflicts within their homes, how children learn to find their way around their neighborhoods, and which furniture arrangements encourage social interaction (Gifford, 2014).

Nevertheless, as mentioned earlier, this chapter considers only a small sample of these efforts: resource dilemmas, social design, and defensible space.

RESOURCE DILEMMAS

As environmental problems and concerns grow, social scientists must learn more about individual and small group contributions to ecological degradation. As humans who dwell in societies, we extract, refine, use, and dispose of many natural resources. However, societies are composed of individuals, and ultimately people make these choices *as individuals and small groups* in their homes, at work, and during their leisure hours.

The crucial aspect of resource management decisions made by each of us is that they sum in ways that are partly rational, partly irrational, and yet all-important, from person to person, across billions of individuals' actions to large-scale effects on the environment and the climate. Mundane everyday choices to turn on the air conditioning, drive the car a short way instead of walking or riding a bike, or take a 15-minute shower instead of a 5-minute shower add up to resource depletion on a larger scale.

Once the macro-environment is affected (e.g., increased CO_2 in the atmosphere, less forest cover, depleted aquifers, more landfills, more pavement), it affects us in return. Most of us realize that we should waste less, but we are tempted to lead lives that use many natural resources (e.g., water, oil, wood). Our divided goals lead us to experience this as a dilemma, that is, one or another of a family called social dilemmas.

A Family of Dilemmas

The focus of this section is on resource dilemmas, which represent one of several kinds of dilemma situations that fall under the general category (family) of social dilemmas. **Social dilemmas** are a group of situations in which individuals face important choices. Sometimes individuals do not realize how important their choices are—or even that they are making choices—but that is a separate problem. In social dilemmas, the rewards to the individual for noncooperation are greater than the rewards for cooperation no matter what others do; however, if most individuals involved fail to cooperate, then everyone receives lower rewards (Dawes, 1980). A simple example would be a person washing a car during a dry spell. This person gains a clean car by using scarce water—the reward (a clean car) seems greater than having no reward (an unclean car)—and this clean car reward occurs, in the short term, regardless of what other community residents do. If this person is one of very few people washing their cars, a clean car reward is gained with little loss to the community water supply. However, if many people wash their cars, serious damage might be done to the water supply, and everyone receives a lower reward—having no water, or perhaps muddy water, from the community supply—and this consequence is worse than merely having a dirty car.

Three main forms of social dilemma are recognized: public goods problems, social traps, and resource (or commons) dilemmas. **Public goods problems** involve dilemmas about whether to contribute (e.g., time, effort, money) to a project that would benefit everyone when

such a contribution is voluntary. For example, one may decide to help (or not help) build a neighborhood children's playground. The dilemma is that contributing costs something (in this case, one's money or time), but if not enough others contribute, the playground project will not be successful.

A person is tempted to *avoid* contributing to the public good (to not cooperate) for two reasons. First, if enough others contribute their time and/or money so that the public good succeeds, the person benefits (gets a neighborhood playground) without having to contribute anything. Second, contributing is risky in that a person might donate money or time, only to find that not enough others do so; if this happens, the project fails, and the person's contribution is wasted.

Of course, the ideal outcome is that everyone helps and the project succeeds. Unfortunately, some do not help, leaving the outcome uncertain, and then each person begins to wonder whether participation is a good idea—this is precisely the public goods dilemma. Public goods dilemmas are surprisingly common in our lives (just look around with the concept in mind). Unfortunately, many worthwhile projects fail.

Social traps are a second form of social dilemma. They involve short-term pleasure or gain that over time leads to pain or loss (Platt, 1973). Some classic social traps include smoking, overeating, and using pesticides. They are dilemmas because individuals must choose between an immediate reward (e.g., the pleasure of smoking, the pleasure of eating an extra dish of ice cream), and the long-term negative outcome to which the reward can lead (e.g., lung cancer, obesity) versus the choice of short-term deprivation (e.g., quitting smoking, refusing to eat the extra dish of ice cream), and the long-term positive outcome to which the deprivation can lead (e.g., a longer life, a slimmer build).

Two problems create the dilemma in a social trap. First, the long-term outcome usually is not certain (e.g., not every smoker dies of smoking-related disease, nor does every person who abstains from smoking live a long time). In the case of the environment, the long-term uncertainty makes it easier to rationalize choosing the environmentally damaging option, for example, using excessive water in the spring when the state of the community reservoir later in the summer is not yet known. Second, individuals tend to *discount* (i.e., downplay) the negative outcomes; for example, pesticide users usually do not think about how their pesticide use can lead to ecological problems in the future, or they believe that their own small contribution does not matter all that much.

Public goods problems and social traps are important social dilemmas that clearly are pertinent to the well-being of the physical environment. All of us must deal with these two forms of dilemma in our lives. However, as noted previously, the focus in this chapter is on a third form of social dilemma, the **resource dilemma,** which is sometimes called the commons dilemma, a term first used by Dawes (1973).

What Is a Resource Dilemma?

Early perspectives on resource dilemmas. The car-washing example given earlier is a specific form of resource dilemma. For a more general understanding, let us start with a little background based on an allegory told long ago by William Lloyd. In some older societies, "the commons" referred to a central open space in the heart of a village. By mutual understanding, this commons was jointly owned by all citizens in good standing without any borders or fences inside it. All citizens were allowed to use its grass and open space to graze their animals. The unwritten rule was that each family could have one cow. There was enough grass for all of the citizens' animals, and the commons worked well for many years (Lloyd, 1837/1968).

However, the day eventually came when one citizen decided to make a little extra money by having a second cow, from which more milk could be produced and sold. There is nothing wrong with "getting ahead," is there? (Another possibility is that more families moved to the village, and each family wanted to add one more cow. Everyone is entitled to one cow,

right?) The problem is that the amount of available grass remained the same; the alternative was to cut down more of the forest surrounding the village, but that is just another form of resource dilemma. Whether someone wanted to get ahead or the number of shareholders in the commons grew, there was more use of the same amount of grass. As demand for a limited resource increases, the issue becomes one of *freedom in the commons,* according to Garrett Hardin. Do citizens have the right to take what they want (individual freedom to get ahead), or to increase the number of families, all of whom want equal grazing rights, or should there be restrictions so that the commons is protected (Hardin, 1968)?

When the supply of a resource seems large or nearly limitless, individuals seem to feel free to exploit the resource as much as possible. One reason for this was advanced by the famous 18th-century economist Adam Smith (1776/1976), who argued that in exploiting a resource for one's own benefit, an individual allegedly is guided by an "invisible hand" to benefit the whole community. For example, a whaler who becomes rich would employ people, buy equipment, and donate to social, educational, and charitable causes—and would generally aid the economy. At one time, the supply of whales seemed nearly endless.

In telling the preceding village allegory, Lloyd (1837/1968), a 19th-century economist, appears to have been the first to see a fundamental problem with Smith's logic. Lloyd recognized that many resources are, in fact, finite and limited. When that is the case, a big problem arises. In a limited commons consisting of some desirable resource, individuals acting in self-interest might lead to a process called the **tragedy of the commons**, which occurs when "each [person] is locked into a system that compels him to increase his [harvesting] without limit—in a world that is limited. Ruin is the destination toward which all [persons] rush, each pursuing his own best interest" (Hardin, 1968, p. 1244).

The classic example of a commons dilemma is grazing land (as in the commons example), but the extreme importance of resource dilemmas is that many other resources are limited and essentially held in common—freshwater, forests, habitat, and even our one and only atmosphere. Resource dilemmas are a *matter of life and death for all life on the planet.*

The conclusion to Lloyd's allegory was that once the commons was overused, the grass ran out and so the cows perished, and then the villagers did not have enough to eat and so they too died. Lloyd's story was an amazingly prescient vision of our modern notion of the limited "spaceship earth," given that he first presented the story more than 175 years ago.

The nature of the dilemma itself. What is a resource dilemma? One occurs each time you want to do something that uses a limited natural resource (e.g., freshwater, oil or gas, wild fish) that would make your life easier, more fun, or more comfortable. Some resources regenerate relatively quickly (e.g., grass for grazing, water in reservoirs), others regenerate not so quickly (e.g., fish, trees), and some regenerate very slowly, or not at all (e.g., oil, endangered species). When resources regenerate more slowly than people can harvest them, the danger of resource exhaustion arises. Users of such resources face a choice: either choose to get ahead quickly at the expense of the commons (the resource and/or the environment) and other harvesters, or choose to restrain harvesting to preserve the commons and increase one's contentment or wealth more slowly. The radical environmentalist Billy Cottrell (opening vignette) apparently believed that oil, from which gas is produced, is a natural resource that is being harvested too quickly.

Not all natural resources are in short supply, even those that are created very slowly (e.g., sand). But, when people are able to harvest a desirable resource faster than it can regenerate through improved technology or sheer person power, the potential dilemma becomes an actual dilemma. Harvesters must choose between rapid, resource-destructive, short-term, self-interested harvesting ("get it while you can"), and restrained, long-term, community- and resource-oriented harvesting.

The consequences of resource dilemmas. Hardin's (1968) article in the journal *Science* on the ultimate consequences of resource dilemmas has been very influential. He concluded that commons dilemmas probably would be fatal to the entire planet eventually. In terms of the enormous environmental social problem called climate change, many tendencies to *not* take appropriate action have been identified. These "dragons of inaction" (Gifford, 2011) include over 30 "species" in seven "genera"—limited cognition, certain ideologies, social norms and comparison, discredence (mistrust of experts), perceived risks (of changing one's behavior), sunk costs (e.g., investments in resource extraction), and limited behavior (e.g., "I recycle, so I have done enough").

However, environmental psychologists have not accepted without question Hardin's tragedy of the commons argument that most (too many) individuals will act in their short-term self-interest. They believe that the issue of how individuals will behave in a limited commons is an open question that will be resolved through empirical research. Hardin was a biologist; he had a fairly pessimistic outlook on the future, based on some clear examples of nonhuman animal populations that followed a tragedy of the commons path to destruction. The growth of the earth's human population over the long term certainly resembles the same pattern observed in some animal populations that collapsed after extremely rapid growth. The explosive growth of the population of humans is depicted in Figure 13.1.

Nevertheless, humans have greater cognitive capacity than other animals, and we can anticipate difficulties and solve problems—usually. Can our species do better, or are we just another animal in the sense that we will not be able to escape the tendency to greed that will eventually destroy us? Social scientists have pursued this question and created sizable bodies of work in their attempts to try to answer it (e.g., Gardner, Ostrom, & Walker, 1990; Gifford, 2014, Chapt. 14; Komorita & Parks, 1994).

The case of water: *A dose of reality.* One of the most important resources in the world is

Figure 13.1 The Growth of the Human Population on Earth

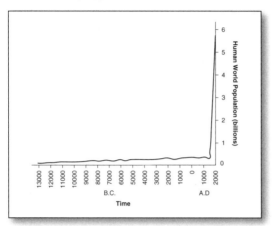

freshwater, and it is bound to become more important in the future. You will recall that Lloyd pointed out a flaw in Adam Smith's 18th-century influential economic theory that was based on the assumption that natural resources are essentially unlimited. It was acceptable—even admirable—for entrepreneurs to use them at will to create wealth because others in society also would benefit. This rationale still is used today to justify the "necessary" growth of business and the economy.

We now know well that at least some natural resources are not unlimited and that people have been fighting over limited natural resources for centuries. In his book *Resource Wars,* Michael Klare recalled the biblical accounts of the Israelites' drive from the desert into the "Promised Land," that is, the fertile valleys of the Jordan River basin that contained good supplies of water (Klare, 2001). This drive involved a successful invasion (led by Moses) of these lands that were held by several groups that the Israelites expelled from the fertile region (e.g., Canaanites, Amorites, Hittites).

Klare (2001) argued that the 1967 Arab–Israeli war essentially was a modern repetition of the same struggle. He quoted former Israeli Prime Minister Yitzhak Rabin who once said, "If we solve every other problem in the Middle East,

but do not satisfactorily solve the water problem, our region will explode." Ancient and modern Egyptian rulers likewise have struggled to control the waters of the Nile, which during modern times flows through nine countries. Boutros Boutros-Ghali, the former Egyptian minister of state for foreign affairs said, "The next war in our region will be over the waters of the Nile, not politics."

Today's natural resource struggles are over oil, fish, and trees as well as water. The ancient legacy of war and armed conflict in the Jordan and Nile regions could well be repeated as sources of water, fish, oil, and trees recede. Indeed, there have already been many oil wars and fish wars during recent times. Thus, cooperation in the use and management of natural resources is not some kind of academic parlor game; it is of vital importance in the real world of politics and war. Lives depend on finding ways of sharing natural resources in equitable ways.

We all play a part in the management of a steady stream of natural resources (e.g., freshwater, oil, wood, fish) that have been converted into products that we use every day. Some of these resources come from limited sources. Commons dilemmas occur when improved technology or increased person power enables the harvesting of resources faster than the resource can regenerate. A special issue of *National Geographic* (Water: Our Thirsty World, 2010) calls our attention to the impending water crisis with the following observations:

- Less than 3% of the Earth's water is fresh (p. 32). Of that amount about 70% is sealed in ice and snow (p. 46).
- The remaining water primarily is in aquifers that are draining faster than nature can replenish them (p. 52). An aquifer is an underground porous deposit of rock, sediment, or soil that can range in area from a few square miles to thousands of square miles.
- Water tables have declined substantially in regions of the Earth that contain half the human population (p. 49).
- People—mostly women—in developing nations must walk on average 3.7 miles to obtain their water (p. 56).

- As approximately 83 million people are added to the Earth's population each year, demand for water continues to increase (p. 52).
- By 2025, nearly 2 billion people will inhabit areas with severe water shortages (p. 56).

As Barbara Kingsolver, an American novelist wrote in that special issue, "We have been slow to give up on the myth of Earth's infinite generosity. Rather grandly, we have overdrawn our accounts. . . . Water is the ultimate commons" (p. 49).

All of us who use natural resources or products derived from them (i.e., everybody) must decide whether to maximize our own gain in the short term, or instead to help maximize the gain over the long term for everyone, including ourselves (and, in the course of so doing, to preserve the resources themselves rather than wiping them out). The crucial aspect of all these individual decisions is that they add up to society's success or failure in managing natural resources. Take a look at Table 13.1, which shows the *virtual water* for a pound of each of several foods, referring to the total amount of water required to produce the pound. To illustrate, in an industrial system, 816,600 gallons of water are needed to raise a cow or steer for three years from birth to market, that is, 808,400 gallons (for pasture, feed, and hay) + 6,300 gallons (for drinking) + 1,900 gallons (for cleaning stables/farmyards). What do the figures in Table 13.1 suggest in terms of the possible decisions that we as individual residents of our planet might consider making as the water crisis intensifies? Also, a tenable explanation for why countries in the Middle East have not been engaged in outright conflicts over water is that they import large quantities of their food, the production of which relies on the consumption of the water of the exporting countries.

Studying Resource Dilemmas

For environmental psychologists, two important questions are as follows. First, under which conditions will individuals act in self-interest to the detriment of others and the resource? Second, under what conditions will individuals not act in self-interest, and thus act to the benefit of others and the resource? The first question

Table 13.1 Number of Gallons of Water Used in the Production of One Pound of a Food Product (Global Average)

Meat and Animal Products		Fruits and Vegetables	
Beef	1,857	Figs	379
Sausage	1,382	Cherries	185
Pork	756	Avocados	154
Processed cheese	589	Corn	109
Chicken	469	Oranges	55
Eggs	400	Beans	43
Fresh cheese	371	Strawberries	33
Yogurt	138	Potatoes	31

SOURCE: Based on data from waterfootprint.org, which appeared in Water: Our Thirsty World [Special Isssue]. (2010, April). *National Geographic*, 217.

concerns understanding the problem, whereas the second question relates to addressing the problem. Often it is easier or more rewarding, at least in the short run, to engage in self-serving behavior than to behave in the public interest. In a limited commons, the cooperative or public-spirited act often is more expensive, difficult, and/or time-consuming and less immediately rewarding than is the self-serving act. As we will see, social factors are among the most important in answering these questions.

More than 100 recent scientific studies have examined many influences on the choices that individuals and groups make in these resource dilemmas. When you think about it, no government or corporation is likely to give anyone, including a social scientist, complete control over any large real resource merely to conduct an experimental study. Thus, we scientists sometimes use **microworlds**, that is, dynamic computer-based virtual environments that exist in laboratories, but reasonably simulate real-world conditions (DiFonzo, Hantula, & Bordia, 1998). It is tempting to think that participants in these simulated environments do not respond in the same way as they do in everyday life, but there is good evidence that a well-constructed microworld will elicit strong emotions that seem to indicate that the participants are taking the microworld as seriously as they would a full-scale resource.

In a typical study, several participants (fishers) might see, in a computer-simulated fishery (i.e., a microworld), that a lake contains 100 fish. They are told that they will receive $5 for each fish they catch, and that they can catch as many as they wish. The fish spawn at the rate of two between seasons, that is, the number of fish left after all the fishers have caught as many fish as they want for a season doubles before the opening of the next season. However, the lake's resources cannot support more than 100 fish, so the spawning can never result in the lake having more than 100 fish. If all the fish are ever taken, they obviously cannot spawn, and the fishery is dead. If you were one of four fishers in this situation, how many fish would you catch in the first

season? Do you wonder how many fish the other three fishers might take? Will the four of you manage this resource in a sustainable way so that the fishery continues indefinitely—or will the four of you extinguish the fish population?

Altogether, perhaps 35 different factors have been found to influence whether harvesters tend to be greedy or cooperative in resource dilemmas (Gifford, 2014, Chapt. 14; Komorita & Parks, 1994). In general, these studies have focused on three kinds of influence on cooperation in the commons. The first is the nature of the resource itself (e.g., how much of it is available, how much of it is certain to exist). For example, in the typical study above, what if the lake contained 1,000 fish, or 25 fish, instead of 100? What if, in the case of a real lake, counting the fish is difficult, so scientists must estimate the fish population? Their best estimate is that the lake contains 50–150 fish. How would that affect the fishers' harvesting? A second factor involves the social conditions or rules surrounding the harvesting (e.g., how well the harvesters know and trust each other; whether a leader exists, is elected, or acts in a certain way). What if the four fishers are all good friends, or all strangers? What if the four have a boss, or they know that a game warden is nearby? The third factor is the characteristics of the harvesters themselves (e.g., their values, their needs, or their experience as fishers). What if one of the fishers has four children and another has none, or two fishers are very aware of the concept of sustainability, and two others have never heard of the idea?

Each study typically examines two or three specific variables at a time. As an example, our own research has focused on the thinking processes of participants as the dilemma evolves over time (Hine & Gifford, 1997), and on the attributions made about the actions of the self and other harvesters (Gifford & Hine, 1997; Hine & Gifford, 1996). In part, decision making and behavior in resource dilemmas depend on what we think about the other harvesters and *their* choices.

Typically these studies are done in laboratories, in order to test hypotheses in a scientifically

Figure 13.2 Screen Shot From FISH 5

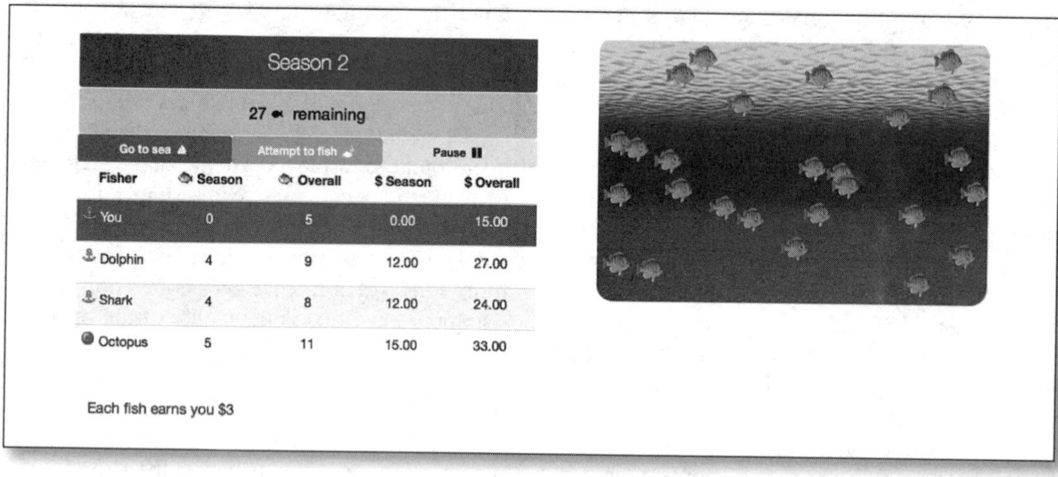

As a participant fisher, you are able to choose, if you wish, to catch fish more quickly than they can spawn. In fact, you can catch all the fish at any time. But if you do that, or another fisher does, the fish will not exist to reproduce in the future, so the quick gain comes at the expense of any future harvests. Therefore, you may also choose to restrain your harvests in the interest of conserving the stock of fish. Each fisher in a fleet (group) has equal and full access to the resource. Thus, one big concern is what the other fishers will do; can they be trusted to restrain their harvests? Figure 13.2 shows a screen shot from FISH 5.

correct way, but the findings do apply to the real world. Not only fish, but water, trees, many species of animals and plants, and other natural resources are valuable, but in short supply. Clearly, the basic idea of the resource dilemma is tied to the fate of many important resources, and therefore, ultimately, to our own fate.

Let us consider an example of a particular microworld called FISH 5 (Gifford & Gifford, 2000), which re-creates in the laboratory the situation faced by actual fishers as they choose how much of a fish stock to harvest. The program creates a context that includes many of the essential elements of a real resource dilemma.

FOCUS ON RESEARCH

Exploring the Thought Processes by Which Fishers Make Harvesting Decisions

Experimental research on resource dilemmas has been very productive and has generated a number of important findings (Komorita & Parks, 1994). Most such studies set up various conditions for their participants and then observe the resulting behaviors. However, more might be learned by examining the "inner" process by which harvesters make their decisions. Grounded theory analysis (Glaser & Strauss, 1967) is an approach that seeks to "get into the heads" of participants, and is useful for this purpose. (Grounded theory analysis was discussed in Chapter 3 as an example of qualitative methods.)

Grounded theory analysis is a sophisticated way of learning how people think about particular issues by asking them what they are doing, and why, as they are considering something like making a decision about using a resource. It uses the **think-aloud procedure**, in which individuals explain their decisions moment by moment as they make them. This procedure enables the researcher to track online cognitive processing as it naturally occurs. As noted earlier, in most resource dilemma studies, researchers simply impose a set of conditions on the harvesters and then observe their resultant decisions. This tells us little about exactly how the decision makers arrived at their decisions because it ignores what goes on in the "black boxes" of the people's minds.

One resource dilemma study used this grounded theory approach to find out what goes on in harvesters' heads (Hine & Gifford, 1997). In this microworld study of fishing, one real participant (at a time) was seated in front of a personal computer and used a tape recorder to collect his or her thoughts. Two computer-simulated fishers also harvested fish, and their harvesting behavior was programmed to range from quite cooperative to quite greedy. The real fishers were faced with a harvest choice: to take fish for which they receive payment, or to leave the fish in the water to reproduce.

Before the fishers fished, and as they fished, the think-aloud technique was used to gather the fishers' action strategies, heuristics, and cues that triggered their decisions about whether to take fish or not. The results showed that several main *action strategies* were employed by harvesters, including the following:

- Close monitoring of others' harvest practices
- Imagining the future harvests of others
- Trying to avoid overuse of the resource
- Attempting to influence the harvests of others through one's own harvest practices (i.e., strategic harvesting)

Notice that three of these goals were social; they related to what other fishers were doing. This shows that social interaction, whether direct or indirect, is an important part of decisions about whether to use natural resources. Interestingly, two of these social strategies—imagining the future harvests of others and strategic harvesting—had received little or no attention previously in the general experimental research literature. By uncovering them, the study helped to point the way toward a fuller understanding of harvesters' decision making, which in turn leads toward improved policy making in real resource dilemmas. The results suggest that when policy makers consider strategies to encourage conservation of natural resources, they should be aware that people do try to imagine or guess what other harvesters might choose to do (a very social factor), and that people use their own harvests to send messages to others (another very social act). How would you turn this knowledge into concrete policy? Now let us leave the lab to consider some programmatic interventions that have been conducted in the field to address how to cause human behavior related to resource dilemmas to become more environment friendly.

Strategies for Inducing Pro-Environment Behavior

Recognizing that a variety of environmental problems represent threats to environmental sustainability and that many problems have their roots in human behavior, Steg and Vlek (2009) delineate four steps to take in the process of promoting pro-environment behavior change. First, choose a specific behavior to be changed that will improve the quality of the environment. Second, examine the primary factors underlying this behavior. Third, design and apply an intervention to change the behavior so as to reduce its environmental impact. Fourth, rigorously evaluate the effects of the intervention on the behavior and also on the quality of environmental and human life. Often, the beginning point of this process is to select a particular group for the intervention, as opposed to changing the behavior of "everyone." The above framework proposed by Steg and Vlek corresponds closely with steps outlined for the design and evaluation of interventions in Chapter 4.

With respect to the second step, what are the main factors that underlie pro-environmental behavior (or the lack of it)? They are a complex mix of values, awareness of the problem, environmental attitudes, a sense of control, moral and social norms, guilt, and attributions about self and others (Bamberg & Möser, 2007). All behavior has multiple determinants; even if one or two influences are investigated in a given study, we must be aware that some influences that are *not* examined also influence the behavior.

What sorts of intervention are used? They fall into two main categories: *antecedent strategies* directed at factors that precede the problem behavior (e.g., behavioral commitment, goal setting, information or education, environmental design), and *consequence strategies* directed at the consequences that follow the problem behavior (e.g., feedback, rewards) (Steg & Vlek, 2009). A widely used antecedent strategy involves providing people with pro-environment information, based on what has been called the *information-deficit model*, which assumes that more information will lead to better behavior. Information-based educational strategies tend to result in greater awareness and knowledge levels, but they often do not lead to actual behavior change. The value of educational campaigns lies in their *priming ability*; that is, they get people ready to make a change rather than actually get them to change. However, information can make a difference. For example, some messages are more effective than others. One study (Gifford & Comeau, 2011) found that empowering messages (e.g., "You can do it!") often produce

stronger intentions to engage in climate-positive behaviors than sacrifice messages (e.g., "You will have to cut back!").

As noted in the preceding example, the way in which information is presented can make a big difference in how effective it is at influencing people's behavior. Cialdini et al. (2006) examined the effectiveness of different forms of messages on preventing people from stealing petrified wood in Arizona's Petrified Forest National Park, a problem that had become so severe that it landed the park on the list of America's ten most endangered parks.

A prominent sign at the park noted that "the park's existence is threatened because so many past visitors have taken pieces of petrified wood from the ground" (p. 5). You'd think a sign like this would be effective at stopping people from stealing the wood, but such a sign might actually be ineffective because it focuses people's attention on undesirable, but apparently common behavior. Behavior is influenced by norms, which you may recall from Chapter 4 are shared beliefs about behavior. You may also recall from Chapter 9 that descriptive norms refer to what most people do in a certain situation (e.g., most people pick up their litter). Such norms indicate how most people act. Injunctive norms refer to what most people approve or disapprove of (e.g., please don't litter). Such norms indicate what people ought to do. In drawing people's attention to the fact that so many visitors had taken wood, the prominent sign new visitors saw at the park might have actually contributed to the problem by inadvertently highlighting the descriptive norm that "everyone is doing it," so you might as well too!

To study this topic the researchers put signs at the start of three popular paths within the park and placed 20 pieces of petrified wood along the paths. To test the effectiveness of the various signs, after 2-hour blocks of time the researchers counted the number of pieces of wood that had been taken from the paths, replaced the pieces, changed the sign, and started again. The signs contained one of four types of messages: those with injunctive versus descriptive norms, mixed with negatively worded versus positively worded messages. The reason for the different valenced messages was to test the idea that negatively worded information has a stronger effect on people than positively worded information. The injunctive signs condition contained a plea to preserve the state of the park. In the negatively worded condition it was phrased as "please don't remove the petrified wood from the park" (Cialdini et al., 2006, p. 8), and included a picture of a person stealing a piece of wood with a circle-and-bar image appearing over his hand. In the positively worded condition, the phrase read "please leave petrified wood in the park" and included a picture of a person photographing a piece of wood. The descriptive norm condition contained information about the behavior of many past visitors to the park. In the negatively worded condition the information was phrased as "many past visitors have removed the petrified wood from the park, changing the state of the Petrified Forest," and included a picture of three people taking some wood. In the positively worded condition, the information was phrased as "the vast majority of visitors have left the petrified wood in the park, preserving the natural state of the Petrified Forest," and included a picture of three people photographing a piece of wood. The researchers hypothesized that the negatively worded injunctive sign would result in the least stealing of wood, whereas the negatively worded descriptive sign would be the worst at curtailing wood theft (because the *in*effectiveness of the descriptive sign would be *intensified* by the negative messaging).

So, what did the researchers find? As predicted, they found that the negatively worded injunctive norm message resulted in the least stealing of petrified wood, and the negatively worded descriptive message resulted in the most stealing of petrified wood. Thus, they found that the prominent sign the park had been using to stop people from taking wood from the forest was, indeed, not as effective as it could be.

As noted by Cialdini et al. (2006), there are numerous examples of public campaigns designed to curtail undesirable behavior that are misguided because they inadvertently include descriptive norms that underscore the popularity of the unwanted behavior. For example, antismoking campaigns that highlight the fact that "there are 3000 new smokers every day" underscore normative information about the popularity of smoking, and thus undermine the intended effect of the message. Successfully changing environmental behavior by drawing on norms may require focusing messages on the injunctive variety. You'll find another example of the value of norms on changing environmental behavior in the Focus on Intervention in this chapter.

Among consequence strategies, rewards often encourage energy conservation, but with short-lived effects. Feedback can be useful, especially if it is given frequently (Abrahamse, Steg, Vlek, & Rothengatter, 2005). Let us consider a small sample of studies that employed intervention strategies directed at encouraging three categories of pro-environment behavior: increased recycling, reduced driving, and reduced home energy usage.

Getting people to recycle. Recycling is a less impactful environmental behavior than transportation or household energy use, but it is easier to adopt, and therefore is environmentally valuable. We might first investigate which factors predict recycling as a behavior. A study in England (Nigbur & Uzzell, 2010) examined various factors, including attitudes, intentions, norms, personal control, identification with one's neighborhood, and self-identity (do persons think of themselves as recyclers?). Attitudes, perceived control, self-identity, and norms predicted the intention to recycle, and these intentions in turn predicted behavior.

However, other research shows that the link between attitudes about recycling and recycling behavior may not be as straightforward as originally believed. Most attitude research examines attitudes on a single dimension from positive (e.g., pro-recycling) to negative (e.g., anti-recycling), but this single dimension may not reflect how people actually feel about recycling. Many people hold ambivalent attitudes about recycling. In other words, they may feel that recycling is important (a positive attitude toward recycling) while simultaneously feeling that recycling is a hassle (a negative attitude). How do ambivalent attitudes toward recycling influence recycling behavior? Ojala (2008) conducted a mixed-methods study to answer this question. You may recall from Chapter 3 that mixed-methods studies involve qualitative and quantitative research methods. Young adults living in Sweden completed a questionnaire measuring their attitudes toward recycling, their recycling behavior, and their worry about the environment. Ojala found that participants who had ambivalent attitudes toward recycling (e.g., they felt that it was important, but also a hassle) were less likely to recycle than those with purely positive attitudes toward recycling.

Although these results are interesting, they don't provide very much detail about the thought processes that people engage in when choosing whether or not to recycle. To find out what motivated people to recycle, Ojala conducted a follow-up qualitative study. In this study, she interviewed 21 participants from the survey study about their recycling attitudes and behaviors. Half of the participants chosen for the interviews were regular recyclers and the other half rarely recycled. The purpose of the study was to gain more in-depth information about the experience of recycling and people's reasons for choosing whether or not to recycle.

Ojala found that the reluctant recyclers (i.e., people who rarely recycled) believed that recycling was important, and that they felt positive emotions when they occasionally recycled, however, the negative aspects of recycling usually outweighed the positive aspects. These negative aspects included viewing recycling as inconvenient, complicated, or disgusting; mistrusting that recycling was actually beneficial; and viewing oneself as too lazy to recycle. In contrast, the regular recyclers were conscious of growing environmental problems, but also felt hopeful that recycling could help the environment. These results suggest that one way to increase recycling behavior is to reduce the perceived barriers to recycling, such as inconvenience, disgust, and

mistrust, while increasing the perceived benefits of recycling. No wonder encouraging people to recycle is not an easy task!

One way to change people's behaviors, for example to increase their level of recycling, is through a social psychological intervention. The effectiveness of several intervention strategies designed to promote recycling was examined in a California community (Schultz, 1998). The researcher attempted to increase residents' recycling behavior by making norms about their own or others' recycling behavior salient to them, thereby highlighting existing discrepancies between the norm (i.e., "I should be recycling every week"), and a resident's actual level of recycling. During an eight-week baseline period, researchers collected and measured the levels of recycling among 480 households. A week after the baseline, a green door hanger was placed on the doorknob of the front door of every household. A message on the hanger indicated to the residents that the household had been chosen to be part of a recycling study and that they should recycle as much as possible. Some households—in the *plea-only condition*—were not contacted again. On one morning of each of the next four weeks (the intervention period), household recycling materials were collected and measured. For each of the remaining three conditions, door hangers were placed on household doorknobs within 24 hours of the collection of the recycling materials. In the *information condition*, the hangers had printed information (varied from week to week) about the recycling process and materials. Households in the *individual feedback condition* received door hangers that provided feedback about their own level of recycling for the previous week, for the current week, and for the course of the study. Households in the *group feedback condition* received information about the level of recycling in the entire neighborhood for the current week, previous week, and course of the study. Levels of recycling also were measured during the four weeks following the intervention period.

Based on theory and evidence regarding the effects of activating norms by providing feedback, Schultz (1998) predicted that feedback of either kind (individual or group) would be more effective in promoting recycling than would either merely providing information or simply making a plea to recycle. The research prediction was supported by the results. During the intervention period and the following four-week period, both the households receiving the individual feedback and those receiving the group feedback significantly increased their amounts of recycling relative to the baseline period. Neither the plea-only condition nor the information condition displayed significant increases.

Schultz's (1998) experimental intervention was by no means a simple field study. Imagine the amount of time and money required to carry out the project. The two norm-based interventions worked, but were they too costly? Schultz took his research a step further by conducting a cost–benefit analysis. He calculated the labor and material costs involved in planning and implementing the intervention, and the short-term financial benefits (e.g., monies received for recycling materials, reduction in funds needed to pay for trash disposal). Schultz determined that if the interventions were implemented on a city-wide basis, the yearly financial gains would exceed the implementation costs of either the individual or the group feedback intervention strategy. He further noted that very important environmental benefits (e.g., conservation of resources, reduced pollution) had not been factored into the benefits of the interventions, but clearly add to their value.

Getting people to drive less. One experimental study designed to get people to drive less involved an online intervention directed at reducing driving in college students (Graham, Koo, & Wilson, 2011). The research was designed and carried out in the context of concern about the pollution caused by the over 240 million registered vehicles in the United States, and the fact that the United States is the world's biggest consumer of energy (although China now uses almost the same amount), of which a substantial proportion is due to the operation of automobiles. Every second day for two weeks, the participants visited a webpage and reported the number of miles they had *avoided* driving (e.g., instead of driving they took a bike, walked, used public transportation). After each session, if participants reported they had avoided using their cars, they received the following feedback depending on the condition: (a) *pollution avoided condition* (i.e., pounds of carbon dioxide, carbon monoxide, hydrocarbons, and nitrogen oxide); (b) *financial gains condition* (i.e., savings on gas and maintenance); (c) *both pollution avoided and financial gains condition*; and (d) *no feedback condition*. The pollution avoided feedback and financial gains feedback were used to connect the decision to drive less to specific goals, a prosocial one—help the environment—in the case of the former, and a personal one—save money—in the case of the latter. There also was a *no-web control condition*; members of this group did not participate in the online phase of the study. Two weeks afterward, students completed an e-mail survey about their driving habits that included a rating scale on which they indicated how much they had used their car during the previous two weeks.

The results showed that students who were in the four conditions in which they reported instances of avoided driving indicated that they had used their cars less than the students in the no-web control group. This result suggests that the process of keeping track of one's driving, independent of the feedback received, served as an effective intervention strategy. As pointed out by the researchers, the finding is consistent with a number of other investigations that have shown the simple act of record keeping alone is effective in reducing the incidence of a variety of undesirable behaviors (e.g., alcohol and drug usage, driving under the influence). In addition, the students in the combined feedback condition reported driving less than those in all of the other conditions. Adding weight to that finding, the students in the combined feedback condition also reported avoiding more miles over the two-week period (mean = 85) than did the students in the monetary feedback, pollution feedback, and no feedback conditions (means 49, 48, and 34, respectively). The researchers concluded their study showed promise of using a cost-efficient means of getting people to drive less, and that the provision of combined prosocial and personal feedback may be effective in overcoming the strong reluctance that many people have about reducing their driving.

Getting people to reduce household energy usage. A third major environmental issue is household energy use, which is a major contributor to the steady increases in greenhouse gas emissions. In 2008, households accounted for about 21% of U.S. carbon dioxide emissions (U.S. Department of Energy, 2009). Therefore, effective interventions aimed at lowering household energy usage can help to ameliorate the negative impact of household energy use on the environment. The Internet has been used as an intervention tool to encourage consumers to use less energy. It was used by Abrahamse, Steg, Vlek, and Rothengatter (2007) in the Netherlands to encourage households to reduce their use of direct energy (gas, electricity, and fuel) and indirect energy (that which is used to produce, transport, and dispose of consumer goods). A combination of three intervention strategies was employed: (a) a list of energy-saving measures with potential savings tailored to each household, (b) a goal-setting request to reduce energy consumption by 5% over five months, and (c) customized feedback about changes in energy use and amount of money saved. The 5% goal was achieved. Households consumed 5.1% less energy, whereas a control group had a slight increase in energy consumption.

FOCUS ON INTERVENTION

Using Normative Messages to Increase Home Energy Conservation

Schultz, Nolan, Cialdini, Goldstein, and Griskevicius (2007) conducted a study of the effect of normative messages in promoting home energy conservation. As the researchers note, there has been a "surge of programs" based on the delivery of normative information to affect changes in behavior related to a variety of social problems (e.g., gambling, drug use, eating disorders, littering). Recall that Chapter 4 reviews social norm–based interventions regarding alcohol consumption on college campuses. The rationale underlying these programs is that many individuals overestimate the prevalence of the target behavior (e.g., believe more people abuse drugs than is actually the case), and they will engage in less of the undesirable behavior once their misperceptions are corrected when provided with information about the actual prevalence. This approach, therefore, relies on the influence of a **descriptive norm** as the actual level of occurrence of the behavior is described. The social norm strategy makes good sense as it draws on the powerful effects that norms have on behavior.

As Schultz and colleagues (2007) point out, whereas many of the social norm–based programs have been successful in accomplishing an overall reduction in undesirable targeted behaviors, other programs have produced only slight reductions in undesirable behavior, and some have produced no behavior change or even increases in the undesirable behavior. Schultz and colleagues reasoned that the occurrence of unintended *boomerang effects* may account for some of the disappointing results. They suggested that the normative information provided might act as a "magnet" for people who engage in more of the undesirable behavior than the norm, *and* also for those who engage in less of the undesirable behavior than the norm. Thus, in shifting their behavior toward greater conformity with the norm, the former individuals will show reductions in the undesirable behavior, whereas, contrary to the objectives of the intervention, the latter individuals will show increases in the undesirable behavior (i.e., the boomerang effect). Needless to say, such increases can undermine program effectiveness. Schultz and colleagues suggested the possible importance of a second type of norm, an **injunctive norm**, that is, a norm that communicates/ defines what is the culturally appropriate and approved behavior. The researchers hypothesized that introducing an injunctive normative message along with a descriptive normative message will prevent the occurrence of a boomerang effect. That is, individuals whose levels of undesirable behavior are already relatively low will be made aware of this fact (by the descriptive norm), but will be less tempted to shift toward the norm because at the same time they will receive a message that approves of their current behavior.

The experimental intervention included 290 households with visible electricity meters. First the researchers took a two-week baseline measure of daily household energy usage. After another two weeks, energy usage was measured again, and door hangers were left on the residents' doors with messages written on them. After another week, energy usage was measured again, and door hangers with messages were left. Three weeks later, energy usage was measured for the last time. In the *descriptive-norm-only condition*, the message indicated the amount of energy (in kilowatt-hours) the household had consumed since the previous reading and descriptive normative information about the actual average consumption of the neighborhood households. In the *descriptive-plus-injunctive-information condition*, the message was the same except the researcher drew a "smiley" face (☺) if the household had consumed less than the average, and a "frowney" face (☹) if the household had consumed more than the average. The valence of the face represented the injunctive norm of approval or disapproval. Households in both conditions also received materials reviewing ways to conserve on energy.

The results were the same whether changes in electricity usage were calculated from one week to the next or across a longer, three-week period. For households in the descriptive-norm-only condition, those who consumed more than average prior to the feedback showed a reduction in electricity consumption, suggesting the constructive influence of descriptive norms. However, the change was in the opposite direction for the households that had been below the average. They showed an increase in electricity consumption, suggesting that descriptive normative feedback can indeed subvert the objectives of a program by producing a boomerang effect. On the other hand, as hypothesized by Schultz and colleagues (2007), the addition of an injunctive normative message eliminated the boomerang effect; no increase in electricity usage occurred in households that initially had been below average in usage. Moreover, the injunctive message had no discernable effect on the above-average-consuming household, which showed a decline in usage, as was the case in the *descriptive-message-only condition*. Assuming replication of the role of injunctive messages, the findings clearly have the potential to help account for the mixed results of many social norm–based interventions and the potential to help design interventions that will reduce the occurrence of boomerang effects and accordingly become more effective in achieving their goals of reducing levels of undesirable behavior.

Environmental audits are another approach to home energy conservation. Energy utility companies and governments have tried to provoke conservation through programs in which a company representative visits a household and examines its energy-wasting capacity. Typically, the auditor points out problems, suggests repairs, offers an attractive grant or loan for major refits, and suggests reputable contractors for doing the needed work. The success of such programs has been variable. For instance, Gonzales, Aronson, and Costanzo (1988) reported that the U.S. national average was approximately 15% of household residents going on to make at least some of the necessary changes to their residences.

The environmental audit program, which on the surface might not seem to have anything to do with social psychology, actually does. Gonzales and colleagues (1988) improved the 15% success rate by training auditors how to communicate more effectively with household residents. Drawing on several established social psychological techniques of persuasion, they instructed auditors to use *vivid examples,* for example, "If you were to add up all the cracks under these doors, it's the same as if you had a hole the size of a basketball in your wall." Also, they told the auditors to *focus on loss rather than gain,* for example, "If you don't fix cracks, it's your hard-earned cash going right out the window." The auditors also were trained to induce residents to invest in the audit process by getting them to follow the auditors around the house, help take measurements, and actually look at the cracks. The researchers reasoned that household residents who personally took part in locating cracks in their homes, and realized that they were playing a role in wasting energy would experience *cognitive dissonance.* They predicted that the residents would be motivated to increase their energy conservation behavior (e.g., fill the cracks) so as to reduce dissonance. Together, the changes to the auditors' social influence strategy produced a cooperation rate of approximately 60%, roughly four times the usual rate and a truly impressive outcome. Imagine the overall impact that the improved communication and

persuasion processes could have if that fourfold improvement were applied to residences on a large-scale basis.

In conclusion, Hardin (1968), whose famous article in *Science Magazine* (a peer-reviewed academic journal of the American Association for the Advancement of Science and one of the world's top academic journals) stimulated monumental modern debate and study on resource dilemmas, was not optimistic that humans can avoid the tragedy of the commons, that is, the complete collapse of our resources, and therefore life as we know it. However, environmental and social psychologists have not accepted without question Hardin's argument that individuals will always act in their short-term self-interest. They consider the issue of how individuals behave in a limited commons to be an open question that will be resolved through empirical research, including implementing and evaluating interventions designed to induce people to put aside self-interest so as to preserve scarce and essential resources before they are destroyed. The material covered in this section has suggested that interventions that draw on social psychological theory and evidence show promise with respect to helping to counter Hardin's very pessimistic position.

THE BUILT ENVIRONMENT

Many aspects of the physical environment have been shown to influence behavior, including lighting, noise, and temperature. This section considers the behavioral effects of the physical design and layout of buildings and neighborhoods. Have you ever had to study, live, or work in a school, home, or workplace that just did not work well and did not foster the types of intended behavior? Certainly, some parts of the built environment need much improvement. One well-known example is a large apartment complex in St. Louis, Missouri, that was completed in 1954. The Pruitt–Igoe project was designed with the admirable intention of replacing deteriorating inner-city housing. The design for this complex, which contained 43 eleven-story buildings to house 12,000 people, was praised in an architectural journal for having vandal-resistant features, individualistic design, and no wasted space (Slum Surgery in St. Louis, 1951).

The Pruitt–Igoe design saved space in part by having elevators stop only at every third floor so that most residents would walk up or down one flight of stairs to their apartments. Pruitt–Igoe cost much less per unit than did comparable buildings. The design changes were considered so admirable that the architect even applied for a patent on the design.

But, problems appeared soon after Pruitt–Igoe opened. The failure to carefully examine its design in relation to human social behavior contributed to high rates of fear, vandalism, serious crime, and vacancy. A particular problem was crime in the stairwells that residents were forced to use caused by the "innovative" elevator savings plan. The situation was so bad that after only 18 years, the city began to demolish the

entire complex. In this example, insufficient consideration of how the physical structure would influence social behavior led to the ultimate failure of the project. Whether the architect ever received his patent is unknown.

Pruitt–Igoe is the most dramatic example of building design failure, but many other buildings also pose problems for their users. Take a look at Figure 13.3 for a different example of architecture that fails to suit human needs. *Hard architecture*, as it is called, is aimed at preventing vandalism, but these benches go so far toward that goal that they are uncomfortable, and therefore rarely used.

Social Design

More humane buildings can be designed. The process for doing so, developed over the past four decades, is called social design (Sommer, 1972, 1983). In general, it involves studying how

Figure 13.3 Hard Benches

settings can best serve human desires and requirements. Social design must be distinguished from **technical design**, that is, the engineering aspects of the building like the performance of building materials. Robert Sommer, a social design pioneer, characterized social design as follows:

> **Social design** is working with people rather than for them; involving people in the planning and management of the spaces around them; educating them to use the environment wisely and creatively to achieve a harmonious balance between the social, physical, and natural environment; to develop an awareness of beauty, a sense of responsibility, to the earth's environment and to other living creatures; to generate, compile, and make available information about the effects of human activities on the biotic and physical environment, including the effects of the built environment on human beings. Social designers cannot achieve these objectives working by themselves. The goals can be realized only within the structures of larger organizations, which include the people for whom a project is planned. (Sommer, 1983, p. 7)

Social design also may be distinguished from formal design, which is the traditional approach (Sommer, 1983). **Formal design** favors an approach that may be described as large scale, corporate, high cost, exclusive, authoritarian, tending to high-tech solutions, and concerned with style, ornament, the paying client, and a national or international focus. In contrast, social design favors an approach that may be described as small scale, human oriented, low cost, inclusive, democratic, tending to appropriate technology, and concerned with meaning and context, the occupant or paying client, and a local focus. Although large building projects lend themselves more naturally to formal design, social design approaches certainly can be employed on an area-by-area approach within a large project. These two approaches to design lead to the construction of buildings that differ dramatically, with important implications for human behavior and welfare inside them.

A growing collaboration. Design education and design competitions often encourage designers to emphasize the aesthetic dimension of architecture at the expense of the setting's functional value. Environments should, of course, be both beautiful and functional for their occupants. Unfortunately, attempts to create fashionable works of art dominated architecture for a long time—and still do. Architectural magazines still use expensive photography and glossy paper to show off buildings, but often no people are even visible in the scenes.

It is tempting to conclude that these "unpeopled buildingscapes" accurately reflect many designers' interests. One of the most influential architects in the world, Philip Johnson, said, "The job of the architect is to create beautiful buildings. That's all" (quoted in Sommer, 1983, p. 4). Where in this view is consideration of the residents' social lives and interpersonal relations? Who will live, work, and learn in the building—the architect or people like you?

But, times are changing. Many architects and designers now recognize the importance of designing for the human use of buildings (without sacrificing technological or aesthetic considerations). For example, decades ago the American Institute of Architects sponsored a conference that served as an early summit meeting between social scientists and designers (Conway, 1973). This conference outlined several key roles that social scientist consultants might play, including evaluating building habitability, defining the psychological needs of occupants, and training occupants in the optimal use of buildings.

Even now, many architects are still mesmerized by the aesthetic properties of geometric space, and mainstream psychology largely neglects the physical context of behavior. However, when architects and social designers do collaborate, they begin to think of architecture as **placemaking**, that is, real people imagined in real spaces (Schneekloth & Shibley, 1993). To "make a place," architects and social designers work together to create an "envelope for behavior," meaning that they think mainly about what people actually do in a building rather than think of the building mainly as a sculptural object without much regard for the people who will be using it.

An example of social design may be offered (Gifford & Martin, 1991). A building that served people with multiple sclerosis (MS) was to be renovated. The social designers interviewed 80 MS patients, their families (who also used the building as visitors), caregivers, and building staff. This resulted in dozens of design recommendations that never would have been incorporated in the renovations had the people who used the building every day not been interviewed. Many of the recommendations were included in the renovation, and an evaluation of the building months later showed that it was greatly appreciated for the way it reduced physical pain for the people with MS and made their use of the building much more convenient and comfortable. The same approach can be used for any group of people, in offices, industrial work sites, public buildings, and even residences.

The social versus formal design dispute need not be adversarial. If formal designers try to make beautiful buildings for the multisensory pleasure of the building's *users,* aesthetic pursuits serve at least part of the social designer's goals (Stamps, 1989). Beautiful buildings may improve our perceptions of each other, facilitate social interaction, and assist occupants in some less direct ways, such as enhancing tourism or a city's reputation.

When and how social design helps. Social design is not *always* needed in the design process. It is not required, for example, in times, places, and cultures where buildings are constructed by small communities in which everyone works together in accordance with a time-tested architectural tradition. These traditions, called **preindustrial vernacular** (Rapoport, 1969), evolved an architecture that already quite well fits community and cultural norms, individual interests, local climate, geography, and building materials. When

Figure 13.4   Vernacular Architecture

community members are both builders and occupants, the design process does not need separate financiers, architects, boards of directors, and construction firms (for an example of vernacular architecture, see Figure 13.4).

In the developed nations of the world, division of labor has produced material benefits for all of us. However, in the design professions (as in other occupations), it has produced considerable role specialization. Because the work of designing and constructing buildings is split more narrowly and each person's entire career is reduced to just one phase of it, communication among the *principal players* in the process tends to diminish. The principal players in building design include the client (who puts up the money), the designer (architect and/or planner), the engineer (on large projects), and (most important) the everyday building user (resident, customer, worker, student, or visitor).

Therefore, social design research has become necessary in industrial and postindustrial societies. Two of its major roles are to both reestablish and facilitate communication among the principal players in the design process. A third role is to remind everyone involved that the everyday building user is one of the principal players.

After the rise of industrialism and before the advent of environmental psychology, the building user was nearly forgotten in architecture. The dazzling technology produced by the industrial revolution provided a vast array of design possibilities—in building materials, construction principles, and international communication among designers. Today, the design of some buildings requires so much attention to technical factors that the future occupants are completely forgotten.

Six goals of social design. Social design researchers and practitioners have six main goals, some are broader than others, and some overlap with others (Steele, 1973):

1. Create physical settings that match the needs and activities of their occupants. *This goal is probably the most important one of all.*

2. Satisfy building users. Occupant satisfaction is important because occupants must spend significant parts of their lives working, residing, or relaxing in the setting.

3. Change behavior. Such changes might include increasing office worker productivity, enhancing social ties among institutionalized elderly people, reducing aggression in a prison, or increasing communication among managers in an administrative office. As we will see, the behavior change goal can be both difficult to attain and controversial.

4. Enhance the building users' personal control (Holahan, 1983). The more building users are able to alter the setting to make it suit their needs, the less stressful that setting will be.

5. Facilitate social support (Holahan, 1983). Designs that encourage cooperation, assistance, and support are desirable primarily for building occupants who are disadvantaged in one way or another, but also for active and successful individuals.

6. Employ "imageability." This refers to the ability of the building to help occupants, and (especially) visitors and newcomers, to find their way around without getting lost or confused.

Let us examine each of these goals more closely by considering the design of buildings.

Matching. How well the occupants' activities and needs are met by the setting is called **matching**. An example of poor matching might be a gymnasium when it is used for a concert. It is done, but gyms are not very well suited to that task. Ideally, of course, buildings should match their occupants' needs and behaviors perfectly. However, whether the degree of match is high or low sometimes depends in part on whose viewpoint is considered (Michelson, 1976). For some, the gym might seem to be a fine place to stage a concert, but for concertgoers and bands, the acoustics and general aesthetics will often be quite inappropriate for a great musical experience.

The early personality theorist Henry Murray and his collaborators distinguished between two forms of **press**, which refers to properties or characteristics of environmental features that shape behavior (Murray, 1938). **Alpha press** refers to actual reality that can be assessed through objective inquiry. **Beta press** refers to people's interpretation of external reality. For example, a person may act toward a conversation partner in an objectively neutral fashion (alpha press), but be perceived by the partner as aggressive (beta press).

Alpha matching, or **congruence**, refers to how well the setting fits the person from an objective point of view. For example, there is a good (objective) height for kitchen counters for persons of different heights. Beta matching, or **habitability**, is "environmental quality as perceived by occupants of buildings or facilities" (Preiser & Taylor, 1983, p. 6). Some kitchen workers might not think that a certain counter height is good for them, even if experts claim that the existing counter height is correct.

Of course, all of the principal players in the design process hope that both perceived and actual matches are good. The possibility remains, however, that a team of design experts could *declare* that matching has been achieved when the occupants believe that it has not. Unfortunately, significant disagreements between experts and users have indeed been demonstrated in several studies of residential environments. For example, one study found that professional planners believed that a high-quality neighborhood was related to how open, interesting, and pleasant it was, whereas neighborhood residents believed that high quality was related solely to how pleasant it was (Lansing & Marans, 1969). Such clashes mean that efforts must be made not only toward improving the fit between users and their environments, but also toward reducing differences between designer and occupant definitions of good design.

When alpha and beta matching are the same, such as when a building user has an objective need on which everyone agrees, the design implications are clear, but the design still does not always meet this need. For example, persons with physical disabilities often have obvious clear-cut needs like smooth ramps for those in wheelchairs. Yet, many buildings still lack ramps even though they are used by people in wheelchairs.

Nevertheless, building design guidelines for individuals with specific characteristics are a good idea, and many lists of guidelines have been prepared. For example, some designers have considered the proper design for relatively able-bodied older people (Hunt, 1991). Children's day care centers are another setting that has been the focus of many design recommendations (Kennedy, 1991).

Satisfaction. Habitability (beta matching) corresponds to occupant satisfaction, the second goal of social design. Congruence (alpha matching) is the expert's opinion that the occupants are satisfied. But, principal players other than the occupants may or may not be satisfied with the project. Some architects, for example, hope that their buildings will work as statements of certain aesthetic design principles. The paying client (the building's developer) might be primarily satisfied if the project is completed within its budget. Most social designers would be happy if their work contributed to a habitable structure. Occupant satisfaction is usually the goal of social design practitioners and other principal players who are particularly sympathetic to the needs of the building users. Some social designers see the process as part of a worldwide concern for human rights; social design began with attempts to provide the benefits of design to the unfortunate (e.g., mental patients), and to the poor (Sommer, 1983). This activist tradition still fuels the efforts of many social designers.

Change behavior. Many projects implicitly or explicitly embody people's hope that occupant behavior will change for the better. When all principal players, including occupants, agree that a certain pattern of behavior needs encouragement or discouragement from the design, the design process may steam merrily ahead. In a New York psychiatric hospital, the violent behavior of some severely regressed psychotic patients was one target when renovation designs were considered

(Christenfeld, Wagner, Pastva, & Acrish, 1989). The new design, which basically made the surroundings more homelike, with shaded lighting, lowered ceilings, and pleasant wall coverings, significantly reduced the incidence of violence. In another study, museum visitors paid more attention to exhibits after careful design changes that increased the visitors' sense of immersion in the exhibit by making the exhibits more dynamic, multisensory, and interactive (Harvey, Loomis, Bell, & Marino, 1998). Sometimes rather simple design modifications can change behavior. For instance, by merely adding tabletop partitions between pairs of students with profound developmental disabilities, researchers increased the amount of on-task behavior of the students (Hooper & Reid, 1985).

Unfortunately, principal players sometimes disagree about who should change which behaviors. Clients who pay for new or renovated workplaces, for example, often expect that the new designs will increase employee productivity. When faced with this expectation, the social researcher is in the uncomfortable position of being asked to use the environment to squeeze productivity out of employees. The very thought of attempting to manipulate employees for the benefit of an organization is unpleasant for many social design practitioners. (Recall the discussion in Chapter 1 of the role of personal values in applied psychology.)

Let us consider an example of how social design can influence performance and behavior in the college classroom. In 1980, Robert Sommer and Helge Olsen redesigned a plain, 30-seat college classroom. With a very small budget, they changed it into a *soft classroom* with semicircular, cushion-covered bench seating, adjustable lighting, a small carpet, and some mobiles. Compared with traditional classrooms of similar size, student participation increased markedly in the classroom. The number of statements per student tripled, and the percentage of students who spoke in class doubled. Students using the soft room wrote many glowing comments about it in a logbook placed in the classroom. The room was still producing

more student participation 17 years later (Wong, Sommer, & Cook, 1992). The research of Sommer and his associates, and others (e.g., Wollin & Montagne, 1981) suggests that college classrooms need not be plain and hard; inexpensive changes to make them more pleasant can have very tangible benefits, including better grades, better discussions, and occupant satisfaction (habitability).

Personal control. Good social design will provide building occupants with real options to control their proximate environment. What does this mean in specific terms? Consider, for example, publicly funded residential space for students (dormitories), and poor people (housing projects). Some buildings, high-rises in particular, seem designed to overload residents with social stimulation. Too few elevators and long, narrow hallways, for example, result in the sense that people are everywhere and inescapable. Residents may develop the feeling that they cannot control the number of social contacts—especially unwanted social contacts—they must face daily. This loss of control can negatively affect feelings of security and self-esteem.

Two other common examples of low-control settings are crowded retail stores and traffic jams. **Crowding** refers to the subjective sense that too many people are around; it may be distinguished from **population density**, which is an objective measure of persons per unit area. High density does not always lead to crowding, and crowding is not always the result of high density. Crowding is caused, in part, by social overload and informational overload, which in turn lead to the sense that one has lost control. Designing *against* crowding is in part designing *for* personal control. Again, simple design changes can be effective. By merely adding a few entrances to a mental health center, clients' sense of freedom (and thus control) was increased. Furthermore, the various treatment units within the center experienced a greater sense of identity because therapists felt as though they had their "own" entrances (Gutkowski, Ginath, & Guttman, 1992).

Stress is often related to lack of personal control over physical and social input. Noise, unwanted social contact, congestion, and a lack of places of refuge are examples of primary sources of stress (Evans & McCoy, 1998). Good social design can anticipate and attempt to overcome such sources, or at least buffer the user from them.

Social support. Personal control is an individual phenomenon, whereas social support is a group phenomenon. **Social support** is a process in which a person receives caring, kind words, and helpfulness from those around him or her. Many social problems would be eased if more and better social support were available. Common psychological problems, such as depression and anxiety have been shown to increase when social support is absent or inadequate. Social support may be seen as an antistress process (Moos, 1981).

What can social design do to facilitate social support? On a small scale, furniture can be arranged in a sociopetal fashion instead of a sociofugal fashion. **Sociopetal arrangements** are those that encourage social interaction (e.g., when people sit facing each other), whereas **sociofugal arrangements** discourage social interaction (e.g., when people sit in rows or even facing away from one another; Mehrabian & Diamond, 1971). At the building level, open-space areas may be arranged to facilitate social interaction (Holahan, 1972). Of course, if the personal control goal as well as the social support goal is to be met, the increased social interaction must be controllable; occupants should be able to find social interaction when and if they want it, but should not be faced with unwanted social encounters.

In office buildings, social support may be fostered through the provision of high-quality lounge space for employees. The mere existence of such space does not guarantee that valuable social support will be available, but with inadequate space for employees to share coffee and conversation, the likelihood of supportive social networks declines.

Finally, in some cases, social support may result from a design that provides optimal privacy (being able to filter one's interactions). Consider shelters for victims of domestic violence. A study of alternative designs for such shelters showed that designs characterized by anonymity and safety were most preferred (Refuerzo & Verderber, 1990). Sometimes social support is maximized when a person simultaneously can be near a helper and far from an abuser. The difference in helpfulness and caring is especially large when the contrast is between a residence that is full of hostility and violence, and one that is dominated by caring and understanding.

Imageability. Buildings should be **imageable** (i.e., clearly understandable or legible) to the people who use them (Hunt, 1985). When you walk into a building, you should immediately be able to find your way around, or in more technical terms be capable of *purposeful mobility*. In simple terms, you should not be confused.

Too often, a person enters a building that is unfamiliar and is unable to figure out where to go next. Unless we realize that buildings should be imageable, there is a tendency to blame ourselves (e.g., "I never did have a good sense of direction"). Sometimes observation reveals that you are not the first to have problems. Perhaps you have seen handmade signs that occupants have made to be helpful and/or to save themselves from answering the same question about where such-and-such is "for the hundredth time." Such signs represent a failure to make the building imageable, either through good signage, or through good and legible design of the building itself.

To conclude this section on building design, social design is architectural design that begins with the principle that the needs and preferences of those who will be working, living, or otherwise using a building are important or even paramount. If a building can also be beautiful, that is a wonderful bonus because people do also need beauty in their lives. By virtue of its effects on the way in which people feel and interact, social design is intimately related to applied social psychology. Slowly, for the past 40 years, social design has increasingly become the goal of most architects. However, goals and reality are not always compatible, and not all new buildings are models of successful social design.

Outdoor spaces. Many of the same social design ideas apply to outdoor public areas, such as plazas, parks, and streets. In one of the most widely used changes wrought by environmental psychology principles, the very fabric of many cities has been changed by a concept called *density bemusing,* which can be traced to the pioneering work of William Whyte (1980). Recognizing the need for some open space in the city core in 1961, the City of New York offered developers a deal: For every square foot of plaza they included in a new project, their new building could exceed normal zoning restrictions by 10 square feet. Developers liked the idea, and this deal certainly increased New York City's supply of open space downtown.

Unfortunately, the new plazas tended to be vast empty spaces, with the developers doing the least possible work to obtain their bonuses. Consequently, New York City revised its offers to developers. It would allow extra floors in new buildings only if developers offered plazas that included many of the amenities identified by Whyte (1980) that are associated with greater use and enjoyment of plazas, such as "sittable space," water (fountains and pools), trees, and accessible food outlets. New plazas based on Whyte's ideas represent marked improvements over the alternatives; that is cities with "canyons," but no open space, or empty concrete spaces. The new plazas have increased the pleasantness not only of New York City, but also of many cities around the world.

A worthwhile exercise is to return to the six goals of social design and consider the extent to which they (some more than others) are served by the implementation of Whyte's thinking. Consider the same exercise with respect to the contributions of Brower (1988), which are reviewed in the following paragraphs.

Sidney Brower has spent years developing and testing ideas for enlivening urban neighborhoods in Baltimore. Two of his key guidelines that have been used to improve the quality of life on the residential streets of that city are (a) keeping the street front alive by encouraging residents to walk, stroll, and play on the sidewalks, and (b) finding a legitimate use for every public space so that people routinely visit all areas of the neighborhood and there are no "dead" or unowned spaces. Once some residents are outside and using the public space, others will feel safe in doing so; security and socializing go hand in hand.

Brower has encouraged more use of the street front by giving residents things to do and places to be. For some, this might mean benches; for others, it might mean horseshoes, hopscotch, bocce, street vendors, or library vans. Recreation on public streets can be encouraged by blocking off streets, alleys, and parking lots to cars. Some areas, such as sidewalks themselves, must be free of fast and rough play by young people so that older people can enjoy walking or watching. At the same time, young people need open space that *can* be used for fast and rough play.

Brower also has reduced the speed and number of cars with speed bumps or temporary barricades. These interventions reduced accidents by up to 30%, and accidents with injuries by roughly 25%. Residents tend to accept the barriers because they feel safer and the neighborhood is quieter and more suitable for walking (Vis, Dijkstra, & Slop, 1992; Zaidel, Hakkert, & Pistiner, 1992).

Defensible Space

As noted previously, in Baltimore, the use of speed bumps and barriers has helped to promote feelings of safety among residents of neighborhoods. How might the physical setting influence the actual likelihood of crime? Most evidence bearing on this question has emerged from the observations and ideas of Jane Jacobs and Oscar Newman that led to **defensible space theory**, which deals with both crime and the fear of crime (Jacobs, 1961; Newman, 1972). This theory proposes that certain design features will increase residents' sense of security and decrease crime in the territory. Some of the features include the use of real or symbolic barriers to separate public territory from private territory, and the provision of opportunities for territory owners to observe suspicious activity in their spaces (surveillance).

Quite a number of field studies have tested defensible space theory, and most of them provide support for it (Schneekloth & Shibley, 1993). For example, one would expect more crime in areas that offer fewer opportunities for surveillance, and do not appear to be controlled by anyone. A study of crime in university residence halls showed that halls with defensible space features (e.g., more areas over which residents could feel some control and exercise more "surveillability") suffered less crime than did halls on the same campus without such features (Sommer, 1987). A survey of 16 well-conducted studies in which multiple design changes were made in accordance with defensible space theory found reductions in robberies of 30% to 84% (Casteel & Peek-Asa, 2000). In what follows, we consider the notion of defensible space in several settings.

Stores and banks. Convenience stores have been frequent robbery targets. Those with smaller parking lots and those that do not sell gas, both of which decrease the surveillability of the stores' interiors, are held up more often (D'Alessio & Stolzenberg, 1990). One chain of stores incorporated a series of changes, such as putting cash registers right in front of windows and removing window ads to make the interior more surveillable. Robberies declined by 30% relative to other stores that were not redesigned (Krupat & Kubzansky, 1987).

A fascinating study of bank robberies found that several design features are related to increased chances of a holdup (Wise & Wise, ca. 1985). Among these, more robberies occur when the bank has a smaller lobby, a compact square lobby (as opposed to a wide rectangular lobby), and larger distances between its teller stations. These features may be influential because they affect surveillability in the bank lobby.

Residences. In a study involving convicted burglars, convicts examined photos of 50 single-family dwellings and rated each one's likelihood of being burglarized (MacDonald & Gifford, 1989). The defensible space features of the houses were then assessed. As the theory predicts, easily surveillable houses were judged to be unlikely burglary targets. However, actual barriers (e.g., fences, visible locks) had no effect on the perceived vulnerability of the houses, although defensible space theory predicts that they should. According to defensible space theory, symbolic barriers, such as extra decorations and fancy gardens are supposed to communicate to criminals that the residents are especially concerned about their property, and therefore more likely to defend it; symbolic barriers should make burglars shy away. However, the burglars saw houses with symbolic barriers as *more* vulnerable to burglary (see Figure 13.5).

Why? Interviews after the study revealed that burglars viewed actual barriers as challenges that they could overcome; most fences and locks were not seen as serious barriers to them. The symbolic barriers were interpreted not as signs that the residents were especially vigilant, but rather as signs that the houses probably contained more than the usual amount of valuables; if the residents have the time and money to decorate their houses and gardens, the burglars reasoned, the houses are probably full of desirable goods. A study of apartment building burglaries confirmed that accessibility (actual barriers) made little difference, but that surveillability reduced burglary (Robinson & Robinson, 1997).

Burglars cannot accurately pick out houses that have been burglarized from those that have not, but they do use social and physical cues in their guesses (Brown & Bentley, 1993). As discussed in the previous study, they do not see

Figure 13.5 An Indefensible House

locks and bars as serious impediments, but they do worry about neighbors seeing them and about the residents' territorial concerns.

Interestingly, research has revealed that residents and police do not use the same house features as do burglars to infer that houses are vulnerable to burglary (Ham-Rowbottom, Gifford, & Shaw, 1999; Shaw & Gifford, 1994). These studies imply that residents and police need to understand burglars' perspective before they can stop burglary through residential design.

As for other features of residences, more crime occurs in taller apartment buildings and in buildings with more than five units per floor or 50 total units (Rand, 1984). This probably occurs because residents of larger buildings are less likely to know one another, tend to treat each other as strangers, and lose the ability to recognize who lives in the building and who does not. This makes entry by criminals easier.

Communities. Crime and vandalism are linked to, or facilitated by, certain aspects of the physical nature of a community.

Defensible space theory asserts that the actions of both the resident and the criminal are affected by defensible space features. Certain streets in St. Louis have defensible space features, including gateway-like entrances, alterations that restrict traffic flow (by narrowing roads or using speed bumps), and signs that discourage traffic (Newman, 1980). Residents who live on such streets are more often seen outside their homes, walking and working in their yards. Such behaviors might not be overtly territorial; residents might not think of themselves as guarding the neighborhood, yet they seem to have the effect of discouraging antisocial activity. Presumably, intruders are discouraged by this naturally occurring surveillance.

One neighborhood with a high crime rate—in Dayton, Ohio—incorporated some defensible space changes (Cose, 1994). Many entrances to the neighborhood were closed, speed bumps were installed to slow down traffic, gates with the neighborhood logo were installed, and the community was divided into five mini neighborhoods with physical barriers. Two years later, traffic was down 67%, violent crime was down 50%, and total crime was down 26%.

When an area seems more residential, with few through streets and little public parking, it usually will experience less crime than will houses on the edges of such areas (Krupat & Kubzansky, 1987). The general principle is to reduce passage by strangers through the area, which increases bonds among residents and helps everyone to spot suspicious activity.

However, some areas that *have* defensible space characteristics still have serious crime problems. That is partly because defensible space (the physical layout) does not necessarily translate into **defended space** (i.e., residents actually acting against crime by keeping an eye out or reporting suspicious activity). This can happen, for example, if the neighborhood is not sufficiently cohesive for residents to act together against criminal elements (Merry, 1981). Defensible space *sets the stage* for crime reduction by making it easier—nearly automatic—for residents to fight crime through visual surveillance of outdoor areas, but if residents are unable or unwilling to act on what they see, crime will not be deterred.

A second reason that defensible space does not guarantee a crime-free neighborhood is that not all criminals pay attention to the environment. Less-experienced criminals who are motivated by thrill-seeking or social approval use less-rational criteria for choosing a target; they may simply not pay attention to defensible space features of the setting (Rand, 1984). Also, some criminals are impaired by drugs or alcohol as they work and pay less attention to the environment.

Researchers in the Netherlands have developed a *checklist for assessing the crime vulnerability of neighborhoods* (van der Voordt & van Wegen,

1990). This checklist consists of six main elements that discourage criminal behavior:

- The potential visibility of public areas (lines of sight)
- The actual presence of residents (to take advantage of these sight lines)
- Social involvement (residents caring enough to maintain buildings and act against criminals)
- Poor access and escape routes for criminals, but good ones for potential victims
- Attractive surroundings that evoke care in residents (with decay informing criminals that residents are not vigilant)
- Structural safeguards or not (e.g., locks, presence of easily vandalized walls, phone booths)

The checklist's primary aim is to identify areas that are susceptible to vandalism, but it may be further developed as a tool against other crimes, such as burglary and violent crime.

Vandalism is a widespread destructive behavior. Not every alteration of public territory is vandalism, of course. We can distinguish between vandalism and *people's art* (Sommer, 1972). Part of the distinction involves motive; the artist's goal is to beautify an ugly environment. Vandals are destructive or egocentric; instead of painting a mural that reflects a social concern, they break off a branch of a young tree or scrawl their own names on a subway wall. In contrast, public artists usually seek anonymity yet creatively enhance a bleak place.

Vandals' motive often may be revenge. **Equity theory** emphasizes the idea that social and other behaviors are influenced by each person's perception that social (or other) rewards and costs should be fair. The theory suggests that vandals often are persons who feel they are dealt with unfairly (Baron & Fisher, 1984). Vandalism may be particularly likely when perceived unfairness is combined with a perceived lack of control, a feeling that the injustice cannot be rectified through normal channels. Whether potential vandals have role models who engage in vandalism may also be important (Baron, 1984).

CULTURE CAPSULE

Cultural Differences in Personal Space

Environmental psychologists are acutely aware that human behavior varies considerably around the world. The ways in which people celebrate birth, teach their children, dress, get married, work, and are treated at death are like a colorful tapestry of swirling colors. Yet, in another way, and at another level, people are the same everywhere. They celebrate births, teach their children, dress, get married, work, and recognize death in some kind of ceremony. Personal space is like that; the distance across which individuals interact with one another varies from culture to culture. Yet, in every culture, there are rules that govern the choice of those interactional distances.

Personal space has been described as hidden, silent, and invisible, yet everyone possesses and uses personal space every day. Personal space stretches and shrinks with circumstances. It is interpersonal, so it depends on the people interacting. It refers to the distance people choose to stay from others, but social interaction, involving angle of orientation and eye contact, is also part of personal space. Finally, personal space can be invaded, although such invasions are a matter of degree (Patterson, 1975). In sum, **personal space** is the geographic component of interpersonal relations, that is, the distance and angle of orientation (e.g., side by side, face to face) between individuals as they interact (Gifford, 2014).

Beyond these within-culture variations, personal space is used differently around the world. In one study, for example, groups of four male students came to the laboratory and were told that they would be observed, but were given no other instructions (Watson & Graves, 1966). Half of the groups were composed of Arabs, and half were composed of Americans. The average interpersonal distance chosen by Arabs was about the length of an extended arm, whereas the average interpersonal distance chosen by Americans was noticeably farther. The Arabs touched one another much more often, and their orientation was much more direct. In general, the Arabs were much more "immediate" (close) with one another than were the Americans.

Such findings might lead to overly simplistic generalizations or stereotypes about cultural differences; for example, that some cultures are "close" and others are "distant." However, two studies (Forston & Larson, 1968; Mazur, 1977) revealed that students from supposedly close cultures (Latin America, Spain, and Morocco) chose seating positions that were farther apart from one another than did students from a supposedly distant culture (United States). Furthermore, not all Latin Americans use the same amount of space (Shuter, 1976). Costa Ricans, for example, choose smaller interpersonal distances on average than Panamanians and Colombians.

Despite some oversimplifications, personal space does vary with culture. In one study, for example, Japanese people used more distance in conversations than did Americans, who in turn used more than did Venezuelans. But, when the same Japanese and Venezuelans spoke English instead of their first languages, their conversational distance moved toward that of the Americans (Sussman & Rosenfeld, 1982). Language, an important part of culture, can modify one's cultural tendencies to use more or less interpersonal distance.

The study of personal space is not merely academic; it also has important implications for cultural understanding and conflict. For example, a researcher taught some English students how to act more like Arabs in their nonverbal behavior (Collett, 1971). Arabs who interacted with the trained students liked them more than they did students who had not received such training. Consider the implications for diplomats or even ordinary tourists.

EPILOGUE

Psychologists have the most difficult scientific job in the world. Natural scientists, even those who study tiny particles or immense galaxies, have the advantage of investigating phenomena that are inherently less complex than they are. Therefore, they can—at least theoretically and at some future time—fully understand the phenomena they study. Psychologists have a more difficult task—to understand entities (people) at their own level of complexity. This is as difficult as frogs trying to understand how and why frogs operate. But beyond that, much of psychology ignores or underplays the important dynamic interaction between people and their physical settings. Thus, environmental psychologists are like frogs trying to understand not only their fellow frogs, but also the manner in which frogs fit into the pond's ecology. No other scientists are faced with a more daunting task.

Nevertheless, for a field of inquiry and action that is only about 50 years old, environmental psychology has made some very significant improvements in the world. One wonders whether other branches of psychology, or even other disciplines, have so positively affected the quality of life of so many people within their first 50 years. From ubiquitous transit maps to international diplomacy, from more humane city plazas to the widespread acceptance of social design principles, from encouraging more environmentally responsible behavior to fighting crime, and from saving lost hikers to facilitating better learning in classrooms, environmental psychology has much to be proud of and can truly say that it has made a difference in the quality of life for millions of people.

SUMMARY

This chapter began by discussing social dilemmas with a particular focus on resource dilemmas that occur in situations where a natural resource may be consumed at a nonrenewable rate, potentially leading to severe environmental and human consequences. The dilemma is that individuals must choose between self-interest (overconsuming the resource), and the interests of the community (cooperating by not overconsuming). Consideration was given to the factors that affect the decisions of people faced with resource dilemmas, with particular emphasis placed on factors including intervention strategies that lead people to avoid acting on the basis of self-interest.

Next, the chapter explored issues related to the built environment. Social design involves the physical design of buildings and outdoor settings, and places an emphasis on the needs and requirements of people as opposed to more technical and stylistic considerations. Social design has six goals: (a) matching the needs of occupants, (b) satisfying building users, (c) changing behavior, (d) enhancing control, (e) facilitating social support, and (f) employing imageability. Of particular importance is the significant role that architecture plays in shaping human behavior, performance, and feelings of well-being. Defensible space theory posits that certain physical design features influence the likely occurrence of crime and feelings of security. We considered the application of the theory to commercial enterprises, residences, and communities.

14

APPLYING SOCIAL PSYCHOLOGY TO DIVERSITY

CATHERINE T. KWANTES

SHERRY BERGERON

When the United States created treaties with indigenous nations during the 1800s, many treaties included the right of the native peoples to continue to hunt and fish on land that they had ceded to the U.S. government. Since that time, many changes have occurred in how these treaties have been interpreted, and the degree to which they have been respected. For example, in some cases, land that was originally ceded to and owned by the government is now owned privately. In other cases, the boundaries of the land allocated for reservations has changed, leading to conflict among native peoples, individual landowners, and the government. The issue of fishing and hunting rights has also become a source of conflict between members of indigenous nations and nonmembers.

The conflicts have generally related to limits for members of indigenous nations in terms of allowed locations, times of the year, and methods of fishing and hunting.

During the late 1980s and early 1990s, intense conflict erupted in Minnesota over fishing and hunting rights claimed by the Ojibwe nation. Native Americans contested their right to use spearfishing while members of the non-Indian community reacted negatively, arguing that this means of fishing constituted harvesting more than fishing, and threatened their ability to engage in sport fishing on lakes where spearfishing took place. In 1988, violence—including rock throwing and attempts to capsize Ojibwe boats—escalated the conflict to the point where Minnesota's attorney general called on the federal government to help deal with the situation. In 1999, the U.S. Supreme Court upheld the rights of the Ojibwe to hunt and fish without state regulation on 13 million acres of public land.

Similarly, in Burnt Church, New Brunswick, clashes occurred over the rights of Mi'kmaq, Maliseet, and Passamaquoddy natives of the Burnt Church area to set lobster traps in accordance with treaty provisions allowing lobster fishing to the extent of earning a moderate living. Nonnative fishers resented these actions, contending that their livelihoods were being threatened. Clashes erupted involving property damage to the lobster traps, boats ramming into each other, and fishers threatening each other with firearms. In 2002, an agreement was reached between the government of Canada and members of the Burnt Church First Nation.

- To what extent do cultural factors play a role in these disputes?
- What aspects of cultural diversity do you think are most important in understanding these issues?
- To what extent do demographic diversity factors play a role in these disputes?
- What aspects of demographic diversity do you think are most important to understanding these issues?

The world is diverse; people have diverse values, diverse behaviors, and diverse customs, and they wear diverse clothing. So, what does it mean to have diversity around us? In this chapter, the approach to understanding diversity and its implications is derived from the discipline of applied social psychology. Applied social psychology is, first and foremost, *psychology*. Therefore, this chapter focuses on the level of the individual and individual experiences, examining the effects of diversity in our lives. Because this is *social psychology*, attention is also paid to the effect that social groups have on individuals, and some of the implications inherent in being an individual who differs in some way from most others with whom he or she interacts. Finally, an emphasis on *applied social psychology* means that the focus of this chapter is on research that can be used by both individuals and groups not only to understand

diversity, but also to deal effectively with issues that result from diversity.

But, what is diversity exactly? The obvious answer is that diversity refers to differences in how people look, how they think, and how they behave. The meaning of the term **diversity** within psychology extends beyond simply acknowledging that differences exist to understanding that diversity can arise from many different sources. Some of the more common sources include ethnicity, nationality, religion, sex, sexual orientation, physical ability, and social class. Differences across these categories reflect the layers that make us who we are, and it is these differences that coexist in each of us. Some aspects of diversity are the result of learned ways of doing things. For example, in some cultures individuals learn that the best way to eat is with a knife and fork, in other cultures chopsticks are favored, and in still other cultures fingers are the utensils of choice. Other aspects of diversity are the result of birth; for example, sex and ethnicity. This chapter takes a look at culture as one source of learned diversity and then focuses on three major domains of demographic diversity: ethnicity, sex, and social class.

Diversity has consequences. Some of these consequences are positive. For example, diversity brings a sense of excitement as we discover new perspectives and ideas. In a sense, creativity itself stems from diversity in viewpoints. Problem solving is enhanced as a diversity of perspectives allows groups to be more flexible. Some consequences of diversity, however, are negative. News stories of individuals and groups who have suffered because they are different in some way are all too commonplace. The final portion of this chapter is devoted to the consequences of diversity—creativity and innovation, then conflict, and then its management and resolution.

SOCIETIES: CULTURAL DIVERSITY

Cultural diversity is increasingly a part of all of our lives. Urban, suburban, and even rural areas are becoming more culturally diverse, and with increased globalization this diversification will continue both in the interactions in our daily lives (e.g., schools, workplaces), and in the broader social structure (e.g., social functions, media). Most urban and suburban schools no longer teach only Christmas songs in December; songs related to Hanukkah and Kwanzaa are also brought into the classroom. Decades ago, a White male entering the workforce could be relatively sure that he would be working with White males in his career; this assumption no longer holds true. Culture has a pervasive influence on the lives of individuals within it. Its reach extends from the more obvious factors, such as values and beliefs, to the less obvious ones, such as nonverbal behavior and communication styles. Broadly speaking, the term *culture* refers to factors, such as race and ethnicity, which exert differential influence over the lives of individuals in different groups. More specifically, culture may be defined as

> a dynamic system of rules, explicit and implicit, established by groups in order to ensure their survival, involving attitudes, values, beliefs, norms, and behaviors shared by a group, but harbored differently by each specific unit within the group, communicated across generations, relatively stable with the potential to change across time. (Matsumoto & Juang, 2004, p. 10)

As you can see by this definition, there are many aspects to culture, and these aspects can result in many differences across groups of people. For example, people from different countries may sometimes be identified by the type of clothing they wear. The photograph in Figure 14.1 was taken by one of the chapter authors in a rural village in India. You can immediately see that the women come from a culture with specific and unique ideas regarding dress and jewelry. Similarly, an individual's religion can sometimes be identified by how the person dresses, such as with some members of the Amish and Islamic communities. Behavioral differences can also result from culture. Although shaking hands when meeting someone is the norm now in many parts of the world, the traditional greeting in Japan is a bow while placing one's hands together in front of the face, whereas nodding is the appropriate greeting in India. However, not all of culture's effects on behavior are as immediately visible as greetings. Think back to the opening vignette. Methods for fishing and gathering food may be culturally based, as may other traditions. In some cultures, it is assumed that a young person will live with his or her parents until marriage, and maybe even after marriage, whereas in North America the norm is for newlyweds to establish a home apart from their parents.

Given the fact that culture is such a multifaceted construct and affects the diversity of values and behaviors in so many ways, it can be difficult to grasp without creating subdivisions within the construct. Developing taxonomies, or classification systems, provides a way in which to examine the influence of culture more effectively. Within the field of social psychology, two taxonomies are currently dominant.

Hofstede's Cultural Taxonomy

The first large-scale study of cultural diversity began roughly 40 years ago. During the 1960s, Geert Hofstede was asked to survey the employees of a large multinational organization. He collected data from individuals in more than 50 countries and realized that there were distinct

Figure 14.1 Women in Rural India

SOURCE: Photo courtesy of Catherine T. Kwantes.

patterns in the data that reflected national cultures. Hofstede (2001) referred to these differences as the "software of the mind," and defined culture as "the collective programming of the mind that distinguishes the members of one group or category of people from another" (p. 9). In other words, humans are born with the same biological brain (the "hardware"), but they learn to value different things and to view the world differently based on the cultures in which they are raised (the "software"). More specifically, Hofstede used a statistical technique called factor analysis to derive four dimensions of culture from his survey data: individualism/collectivism, power distance, masculinity/femininity, and uncertainty avoidance. He later added one more dimension based

on work by Bond (1988): long- or short-term orientation. Each of these dimensions is related to diversity among humans. Cultures differ along these dimensions, and each of these differences results in different learned values and preferences.

Individualism and collectivism. When you have a major decision to make, do you discuss it with anyone? Do you turn to family or friends? And if their advice does not match what you want to do, would that affect your decision? Would you opt for what you want to do, or would you conform to what your family or friends think is best? The way in which an individual answers these questions is at the heart of **individualism and collectivism**. Someone with an individualistic orientation, an **idiocentric**, will tend to follow his or her own goals regardless of the opinions of family or friends. On the other hand, someone with a collectivistic orientation, an **allocentric**, will tend to do what is seen as best for the group, even if it means giving up personal goals (Oyserman & Lee, 2008; Triandis, 1995).

Every person grows up in a society that reflects certain values and preferences. Individualism and collectivism refer to the values that society places on the group as opposed to the individual, and these values are taught to most individuals within the society. Harry Triandis (1994) pointed out that in individualistic societies, social experiences are structured around individuals, whereas in collectivistic societies, social experiences are structured around social groups. For example, in societies with individualistic tendencies, such as the United States and Canada, marriage has traditionally been viewed as the choice of the couple; two people fall in love and then get married. However, in collectivistic societies, such as Japan and India, marriages were traditionally arranged by the parents or other elders in the family, and in some cases they still are. The purpose of marriage is not viewed as providing happiness to the two individuals involved; rather, it is viewed as developing alliances between families. Differences on this dimension not only are found between nations, but also may be found between regions within countries. Vandello and Cohen (1999), for example, found that within the United States there are striking regional differences in individualism and collectivism, with individualism being more predominant in the North and East and collectivism being more predominant in the South and West. Individualism/collectivism and power distance are the cultural dimensions that have been most widely examined in research. The degree to which a person is from a culture that emphasizes individualism or collectivism has been shown to make a difference in many of that person's attitudes and behaviors. For example, differences have been found in work behaviors, such as one employee looking for another job, and another doing little "extras" to help out the organization in which one works—even without added pay. In the United States, an individualistic country, the intensity with which an employee looks for a new job, or how much extra the employee does for his or her company, depends on how much the person likes the company. However, in India, a collectivistic country, these behaviors depend not only on how much an employee likes his or her company, but also on the extent to which the employee feels obligated to the company (Kwantes, 2003).

In the intergroup and interpersonal arena, Gelfand and colleagues (2001) suggested that in collectivistic countries like Japan, conflict is viewed and experienced more as a situation that calls for compromise, whereas in more individualistic countries like the United States, conflict is experienced more as a win–lose situation. Even children show noticeable differences on this dimension. For example, Barbopoulos, Fisharah, Clark, and El-Khatib (2002) found that children in Canada, an individualistic culture, exhibited more independent attitudes than did children from Egypt, a more collectivistic culture. Other more global attitudes may also be related to these cultural dimensions. Accordingly, people in collectivistic societies are more likely to view the thoughts and business of others in their group as their own business, whereas people in individualistic societies are more likely to desire privacy (Triandis, 1995).

Power distance. **Power distance** refers to the extent to which people in a society accept inequalities based on social status, wealth, power, laws, and/or physical characteristics (Robert, Probst, Martocchio, Drasgow, & Lawler, 2000). In countries with high power distance, such as Malaysia, Guatemala, the Philippines, and many Arab countries, it is normal to find conformity among the people, and to find that most power is held by a small group of individuals with authoritarian values. It is not uncommon for individuals with this value orientation to view those who have a high status in society as fundamentally different from other humans. Because of this, the inequality is accepted. In contrast, those in countries with low power distance, such as New Zealand, Germany, Great Britain, and the Scandinavian countries view individuals as essentially equal. In such countries, the exercise of power is accepted only if there is agreement with the rationale behind it (e.g., as with elected officials), and independence of thought is valued over conformity. You can sometimes see the effects of power distance in how people address each other. In low–power distance societies, people tend to use first names very quickly regardless of whether the other person is senior in position. In high–power distance societies, titles are used for those who are senior in position by virtue of either employment (e.g., one's boss), or age (e.g., an elderly neighbor). There tends to be a strong relationship across cultures between power distance and individualism/collectivism, with high power distance correlating with collectivism and lower power distance correlating with individualism (Triandis, 1994).

Masculinity and femininity. The name for this dimension comes from different values placed on work goals. Hofstede (2001) noted that surveys on work goals nearly universally indicate that women place higher values on social goals, such as relationships and helping others, whereas men place higher values on what Hofstede called "ego goals" (p. 279) that relate to money and careers. Hofstede applied this **masculinity/femininity** distinction to differences in values among countries. Individuals in cultures high in femininity are taught to value relationships and harmony, whereas those in cultures high in masculinity are encouraged to emphasize competition, advancement, and recognition in jobs. Societies that emphasize masculinity, such as Japan, Venezuela, Italy, and Mexico, often exhibit great differences between men and women in the values they endorse. Men, for example, place much stronger emphasis on ambition and career goals than do women (Hofstede, 1997). Societies that emphasize femininity, such as Sweden, Norway, the Netherlands, and Costa Rica, generally do not demonstrate large differences in values between men and women. Hofstede further pointed out that in feminine countries, both males and females are expected to be modest and nonassertive.

Uncertainty avoidance. High levels of uncertainty can lead to anxiety and stress. Common ways of dealing with uncertainty can characterize cultures because each society teaches that some ways of coping are more acceptable than others. Technology, religion, social customs, and even family customs are used to help cope with uncertainty. For example, individuals from societies with low **uncertainty avoidance**, such as Singapore and Jamaica, generally accept the fact that some uncertainty is unavoidable (Hofstede, 2001). These individuals believe that it is important to "go with the flow," and are often willing to take a certain amount of risk. On the other hand, individuals from cultures characterized by high uncertainty avoidance, such as Portugal and Greece, learn to feel threatened by uncertainty; thus, these individuals tend to take fewer risks, behave more carefully regarding laws, and avoid things (and people) that are different from their accustomed ways.

Long- or short-term orientation. After Hofstede's original research, other psychologists also began to investigate how culture affects diverse values, attitudes, and behaviors. Because Hofstede's survey research was carried out in one organization, namely IBM, most of his survey questions were developed from a Western cultural perspective, and therefore did not capture some cultural values that might be more immediately obvious to someone from an Eastern cultural perspective. A fifth classification, **long- or short-term orientation**, was added to the original four based on values in a Chinese context (Bond, 1988). In cultures with a long-term orientation, such as Taiwan, Japan, and South Korea, individuals learn to value future rewards, thereby placing an emphasis on persistence, thrift, patience, and harmony. On the other end of the spectrum, cultures that emphasize a more short-term orientation, such as Canada and the United States, place value on short-term rewards and emphasize immediate gratification over long-term considerations (Hofstede, 2001).

Hofstede's taxonomy has made possible comparisons of cultures along specific dimensions. Using his original data (Hofstede, 2001), an example comparing the three North American countries employing Hofstede's original four dimensions is illustrated in Figure 14.2. You can see how each country has a different profile on the graph, indicating different value emphases. For example, people in Mexico place a much stronger emphasis on uncertainty avoidance and power distance than do people in Canada and the United States. In contrast, people in Canada and the United States emphasize individualism more than people in Mexico. There is very little difference among these three countries, however, in terms of the emphasis that people place on the masculinity/femininity dimension of culture. Using these dimensions, it is possible to acquire a quick "snapshot" of some of the values in a culture, and to be able to compare and contrast different cultures in terms of these values.

Although this taxonomy has stimulated a lot of research and has provided a useful perspective for understanding the effects of culture on values, attitudes, and behaviors, not everyone agrees with Hofstede that this taxonomy is universal and that it can be used to describe all cultures. The sample that was used in the original research constituted individuals who were all working for the same company, and so it was not necessarily representative of all individuals in a given culture. Also, the kinds of people that worked in those types of jobs (e.g., educated men) limited the range of characteristics represented in the group. However, psychologists do agree that this work is extremely important because it represents the first attempt to examine global cultural differences and to look for dimensions appropriate to contrast and compare cultures. Hofstede (2010) himself notes that "over the past 30 years, the nomological network of the five dimensions . . . has continued to expand . . . to a surprising variety of disciplines, and new applications keep appearing"

Figure 14.2 Hofstede's Cultural Dimensions

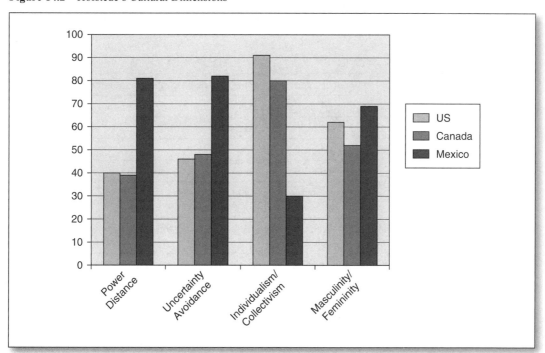

SOURCE: Data gathered from http://www.geert-hofstede.com/.

(p. 1345). The taxonomy proposed by Hofstede has been successfully used to help explain a wide variety of differences in social phenomena across cultures, such as gender role attitudes (Chang, 1999); workplace stress and intercultural communication (Redmond, 2000); employee service behavior (Kim & Lee, 2009); and consumer behavior and marketing (Biswas, Hussain, & O'Donnell, 2009).

Schwartz's Values Framework

Rather than looking for ways to find differences between cultures, it is possible to look for ways that culturally learned values, and therefore cultures may be similar. Shalom Schwartz developed a theoretical framework that may be used to understand the content and structure of value systems in cultures, and how these values affect the ways in which individuals in different groups organize their understanding of the world around them (Schwartz, 1992; Schwartz, Lehmann, & Roccas, 1999). In research spanning 20 countries, Schwartz has established that

a set of ten value types is comprehensive enough to be useful in a global context. In other words, the value types are universal, and different groups agree on their meanings. Core values have been grouped into value types that encompass an overarching or defining feature. For example, the value type termed *tradition* is based on the core values of respect and commitment (see Table 14.1).

A great deal of research has shown that this framework holds across numerous cultures and can be used to predict attitudes and behaviors. For example, values have been found to be important predictors in determining the degree to which Israeli Jews, Israeli Arab Muslims, and Israeli Christians would be willing to engage in contact with individuals outside their own cultural groups (Sagiv & Schwartz, 1995). Similarly, in their sample of more than 150 teachers, Sagiv and Schwartz (1995) found that values predicted willingness to engage in contact with dissimilar others. Specifically, those who scored higher on universalism demonstrated more of a willingness to engage in contact with dissimilar others

Table 14.1 Definitions of Motivational Types of Values and How They Affect Behavior

Power	Social status and prestige, control or dominance over people and resources
Achievement	Personal success through demonstrating competence according to social standards
Hedonism	Pleasure and sensuous gratification for oneself
Stimulation	Excitement, novelty, and challenge in life
Self-direction	Independent thought and action, choosing, creating, and exploring
Universalism	Understanding, appreciation, tolerance, and protection for the welfare of all people and for nature
Benevolence	Preservation and enhancement of the welfare of people with whom one is in frequent personal contact
Tradition	Respect for, commitment to, and acceptance of the customs and ideas that traditional culture or religion provides
Conformity	Restraint of actions, inclinations, and impulses likely to upset or harm others and to violate social expectations or norms
Security	Safety, harmony, and stability of society, relationships, and self

SOURCE: Adapted from Schwartz, Lehmann, and Roccas (1999, p. 109).

than did those who scored higher on tradition or conformity. As another example, in research focusing on values and worries, Schwartz, Sagiv, and Boehnke (2000) found that there were few differences between respondents in Israel and Germany in the relationships between specific values and the types of worries they had. An emphasis on power, for example, correlated with "micro-worries," that is, worries related to the self or the group to which a person belongs (Boehnke, Schwartz, Stromberg, & Sagiv, 1998). Fear of war has been found to be greater in individuals from both Germany and Israel who attach a high priority to values related to concern for others like benevolence, and who attach importance to issues of equality and social justice (Boehnke & Schwartz, 1997). More recently, Cohen (2010) was able to use the Schwartz Value Survey to explain different levels of commitment in Arab teachers working in Israel.

Social Axioms Approach

In 2002, a group of researchers led by Kwok Leung and Michael Bond devised a new way to look at culture. Previous work by Hofstede and Schwartz focused on differences in *values*. That is, they focused on what people thought was important and that guided their actions. Leung, Bond, and colleagues (2002) instead took the approach that while values are important, people also use their expectations of what will happen if they take a certain action as a guide to choosing behaviors in any given situation. They called these expectations *Social Axioms*. It has been suggested that this way to look at culture is a way to look at "what is" (beliefs or understandings) in a culture rather than "what should be" (values) in a culture (Boehnke, 2009).

Axioms refer to ideas that individuals think are very obvious—so obvious that they do not need to be proven. They are implicit understandings of how the world works. What Leung, Bond et al. (2002) pointed out is that many of the axioms held by individuals come from his or her contextual experience, and therefore societal culture shapes these understandings both directly

and indirectly. Directly, children are taught by their families and by their communities what their given society feels they should know, and how they should behave. Indirectly, as children and as adults, each individual in a society sees the consequences of his or her actions. So, for example, a societal culture may emphasize that the world is a complex place, and that there are many different ways that one can approach problems, and different ways that issues can be resolved. Individuals within that culture will then also see that different people do things in different ways, and that these different ways of doing things can still all lead to successful outcomes. In this way, a culture teaches *social axioms* to its members, therefore someone who lives in a context with others who believe the same thing, and further sees how particular actions are rewarded or punished within a particular context can come to the conclusion that "this is how the world works." Leung, Bond et al. (2002) further defined social axioms as "generalized beliefs about oneself, the social and physical environment, or the spiritual world, [which] are in the form of an assertion about the relationship between two entities or concepts" (p. 289).

To find out what social beliefs might exist, a wide variety of literature was used. Leung, Bond and colleagues looked at previous research that measured different beliefs—over 300 different belief scales. As this research was predominantly English and undertaken in Western cultural contexts, the research team also conducted interviews in both Hong Kong and Venezuela with individuals in both urban and rural settings, asking them about the beliefs they had which guided their behavioral choices in a number of different areas of life, such as interpersonal interactions, marriage, health, politics, and the environment. The research team then searched out proverbs and axioms in both Hong Kong and Venezuela by examining literature anthologies, popular songs, newspapers, advertising, magazines, and other commonly available material. Similar to the approach Hofstede used that was described above, Leung and his fellow researchers (2002) used factor analysis to find clusters; five pancultural (that is, existing across all cultures) social beliefs emerged from this extensive work. The five are named: social complexity (also sometimes called social flexibility); social cynicism; reward for application; fate control; and spirituality (later renamed religiosity).

Social Flexibility. As described above, someone who holds this belief views the world in ways that suggest that there are many different and likely equally appropriate ways to achieve a given end. If you believe that there are many possible good options for getting things done, and that there are no rigid rules for how to do things, then you may score high on Social Flexibility. People in this high ranking also may view that there is no single "right" way to achieve goals, and therefore also have an expectation that human behavior should be consistent.

Social Cynicism. In many cultures, people are skeptical of the institutions in their country, having the sense that it would be foolish to expect organizations and institutions to behave fairly or ethically. This belief reflects a level of cynicism consistent with what Leung and his co-researchers (2002) labeled Social Cynicism. People who feel that they cannot trust social or business institutions also tend to be defensive and to hold biases against people in other groups. Further, there is often a sense that if one cannot trust governments, social institutions, or organizations to behave ethically and appropriately, then there is no need to follow those sorts of guidelines oneself either. This particular aspect of culture has been shown in research to be related to many different behaviors and attitudes. For example, people who have less cynical attitudes tend to be more favorably inclined toward the idea of seeking psychological help if needed (Kuo, Kwantes, Towson, & Nanson, 2006). In organizational settings, people who have less cynical beliefs tend to also view organizational behaviors that help out the organization and coworkers as part of an employee's job rather than as activities that are discretionary (Kwantes, Karam, Kuo, & Towson, 2008).

Reward for Application. People who believe that hard work pays off would likely score high on a measure of Reward for Application. This

dimension reflects a belief that if one gets the information one needs and then plans carefully, positive results will follow. This dimension is one where it is quite easy to see how culture can affect the extent to which one believes this axiom. In the United States and Canada, for example, there are many resources and many social systems in place to support individual efforts. Early settlers from Europe who could not own land in the countries of their birth came to claim large tracts of land that they could farm. Both countries have stories of early immigrants who came from other countries with nothing but determination, and managed to succeed in many different ways. While these experiences are certainly not part of every person or group's experience in these cultures (e.g. First Nations individuals, Native Americans, and enslaved Africans) the idea that hard work will have a good outcome has become a social axiom endorsed by many Canadians and Americans.

Fate Control. If you have heard the term "karma" or "kismet" then you are already familiar with some variations of the belief that many aspects of life are determined by fate or some other impersonal forces. "Kismet" for example, refers to the idea that our lives are governed by destiny to an extent, while "karma" refers to the idea that an action or behavior now will lead to a consequence at some time in the future. The social axiom of fate control, therefore, measures the extent to which a person believes that chance, or luck, affects a person, or believes that somehow behaviors have predetermined consequences.

Religiosity. Religiosity refers to a belief that there is a supreme being or beings interested in human activities, with whom an individual can have a personal relationship. It tends to reflect a belief in some of the major world religions, and is distinct from the idea of luck, fate, or fortune determining one's destiny (Hui & Hui, 2009). Further, it is a belief that social institutions based on religious beliefs are beneficial to individuals and societies. Thus, someone who has a strong sense of religiosity would generally support the existence of churches, temples, mosques, and other organized bodies of worship as well as believe that the moral rules established by these religions have a positive effect on society.

As you can see, by developing dimensions of culture, researchers have tried to reduce the complex notion of the effect of culture on values and behaviors, allowing us to look at some aspects of diversity that are learned by individuals within groups and societies. Do you see any of these ways of viewing cultural differences as being able to explain the tensions and conflicts related to the hunting and fishing rights of native and nonnative peoples? Are there fundamental learned value or belief differences between the two groups that might explain some of the differences in perspective?

There is always a bit of danger, however, in looking to large groups for explanations of differences in individual behavior. One reason for this is that groups, and especially large groups, are never completely homogeneous, and individual differences, such as ethnic background, sex, and social class, can also contribute to individual experiences related to diversity.

DEMOGRAPHICS: PERSONAL DIVERSITY

Just as cultural diversity reflects complex phenomena, demographic diversity is also complex. People differ on core characteristics that are key determinants of life experiences. These characteristics and experiences affect how we see ourselves and create different pieces of identity that are like links on a chain; one never exists without the others. A man from an upper-class background cannot necessarily differentiate the parts of his experience that are related to being upper class from the parts that are related to being male. Similarly, our own experiences are intertwined with our own characteristics. People respond to us because of a combination of these factors and rarely to any one factor alone. Our life experiences are affected by these largely socially constructed factors stemming from both visible aspects (e.g., race, gender, social class) and in-/nonvisible aspects (e.g., sexual identity,

religion) (Bierema, 2010; Mannix & Neale, 2005; Wilton, Moss-Racusin, Good, & Sanchez, 2015). When examining the sources of diversity and how these affect individual experience, it is important to remember that these sources typically do not operate in isolation from each other, nor do they necessarily affect everybody in the same way. Rather, these different aspects of identity become important to us at different times depending on the context or circumstances (Bierema, 2010; Kawakami & Dion, 1995; Roberson & Kim, 2014).

Is differential treatment based on one's race, sex, or class (e.g., racism, sexism, classism) still a problem in our society? Do you think that your own race, sex, or social class affects how you would answer this question? Some people believe that North American societies provide equal opportunities for all of their citizens, skin color does not create advantages or disadvantages, gender makes no difference, and equal opportunity exists for all regardless of social class. Admittedly, blatant discrimination rarely occurs today, but discrimination and bias continue to exist in more sophisticated, convoluted, and subversive ways. Racial segregation of schools is no longer an official policy, although in many areas it continues to be a practical reality. Women have penetrated the borders of many traditionally male workplaces, yet are still drastically underrepresented in the upper echelon of the corporate world (Catalyst, 2010); social class still has an effect on the availability of educational and occupational opportunities. This section takes a closer look at gender, race, and social class, each of which continues to influence one's experiences and opportunities.

Gender

Although many people use the terms *sex* and *gender* to mean the same thing, there is actually a difference between them. The term **sex** refers to the biological distinction of being male or female, whereas the term **gender** refers to the social or learned characteristics that are associated with being male or female. Unlike sex, gender is the result of sociocultural influences throughout an individual's development. Boys are molded to become what society considers to be masculine (e.g., independent, assertive), whereas girls are molded to become what society considers to be feminine (e.g., caring, dependable). Behaviors that match these expectations are often associated with rewards (Robinson & Howard-Hamilton, 2000) while behaviors that violate these expectations are often associated with costs (Good & Sanchez, 2010).

An individual's sex is often used as a primary source of social categorization, or more simply, as a way in which to place people into groups. From the beginning, babies are wrapped in the color of blanket that is matched with their sex—blue for boys and pink for girls. Descriptors of behaviors are also often gender typed from birth. For example, early research by Condry and Condry (1976) found that when a male child cries, people will often explain the behavior by saying that he is angry, whereas when a female child cries, they will often describe her as frightened. This process continues as an individual grows into adulthood, where descriptors are often still distributed differentially based on sex. In fact, a well-known study by Williams and Best (1982) not only demonstrated that adjectives were viewed as being differentially associated with men and women, but also revealed that this happened with a surprising amount of consistency across participants from the 30 countries represented in their sample. Men, for example, were more frequently associated with descriptors such as *aggressive, capable,* and *rational,* whereas women were more frequently associated with descriptors such as *affectionate, dependent,* and *emotional.*

Are women and men actually more similar than they are different, or are they more different than they are similar? Do any differences across the sexes justify social inequalities? Early research on sex differences held men as the standard to which women were compared. Differences between the sexes were put up as evidence of the innate superiority of men, and thus were used to justify differences in social

power. For example, the sizes of male and female brains were compared, and when male brains were found to be larger, this data was used to explain the superior intellect of men (instead of the equally plausible, but politically incorrect proposition that women's brains were more efficient). The greater social power held by men was merely a natural derivative of this superior intellect (Shields, 1975).

Although things have changed from the time when women were thought to be too intellectually inferior or too weak and frail to participate in many aspects of society, a belief in the fundamental difference between the sexes is still evident in modern cultures (Benokraitis & Feagin, 1995). Even in presumably advanced societies, books that suggest that women and men are seen not only as different, but as (figuratively) coming from different planets (Mars and Venus) can become best sellers.

The focus on differences and the ignoring of similarities have been the basis of much of the feminist critiques of research on gender (Hyde, 1991). If differences do exist, what do they really mean, and are they substantial enough to be weighted more heavily than the similarities? One of the responses to gender diversity or the differences between the sexes (whether real or perceived) is **sexism**, that is, differential and often detrimental treatment of a person based on that person's sex. The term *sexism* likely brings to mind thoughts of negative or demeaning attitudes toward women. Negative comments, such as "a woman's place is in the home," and "women are bad drivers," are frequently assumed to be the only way in which sexism can be expressed. However, this is not the case.

An article by Peter Glick and Susan Fiske explored the concept of sexism and revealed some of its more complex and subtle nature. In its purest sense, **sexism** refers to any bias against an individual or a group of individuals based on the individual's or group member's sex. That bias does not necessarily have to be expressed in the form of negative attitudes or behaviors. Glick and Fiske (1996) proposed a tripartite, or three-part, understanding of the different forms of sexism.

Negative expressions, or behaviors that reflect negative attitudes toward women, are referred to specifically as **hostile sexism**. Some forms of sexism, however, involve the attribution of typically positive traits or qualities. This is referred to as **benevolent sexism**. Although this might seem to be a contradiction in terms, the problem (according to Glick and Fiske) is that the attributions associated with benevolent sexism, even though they sound positive, are derived from stereotypes that see women in limited ways and often stem from a male-centered perspective. Imagine for a moment that a female executive is about to sit down at a negotiation table when a male coworker comments, "You look very good in that suit." Glick and Fiske suggested that although the comment might not be intended as negative or hostile, it is nonetheless sexist. The remark sounds pleasant, but in effect emphasizes traditional stereotypic notions of women and trivializes the fact that competence rather than beauty was behind the executive's promotion to her current position. According to Glick and Fiske, not only can people hold both hostile and benevolent sexist attitudes, but also these attitudes and beliefs can be held simultaneously. They named this **ambivalent sexism**. An illustration of ambivalent sexism, they suggested, is when an individual believes both that women need to be protected by men (benevolent— helping those who are perceived to need help), and that women are incompetent (hostile).

FOCUS ON RESEARCH

Women's Responses to Sexist Comments

These different forms of sexism can play out in many different ways. Imagine, for example, a woman standing with a group of men at a social gathering. One of the men in the group makes a comment that is clearly sexist and derogatory toward women. What does she have to gain or lose by responding? What does she have to gain or to lose by choosing not to respond? Do you think that she would be more or less likely to respond if there were other women present?

A recent series of experiments by Janet Swim and Lauri Hyers examined how women would respond both publicly (what they said or did), and privately (what they thought) in such a situation. When women encounter sexism, Swim and Hyers (1999) suggested they must decide not only how to respond, but also more fundamentally, whether to respond at all. Although there are things to be gained by responding, there are also potential costs associated with speaking up against sexism. In their first experiment, Swim and Hyers recruited from a pool of female students in an introductory psychology class. Participants were told that the study was on group decision making and were placed into groups of four, where the other three people were actually experimental confederates. In the "solo" condition, the participant was placed with three male confederates. In the "nonsolo" condition, two of the confederates were female and one was male. The apparent group task was to choose from a list of 15 women and 15 men with different occupations, the 12 people whom group members felt would be most able to survive on a deserted island. The four group members were seated in a predetermined order, and each member was asked to give reasons for inclusion or exclusion of each of the 30 people listed. Each group member made comments in a clockwise direction. A male confederate who was seated to the participant's right made scripted responses to each of the hypothetical candidates. In the sexist condition, three of the comments directed at female candidates

(Continued)

(Continued)

were sexist. In the nonsexist condition, three similar comments were made, but the sexism was removed. For example, when discussing whether to include a man whose occupation was a chef, in the sexist condition, the confederate said, "No, one of the women can cook" (Swim & Hyers, 1999), whereas in the nonsexist condition, the confederate said, "No, one of the others can cook." The participants' actual responses to the sexist remarks formed the basis of the public response measure. After the group had made all of the choices, the experimenter directed each of the group members to a private room; at this point, the participant was asked to complete a questionnaire. After completing the questionnaire, the participant was taken to another room where she was told that the group decision-making task had been videotaped. The participant was then asked to watch the tape to improve her recall of her thoughts and feelings during the task. She was instructed to stop the tape whenever she remembered something that she was thinking or feeling at that particular time and to write down what she remembered. This formed the basis of the private response measure. Finally, the participant rated her feelings toward each of the experimental confederates.

After analyzing the women's public responses to the sexist remarks, Swim and Hyers (1999) reported that 45% of the women confronted the men who made the sexist remarks in some way (e.g., using humor or sarcasm, questioning the person who made the comment, displaying exclamations of surprise), but that only 16% directly confronted the men with verbal responses that challenged the stated reasons for the candidate choice (e.g., "You can't pick someone for that reason. Pick another person" [p. 76]). Interestingly, when the participant was the only woman among three male confederates, she was more likely to respond to the initial sexist remark than when other women were present.

Using social psychological theory, Swim and Hyers (1999) offered an explanation for this seemingly curious finding. If more than one woman is present when the sexist remark is made, each woman may look to the other women to respond and might feel that the responsibility for addressing the comment does not fall on her shoulders alone. This concept is termed the **diffusion of responsibility** and is useful for providing insight into the response patterns of the women in this study.

Examination of the participants' private responses (what they reported thinking or feeling during the group discussion) revealed that the absence of public responses did not mean that the participants did not notice or did not disagree with the sexist comments. Of the 55% of women who did not publicly respond, 75% rated the confederates who made the comments as prejudiced, and nearly all of them (91%) viewed the confederates negatively.

In a follow-up study performed by Swim and Hyers, an identical situation was described to female participants, and they were asked to indicate how they thought that they would respond in that situation. Not surprisingly, far more women indicated that they would respond publicly and directly than those who actually did in the first study. In fact, only 1% of the respondents indicated that they would ignore the comments, whereas 55% actually did ignore the comments in the first study. Swim and Hyers proposed that these two studies suggest that most women might not be responding to the sexist comments they encounter in their everyday lives in the way they would like. The social situation, they suggested, controlled not only *whether* the women would respond, but also *how* the women would respond. For example, even when women did choose to respond, they typically did so in a polite, and more socially acceptable, manner. Awareness of the powerful impact of the situation on our behavior can help us to understand reactions to sexism, but also provide us with clues on how to effect change.

In a recent study examining the consequences of verbal as well as nonverbal expressions of both hostile and benevolent sexism, the authors suggest that benevolent sexism may—counter to what one may think—be more facilitative of sustained gender inequality than hostile sexism (Goh & Hall, 2015). Offering a "wolf in sheep's clothing" analogy, Goh and Hall explain that the seeming harmless, even appealing, comments characteristic of benevolent sexism may lull women into accepting the societal status quo and therefore leaves the "driving forces" of inequality unanswered.

Ethnic Background

Another domain of diversity is ethnic diversity. Like gender, ethnicity is often used as a way in which to group people together. Unfortunately, a common response to ethnic diversity is racism. **Racism** can be defined as bias against an individual or a group of individuals based on the individual's or group members' race/ethnicity. It may seem likely that racism no longer exists given that official policies that condone overt discrimination rarely exist. However, reality tends to show otherwise. For example in 1997, Jones pointed out that the United States ranked 6th in the world on the Human Development Index, a United Nations (UN) index based on measures of life expectancy at birth, literacy, years of schooling, and economic data. He further noted that if this index were computed based on data from African Americans alone, the United States would rank 31st; if data from Hispanic Americans alone were used, the ranking would be 34th globally. In 2014, the U.S. ranked 5th (United Nations Human Development Reports, 2014). Unfortunately, the negative effects of racism are still prevalent in American society today.

In North America, modern forms of racism are often difficult to measure because most displays of bias or negative attitudes have become very subtle and might not match our common understanding of the term. Typically, people's beliefs about minorities appear to be positive, or at least do not appear to be overtly negative. In most (but not all) situations, it is no longer considered acceptable to make directly racist comments, and so racism tends to reveal itself in indirect ways. Direct and blatant attacks on minority group members have become less frequent in North America, and negative attitudes are expressed only if situations are ambiguous or if the attitude can be attributed to something other than a response to the target group (Nelson, 2002). It is obvious that among many other historic examples, the persecution of Jews in Nazi Germany and the lynching of Blacks by the Ku Klux Klan constitute prejudice, racism, and discrimination. The fact that nearly all of the professors in a given psychology department are White, or that nearly all of the chief executive officers of the major corporations across North America are White, might not strike you as indicative of prejudice or discrimination, yet such situations also may be the result of some form of racism.

What most people commonly understand to be racism is actually more similar to the **blatant racism** that was more common in the past than to modern forms of racism. Racism in the past was often blatant in that it took obvious forms, such as segregation and clear differential treatment based on skin color. Blatant racism is easier to measure than more contemporary forms of racism because blatant racists will usually admit to holding negative attitudes and beliefs. Accessing this information may be as simple as asking.

During more recent years, other forms of racism have been identified. In many cases, people do not believe that they are racist or that they hold prejudiced attitudes toward specific racial/ ethnic groups. In other cases, perceived social norms against racism inhibit the likelihood that someone will admit to racist attitudes or beliefs. As such, these forms of prejudice may be more subtle and indirect. An example of a form of modern racism is **aversive racism** (Gaertner & Dovidio, 1986). Despite holding racist beliefs, aversive racists believe that they are not prejudiced against people from races other than their own. They do not acknowledge their racial biases because this perspective is inconsistent with their view of themselves as egalitarian. Therefore, although racism is present, the racist attitudes are not conscious (Nelson, 2002).

Similarly, **symbolic racism** (Sears, 1988) also does not manifest itself in obvious ways. In instances of this type of racism, a negative attitude is associated with something other than the target. For example, an individual may insist that he or she is not racist and has "nothing against Blacks." However, the individual may also say that there is a problem with affirmative action, something that he or she believes gives an unfair advantage to Blacks over Whites in hiring practices. Aversive racism and symbolic racism are similar concepts in that people who manifest either type do not acknowledge racism explicitly. That is, the actual negative attitudes are associated with some other proxy type factor (e.g., affirmative action) and not with the target. So, the attitudes appear as though they are tied to politics rather than to groups of people (Hilton & von Hipple, 1996).

Ambivalent racism (Hass, Katz, Rizzo, Bailey, & Eisenstadt, 1991), like ambivalent sexism, contends that people can simultaneously hold two attitudes that are inconsistent with each other. With this type of racism, people are not overtly prejudiced and do recognize the unfair treatment of minorities and racial disparities, but at the same time they believe that the system is based on meritocracy, that is, the principle that hard work will pay off—the "American Dream" (Hilton & von Hipple, 1996). As a result of holding this attitude, these individuals are more willing to accept different outcomes for people of different races/ethnicities in the belief that everyone has had the same opportunities, but that individuals from some groups have not taken full advantage of the opportunities available to them.

Despite the many obvious visible changes since the time when it was acceptable to have "Whites only" drinking fountains and bus seats, racism does still exist. Its expression has changed to more subtle forms, but racism has not yet been eradicated. The good news is that this may be slowly changing. In 2000, researchers examined how the expression of aversive racism had shifted over the 10-year period between 1989 and 1999 (Dovidio & Gaertner, 2000). Coinciding with their expectations, self-ratings of prejudice were much lower in 1999 than in 1989. In addition to self-reports of racial prejudice, participants were asked to engage in a simulated employment situation and make selection decisions. The researchers found that in situations where candidates presented with strong credentials, no prejudice or discrimination was shown to Black candidates. Black candidates whose credentials were not as strong, however, were still selected for employment at a lower rate than were White candidates with the same credentials. This study is optimistic in that some things do appear to be changing, but it is also pessimistic in the sense that in many ways real change is making only very slow progress.

Social Class

Issues relating to social class constitute another example of how the ideal of equal opportunity, and the belief that individual effort always pays off pervades many Western societies, allowing people to avoid acknowledging structural and systemic inequalities.

Those who are economically disadvantaged have historically been described as belonging to a culture of poverty (Mincy, 2000). This culture has been assumed to be the result of values and attitudes held by impoverished individuals and is viewed as part of what separates those in the lower socioeconomic strata from those in other strata. Research suggests that social class is indeed a determinant of how we "size people up." For example, Kirby (1999) found that class bias was involved in people's impressions of new neighbors. She found that people were more likely to object to their new neighbors if they believed that the neighbors were receiving public assistance, and that this bias was one that participants expressed candidly.

Issues related to poverty and social class have been likened to an elephant in the room that everyone knows is there, but that nobody wants to talk about (Younge, 2003). The huge economic disparities in the lives of people across North America are undeniable, and the United States has been described as the most stratified industrial society in current times (Mantsios, 2000). Because this inequity is undeniable, it is often justified or excused.

Younge (2003) suggested that the notion of equal opportunity is often used to excuse the huge disparity in economic realities. The concepts of the deserving poor and the undeserving poor are rooted in people's perceptions of those who comprise the lowest socioeconomic classes (Mincy, 2000). The **undeserving poor** are those whose economic conditions are assumed to be through no fault of their own. For example, individuals who are handicapped, are mentally ill, or have some other life circumstances that have clearly affected their ability to earn a living are often given sympathy, and we are less likely to hold their economic circumstances against them. However, most individuals are assumed to have equal opportunity and equal access to earning a living. Those who fall into the **deserving poor** category are those whom others think should have taken advantage of the supposed opportunities, but have not done so due to their own lack of initiative. This artificial and frequently erroneous pattern of assumptions allows others, especially those who are more privileged, to justify the existence of social class inequalities. In fact, a recent study by Fiske, Xu, and Cuddy (1999) conducted with a sample of university students indicated that among the 16 groups in their analysis (Asians, African Americans, Latinos, Jews, gay men, feminists, rich people, businesswomen, disabled people, blind people, retarded people, northerners, southerners, migrant workers, house cleaners, and housewives), those who received welfare were the only group of people who were rated as both disliked and disrespected.

Unfortunately, these assumptions about equal opportunity are so deep-seated that they are difficult to overcome, even for the people who are the most disadvantaged by societal inequalities. Duck (2012) conducted an ethnographic study of a poor African-American single mother ("Benita") living in a small city in the northeastern United States. You may remember from Chapter 3 that **ethnography** involves describing and interpreting the

shared values, beliefs, behaviors, and languages of a specific intact cultural group. In this study, Duck (2012) focuses on telling the story of one woman, but he argues that her experience mirrors that of other poor families. Duck immersed himself in Benita's community for five years and used research methods typical to ethnography, including in-depth interviews, observation, and volunteering in the community to gain extensive insights into her life. Benita experienced many systemic barriers to economic success, such as the city's flourishing drug trade, high unemployment rate, and a lack of affordable housing. Even social policies that are intended to help the poor often backfire, resulting in more financial hardship. For example, affordable social housing is all but impossible to receive, forcing Benita to "float" from residence to residence in a cycle of eviction. Other hardships included receiving only sporadic child support payments from her children's father, and having to use an expensive payday loan service to cover basic living expenses, resulting in Benita getting deeper and deeper into debt. Despite these barriers, Duck reports that Benita attributes her problems to poor decisions that she has made in her life. This internalization of the assumption of equal opportunities demonstrates the power of the belief that poor people are somehow deserving of their circumstances.

Gender, ethnicity, and social class constitute three of the many ways in which we are demographically diverse. As mentioned at the beginning of this section, each of these differences does not operate in isolation; we are complex individuals with many different aspects to our identities. Do you think that any of these aspects of demographic diversity might help to explain the conflict described in the opening vignette? Might race and/or social status have played a role?

CONSEQUENCES OF DIVERSITY: OPPORTUNITIES AND CHALLENGES

Opportunities. Although cultural diversity may foster misunderstandings and xenophobia, and demographic diversity may give rise to social problems, such as sexism, racism, and classism, diversity has the potential to produce positive results as well. Research on the positive effects of diversity has focused mainly on how diversity enhances group processes. The logical question to ask, then, is what aspects of diversity affect how people behave in groups? To answer this, a distinction needs to be made between functional diversity and the other types of diversity that we have been discussing. **Functional diversity** refers to the fact that each person in a group brings different strengths and talents to the group process. Although a greater number of people working on a problem provides more chances for important information to be brought to light than an individual working alone on a problem (Triandis, Kurowski, & Gelfand, 1994), functional diversity enhances group effectiveness even further by contributing to a group's ability to be innovative and creative (Amabile, 1983; Zhang, 2015). Functional diversity is related to both cultural and demographic diversity. When groups are composed of members who belong to different cultures or demographic categories—whether ethnic background, sex, or other categories—they have built-in functional diversity (Schneider & Northcraft, 1999) simply as a result of having members with diverse experiences and being exposed to different perspectives from their own in-groups. For example, a Hispanic individual who grew up in an urban neighborhood will have different experiences, and therefore will bring different insights to an issue than an Asian individual who grew up in a suburban neighborhood.

Just having diversity, however, does not necessarily guarantee positive results. Roberge and van Dick (2010) point out that diverse groups can have difficulties with cohesion, reducing group members' satisfaction with the group, and in organizational settings, also reducing the productivity of the group. Generally speaking, the literature suggests that when groups are diverse there is decreased communication and social interaction within the group, and differences about how to accomplish tasks are increased (Williams & O'Reilly, 1998). Roberge and van

Dick propose that diversity leads to opportunities rather than challenges most frequently when there is good communication in the group, when individuals in the group interact frequently, and when there is trust between group members. In other words, when group members have a meaningful group identity, have created a psychologically safe group climate, and feel that they can express their thoughts and opinions without being judged or rejected for those thoughts and opinions, then the chances that diversity will bring about positive results are the greatest.

Creativity and Innovation

These different perspectives can lead group members to rely less on past ways of dealing with things and may result in a reduced emphasis on conformity to the group. Some of the positive outcomes related to diversity within groups include creativity, innovation, and potentially improved problem solving (Cox, 1991). It has also been suggested that minority points of view can challenge the prevailing way of thinking, and therefore can stimulate greater creativity (Nemeth, 1986).

In a study of university teachers, those who described their working environment as diverse were the ones who were the most creative (Ryhammer & Smith, 1999). Of course, diversity may take many forms, and some differences may matter more than others. In a laboratory experiment, it was found that more creative solutions to problems emerged when groups were composed of both men and women than when they were composed of just men or just women (Schruijer & Mostert, 1997). The research of McLeod, Lobel, and Cox (1996) found that groups composed of only Anglo-Americans came up with less effective solutions in a brainstorming task than did groups composed of multiple ethnicities. In Korea, researchers found that groups of students who were diverse with respect to nationality, chosen major in school, and years of education became more creative and more productive as they worked together on term projects (Santandreau Calonge & Safiullin, 2015). Despite these findings, the effect of diversity on creativity and innovation may not always be so positive. A study conducted with 50 work teams from a Fortune 500 company indicated that diversity in the teams related to age, sex, and race had no effect on the innovative quality of group-generated solutions (Cady & Valentine, 1999). On the other hand, they found that sex diversity had a negative impact on the number of innovative ideas generated in response to a given problem, whereas racial diversity had a positive impact. Other research has found that diversity leads to feelings of exclusion and conflict rather than positive outcomes (Mannix & Neale, 2005). It seems that there must be a balance between the diversity of the group members and the similarity of their values and goals (Ofori-Dankwa & Julian, 2002). Research is continuing in this area to try to untangle just what aspects of diversity are important to creativity and innovation in groups, and how the different aspects of diversity interact. For example, some researchers have found that diversity training can be effective in some circumstances (Homan, Buengeler, Eckhoff, van Ginkel, & Voelpel, 2015).

Problem Solving

Problem solving tends to be better when groups are of diverse backgrounds and abilities (Cox & Blake, 1991). When a group can draw on a rich variety of perspectives and experiences, decision making can be of higher quality than if the perspectives and experiences shared by the group members are similar. Yet, as was the case with creativity and innovation, the most effective problem solving emerges when a balance of diversity exists. Diversity without any shared values and goals is likely to break a group apart; however, shared values and goals may lead to what Irving Janis has termed *groupthink*. As you may recall from Chapters 2 and 10, groupthink describes what happens when groups converge on a single answer to a problem, and rather than critically evaluating the solution, they convince themselves and each other that the

solution they came up with is the best one (Janis, 1983, 1996). As discussed in earlier chapters, this type of decision making can have disastrous consequences. Unfortunately, group homogeneity may exacerbate the likelihood of groupthink occurring. For example, during the Bay of Pigs fiasco, the similarity of the individuals within John F. Kennedy's presidential advisory council fostered a high degree of group cohesion, and shared values and goals helped to intensify this cohesion. In contrast, diverse groups are much less likely to have this sort of cohesion, thereby minimizing the likelihood that groupthink will occur (Cox, 1991), and maximizing the likelihood that many different possible solutions will be examined.

However, the differences in perspectives, opinions, and other variables that are present in diverse groups and enhance their creativity can also be an impediment to problem solving. Although diverse groups may be more creative (a divergent task), the differences among people that generate diversity may also produce difficulty in agreeing on how to implement solutions to address the problems they're considering (a convergent task). Thus, problem solving may not be enhanced in diverse groups unless facilitating conditions are present, such as training in diversity management and a group culture that embraces diversity (Scott, Heathcote, & Gruman, 2011).

Challenges. Although diversity presents many opportunities, there are also a number of challenges present when individuals with diverse backgrounds and experiences interact.

Prejudice and Discrimination

One challenge related to diversity is dealing with prejudice and discrimination against those who are in some way different. **Prejudice** is "an attitude toward others based solely on group membership" (Moghaddam, 1998, p. 330). When prejudiced attitudes get translated into behavior, discrimination results. So, the term **discrimination** is reserved for use when referring to the "actual behavior directed at others on the basis of category membership" (p. 332). Challenges often result when considering the consequences of confronting prejudice and discrimination (Becker, Zawadzki, & Shields, 2014).

Social psychology has played a prominent role in research on both prejudice and discrimination. For example, early research on racism and discrimination focused on the characteristics of people who are prejudiced, or who discriminate against others based on their race or ethnicity (Dovidio, 2001). More recently, many social psychologists have begun to include an examination of the effects that prejudice and discrimination have on the targets of these attitudes or behaviors. For example, how does being a target of discrimination affect the way in which people feel about themselves? The scope of interest has also expanded beyond racism to include other types of diversity, including the sexism and classism mentioned earlier in this chapter.

Where does prejudice originate? Some believe that prejudice stems from our thoughts and belief systems, or from cognitive sources (Nelson, 2002). The mistaken belief that two things are related simply because they are seen as occurring together is one cognitive process that contributes to the formation of stereotypes (Jones, 1997). So, for example, you may begin to believe that all people with red hair have terrible tempers because the last several times you saw someone yelling and was upset in a restaurant, the person having the tantrum had red hair. Another perspective on the origins of prejudice suggests that we are motivated to hold particular beliefs. Examples of this view would be illustrated in some theories of conflict that are discussed later in the chapter (e.g., social identity theory, realistic group conflict theory, theory of relative deprivation).

Prejudice also arises because of in-group bias. As suggested earlier, we tend to think of some people as part of our in-group (we perceive them as like us), and others as part of an out-group (perceived as unlike us). Prejudice is a form of discrimination aimed at people in outgroups. In-group bias may have partly biological origins. In our evolutionary past, resources like food were commonly scarce. During those times, groups of individuals who shared their food with people they considered more "like them" were more likely to share food with relatives, and thus more likely to successfully pass on familial genes. Intensifying this potentially adaptive tendency to like others who are similar to us would be to dislike others who are dissimilar. Consequently, although we don't condone it, we have inherited a tendency to be prejudiced against others because the in-group bias that underlies prejudice may have certain genetic and evolutionary advantages (e.g., Correll & Park, 2005; Scheepers, Spears, Doosje, & Manstead, 2006). We should note how subtle such biases can be. Clearly, overt prejudice based on stereotypes can be considered an example of bias, but so can much more apparently benign behavior, such as when a news broadcaster reports that "seven Americans were killed in a plane crash." Many of the same psychological processes that underlie prejudice underlie our interest in knowing the nationality of crash victims (i.e., were they like me?).

Stereotypes are "beliefs about the characteristics, attributes, and behaviors of members of certain groups" (Hilton & von Hipple, 1996, p. 240), and many stereotypes are culturally based (Moghaddam, 1998). Within social psychological research, stereotypes have been studied as a process (how people come to believe what they do), as content (what traits comprise a particular stereotype), and as varying in their strength or intensity (how firmly people believe what they do about particular social groups), as well as in their consequences (Madon, 1997). Over the past few decades, process and consequence issues have dominated researchers' attention, and it is only recently that there has been a shift in focus to return to analysis of stereotype content (Madon, 1997). Knowledge of the content of stereotypes is important both because of real-life implications (Fitchen & Amsel, 1986), and because of the potential that this information holds for providing insight into possible avenues of social change for stigmatized groups.

Stereotype content may affect the target in many different ways. One of the more subtle effects is stereotype threat, which was discussed in Chapter 9. You'll recall that **stereotype threat** is a fear or nervousness that your behavior will exemplify a negative stereotype about your in-group, thereby in essence confirming the accuracy of the stereotype. Unfortunately, this may capture some of the attention of the target and affect the target's performance on the task at hand (Steele & Aronson, 1995). Performance deficits are a well-documented result associated with stereotype threat (Kalokerinos, von Hipple, & Zacher, 2014). For example, if a woman was due to take a math exam and she knew that women are not expected to perform well in math, she might get nervous about her performance (see Figure 14.3). The nervousness may negatively affect her score by affecting her level of concentration, thereby contributing to the stereotype. Speaking to its generalizability, this phenomenon is found across multiple groups in many countries (Roberson & Kim, 2014). Moreover, the authors warn that since we all have many social identities, anyone can be subjected to the consequences of stereotype threat. Recognition that stereotypes are not always exclusively negative, and that in fact positive traits (e.g., Africans are good dancers, Asians are good at math, gay men are good at decorating) are included in the stereotypes of many social groups, is central to further enhancing our understanding of the complexity of stereotype content and the effects that stereotypes may produce.

Figure 14.3 Women Who May Be Likely to Experience Stereotype Threat

SOURCE: Photo Courtesy of Centre for Flexible Learning, University of Windsor.

FOCUS ON INTERVENTION

Helping Children Decategorize Others

Stereotypes can help us to organize the world around us, but we must be careful about the negative effects that they have for relationships between groups and for our society. They can make it seem as though the differences that exist between certain people, or groups of people, are larger than the similarities, or that these differences are larger than they really are. This perception of differences can sometimes lead to problems. This idea is at the crux of a recent intervention designed to reduce stereotyping and increase tolerance of diversity through educating children to decategorize their perceptions of people from diverse ethnic backgrounds (Jones & Foley, 2003). In general, decategorization involves changing how we categorize people so that the new categories emphasize similarities rather than differences.

In this experiment, 65 fourth graders were randomly assigned to either a control condition where they were read a story, or an experimental group where they were read a presentation with material that focused on various topics related to diversity. Specifically, the presentation covered the topics of anthropology (emphasizing our common human ancestry), biology (emphasizing our common genetic background), and the "melting pot" (emphasizing that most people living in the United States are from immigrant families). All children were asked to complete an adapted version of the Racial Decategorization Scale, a 30-item questionnaire designed to assess their feelings and beliefs about people of diverse ethnic backgrounds and stereotypes, and a questionnaire assessing their knowledge about anthropology, biology, and diversity in the United States. Responses to the questions were recorded on a 5-point Likert scale (1 = *strongly agree*, 5 = *strongly disagree*), with higher scores indicating more racial categorization and negative perceptions of diverse ethnic groups. Study results demonstrated that the experimental group scored lower on the Racial Decategorization Scale than did the control group (*Ms* = 50.4 and 58.9, respectively). These findings support the assertion that children can and do benefit from material that stresses decategorization, and that shifting the focus to emphasizing similarities across groups rather than differences is potentially useful. This has implications for the reduction of prejudice in children. Often, biases that form the basis of prejudice are developed early in life. To combat them, interventions aimed at reducing or correcting these biases should be put into place as early as they are observed, if not earlier. Perhaps if we spend more time emphasizing the overlap between ethnic groups, we will make it harder for people (especially children) to treat people differentially based on race. At the very least, making use of interventions like these would be another step toward fostering an increased tolerance for diversity.

Conflict (coauthored with Ritu Kaushal)

Ideally, society would recognize, appreciate, and even celebrate its diversity by acknowledging the richness and value that diversity brings, but this is not always the case. Attention to diversity and misperceptions involving the people around us often brings the threat of **conflict**, which has been defined as "a perceived incompatibility of interests" (Moghaddam, 1998, p. 513). Often the person or group is competing for limited resources with another person or group that holds incompatible goals. Examples seem to be in the news on a constant basis—ISIS in the Middle East, drug wars in Mexico, civil war in Iraq, ethnic clashes in the Balkans and Rwanda, and angry clashes between natives and nonnatives over fishing rights. Conflicts inevitably arise out of clashes of values, attitudes, and/or behaviors, and these conflicts must be dealt with effectively.

This definition of conflict is not the only one. In fact, Deutsch (1973) suggested that conflict may occur when persons or groups hold either competitive or cooperative interests. For example, consider school projects in which two students are asked to work together. Both students may be motivated to do a good job, but may disagree on how to go about this. One student may want to use information collected from interviews about personal experiences, whereas the other student may want to use more general information collected from magazines, books, and research journals. Despite the fact that both students have compatible goals and an equal desire to succeed, conflict can still result. In this scenario and others like it, the competitive interests produce the conflict ("I want the project to be done my way"), and the cooperative interests serve as motivation to reach an agreement ("I want the teacher to be impressed with our work").

It is often assumed that conflict is always a bad thing. Because of this, conflict is often given a bad name. Granted, most conflict that we hear about is of the negative variety. Negative conflict may waste both time and valuable resources, and it can result in resentment and animosity. It can increase emotional exhaustion and even have negative physiological effects (Dijkstra, De Dreu, Evers, & van Dierendonck, 2009; Wright & Loving, 2011). However, conflict is not necessarily negative. Conflict can represent honest differences of opinion and may be healthy or functional when people take the opportunity to express themselves assertively yet respectfully, and thus open the lines of communication. This type of conflict can serve as the basis for the creativity and innovation discussed earlier. Viewed from this perspective, conflict provides a stimulus to foster positive change.

Despite the fact that conflict may be beneficial in the sense that it stimulates needed change, it can also become a very serious problem with enormous implications across organizational, community, and national settings (Fisher, 1990). Within organizational settings, conflict has the potential to decrease the effectiveness of employees through lost work time, lowered morale, wasted energy, and various other negative effects. Within the community, it may lead to increased levels of prejudice and discrimination among groups. At the international level, conflict can be even more dangerous, as demonstrated by numerous armed conflicts throughout human history.

As noted in earlier chapters, we often see others and ourselves as members of groups; that is, members of in-groups and out-groups. Usually such perceptions are harmless and often work to increase group cohesiveness. At a football game between rival universities, for example, the fact that you attend one of the universities is much more important than your major (a sense of cohesion exists across majors, ages, fraternities, and other groups). You quickly identify with your own team and university, and you view people from the other university as the out-group. Focusing on groups rather than individuals, however, also leads to the perception of exaggerated group differences, and thus creates the potential for conflict. In situations like those described earlier in New Brunswick and Minnesota, reports of the conflicts quickly come to include comments by those involved that refer to "them"—meaning members of the other group. These comments are rarely positive and typically apply a characteristic (e.g., stubborn) to everyone in the other group simply on the basis of group membership. Understanding the dynamics of group interaction is important for understanding the development of conflict as well as its management and resolution. Some of the relevant theories of intergroup relations with respect to conflict and conflict management include social identity, relative deprivation, and realistic group conflict.

Theories of Conflict

Social identity theory. **Social identity theory** (SIT) is a popular theory in the study of intergroup behavior (Karasawa, 1991). Although SIT was not developed as a theory of conflict, it does provide insight into how conflict may arise from relations between groups. SIT posits that an individual's self-knowledge is based on two types of identity (Tajfel & Turner, 1986). One type, known as *personal identity,* reflects an individual's sense of his or her own personal qualities and characteristics. Personal identity, for example, may be reflected by characterizations of the self as smart, outgoing, and funny. The other type, *social identity,* reflects a sense of identity based on the social groups to which individuals belong or with which they identify. Being a student, a woman, and an American could reflect a person's social identity. Which identity is expressed at any given time is often determined by the situation or the context within which a given behavior occurs. For example, going to a movie with a friend or out to dinner with a date brings personal characteristics, and hence personal identity, to the fore. On the other hand, marching in a student protest against tuition hikes, playing basketball against a rival university team, or becoming involved in a dispute over native fishing rights could evoke one's sense of social identity. Think about this: Would you fail to notice if you were the only person of color in a room full of White people, or if you were the only woman in a room full of men? In essence, SIT suggests that it is the context within which individuals find themselves that determines which type of identity—personal or social—will predominate.

A fundamental assumption of SIT is that people want to feel good about who they are and about the groups to which they belong; that is, they strive toward achieving (or maintaining) a positive social identity (Tajfel & Turner, 1986). So, as an American, a person might think great things about people from the United States because these positive comments also apply to him or her as a member of that category. Although this is true in some cases, it is especially so in situations involving intergroup relations. When in a group, being motivated to feel good about oneself and one's group often goes hand in hand with being motivated to evaluate members of the other group negatively. This is where the danger lies.

Awareness and critical evaluation of group membership forms the basis of the social identity process in that there must be an awareness that one belongs to a particular group. Then, through a social comparison process, evaluation of group status occurs. This evaluation results in a negative social identity (i.e., a status differential exists between an individual's group and the comparison group, with one's own group comparing unfavorably), or a positive social identity (i.e., either no status differential exists, or one's own group compares favorably with the comparison group). Thus, perception of group differences and status differentials play an important role in the potential for conflict by setting the stage for "us versus them" comparisons. In situations where there is high tension between groups, such as in the opening vignette, the differences between "my" group and the "other" group become even more exaggerated.

It is important to note that the categorization of groups does not have to be based on real or observable between-group differences, and that one needs only to perceive oneself as being part of a particular group and different from another group to induce a sense of group membership. Such comparisons, if left unchallenged, may be the building blocks for stereotypes and other forms of prejudice and discrimination.

Relative deprivation. Like SIT, the **theory of relative deprivation** acknowledges the importance of both perceptual comparative processes and social comparative processes between groups in conflict. Originally developed by Stouffer, Suchman, DeVinney, Star, and Williams (1949), the theory of relative deprivation suggests that a person may feel deprived of some desirable thing relative to his or her own past; or to another person(s), group, or ideal; or to some other social category. It is important to note that this sense of deprivation is based on a relative comparison with some "other" thing, and that the person does not have to be "deprived" in the absolute sense of the word (Runciman, 1972). For example, even if an individual has received what would be considered a "fair share," conflict may still occur as a result of the perception that one has received less than the individual believes he or she is due. Thus, conflict arises only after individuals have compared themselves with some standard and judged themselves to be deprived.

Although the theory of relative deprivation has its limitations, it can provide a useful framework for understanding some types of conflict. When individuals experience relative deprivation, they are motivated to act in a way that serves to reduce or eliminate the deprivation. This action may sometimes result in conflict. The theory of relative deprivation may be used to explain the origins of many political conflicts because individuals believe that this relative deprivation is the result of social injustice (Auvinen & Nafziger, 1999). This theory also helps to explain conflicts over fishing and hunting rights between native and nonnative peoples. When native and nonnative fishers have different restrictions placed on them, it is understandable that the more restricted group feels deprived in comparison with the other group. Similarly, when native people believe that restrictions are being placed on activities where no restrictions existed previously, a sense of relative deprivation may occur.

Realistic group conflict theory. In essence, **realistic group conflict theory** (RGCT) suggests that intergroup hostility is produced by competition in the form of conflicting goals. Basing their theory on the work of Sherif (1966a), LeVine and Campbell (1972) suggested that conflict is reduced by cooperation in the form of common goals that are attainable only through cooperation. The basic premise of this theory is that conflict between groups is a result of real conflicts of interest. Unlike the theories of social identity and relative deprivation (where perception plays a central role), RGCT suggests that perception is not enough and that a real and immediate conflict of interest must exist for actual conflict to occur. Once in-group identity is threatened, awareness of in-group identity is heightened, and feelings of in-group solidarity are increased along with negative feelings toward those in the out-group. The presence of all these factors can be clearly seen in the ongoing conflict over fishing rights in the United States and Canada.

The basis for RGCT was the classic field experiment conducted by Muzafer Sherif (1966b) that was discussed in Chapter 1. You may recall that the study, known as the Robbers Cave Experiment, involved boys at a summer camp and consisted of three phases: a *group formation* phase during which groups with distinct norms formed, an *intergroup conflict* phase during which conflict between groups and the denigration of out-group members surfaced, and a *reduction of conflict* phase during which the introduction of superordinate goals led to the reduction of conflict between the groups (Fisher, 1990; Sherif, Harvey, White, Hood, & Sherif, 1961).

In Sherif's field study, the boys were ultimately able to reduce (if not eliminate) their out-group biases and eventually get along. This study provided some definite insights into the consequences of conflicts of interest and the development and resolution of intergroup conflict. Furthermore, this study provided clear evidence that superordinate goals play a key role in conflict management and that the resolution of conflict takes more than mere contact with out-group members.

As mentioned in earlier sections of this chapter, it is simply human nature to categorize people into different groups. From an early age, individuals learn to place people into groups based on obvious differences, such as gender, ethnic background, and social class. In fact, Sherif and colleagues' (1961) pioneering field studies have demonstrated that even when the differences are completely arbitrary, people still categorize others into groups and behave in ways that correspond with in- and out-group membership. Thus, the work of Sherif and colleagues emphasized the importance of "self–other" differences, whether concrete or perceived, when establishing group or social identity.

Although the experimental work that has been done in the area of conflict management is important, it must be noted that such experimental work is of limited value if it cannot be applied to real-world situations. In this way, the work of Sherif and colleagues has greatly helped to identify some of the conflict management and resolution strategies that could be applied in settings ranging from home and school to the workplace. It has been used, for example, to explain why prejudiced attitudes may exist in the workplace, even if employees come from an ethnically diverse community (Brief et al., 2005).

RGCT has also been used successfully to understand the effectiveness of team-based organizations. Hennessy and West (1999) looked at the effects of identification with a work group and perceptions of competition between groups at a community health care hospital in England. The teams used in the research were composed of individuals working at 17 different day care centers of the hospital. As part of the survey, participants were given scenarios where they were asked to make decisions on how they would distribute a pool of funds between the day care centers. They found that participants who strongly identified with their team and who perceived some competition between groups made decisions that benefited their team at the expense of the other teams, allocating significantly more money to their team than to the others. RGCT provides a useful tool to understand how individuals and groups may, even unintentionally, initiate conflict situations when limited resources are available. The health care workers in this research were more concerned with their own needs and the benefits that the additional funding could provide for patients in their own program than with equitable distribution among the day care centers.

This type of situation is often the beginning of conflict, even if nobody is behaving maliciously or even intending for conflict to occur. This is especially true in cross-cultural situations where there may be great differences in expectations for how resources ought to be divided (Fischer & Smith, 2003). In collectivistic countries, for example, norms typically dictate that resources be distributed equally; everyone gets the same regardless of how hard they worked or their rank. In individualistic countries, however, the norm is for rewards to be equity based; the more one puts into a project in terms of work, materials, and so forth, the more of the reward that person receives. It is extremely difficult to reach a consensus on reward allocation when individuals from both cultural perspectives must arrive at a solution, and this sets the stage for conflict (Leung, 1988). Let us reflect back for a moment on the intervention example used for prejudice reduction. How would you extend these techniques from simple prejudice reduction to conflict management and resolution?

Conflict Management and Resolution

Although understanding the causes of conflict is extremely important, understanding the ways in which we can manage and potentially resolve conflict is perhaps more so. At the group level, two promising theories of conflict management and resolution are the contact hypothesis and coalition building.

The contact hypothesis. In his classic book *The Nature of Prejudice* (1954), Gordon Allport suggested that negative intergroup relations could be improved by increasing positive contact between members of two groups. Known as the **contact hypothesis**, the assumption was that positive contact with members of an out-group could decrease negative stereotyping of the out-group by the in-group and lead to improved intergroup relations. However, Allport pointed out that contact in and of itself is insufficient to produce positive change without other important criteria being met. For example, improvement can be anticipated only if both the in-group and the out-group are perceived as relatively equal in status and power. Here, even the perception of status equality between the groups is enough to help resolve a conflict situation. In addition, a perception that the two groups share a common goal should exist along with a perception that their environments support their movement toward that goal. When attempting to reach a desired outcome that is common to both groups, it is necessary for them to work together to achieve this. The interaction that occurs as a result of working together helps to overcome some of the barriers that caused the conflict in the first place. However, if two groups have a common goal and yet engage in competition rather than cooperation with one another, this will serve to impede the process of conflict resolution. For example, if two groups are competing for the same limited resources, prejudice will increase rather than decrease, as was the case during the early phases of the situations described in the opening vignette. This theory has been the basis for attempts to minimize conflicts between groups in a number of settings. Many attempts to reduce conflict in Israel have begun by bringing together young Israelis and Arabs. However, a high degree of interaction does not always occur when groups are brought together (Maoz, 2002), and more than mere contact seems to be required for meaningful change.

One example of a conflict intervention that uses the preceding principles in a group setting is the "graduated and reciprocated initiatives in tension reduction" (GRIT) strategy, which involves building on successive attempts at conciliation (Osgood, 1962). The initiation of the GRIT strategy involves one "side" or party taking the first step by engaging in a few de-escalatory actions to demonstrate an attempt at conciliation. This step is meant to notify the opposing party of the initiating party's intent to de-escalate conflict as well as to invite the opposing party to respond by taking its own steps to de-escalate the conflict. This first step serves two purposes: (a) to clarify the intent of the initiating group (so as to make clear that this is a step toward peace and not a trick), and (b) to publicly demonstrate the attempt at conciliation in such a way as to allow for external pressure (by the public, the media, or the international community) to be placed on the opposing party to reciprocate. If the opposing party responds in kind, step-by-step the conflict can be reduced. Osgood (1962) suggested that if the opposing party does not respond in kind, the initiating party should try again to make a small concession a second or third time.

The GRIT strategy will be successful only if each of the conflicting parties responds appropriately, and if a certain degree of trust can be developed (Lindskold, 1978). However, the potential remains for the initiating party to take a conciliatory step, and if the opposing party chooses not to respond, to leave itself vulnerable to being taken advantage of by the opposing party. In this respect, the GRIT strategy also emphasizes the need for both conflicting parties to protect their own interests by ensuring that they are capable of retaliation if the need arises. The nature of the GRIT strategy is such that it encourages gradual steps in tension reduction, a process that ensures the safety of both parties because it does not leave any one party more vulnerable than another party. Given what you know about the groups described in the opening vignette, do you think that those interested in decreasing conflict would be wise to try to increase contact between the two groups?

Coalition building. Research on **coalition building** has identified a set of pivotal factors required for making positive changes to intergroup relations. These factors include acquaintance potential, social norms, cooperative tasks and reward systems, and the characteristics of individuals (Fisher, 1982, 1990).

A high *acquaintance potential,* meaning a greater opportunity for personal and informal interaction between groups, would serve to help members of different groups to get to know each other. This would increase the potential for positive interaction between groups. Also, *social norms* that encourage positive intergroup interaction would allow for more accepted relations between groups. If such norms were institutionalized, communication between groups would become more commonplace because it would not be looked on so negatively. As mentioned previously, introducing *cooperative tasks* and *reward systems* would also create common cooperative goals that members of different groups could work together to achieve. Having to work together often starts off feeling like forced inter-action, but as people get to know each other on a more personal level, relations between them start to change and become more positive in nature (Fisher, 1982, 1990). Efforts to resolve conflicts like the fishing disputes described earlier often involve creating coalitions with members from both groups convening to seek solutions to the problem that would aid members of both groups. This approach to conflict resolution has been cited as a critical factor in the peace treaty signed in 2005 that ended a conflict of over 30 years between the Indonesian government and the Free Aceh Movement (Schiff, 2014).

Finally, *individual characteristics* also serve to influence intergroup interactions—both the individual who may hold a negative attitude and the target of that attitude. The strength with which people hold prejudicial ideas may deter-mine how open they are to changing their stereotypes of people from other groups. For example, being introduced to a member of a minority group who is highly competent may make a person think about the stereotypes that he or she holds about that particular group, and might even motivate the individual to change his or her thinking (Fisher, 1982, 1990).

Desforges and colleagues (1991) investigated the effects of different types of social contact with a former mental patient (two types of struc-tured cooperative contact and a control condition) on attitudes toward former mental patients and found support for the contact hypothesis as a way in which to reduce conflict. Specifically, the study explored the potential for attitude change as a result of contact with a representative from a stigmatized social group. The results demon-strated that attitudes toward former mental patients changed from being negative to being more positive in nature after individuals engaged in a cooperative task with a confederate playing the role of a former mental patient. In addition, contact was linked to more positive attitudes regarding the typical former mental patient and to more positive general attitudes toward former mental patients. Thus, as Desforges and

colleagues demonstrated, contact may indeed foster a change in negative attitudes toward mental patients and other stigmatized social groups, a finding that has several implications for the reduction of prejudice through contact.

Another example of a conflict intervention is illustrated by the United Nations' efforts in developing peace-building support offices in postconflict areas where help is needed to restore a sense of balance in the legal, political, eco-nomic, and/or social systems of the regions. The UN website is a great source of information regarding the peace-building support offices as well as other interventions aimed at reducing ten-sions between conflicting groups. The aim of these peace-building offices is to provide support throughout the peace process, essentially helping to prevent further conflict. The mandate of such offices is often part of a "disarmament–demobilization–reconciliation" (DDR) process in which the primary aim of peace building is to encourage conflicting parties to disarm, demobi-lize, and reconcile their differences. Each peace-building office is headed by a representa-tive of the Secretary-General who is responsible for overseeing each peace-building initiative. Often these individuals serve as negotiators between the government and the international community. Although they are responsible for encouraging and monitoring communication between conflicting parties, they must take care not to cross the boundary between helping and interfering with the internal affairs of the region.

Peace-building offices have come into exist-ence only during recent years and can be found in regions that have recently dealt with conflict, such as Liberia, Tajikistan, Nepal, Burundi, Comoros, Guinea, Guinea-Bissau, Côte d'Ivoire, Sierra Leone, and the Central African Republic. In each of these areas, the nature of the peace-building activities taking place is different, although the function of such activities remains the same. For example, peace-building activities monitored by the offices may range from monitoring elections and cease-fire agreements to temporarily taking over the functions of government.

Headed by Felix Downes-Thomas, the peace-building office in the West African nation of

Liberia is one such attempt at rebuilding a region recovering from civil war. In Liberia, some disarmament and demobilization goals have been met, but the goals of reconciliation still remain. To this end, Downes-Thomas has facilitated meetings between government and rebel leaders, advising the two groups on ways in which they can improve their economic cooperation. In addition, the country's president recently released some political prisoners from jail. Such efforts at peace building help to encourage reciprocal actions that, in turn, help to de-escalate the conflict. So far, these peace-building efforts have been maintained successfully. However, as with any peace-building initiative, any progress that has been achieved can be undone just as quickly. In Liberia, less than a year later, clashes re-erupted in the North as a result of dissident groups whose members felt that their needs were not being met during the process of conflict resolution. This highlights the need, during the postconflict phase, for the UN peace-building support offices to do their job and help to reestablish a sense of peace within the region. How might one use this approach to help reduce the conflict discussed in the vignette at the beginning of the chapter?

Throughout this section, much of the focus has centered on conflict at the group level. However, we also experience conflict in our daily interactions with others; that is, at an interpersonal level. Understanding interpersonal conflict can provide insight into group processes and improve conflict management skills. At the interpersonal level, Rahim and Bonoma (1979) provided an understanding of the different styles of managing conflict.

Interpersonal conflict management. The contact hypothesis and coalition building focus on strategies for managing conflict between groups (intergroup conflict). However, conflict also occurs between individuals (interpersonal conflict). According to Rahim and Bonoma (1979), interpersonal conflict is best managed when individuals balance their personal goals and the requirements of the task in such a way as to meet both personal and group goals. The most

effective strategy in a given situation depends on specific factors embedded in the situation. Rahim and Bonoma identified distinct styles of conflict management, each of which can be placed on two dimensions: concern for the self and concern for others. The dimension called *concern for self* represents the extent to which individuals are motivated to look out for themselves. In contrast, the *concern for others* dimension represents the extent to which individuals place the needs of others before those of themselves. Figure 14.4 graphically represents each style as a function of the degree of concern for self and the degree of concern for others.

The *integrating* style of conflict management involves problem solving through the exchange of information. Individuals who handle conflict in this way make use of any and all information provided to them about the context of the conflict and attempt to achieve an agreement on a particular course of action that fully satisfies the interests of both parties. This style of managing conflict reflects an attempt to balance a high concern for one's own needs with a high concern for the perceived needs of others. Rahim and Bonoma (1979) suggested that this strategy is most useful in dealing with issues that are complex in nature.

The *obliging* style of handling conflict involves making adjustments to satisfy others. Individuals who manage conflict with this style try to emphasize any and all common ground while ignoring differences, emphasizing the concern for others more strongly than the concern for self. This strategy is most useful when someone believes that he or she may be incorrect or that he or she cares much less about the outcome than do others.

Forcefully controlling the behavior of others to get what one wants is the focus of the *dominating* style of conflict management. When using this strategy, individuals effectively focus only on their own goals without much concern for others. Individuals who are dominating are often willing to "risk it all" to gain an unfair advantage against others. This conflict management style is most useful in situations where a decision needs to be made under pressure of time.

Figure 14.4 Rahim and Bonoma's Interpersonal Conflict Management Styles

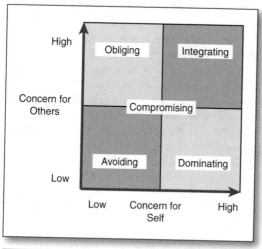

SOURCE: Based on Rahim and Bonoma (1979). Reprinted with permission.

Rahim and Bonoma (1979) suggested that when an issue is simple and insignificant, *avoidance* is the most effective way of managing conflict. Neither concern for self nor concern for others comes into play because the conflict is basically ignored. Handling conflict through avoidance usually involves some form of denial or distraction. The inherent risk in this strategy is that if the conflict is not minor or insignificant, individuals who select this strategy often end up disappointing themselves as well as others.

The *compromising* style of conflict management involves reaching an agreement that is mutually satisfactory to the self as well as to others. Individuals who make use of this style of conflict management are willing to give in a little bit to achieve a common goal. There is a moderate focus on their own needs and goals as well as a concern about the needs of others.

FOCUS ON INTERVENTION

Diversity Training

In an attempt to encourage some much needed dialogue concerning diversity-related issues, implementation of various diversity training initiatives has become increasingly popular. These initiatives are often educational programs designed to increase awareness about diversity through the use of readings, workshops and presentations, group exercises, writing assignments, and open discussions. They are meant to foster interaction between members of different groups (cultures, classes, genders, sexual orientations, etc.), and encourage critical thinking about diversity and its influences. In recent years, diversity training efforts have been geared toward multiple audiences, ranging from employees working in various organizations to students attending high schools, colleges, and universities. Targeting academic environments has proven particularly effective as diversity training initiatives have not only helped to shape the thinking of our future leaders, but have also allowed for the study of such initiatives and their effects on the student population.

As an intervention, some diversity training initiatives focus solely on the development of critical thinking about the students' own attitudes, values, beliefs, and/or stereotypes. To this end, some university-based programs have introduced diversity training into the core curriculum by incorporating the training into course material, designing specific courses, or conducting workshops solely dedicated to diversity. The University of Windsor in Canada, and the University of Wisconsin, Madison, in the United States are two examples of academic environments that use diversity training initiatives as a teaching tool that makes use of social psychological principles (such as the contact hypothesis and coalition building theories discussed earlier in this section) in order to promote tolerance and understanding of diversity. Yet, other university-based programs have also included an evaluative component in the diversity-training process, aimed at measuring the short-term and long-term effects of diversity training initiatives. This added research component allows for evaluation of the programs using methodologically sound, credible research (Gottfredson et al., 2008). The Multiversity Intergroup Dialogue Research Project is one such program developed at the University of Michigan and implemented at nine universities across the United States (Arizona State University; Occidental College; Syracuse University; the University of California, San Diego; the University of Maryland; the University of Massachusetts, Amherst; the University of Texas, Austin; and the University of Washington, Seattle). Implementing a randomized, multi-study design, these nine campuses use diversity training initiatives as both a means for educating students about diversity and a measure of the effectiveness of such programs, thus allowing for both research and intervention to occur together (DeAngelis, 2009). To date, some support has been demonstrated for the beneficial impact of diversity training initiatives in higher education through the aforementioned teaching tools (Sorensen, Nagda, Gurin, & Maxwell, 2009). Educational benefits, such as enhanced skills in communication, perspective taking, critical thinking, and conflict management are outcomes that have been reported in previous research, and give reason to support the development and implementation of such initiatives with the hope that these benefits may be transferable across the numerous spheres of our lives (Sorensen et al., 2009).

The above examples of diversity training initiatives and others like them are an important application of the theories of conflict management and resolution. Integrating theory, research, and practice within the realm of social psychology, these initiatives teach important skills that can be generalized to a number of settings ranging from the classroom to the workplace, with great implications for both programming and policy building (Sorensen et al., 2009). Such efforts to teach students about diversity are necessary if we want to promote tolerance, understanding, and critical thinking when it comes to diversity-related issues.

SUMMARY

Anywhere humans exist, diversity will exist; people differ in how they look, how they feel, and how they behave. Some of these differences are the result of learning. The social culture in which an individual grows up teaches its members to value certain behaviors or perspectives over others. Other differences are not the result of learning, for example, differences in sex, ethnic background, and socioeconomic status. None of these aspects of diversity operates in isolation from the others, and all of these differences have implications for how the world is experienced.

Some of the implications of diversity are positive and some are negative, and there is much yet to learn about how diversity affects individual and group behavior (van Knippenberg & Schippers, 2007). Diversity brings about the opportunity to learn new perspectives, and in so doing to increase creativity and innovativeness for both individuals and groups. However, it can also lead to negative effects, such as prejudice, discrimination, and even conflict. A clear understanding of when diversity leads to conflict is important because conflict itself may be beneficial or harmful. It can move us toward innovation and change, but it can hinder such efforts as well. Research and theories relating to conflict management and resolution offer ways in which to deal with conflict constructively so that negative outcomes are minimized and positive outcomes are maximized.

PART III

APPLYING SOCIAL PSYCHOLOGY TO ONE'S OWN LIFE

15

APPLYING SOCIAL PSYCHOLOGY TO PERSONAL RELATIONSHIPS

ANN L. WEBER

JENNIFER DOBSON

Chris dreads the end of the semester. A transfer student, Chris had struggled to adapt to a new campus and to keep up with a more demanding curriculum. Some things were the same, of course: reading assignments were excessive; tests were all scheduled at once; and professors still seemed to be in a different world, and to think very differently from students. It took constant effort to figure out how to play the game at the new campus.

But, other challenges were new and daunting: Chris felt lonely and even shy, a rare and unwelcome experience. At Chris's hometown campus, there had been familiar faces and old friends to ease the adjustment to college life. But, now far away from the familiar environment, this "better" school felt surprisingly isolated. Chris had felt excluded and a little lost, going through the motions of classes and studying, but with no direction or optimism.

Until Lee, that is. From the first time they sat beside each other in psych class, Chris and Lee had easily fallen into conversation. Lee was also an active participant in class, and chatted easily with other students—a social ease and self-confidence that Chris envied and admired. Lee had a year's more experience on campus than Chris, and offered good advice about getting around and fitting in. Where Chris frequently felt self-conscious, Lee seemed relaxed and spontaneous. For his part, Chris was more scholarly, and helped Lee to study better—and to enjoy it.

They found much in common. They liked the same courses, shared the same jokes about some professors' idiosyncrasies, and enjoyed the same sports and movies. They both loved hiking and outdoor activities. As they shared talk, time, and pastimes, they soon became close friends. Helping each other, they grew even closer. As months passed, they also felt personally attracted to each other, and friendship soon included romantic closeness.

Lee and Chris became inseparable partners. Chris began to feel confident and socially comfortable. Lee enjoyed academic success and worried less about grades. Superficial differences made their relationship interesting, which sometimes surprises those who know them both. Lee is the talker, telling the stories and getting the laughs; Chris is the quiet one who chimes in less often, but pays close attention to the goings-on. Friends call them "the odd couple," and joke that it must be true that opposites attract. But, despite some contrasting habits and traits—or maybe because of them—Chris and Lee feel content and well matched. They feel better together than either does apart.

Now, as summer break approaches, Chris realizes that so much remains unsaid. Soon they'll part ways and travel back to their different homes and summer jobs. In one sense, it's only a few months apart; but in another sense, that's equal to almost half the time they have already been together. Visits will cost too much, so they must rely on e-mail, phone calls, and texting. Now Chris can picture being back at home, keeping busy, but missing Lee—and losing a little of that recently won self-confidence.

Feeling depressed at the thought, Chris frowns—only to be interrupted by Lee's familiar voice: "Hey, didn't you see me? I've said your name twice. You're lost in thought. So what's the matter? You look like you've lost your best friend." Startled by Lee's apparent mind reading, Chris laughs and shakes off the concern for now. Together they walk off in search of coffee. Chris considers: "Now might be a good time to talk it out. But, then again, why spoil the moment with heavy conversation? Let's just enjoy the time we have together."

The above vignette serves as a means of introducing you to the focus of this chapter, which is about personal relationships and how you can use a social psychological perspective to help accomplish your goals in the world of interpersonal relationships. Here are a few questions that stem from the vignette and are addressed in the chapter.

- What leads people like Chris and Lee to get together in the first place?
- What factors account for the strengthening of relationships like Chris and Lee's?
- Nothing was said about how physically attracted the two students were to each other. How important

is physical attractiveness in the development of personal relationships?

- What do his worries about the effect of the summer separation on their relationship tell us about Chris's attachment needs?

The story of Chris and Lee, as even Chris realizes, is not the kind of grand romance that makes a good movie plot. Their love began with friendship, not the heavy looks and passionate clutches portrayed by gorgeous actors on screen. Their good times are not scripted; their laughter is neither great wit nor wacky comedy. And the challenge they face, of parting for summer break, is hardly the stuff of Shakespearean tragedy.

Figure 15.1 Love and Friendship

Most of us don't lead the magical lives of fictional characters; your romantic experiences may not seem as thrilling—or as traumatic—as those of characters in movies and books. But, love and friendship are necessarily important to you, and that partly explains why romantic tragedies and comedies are so appealing to wide audiences. Like Chris and Lee, Romeo and Juliet, Brad and Angelina, you too need closeness and passion in your life. And you too risk challenge, conflict, and disappointment (see Figure 15.1).

To apply social psychology to your relationship experiences, begin by recognizing two practical realities: First, human beings are social creatures who cannot live without closeness to others. Second, the skills we need to succeed in relationships do not come naturally. Like other social skills, relationship behaviors must be learned. This means effort, mistakes, trial and error—and a certain amount of luck!

Let's begin this chapter with the very human need to affiliate with and become close to others, which is where relationships themselves usually begin. In the next section, we consider the topic of interpersonal attraction, including what it means to feel attracted to specific others and some of the major determinants of attraction, such as proximity, familiarity, and physical attractiveness. In infancy, the process of attachment (the focus of the third section) might become our blueprint for developing later adult intimacy. The final section covers the selection process, which explores the qualities and experiences that draw us to others, what makes others seem attractive, and how we become closer.

Circumstances sometimes throw people together. Simply enrolling in the same class as someone else, or happening to sit beside him or her can prompt interaction and liking, eventually friendship, and even love. Social psychology offers several principles to account for such transformations. The most consistent lesson of social psychology is the power of *situational influences* (see Chapter 1). Circumstances affect you. You live your life in a social context, considering and reacting to the events and conditions surrounding you. In human experience, thoughts, feelings, and actions are shaped, at least in part, by the social environment. Someone you run into frequently becomes more familiar—and more likable. Chris and Lee were *pushed* together by common circumstances (a small campus, the same class), and *pulled* together by mutual interests (perceiving common preferences in pastimes, developing shared friendships). Once attracted, they selectively perceived what they liked in each other and downplayed their differences. For example, Chris saw Lee as socially confident and skilled; only later did Chris recognize that Lee too had needs for reassurance and social acceptance. In addition to individual differences and personality characteristics (the subject matter of personality psychology), their fate is also shaped by situational influences and the social perceptions they support. What circumstances have brought you into contact with others? How have your social perceptions and even wishful thinking shaped your social life as it is today?

THE NEED TO BE CLOSE

How much do you value relationships? How important is it for you to get close to others? Look at Table 15.1, a listing of several pairs of personal qualities. Suppose you could possess only one of the traits in each pair; which would you rather be? Make your choices before continuing.

This forced-choice task requires you to make a series of decisions that may be difficult in some cases. All of these traits are desirable qualities, but one quality in each pair reflects more of a *social orientation;* that is, a greater interest in relating to others (e.g., kindness) than in developing a personal ability or talent (e.g., strength). (In real life, of course, there is no reason why you should not cultivate both qualities in each pair.)

Table 15.1   Personal Qualities Menu

> *Instructions:* If you could have only one personal quality from each pair, circle the one you would choose. (An explanation of scoring is provided in text.)
>
> 1. Strong or kind?
> 2. Intelligent or generous?
> 3. Friendly or brave?
> 4. Helpful or artistic?
> 5. Popular or sympathetic?

To score yourself on this simple assessment of social interest, give yourself one point for choosing each of the following: *kind, generous, friendly, helpful,* and *sympathetic.* Each of these qualities requires a partner or recipient—someone to whom you can be kind or generous. Such qualities can be expressed only in a social situation. If you selected all or most of these traits, this (very crude) assessment suggests a stronger social orientation than if you selected none or very few of them.

Some people are more skilled at social interaction than others. But, all human beings are social creatures (Aronson, 2007). Human beings did not evolve to survive alone. Our earliest human ancestors lived in groups, cooperating in their efforts to obtain food and shelter and raise their offspring. Without your clan or community, you would be vulnerable, homeless, and hungry. For this reason, the ancient practice of punishing an offender by exile was often a death sentence. Recent research confirms a neurological basis for "social pain," the suffering that ensues as a result of rejection, loss, or group ostracism (MacDonald & Jensen-Campbell, 2010).

As social animals, all humans need social relationships, and we express this need in different ways. In his classic theory of a hierarchy of needs and motives, humanistic psychologist Abraham Maslow (1970) listed "belongingness" as the third most important motive after physiological and safety needs. Not far from food, water, and safety, one's closeness to others is vital to one's survival and well-being.

Losing a relationship means losing the resources it provides. In the opening story, Chris worries about the possibility of being separated from Lee—losing their connection and the unique pleasures of their intimacy. Obviously the closer the relationship, the more it means, and the greater the loss would be. In fact, research on regret shows that people's greatest regrets in life involve mistakes or missed opportunities in close social relationships, such as missing out on time with family, or cheating on a romantic partner, as opposed to nonsocial domains, such as work or school (Morrison, Epstude, & Roese, 2012). The research supports the importance of close social relationships for well-being, and the lifelong impact of losing or damaging such relationships. But, even the most casual connections with others provide benefits. Great loves begin with simple connections to others. Closeness begins with the most casual contact.

You meet and interact with many people before you form a single close relationship. Long before people form particular friendships or romances, they seek out the company of others, whether strangers or acquaintances. The presence of any warm body can seem reassuring and soothing. You are not alone; you face your fate with others of your own kind. Affiliating also provides unique rewards, including information about what's going on, strategies for how to behave and what to do, companionship, and humor. Imagine the casual conversation and joking that can erupt among the people seated in a dentist's waiting room. Ominous sounds that make a lone patient fearful can prompt laughter and social support in a group, even though the patients don't know each other.

In a classic social psychology experiment, Stanley Schachter (1959) investigated whether fear increases the desire to affiliate. He recruited women attending the University of Minnesota as participants. Students in one of two randomly assigned groups met with an "experimenter," clad in lab coat and stethoscope, who explained the procedure to come. In fact, he advised, this was a study of the effects of electric shock. Each volunteer would receive a series of electric shocks, and the physical effects would be measured. One group (the *low-fear* condition) heard reassurance that the shocks would be mild, resembling a tickle or tingle. But, women in the *high-fear* condition were specifically warned that the shocks would be severe—they would be painful and would hurt.

As the women pondered what was to come, they were asked to wait elsewhere while the menacing-looking equipment was set up. Each woman was then asked to indicate in writing one of three preferences: (a) She would wait alone, individually in her own comfortable room; (b) she would wait with some of the other women in a larger room; or (c) she didn't care. In fact, here the experiment ended. No shocks were ever administered.

Schachter's (1959) experiment examined not the effects of shock, but rather the effects of fear on preferring to affiliate. Indeed, the results indicated that fear did affect affiliative behavior. Some 63% of the women in the high-fear condition preferred to wait with others, whereas only 37% of those in the low-fear condition preferred to wait with others. The effect is summed up in a familiar aphorism: "Misery loves company."

Schachter (1959) concluded that fear motivates individuals to affiliate with others. Affiliation reduces the feeling of being alone, provides comfort, and even demonstrates how others are coping with a common threat. Everyone has moments of anxiety and fear, times when one would feel better with others around, even mere strangers. If you felt nervous about receiving treatment at the dentist's office, would you rather be alone beforehand or share the waiting room with other patients? To meet our social needs, we affiliate with others, endeavoring to become close with some of them.

ATTRACTION

Affiliation is a search for any "warm body"; in contrast, attraction is a pickier process. *Feeling attracted to someone* means knowing that not just anyone will do; you want especially to be with that particular person.

What is it that attracts you to someone else? The very term *attraction* suggests almost a force of physics, powerfully drawing you to another person, regardless of your conscious wishes or circumstances. In fact, some factors in interpersonal attraction are not a matter of taste or choice. Such factors as *proximity* and *familiarity* demonstrate social psychology's lesson on the power of situations. Let's briefly examine these factors in attraction and apply their lessons in everyday life.

Proximity and Familiarity

Most relationships begin with **physical proximity**; that is being near or accessible to another person. In the opening vignette, Chris reflects on having first met Lee when they sat next to each other in class. Being near someone makes eye contact easy and conversation natural. When two people sit near enough to learn about each other—their clothing preference, their voice and accent, when and how they laugh, other classes they are taking—they know when they are likely to see each other again. In just this way, the beginning of Chris and Lee's relationship lay in their proximity, in other words their nearness and frequent interaction and what they could therefore learn about each other.

With proximity comes interaction and the possibility of a relationship. Like many students, you might uncover the effects of proximity in relationship formation by considering your friendships. Think of your friends, especially childhood friends. Jot down the initials of their (original) last names. Are many of them "from" the same region of the alphabet as the initial of your own original last name? If so, proximity may have determined some of your friendships. In grade school and later, pupils are often assigned classroom seats on an alphabetical basis, so you tend to get to know best those who sit near you: *Ts* meet other *Ts*, and *Ss* and *Us*, and so forth. Thus, proximity might affect early, even lifelong, relationships.

The **proximity effect**—the tendency for physical and psychological nearness to increase interpersonal liking—was identified in a classic study by Leon Festinger and his colleagues (Festinger, Schachter, & Back, 1950). The researchers asked students in a large university housing complex to name their closest friends. Although the students had been assigned living spaces randomly, they overwhelmingly identified as their friends students who lived nearby, and with whom they had the most frequent contact rather than others with the same hometown, same major, or pastimes. Some locations make people more approachable or likable than others. For example, if you live near an exit or elevator, more people will pass your door than if you live at the far end of a hall. Even such accidental interactions facilitate people's liking for each other. It isn't your nearness to the exit that makes you appealing; it's the fact that using the exit brings you and others into regular contact with each other.

A more recent study by Back, Schmukle, and Egloff (2008) confirms the importance of proximity for attraction. In this study, students in a first year psychology course were randomly assigned seats in the classroom and instructed to introduce themselves to the other students in their row. One year later, the students were contacted again and asked to rate the intensity of their current friendships with the other students in the class. Even a full year after the initial seating arrangement, participants rated students who were randomly assigned to sit beside them as closer friends than students who did not sit nearby. This research shows the powerful effects of proximity in friendship formation. Sometimes friendships (and perhaps romantic relationships) can develop not because of shared interests, but simply as a matter of proximity brought about by chance.

Applying the proximity effect. This research suggests one obvious application of the proximity effect: If you want to meet people and form friendships, try to secure a living space, work space, or even parking space that brings you into contact with as many people as possible. At least some people may be regular passers-by, and more frequent interactions with them could be the beginning of something more. In effect, you can use the power of the situation by deliberately manipulating the locations you frequent and then enjoying the social benefits of situational influence. As shown in the study by Back and colleagues (2008), your proximity to others can have long-lasting effects.

Familiarity breeding contentment. Why should proximity and contact make someone likable in the first place? It doesn't always work that way. The more contact you have with an unpleasant person, the more you will dislike him or her—an effect known as **environmental spoiling** (Ebbeson, Kjos, & Konecni, 1976). Ebbeson and colleagues (1976) surveyed residents of a condominium complex, asking them how much they either liked or disliked fellow residents. Each respondent's list of those he or she liked or disliked in particular singled out neighbors living in the same section of the complex as the respondent.

Increased exposure to someone generally enhances preexisting feelings toward that person, whether positive *or* negative (Zajonc, 1968). In the absence of any prejudgment, however, frequent contact usually increases positive affect. This may be because mere exposure increases another's *familiarity*, a quality most people find reassuring and pleasant. Familiar faces are comforting; familiar people seem predictable, even after only superficial contact. And predictability offers a sense of order and control in an age of uncertainty and anxiety. Since the original research on familiarity and attraction in the 1960s, dozens of studies have tested this effect. Most studies have supported the claim that familiarity promotes attraction (e.g., Reis, Maniaci, Caprariello, Eastwick, & Finkel, 2011).

Frequent contact also increases *perceived similarity* (Moreland & Zajonc, 1982). Suppose you visit the library to search for a journal article and find another student searching the same part of the stacks. You make eye contact, nod, and smile, but don't speak. Another day you visit your favorite coffee shop, and notice that same student sitting at a table reading. Still another day, you go to a movie, and there is that same person standing in line for the same feature. By this time, you are making assumptions that you and the stranger have several things in common—courses, restaurant preferences, and taste in movies. The stranger seems less strange; each time you notice each other, you feel more comfortable, warmer in your greeting, and closer to making conversation.

Applying the familiarity effect. How can you apply the familiarity effect in your own life? If you want an appealing stranger to like you, make yourself *familiar* somehow. Don't "stalk" him or her! Contrived encounters may seem deceptive, if not threatening. But, when your contact is spontaneous express recognition; make eye contact. If the other person returns eye contact, smile—but don't push it. If you begin to talk, keep it pleasant. If possible, be the first one to end the conversation, and do so positively (e.g., "I hope to see you again"). Your goal is to become associated with all that is good about familiar others: pleasantness, friendliness, predictability, safety, and so forth. As noted by Zajonc (1968) and Ebbeson and colleagues (1976), exposure has an amplifying effect and can increase preexisting negative as well as positive attitudes: under certain circumstances, familiarity can indeed also breed contempt (Norton, Frost, & Ariely, 2007). But, keep in mind that the more common outcome of familiarity is liking (Zajonc, 1968, 2001). Familiarity alone is not enough for true closeness, but it is a vital first step in intimacy. It generally breeds not contempt, but increased contentment and acceptance, and it paves the way for real interaction and communication.

Physical Attractiveness

Once you have made contact with someone, how do you know whether this is a relationship you want to pursue? In addition to words and actions, most people judge each other to some extent by their looks. This reliance on physical attractiveness may be a form of the **primacy effect**, the tendency to be especially influenced by information that is presented first. Physical appearance is usually the earliest information you get about another person, someone you have seen, but not yet met. Even if you hear someone's voice on the phone first or meet through e-mail or web connections before you ever see each other, it is difficult not to imagine what the other person looks like.

But, what if instead of forming impressions based on scanty data, you had an early opportunity to get to know the person? Can genuine interaction overcome the primacy of looks alone? To study this question, researchers had to "rearrange" reality somewhat so that prospective dates would meet to interact on the basis of something other than evaluating each other's physical attractiveness.

The computer-match study. More than 40 years ago, researchers at the University of Minnesota explored reasons for dating choices by inviting new students to a Welcome Week dance (Walster, Aronson, Abrahams, & Rottmann, 1966). Several hundred first-year student volunteers signed up to attend. They were told (deceptively) that a computer would use each student's personal data to effect the best match for the evening. On arriving at the dance, the students were paired up for the evening. In exchange for free entertainment and soft drinks, participants were asked to check in a couple of times during the dance to complete a few forms. These questionnaires asked the students to provide self-ratings (e.g., about their self-esteem), and ratings of their partners (e.g., about their physical attractiveness, about how similar they were to themselves). At the end of the evening participants privately reported whether they would like to see their "matched" dates again.

When the data were analyzed, only one variable predicted whether a given person wanted to see his or her date again: the date's physical attractiveness! Not the date's conversational skills, not the two persons' similarity to each other, and not the respondent's own self-esteem. This surprising finding (at the time), confirming a human preference for looks over other qualities has been reported countless times in psychology

texts and classrooms. In the decades since the computer-match study, the power of looks in selecting dates and mates has been supported (e.g., Hatfield & Sprecher, 1986; Sprecher, 1989), although with some qualifications. For example, men seem to value looks more than women (Feingold, 1990). Recent research using data gathered from online dating sites also demonstrates the power of physical attractiveness in attracting dating interest (e.g., Brand, Bonatsos, D'Orazio, & DeShong, 2010). What then does physical attractiveness "mean" to us?

Looks matter. Physical attractiveness does matter. Attractive people are pleasing to look at. But, the importance of looks extends well beyond the gratifying experience of finding another person attractive. People associate good looks with other good things about the person. In a seminal study, Dion, Berscheid, and Walster (1972) found that attractive people are expected, purely on the basis of their looks, to be better people: sensitive, sexually responsive, interesting, and sociable. Three decades later meta-analyses of a large number of studies confirmed Dion and colleagues' initial finding that attractive people are judged more positively than unattractive people (Langlois et al., 2000); in sum, attractive people are regarded as having better social appeal, interpersonal competence, occupational competence, and adjustment. Such common assumptions about looks make up the ***physical attractiveness stereotype***: the general expectation that a physically attractive person has positive qualities while an unattractive person has negative qualities. The physical attractiveness stereotype can have powerful consequences. For example, employers who are offered similar résumés from two people, one good-looking and the other not, generally prefer attractive job applicants, inferring that they will be better employees (e.g., Hamermesh & Biddle, 1994). Also, good-looking people tend to get higher job evaluations than their less attractive peers (Hamermesh & Parker, 2005). The physical attractiveness stereotype also plays into political decisions. Research shows that uninformed voters (that is, voters who are not knowledgeable about the political issues) are more likely to vote for attractive political candidates than unattractive candidates (Stockemer & Praino, 2015). In contrast, people considered unattractive can be passed over for job advancement, and in legal proceedings can even be assumed to be more capable of criminal behavior (e.g., Efran, 1974; Esses & Webster, 1988; Hatfield & Sprecher, 1986).

However, a bias is not a rule, and in the case of the physical attractiveness stereotype it isn't even accurate. Ample research shows that despite expectations, for virtually every quality and virtue measured (e.g., intelligence, friendliness, honesty), better-looking people are no better or worse than people of average looks (e.g., Miller & Perlman, 2009). Still, the attractiveness stereotype is a very strong bias, as demonstrated in the "computer-match" dance study. Must only the best-looking people win the competition for closeness? Apparently not. Looks matter, but in the long run most of us are looking not so much for a prize as for a match.

The matching phenomenon. Think of some celebrities—movie stars, singers, politicians, athletes, and so forth—and list several whom you consider extremely physically attractive. Then on a scale from 1 *(very unattractive)* to 10 *(very attractive),* assign each celebrity a rating. Now, what rating would you give yourself? If you rated the celebrities higher than average, but yourself low (compared to them), how does this make you feel? What are your chances of being attractive to the sort of person you consider most physically attractive?

It can be sobering for many of us to realize that our looks sometimes do not match the looks of the persons we find desirable. If you rated yourself a five—maybe a six on a good day— how can you capture the heart of a nine or ten, even one you know and have things in common with (e.g., an extremely good-looking classmate)? Fortunately, despite any evolutionary preferences for beauty, most people seek long-term partners who do not exceed, but rather *match* their own perceived level of attractiveness.

If a five asks a ten for a date, what are the chances the ten will accept? You're more likely to be rejected if you aim too high; but you'll be disappointed and dissatisfied with your partner if you keep thinking you aimed too low and could do better. The *matching phenomenon,* preferring a long-term partner who is similar to oneself in looks (and other qualities), reduces the chances of either rejection or dissatisfaction (Folkes, 1982; Hitsch & Ariely, 2007; Shaw Taylor, Fiore, Mendelsohn, & Cheshire, 2011).

Test the matching phenomenon yourself. Take a good look at the long-term couples you know. Do they seem to "belong" together, looks-wise? Now, look at couples who have not been together very long. Could you predict on the basis of whether their attractiveness levels match, whether they are likely to stay together?

A recent experimental investigation in the Netherlands by Van Straaten, Engels, Finkenauer, and Holland (2009) had university students converse with an other-sex confederate whose physical attractiveness was varied (high vs. low). Consistent with the matching phenomenon (and evidence of cross-cultural generalizability), after the conversation, participants indicated more interest in dating the confederate when they were similar in attractiveness to the confederate (either both were low or both were high in attractiveness) than when they were dissimilar (low and high or high and low).

However, Van Straaten and colleagues (2009) went beyond other research by content analyzing the conversations to determine the degree to which participants engaged in *approach behaviors* suggestive of investment in the relationship with the confederate (i.e., behaviors reflecting interpersonal warmth, interest, attraction, and responsiveness). The analyses showed that the attractive men acted in a manner consistent with the matching phenomenon. They displayed more approach behavior with the attractive confederate than with the less attractive confederate, whereas the less attractive men displayed more approach behavior with the less attractive confederate than with the attractive confederate. This finding is indeed significant because it provides the first experimental demonstration of how in the very early stages of a relationship, men will engage in behaviors that signal to a potential mate their interest in having the relationship develop further. On the other hand, although as noted above the women's dating interests corresponded with the matching phenomenon, their approach behaviors did not correspond with whether or not the confederate's attractiveness matched their attractiveness. The researchers interpreted this finding as consistent with the evidence (e.g., Baumeister & Vohs, 2004) that "women are more reserved in the communication of attraction to potential mates" (p. 693).

Applying the lessons of looks. So much research and writing has been done on the power of physical appearance that it is difficult to choose any single application. Knowing that looks matter, you should take your appearance seriously especially when others will be evaluating you, for example, as a potential date, friend, partner,

or employee. If you think of yourself as rather low in physical attractiveness, identify your other fine qualities and emphasize them. Make them visible and act on them; demonstrate your kindness, wit, generosity, humor, and so forth. Unlike the women in the Van Straaten and colleagues study (2009), if you are a woman and wish to have more control of the people you select to develop new relationships, consider being more discriminating in your display of approach (relation-promoting) behaviors.

Keep the importance of looks *in perspective.* Evolutionary forces have shaped many of our own (and other species') preferences for the health and fertility promised by good looks (Buss, 2008). However, human behavior is complex, influenced by biology, but not driven by instinct. The looks and qualities people find attractive differ across cultures around the world. See the Culture Capsule box for a perspective on how interpersonal attraction varies from one culture to another.

CULTURE CAPSULE

Culture and Interpersonal Attraction

Who attracts you? Your preferences may seem personal, unique to your personal history, needs, and taste. But, much of what you find appealing about someone else is determined by your culture—what you have *learned* to value and seek. Mate preference is more strongly associated with one's culture than with one's sex (male or female), or gender (masculine or feminine) (Goodwin, 1999).

Ours is an *individualistic* culture where personal successes and accomplishments are valued. We like winners, people who stand out and people whom others will prize, admire, and even desire. But, a different set of values emerges in cultures that value group success over individual achievement. In *collectivist* cultures, such as China and India where community cooperation is valued more than individual distinction, a potential mate is especially prized for practical virtues, such as possessing money and household-management skills (Goodwin & Tang, 1991; Sprecher & Chandak, 1992). Western cultures emphasize autonomy and encourage young adults to develop independent lives and find mates of their own choosing. But, in traditional Eastern societies, such as Pakistan, India, and Nepal the goal of marriage is social order, and thus intimate relationships are a means to preserve family unity and social order (Goodwin, 1999; Hamon & Ingoldsby, 2003).

A culture's economic and family values affect each of its members' relationship values. In urban mobile cultures, such as those in the United States and Canada, a given individual seeking a friend or partner has available a much larger "pool," and might have the luxury of choice. In contrast, individuals in developing economies, or in rural and isolated regions, have far less choice. In such places, close relationships depend greatly on proximity and availability, and therefore once formed, they are hard to replace. For someone in a subsistence economy, an arranged marriage is greeted not with scorn but with gratitude; if not for the arrangement, how else would this individual even find a mate (Moghaddam, Taylor, & Wright, 1993)? In this sense, culture is a very large-scale version of "situational influence" on relationship choices! How would you react if an arranged marriage were advised for you? Your likely reaction gives apt testimony to the extent to which we truly are products of our cultures.

ATTACHMENT

Have you ever had your heart broken? The loss of a close relationship is universally painful. How did you feel and behave? Common reactions are distraction, anger, sadness, despair, loss of sleep, and loss of the ability to concentrate. Perhaps you argued or wept. Compare these reactions to those of a baby whose mother leaves, even briefly. The child is placed in a crib or in the arms of the babysitter and watches as the mother walks away. (If you have ever cared for younger siblings or other children, you may have been the "villain" in a similar scenario.) The baby cries out wailing in apparent sadness, or screaming in what certainly seems like rage.

Infant Attachment

What is happening in these interactions? The child is reacting to *separation,* in this case to the loss of the most important person in his or her life. In the process of *attachment,* the human infant associates satisfaction and need gratification with only one or two specific others (Bowlby, 1969/1982). Many years later, the human adult similarly sees an intimate partner as essential to well-being and happiness and becomes attached to that individual. If that relationship ends, the adult is likely to express grown-up versions of the symptoms of infantile **separation distress**; that is attention focused on the lost other and

extreme discomfort at that person's inaccessibility (Weiss, 1975).

Many psychologists argue that the blueprint for later life relationships is drawn when you are still a baby, by your first experience of being cared for by your parents, particularly your mother or primary caregiver. To be fed, cuddled, and protected, you must be sure your caregiver is near or signal your need for that person. Missing or losing your attachment figure triggers a series of attachment behaviors, including looking for the person, pleading for contact, moving toward him or her, or clinging to prevent abandonment (Shaver & Hazan, 1994). This action pattern evolved as an effective way to bring back a too-distant caregiver.

Individuals differ in how they express separation distress. For all our variety, however, attachment behaviors have been found to fall into a few basic patterns. Understanding these patterns—your own as well as other people's—can help you to achieve more satisfactory relationships.

Research among infants by developmental psychologist Mary Ainsworth and her colleagues (Ainsworth, Blehar, Waters, & Wall, 1978) identified three patterns of attachment behavior. Infants were separated from their mothers by barriers, or were introduced to a strange person, or environment—all situations that triggered separation distress. Although the trigger situation was similar for all the babies, reactions reflected one style of secure attachment and two styles of insecure attachment.

1. *Secure attachment style:* Most infants were unhappy while the attachment figure was away, but were quickly soothed when she returned.

2. *Insecure attachment style, anxious/ambivalent:* A minority of insecure infants acted unhappy about being separated, but were still fretful and clingy when the attachment figure returned.

3. *Insecure attachment style, avoidant:* Most insecure infants behaved as if they were unconcerned with the presence or absence of the attachment figure. They did not cry when she left and avoided contact when she returned.

Why the differences? Children's attachment patterns most likely develop from a combination of biological influences (e.g., inherited traits) and social learning (e.g., the attachment figure's responsiveness to the child's actions, like giving insufficient attention). A nervous or unwell child with a stressed or overworked parent is likely not to receive "enough" attention, contributing to an insecure style (Shaver & Hazan, 1994). Set in place early in life, the attachment categories of infancy appear to endure as attachment styles in adult relationships. Secure babies grow to be secure adults, with measurably different relationship choices and experiences, which we now consider and review.

Adult Attachment Styles

Your infantile attachment was not a matter of choice for you; you were born into a particular family arrangement. But, as an adult you are not assigned friends and partners; you must choose them. As an adult making such choices, you know that every relationship entails risks; to get close to someone else, you must open up, self-disclose, and become vulnerable. In developing closeness with someone, you run two great risks: rejection and betrayal. Another person may reject you, that is, refuse to become close to you. Or once a person is close, he or she might betray you; that is, deceive or harm you. Is intimacy worth such a risk? Based on experience, do you feel you can count on people, or do you mistrust them? Are you optimistic about love, or do you expect others sooner or later to abandon you?

Infants' distinctive patterns of attachment appear to continue into childhood, and later to characterize adults' reactions to love, threat, and loss in their romantic experiences. Shaver, Hazan, and their colleagues invited adults to provide descriptions of their attachment behaviors in response to newspaper questionnaires about life, love, and work. The participants' attachment patterns fell into patterns similar to those of secure and insecure infants (e.g., Shaver & Hazan, 1994; Shaver, Hazan, & Bradshaw, 1988).

At about the same time, Main, Kaplan, and Cassidy (1985) used interviews to assess the attachment styles of parents and to relate these to their infants' response styles. Combining such techniques as those used by Main and colleagues and those used by Shaver and colleagues, attachment researchers have confirmed that in our adult relationships, we replay early-life patterns of dealing with closeness, separation, and loss. In 1990, Bartholomew developed more complex assessment techniques, identifying not three, but four styles of adult attachment.

Assess Your Attachment Style

Before reading further, see if you can *identify your own attachment style.* First, reflect for a moment on your own adult relationship experiences. Now examine Table 15.2 and review the different patterns found in people's attitudes toward closeness. Choose the one pattern that best sums up your particular approach to being close. Then we'll examine how to interpret your choice.

The four patterns described in Table 15.2 refer to four patterns of adult attachment identified by Bartholomew (1990; see also Miller & Perlman, 2009):

1. *Secure:* trusting, comfortable with closeness and interdependence

2. *Preoccupied:* needful of closeness, worried about abandonment

3. *Fearful:* afraid of rejection, mistrustful, shy

4. *Dismissing:* self-reliant, independent, uninterested in intimacy

Table 15.2   Views of Self and Others

> *Instructions:* Choose the statement that best reflects your attitude toward close relationships. (See text for interpretation and explanation.)
>
> 1. I am comfortable being emotionally close to another person. I enjoy depending on others and having them depend on me. I enjoy socializing with others. I feel optimistic about my close relationships.
>
> 2. I need a close relationship to feel good about myself. I often find that others don't want to get as close as I want to get. I worry about losing my partner. I feel jealous if our relationship seems to be threatened.
>
> 3. I generally feel shy in social situations. I have difficulty trusting others or depending on them. I fear being hurt or rejected by others if I attempt to become close to them.
>
> 4. I do not need close relationships and prefer to rely on myself. I would rather have independence than intimacy. Getting close to someone just isn't worth the trouble involved.

SOURCE: Adapted from Bartholomew (1990); Miller & Perlman (2009).

Each of these adult attachment styles balances one's view of oneself with one's view of others. Secure individuals have positive views of both themselves, and the trustworthiness of close others. Preoccupied individuals have poor views of themselves, but want to be close to others. Fearful persons are unhappy with themselves, and do not trust closeness. And dismissing individuals see themselves as all right, especially if they are untroubled by closeness with others.

Applying Attachment Lessons

You can apply research on attachment by considering the dynamics of different combinations of attachment styles. Suppose, in one couple, a man has developed a preoccupied attachment style, whereas his female partner is more dismissing. He seeks her presence, reaching for her and making plans for their time together. But, she feels uncomfortable with that much closeness and pulls away in order to feel more independent. As she does so, canceling plans or behaving coolly, he feels threatened and needy. He becomes more clinging, hoping for warmth and contact—but she only pulls away that much more. Both are unhappy, but perhaps they are unable to explain their unhappiness or what to do about it.

In your own life, you can be more practical in identifying what you need in a relationship and how best to interact with others. Identify your feelings about yourself and others, and be realistic about how to meet both your own and others' complex needs. Begin a relationship by being honest in your early interactions, and communicating your needs and goals as best you can. If you need reassurance in relationships, communicate this clearly to the other person; don't expect anyone to read your mind. Listen carefully to what your partner says and seeks. The combination or confrontation of your two styles is also important. If one of you needs reassurance, but the other does not or even cannot make eye contact, both of you will suffer.

Suppose that you have identified yourself as possessing a particular attachment style, for example, an insecure style, but you want to act and feel secure. Is change possible? A recent meta-analysis (i.e., a study that statistically combines the results of several separate studies) of attachment stability found a moderate correlation between attachment style in early childhood and attachment style later in life, but no relationship between attachment styles measured more than 15 years apart (Pinquart, Feubner, & Ahnert, 2013). Therefore, attachment styles can and do change. Attachment itself is shaped by experience.

Unsuccessful relationship behaviors can be unlearned, and more successful ones can be tried and reinforced to replace them. But, before you can alter your patterns, you must know what you are starting with, where you want to go, and how to close the gap. This journey begins with self-awareness, so keep in mind that you and everyone else need attachments, and that your life experience led you to develop a distinctive style, which may be amenable to change.

THE SELECTION PROCESS

We have already considered some factors that serve as important positive influences on people's desire to approach others for the purpose of establishing a relationship, including familiarity and physical attractiveness. Decades of research have identified several other such factors, including shared values, beliefs, interests, and certain personality characteristics, such as warmth, trustworthiness, and vitality (Finkel & Baumeister, 2010). Another important factor influencing relationship formation and satisfaction is **social network approval**, which refers to perceived approval of a romantic relationship by friends and family (Felmlee, 2001). So, in contrast to Shakespeare's Romeo and Juliet, if your parents and friends disapprove of your choice in romantic partners, this disapproval is likely to lead to less satisfaction and commitment in your relationship, and to not bring you and your partner closer together (Sinclair, Hood, & Wright, 2014).

Whatever the mix of factors, most people do find at least some others attractive and then face the next hurdle: establishing actual closeness; that is an interaction or a relationship that is real for both parties, not just a fantasy in the mind of the one who feels attracted to the other. Keeping your attraction to yourself gets you nowhere. Similarly, finding another person appealing to look at, without knowing more about the person's personality and whether you have important values and interests in common, leaves much yet to be done: You must meet, interact, and assess the desirability of getting closer. This process risks rejection or the possibility of desiring no further interaction because "there is nothing there." How does one begin?

The T-Shirt Study

Long before the Internet made it possible to "meet" others in cyberspace via online dating sites, people relied on other strategies: blind dates, friends' recommendations, and personal ads. Alan Gross (1983) and his colleague India McHale created an ingenious low-tech study of the first meeting between prospective dates, combining strategies of two popular sources of information: parties and personal ads. The 200 participants for this study were single, straight college men and women, who first provided information that a prospective date might want to know, such as their college major, religion, sports and music preferences, drinking and smoking habits, and personality traits. The participants attended a mixer, with each donning a T-shirt (yellow for women and blue for men) custom-printed with his or her own "personal ad" and identifying number. The ad included the student's first name, his or her major, and some personal information/preferences, something like the following:

(19)

Alex

Psychology

Soccer, Rock, Jewish

Movies, Sense of humor!

Each participant's goal was to speak with as many participants of the other sex as possible and to identify possible dates. Each was required to interact for no more than five minutes and then move on. After an hour of excited number seeking, participants made their final rankings of those they would most like to date. They were permitted to exchange contact information if they hit it off during their five-minute meetings.

(Keep in mind that this innovative approach to attraction research was devised three decades before today's real-life "speed dating" programs became popular.)

Among other findings, Gross (1983) discovered that once his participants had engaged in all their face-to-face "minidates," physical attractiveness actually *lost* much of its selection power. It turned out that participants did not use looks to select each new date—they didn't need to. Because each T-shirt displayed the personal information necessary to decide whether to initiate interaction and what they could talk about; it was not necessary to rely on physical appearance as an indicator of each person's date potential. Conversations were easier because the T-shirts were the introductions. A person's looks are usually the first information you get about him or her, so you rely on physical appearance as a *filter* for choosing others and forming impressions. But, here participants could consult others' "labels" as a guide to their "contents"—eerily similar to deciding what brand to buy based on the information, not the visual design, of the packaging.

Drawing on these findings, Gross (1983) "envision[s] rooms throughout the social world filled with singles sporting descriptive T-shirts— or at least lengthy nametags." Now the web offers us just such lengthy "name tags" in the form of social network profiles, online dating sites, chat rooms, and other shortcuts to making friends and dates. Just like live interactions, most of the resulting virtual meetings take place because similar interests and attracting forces bring people together. The protagonists in the 1998 movie *You've Got Mail* first meet in a chat room for book lovers, not realizing they are both in the bookselling business—and are in fact archrivals for the same customers. Their similarities have drawn and kept them together long before they discover and deal with their differences.

If you've seen *You've Got Mail,* you might have wondered what would happen to the characters played by Tom Hanks and Meg Ryan after the credits rolled. In other words, do online relationships last and are couples who meet online just as likely to be satisfied as couples who meet

in more traditional ways? Researchers in the United States conducted an online survey using a nationally representative sample of 19,131 people who got married between 2005 and 2012 to address these questions (Cacioppo, Cacioppos, Gonzaga, Ogburn, & VanderWeele, 2013). Participants indicated how they met their spouse (e.g., online or offline), whether they were still married, and their level of marital satisfaction. Approximately one third of participants indicated that they had met their spouse online. Surprisingly, participants who met online reported feeling slightly more satisfied with their marriages, and were slightly more likely to still be married than participants who met through traditional venues like work or school. Relationships that begin online may be stronger and longer lasting because people often feel more comfortable expressing their true selves to others online (McKenna, Green, & Gleason, 2002), and greater self-disclosure has been shown to lead to greater relationship satisfaction. It is also possible that people who meet online end up in more satisfying marriages because they have access to a larger "pool" of potential dates to choose from, resulting in more compatible matches. Either way, it is clear that the Internet is changing the way that people date and find spouses, possibly for the better.

Qualitative research on online dating shows that people put a lot of effort into crafting their online profile to make themselves appear desirable to others. In one study of online dating profiles, Manning (2014) conducted a content analysis of how people construct (using language and photos) their profiles. In this study, Manning (2014) interviewed 30 people about their online dating profiles, asking participants to describe themselves and what they were looking for in a dating partner. The researcher then asked participants to discuss discrepancies between their stated values, attitudes, and beliefs, and what they had written in their profiles. Manning studied the **rhetorical devices** (i.e., the language used to convey a certain message to persuade the listener or reader) that participants used in their online profiles, and in the interviews to attract a partner and to present themselves in a positive light. Not surprisingly, he found that participants wanted to find a romantic partner who was laid back, good looking, financially stable, and funny (among other positive traits). However, many of these characteristics were not specifically stated in the online ads. Manning concluded that including certain information in an online ad (such as a desire for an attractive or financially stable partner) is off-limits because it makes the writer appear desperate, or as though he or she doesn't know how to "play the [dating] game." Participants also used vague language in their online ads, and avoided including certain information about themselves, such as recent life changes like divorce (does this remind you in any way of our discussion about stigma in Chapter 12?). Manning argued that this strategy allowed participants to present themselves in a positive light. This research comparing online dating profiles with interviews with the people who created the profiles allows researchers to learn more about *how* people construct themselves and their desired dating partners. The results of this study suggest that looking for a romantic partner online may be similar to other forms of online "shopping." In both cases, the cliché "buyer beware" rings true.

Selection Process Lessons and Applications

Selection of dating or mating partners is a process. Conversations don't just "happen"—people must create and join them. However much one longs for attachment and however appealing you find another person, you or the other person must do or say something to establish a connection. After all, the T-shirt study suggests that once you learn to enjoy each other's company, you can overlook the fact that the other person's looks rate somewhat less than a perfect ten.

Yet, even when you do feel well matched to the person who interests you—another six to your own six, for example, or someone who shares your passion for the same social causes—you may

still hesitate to express your interest. Fear of rejection can overwhelm desire. The longer it takes for either person to express interest, the less likely anything will happen at all—an opportunity lost, a road not taken. That "first move" is difficult for both men and women to make—yet each wishes the other would make it (Regan, 2003). For example, Vorauer and Ratner (1996) asked men and women to imagine meeting an attractive person and having a really good conversation, after which neither expressed interest in seeing the other again. How, the researchers asked their respondents, did they explain this failure to follow up? Participants generally blamed their own inaction on fear of rejection, but blamed the other person's inaction on lack of interest. Note that this is a classic case of negative attribution bias. The participants fully blamed themselves (not the other person) for the negative outcome (no follow-up) by seeing themselves as fearful, and also as not encouraging the interest of the other person. This likely reflects an all too common scenario consisting of an unfortunate set of relationship undermining negative attributions possessed by two individuals who have missed a promising opportunity to get to know each other.

Unfortunately, when you assume the other person is simply not interested in you (when in fact he or she may be just as afraid of rejection as you are), your silence guarantees the relationship will stop before it ever gets started. The lesson? Avoid making assumptions, except to infer that the other's concerns and motivations are likely a lot like yours. Learn to express interest while still saving face. The next time both of you fear rejection, take responsibility yourself, and say something!

Also, you should keep in mind that although you may worry about (even fear) the possibility of rejection, you may overestimate the impact of rejection on you. This is suggested by the rather counterintuitive findings of a meta-analytic review of over 100 experimental studies on the psychological effects of social exclusion (e.g., rejection, ostracism) (Blackhart, Nelson, Knowles, & Baumeister, 2009). The results indicated that when participants experienced an act of rejection, their emotional states did shift in a negative direction (most starting in the positive range); however, the resulting emotions were not negative, but were neutral or slightly positive. According to the researchers, the rejected people generally did not report feeling badly, but they "did not on average report affective states that could be described as negative, distress, or upset" (Blackhart et al., p. 300). Similarly, rejection produced no detectable drop in self-esteem. Consider drawing on Blackhart and colleagues' results to overcome any hesitation you might have the next time you want to reach out to establish contact with someone who has just happened to catch your eye.

As you are aware, making that initial connection with someone is only the first step in a relationship that may run its course in no time, or may last a lifetime. The development of relationships is a broad and complex topic and extends well beyond the scope of this chapter. But, here is one thing to contemplate as you anticipate future relationships, or are involved with current ones. Most people understand, and the research evidence shows, that one key to better functioning and more satisfying relationships is when the individuals are there to provide support and comfort in difficult and stressful times when negative events occur. But, what many people fail to recognize is the importance of how individuals respond to good events. In an article titled "Will You Be There for Me When Things Go Right?" Gable, Gonzaga, and Strachman (2006) found in dating couples that supportive reactions to positive events (e.g., showing interest, enthusiasm, pleasure) were more strongly associated with relationship well-being and relationship endurance (no breakup) than were responses to negative events.

CONCLUSION: THE SCIENCE OF CLOSENESS

Relationships are important. Humans are social creatures; we need each other to survive and thrive. Beyond our family attachments, we must

learn to make intelligent choices in partners. The study of our relationships is also very important and useful. Our understanding of how we influence and care about each other is vital to life and happiness. If successful closeness is your goal, then applied social psychology is an excellent tool. *Use* social psychology to achieve an understanding of the situational forces that affect your closeness to others. What you learn will enable you to act more effectively in determining your experiences, and in beginning and developing your social and personal relationships.

Above other fields in psychology, social psychology confronts the power of the situation—a power to which no one is immune. Circumstances can throw people together and offer (or deny) attractions and opportunities for friendship and passion. But, we should not be victims of these influences. By learning about them, we learn how to actively apply them. Anticipate these influences and work with situations, and you will lead your life instead of being led by it. Will your personal relationships be shaped more by chance or by choice? That may be up to you! If you opt for choice, not chance, then happy choices are those that are *informed*. So begin simply by appreciating the value of applied social psychology in your everyday life. You will find that the more you come to understand and apply the social psychology of personal relationships, the better and more fulfilling yours will become.

SUMMARY

The need to be close to others varies among people. You may express this need differently than other people you know. Being attracted to another person is a function of several factors, including proximity, familiarity, and physical attractiveness. We tend to be attracted to physically attractive people, although we are more likely to look for a long-term partner who is equal to us in physical attractiveness. The types of attachment patterns we have as children with our caregivers seem to continue into adulthood and affect our adult relationships. In the context of the host of factors that affect relationships, people must still act on their attractions and desires. In order to select a partner, a person must be aware of the individual and then interact with and assess the likelihood of establishing a relationship with him or her. The chapter reviewed some lessons from social psychology that if appropriately applied can help you to function more effectively in your interpersonal world.

16

APPLYING SOCIAL PSYCHOLOGY TO THE CLASSROOM

RANDOLPH A. SMITH

CHAPTER OUTLINE

Robert is confused about school and things that he sees going on in that environment. For example, his psychology teacher mentions Freud almost every week—Robert wonders how anyone so smart can possibly believe in Freud's ideas. Robert is also confused about his performance in the class. Although he always makes plans to begin studying several days in advance of the exam, he inevitably finds himself doing other things such as going out for pizza with friends, updating his Facebook page, or playing video games so that he ends up having to cram the night before the exam. Still, after taking the exam, Robert believes that he has done pretty well until he gets his grade back; he usually has scored considerably lower than he thought he had.

Juliane is Robert's psychology teacher—she, too, is mystified about events taking place in her class. As a new teacher, Juliane had looked forward to interacting with students, becoming partners in the learning enterprise. Instead, she finds herself thinking about "those darn students" who want to argue over points, seem bored and disinterested, and are more interested in grades than learning.

She wonders why the students aren't as interested in the material as she is. Finally, although psychology provides many insights into human behavior, Juliane finds that students will learn an answer for the test, but will not change their preexisting opinions.

- Why is Robert prone to think that his teacher believes Freud's ideas when she teaches about Freud?
- Why does Robert tend to avoid studying as hard as he could for his exams?
- Why does Robert usually overestimate his exam performance?
- Why do Juliane and her students seem to be at odds with each other?
- Why does Juliane often find that her students are disinterested in the course material?
- Why are Juliane's students stubborn about changing their ideas about topics she covers in class?

Although many social psychology texts examine the application of social psychological knowledge to various arenas of life, such as education, law, health, and the environment, no leading texts come down to a more personal level by systematically addressing an arena that so greatly affects (and perhaps interests) you: the classroom. You have plenty of experience with school; after all, you have been attending school since you were a young child. However, aspects of school may have been confusing or mysterious to you. This chapter may provide you with answers to some of those mysteries and, perhaps, make dealing with your academic life a bit easier in the future. The chapter focuses in particular on how students and instructors think about and relate to each other. The neglect of the classroom as a "social psychology laboratory" in social psychology texts seems unusual because the classroom dynamics between student and teacher involve many important social psychology phenomena and accordingly many opportunities for students to draw on those phenomena for their own personal uses/interventions.

This chapter delineates several classic social psychological findings and demonstrates how they apply to your classroom experiences and interactions. One thing this chapter requires of you is to recognize that to understand the dynamics of the classroom, you must take into account two main perspectives: that of the student and that of the instructor (see Figure 16.1).

Furthermore, be advised that several of the phenomena that we review can interfere with how effectively you deal with your academic life (as well as your life beyond academia). If being forewarned is being forearmed, the material considered may help you to anticipate these social psychological patterns and, perhaps, to take steps to minimize their negative impact on you. For example, Beaman, Barnes, Klentz, and McQuirk (1978) found that undergraduate students' rates of helping could be increased by alerting students to the bystander effect, which, as noted in Chapter 1, refers to the finding that a person is less likely to help in an emergency with other bystanders present. Other research evidence likewise has shown that alerting an audience to social psychological phenomena may help its members to avoid mistaken judgments. In examining social psychology concepts at work in the classroom, you will find two major categories of phenomena: cognitive errors and self-perceptions.

Cognitive Errors and Student–Teacher Relations

Cognitive errors are errors that people make in their thought processes. Because of these errors, people make predictable mistakes when interacting with and judging others. This section discusses three common cognitive errors. It is quite likely that you will recognize yourself in some of the descriptions of these errors. If so, do not worry; they are quite common. However, do pay attention to these errors so that you may be in a position to try to minimize them in the future.

Figure 16.1   Different Perspectives in the Classroom

SOURCE: Photos Courtesy of Centre for Flexible Learning, University of Windsor.

Fundamental Attribution Error

Have you ever found yourself wondering why a teacher holds a belief that you think is outlandish? For example, you may have listened to a professor talk about Sigmund Freud and wondered to yourself, "How can an educated person believe that stuff?" If so, you may have been guilty of making the fundamental attribution error, which was first introduced in Chapter 1, and as a concept of widespread relevance, appears in several other chapters in this book.

Classic study of the fundamental attribution error. Much social psychology research has dealt with the **fundamental attribution error**, that is, the tendency people have to focus on personal causes of other people's behavior (i.e., to make internal attributions) and to downplay the influence of situational causes (i.e., to not make external attributions). Thus, to put a different spin on the example provided in Chapter 1, if you walk into class late because you had a flat tire on the way to school, and your teacher concludes that your tardy behavior is due to the fact that you are a lazy student who overslept, then your teacher is guilty of making a fundamental attribution error. Jones and Harris (1967) conducted a classic study on the fundamental attribution error. They had college students read either pro-Castro or anti-Castro essays dealing with Fidel Castro's rule of Cuba and told the students that the writer either had chosen the position, or had been assigned the position (as in a debate). Then, the researchers asked the students to infer the attitudes of the writers. The results showed that students made pro- or anti-Castro attributions based solely on the content of the essays. For example, if an essay was pro-Castro, the students assumed that the writer held pro-Castro attitudes *regardless* of whether the writer had chosen the position or the position had been determined by an external situational factor (i.e., being assigned to the writer). Assuming that someone assigned to write an attitudinal essay actually holds that attitude illustrates making a fundamental attribution error.

The research on fundamental attribution error is supported by Lassiter's research in the legal system. Lassiter and colleagues (Lassiter, Ware, Ratcliff, & Irvin, 2009; Snyder, Lassiter, Lindberg, & Pinegar, 2009) have found that simulated jurors who watch videotaped confessions (either simulated or actual) that focused on the alleged perpetrator were more likely to return guilty verdicts than jurors who watched taped confessions that focused on the interrogator, or on both the perpetrator and the interrogator equally. Thus, it appears that jurors make the fundamental attribution error by focusing on the person (alleged criminal) rather than the situation (the interrogation system).

Interestingly, people believe that they are *less* prone to making the fundamental error than other people; in other words, we believe that we take situational factors into account more than do our peers. Van Boven, White, Kamada, and Gilovich (2003) asked subjects about factors that contributed to the Columbine shootings in which two boys shot and killed 12 classmates and a teacher before committing suicide. The researchers had subjects rate the relative weight of four factors: the boys' cruel and hateful personalities, their evil natures, inadequacies within the boys' families, and the boys having been hassled and rejected by their classmates. The first two factors denoted personal characteristics whereas the last two indicated situational factors. Subjects also estimated how they thought their classmates would rate the same four factors. The subjects responded that they would weight situational factors more heavily than personal factors, but that their peers would weight these two types of factors more equally. Thus, people believed that they were less likely than their peers to fall victim to the fundamental attribution error.

Attributions based on lectures. Coren (1993) had college students read hypothetical lectures and make attributions about the professors' attitudes and motivations for lecturing on the specific topics. Coren found that students made negative attributions about professors who lectured that genetic factors could explain some racial differences in IQ scores (e.g., that the professor was racist), and that sex differences in cognitive skills could be due to genetic factors (e.g., that the professor was sexist). This evidence supports the notion that students think that faculty members necessarily believe everything they teach. However, consider this situation logically. Teachers have to cover a good deal of material that may very well include some ideas or theories that are controversial, or seem foolish or inappropriate to you. To do an effective job of teaching, faculty members must be evenhanded in their coverage, seeming to give equal weight and emphasis to a diversity of topics and viewpoints. Also, to challenge students' thinking, instructors may purposely express controversial ideas that they may not personally agree with (i.e., they play the devil's advocate). Thus, to assume that faculty members are proponents of virtually everything they say may be viewed as making the fundamental attribution error.

The vignette that opened this chapter revealed an instance in which Robert committed the fundamental attribution error about his psychology teacher. Robert observed Juliane covering Freud in class interactions and attributed that coverage to Juliane liking or believing Freud's ideas. It turns out that Juliane's covering Freud was not so much direct reflections of her likes and dislikes as it was *a function* of the class context. Robert saw Juliane talking about Freud in class, but did not realize that the department had guidelines about the course that mandated covering Freud's ideas. Robert's selective observations led to an impression of Juliane as someone who had favorable opinions about Freud, but this impression was not entirely accurate.

Overcoming the fundamental attribution error. Is there a "cure" for the fundamental attribution error? Certainly, if people could somehow learn how to guard against a biased mode of viewing others that involves insufficiently recognizing possible situational determinants of their actions, their interpersonal understanding and relations would improve. For help, we look to a study by Gilbert, Pelham, and Krull (1988), who had college students watch a silent video of a woman talking with a stranger. The woman exhibited several anxious behaviors, such as twirling her hair and biting her fingernails. The experimenter told half of the participants that the woman was discussing an "anxious topic" (e.g., sexual fantasies, secrets), and told the other half that the woman was discussing a "relaxing topic" (e.g., vacations, hobbies).

The participants who believed that the woman was discussing an anxious topic rated her lower on the trait of anxiety than did those who thought that she was discussing a relaxing topic. Thus, participants made the attribution of "anxious person" when they thought that the woman should not be anxious. Those participants who believed that the woman was discussing a sensitive topic apparently attributed her anxiety to the topic (situation) rather than to her personality. Gilbert and colleagues (1988) hypothesized that the fundamental attribution error occurs automatically and that people have to devote cognitive effort to overcome it, for example, by getting additional information or being thoughtful about the situation. That is, the participants had to make extra effort to look past the woman's behavior and take the topic into account. Thus, if you wish to avoid making the fundamental attribution error about people, try to find out more about their situations, or try to think of reasons why they might behave the way they do. Teachers should attempt to find out why their students enter class late, fall asleep in class, and do not turn in assignments so as to avoid unfairly drawing negative conclusions about them. Perhaps the undesirable behavior was due to situational factors that were largely or entirely beyond the students' control; for example, the tardiness due to a flat tire, the sleepiness due to holding a night job, and the late assignment due to caring for a sick child. Likewise, students should attempt to discover teachers' motivations for covering class material that seems to indicate a certain set of attitudes. Although a teacher may lecture on Freud or race differences in aptitude test performance, such a lecture does not make the teacher a Freudian or a racist.

CULTURE CAPSULE

Culture and the Fundamental Attribution Error

The evidence for the fundamental attribution error reported in this chapter is based on research conducted in the United States and Canada. This begs the question about possible cultural variations

(Continued)

(Continued)

in the expression of this cognitive error. In fact, there is some evidence that this type of error in attribution depends on the culture in which we live.

The United States and Canada are **individualistic cultures** where people tend to value personal successes and accomplishments. We like winners and people who stand out, and we tend to give them personal credit for their successes. Similarly, we tend to blame people for their personal failures. However, cultures that value group success over individual achievement have a different set of values. In **collectivistic cultures**, such as China and India, community cooperation is valued more than individual distinction, and people from those countries tend to favor external rather than internal attributions (Lee, Hallahan, & Herzog, 1996).

Two studies clearly illustrate this cultural difference in making attributions. Smith and Whitehead (1984) had participants from the United States and India rate possible reasons for a person's promotion or demotion. The American participants rated levels of skill and effort higher than did the Indian participants. On the other hand, the Indian participants rated potential factors, such as the difficulty level of the job, a relationship with someone on the job, and corruption in the situation, higher than the American participants. Thus, Americans tended to favor internal explanations, and Indians tended to favor external explanations. In a study also involving people from the United States and India, Miller (1984) had participants generate explanations for things that people had done wrong and for behaviors people had exhibited that benefited someone else. Although children from the two countries showed few differences in attributions, there were marked differences for adults. American adults tended to favor people's general dispositions to explain both positive and negative behaviors, whereas Indian adults tended to favor contextual explanations for both.

Apparently, growing up in an individualistic culture predisposes people to look for personal internal explanations for behavior. On the other hand, living in a collectivistic culture makes external attributions more likely. As with most psychological differences, it is not impossible to see examples that run contrary to a finding, but generally speaking, social psychologists would predict a lower tendency for people from collectivistic cultures to fall victim to the fundamental attribution error and by extension for the error to show up in the classroom.

Belief Perseverance

Belief perseverance means that people tend to maintain their initial ideas or beliefs despite exposure to disconfirming evidence. They may discredit, ignore, misinterpret, or give the disconfirming information little weight, but the effect is the same in that their ideas or beliefs persist.

Classic study of belief perseverance. Wegner, Coulton, and Wenzlaff (1985) had college students (referred to as "actors") read 25 pairs of suicide notes and guess which one of each pair was genuine. Half of the actors received success feedback (24 of 25 correct), and half received failure feedback (10 of 25 correct). While each actor was working, another student observed. Afterward, the actor and observer were informed that the feedback was not genuine; that is, it had been predetermined and did not reflect the actor's actual performance. Then, both the actor and the observer were asked to predict how well the actor would perform on an additional 25 trials. Curiously, their predictions were not affected by learning that the feedback was false. Instead, both actors and observers predicted that "successful" actors would perform better than "failure" actors. Their initial beliefs about the actors' ability had persevered and led them to predict future behavior despite the evidence that their initial beliefs had been based on erroneous information. The participants' failure to factor into their predictions the fact that the initial feedback had been predetermined is similar to what happens with the fundamental attribution error in which the role of the situation is downplayed.

Lewandowsky, Stritzke, Oberauer, and Morales (2005) provide a more recent experimental example of belief perseverance. They examined memory for events during the Iraq War that were initially reported and later retracted, such as Iraqi troops killing Allied troops who were captured. Lewandowsky and colleagues found that Americans had maintained belief in events that had been retracted, presumably because those events fit their preconceptions. On the other hand, Germans and Australians, who were more skeptical than Americans about the war, showed much lower memory for the retracted events.

Belief perseverance in the classroom. Unfortunately, belief perseverance also takes place in the classroom. If you have used a word for many years to mean one thing, it may be difficult to learn a different or more specific meaning for it in a class. For example, psychology students often confuse *negative reinforcement* and *punishment*, despite having encountered the terms since their first psychology course. Having entered a psychology program with a long-held belief that negative reinforcement entails the use of punishment, they cling to that belief despite disconfirmations revealed in lectures and textbooks. In an academic example, Prohaska (1994) found that students with medium or low grade point averages (GPAs) were prone to overestimate their future grades. Thus, despite their unsatisfactory performance in the past, low-achieving students continued to believe that they would get good grades in the future.

Lepper, Ross, and Lau (1986) demonstrated some negative implications of belief perseverance in their high school classroom research.

They presented subjects with either highly effective or highly ineffective filmed instruction about how to solve certain math problems. Not surprisingly, students who got the effective instruction performed better on four such math problems than students who received the ineffective instruction. However, in one condition, Lepper et al. actually showed the students the film that they did not view after they had attempted to solve the math problems. In other words, the students who had received the effective instruction attempted to solve problems, and then saw the ineffective film instruction, and vice versa. Thus, each group received evidence that their performance was mostly dependent on which film they viewed rather than on their personal math ability. Three weeks after the initial research session just described, all students at the school (not only the ones who participated in the original research) took a survey about three proposed future units for math courses at the school—there was no obvious link between this survey and the prior research. One of the three proposed units was described in terms to make it seem similar to the types of problems the research participants had previously encountered. When asked how they believed they would perform in the proposed unit that was similar to the research problems, students who had received the effective instruction film believed that they would perform well, whereas students who had viewed the ineffective instruction film predicted that they would perform poorly on the material. Thus, despite having learned (during the research study) that their performance was due to an external factor (the particular type of instructional film they watched), students' ratings of their future math ability was dependent on how they had scored on the math questions during the research. These results tell us that students apparently discounted the true reason that they performed well or poorly, and instead credited or blamed themselves for being good or bad at math. Belief perseverance was beneficial for the students who received the effective instruction, but was detrimental for the students who received the poor instruction—they blamed themselves and believed they would continue to do poorly in a similar situation in the future. These results show just how strong belief perseverance can be.

There is substantial literature dealing with popular misconceptions about psychology. Much of the research shows that taking a psychology course does not remove those misconceptions (e.g., Vaughan, 1977). When students have completed a course, but still hold the misconceptions with which they entered the course, this problem illustrates belief perseverance. Gardner and Dalsing (1986) administered a 60-item "test of common beliefs" (which were actually incorrect) to more than 500 students taking psychology courses (e.g., "To change people's behavior toward members of ethnic minority groups, we must first change their attitudes"; "In love and friendship, more often than not, opposites attract"). On average, students agreed with more than 20% of the misconceptions. The only significant drop in misconceptions occurred for students who had taken at least six psychology courses. Thus, it appears to take repeated exposure to disconfirming information for students to overcome belief perseverance.

Reducing belief perseverance. By now, you may have recognized that belief perseverance is not necessarily a good thing. In fact, more often than not, it is maladaptive for the individual who steadfastly clings to beliefs in the face of information suggesting that the beliefs may be, or in fact are, wrong. Is it possible to overcome belief perseverance? An experiment by Hirt and Markman (1995) shed some light on how it can be done. Hirt and Markman gave introductory psychology students one of several hypothetical relations (e.g., risky firefighters are more successful than less risky firefighters, or the exact opposite), and asked them to generate an explanation for the relationship. Afterward, the experimenters told the participants that the relationship they had given them was bogus; that is, there was no truth to it. Then, they asked the participants to decide what the true relation was between risk-taking behavior and firefighting ability. As you would probably predict from the concept of

belief perseverance, the participants tended to presume that the true relation was the one they previously had heard and explained. In a second study, Hirt and Markman sought to prevent belief perseverance from occurring. They presented one of the same hypothetical relations (e.g., risky firefighters are better), and asked the participants to generate an explanation for it, *and* an explanation for any alternative relation (e.g., risky firefighters are not better). When these participants learned that the original relation was not true, they were less likely to stick with their first impressions when choosing what they believed to be the true relation. Thus, they showed much lower levels of belief perseverance.

You might wish to guard against belief perseverance when you encounter new ideas or information in class, both because an open mind better facilitates learning, and to prepare for upcoming tests. If so, the results of the research by Hirt and Markman (1995) suggest that you should listen carefully to the instructor's account of the new information even though it may conflict with your viewpoint. Then, try to think of an explanation as to why that new information is correct and why the old information you believed is incorrect. Hirt and Markman refer to this as adopting an **alternative strategy**. Considering an alternative should reduce the tendency to cling to your former belief. For example, you may cover interpersonal attraction in your social psychology class. Suppose that all your life, you have believed that "opposites attract" because you have heard that phrase so often. However, extensive social psychology research has not supported this notion; David Buss (1985) wrote that this tendency for opposites to marry or mate "has never been reliably demonstrated" (p. 47). To get rid of this belief and to avoid belief perseverance, you should read the available evidence, *and* think about why "opposites attract" could be wrong.

It would not be surprising if your belief still is struggling to persevere; that is, if you still have difficulty believing that opposites do *not* attract. It is true that someone who is *different* than you in some ways can be especially attractive, but "different" is hardly the same as "opposite." If opposites truly attracted, then rich people would be attracted to poor people and smart people would want dumb partners, but these outcomes seldom happen in real life. Indeed, if your confidence in the opposites-attract notion continues to persevere, you are encouraged to look through a fascinating book by Lilienfeld, Lynn, Ruscio, and Beyerstein (2010) titled *50 Great Myths of Popular Psychology: Shattering Widespread Misconceptions About Human Behavior*. In this book the authors draw on existing evidence to systematically dispel "Myth #27, Opposites Attract," as well as numerous other misconceptions that persevere in the minds of many people.

Social Categorization

Do you ever find yourself in a gripe session with other students complaining about "those professors"? Does it sometimes seem like school turns into mini battles between students and teachers? Unfortunately, what should be a mutual adventure of learning between two groups interacting in a positive manner sometimes can seem like an adversarial experience.

Classic study of social categorization. According to the principle of **social categorization**, we tend to classify other people into groups on the basis of certain social characteristics (e.g., race, gender, status, occupation). Because of social categorization, as soon as the sorting process begins, we form in-groups and out-groups (discussed in Chapter 1 in the context of how intergroup attitudes form). These groupings, in turn, often create an "us versus them" mentality. In a school setting, one logical set of categories is students and teachers. Which group is the in-group and which is the out-group depends on the group to which you belong. From this perspective, if you were at the chapter author's university, then for you I would be the out-group, and for me you would be the out-group.

One vivid example of social categorization occurred in a study by Rabbie and Horwitz (1969) in which the researchers simply flipped a coin to divide junior high school participants into two groups. Then, they had the participants rate both the groups and the individuals in the groups on eight characteristics (e.g., responsibility, consideration, fearfulness, openness, etc.). Rabbie and Horwitz found evidence of **in-group/ out-group bias**; that is, students rated their own group more favorably on the characteristics than they did the other group, and they rated individuals in their group more favorably than they did individuals in the other group. These ratings occurred despite the fact that the participants had been divided into groups by the mere flip of a coin. There is considerable laboratory research and anecdotal evidence of the divisive role of in-group/out-group biases in intergroup relations (e.g., Brewer & Brown, 1998). It is certainly likely that social categorization is pertinent to the relations between faculty members and students.

Another outcome of social categorization is the **out-group homogeneity bias**, which is the tendency to perceive less variability among members of an out-group than among members of the in-group. Thus, when we look at out-groups, we tend to think that all of their members are similar; they act alike and possibly even "look alike." Bernstein, Young, and Hugenberg (2007) showed student participants pictures of people described as students from the same or a different university as the participants. When given a picture recognition test later, participants recognized more of the students who were allegedly from their university than from the other university. Linville, Fischer, and Salovey (1989) asked undergraduates and people living in a retirement community to rate 100 hypothetical elderly people and 100 hypothetical college students on eight attributes (e.g., friendliness, motivation, interestingness, irritability, attractiveness, etc.). Each group gave less variable ratings to the other age group than to their own age group, meaning that they saw the out-group members as more similar than the in-group members. Thus, the out-group homogeneity effect could lead to the similar refrain, "They're all alike." For example, teachers may tend to see fewer differences among students, and students may tend to see fewer differences among faculty members.

DeSteno, Dasgupta, Bartlett, and Cajdric (2004) examined the effects of emotion on prejudice toward out-groups. They artificially created in-groups and out-groups based on scores from a bogus personality test. They then induced an emotion in the participants by having them write about an episode in their life that made them very angry, very sad, or emotionally neutral. The researchers found that subjects experiencing anger (through the writing task) showed evidence of negative attitudes toward the out-group, but not toward the in-group. Neither the sad nor emotionally neutral groups showed negative attitudes toward either group. Thus, DeSteno et al. concluded that the emotion of anger created automatic prejudice toward out-groups. This research has direct relevance to the classroom situation. If students and faculty already automatically perceive each other as out-groups, any experience of anger could create negative attitudes toward the other group. It is likely the case that students may get angry when they get grades that are lower than they expect, and faculty may get angry at students who are pushy, rude, or belligerent. Thus, the situation is ripe for both groups to form negative attitudes (and probably stereotypes) of the other group. This result would not be ideal for a learning situation!

Reducing in-group/out-group biases. There is an extensive research literature that addresses how to ameliorate the negative effects of in-group/out-group biases, and other factors relevant to intergroup attitudes and relations (see, for example, Chapter 14). Here, we briefly consider the implications of an experiment by Gaertner and colleagues (1999) and the evidence on cooperative learning. Cooperative learning typically refers to having small groups of students work together and gain information from each other (Vazin & Reile, 2006).

Gaertner and colleagues (1999) had groups of three college students who shared similar political preferences (i.e., all three were Republican or Democrat) work together on a problem-solving task dealing with survival after a plane crash. After a group had completed the task, the

experimenters had the same group of students work on a new problem, this time with another group whose members had the opposite political preference to theirs. Each of the groups was able to win money for good solutions. Gaertner and colleagues varied the amount of interaction the two groups could have as they worked on the new problem: full interaction or no interaction (i.e., the groups could see each other, but could not communicate). Also, with regard to the monetary reward, some groups had a common fate (both groups won the same amount of money), and some did not have a common fate (each group could win differing amounts of money). After all of the various pairings of groups had completed the experiment, Gaertner and colleagues found that interaction was a more important variable than was common fate given that the groups having full interaction performed the best. Thus, for groups composed of different types of people, it is to their benefit to overcome those differences and communicate with each other fully as they work together to achieve the best outcomes. In another classic study, Sherif, Harvey, White, Hood, and Sherif (1961) divided 22 boys, all age 11, into two groups (Eagles and Rattlers) at a summer camp. After a week of working in their groups, the two groups came together for athletic contests. Predictably, introducing competition created negative attitudes within each group toward the other. The researchers then introduced a problem (broken water supply) that both groups had to work together to solve (a superordinate goal). Once the two groups worked together to solve the problem, their rivalry, and thus the negative attitudes, disappeared.

In terms of the interaction between students and teachers, the preceding results imply that the parties should focus on interaction and communication in an attempt to overcome their differences in perspective, and to find common ground to have the best possible class. A cooperative learning relationship between students and faculty members should facilitate the achievement of this goal. Rather than viewing the teacher–student relationship as adversarial, students and faculty should work as partners in learning (see Ferris, 2002, for an application of this approach in a business school environment). In all aspects of a course (e.g., syllabus, lectures, interactions with students in class and during office hours), instructors should embrace and reinforce the concept of a cooperative relationship. Students, as well, should embrace the idea and take responsibility for engaging in constructive interactions with instructors both in and out of class. Both parties should understand that they have common goals (e.g., having students do well in the course), and must work toward the same ends (i.e., student learning and achievement). On the other hand, if teachers and students find themselves in an antagonistic "us versus them" situation, the atmosphere of the class will suffer, and learning (and satisfaction) will be lower.

In graduate school the working relationship between professors and students often changes. Students typically work closely with one professor, who acts as his or her advisor and is expected to provide guidance about research, course work, and career development. Although graduate students are expected to act professionally, and are often treated as colleagues by faculty members, problems in professor-student relationships still occur. Knox, Schlosser, Pruitt, and Hill (2006) conducted a qualitative interview study of the advisor-student relationship in graduate school. They interviewed 19 advisors in a Counselling Psychology program about their thoughts on the advisor-student relationship in general. Participants were also asked to describe an advisor-student relationship that they felt had been positive, and one that they felt had been negative. The researchers coded the interview transcripts by identifying common themes in the interviews. They found that advisors cited mutual respect, good communication, and similar career paths as an important characteristic of positive relationships. In negative relationships, in contrast, advisors reported a lack of respect from their students. Open communication was also listed as an important characteristic of positive advisor-student relationships. For example, one advisor described a negative relationship with a student that was characterized by poor communication. In this case, the advisor felt that she was among the last to find out that her student was switching to another advisor. In both good and poor relationships, when conflict occurred, it was addressed directly, and not swept under the rug. The results of this study suggest that the issues that exist between students and professors can sometimes persist in graduate school. These issues can often be overcome by clear communication and mutual respect.

SELF-PERCEPTIONS AND THEIR ACADEMIC CONSEQUENCES

In addition to cognitive errors that we make in dealing with other people, social psychological research has shown that we also make certain predictable *errors in thinking about ourselves.* Most of these errors show that we tend to misjudge our motivations or ourselves. Not surprisingly, in many cases we judge ourselves more favorably than we should.

Self-Handicapping

Have you ever found yourself walking into an exam knowing that you studied less than you should have, or that you spent time with friends instead of studying the night before the exam? Similarly, have you ever begun a competition (athletic or otherwise) knowing that you did not prepare enough? If any of these situations describes you at some point in your life, you may have been guilty of self-handicapping. According to the social psychological concept of **self-handicapping**, people act in ways that may undermine their subsequent performances, thereby having anticipatory excuses for potential failures. In other words, if you studied less than you know you should have, you have a handy excuse in case your grade is lower than you would prefer. Table 16.1 includes items from a self-handicapping scale. A person who

Table 16.1   Items Indicating Self-Handicapping

1. When I do something wrong, my first impulse is to blame circumstances.

2. I tend to put things off until the last moment.

3. I suppose I feel "under the weather" more often than most people do.

4. I am easily distracted by noises or my own creative thoughts when I try to read.

5. I would do a lot better if I tried harder.

6. I sometimes enjoy being mildly ill for a day or two because it takes off the pressure.

7. Sometimes I get so depressed that even easy tasks become difficult.

SOURCE: Rhodewalt (1990).

tends to engage in self-handicapping would endorse these kinds of items.

Classic study of self-handicapping. Berglas and Jones (1978) conducted the classic study of self-handicapping. The experimenters gave college students analogies to solve, after which all participants were told that they had performed well—although some of the analogies were unsolvable. Before working on a second set of analogies, the students had the choice of taking a performance-enhancing drug, or a performance-impairing drug. Men (but not women) who had been told they had done well on the unsolvable analogies chose the drug that would hinder their performance, presumably because they had no confidence that they would continue to perform well (see Figure 16.2). According to Hirt, McCrea, and Kimble (2000), subsequent research has shown that men (but not women) tend to self-handicap through strategies that will actually hamper their performance (e.g., by failing to practice or study). On the other hand, the research shows that both men and women tend to claim excuses ahead of time; for instance, prior to the time of performance, they may point to potentially debilitating stress, or physical illness. Relatedly, Mello-Goldner and Jackson (1999) discovered that female college students who reported premenstrual syndrome (PMS) symptoms scored higher on a self-handicapping measure than did women who did not report such symptoms.

Self-handicapping and academics. There is ample research evidence that self-handicapping takes place in academic settings. Beck, Koons,

Figure 16.2   Results Indicating That Men (but Not Women) Self-Handicapped (Chose a Performance-Impairing Drug) on Very Hard Tasks

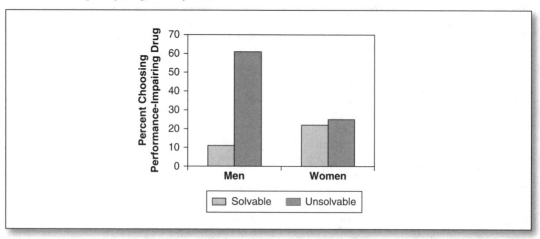

SOURCE: Results From Berglas and Jones (1978).

and Milgrim (2000) administered self-report measures of self-handicapping (as illustrated in Table 16.1) and procrastination to more than 400 college students, and found that self-handicapping and procrastination were positively correlated. They also found that self-handicappers (i.e., those who scored high on the self-handicapping measure) not only began studying for tests later than non-self-handicappers, but also earned lower grades. Similarly, Zuckerman, Kieffer, and Knee (1998) found that among college students, higher self-handicapping scores were directly correlated with lower GPAs, less time spent on academic work, and less efficient exam preparation. Elliot and Church (2003) found that self-handicapping was positively correlated with fear of failure and negatively correlated with need for achievement. This finding means that students who scored higher on self-handicapping tended to be more afraid of failing, but they had lower drive for accomplishment. More importantly, self-handicapping was associated with not only lower exam scores, but also with lower GPAs. Thus, it appears that seeking to avoid failure is not an adequate motivator to perform well in classes. Sikorski and colleagues (2002) found that roughly 20% of students at two universities admitted to not buying a textbook for an introductory college course, whereas nearly 80% reported either not reading or reading only sparingly a text they had bought for an introductory course. Clearly, self-handicapping can be a problem for college students, as it actually results in reducing one's chances of future success.

Why might students self-handicap regarding classes and exams? To answer this question, consider the consequences of *not* self-handicapping. Suppose that a student prepares as well as he or she can for an exam and then fails the exam (or earns a grade that is below expectations). How can this student explain this outcome? Having studied hard, a logical and disturbing answer goes something like "I'm stupid," or "I'm not smart enough to handle that kind of exam." On the other hand, if the student waits until the night before the exam to begin studying, or goes out for pizza instead of studying, he or she has a ready-made excuse for not doing well on the exam. In other words, self-handicapping prevents a blow to the student's self-image. In some cases, faculty members might also try to protect their self-images. You might be surprised to know that many faculty members would admit that they have waited until the last minute to begin working on an important paper or grant application. Perhaps some are motivated by the ego-protective function of self-handicapping.

Reducing self-handicapping. Clearly, not everyone is a self-handicapper, although we imagine that most people can recall at least one or two times when what they did (actually, what they did not do) fit the meaning of the term. The problem, of course, is that whereas self-handicapping might protect one's self-image on a particular occasion, it clearly undermines the possibility of performing at an optimal level on that occasion. Moreover, people should recognize that self-handicapping is self-defeating in the long run. Also, other people might not respond to self-handicapping in a positive manner. For example, Rhodewalt, Sanbonmatsu, Tschanz, Feick, and Waller (1995) asked college students to evaluate a hypothetical coworker who gave one of three excuses for performing poorly on a task. The students consistently evaluated persons making self-handicapping excuses lower on ability, on actual performance, and on 20 different personality traits (e.g., friendly, pleasant, egotistic, etc.). Thus, if you do tend to self-handicap and give excuses for your poor performance in hopes of getting other people to "cut you some slack" in their evaluations of you, that type of behavior may boomerang on you. Instead of creating more positive evaluations of you, you may actually be creating more negative evaluations.

Is there anything that might lessen self-handicapping? It is important to recognize the short- and long-term self-defeating aspects of self-handicapping. Even the short-term protection of one's self-image is soundly offset by the long-term havoc brought on by repeated underperformance experiences. Therefore, people with self-handicapping tendencies would be better off devoting their energies to preparing for major events than to making excuses ahead of time for potential poor performances. Siegel, Scillitoe, and Parks-Yancy (2005) found that students who engaged in a high self-affirming task (writing about values important to them) were less likely to engage in self-handicapping on a subsequent test than students who engaged in a low self-affirming task (writing about an unimportant value). Thus, as students prepare for exams, they should bring to mind their high value for education and valued career goals—intentionally thinking about how important school and academic achievement are might help stop a student from making that late-night pizza run before an exam. Students also might remember the possible constructive role of social influences and consider surrounding themselves with conscientious and achievement focused (clearly non-self-handicapping) classmates, especially with the approach of important assignments and exams.

Self-Serving Bias

It may be expected that, from time to time, you will receive an exam grade that is lower than you had anticipated. In such a case, whom do you tend to blame for the low grade? Do you own up to not knowing the material and not studying enough, or do you perhaps blame the teacher for making an unfair or too difficult exam? Here is a different scenario. Do you ever get a higher grade on an exam than you expected? If so, whom do you credit for the high grade? Do you decide that you must have really known the material and did an excellent job of studying, or do you decide that the teacher made an exam that was too easy or you just "lucked out"? If you are like most people, you are more likely to blame the teacher for the low grade, but take personal credit for the high grade. This pattern of explanation for good and bad performances exemplifies the self-serving bias.

Classic study of the self-serving bias. According to the principle of the **self-serving bias**, we have a tendency to attribute our positive outcomes to internal causes (e.g., our traits or characteristics), but to attribute our negative outcomes to external causes (e.g., chance, difficulty of a task). Thus, we are likely to take credit for our successes, but blame others or circumstances for our

Figure 16.3   Results Indicating That Participants Tend to See Their Own Team as Responsible for Its Success, but Tend to See the Other Team as Responsible for Its Failure

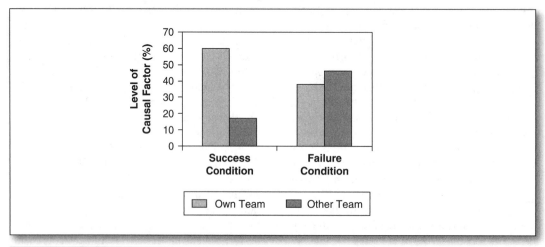

SOURCE: Results From Streufert and Streufert (1969).

shortcomings. For example, in an experiment by Streufert and Streufert (1969), pairs of undergraduate students played a tactical economics game against what they thought was another team. The other team was actually a computer that was used to provide standardized success or failure feedback regarding game performance. After playing the game, participants rated how much of their performance was due to their team or to the other team. Streufert and Streufert found that participants who had been informed that they succeeded at the game gave the lion's share of the credit to their team. Participants who had been informed that they failed, however, tended to say that the other team was responsible for the outcome, thereby deflecting the blame for poor play (see Figure 16.3).

Self-serving attributions in academics. There are several findings in research on the self-serving bias that can spell trouble for students. Baumeister and Cairns (1992) found that people remembered and paid more attention to favorable information about themselves than unfavorable information. Wills (1981, p. 245) described a theory of downward comparison in which "persons can increase their subjective well-being through comparison with a less fortunate other." Campbell (1986) found that people tend to convince themselves that their good traits are unusual and their shortcomings are common in others. When we combine these results, we can see that students would tend to remember their academic successes more than their failures, favorably compare themselves to weaker students, and believe that their positive academic behaviors are rare compared to peers. All of these self-serving attributions would tend to lead students to believe that they are better students than they might actually be.

In two studies, McAllister (1996) looked for evidence of the self-serving bias in the academic arena. First, in a laboratory experiment, he paired introductory psychology students and had them engage in a teacher–learner interaction about reading an article in a psychology journal. In each student pair, one student was assigned the role of the teacher, who read and wrote notes on the article, and the other was assigned the role of the learner, who studied from the notes and took a test about the article. The learners received false feedback of either failure (50% correct), or success (90% correct). In their attributions for their performance, learners took credit for their performance in the success condition and blamed the teachers in the failure condition. In the second study, McAllister asked students to think about the most recent courses in which they had received an *A* and an *F* (or their best and worst grades) and to write down the most likely cause of their performance. The results were virtually identical to those of the laboratory experiment in that students indicated they had deserved (earned) the high grade, but that the instructor was the cause of the low grade.

In the same two studies, McAllister (1996) also examined the teacher's perceptions. In the laboratory study, the students who served as the teacher in the success conditions believed that they had played a large role in the student learners' success. However, teachers who were in the failure condition believed that the student learners were more responsible for their poor performance. In the second study, McAllister asked actual college faculty members to think of the most recent courses in which they had graded students as receiving an *A* or an *F* and to make attributions for those grades. Again, the reversal was present such that instructors believed that they played a large role in students' successes, but that the students were to blame for their failures.

Adaptive nature of the self-serving bias. Just as with self-handicapping, the self-serving bias can be an adaptive mechanism in terms of guarding one's self-image. If we take credit for our successes, but explain away our failures, our self-esteem is left intact. In fact, our self-esteem probably becomes somewhat inflated: Most of us view our lives through rose-colored glasses believing that we are better than we actually are. Thus, it is a simple matter for faculty members to believe that they are effective teachers, and that their students should work harder. By the same token, students tend to think that they are smart and hardworking, but that faculty members could teach better, or be fairer in their grading.

The self-serving bias can be maladaptive for many students. Often, students believe that they are quite prepared for an exam until *after* they have taken the exam. This type of experience is likely due to self-serving bias, as students overestimate how well they know the material beforehand. For example, Prohaska (1994) found that low-GPA students overestimated their future grades to a greater degree than either medium- or high-GPA students.

Reducing self-serving bias. Norem has written about defensive pessimism in which people are pessimistic about their potential outcomes in a given situation, and are worried and anxious about how they will perform. Rather than letting the worry and anxiety debilitate their performance, however, defensive pessimists take steps to reduce their worry and anxiety by coping effectively with the situation (Norem & Smith, 2006). Eronen, Nurmi, and Salmela-Aro (1998) compared Finnish college students with four different achievement strategies (optimism, defensive pessimism, impulsiveness, self-handicapping) and found that defensive pessimists completed more courses than all groups other than the optimists. However, the defensive pessimists performed better in their courses than the other groups. Cantor (1990) summarized similar findings with American college students. Thus, to avoid self-serving bias with regard to academic performance, it seems wise to avoid the unfounded optimism about grades that most students maintain. Instead, it would be best to worry about your upcoming performance, but then ensure that you act on that worry by studying, writing your paper well ahead of time, or whatever strategy helps reduce your worry in a constructive fashion.

Overjustification Effect

Have you ever wondered why your teachers seem so excited about classroom material that you *have* to absorb for the course, but find boring?

Have you ever read a textbook and thought, "This might be a good book if I didn't *have* to read it?" Or, have you ever been aware that people were raving about a certain book or movie, but when you read or watched it as a course requirement, you thought it was a drag? If you have ever had these kinds of experience, you have experienced the overjustification effect.

According to the **overjustification effect**, if people see an external reason (e.g., reward or punishment) for their behavior, they may view the behavior as controlled by the external reason (i.e., the reward or punishment) rather than see it as intrinsically appealing (i.e., something they just like to do). Thus, it is possible that students by virtue of *having* to learn about psychology for a course might find the content of psychology less enjoyable than if they learned about it on their own.

Classic studies of the overjustification effect. Lepper, Greene, and Nisbett (1973) conducted an oft-cited experiment of the overjustification effect. They matched preschool children on their interest in drawing and divided them into three groups. All children had the opportunity to draw pictures with markers. One third of the children were shown an award they could win by drawing good pictures, one third were given an unanticipated award after drawing a picture, and the other third got no award. Judges, who were unaware of the three conditions, rated the children's pictures for quality. Lepper and colleagues found that the children drawing to win an award somewhat counterintuitively drew lower-quality pictures. In a follow-up session one to two weeks later, the experimenters observed the children during free play time (drawing with markers was one of the free play choices). Children who had originally drawn pictures to win awards spent less time drawing during this subsequent period. Thus, rewarding the children for something they already enjoyed doing produced lower-quality output and undermined subsequent motivation to engage in the activity.

Deci (1971) found similar results in an experiment where undergraduates first solved puzzles;

then some, but not all of the students were paid to solve puzzles; and finally all students returned to the original condition where nobody was paid. In this condition, the students worked longer on the puzzles if they had not been paid to solve puzzles. Are faculty members any different? Perhaps not. At the former college of the chapter author a few years ago, faculty members formed a voluntary reading group. The group met once a month to discuss a book of mutual interest. Each month, the leader of the group would bring the next month's book to pass around, presumably to pique the members' interest and curiosity. Within a matter of a few months, the group members acted just like the examples at the beginning of this section, where *having* to engage in an activity required for a course seemed to sabotage student interest in the activity. They quickly examined each book to see how large or small the print was and to find out how many pages it had, complaining if the print was too small, or the book was too long. *Having* to read made it less fun.

Unfortunately, parents appear to be unaware of the overjustification effect. Boggiano, Barrett, Weiher, McClelland, and Lusk (1987) had parents read scenarios in which elementary school children showed either high interest or low interest in academic activities. Then the parents rated several social control techniques as to how good they would be to maintain the children's enjoyment or interest in an activity. The parents did not differentiate between high- and low-interest scenarios; in either case, they opted for the use of reward as the control technique of choice. The research on overjustification clearly indicates that reward would be a bad choice for children who already have high interest in academics.

Immunization against overjustification. There is hope, however, for mitigating the overjustification effect. Hennessey and Zbikowski (1993) attempted to immunize fourth-grade children against the effect by showing them videotapes of target children discussing their work at school. The target children said that getting rewards was nice, but that the real reason they did their schoolwork was because of how much they enjoyed it. A day later, the children and a control group whose members had not seen the videotapes, took part in an apparently unrelated study. A researcher asked the children to make up a story to accompany a picture book with no words (a measure of creativity). Half of the children from the treatment group and the control group were offered a reward and half were not. The children who had watched the videotapes of the target children showed higher creativity scores than did those in the control group. The control group children who had been offered a reward produced the least creative stories, demonstrating the overjustification effect. Therefore, it appears that focusing on intrinsic motivation may reduce or eliminate the overjustification effect.

Tang and Hall (1995) reviewed MANY studies of the overjustification effect, and concluded that *contingent* reward (reward given only for good performance) can mitigate the overjustification effect. Wimperis and Farr (1979) conducted a study with college students as subjects in which they had both contingent and noncontingent reward situations. Indeed, they found that subjects who received a reward only if they performed well outperformed subjects in the noncontingent condition, thus avoiding the overjustification effect. Being rewarded regardless of how well you perform may be the root cause behind the overjustification effect. Therefore, sports leagues in which all children receive trophies regardless of their performance may actually undermine intrinsic motivation of the children.

What should people do to avoid the overjustification effect? As an example, let us consider individuals who may have suffered a decline in enthusiasm for the content of the courses they are taking. First, they should remind themselves why they have chosen to go to college. Presumably, they are in college because they are interested in learning new information. If they behave like they did when they were children—full of curiosity about the world—they should be able to avoid the negative effects of overjustification. On the other hand, if they find themselves working for grades rather than knowledge, overjustification becomes more likely. Along the same lines, if you are studying psychology because it interests you, remind yourself of that intrinsic interest when the going gets tough. Focusing on your internal reasons for studying and learning will help you to avoid focusing on the external factors that could lead to the overjustification effect.

CONCLUSION: SOCIAL PSYCHOLOGY IN THE CLASSROOM

The interaction patterns that take place in the classroom reflect predictable social psychology phenomena. This section has spotlighted several of those phenomena. As a psychology student, you are well qualified to notice the occurrence of these and other phenomena and understand them. Coping more successfully with your classroom experiences may be easier as a result of knowing and applying the social psychological processes at work in the classroom.

SUMMARY

This chapter has dealt with an important topic to most college students: the classroom environment,

and although this topic is complex, social psychology provides some valuable insights into it. Social psychology plays important roles in the classroom in terms of cognitive errors and self-perceptions. The chapter considered three basic cognitive errors that are relevant to student–teacher relations: fundamental attribution, belief perseverance, and social categorization. When making the fundamental attribution error, students may assume that faculty members are proponents for all of the positions they present in the classroom. The error of belief perseverance may lead students to continue to hold beliefs that have been shown to be incorrect in a class. Social categorization makes it likely that students and faculty members will see each other as opposing groups (us vs. them) rather than as cooperating teammates in the educational venture. There are also three problematic self-perceptions: self-handicapping, self-serving bias, and the overjustification effect. Students may self-handicap by giving less effort in a class so as to have an excuse for a less than stellar performance. Self-serving bias can occur when students take credit for good performance, but blame faculty members for poor performance. The overjustification effect predicts that because students *have* to read or study class material, they will tend to like it less than if they simply chose to learn about it.

17

APPLYING SOCIAL PSYCHOLOGY TO THE GOOD LIFE: BALANCING OPTIMISM AND PESSIMISM

JAMIE A. GRUMAN

KENNETH E. HART

PHILLIP A. IANNI

You may recall the story of Deena, whom we introduced in Chapter 5 to illustrate the application of social psychology to clinical psychology. We continue with her story to illustrate some of the content of this chapter. The story resumes with Deena about to go on her first date with the guy named Jim, whom she just met at the library. Recall that Deena immediately was very attracted to Jim, but she was overwrought with worry and anxiety about the impression she made. She felt so skeptical about what might happen that she even thought about calling off the date. Now, while she was looking forward to the evening, she also thought about the times when she had screwed up first dates. She waited outside her dorm for Jim who said he'd pick her up in his car at 6:00 p.m. to go out for dinner and a movie. Deena soon became anxious as 6:00 p.m. came and went, and Jim failed to show up. As she continued to wait, Deena considered the possibilities of what could have happened, including that perhaps Jim had second thoughts about the date with her. She remembered feeling awkward and uncomfortable when Jim had approached her in the library, and that she hadn't washed her hair that morning. She wondered if she should be interested in him at all. As the minutes passed, the more she thought about it, the more negative Deena became about this evening working out well. Then, at 6:15 Deena's cell phone rang. It was Jim. He explained apologetically that he'd been stuck in a traffic jam for the last half hour and would be late for the date. Deena was relieved, but still wondered if that was the real reason Jim was late. Finally, when on the date, Deena had a fun time with Jim and clearly was drawn to his looks and personality. They shared a bottle of wine and enjoyed good conversation. They laughed together, especially at the movie, which was very funny. The evening ended with Jim saying that he had a really good time and maybe they could get together again.

Once home after the date, Deena reflected on the evening. Yes, it was a fun date, but she really didn't think that she had done much to make it fun. Mostly it was the wine, the movie, and Jim's sense of humor that carried the evening. The wine surely helped to overcome her usual awkwardness. Deena thought she would like to date Jim again, but despite what he said at the end of the date, she doubted if he would call her. She also thought that if she and Jim did go on a second date, it probably would not go as well, and more of its success would rest on her shoulders, putting even more pressure on her.

- If you were in the same situation as Deena, what would your initial thoughts be about the reason why your date didn't show up on time? How you would explain his or her tardiness is important. As you read through the chapter, you learn how causal attributions can influence how upset you might get in this situation, and whether you are likely to expect good or bad things to happen in future relationship events.
- How might psychology be applied to helping people like Deena to upgrade the quality of their interpersonal relationships?

INTRODUCTION TO POSITIVE SOCIAL PSYCHOLOGY

Historically, the science and profession of psychology has been negative in orientation. Until recently, it has focused much of its attention on human weaknesses, liabilities, and negative mental health. This lopsided and pessimistic view of human nature is especially true of the subfields known as abnormal psychology and clinical psychology. Over the last 50 years, these two subfields have expended a huge amount of energy

to understanding psychopathology and repairing what is wrong with people. This work (considered in Chapter 5) has produced a number of benefits. We know more today than we did previously about why people become depressed, why they become anxious, and why they suffer from other forms of negative mental health. In terms of treatment, we have also learned new methods of intervening to remediate such problems.

Unfortunately, the tremendous emphasis placed on understanding and treating negative mental health has come at a cost. We know little about the psychology of flourishing and thriving in life. The current chapter seeks to help fill the gap left open by the field's neglect of the positive side of human nature. In particular, you learn about the new field of positive psychology, which emphasizes well-being. **Well-being** may be defined as optimal adjustment to life and positive mental health. There are many examples of well-being. Perhaps the most studied of these is the subjective sense of satisfaction and happiness with the quality of one's life.

Relative to abnormal and clinical psychology, social psychology has been somewhat more balanced in terms of its concern with the negative and positive sides of human nature. Although it is true that social psychologists have given attention to harmful and destructive aspects of the human condition, they have also studied the positive side of it. Because of this two-pronged approach, we currently know a lot about social psychological factors that cause or contribute to prejudice, discrimination, and aggression. Knowledge of variables that influence these phenomena has led to initiatives designed to lessen or prevent social inequity and other types of hurtful actions. In addition, social psychologists have improved understanding of positive and constructive processes, such as altruism, helping, liking, and loving.

That said, like most other areas of psychology, social psychology has been somewhat biased by focusing largely on the negative. Krueger and Funder (2004) note that some of the most seminal studies in social psychology focus on negative phenomena, much of which has been discussed in this book: such as how people betray their own beliefs to conform to erroneous public opinion, obey orders that harm other people, fail to intervene to help others in need, and fall victim to cognitive biases like the fundamental attribution error. This type of research might lead us to believe that the power of the situation typically leads people to engage in negative, less than ideal behavior. However, as elaborated by Kruger and Funder (2004), this conclusion is likely misplaced given that the seemingly irrational, bad behavior often elicited in social psychological research settings may, over the long term, produce adaptive and effective social behavior in everyday circumstances.

Toward the end of the last century, and to remedy psychology's historical overreliance on studying negative phenomena, then President of the American Psychological Association, Martin Seligman, advanced the idea of positive psychology (Seligman, 1999). Whereas traditional psychology overemphasizes the negative side of life, positive psychology generally focuses on optimal human functioning, well-being, and the positive side of life (Linley, Joseph, Harrington, & Wood, 2006). Importantly, positive psychology includes the study of how social phenomena like

institutions help to promote positive outcomes (Seligman & Csikszentmihalyi, 2000). We refer to the emerging specialized branch of scholarship that studies how social psychological phenomena promote the best things in life as **positive social psychology**. Recently, a small cadre of research psychologists has begun to study the relevance of social psychological theories and concepts to understanding well-being. For example, building on Bronfenbrenner's (1977) experimental ecology, Lomas (2015) discusses how well-being can be promoted through interventions at various levels of the social environment. The microsystem level focuses on a person's immediate social environment, such as school or work. At this level positive outcomes can be promoted by positive parenting programs and positive workplace programs. The mesosystems level focuses on the interaction of microsystems. At this level, positive outcomes can be promoted by work-life balance programs, and school-family programs. The exosystem level focuses on social structures, such as community or mass media. At this level, well-being can be promoted by community-based programs, such as healthy eating and crime prevention initiatives. The macrosystem concerns overarching institutional patterns, such as economics and politics. At this level, well-being is promoted by initiatives like measuring "Gross National Happiness," instead of just GDP (gross domestic product). Finally, at the ecosystem level it is promoted by initiatives that sustain the planet, like programs to support energy consumption. All of these initiatives can be considered forms of positive social psychology.

In the current chapter, you learn more about this specialization, which has also been referred to as the interface of social psychology and positive psychology. Our general goal is to help you to better understand social-cognitive processes that make it more likely that a person will truly thrive and flourish in life. Our specific aim is to describe theory, research, and practical applications of *the expectancy construct;* that is, the role that expectations play in the lives of people. As such, we concentrate on the social psychology of optimism and pessimism. First, we define and describe the nature of optimism, and then identify its causes and its benefits. Consistent with the theme of this part of the book, special attention is given to showing students how they can put their knowledge of optimism and pessimism to use for purposes of improving the quality of their lives. Thus, in addition to describing theory and research, a major purpose of this chapter is to identify the practical relevance of this scholarship. To this end, we suggest techniques that people can use to enhance their ability to think adaptively. The specific technique or strategy we focus on is called attribution retraining (Forsterling, 2001). The more general term, *positive psychology coaching* is the name given to positive psychology technology as a whole (Biswas-Diener, 2010). This term has nothing to do with coaching in the context of athletics. It is more relevant to "life coaching." Essentially, coaching techniques are self-help strategies that research has shown are effective in helping to upgrade a person's well-being.

After learning about the relevant scholarship and trying out some of the positive coaching techniques, you learn that positive social psychology concerns itself with more than telling people to "don't worry, be happy." Using your own life as a case study, we believe you will see how positive social psychology can help you feel a greater sense of satisfaction with your life. Consistent with the emphasis in the positive psychology literature, our discussion focuses mostly on optimism, but we also discuss pessimism, and how a balanced perspective that incorporates both optimism and pessimism may offer you the best roadmap for producing your own well-being. At the end of the chapter, we broaden the discussion to give a brief overview of other areas that fall under the umbrella of the rapidly emerging field of positive social psychology.

OPTIMISM

Introduction to Optimism–Pessimism

Imagine a science fiction movie where people live in a world with no future. In such a world,

there is no such thing as optimism. By definition, optimism is a type of thinking that requires a person to be mindful about his or her future goals. How optimistic are you that you will get an *A* on your next exam in this course? Would you say your chances are 80% or above? Maybe you have serious doubts and would say your chances are below 25%. Generally speaking, social psychologists would call you optimistic in the first case, and pessimistic in the second case. From this example, you can see that optimism has to do with estimates of the future probability of reaching an important goal.

Outcome expectancies of optimists and pessimists. People who look forward to the future and see it as rosy differ from those who see it as bleak. The former (i.e., **optimists**) believe that good things are very likely to happen. Technically speaking, these people have *positive outcome expectancies* that significantly influence both their thinking and their approach to the world. The belief that a desirable goal in life (e.g., getting good grades) is attainable can have incentive value for the individual; that is, it can stimulate or energize both one's goal-directed thinking and one's goal-directed action. Positive expectancies also cause people to be more persistent when pursuing their goals. Persistence or "grit" helps to inoculate people against caving in to the temptation to give up on their efforts to attain their goals. Whereas optimistic expectancies can facilitate constructive actions that are goal congruent, negative expectancies—those held by **pessimists**—can have the opposite effect. People who doubt their chances of attaining desirable goals often withhold effort. Negative outcome expectancies can act as disincentives. They can demotivate people and produce destructive actions that are goal incongruent. This is why pessimists are sometimes more likely to quit or give up when faced with obstacles that block their progress toward goals.

People have expectancies for attaining a variety of valued goals in many different areas of their lives. It will come as no surprise that in addition to having academic aspirations and expectancies, students have aspirations and expectancies for their romantic lives, social lives, and family lives. They also have career goals and goals for their physical and mental health. From your own personal experience, you probably know students who have strong convictions that they will reach most of their goals in most spheres of their lives. On balance, their faith outweighs their doubt. You may also know a few people who harbor more doubt than conviction. Think about yourself and all the different goals in life that you aspire to reach. On balance, which are you: an optimist or a pessimist? Does it really matter? Why should you care? The previous paragraph clearly suggests whether a person is more of an optimist or a pessimist matters a great deal. Next we consider in what ways it matters.

Consequences of outcome expectancies. One of the main reasons that positive social psychologists study optimists and pessimists is that particular expectancies for the future can affect the outcomes people achieve and the quality of their lives. As you see later in the chapter, research shows a person's level of optimism influences a wide range of life outcomes. To give you a "trailer" of "coming attractions," research shows that compared with their pessimistic counterparts, people who hold optimistic expectancies generally enjoy better emotional well-being, better medical health, and better academic performance. Occupational research also shows that optimists outperform and even outearn pessimists in work-related achievement domains. Last, but not least, optimists have people in their lives who give them more social support, and they also enjoy more satisfying romantic relationships. In general, research suggests that optimists thrive and flourish in a greater number of life domains. However, as we see, this is not always the case. There can sometimes be value in pessimism, too. The good life may best be achieved by adopting a balanced approach between optimism and pessimism.

But, we're getting ahead of ourselves. For now, as an example of the value of optimism in the educational domain, let's take the case of a student who is attending the last year of high school, but who is (unrealistically) pessimistic about getting into college despite having good grades. Because of the negative expectancies, the student feels demoralized and does not bother to apply for higher education. This example illustrates a **self-fulfilling prophecy**: when the way you imagine the future leads you to behave in a manner that causes the imagined future to come true. Action (or inaction) follows belief (or disbelief). Self-fulfilling prophecies can have real-life consequences. For the student in question, making a pessimistic prediction about goal attainment easily could have long-term detrimental effects because it can curb educational advancement, which in turn will likely limit career options, and future earnings potential. Thankfully, when you were in your last year of high school, you were likely more optimistic about your future in education. Your positive expectancies motivated you to actively pursue postsecondary school education. Happily, the optimistic prediction you had about your life paid off, and you are on the way to earning your degree.

Let's review the self-fulfilling prophecy process as it is relevant to any sphere of life in which people may or may not strive for valued goals. People—optimists—who believe their futures will be rosy in a given domain of life (e.g., relationships, career) are likely to actually take steps toward realizing their desired futures. For pessimists, however, negative expectancies can act as disincentives, which demotivate them. As a result, people who believe the future will be dark, cold, and wet tend to withhold effort, thereby increasing the chances that the undesirable future will actually happen. If you forecast warm and sunny "relationship weather," you increase your chances of making this happen. The reason is simple enough. The greater motivation of optimists leads them to make a greater number of constructive efforts that move them closer and closer to their desired futures.

Self-Assessment of Optimism–Pessimism

To facilitate your understanding of the conceptual information in this chapter, we encourage you to pause for a moment now and respond to a series of questions that we refer to as the self-assessment inventory. The questions are designed to help you reflect on the future and the outcomes you expect to attain.

From a positive social psychological perspective, optimism is a domain-specific way of perceiving the future. You may be optimistic about some spheres of your life, but fall on the pessimistic side when thinking about other spheres. The self-assessment inventory is designed to help you to become more mindful of whether you are optimistic or pessimistic in several life domains.

Interpretation of your results is straightforward. If, for example, your overall optimism score is somewhere in the 60 to 79 range, the measure suggests that you have an overall moderate level of optimism, whereas if your overall score is in the 20 to 39 range, a moderate level of pessimism is suggested. Thus, the average score that you receive across the five domains of optimism gives you some indication of the extent to which you are in general either optimistic or pessimistic. Recognize that the self-assessment scale was developed specifically for the purpose of this chapter and may

not meet the psychometric criteria that are required of established personal assessment measures. For instance, no attempt has been made to systematically determine various indices of reliability and validity. Nonetheless, to the extent that you conscientiously and candidly answer the five questions, the exercise may be regarded as providing personally relevant feedback concerning your level of optimism–pessimism.

Furthermore, we should also recognize that there are many spheres of life in which optimism plays a role, some of which are not tapped by the self-assessment scale (see if you can add a few to the list of five), and therefore the overall score is far from inclusive. Also, what may be of more pertinence and interest to you than the overall score are the indices of optimism–pessimism with respect to specific domains of life. As we noted earlier, for some people, optimism levels can vary substantially, including from one domain of life to the next. You can use the same classification scheme to identify your level of optimism–pessimism for each of the five domains.

SELF-ASSESSMENT INVENTORY

We invite you to reflect on your future with respect to five domains of life. For each domain, a positive outcome is indicated. You are to think forward to a year after you graduate and use the following probability rating scale to indicate what you believe is the probability that you will actually achieve the positive outcome as stated.

| 0% | 10% | 20% | 30% | 40% | 50% | 60% | 70% | 80% | 90% | 100% |

For each domain, select a probability between 0% and 100%. For instance, if you choose 10%, it means you believe there is very little likelihood that your life will be this way one year after graduation. The only requirement is to be honest with yourself. When answering, avoid giving in to the temptation to be unrealistically optimistic (i.e., avoid wishful thinking).

Write the probabilities that you select on a piece of paper. Carefully consider each question and select the probability that you will attain the stated outcome one year after graduation. Now please begin.

1.   What are the chances you will be in a satisfying and fulfilling romantic relationship?

2.   What are the chances you will be doing fun things with good friends?

3. What are the chances you will have excellent medical health?

4. What are the chances you will be very happy with your life?

5. What are the chances you will have a satisfying job, or be working for an advanced degree that meets with your satisfaction?

Once you have answered all five questions, you can calculate your overall level of optimism by adding up the five selected probability scores and dividing by 5. Then you can identify your level of optimism–pessimism in accordance with the following classification:

80–100   high optimism

60–79   moderate optimism

40–59   neutral

20–39   moderate pessimism

0–19   high pessimism

If the results suggest that you have a mixed profile, we invite you to think of reasons why you might be more optimistic (or pessimistic) in one or more of the domains than in others. Use this self-assessment exercise as a means of helping you to explore this very important aspect of well-being—optimism—as it pertains to you. Later, we identify some factors that affect why people tend to be optimistic or pessimistic.

In the next section, we provide a fuller examination of the nature of optimism. We also show how social psychological theory is relevant to a scientific understanding of optimism. We discuss prominent theories used to explain optimism, and we apply the theories to the vignette at the beginning of this chapter.

The Social Psychology of Optimism

Social psychologists have developed several theories to describe the processes underlying optimism and pessimism. Two theories are described here: Carver and Scheier's (2009) expectancy theory, and Seligman's (2011) learned optimism theory. Common to both theories is the idea that optimism has little to do with

the objective characteristics of the situation, which can range from dire to ideal. Instead, optimism is a largely subjective perceptual phenomenon. As a mini learning exercise, we invite you to obtain and fill to the halfway mark two identical juice glasses. Be sure to fill both glasses exactly halfway. Set them side-by-side and focus your attention on the glass on the left. Using the power of your mind, see the glass as being half full. Try to sense, to experience, its fullness. This is how optimists experience the world. Now shift your gaze to the glass on the right. Focus your mind on the fact it is half empty. Experience its emptiness. If you can actually experience its emptiness, you now know how many pessimists tend to think when considering their future lives (see Figure 17.1). Do you generally see glasses as half-empty or half-full?

In their conception of optimism, Scheier and Carver (1992) maintain that optimism presupposes that people are able to identify goals that exist in the future. There are *two basic kinds of goal:* things we want to happen (approach goals), and things we don't want to happen (avoidance goals). When thinking about the future, optimists believe that good things will be plentiful and that bad things will be rare. For instance, you might

Figure 17.1   Is the Glass Half Empty or Half Full?

think it is important to get high marks on your future exams. According to Scheier and Carver, there are individual differences in the subjective probability that positive-valued goals will be realized and negative-valued goals will be averted. If you are an optimist, you will believe there is a high probability that you will both obtain high marks and avoid failing exams. On the other hand, if you are a pessimist, you will believe the probability is low that you will achieve high marks and avoid failing exams. By definition, optimists strongly expect good things will happen in the future. They believe they will get what they want. Conversely, pessimists strongly expect bad things will happen in the future. They believe they will get what they fear.

Using the power of your imagination, think forward to your next exam in this course and about the exercise involving the two juice glasses. With regard to what you expect as a grade on your next exam, which glass do you most closely identify with? Does the "empty" glass come to mind, or are you thinking about the "full" glass? Keep in mind that it matters a lot whether you see life through the eyes of an optimist or a pessimist. During times of difficulty or

goal frustration, optimistic thinking can lead to continued efforts in the service of goal pursuit. In contrast, when the going gets tough, negative thinking can undermine effort.

What determines if a person is an optimist or a pessimist? There are many reasons why someone might see his or her glass as being half full or half empty. You may recall that in Chapter 5 we mentioned Seligman's learned helplessness theory of depression (Abramson, Seligman, & Teasdale, 1978). Seligman (2011) has modified that theory. His modification is called **learned optimism theory**. This theory identifies factors that determine whether someone is likely to think about the future in ways that are optimistic or pessimistic. According to Seligman, your expectancies for the future depend on the kinds of attributions you make. An **attribution** is an inference about why something happened (also for example, see Chapter 10). Seligman's learned optimism theory classifies attributions along three dimensions: internal/external, stable/unstable, and global/specific. The types of attribution that people make affect the degree of optimism that they have for the future.

Internal attributions occur when individuals attribute events that happen to them internally, that is, to self-related causes. In contrast, **external attributions** occur when individuals attribute such events externally, that is, to things that are outside of themselves and often out of their control, such as luck or other people. Optimists tend to make internal attributions for positive events like receiving a good mark ("I am responsible; something about me caused the good mark"), and they make external attributions for negative events like receiving a poor mark ("I am not responsible; something else caused the bad mark"). On the other hand, pessimists tend to infer the opposite: They make external attributions—shun responsibility—for good events, and make internal attributions—assume responsibility—for bad events.

Stable attributions are made when people attribute events to things that are not likely to change (e.g., level of intelligence, discriminatory practices). In contrast, **unstable attributions** are made when people attribute events to factors that are temporary (e.g., a head cold, bad weather). In this case, the event is explained as being due to a cause that is unusual and/or unlikely to occur often. Optimists tend to make stable attributions for good things that happen (i.e., the cause of this good event will continue to benefit me), and unstable attributions for bad things that happen (i.e., the cause is temporary, and thus unlikely to harm me again). The attributions of pessimists reflect the opposite pattern where they see the cause of positive events as unstable, and the cause of negative events as stable. Last, **global attributions** are made when people believe that the cause of an event will have wide-ranging effects. **Specific attributions** are made when people believe that the cause of an event will be limited to that area of life. Optimists tend to make global attributions for good events (i.e., the cause has benefited me in this area, and also can benefit me in other areas), whereas they tend to make specific attributions for negative events (i.e., the cause has harmed me in this area, but will not in other areas). As you might expect, pessimists tend to explain good and bad things that happen to them with the opposite pattern of attributions.

Peterson and Seligman (1984) suggest that people tend to adopt habitual ways of explaining why things happen in their lives. Consistent differences in the types of causal attributions that people make have been termed **explanatory style**. According to this framework, *differences in explanatory style can help to account for how people become optimists and pessimists.* You may have anticipated which pattern of causal attributions is associated with optimists and which pattern is associated with pessimists. An **optimistic explanatory style** (also called positive explanatory style) involves the following: Individuals make internal, stable, and global attributions to account for why good things happen to them. For example, "I got a good mark because I am smart." This explanation involves an internal attribution (my intelligence is the cause), a stable attribution (level of intelligence does not change), and a global attribution (high intelligence affects performance in other courses and areas of life). On the other hand, when bad things happen, the optimistic explanatory style involves external, unstable, and specific attributions. For example, "I got a poor mark because my neighbor had an all-night engagement party." This is an external attribution (the neighbor's party was the cause), an unstable attribution (engagement parties do not happen often), and a specific attribution (the negative effect of the party pertains only to this one exam).

Now a **pessimistic explanatory style** (also called negative explanatory style) involves a very different set of attributions than an optimistic explanatory style. The individual uses external, unstable, and specific attributions to explain good things that happen to him or her. For example, "I received a good mark because I got lucky." This is an external attribution (good performance was seen as due to something outside of the self), an unstable attribution (luck changes), and a specific attribution (the luck helped with the exam performance, but not with anything else). When bad things happen to the pessimist, he or she accounts for them by making internal, stable, and global attributions. For example, "I got a poor mark because I am not smart." This is an internal attribution (my low intelligence is the cause), a stable attribution (intelligence level does not change), and a global attribution (low intelligence negatively influences performance in other courses and areas of life).

Having considered the different explanatory styles of optimists and pessimists, including the examples provided, we expect that you have a clearer understanding of how optimists think and how pessimists think and in particular of the marked differences in how they account for the good and bad things that happen to them. When a good thing occurs, optimistic people lay claim to it, see themselves as responsible for its occurrence, expect to be able to accomplish it again, and expect to accomplish similar good things in other areas of their lives. Pessimists, on the other hand, see something or someone other than themselves as responsible for the occurrence of the good thing, and think it is unlikely to occur again (or often) in similar or different situations. Optimists and pessimists "trade" patterns of attributions when a bad thing happens. Simply put, pessimists blame themselves; optimists do not.

Case example of a pessimist. Recall the vignette about Deena at the beginning of the chapter. Even before reading any more of this chapter, it is quite likely that you identified Deena as a pessimistic thinker. If you had done so, you would have been correct. Let us analyze that scenario from the standpoint of the social psychological concepts that we have considered.

The vignette begins with Deena waiting for Jim to pick her up for their first date. On the surface, this had the potential to be a good date. Deena was an attractive young woman (as described in the Chapter 5 vignette), was very attracted to Jim, and on at least one level was excited about the date with Jim. However, leading up to the date, Deena was plagued by negative outcome expectancies (e.g., about the impression she would make, and how she often "screwed up first dates"). The negative expectancies, as a form of self-fulfilling prophecy, set in motion negative thoughts that threatened to sabotage the date (thoughts about calling it off), even before it had begun.

We see evidence of Deena's attributional style. As noted, she made internal attributions for previous unsuccessful first dates. Also notice when a seemingly minor negative event occurred, Jim not arriving exactly on time, Deena overreacted by entertaining the possibility that once again she may have done something—behaved awkwardly, hadn't washed her hair—to undermine a date (this time even before it happened). Jim's tardiness triggered other pessimistic thoughts, including assuming he might be having second thoughts, and not be interested in her; Deena even questioning her own interest in him. We see further evidence of Deena's pessimistic explanatory style when after the date she reflected on the evening with Jim, which involved the two having a fun time together (e.g., good conversation, lots of laughter). In typical pessimistic fashion, Deena explained this positive event (a good thing that happened to her) by disclaiming responsibility for causing it (she hadn't "done much to make it fun"), and pointing to external, largely temporary (unstable) and situation-specific causes, including the wine, the movie, and Jim's sense of humor. Furthermore, we can see that Deena's negative thinking and attributions throughout the scenario served to reinforce her negative outcome expectancies for the future; she doubted that Jim would call her, but if he did, it would be unlikely that a second date would be as successful as the first.

If Deena was an optimist instead of a pessimist, imagine the same scenario involving Deena and Jim, but with positive outcome expectancies and an optimistic explanatory style that guided her thinking and actions. We expect that she would have eagerly, and with few if any concerns, looked forward to the date with Jim. She would have barely given a thought to his not arriving exactly on time; freely enjoyed the evening with Jim (even more so than pessimist Deena); never questioned her contribution to the date's success; expected to receive a call from Jim; and looked forward to another fun time with him. It is apparent there is quite a difference in the romantic relationship lives of the two Deenas. Clearly, there are benefits that stem from being an optimist. In the next section, we consider some of the benefits.

The Benefits of Optimism

There is an abundance of research that suggests optimism facilitates adjustment (social, psychological, physical) across a variety of spheres of life (Carver, Scheier, & Segerstrom, 2010). We consider the benefits of optimism in six spheres: romantic relationships, friendships, biomedical health, mental and emotional health, work, and college. In this section, we review a small portion of the large body of research that points to the advantages of optimistic thinking. Some of the studies used an overall (dispositional) measure of optimism, whereas other studies used a domain-specific measure. Regardless of the kind of measure used, the research generally points to the benefits of optimistic thinking. In some cases, we indicate what the study suggests about why and how optimism exerts its beneficial influence.

Romantic relationships. Research suggests that optimism has positive effects on the well-being of couples involved in dyadic romantic relationships. In one study (Assad, Donnellan, & Conger, 2007), greater optimism among relationship members was associated with better relationship satisfaction, happiness, and functioning. The findings suggest that the positive outcomes might be due to the fact that optimistic couples tend to engage in more cooperative problem solving than pessimistic couples. Another study involved couples in which the woman was being treated for breast cancer (Abend & Williamson, 2002). Compared with more pessimistic women, optimistic women reported that their partners found them to be more physically attractive, and were more available to give support and nurturance. Also, relationship disagreement levels were lower in couples with more optimistic women.

Friendships. The quality of nonromantic friendships has also been found to be higher in friendships consisting of optimists compared with pessimists. For example, optimism among friends has been shown to be positively correlated with the perceived availability of social support and with support reciprocity, and negatively correlated with levels of interpersonal conflict (Friedman et al., 2006; Sumi, 2006).

Biomedical health. There is an extensive base of evidence suggesting optimism generally contributes to positive biomedical health outcomes. In a study of psychological factors that influence women's biological responses (e.g., estradiol levels) to fertility treatment, Lancastle and Boivin (2005) found that optimism is associated with a better response and that this effect is explained as likely due to optimists' higher levels of emotional calm, and lower levels of negative emotional reactivity. Mulkana and Hailey (2001) investigated why lower levels of medical symptoms are found in persons who score high on optimism. Among university students, they found better health-related lifestyle habits in optimists, and suggested that health-enhancing lifestyle behaviors likely serve to protect and preserve the health of optimists.

Mental and emotional health. Similarly, the evidence supporting a link between optimism and mental health is convincing. Affleck, Tennen, and Apter (2001) investigated emotional well-being in persons suffering from rheumatoid arthritis, asthma, and fibromyalgia. Their results indicated that day-to-day levels of happiness were positively related to optimism, whereas levels of sadness were inversely related to optimism. The authors suggested that optimists are better able to regulate their moods than are pessimists. Similar results have been found with healthy employed adults. For example, a Finnish study showed that optimistic employees suffered from less emotional exhaustion (burnout) and mental distress than pessimistic employees (Makikangas & Kinnunen, 2003).

Work. Research has strongly suggested optimism contributes to better performance and better adjustment in occupational settings. In a study by Segerstrom (2007), former law students were followed for over ten years after they graduated. The results showed that more optimistic first-year law students made more money ten years later. It was suggested that this effect can be explained by higher levels of effort and persistence. Other research has shown that in work situations, job satisfaction, work happiness, and organizational commitment are all higher in optimists (Youssef & Luthans, 2007), whereas distress symptoms and burnout are lower (Kluemper, Little, & DeGroot, 2009).

College. Of immediate relevance to you is evidence that indicates an appreciable connection between the levels of optimism and college student performance and retention. Chemers, Hu, and Garcia (2001) demonstrated a direct relationship between positive outcome expectancies (optimism) and college grades. In addition, Nes, Evans, and Segerstrom (2009) explored the role that optimism might play with respect to college retention, noting that predictors of retention are especially important to identify given the fact that the average annual income of adults with a bachelor's degree is almost 90% greater than that of adults with a high school diploma. The researchers found support for their prediction that students with high scores on optimism would be less likely to drop out of college than students with low scores.

What makes optimism more beneficial than pessimism in the context of being a full-time student who is studying for a degree? Some answers to this question were hinted at in the research covering the benefits of optimism earlier in this section. At this point, let us examine the idea that optimistic students cope with the stresses of their education more effectively. A number of studies have examined the roles of optimism and pessimism in the employment of two basic types of coping strategy: problem-focused coping (also known as approach-oriented coping), and emotion-focused coping (also known as avoidance-oriented coping). **Problem-focused coping** involves engaging in behaviors (words, deeds, cognitions) that are aimed at modifying a stressful situation that is perceived by the individual to be controllable and amenable to change. **Emotion-focused coping** involves behaviors and cognitions that do not directly address the source of stress; instead they aim to reduce the individual's level of emotional distress. Avoidance strategies involve cognitive or behavioral distraction or withdrawal.

Aspinwall and Taylor (1992) studied approach- and avoidance-oriented coping in university students who were undergoing a high degree of academic stress. Their findings showed that optimistic students coped better than pessimistic students. In particular, optimists were more likely to use direct, problem-focused coping strategies. The optimists were more likely to seek out and find new friends, and to ask other students for help. Also, they studied harder for exams and were less likely to report wanting to give up. Pessimistic students, on the other hand, were more likely to employ emotion-focused coping strategies, including the following kinds of behavior: They avoided thinking about deadlines, disengaged from studying and preparing for classes, procrastinated, and became distracted by irrelevant (to academic progress) social activities. Pessimists also engaged in more wishful-thinking coping, which tends to be passive and not very constructive. As a result of their different modes of coping, the problems faced by pessimists were more likely to fester and get worse, whereas the problems confronted by optimists tended to be taken care of more effectively. Because this study by Aspinwall and Taylor tracked students' emotional well-being/adjustment over time, it provides evidence consistent with the following causal chain of influence: Initial optimism leads to the use of effective coping responses, which in turn contribute to both better psychological well-being/adjustment and better academic performance.

Positive Coaching Exercises

A wide variety of coaching techniques has been studied by scholars who conduct research at the interface of social psychology and positive psychology. These techniques tend to be brief and psychoeducational in nature, and when they are enacted by individuals themselves, they represent personal interventions—the focus of this part of the book. That is, individuals draw on social psychological theory and evidence to develop a strategy directed at improving their functioning in some area of life. Coaching exercises that involve disputing pessimistic causal attributions (i.e., maladaptive attributions), and replacing them with optimistic attributions (i.e., adaptive attributions) are commonly referred to as **attribution retraining interventions**. Attribution retraining has been shown to improve many aspects of human functioning: for example, prevention of depression (Reivich, Gillham, Chaplin, & Seligman, 2005); increase in academic performance (Berkeley, Mastropieri, & Scruggs, 2011); improvement in benefits from couples and family therapy (Hilt, 2003); increase in happiness (Shapira & Mongrain, 2010); reduction in aggressive behavior (Hudley, Graham, & Taylor, 2007); increase in achievement motivation (Perry, Hechter, Menec, & Weinberg, 1993); and enhanced consideration of career goals (Szabo, 2006).

In this section of the chapter, we invite you to take advantage of the opportunity to upgrade your quality of life by engaging in an attribution retraining exercise. The concepts and theories discussed so far will have no practical benefit in terms of upgrading the quality of your life unless you make an effort to put them into action. This means you need to find time to practice the techniques. Some students may only want "head knowledge" of the principles we discussed. If this is true in your case, you can read through the rest of this section to achieve an understanding of the process of attribution retraining, and then move on to the rest of the chapter. However, before doing so, remember the section on the benefits of optimism and the compelling advantages that people who think optimistically often have over people who think pessimistically in a wide diversity of areas of life. We believe that virtually anyone has something to gain from supplementing his or her cognitive understanding with "experiential understanding."

It is perhaps an oversimplification, but we distinguish between three categories of people who may be involved in attribution retraining:

those who are pessimists (moderate or high); those who are on the border between optimism and pessimism; and those who are optimists (moderate or high). The self-assessment inventory that you completed earlier in the chapter may help you identify your category either for the overall score, or for each individual domain. However, regardless of a person's category, the overriding goal is the same—to have positive (and realistic) outcome expectancies with respect to an important domain of life, or important domains of life. This is the key to becoming involved in attribution retraining. You must acknowledge the importance and benefits to you of thinking as an optimist (i.e., having positive outcome expectancies) with regard to significant areas of your life. Remember that positive expectancies can energize and motivate the individual to expend effort toward the achievement of goals, whereas negative outcome expectancies can do the opposite—de-energize and demotivate the individual. Also, you must remember that a person's explanatory style has a significant influence on his or her outcome expectancies; specifically, a positive explanatory style contributing to and undergirding positive expectancies, and a negative explanatory style undermining them and supporting the development and maintenance of negative expectancies.

At the heart of the process of attribution retraining is changing (i.e., retraining) the causal attributions that people make for positive and negative things that happen to them in particular domains of their lives. As you would expect, pessimists must undergo more change in their attribution styles than those who are somewhere between optimism and pessimism. In the case of high optimists, the term *retraining* may not be especially applicable; for the most part, these individuals may have to simply review and verify their attribution styles and recommit to them. Needless to say, structured attribution retraining programs do not routinely involve people who have positive outcome expectancies with respect to the domain area in question. To provide you with guidance about attribution retraining, we briefly consider two domains as a means of illustrating the process of attribution retraining: education and romantic relationships. However, the process and principles that are illustrated also are relevant to attribution retraining in other spheres of life.

Attribution retraining in the academic domain. With regard to the domain of concern (in this case the academic domain), the first step is to take some time to examine the kinds of attribution that you typically make when you experience successful outcomes (e.g., satisfactory grades), and unsuccessful outcomes (e.g., unsatisfactory grades). As you carry out this retraining exercise, you may find it helpful to write down the ideas that come to your mind. Think of a few successful academic outcomes that you have had in the recent past, and the causal attributions that you may have made at the time, or now make. If you make an external and unstable attribution (i.e., accrediting good luck, or assigning success to an unusually easy test, this is undesirable because you are not assigning responsibility for the positive event to yourself. Do your best to identify an internal and potentially stable cause, such as the good grade being a reflection of your ability and knowledge or your effort and hard work. Such explanations help to encourage expectations of continued success (i.e., stability), possibly enhancing your performance in other courses as well (i.e., global attribution).

Likewise, think of some unsuccessful academic outcomes that you had in the recent past and attributions that you made (or now make) in explaining them. It is especially undesirable if you tend to explain negative academic outcomes as the result of lack of ability because a person has little or no control over such a stable factor, and as such the attribution merely reinforces and sustains negative outcome expectations. Be very careful not to assume that you have low ability for the subject matter of a course because admission to your school signifies that the admissions staff evaluated your intelligence as sufficient to succeed and graduate from their institution. More than likely there are other students whose ability level is at your ability level or lower and

who have achieved quite satisfactorily in the course in question.

Do your best to change the attribution from ability/intelligence to either bad luck or lack of effort (unstable causes), because both leave open the possibility of improved performance in the future. Now that you have taken a first step in changing your explanatory style regarding academic performance, periodically repeat the exercise, which is especially valuable when newly relevant academic outcomes occur. With time, you should experience movement toward a more functional (i.e., optimistic) explanatory style, and accordingly more positive outcome expectancies with their self-fulfilling properties, including increased motivation, effort, persistence, and rewards.

Attribution retraining in the romantic relationship domain. The relationship between Deena and Jim, described in the opening vignette, falls into this domain category as a new romantic relationship. Recall that at one point Deena had apparently thought of Jim as possibly her "Mr. Right." At the end of the section, "The Social Psychology of Optimism," we included a social psychological analysis of that early stage of Deena and Jim's relationship, which revealed Deena's pessimistic outcome expectancies and explanatory style. We do not repeat that information here, but suggest that Deena is a prime candidate for attribution retraining in that her maladaptive attributions are seriously interfering with her ability to adjust well to her social world. The objective of attribution retraining is to help her alter her attributions for bad and good relationship events in such a way that she doesn't readily see herself as the cause of negative events, which prohibits her from seeing herself as a significant causal factor with regard to positive events.

Now we ask you to think back to a time when you were in a romantic relationship that ended poorly with your partner initiating the breakup, and leaving you with angry and/or hurt feelings. If this kind of situation has not happened to you, use the power of your imagination to think up a likely scenario. (Another possibility is for you to think in terms of a friendship relationship that ended with the other person severing the ties.) Reflect for a few moments about the reason(s) for the breakup, including what you regard is the single most important cause of the relationship breakdown. Conduct an analysis of the attributions you have made. If you made an internal attribution and believe that something about you caused the breakup, we caution that certain kinds of internal attribution will tend to dampen your optimism, and increase your pessimism about future romantic relationships. Attributions for past negative events, such as a partner-initiated breakup that are both internal and stable (thus not under your control), should be avoided because they hinder optimism and breed pessimism. For example, you may think the relationship ended because you are unlovable or not sufficiently attractive. Your cognition is that you caused the breakup due to a characteristic of yours that will continue to threaten future romantic relationships. Such a cognition promotes and reinforces pessimistic outcome expectancies.

If you make an internal attribution for the breakup, an unstable cause is preferable because you may see yourself at fault, but a reoccurrence of the cause having a similar effect is not necessarily likely to happen. This is closer to the way optimists think. For example, maybe you made some faulty choices. Bad decision making identifies you as the cause, but future decisions do not have to continue to be problematic. Moreover, try to come up with an attribution that is even more consistent with the optimistic explanatory

style. Optimists tend to make external attributions for bad events. For example, if you attributed the breakup to a change in life circumstances of your partner (he or she had to move to a distant city), we would classify this as both an external attribution and one that is unstable. Take a moment to reflect on other aspects of the explanation you offered for the breakup. If you made stable attributions, think again. Finally, if you made a global attribution, think again. Try to come up with a specific attribution that is potentially true. The goal is to tilt the balance so that optimism tends to outweigh pessimism.

Now that you have engaged in some attribution retraining concerning your academic performance and your romantic relationships, consider how you can extrapolate the approach to explaining good and bad events in other domains of your life. To improve the breadth of your optimism for the future, try to reexplain your past failures (and successes) in other spheres of life. Ask yourself why bad things happened, and why good things happened. Write down explanations for why these things happened. The more time you can spend questioning and disputing negative attributions, the better. By getting enough practice replacing negative attributions with positive ones, you will be able to teach yourself how to be more optimistic about the future. While it is impossible to always be 100% optimistic in all domains of your life, it is possible to eliminate stubborn patterns of habitual pessimism, patterns that are self-limiting and self-defeating. Research suggests the payoff is an upgraded quality of life.

CULTURE CAPSULE

East–West Differences in the Optimistic Bias

Are North Americans more prone to optimism than people from the Far East? People who believe good things are more likely to occur in their own lives relative to the lives of others (and who think bad things are relatively less likely) may be said to score high on optimism. Some scholars use the

(Continued)

(Continued)

term **optimistic bias** to describe skewed results of comparative judgments. For instance, people who score high on optimistic bias would think their chances of winning the Powerball lottery in the future are better than the comparative chances of others, and also would believe they are less likely than others to get into a serious car accident. In contrast, when thinking about their futures, people who believe bad things are more likely to occur (and who thereby think good things are less likely) are said to score low on optimistic bias. In other words, some people have a **pessimistic bias**. Such people would tend to believe their own chances of winning the lottery and getting into a car accident are lower and higher, respectively, than the comparative chances of others.

Research by Chang, Asakawa, and Sanna (2001) examined the question of cultural differences in optimistic bias. In their study, Japanese (representing Easterners) were compared to European Americans (representing Westerners). Based on the evidence that Westerners are more sensitive to positive information about themselves (i.e., in line with the Western cultural norm supporting self-enhancement), and Easterners are more sensitive to negative information about themselves (i.e., in line with the Eastern cultural norm supporting self-criticism), the authors hypothesized that Westerners would show an optimistic bias for both positive and negative events, and Easterners would show a pessimistic bias for both positive and negative events.

In two studies, students at the University of Michigan (the Westerners), and students at Shikoku Gakuin University (the Easterners) filled out self-report questionnaires that measured degrees of optimistic bias and pessimistic bias. As predicted, the Westerners believed that it was less likely that bad things would happen to them relative to others. This finding was interpreted as evidence of an optimistic bias for negative events. It is easy to see how such a "bias" might help give a person a subjective sense of safety and security. Contrary to prediction, Easterners also believed that it is less likely that negative events would happen to them. This unexpected finding suggests there was no East–West difference in people's optimistic bias for negative events—both groups showed an optimistic bias.

However, a cultural difference was found for positive events. As hypothesized, the Easterners showed a pessimistic bias for future good events—they tended to believe that good things are more likely to happen to others than to themselves. Curiously, when forecasting the chances of good things happening in the future, Westerners had neither an optimistic (which had been hypothesized), nor a pessimistic bias. In sum, the results provided evidence of a cultural difference, but only in pessimistic bias regarding positive events.

It should be noted the study entailed a correlational research design; thus, inferences about cause-and-effect relationships must remain tentative. That is, we cannot conclude that the American–Japanese difference in pessimistic bias concerning positive events was caused by differences in culture. Also, stronger conclusions about East–West differences must await replication of the results in a wider representation of cultural groups.

PESSIMISM

Now that we have likely sold you on the value of optimism, we want you to apply the brakes a little bit. It turns out that the wholehearted adoption of an exclusively optimistic outlook may not be what best promotes your well-being and the good life. For example, what if you're not performing well in school because you're not studying hard enough? Simply adopting an optimistic perspective isn't going to help you perform better, succeed in life, or enhance your well-being. Consider Deena again. What if she's pessimistic about screwing up her first few dates because she's genuinely socially awkward, and commits faux pas in her interactions that lead her dates to be less enamored of her than they would be otherwise? Attribution retraining isn't going to help her succeed on her dates if she continues to commit social blunders. It might actually be better for Deena to believe that she is in fact likely to mess up her dates, and then take steps to mitigate such negative outcomes. People who think this way are known as defensive pessimists.

Defensive pessimism is "a cognitive strategy in which people set low expectations and reflect extensively on possible outcomes prior to an event, situation, or performance" (Norem & Illingsworth, 2004, p. 352). For example, someone who is optimistic about passing an upcoming test may not invest much effort in studying because they feel they'll perform adequately. However, someone who is defensively pessimistic and anxious because they expect to fail an upcoming test may be motivated to try to search for ways to avoid failing. Somewhat paradoxically, given our prior discussion of the advantages of optimism, the defensive pessimist may actually outperform the optimist on the test. Indeed, research demonstrates that defensive pessimists sometimes outperform optimists (Norem & Illingsworth, 2004).

Defensive pessimism typically occurs among people who tend to be anxious. The anxiety that defensive pessimists experience is not an outcome of their pessimistic thinking style, but is in fact part of what drives them to consider ways to mitigate negative outcomes. Put another way, they can reduce their anxiety if they plan for how to deal with negative outcomes so that such outcomes can be avoided or minimized. Because of this, asking defensive pessimists to think optimistically actually harms them (Norem & Chang, 2002).

So, it seems that the relationship between optimism, pessimism, and "the good life" is more complicated than we led you to believe in the earlier part of this chapter. In addition to there being some potential advantages to being pessimistic, at least sometimes and for some people, there are also potential disadvantages to being optimistic, sometimes and for some people. Promoting well-being may be best achieved not by always adopting an optimistic outlook, but by adopting a more balanced outlook. Remember when we asked you to consider whether you generally see glasses as half empty or half full? Maybe it's best to generally see them as both half full *and* half empty at the same time. That's balance.

A BALANCED VIEW OF OPTIMISM AND PESSIMISM

In a review of the literature, Gruman, Lumley, and Gonzalez-Morales (2016) suggested that research and writing in the area of positive psychology generally presents an overly positive, and thus slanted, view of the good life. To correct this, Gruman et al. (2016) presented a conceptual framework explicitly based on balance, and discussed a number of ways in which balance can be considered to better promote well-being and other positive outcomes. We apply this framework in the present chapter to provide a more balanced view of the role of optimism and pessimism in promoting the good life.

One way to consider balance is *balance as mid-range*. Balance as mid-range suggests that the good life is often best achieved by manifesting moderate, not extremely high levels of positive constructs. Indeed, there is research showing that too much optimism can be bad for you. In a longitudinal study with inner-city women, Devine et al. (2000) found that moderate levels of optimism at Time 1 were subsequently associated with low levels of depression, but that higher levels of optimism at Time 1 were subsequently associated with higher levels of depression. They noted that their results call into question the idea that greater optimism produces better functioning, and concluded that excessive optimism can be detrimental. Similar results were obtained by Milam, Richardson, Marks, Kemper and McCutchan (2004) who found that after controlling for disease status at baseline, HIV-infected individuals who displayed moderate levels of optimism had higher CD4 counts (a marker of relative health) months later compared to those with low or high levels of optimism. Milam et al. (2004) concluded that high levels of optimism do not protect against HIV disease progression, speculating that high optimism might induce stress when desired positive health outcomes can't be achieved. Milam et al. (2004) also suggested that there might be an "optimal margin of optimism" (p. 177). Thus, achieving well-being and success may be best accomplished by having some, but not too much optimism.

A second way to consider balance is *balance as synthesis*. Balance as synthesis involves considering how multiple variables operate jointly in promoting the good life. In our case, it means considering how optimism and pessimism may operate in tandem. At first, the idea of optimism and pessimism operating jointly may seem odd because we tend to regard them as opposite ends of a single pole, as suggested in the scale you completed earlier in the chapter. However, there is research suggesting that optimism and pessimism may be effectively thought of as distinct systems that exist on two independent poles (Herzberg, Glaesmer, & Hoyer, 2006; Peterson, 2000). This means you can be high on optimism and pessimism, or low on both, or high on one and low on the other, at the same time. For example, Herzberg et al. (2006) showed that after taking optimism into account, people's quality of life could be better predicted by also including their level of pessimism. That is, quality of life is not determined by how you score on optimism versus pessimism, but by how you score on both simultaneously. Similarly, in a sample of people suffering from arthritis, Benyamini (2005) found that optimism and pessimism interacted such that those with high scores on both constructs were most likely to use coping strategies to deal with their pain. The good life may also sometimes be

promoted by another form of synthesis—switching between optimism and pessimism to foster goals that involve achieving gains versus protecting against losses, respectively (Hazlett, Molden, & Sackett, 2011). Thus, the good life may require that we synthesize optimism and pessimism, and not just focus on being optimistic all the time.

The third way to conceptualize balance is *balance as tempered view*, which asks us to recognize that what we regard as positive and negative may be more ambiguous than we initially think. Is optimism a good thing? Is pessimism a bad thing? Thinking this way may be overly simplistic. As noted by Peterson and Chang (2003) "optimism and pessimism are complex constructs and it makes no sense to speak of the former as always desirable and the latter as always undesirable" (p. 64). For example, although we tend to think of it as a good thing, optimism may contribute to gambling problems, and lead people to downplay the importance of health threats (Carver, Scheier, & Segerstrom, 2010). By contrast, as we saw earlier, although we tend to think of it as a bad thing, pessimism can sometimes lead to high performance. If we closely examine the research on these topics, the overall picture does point to the general desirability of optimism. However, it's important to note that optimism can have a downside, and pessimism can sometimes confer benefits (Carver et al., 2010; Chang, Chang, & Sanna, 2009).

The final way to conceptualize balance is *balance as contextual sensitivity*. This form of balance recognizes that constructs may be more or less desirable or undesirable depending on the situations in which they occur. In terms of the present discussion, balance as contextual sensitivity recognizes that optimism and pessimism may be advantageous or disadvantageous in different situations. For example, research has shown that optimism maintains marital satisfaction among spouses who abstain from criticism, and make benevolent attributions for each other's undesirable behavior, but compromises satisfaction among spouses deficient in these skills (McNulty & Fincham, 2012). Similarly, Segerstrom (2005) has shown that optimism is positively associated with cellular immunity when people are exposed to easy stressors, but negatively associated in the face of difficult stressors. Optimism may also produce negative outcomes in situations that require that you engage in a thorough review of all the possible contingencies in order to assess and address potential difficulties before they occur (Norem & Chang, 2004). In short, whether or not optimism helps to promote well-being may depend on the situation you're facing.

The picture about optimism and pessimism is complex. This is partly because, as noted by Norem and Chang (2004), there are numerous way to think about these constructs, including attributional styles, dispositional optimism and pessimism, naïve optimism, realistic and unrealistic optimism and pessimism, optimistic and pessimistic biases, strategic optimism, and defensive pessimism. It is too simple to think about optimism as positive and pessimism as negative. The balanced approach outlined above will help you better appreciate the nature of optimism and pessimism, and understand when attribution retraining may be warranted as a means of improving your life, and when other approaches, such as planning to avoid failure, might prove more fruitful. Which approach would you recommend to Deena?

BROADENING THE PERSPECTIVE ON WELL-BEING

The purpose of this section is to help to expand your awareness of the scope of positive psychology beyond the topic of optimism. In the beginning of this chapter, we suggested that many of the theories and concepts currently studied in the field of positive psychology have their origins in the field of social psychology. One of the more obvious examples of this cross-fertilization involves the branch of attribution theory that was originally concerned with understanding why some people are particularly vulnerable to depression. What started as research on the depressogenic explanatory style morphed, over time, into research on learned optimism. The person who was chiefly responsible

for this transformation is social psychologist Martin Seligman. His most recent book on positive psychology is titled *Flourish* (2011). We recommend the book to people who are interested in maximizing their potential to thrive and upgrade the quality of their lives.

Hart and Sasso (2011) have identified four broad themes that define the subject matter of concern to positive psychology. Because research shows optimism can upgrade the quality of a person's life in a number of ways, it is a topic that attracts a great deal of scholarly attention. By itself, however, optimism is not one of the four main themes that describe the field of positive psychology. Instead, it is a member of a close-knit family that consists of a constellation of positive personality traits, such as hardiness, sense of coherence, emotional intelligence, gratitude, and hope. The name of the theme of this cluster is *character, strengths, and virtues.* Let us briefly consider the topic of hope, which in addition to optimism is one of the positive personality traits.

Research on hope has become very popular due to the work of C. R. Snyder, who is well known for pioneering scholarship at the interface of social psychology and clinical psychology. Snyder (2002) has defined hope as the positive personality trait that arises when two psychological conditions (see below) coexist simultaneously. When these conditions converge, a person is apt to experience strong positive expectancies concerning the occurrence of future events or situations. You will recognize this type of expectancy as optimism. As a member of the family of positive personality traits, hope is a "sister" to optimism. Similar to the concept of optimism, the concept of hope assumes that high-functioning people organize their lives around the pursuit of important goals.

According to Snyder (2002), hope arises in people when they score above average on two kinds of thinking. The first kind is called **pathway thinking**. People score high on pathway thinking when they know what steps to take to reach a goal. Not only do they know the means to reach the goal; they see many workable routes. Thus, if one route is blocked, they find it easy to think outside the box in order to identify creative alternative solutions. The second kind of thinking that gives rise to hope is called **agency thinking**. Snyder describes this as a blending of willpower and sense of mastery. People who score high on agency thinking are very strongly committed to achieving goals that they see as being important (i.e., have willpower). In addition to having very high levels of energy/motivation, these people also have high self-efficacy (i.e., sense of mastery). In other words, they feel confident in their ability to implement the steps that they believe will lead to goal attainment. People who score above average on *both* pathway thinking and agency thinking are said to have high levels of hope. When these two elements converge, all sorts of benefits are likely to result. Research shows these benefits rival those that are enjoyed by optimists (e.g., Gillham, 2000).

In addition to the theme of positive personality traits, the three other themes that define the content of the field of positive psychology as identified by Hart and Sasso (2011) are (a) resilience and positive coping under conditions of adversity, (b) subjective happiness and life satisfaction, and (c) the developmental process of self-actualization and personal growth. To learn more about the four content areas of positive psychology, we encourage you to read *Positive Psychology: The Scientific and Practical Explorations of Human Strengths* (Snyder, Lopez, & Pedrotti, 2011), which reviews theories related to positive psychology and provides practical advice on how to implement a number of positive coaching techniques.

SUMMARY

This chapter serves as an introduction to positive psychology, the branch of psychology that emphasizes well-being, and optimal human functioning. There is a close connection between positive psychology and social psychology in that theory and research in social psychology have contributed considerably to understanding well-being. At the intersection between positive psychology and social psychology is the study of optimism and pessimism, which represents the main focus of this chapter. Positive social psychology can be considered as the study of how social psychological phenomena can help to promote the best things in life.

The nature of a person's outcome expectancies is central to the definitions of optimism and pessimism. Optimists expect their futures will bring them positive outcomes (good things will happen to them), whereas pessimists believe their futures will bring negative outcomes (bad things will happen to them). Outcome expectancies significantly guide and influence individuals' thinking and approach to the world, and can act as self-fulfilling prophecies. Research indicates that people who hold optimistic outcome expectancies often enjoy well-being in many domains of life, but it is a mistake to blindly assume that optimism is always desirable and pessimism is always undesirable. A more balanced approach is required.

An important distinction is between an optimistic (positive) explanatory style and a pessimistic (negative) explanatory style. Individuals who use the optimistic style make internal, stable, and global attributions to explain the causes of good things that happen to them, and make external, unstable, and specific attributions to account for bad things that happen. People who use the pessimistic explanatory style demonstrate the opposite pattern, that is, external, unstable, and specific attributions for the good things, and internal, stable, and global attributions for the bad things. Not surprisingly, people who use the optimistic explanatory style and those who use the pessimistic explanatory style are likely to become optimists and pessimists, respectively. Attribution retraining is an intervention designed to help a pessimist replace his or her maladaptive pessimistic explanatory style with a more adaptive optimistic explanatory style. The reader is provided with guidance on how to carry out attribution retraining with respect to any sphere of life about which he or she has negative outcome expectancies. However, it should be remembered that when successfully managing situations calls for a change in behavior, or anticipating future problems in order to deal with them, attribution retraining may not be the optimal way to promote the good life.

REFERENCES

Abela, J. R. Z., Gagnon, H., & Auerbach, R. P. (2007). Hopelessness depression in children: An examination of the symptom component of the hopelessness theory. *Cognitive Therapy and Research, 31*(3), 401–417.

Abelson, R. P., Aronson, E., McGuire, W. J., Newcomb, T. M., Rosenberg, M. J., & Tannenbaum, P. H. (Eds.). (1968). *Theories of cognitive consistency: A sourcebook.* Chicago, IL: Rand McNally.

Abend, T. A., & Williamson, G. M. (2002). Feeling attractive in the wake of breast cancer: Optimism matters, and so do interpersonal relationships. *Personality and Social Psychology Bulletin, 28,* 427–436.

Abfalter, D., Zaglia, M. E., & Mueller, J. (2012). Sense of virtual community: A follow up on its measurement. *Computers in Human Behavior, 28*(2), 400–404.

Abrahamse, W., Steg, L., Vlek, C., & Rothengatter, T. (2005). A review of intervention studies aimed at household energy conservation. *Journal of Environmental Psychology, 25,* 273–291.

Abrahamse, W., Steg, L., Vlek, C., & Rothengatter, T. (2007). The effect of tailored information, goal setting, and tailored feedback on household energy use, energy-related behaviors, and behavioral antecedents. *Journal of Environmental Psychology, 27,* 265–276.

Abramson, L. Y., Metalsky, G. I., & Alloy, L. B. (1989). Hopelessness depression: A theory-based subtype of depression. *Psychological Review, 96,* 358–372.

Abramson, L. Y., Seligman, M. E. P., & Teasdale, I. (1978). Learned helplessness in humans: Critique and reformulation. *Abnormal Psychology, 87,* 49–74.

Adams, J. S. (1965). Inequity in social exchange. In L. Berkowitz (Ed.), *Advances in experimental psychology* (Vol. 2, pp. 267–299). San Diego, CA: Academic Press.

Adler, N. E., Boyce, T., Chesney, M. A., Cohen, S., Folkman, S., Kahn, R. L., & Syme, S. L. (1994). Socioeconomic status and health: The challenge of the gradient. *American Psychologist, 49,* 15–24.

Adler, N. E., & Snibbe, A. C. (2003). The role of psychosocial processes in explaining the gradient between socioeconomic status and health. *Current Directions in Psychological Science, 12*(4), 119–123.

Affleck, G., Tennen, H., & Apter, A. (2001). Optimism, pessimism, and daily life with chronic illness. In E. C. Chang (Ed.), *Optimism and pessimism: Implications for theory, research, and practice* (pp. 147–168). Washington, DC: American Psychological Association.

Ainsworth, M. D., Blehar, S. D., Waters, E., & Wall, S. (1978). *Patterns of attachment.* Hillsdale, NJ: Erlbaum.

Ajzen, I. (1985). From intentions to actions: A theory of planned behavior. In J. Kuhl & J. Beckmann (Eds.), *Action control: From cognition to behavior* (pp.11–39). New York, NY: Springer.

Ajzen, I. (1991). The theory of planned behavior. *Organizational Behavior and Human Decision Processes, 50,* 179–211.

Ajzen, I. (1998). Models of human social behavior and their application to health psychology. *Psychology and Health, 13,* 735–739.

Ajzen, I. (2002). Perceived behavioral control, self-efficacy, locus of control, and the theory of planned behavior. *Journal of Applied Social Psychology, 32,* 665–683.

Ajzen, I. (2011a). Behavioral interventions: Design and evaluation guided by the theory of planned behavior. In M. M. Mark, S. I. Donaldson, & B. Campbell (Eds.), *Social psychology and evaluation* (pp. 74–100). New York, NY: The Guilford Press.

Ajzen, I. (2011b). The theory of planned behavior. In P. A. M. Van Lange, A. W. Kruglanski, & E. T. Higgins (Eds.), *Handbook of theories of social psychology: Volume one* (pp. 438–459). Thousand Oaks, CA: SAGE.

Akehurst, L., & Vrij, A. (1999). Creating suspects in police interviews. *Journal of Applied Social Psychology, 29,* 192–210.

Albright, J. M. (2008). Sex in America online: An exploration of sex, marital status, and sexual identity in Internet sex seeking and its impacts. *Journal of Sex Research, 45,* 175–186.

Alinsky, S. (1971). *Rules for radicals.* New York, NY: Random House, Vintage Books.

Allen, M., D'Alessio, D., & Brezgel, K. (1995). A meta-analysis summarizing the effects of pornography II: Aggression after exposure. *Human Communication Research, 22,* 258–283.

Allen, M., D'Alessio, D., Emmers, T. M., & Gebhardt, L. (1996). The role of educational briefings in mitigating effects of experimental exposure to violent sexually explicit material: A meta-analysis. *Journal of Sex Research, 33,* 135–141.

Allen, M., Emmers, T., Gebhardt, L., & Giery, M. A. (1995). Exposure to pornography and acceptance of rape myth. *Journal of Communication, 45,* 5–25.

Allen, V. L., & Wilder, D. A. (1975). Categorization, belief similarity, and intergroup discrimination. *Journal of Personality and Social Psychology, 32,* 971–977.

Alloy, L. B., & Clements, C. M. (1998). Hopelessness theory of depression: Tests of the symptom component. *Cognitive Therapy and Research, 22,* 303–335.

Allport, G. W. (1954). *The nature of prejudice.* Reading, MA: Addison-Wesley.

Amabile, T. M. (1983). The social psychology of creativity. *Journal of Personality and Social Psychology, 45,* 357–376.

American College of Emergency Physicians. (2001). NHTSA update on safety belt effectiveness: Crowded emergency departments urged to prepare for mass casualty incidents. *Annals News Release.* Retrieved from http://www.acep.org/1,2727,0.html

American Psychiatric Association. (2013). *Diagnostic and statistical manual of mental disorders.* (5th ed.). Arlington, VA: Author.

American Psychological Association. (2010). *American Psychological Association ethical principles of psychologists and code of conduct.* Retrieved from http://www.apa.org/ethics/code/index.aspx

American Psychological Association Committee on Accreditation. (2007). *Guidelines and principles for accreditation of programs in professional psychology.* Retrieved from http://www.apa.org/ed/accreditation/about/policies/guiding-princi ples.pdf

Anderson, A. H., McEwan, R., & Carletta, J. (2007). Virtual team meetings: An analysis of communication and context. *Computers in Human Behavior, 23,* 2558–2580.

Anderson, C. A. (2004). An update on the effects of playing violent video games. *Journal of Adolescence, 27,* 113–122.

Anderson, C. A., & Bushman, B. J. (2001). Effects of violent video games on aggressive behavior, aggressive cognition, aggressive affect, physiological arousal, and prosocial behavior: A meta-analytic review of the scientific literature. *Psychological Science, 12,* 353–359.

Anderson, C. A., & Bushman, B. J. (2002). Human aggression. *Annual Review of Psychology, 53,* 27–51.

Anderson, C. A., Gentile, D. A., & Buckley, K. E. (2007). *Violent video game effects on children and adolescents: Theory, research, and public policy.* Oxford, UK: Oxford University Press.

Andrews, D. A., & Bonta, J. (2016). *The psychology of criminal conduct* (6th ed.). Abingdon, UK: Taylor & Francis.

Andrews, D. A., Leschied, A. W., & Hoge, R. D. (1992). *The prediction and assessment of youth at risk: A social psychological approach.* Toronto, ON: Ministry of Community and Social Services.

Ansolabehere, S., & Iyengar, S. (1996). *Going negative: How political advertisements shrink and polarize the electorate.* New York, NY: Free Press.

Aos, S., Phipps, R., Barnoski, R., & Lieb, R. (2001). *The comparative costs and benefits of programs to reduce crime, Version 4.0.* Olympia, WA: Washington State Institute for Public Policy. Retrieved from http://www .wsipp.wa.gov/rptfiles/costbenefit.pdf

Apple, K. S. (1993). *The antecedents and consequences of multidimensional cohesion throughout an intercollegiate baseball season.* Unpublished master's thesis, Purdue University, West Lafayette, Indiana.

Argote, L., Seabright, M. A., & Dyer, L. (1986). Individual versus group use of base-rate and individuating information. *Organizational Behavior and Human Decision Processes, 38,* 65–75.

Armitage, C. J., & Conner, M. (2001). Efficacy of the theory of planned behaviour: A meta-analytic review. *British Journal of Social Psychology, 40,* 471–499.

Arnett, J. J. (2008). The neglected 95%: Why American psychology needs to become less American. *American Psychologist, 63,* 602–614.

Aronson, E. (1968). Dissonance theory: Progress and problems. In R. P. Abelson, E. Aronson, W. J. McGuire, T. M. Newcomb, M. J. Rosenberg, & P. H. Tannenbaum (Eds.), *Theories of cognitive consistency: A sourcebook* (pp. 5–27). Chicago, IL: Rand McNally.

Aronson, E. (1992). Stateways can change folkways. In R. Baird & S. Rosenbaum (Eds.), *Bigotry, prejudice and hatred: Definitions, causes and solutions* (pp. 185–201). Buffalo, NY: Prometheus Books.

Aronson, E. (1999). Dissonance, hypocrisy, and the self-concept. In E. Harmon-Jones & J. Mills (Eds.), *Cognitive dissonance: Progress on a pivotal theory in social psychology* (pp. 103–126). Washington, DC: American Psychological Association.

Aronson, E. (2002). Building empathy, compassion, and achievement in the jigsaw classroom. In J. Aronson (Ed.), *Improving academic achievement: Impact of psychological factors on education* (pp. 209–225). New York, NY: Academic Press.

Aronson, E. (2007). *The social animal* (10th ed.). New York, NY: Worth.

Aronson, E., Fried, C., & Stone, J. (1991). Overcoming denial and increasing the intention to use condoms through the induction of hypocrisy. *American Journal of Public Health, 81,* 1636–1638.

Aronson, E., & Mills, J. (1959). The effect of severity of initiation on liking for a group. *Journal of Abnormal and Social Psychology, 59,* 177–181.

Aronson, E., Stephan, C., Sikes, J., Blaney, N., & Snapp, M. (1978). *The jigsaw classroom.* Beverly Hills, CA: SAGE.

Arvey, R. D., Bouchard, T. J., Segal, N. L., & Abraham, L. M. (1989). Job satisfaction: Environmental and genetic components. *Journal of Applied Psychology, 74,* 187–192.

Asch, S. E. (1946). Forming impressions of personality. *Journal of Abnormal and Social Psychology, 41,* 258–290.

Asch, S. E. (1951). Effects of group pressure upon modification and distortion of judgements. In H. Guetzkow (Ed.), *Groups, leadership, and men* (pp. 177–190). Pittsburgh, PA: Carnegie Press.

Asch, S. E. (1955). Opinions and social pressure. *Scientific American, 193*(5), 31–35.

Asp, E., & Garbarino, J. (1988). Integrative processes at school and in the community. In T. D. Yawkey & J. E. Johnson (Eds.), *Integrative processes and socialization: Early to middle childhood* (pp. 167–183). Hillsdale, NJ: Erlbaum.

Aspinwall, L. G., & Taylor, S. E. (1992). Modeling cognitive adaptation: A longitudinal investigation of the impact of individual differences and coping on college adjustment and performance. *Journal of Personality and Social Psychology, 61,* 755–765.

Assad, K. K., Donnellan, M. B., & Conger, R. D. (2007). Optimism: An enduring resource for romantic relationships. *Journal of Personality and Social Psychology, 93,* 285–297.

Auvinen, J., & Nafziger, E. W. (1999). The sources of humanitarian emergencies. *Journal of Conflict Resolution, 43,* 267–290.

Avolio, B. J. (2007). Promoting more integrative strategies for leadership theory-building. *American Psychologist, 62,* 25–33.

Avolio, B. J., Walumbwa, F. O., & Weber, T. J. (2009). Leadership: Current theories, research, and future directions. *Annual Review of Psychology, 60,* 421–449.

Axsom, D. (1989). Cognitive dissonance and behavior change in psychotherapy. *Journal of Experimental Social Psychology, 25,* 234–252.

Axsom, D., & Cooper, J. (1985). Cognitive dissonance and psychotherapy: The role of effort justification in inducing weight loss. *Journal of Experimental Social Psychology, 21,* 149–160.

Babbie, E., & Benaquisto, L. (2002). *Fundamentals of social research.* Toronto, ON: Thomson-Nelson Canada.

Back, M. D., Schmukle, S. C., & Egloff, B. (2008). Becoming friends by chance. *Psychological Science, 19*(5), 439–440.

Baer, J. L., Kohut, T., & Fisher, W. A. (2015). Is pornography use associated with anti-woman aggression? Re-examining the Confluence Model with third variable considerations. *The Canadian Journal of Human Sexuality, 24(2),* 160–173.

Bales, R. F. (1950). *Interaction process analysis.* Reading, MA: Addison-Wesley.

Balsis, S., Woods, C. M., Gleason, M. E. J., & Oltmanns, T. F. (2007). Overdiagnosis and underdiagnosis of personality disorders in older adults. *American Journal of Geriatric Psychiatry, 15*(9), 742–753.

Baltes, B. B., Marcus, W. D., Sherman, M. P., Bauer, C. C., & LaGanke, J. S. (2002). Computer-mediated communication and group decision making: A meta-analysis. *Organizational Behavior and Human Decision Processes, 87,* 156–179.

Bamberg, S., & Möser, G. (2007). Twenty years after Hines, Hungerford, and Tomera: A new meta-analysis of psycho-social determinants of pro-environmental behaviour. *Journal of Environmental Psychology, 27,* 14–25.

Banaji, M. R., & Heiphetz, L. (2010). Attitudes. In S. T. Fiske, D. T. Gilbert, & G. Lindzey (Eds.), *Handbook of social psychology* (5th ed., Vol. 1, pp. 353–393). Hoboken, NJ: Wiley.

Bandura, A. (1965). Influence of models' reinforcement contingencies on the acquisition of imitative responses. *Journal of Personality and Social Psychology, 1,* 589–595.

Bandura, A. (1977a). Self-efficacy: Toward a unifying theory of behavioral change. *Psychological Bulletin, 84,* 191–215.

Bandura, A. (1977b). *Social learning theory.* Englewood Cliffs, NJ: Prentice Hall.

Bandura, A. (1983). Psychological mechanisms of aggression. In R. G. Geen & E. I. Donnerstein (Eds.), *Aggression: Theoretical and empirical reviews* (Vol. 1): *Theoretical and methodological issues* (pp. 1–40). New York, NY: Academic Press.

Bandura, A. (1986). *Social foundations of thought and action: A social cognitive theory.* Englewood Cliffs, NJ: Prentice Hall.

Bandura, A. (1997). *Self-efficacy: The exercise of control.* New York, NY: Freeman.

Bandura, A. (2009). Social cognitive theory of mass communication. In J. Bryant & M. B. Oliver (Eds.), *Media effects: Advances in theory and research* (3rd ed., pp. 94–124). New York, NY: Routledge.

Bandura, A., Ross, D., & Ross, S. A. (1963). Imitation of film-mediated aggressive models. *Journal of Abnormal and Social Psychology, 66,* 3–11.

Bandura, A., & Walters, R. H. (1963). *Social learning and personality development.* New York, NY: Holt, Rinehart & Winston.

Barak, A., & Fisher, W. A. (1989). Counsellor and therapist gender bias? More questions than answers. *Professional Psychology: Research and Practice, 20,* 377–383.

Barbopoulos, A., Fisharah, F., Clark, J., & El-Khatib, A. (2002). Comparison of Egyptian and Canadian children on a picture apperception test. *Cultural Diversity and Ethnic Minority Psychology, 8*(4), 395–403.

Barker, R. G. (1968). *Ecological psychology: Concepts and methods for studying the environment of human behavior.* Stanford, CA: Stanford University Press.

Barnard, N., & Kursban, M. (2002, August 4). Why fast-food lawsuit is good news. *Physicians Committee for Responsible Medicine Commentary.* Retrieved from http://www.pcrm.org/health/Commentary/commentary020804.html

Baron, R. A., Branscombe, N. R., & Byrne, D. (2008). *Social psychology* (12th ed.). Boston, MA: Allyn & Bacon.

Baron, R. M. (1984, August). *A social-psychological perspective on environmental issues.* Paper presented at the annual meeting of the American Psychological Association, Toronto, ON.

Baron, R. M., & Fisher, J. D. (1984). The equity-control model of vandalism: A refinement. In C. Lévy-Leboyer (Ed.), *Vandalism: Behaviour and motivation* (pp. 63–75). Amsterdam: North Holland.

Baron, R. S. (2005). So right it's wrong: Groupthink and the ubiquitous nature of polarized group decision making. *Advances in Experimental Social Psychology, 37,* 219–253.

Bartholomew, K. (1990). Avoidance of intimacy: An attachment perspective. *Journal of Personal and Social Relationships, 7,* 147–178.

Bateson, M., Nettle, D., & Roberts, G. (2006). Cues of being watched enhance cooperation in a real-world setting. *Biology Letters, 2,* 412–414.

Baumeister, R. F., & Cairns, K. J. (1992). Repression and self-presentation: When audiences interfere with self-deceptive strategies. *Journal of Personality and Social Psychology, 62,* 851–862.

Baumeister, R. F., & Scher, S. J. (1988). Self-defeating behavior patterns among normal individuals: Review and analysis of common self-destructive tendencies. *Psychological Bulletin, 104,* 3–22.

Baumeister, R. F., & Vohs, K. D. (2004). Sexual economics: Sex as female resources for social exchange in heterosexual interactions. *Personality and Social Psychology Review, 8,* 339–363.

Beal, A. C., Ausiello, J., & Perrin, J. M. (2001). Social influences on health-risk behaviors among minority middle school students. *Journal of Adolescent Health, 28,* 474–480.

Beaman, A. L., Barnes, P. J., Klentz, B., & McQuirk, B. (1978). Increasing helping rates through information dissemination: Teaching pays. *Personality and Social Psychology Bulletin, 4,* 406–411.

Beck, A., & Katcher, A. (1996). *Between pets and people.* West Lafayette, IN: Purdue University Press.

Beck, A. T. (1976). *Cognitive therapy of depression.* New York, NY: Guilford Press.

Beck, B. L., Koons, S. R., & Milgrim, D. L. (2000). Correlates and consequences of behavioral procrastination: The effects of academic procrastination, self-consciousness, self-esteem and self-handicapping. *Journal of Social Behavior and Personality, 15*(5), 3–13.

Becker, J. C., Zawadzki, M. JU., & Shields, S. A., (2014). Confronting and reducing sexism: A call for research on intervention. *Journal of Social Issues, 70*(4), 603–614.

Becker-Blease, K. A., & Freyd, J. J. (2006). Research participants telling the truth about their lives: The ethics of asking and not asking about abuse. *American Psychologist, 61,* 218–226.

Beer, M., Ruh, R., Dawson, J. A., McCaa, B. B., & Kavanagh, M. J. (1978). A performance management system: Research, design, introduction and evaluation. *Personnel Psychology, 31,* 505–535.

Behr, R. L., & Iyengar, S. (1985). Television news, real-world cues, and changes in the public agenda. *Public Opinion Quarterly, 49,* 38–57.

Benbenishty, R., & Astor, R. A. (2005). *School violence in context: Culture, neighborhood, family, school, and gender.* New York, NY: Oxford University Press.

Benjamin, L. T., Jr., & Crouse, E. M. (2002). The American Psychological Association's response to *Brown v. Board of Education. American Psychologist, 57,* 38–50.

Bennett, W. W., & Hess, K. M. (2001). *Criminal investigation.* Belmont, CA: Wadsworth.

Bennington, A. J., Shetler, J. C., & Shaw, T. (2003). Negotiating order in interorganizational communication: Discourse analysis of a meeting of three diverse organizations. *The Journal of Business Communication, 40*(2), 118–143.

Benokraitis, N. V., & Feagin, J. R. (1995). *Modern sexism: Blatant, subtle, and covert discrimination* (2nd ed.). Upper Saddle River, NJ: Prentice Hall.

Benson, E. (2003). Psychology and the prison system: Rehabilitate or punish? *APA Monitor, 34*(7), 46–47.

Benyamini, Y. (2005). Can high optimism and high pessimism co-exist? Findings from arthritis patients coping with pain. *Personality and Individual Differences, 38,* 1463–1473.

Beranek, P. M., & Martz, B. (2005). Making virtual teams more effective: Improving relational links. *Team Performance Management, 5/6,* 200–213.

Berglas, S., & Jones, E. E. (1978). Drug choice as a self-handicapping strategy in response to non-contingent success. *Journal of Personality and Social Psychology, 36,* 405–417.

Berkeley, S., Mastropieri, M. A., & Scruggs, T. E. (2011). Reading comprehension strategy instruction and attribution retraining for secondary students with learning and other mild disabilities. *Journal of Learning Disabilities, 44,* 18–32.

Berkowitz, A. D. (2004). *The social norms approach: Theory, research, and annotated bibliography.* Retrieved from http://www.alanberkowitz.com/articles/social_norms.pdf

Berkowitz, L. (1984). Some effects of thoughts on anti- and prosocial influences of media events: A cognitive-neoassociationistic analysis. *Psychological Bulletin, 95,* 410–427.

Berkowitz, L. (1989). Frustration-aggression hypothesis: Examination and reformulation. *Psychological Bulletin, 106,* 59–73.

Berkowitz, L., & LePage, A. (1967). Weapons as aggression-eliciting stimuli. *Journal of Personality and Social Psychology, 7,* 202–207.

Berkowitz, L., & Powers, P. C. (1979). Effects of timing and justification of witnessed aggression on the observers' punitiveness. *Journal of Research in Personality, 13,* 71–80.

Berman, H., Ford-Bilboe, M., Moutrey, B., & Cekic, S. (2001). Portraits of pain and promise: A photographic study of Bosnian youth. *Canadian Journal of Nursing Research, 32,* 21–41.

Bernstein, M. J., Young, S. G., & Hugenberg, K. (2007). The cross-category effect: Mere social categorization is sufficient to elicit an own-group bias in face recognition. *Psychological Science, 18,* 706–712.

Bickman, L. (1981). Some distinctions between basic and applied approaches. In L. Bickman (Ed.), *Applied social psychology annual 2* (pp. 23–47). Beverly Hills, CA: SAGE.

Bierema, L. L. (2010). Diversity education: Competencies and strategies for educators. *Advances in Developing Human Resources, 12(3),* 312–331.

Biglan, A., Mrazek, P. J., Carnine, D., & Flay, B. R. (2003). The integration of research and practice in the prevention of youth problem behaviors. *American Psychologist, 58,* 433–440.

Bishop, G. D. (1994). *Health psychology: Integrating mind and body.* Needham Heights, MA: Allyn & Bacon.

Biswas-Diener, R. (2010). *Practicing positive psychology coaching: Assessments, activities and strategies for success.* Hoboken, NJ: Wiley.

Biswas, S., Hussain, M., & O'Donnell, K. (2009). Celebrity endorsements in advertisements and consumer perceptions: A cross-cultural study. *Journal of Global Marketing, 22*(2), 121–137.

Bjork, R. (2000). Giving away and selling the behavioral sciences. *Monitor on Psychology, 9*(11), 27.

Black, M., & Krishnakumar, A. (1998). Children in low income, urban settings: Interventions to promote mental health and well-being. *American Psychologist, 53*(6), 635–646.

Blackhart, G. C., Nelson, B. C., Knowles, M. L., & Baumeister, R. F. (2009). Rejection elicits emotional reactions, but neither causes immediate distress nor lowers self-esteem: A meta-analytic review of 192 studies on social exclusion. *Personality and Social Psychology Review, 13,* 269–309.

Blackman, M. (2002). The employment interview via the telephone: Are we sacrificing accurate personality judgements for cost efficiency? *Journal of Research in Personality, 36,* 208–223.

Blanchard, A. L. (2008). Testing a model of virtual community. *Computers in Human Behavior, 24*(5), 2107–2123.

Blanton, H., Buunk, B. P., Gibbons, F. X., & Kuyper, H. (1999). When better-than-others compare upward: Choice of comparison and comparative evaluation as independent predictors of academic performance. *Journal of Personality and Social Psychology, 76,* 420–430.

Blass, T. (2004). *The man who shocked the world: The life and legacy of Stanley Milgram.* New York, NY: Basic Books.

Blue, C. L. (1995). The predictive capacity of the theory of reasoned action and the theory of planned behavior in exercise behavior: An integrated literature review. *Research in Nursing and Health, 18,* 105–121.

Boehnke, K. (2009). Are parents decisive? The intergenerational transmission of social axioms under conditions of rapid social change. In K. Leung, & M. Bond (Eds.), *Psychological aspects of social axioms: Understanding global belief systems.* New York, NY: Springer.

Boehnke, K., & Schwartz, S. (1997). Fear of war: Relations to values, gender, and mental health in Germany and Israel. *Peace and Conflict: Journal of Peace Psychology, 3*(2), 149–165.

Boehnke, K., Schwartz, S., Stromberg, C., & Sagiv, L. (1998). The structure and dynamics of worry: Theory, measurement, and cross-national replication. *Journal of Personality, 66*(5), 745–782.

Boggiano, A. K., Barrett, M., Weiher, A. W., McClelland, G. H., & Lusk, C. M. (1987). Use of the maximal-operant principle to motivate children's intrinsic interest. *Journal of Personality and Social Psychology, 53,* 866–879.

Boissicat, N., Pansu, P., Bouffard, T., & Cottin, F. (2012). Relation between perceived scholastic competence and social comparison mechanisms among elementary school children. *Social Psychology of Education, 15,* 603–614.

Bond, M. H. (1988). Finding universal dimensions of individual variation in multicultural studies of values: The Rokeach and Chinese value surveys. *Journal of Personality & Social Psychology, 55,* 1009–1015.

Boon, S. (2005). [Review of the book *Applied social psychology*: *Understanding and addressing social and practical problems*]. *Canadian Psychology, 46,* 251–252.

Bordia, P. (1997). Face-to-face versus computer-mediated communication: A synthesis of the experimental literature. *The Journal of Business Communication, 34,* 99–120.

Borduin, C. M., Cone, L. T., Mann, B. J., Henggeler, S. W., Fucci, B. R., Blaske, D. M., & Williams, R. A. (1995). Multisystemic treatment of serious juvenile offenders: Long-term prevention of criminality and violence. *Journal of Consulting and Clinical Psychology, 63,* 569–578.

Börkan, B. (2010). The mode effect in mixed-mode surveys: Mail and web surveys. *Social Science Computer Review, 28,* 371–380.

Bowlby, J. (1982). *Attachment and loss: Vol. 1: Attachment* (2nd ed.). New York, NY: Basic Books. (Original work published in 1969)

Bracken, C. C. (2005). Presence and image quality: The case of high-definition television. *Media Psychology, 7,* 191–205.

Bracken, C. C., & Botta, R. A. (2010). Telepresence and television. In C. C. Bracken & P. D. Skalski (Eds.), *Immersed in media: Telepresence in everyday life* (pp. 39–62). New York, NY: Routledge.

Bradley, S. D., Angelini, J. R., & Lee, S. (2007). Psychophysiology and memory effects of negative political ads. *Journal of Advertising, 36,* 115–127.

Braithwaite, J. (2000). Shame and criminal justice. *Canadian Journal of Criminology, 42,* 281–298.

Brand, R. J., Bonatsos, A., D'Orazio, R., & DeShong, H. (2010). What is beautiful is good, even online: Correlations between photo attractiveness and text attractiveness in men's online dating profiles. *Computers in Human Behavior, 28,* 166–170.

Brannon, L., Feist, J., & Updegraff, J. A. (2014). *Health psychology: An introduction to behaviour and health* (8th ed.). Belmont, CA: Wadsworth Cengage Learning.

Brawley, L. R., Carron, A. V., & Widmeyer, W. N. (1992). The nature of group goals in sport teams: A phenomenological analysis. *The Sport Psychologist, 6,* 323–333.

Brawley, L. R., & Paskevich, D. M. (1997). Conducting team building research in the context of sport and exercise. *Journal of Applied Sport Psychology, 9,* 11–40.

Bray, C. D., & Whaley, D. E. (2001). Team cohesion, effort, and objective individual performance of high school basketball players. *The Sport Psychologist, 15,* 260–275.

Brehm, J. W. (1956). Postdecision changes in the desirability of alternatives. *Journal of Abnormal and Social Psychology, 52,* 384–389.

Brehm, J. W., & Cohen, A. R. (1962). *Explorations in cognitive dissonance.* New York, NY: Wiley.

Brehm, S., & Brehm, J. W. (1981). *Psychological reactance: A theory of freedom and control.* New York, NY: Academic Press.

Brehm, S. S., Kassin, S. M., & Fein, S. (1999). *Social psychology* (4th ed.). Boston, MA: Houghton Mifflin.

Bresnahan, M., Begg, M. D., Brown, A., Schaefer, C., Sohler, N., Insel, B. . . . Susser, E. (2007). Race and risk of schizophrenia in a U.S. birth cohort: Another example of health disparity? *International Journal of Epidemiology, 36*(4), 751–758.

Brewer, M. B., & Brown, R. J. (1998). Intergroup relations. In D. T. Gilbert, S. T. Fiske, & G. Lindzey (Eds.), *The handbook of social psychology* (Vols. 1 & 2, 4th ed., pp. 554–594). New York, NY: McGraw-Hill.

Brief, A. P., Umphress, E. E., Dietz, J., Burrows, J. W., Butz, R. M., & Scholten, L. (2005). Community matters: Realistic group conflict theory and the impact of diversity. *Academy of Management Journal, 48*(5), 830–844.

Bronfenbrenner, U. (1977). Toward an experimental ecology of human development. *American Psychologist, 32,* 513–531.

Brophy, J. E. (1983). Research on the self-fulfilling prophecy and teacher expectations. *Journal of Educational Psychology, 75,* 631–661.

Broverman, I. K., Broverman, D. M., Clarkson, F. E., Rosenkrantz, P. S., & Vogel, S. R. (1970). Sex role stereotypes and clinical judgments of mental health. *Journal of Consulting and Clinical Psychology, 34,* 1–7.

Brower, S. (1988). *Design in familiar places: What makes home environments look good?* New York, NY: Praeger.

Brown, B. B., & Bentley, D. L. (1993). Residential burglars judge risk: The role of territoriality. *Journal of Environmental Psychology, 13,* 51–61.

Brown, S. P., Cron, W. L., & Leigh, T. W. (1993). Do feelings of success mediate sales performance-work attitude relationships? *Journal of the Academy of Marketing Science, 21,* 91–99.

Brown, S. P., & Peterson, R. A. (1994). Effects of effort on sales performance and job satisfaction. *Journal of Marketing, 58,* 70–80.

Bruns, E. J., & Walker, J. S. (2008). *The resource guide to wraparound.* Portland, OR: National Wraparound Initiative, Research and Training Center for Family Support and Children's Mental Health.

Bryant, J., Carveth, R. A., & Brown, D. (1981). Television viewing and anxiety: An experimental examination. *Journal of Communication, 31*(1), 106–119.

Brydon-Miller, M. (1993). Breaking down barriers: Accessibility self-advocacy in the disabled community. In P. Park, M. Brydon-Miller, B. Hall, & T. Jackson (Eds.), *Voices of change: Participatory* research in the United States and Canada (pp. 125–144). Westport, CT: Bergin & Garvey.

Bryman, A. (2006). Integrating quantitative and qualitative research: How is it done? *Qualitative Research, 6*, 97–113.

Buchanan, G. M., & Seligman, M. E. P. (1995). *Explanatory style.* Hillsdale, NJ: Erlbaum.

Bukszar, E., & Connolly, T. (1988). Hindsight bias and strategic choice: Some problems in learning from experience. *Academy of Management Journal, 31*, 628–641.

Bullock, J. R. (1992). Children without friends: Who are they and how can teachers help? *Childhood Education, 69*, 92–96.

Burger, J. M. (2009). Replicating Milgram: Would people still obey today? *American Psychologist, 64*, 1–11.

Burgoon, J. K. (1994). Nonverbal signals. In M. L. Knapp & G. R. Miller (Eds.), *Handbook of interpersonal communication* (pp. 229–285). Thousand Oaks, CA: SAGE.

Burk J. P., & Sher, K. J. (1990). Labeling the child of an alcoholic: Negative stereotyping by mental health professionals and peers. *Journal of Studies on Alcohol, 51*, 156–163.

Burnam, A., Komarraju, M., Hamel, R., & Nadler, D. R. (2014). Do adaptive perfectionism and self-determined motivation reduce academic procrastination? *Learning and Individual Differences, 36*, 165–172.

Burnstein, E., & Vinokur, A. (1977). Persuasive argumentation and social comparison as determinants of attitude polarization. *Journal of Experimental Social Psychology, 9*, 236–245.

Burton, D. (1989). Winning isn't everything: Examining the impact of performance goals on collegiate swimmers' cognitions and performance. *The Sport Psychologist, 3*, 105–132.

Bushman, B. J., & Anderson, C. A. (2001). Media violence and the American public: Scientific facts versus media misinformation. *American Psychologist, 56*, 477–489.

Bushman, B. J., Huesmann, L. R., & Whitaker, J. L. (2009). Violent media effects. In R. L. Nabi & M. B. Oliver (Eds.), *The SAGE handbook of media processes and effects* (pp. 361–376). Thousand Oaks, CA: SAGE.

Bushman, B. J., & Stack, A. D. (1996). Forbidden fruit versus tainted fruit: Effects of warning labels on attraction to television violence. *Journal of Experimental Psychology: Applied, 2*, 207–226.

Buss, D. M. (1985). Human mate selection. *American Scientist, 73*, 47–51.

Buss, D. M. (2008). *Evolutionary psychology: The new science of the mind* (3rd ed.). Boston, MA: Allyn & Bacon.

Cacioppo, J. T., Cacioppo, S., Gonzaga, G. C., Ogburn, E. L., & VanderWeele, T. J. (2013). Marital satisfaction and break-ups differ across on-line and off-line meeting venues. *Proceedings of the National Academy of Sciences, 110*(25), 10135–10140.

Cady, S. H., & Valentine, J. (1999). Team innovation and perceptions of consideration: What difference does diversity make? *Human Relations, 30*, 730–750.

Calhoon, M. B. (2005). Effects of a peer-mediated phonological skill and reading comprehension program on reading skill acquisition for middle school students with reading disabilities. *Journal of Learning Disabilities, 38*, 424–433.

California Youth Authority. (1997). *LEAD: A boot camp and intensive parole program: Final impact evaluation.* Sacramento, CA: Department of the Youth Authority.

Campbell, D. T. (1969). Reforms as experiments. *American Psychologist, 24*, 409–429.

Campbell, J. D. (1986). Similarity and uniqueness: The effects of attribute type, relevance, and individual differences in self-esteem and depression. *Journal of Personality and Social Psychology, 50*, 281–294.

Canadian Psychological Association. (2000). *Canadian code of ethics for psychologists* (3rd ed.). Ottawa, ON: Author.

Cancian, F. M. (1993). Conflicts between activist research and academic success: Participatory research and alternative strategies. *The American Sociologist, 24*(1), 92–106.

Cantor, J. (2009). Fright reactions to mass media. In J. Bryant & M. B. Oliver (Eds.), *Media effects: Advances in theory and research* (3rd ed., pp. 287–303). New York, NY: Routledge.

Cantor, J., Harrison, K., & Nathanson, A. I. (1998). Ratings and advisories for television programming. In *National television violence study* (Vol. 2, pp. 269–322). Thousand Oaks, CA: SAGE.

Cantor, J., Kester, D., & Miller, A. (2000). *Amazing results! Teacher expectations and student achievement (TESA) follow-up survey of TESA-trained teachers in 45 states and District of Columbia.* Paper presented at the Annual Meeting of the California Educational Research Association, Santa Barbara, CA.

Cantor, J., & Nathanson, A. I. (1996). Children's fright reactions to television news. *Journal of Communication, 46*(4), 139–152.

Cantor, J., & Sparks, G. G. (1984). Children's fear responses to mass media: Testing some Piagetian predictions. *Journal of Communication, 34*(2), 90–103.

Cantor, J., Wilson, B. J., & Hoffner, C. (1986). Emotional reactions to a televised nuclear holocaust film. *Communication Research, 13,* 257–277.

Cantor, N. (1990). From thought to behavior: "Having" and "doing" in the study of personality and cognition. *American Psychologist, 90,* 735–750.

Cantril, H., Gaudet, H., & Herzog, H. (1940). *The invasion from Mars: A study in the psychology of panic.* Princeton, NJ: Princeton University Press.

Cappella, J. N., & Jamieson, K. H. (1997). *Spiral of cynicism: The press and the public good.* New York, NY: Oxford University Press.

Carlson, M., Marcus-Newhall, A., & Miller, N. (1990). Effects of situational aggression cues: A quantitative review. *Journal of Personality and Social Psychology, 58,* 622–633.

Carnahan, T., & McFarland, S. (2007). Revisiting the Stanford prison experiment: Could participant self-selection have led to the cruelty? *Personality and Social Psychology Bulletin, 33,* 603–614.

Carpentier, F. D., Roskos-Ewoldsen, D. R., & Roskos-Ewoldsen, B. (2008). A test of network models of political priming. *Media Psychology, 11,* 186–206.

Carron, A. V., & Ball, J. R. (1977). Cause-effect characteristics of the cohesiveness and participation motivation in intercollegiate hockey. *International Review of Sport Sociology, 12,* 49–60.

Carron, A. V., Brawley, L. R., & Widmeyer, W. N. (1997). The measurement of cohesiveness in sport groups. In J. L. Duda (Ed.), *Advances in sport and exercise psychology measurement.* Morgantown, WV: Fitness Information Technology.

Carron, A. V., Colman, M., Wheeler, J., & Stevens, D. (2002). Cohesion and performance in sport: A meta-analysis. *Journal of Sport and Exercise Psychology, 24,* 168–188.

Carson, E. A. (2014). *Prisoners in 2013.* Washington, DC: U.S. Department of Justice. Office of Justice Programs. Bureau of Justice Statistics. Retrieved from http://www.bjs.gov/content/pub/pdf/p13.pdf

Cartwright, E. (Ed.). (1951). *Field theory in social science: Selected theoretical papers by Kurt Lewin.* New York, NY: Harper & Brothers.

Carver, C. S., & Scheier, M. F. (2009). Optimism. In M. R. Leary & R. H. Hoyle (Eds.), *Handbook of individual differences in social behavior* (pp. 330–342). New York, NY: Guilford Press.

Carver, C. S., Scheier, M. F., & Segerstrom, S, C. (2010). Optimism. *Clinical Psychology Review, 30,* 879–889

Casey-Campbell, M., & Martens, M. L. (2009). Sticking it all together: A critical assessment of the group cohesion-performance literature. *International Journal of Management Reviews, 11,* 223–246.

Casteel, C., & Peek-Asa, C. (2000). Effectiveness of crime prevention through environmental design (CPTED) in reducing robberies. *American Journal of Preventive Medicine, 18,* 99–115.

Castelli, L., De Dea, C., & Nesdale, D. (2008). Learning social attitudes: Children's sensitivity to the nonverbal behaviors of adult models during interracial interactions. *Personality and Social Psychology Bulletin, 34,* 1504–1513.

Catalani, C., & Minkler, M. (2010). Photovoice: A review of the literature in health and public health. *Health Education and Behavior, 37*(3), 424–451.

Catalino, L. I., Furr, R. M., & Bellis, F. A. (2012). A multilevel analysis of the self-presentation theory of social anxiety: Contextualized, dispositional, and interactive perspectives. *Journal of Research in Personality, 46,* 361–373.

Catalyst. (2010). *Quick takes: Statistical overview of women in the workplace.* New York, NY: Author.

Center for Consumer Freedom. (2002). *Special report: "The first thing we do, let's kill all the lawyers."* July 26. Retrieved from http://www.consumerfreedom.com/news_detail.cfm/h/1500-special-report-the-first-thing-we-do-lets-kill-all-the-lawyers

Centerwall, B. S. (1989). Exposure to television as a cause of violence. In G. Comstock (Ed.), *Public communication and behavior* (Vol. 2, pp. 1–58). San Diego, CA: Academic Press.

Chan, R. Y. K., & Lau, L. B. Y. (2002). Explaining green purchasing behavior: A cross-cultural study on American and Chinese consumers. *Journal of International Consumer Marketing, 14*(2–3), 9–40.

Chang, E. C., Asakawa, K., & Sanna, L. J. (2001). Cultural variations in optimistic and pessimistic bias: Do Easterners really expect the worst and

Westerners really expect the best when predicting future life events? *Journal of Personality and Social Psychology*, *81*, 476–491.

Chang, E. C., Chang, R., & Sanna, L. J. (2009). Optimism, pessimism, and motivation: Relations to adjustment. *Social and Personality Psychology Compass, 3/4*, 494–506.

Chang, L. (1999). Gender egalitarian attitudes in Beijing, Hong Kong, Florida, and Michigan. *Journal of Cross-Cultural Psychology, 30,* 722–742.

Chansky, T. E., & Kendall, P. C. (1997). Social expectancies and self-perceptions in anxiety-disordered children. *Journal of Anxiety Disorders*, *11*, 347–363.

Charlton, T., Gunter, B., & Hannan, A. (2002). *Broadcast television effects on a remote community.* Mahwah, NJ: Erlbaum.

Chase, M. A., Feltz, D. L., & Lirgg, C. D. (2003). Sources of collective and individual efficacy of collegiate athletes. *International Journal of Sport and Exercise Psychology, 1,* 180–191.

Cheavens, J. S., Feldman, D., Gum, A., Michael, S. T., & Snyder, C. R. (2006). Hope therapy in a community sample: A pilot investigation. *Social Indicators Research, 77,* 61–78.

Checkoway, B. (1995). Six strategies of community change. *Community Development Journal, 30*(1), 2–20.

Chemers, M. M., Hu, L., & Garcia, B. F. (2001). Academic self-efficacy and first-year college student performance and adjustment. *Journal of Educational Psychology, 93*, 55–64.

Chen, M. -W., Froehle, T., & Morran, K. (1997). Deconstructing dispositional bias in clinical inference: Two interventions. *Journal of Counseling & Development, 76*, 74–81.

Cheung, S. F., & Chan, D. K. -S., & Wong, Z. S. -Y. (1999). Reexamining the theory of planned behavior in understanding wastepaper recycling. *Environment and Behavior*, *31*(5), 587–612.

Choy, O., Farrington, D. P., & Raine, A. (2014). The need to incorporate autonomic arousal in developmental and life-course research and theories. *Journal of Developmental and Life-Course Criminology, 1,* 189–207.

Christenfeld, R., Wagner, J., Pastva, G., & Acrish, W. P. (1989). How physical settings affect chronic mental patients. *Psychiatric Quarterly, 60*, 253–264.

Christensen, L. B. (2004). *Experimental methodology* (9th ed.). Boston, MA: Pearson.

Cialdini, R. B., Cacioppo, J. T., Bassett, R., & Miller, J. A. (1978). Low-ball procedure for producing compliance: Commitment then cost. *Journal of Personality and Social Psychology, 36,* 436–476.

Cialdini, R. B., Demaine, L. J., Sagarin, B. J., Barrett, D. W., Rhoads, K., & Winter, P. L. (2006). Managing social norms for persuasive impact. *Social Influence, 1*, 3–15.

Cialdini, R. B., & Goldstein, N. J. (2004). Social influence: Compliance and conformity. *Annual Review of Psychology, 55,* 591–621.

Cialdini, R. B., Kallgren, C. A., & Reno, R. R. (1991). A focus theory of normative conduct: A theoretical refinement and reevaluation of the role of norms in human behavior. *Advances in Experimental Social Psychology, 24,* 201–234.

Cialdini, R. B., Trost, M. R., & Newsom, J. T. (1995). Preference for consistency: The development of a valid measure and the discovery of surprising behavioral implications. *Journal of Personality and Social Psychology, 69,* 318–328.

Classification and Rating Administration. (2011). *Rating rules.* Retrieved from http://www.filmratings .com/filmratings_cara/#/ratings/rules

Cline, R. J. W., & Haynes, K. M. (2001). Consumer health information seeking on the internet: The state of the art. *Health Education Research, 16*(6), 671–692.

Coates, R., Miller, A., & Ohlin, L. (1978). *Diversity in a youth correctional system.* Cambridge, MA: Ballinger.

Cobb, H. C., Reeve, R. E., Shealy, C. N., Norcross, J. C., Schare, M. L., Rodolfa, E. R. . . . Hall, M. (2004). Overlap among clinical, counseling, and school psychology: Implications for the profession and combined-integrated training. *Journal of Clinical Psychology, 60*, 939–955.

Cohen, A. (2010). Values and commitment: A test of Schwartz's human values theory among Arab teachers in Israel. *Journal of Applied Social Psychology, 40*(8), 1921–1947.

Cohen, A. K. (1960). *Delinquent boys.* New York, NY: The Free Press.

Cohen, S., & Wills, T. (1985). Stress, social support, and the buffering hypothesis. *Psychological Bulletin, 98,* 310–357.

Cokley, K. (2000). An investigation of academic self-concept and its relationship to academic achievement in African American college students. *Journal of Black Psychology, 26,* 148–164.

Cokley, K. (2002). Ethnicity, gender, and academic self-concept: A preliminary examination of academic disidentification and implications for psychologists. *Cultural Diversity and Ethnic Minority Psychology, 8,* 378–388.

Cokley, K., McClain, S., Jones, M., & Johnson, S. (2011). A preliminary investigation of academic disidentification, racial identity, and academic achievement among African American adolescents. *The High School Journal, 95,* 54–68.

Cokley, K., & Moore, P. (2007). Moderating and mediating effects of gender and psychological disengagement on the academic achievement of African American college students. *Journal of Black Psychology, 33,* 169–187.

Cokley, K., & Patel, N. (2007). A psychometric investigation of the academic self-concept of Asian American college students. *Educational and Psychological Measurement, 67,* 88–99.

Cole, E. R. (2009). Intersectionality and research in psychology. *American Psychologist, 64*(3), 170–180.

Collett, D. (1971). Training Englishmen in the nonverbal behavior of Arabs. *International Journal of Psychology, 6,* 209–215.

Condry, J. C., & Condry, S. (1976). Sex differences: A study of the eye of the beholder. *Child Development, 47,* 812–819.

Conger, J. A. (1991). Inspiring others: The language of leadership. *Academy of Management Executive, 5,* 31–45.

Conner, M., & Armitage, C. J. (1998). Extending the theory of planned behavior: A review and avenues for further research. *Journal of Applied Social Psychology, 28*(15), 1429–1464.

Connolly, J. J., & Viswesvaran, C. (2000). The role of affectivity in job satisfaction: A meta-analysis. *Personality and Individual Differences, 29,* 265–281.

Converse, P. D., Wolfe, E. W., Huang, X., & Oswald, F. L. (2008). Response rates for mixed-mode surveys using mail and e-mail/web. *American Journal of Evaluation, 29,* 99–107.

Conway, D. (1973). *Social science and design: A process model for architect and social scientist collaboration.* Washington, DC: American Institute of Architects.

Cook, T. D., & Campbell, D. T. (1979). *Quasi-experimentation: Design and analysis issues for field settings.* Boston, MA: Houghton Mifflin.

Cooper, J., & Axsom, D. (1982). Effort justification in psychotherapy. In G. Weary & H. Mirels (Eds.), *Integrations of clinical and social psychology* (pp. 214–230). New York, NY: Oxford University Press.

Copeland, B. L., & Straub, W. F. (1995). Assessment of team cohesion: A Russian approach. *Perceptual and Motor Skills, 81,* 443–450.

Coren, S. (1993). When teaching is evaluated on political grounds. *Academic Questions, 6,* 73–79.

Correll, J., & Park, B. (2005). A model of the ingroup as a social resource. *Personality and Social Psychology Review, 9,* 341–359.

Corrigan, P., & Penn, D. (1999). Lessons from social psychology on discrediting psychiatric stigma. *American Psychologist, 54,* 765–778.

Corrigan, P. W. (2007). How clinical diagnosis might exacerbate the stigma of mental illness. *Social Work, 52*(1), 31–39.

Cose, E. (1994, July 11). Drawing up safer cities. *Newsweek,* p. 57.

Cotton, J. L., & Tuttle, J. M. (1986). Employee turnover: A meta-analysis and review with implications for research. *Academy of Management Review, 11*(1), 55–70.

Cottrell, W. (2011). In *Wikipedia, The Free Encyclopedia.* Retrieved from http://en.wikipedia.org/w/index.php?title=William_Cottrell&oldid=411990111

Couper, M. P. (2000). Web surveys: A review of issues and approaches. *Public Opinion Quarterly, 64,* 464–494.

Couper, M. P., & Miller, P. V. (2008). Web survey methods: Introduction. *Public Opinion Quarterly, 72,* 831–835.

Couper, M. P., Tourangeau, R., & Conrad, F. G. (2004). What they see is what they get: Response options for web surveys. *Social Science Computer Review, 22,* 111–127.

Cox, T. H. (1991). The multicultural organization. *Academy of Management Executive, 5,* 34–44.

Cox, T. H., & Blake, S. (1991). Managing cultural diversity: Implications for organizational competitiveness. *Academy of Management Executive, 5,* 45–56.

Cozby, P. C. (2009). *Methods in behavioral research* (10th ed.). Boston, MA: McGraw-Hill.

Cramer, K. M., & Lafreniere, K. D. (2003). Wedding preparation stress: Results of a pilot study. *Guidance and Counselling, 19,* 18–27.

Crano, W. D., & Brewer, M. B. (2002). *Principles and methods of social research* (2nd ed.). Mahwah, NJ: Erlbaum.

Crawford, N. (2003). Web site puts out information on reproductive health. *Monitor on Psychology, 34*(2), 17. Retrieved from http://www.apa.org/monitor/feb03/website.html

Crenshaw, K. (1989). Demarginalizing the intersection of race and sex: A Black feminist critique of antidiscrimination doctrine, feminist theory and antiracist politics. *University of Chicago Legal Forum, 140*, 139–167.

Creswell, J. W. (2007). *Qualitative inquiry and research design: Choosing among five approaches* (2nd ed.). Thousand Oaks, CA: SAGE.

Creswell, J. W. (2009). *Research design: Qualitative, quantitative and mixed methods approaches* (3rd ed.). Thousand Oaks, CA: SAGE.

Crisp, R. J., & Turner, R. N. (2009). Can imagined interactions produce positive perceptions? Reducing prejudice through simulated social contact. *American Psychologist, 64*, 231–240.

Crocetti, G., Spiro, H., & Siassi, H. (1973). *Contemporary attitudes toward mental illness.* Pittsburgh, PA: University of Pittsburgh Press.

Crowell, D. H. (1987). Childhood aggression and violence: Contemporary issues. In D. H. Crowell, I. M. Evans, & C. R. O'Donnell (Eds.), *Childhood aggression and violence: Sources of influence, prevention, and control* (pp. 17–52). New York, NY: Plenum.

Cunha, M., Jr., & Caldieraro, F. (2009). Sunk-cost effects on purely behavioral investments. *Cognitive Science, 33,*105–113.

Cunningham, I. J., & Eys, M. A. (2007). Role ambiguity and intra-team communication in interdependent sport teams. *Journal of Applied Social Psychology, 37*, 2220–2237.

Dabbs, J. M., Carr, T. S., Frady, R. L., & Riad, J. K. (1995). Testosterone, crime, and misbehavior among 692 male prison inmates. *Personality and Individual Differences, 18*, 627–633.

Dale, G. A., & Wrisberg, C. A. (1996). The use of a performance profiling technique in a team setting: Getting athletes and coaches on the "same page." *The Sport Psychologist, 10*, 261–277.

D'Alessio, S., & Stolzenberg, L. (1990). A crime of convenience: The environment and convenience store robbery. *Environment and Behavior, 22*, 255–271.

Dalton, J., Elias, M., & Wandersman, A. (2007). *Community psychology: Linking individuals and communities* (2nd ed.). Belmont, CA: Wadsworth.

Danzinger, P. R., & Welfel, E. R. (2000). Age, gender and health bias in counselors: An empirical analysis. *Journal of Mental Health Counseling, 22*, 135–149.

Darcy, K., Davila, J., & Beck, J. G. (2005). Is social anxiety associated with both interpersonal avoidance and interpersonal dependence? *Cognitive Therapy and Research, 29*(2), 171–186.

Darley, J., & Latané, B. (1970). *The unresponsive bystander: Why doesn't he help?* New York, NY: Appleton Century Crofts.

Darley, J. M., & Latané, B. (1968). Bystander intervention in emergencies: Diffusion of responsibility. *Journal of Personality and Social Psychology, 8*, 377–383.

Das, E., Bushman, B. J., Bezemer, M. D., Kerkhof, P., & Vermeulen, I. E. (2009). How terrorism news reports increase prejudice against outgroups: A terror management account. *Journal of Experimental Social Psychology, 45*, 453–459.

Davis, J. H. (1992). Some compelling intuitions about group consensus decisions, theoretical and empirical research, and interpersonal aggregation phenomena: Selected examples, 1950–1990. *Organizational Behavior and Human Decision Processes, 52*, 3–38.

Davison, K., Pennebaker, J., & Dickerson, S. (2000). Who talks? The social psychology of illness support groups. *American Psychologist, 55*, 205–217.

Dawe, S. W. L., & Carron, A. V. (1990, October). *Interrelationships among role acceptance, role clarity, task cohesion, and social cohesion.* Paper presented at the Canadian Society for Psychomotor Learning and Sport Psychology, Windsor, Ontario.

Dawes, R. M. (1973). The commons dilemma game: An N-person mixed motive game with a dominating strategy for defection. *ORI Research Bulletin, 13*, 1–12.

Dawes, R. M. (1980). Social dilemmas. *Annual Review of Psychology, 31*, 169–193.

DeAngelis, T. (2008). Psychologists' expertise in human behavior is increasingly welcomed in many nontraditional career settings. *Monitor on Psychology, 39*(4), 65–71.

DeAngelis, T. (2009). Changing the way we see one another. *Monitor on Psychology, 40*, 54–57.

Dearing, J. W., & Rogers, E. M. (1996). *Agenda setting.* Thousand Oaks, CA: SAGE.

Deci, E. L. (1971). Effects of externally mediated rewards on intrinsic motivation. *Journal of Personality and Social Psychology, 18,* 105–115.

Deci, E. L., & Ryan, R. M. (1985). *Intrinsic motivation and self-determination in human behavior.* New York, NY: Plenum Press.

Deci, E. L., & Ryan, R. M. (2012). Self-determination theory. In P. A. M. Van Lange, A. W. Kruglanski, & E. T. Higgins (Eds.), *Handbook of theories of social psychology, Volume one* (pp. 416–437). Thousand Oaks, CA: SAGE.

DeLeon, P. H. (2002). Presidential reflections: Past and future. *American Psychologist, 57,* 425–430.

Dennis, A. R., Rennecker, J. A., & Hansen, S. (2010). Invisible whispering: Restructuring collaborative decision making with instant messaging. *Decision Sciences, 41,* 845–886.

DePaulo, B. M., Kenny, D. A., Hoover, C. W., Webb, W., & Oliver, P. (1987). Accuracy of person perception: Do people know what kinds of impressions they convey? *Journal of Personality and Social Psychology, 52,* 303–315.

DePaulo, B. M., Lindsay, J. J., Malone, B. E., Muhlenbruck, L., Charlton, K., & Cooper, H. (2003). Cues to deception. *Psychological Bulletin, 129,* 74–112.

DePaulo, P. (1992). Applications of nonverbal behavior research in marketing and management. In R. Feldman (Ed.), *Applications of nonverbal behavioral theories and research* (pp. 63–87). Hillsdale, NJ: Erlbaum.

DeSanctis, G., & Monge, P. (1999). Introduction to the special issue: Communication processes for virtual organizations. *Organization Science, 10*(6), 693–703.

Desforges, D. M., Lord, C. G., Ramsey, S. L., Mason, J. A., Van Leeuwen, M. D., West, S. C., & Lepper, M. R. (1991). Effects of structured cooperative contact on changing negative attitudes toward stigmatized social groups. *Journal of Personality and Social Psychology, 60,* 531–544.

Deshpande, S., Basil, M. D., & Basil, D. Z. (2009). Factors influencing healthy eating habits among college students: An application of the health belief model. *Health Marketing Quarterly, 26,* 145–164.

DeSteno, D., Dasgupta, N., Bartlett, M. Y., & Cajdric, A. (2004). Prejudice from thin air: The effect of emotion on automatic intergroup attitudes. *Psychological Science, 15,* 319–324.

Deutsch, M. (1969). Socially relevant science: Reflections on some studies of interpersonal conflict. *American Psychologist, 24,* 1076–1092.

Deutsch, M. (1973). *The resolution of conflict.* New Haven, CT: Yale University Press.

Deutsch, M., & Gerard, H. B. (1955). A study of normative and social influences upon individual judgment. *Journal of Abnormal and Social Psychology, 51,* 629–636.

Devellis, B. M., Blalock, S., & Sandler, R. (1990). Predicting participation in cancer screening: The role of perceived behavioral control. *Journal of Applied Social Psychology, 20,* 639–660.

Devine, D., Forehand, R., Morse, E., Simon, P., Clark, L., & Kernis, M. (2000). *International Journal of Rehabilitation and Health, 5,* 141–156.

de Visser, R. O., Graber, R., Hart, A., Abraham, C., Scanlon, T., Watten, P., & Memon, A. (2015). Using qualitative methods within a mixed-methods approach to developing and evaluating interventions to address harmful alcohol use among young people. *Health Psychology, 34,* 349–360.

Devos-Comby, L., & Salovey, P. (2002). Applying persuasion strategies to alter HIV-relevant thoughts and behavior. *Review of General Psychology, 6,* 287–304.

De Vries, H., Backbier, E. H., Kok, G., & Dijkstra, M. (1995). The impact of social influences in the context of attitude, self-efficacy, intention, and previous behavior as predictors of smoking onset. *Journal of Applied Social Psychology, 25*(3), 237–257.

Diamond, S. S., Peery, D., Dolan, F. J., & Dolan, E. (2009). Achieving diversity on the jury: Jury size and the peremptory challenge. *Journal of Empirical Legal Studies, 6,* 425–449.

DiBerardinis, J. D., Barwind, J., Flanningam, R. R., & Jenkins, V. (1983). Enhanced interpersonal relation as predictor of athletic performance. *International Journal of Sport Psychology, 14,* 243–251.

Dickerson, C., Thibodeau, R., Aronson, E., & Miller, D. (1992). Using cognitive dissonance to encourage water conservation. *Journal of Applied Social Psychology, 22,* 841–854.

Diefenbach, D. (1997). The portrayal of mental illness on prime time television. *Journal of Community Psychology, 25,* 289–302.

DiFonzo, N., Hantula, D. A., & Bordia, P. (1998). Microworlds for experimental research: Having your (control and collection) cake, and realism too. *Behavior Research Methods, Instruments, & Computers, 30,* 278–286.

Dijkstra, M., De Dreu, C., Evers, A., & van Dierendonck, D. (2009). Passive responses to interpersonal conflict at work amplify employee strain. *European Journal of Work and Organizational Psychology, 18*(4), 405–423.

Dijkstra, P., Kuyper, H., van der Werf, G., Buunk, A. P., & van der Zee, Y. G. (2008). Social comparison in the classroom: A review. *Review of Educational Research, 78,* 828–879.

Dillman, D. A. (2000). *Mail and Internet surveys: The tailored design method* (2nd ed.). New York, NY: Wiley.

DiMatteo, M. R., & Martin, L. R. (2002). *Health psychology*. Boston, MA: Allyn & Bacon.

Dion, K. K., Berscheid, E., & Walster, E. (1972). What is beautiful is good. *Journal of Personality and Social Psychology, 24,* 285–290.

Dishion, T. J., & Piehler, T. F. (2007). Peer dynamics in the development and change of child and adolescent problem behavior. In A. S. Masten (Ed.), *Multilevel dynamics in developmental psychopathology: Pathways to the future. Minnesota symposia on child psychology* (pp. 151–180). New York, NY: Taylor & Francis Group/Erlbaum.

Dishion, T. J., Spracklen, K. M., Andrews, D. W., & Patterson, G. R. (1996). Deviancy training in male adolescent friendships. *Behavior Therapy, 27,* 373–390.

Donaldson, G., & Lorsch, J. (1983). *Decision making at the top.* New York, NY: Basic Books.

Donnerstein, E., & Berkowitz, L. (1981). Victim reactions in aggressive erotic films as a factor in violence against women. *Journal of Personality and Social Psychology, 41,* 710–724.

Doornwaard, S. M., Bickham, D. S., Rich, M., ter Bogt, T. F. M., & van den Eijnden, R., J. J. M. (2015). Adolescents' use of sexually explicit internet material and their sexual attitudes and behavior: Parallel development and directional effects. *Developmental Psychology, 51*(10), 1476–1488.

Dovidio, J. F. (2001). On the nature of contemporary prejudice: The third wave. *Journal of Social Issues, 57,* 829–849.

Dovidio, J. F., & Gaertner, S. L. (2000). Aversive racism and selection decisions: 1989 and 1999. *Psychological Science, 11,* 315–319.

Dowling, C. G. (2000, August 14). Mistaken identity. *People,* pp. 50–55.

Drabman, R. S., & Thomas, M. H. (1974). Does media violence increase children's toleration of real-life aggression? *Developmental Psychology, 10,* 418–421.

Drapaski, A. L., Lucksted, A., Perrin, P. B., Aakre, J. M., Brown, C. H., DeForge, B. R., & Boyd, J. E. (2013). A model of internalized stigma and its effects on people with mental illness. *Psychiatric Services, 64,* 264–269.

Driskell, J. E., Radtke, P. H., & Salas, E. (2003). Virtual teams: Effects of technological mediation on team performance. *Group Dynamics: Theory, Research and Practice, 7,* 297–323.

Dryburgh, H. (2001). Changing our ways: Why and how Canadians use the internet. Retrieved from http://www.statcan.gc.ca/pub/56f0006x/56f 0006x2000001-eng.pdf

Duck, W. O. (2012). An ethnographic portrait of a precarious life: Getting by on less. *The Annals of the American Academy of Political and Social Science, 642,* 124–138.

Duffy, K. G., & Wong, F. Y. (2003). *Community psychology* (3rd ed.). Boston, MA: Allyn & Bacon.

Dunham, P., Hurshman, A., Litwin, E., Gusella, J., Ellsworth, C., & Dodd, P. (1998). Computer mediated social support: Single young mothers as a model system. *American Journal of Community Psychology, 26,* 281–290.

Dunkerley, K. J., & Robinson, W. P. (2002). Similarities and differences in perceptions and evaluations of the communication styles of American and British managers. *Journal of Language and Social Psychology, 21*(4), 393–409.

Dunn, S. W. (2009). Candidate and media agenda setting in the 2005 Virginia gubernatorial election. *Journal of Communication, 59,* 635–652.

DuPaul, G. J., Ervin, R. A., Hook, C. L., & McGoey, K. E. (1998). Peer tutoring for children with attention deficit hyperactivity disorder: Effects on classroom behavior and academic performance. *Journal of Applied Behavior Analysis, 31,* 579–592.

Eagly, A. H., & Chaiken, S. (1993). *The psychology of attitudes.* Fort Worth, TX: Harcourt Brace Jovanovich College Publishers.

Ebbeson, E. B., Kjos, G. L., & Konecni, V. J. (1976). Spatial ecology: Its effects on the choice of friends and enemies. *Journal of Experimental Social Psychology, 12,* 505–518.

Eccles, D. W., & Tenenbaum, G. (2007). A social cognitive perspective on team functioning in sport. *Handbook of Sport Psychology* (3rd ed.). Hoboken, NJ: Wiley.

Eddy, J. M., Reid, J. B., & Fetrow, R. A. (2001). An elementary school-based prevention program targeting modifiable antecedents of youth delinquency and violence: Linking the interests of families and teachers (LIFT). In H. M. Walker & M. H. Epstein (Eds.), *Making schools safer and violence free: Critical issues, solutions, and recommended practices* (pp. 128–139). Austin, TX: Pro-Ed.

Edley, N. (2001). Unravelling social constructionism. *Theory and Psychology, 11*(3), 433–441.

Edwards, D. L., Schoenwald, S. K., Henggeler, S. W., & Strother, K. B. (2001). A multilevel perspective on the implementation of multisystemic therapy (MST): Attempting dissemination with fidelity. In G. A. Bernfeld, D. P. Farrington, & A. W. Leschied (Eds.), *Offender rehabilitation in practice: Implementing and evaluating effective programs* (pp. 97–120). New York, NY: Wiley.

Edwards, J. R. (1991). Person-job fit: A conceptual integration, literature review, and methodological critique. In C. L. Cooper & I. T. Robertson (Eds.), *International review of industrial and organizational psychology* (pp. 283–357). Chichester, UK: Wiley.

Efran, M. G. (1974). The effects of physical appearance on the judgment of guilt, interpersonal attraction, and severity of recommended punishment in a simulated jury task. *Journal of Research in Personality, 8,* 45–54.

Elliot, A. J., & Church, M. A. (2003). A motivational analysis of defensive pessimism and self-handicapping. *Journal of Personality, 71,* 369–396.

Elliot, A. J., & McGregor, H. A. (2001). A 2 × 2 achievement goal framework. *Journal of Personality and Social Psychology, 80,* 501–519.

Ellis, A. (1962). *Reason and emotion in psychotherapy.* New York, NY: Lyle Stuart.

Ellsworth. P. C. (1991). To tell what we know or wait for Godot? *Law and Human Behavior, 15,* 205–224.

Ellsworth, P. C., & Mauro, R. (1998). Psychology and law. In D. T. Gilbert, S. T. Fiske, & G. Lindzey (Eds.), *The handbook of social psychology* (pp. 684–732). Boston, MA: McGraw-Hill.

Emrich, C., Brower, H. H., Feldman, J. M., & Garland, H. (2001). Images in words: Presidential rhetoric, charisma, and greatness. *Administrative Science Quarterly, 46,* 527–557.

Engel, G. L. (1977). The need for a new medical model: A challenge for biomedicine. *Science, 196,* 129–136.

Engelhardt, C. R., Bartholow, B. D., Kerr, G. T., & Bushman, B. J. (2011). This is your brain on violent video games: Neural desensitization to violence predicts increased aggression following violent video game exposure. *Journal of Experimental Social Psychology, 47,* 1033–1036.

Eronen, S., Nurmi, J.-E., & Salmela-Aro, K. (1998). Optimistic, defensive-pessimistic, impulsive and self-handicapping strategies in university environments. *Learning and Instruction, 8,* 159–177.

Erturan-İlker, G. (2014). Effects of feedback on achievement goals and perceived motivational climate in physical education. *Issues in Education Research, 24,* 152–161.

Esses, V. M., & Webster, C. D. (1988). Physical attractiveness, dangerousness, and the Canadian Criminal Code. *Journal of Applied Social Psychology, 18,* 1017–1031.

Evans, G. W., & McCoy, J. M. (1998). When buildings don't work: The role of architecture in human health. *Journal of Environmental Psychology, 18,* 85–94.

Evans, M. J., & Moore, J. S. (2013). Peer tutoring with the aid of the Internet. *British Journal of Educational Technology, 44,* 144–155.

Ewoldsen, D. R., Eno, C. A., Okdie, B. M., Velez, J., Guadagno, R. E., & DeCoster, J. (2012). Effect of playing violent video games cooperatively or competitively on subsequent cooperative behavior. *Cyberpsychology, Behavior, and Social Networking, 15,* 277–280.

Eys, M. A., Patterson, M. M., Loughead, T. M., & Carron, A. V. (2006). Team building in sport. In J. Duda, D. Hackfort, & R. Lidor (Eds.), *Handbook of research in applied sport psychology: International perspectives* (pp. 219–231). Morgantown, WV: Fitness Information Technology.

Farina, A., & Felner, R. D. (1973). Employment interviewer reactions to former mental patients. *Journal of Abnormal Psychology, 82*(2), 268–272.

Farina, A., & Ring, K. (1965). The influence of perceived mental illness on interpersonal relations. *Journal of Abnormal Psychology, 70*(1), 47–51.

Feingold, A. (1990). Gender differences in effects of physical attractiveness in romantic attraction: A comparison across five research paradigms. *Journal of Personality and Social Psychology, 59,* 981–993.

Felmlee, D. (2001). No couple is an island: A social stability network perspective on dyadic stability. *Social Forces, 79,* 1259–1287.

Feltz, D. L., & Chase, M. A. (1998). The measurement of self-efficacy and confidence in sport. In J. L. Duda (Ed.), *Advancements in sport and exercise psychology measurement* (pp. 65–80). Morgantown, WV: Fitness Information Technology.

Feltz, D. L., & Lirgg, C. D. (1998). Perceived team and player efficacy in hockey. *Journal of Applied Psychology, 83,* 557–564.

Fenton, R., & O'Leary, N. (1990, February). *Improving student achievement through enhancing the instructional communication competence of teachers*. Paper presented at the Annual Meeting of the Communication and Instruction Division of the Western States Communication Association, Phoenix, Arizona.

Fernández, M. J., Guàrdia-Olmos, J., & Peró-Cebollero, M. (2014). Qualitative methods of data analysis in psychology: An analysis of the literature. *Qualitative Research, 14*, 20–36.

Ferrari, J. R. (2001). Procrastination as self-regulation failure of performance: Effects of cognitive load, self-awareness, and time limits on "working best under pressure." *European Journal of Personality, 15,* 391–406

Feshbach, S. (1961). The stimulating versus cathartic effects of vicarious aggressive activity. *Journal of Abnormal and Social Psychology, 63,* 381–385.

Fessel, F., Epstude, K., & Roese, N. J. (2009). Hindsight bias redefined: It's about time. *Organizational Behavior and Human Decision Processes, 110*, 56–64.

Festinger, L. (1954). A theory of social comparison processes. *Human Relations, 7,* 117–140.

Festinger, L. (1957). *A theory of cognitive dissonance.* Stanford, CA: Stanford University Press.

Festinger, L. (1999). Reflections on cognitive dissonance 30 years later. In E. Harmon-Jones & J. Mills (Eds.), *Cognitive dissonance: Progress on a pivotal theory in social psychology.* Washington, DC: American Psychological Association.

Festinger, L., & Carlsmith, J. M. (1959). Cognitive consequences of forced compliance. *Journal of Abnormal and Social Psychology, 58,* 203–210.

Festinger, L., Schachter, S., & Back, K. W. (1950). *Social pressures in informal groups: A study of human factors in housing.* New York, NY: Harper.

Filstead, W. J. (1979). Qualitative methods: A needed perspective in evaluation research. In T. D. Cook & C. S. Reichardt (Eds.), *Qualitative and quantitative methods in evaluation research* (pp. 33–48). Beverly Hills, CA: SAGE.

Finkel, E. J., & Baumeister, R. F. (2010). Attraction and rejection. In R. F. Baumeister & E. J. Finkel (Eds.), *Advanced social psychology: The state of the science* (pp. 419–459). New York, NY: Oxford University Press.

Fischer, R., & Smith, P. B. (2003). Reward allocation and culture: A meta-analysis. *Journal of Cross-Cultural Psychology, 34*(3), 251–268.

Fischoff, B. (1975). Hindsight is not foresight: The effect of outcome knowledge on judgment under uncertainty. *Journal of Experimental Psychology: Human Perception and Performance, 1,* 288–299.

Fisher, B. A. (1978). *Perspectives on human communication.* New York, NY: Macmillan.

Fisher, R. J. (1982). *Social psychology: An applied approach.* New York, NY: St. Martin's Press.

Fisher, R. J. (1990). *The social psychology of intergroup and international conflict resolution.* New York, NY: Springer-Verlag.

Fisher, R. P. (2010). Interviewing cooperative witnesses. *Legal and Criminological Psychology, 15*(1), 25–38.

Fisher, R. P., & Geiselman, R. E. (1992). *Memory-enhancing techniques in investigative interviewing: The cognitive interview.* Springfield, IL: Charles C. Thomas.

Fisher, R. P., Geiselman, R. E., & Raymond, D. S. (1987). Critical analysis of police interview techniques. *Journal of Police Science and Administration, 15*, 177–185.

Fisher, R. P., & Schreiber, N. (2007). Interviewing protocols to improve eyewitness memory. In M. Toglia, J. Reed, D. Ross, & R. Lindsay (Eds.), *The handbook of eyewitness psychology: Volume 1. Memory for events* (pp. 53–80). Mahwah, NJ: Erlbaum.

Fiske, S. T. (1993). Social cognition and social perception. In E. W. Porter & M. R. Rosenzweig (Eds.), *Annual review of psychology* (pp. 155–194). Palo Alto, CA: Annual Reviews.

Fiske, S. T., Xu, J., & Cuddy, A. C. (1999). (Dis)respecting versus (dis)liking: Status and interdependence predict ambivalent stereotypes of competence and warmth. *Journal of Social Issues, 55*, 473–489.

Fitchen, C. S., & Amsel, R. A. (1986). Trait attribution about college students with a physical disability: Circumplex analyses and methodological issues. *Journal of Applied Social Psychology, 16*(5), 410–427.

Fitzpatrick, S. E., Reddy, S., Lommel, T. S., Fischer, J. G., Speer, E. M., Stephens, H., Park, S., & Johnson, M. A. (2008). Physical activity and physical function improved following a community-based intervention in Georgia senior centers. *Journal of Nutrition for the Elderly, 27*, 135–154.

Flanagan, E. H., Blashfield, R. K. (2005). Gender acts as a context for interpreting diagnostic criteria. *Journal of Clinical Psychology, 61*(12), 1485–1498.

Foa, U. G., & Foa, E. B. (1974). *Societal structures of the mind.* Springfield, IL: Charles C. Thomas.

Fointiat, V. (2004). 'I know what I have to do, but. . .' When hypocrisy leads to behavioral change. *Social Behavior and Personality, 32*(8), 741–746.

Folkes, V. S. (1982). Forming relationships and the matching hypothesis. *Personality and Social Psychology Bulletin, 8,* 631–636.

Forsterling, F. (2001). *Attribution: An introduction to theories, research and applications.* New York, NY: Psychology Press.

Forston, R. F., & Larson, C. U. (1968). The dynamics of space: An experimental study in proxemic behavior among Latin Americans and North Americans. *Journal of Communication, 18,* 109–116.

Forsyth, D. R. (1999). *Group dynamics* (4th ed.). Belmont, CA: Brooks/Cole.

Foster-Fishman, P., Nowell, B., Deacon, Z., Nievar, M. A., & McCann, P. (2005). Using methods that matter: The impact of reflection, dialogue, and voice. *American Journal of Community Psychology, 36*(3/4), 275–291.

Fournier, D. M. (2005). Evaluation. In S. Mathison (Ed.), *Encyclopedia of evaluation* (pp. 139–140). Thousand Oaks, CA: SAGE.

Fowler, F. J. (1998). Design and evaluation of survey questions. In L. Bickman & D. J. Rog (Eds.), *Handbook of applied social research methods* (pp. 343–374). Thousand Oaks, CA: SAGE.

Freedman, J., Cunningham, J., & Krismer, K. (1992). Inferred values and the reverse-incentive effect in induced compliance. *Journal of Personality and Social Psychology, 62,* 357–368.

Freijy, T., & Kothe, E. J. (2013). Dissonance-based interventions for health behaviour change: A systematic review. *British Journal of Health Psychology, 18,* 310–337.

Freire, P. (1970). *Pedagogy of the oppressed.* New York, NY: Seabury.

Freud, S. (1935). *A general introduction to psychoanalysis.* New York, NY: Liveright.

Fried, C., & Aronson, E. (1995). Hypocrisy, misattribution, and dissonance reduction: A demonstration of dissonance in the absence of aversive consequences. *Personality and Social Psychology Bulletin, 21,* 925–933.

Fried, Y., & Ferris, G. R. (1987). The validity of the job characteristics model: A review and meta-analysis. *Personnel Psychology, 40,* 287–322.

Friedlander, M. L., & Stockman, S. J. (1983). Anchoring and publicity effects in clinical judgment. *Journal of Clinical Psychology, 39,* 637–643.

Friedman, H. S. (2002). *Health psychology* (2nd ed.). Upper Saddle River, NJ: Prentice Hall.

Friedman, L. C., Kalidas, M., Elledge, R., Chang, J., Romero, C., Husain, I., . . . Liscum, K. R. (2006). Optimism, social support and psychosocial functioning among women with breast cancer. *Psycho-Oncology, 15,* 595–603.

Frisco, M. L. (2005). Parental involvement and young women's contraceptive use. *Journal of Marriage and Family, 67,* 110–121.

Frye, C. M. (1996). *New evidence for the job characteristics model: A meta-analysis of the job characteristics-job satisfaction relationship using composite correlations.* Paper presented at the 11th Annual Meeting of the Society for Industrial and Organizational Psychology, San Diego, CA.

Funder, D. C., & Ozer, D. J. (1983). Behavior as a function of the situation. *Journal of Personality and Social Psychology, 44,* 107–112.

Funk, J. B., Baldacci, H. B., Pasold, T., & Baumgardner, J. (2004). Violence exposure in real-life video games, television, movies, and the Internet: Is there desensitization? *Journal of Adolescence, 27,* 23–39.

Furlong, M., & Morrison, G. (2001). The *school* in school violence: Definitions and facts. In H. M. Walker & M. H. Epstein (Eds.), *Making schools safer and violence free: Critical issues, solutions, and recommended practices* (pp. 5–16). Austin, TX: Pro-Ed.

Gable, S. L., Gonzaga, G. C., & Strachman, A. (2006). Will you be there for me when things go right? Supportive responses to positive event disclosures. *Journal of Personality and Social Psychology, 91,* 904–917.

Gadd, J. (2003, June 3). Matti kicked like a "rag doll," trial told. *The National,* p. A11.

Gaertner, S. L., & Dovidio, J. F. (1986). The aversive form of racism. In J. F. Dovidio & S. L. Gaertner (Eds.), *Prejudice, discrimination and racism* (pp. 61–81). San Diego, CA: Academic Press.

Gaertner, S. L., Dovidio, J. F., Rust, M. C., Nier, J. A., Banker, B. S., Ward, C. M., . . Houlette, M. (1999). Reducing intergroup bias: Elements of intergroup cooperation. *Journal of Personality and Social Psychology, 76,* 388–402.

Gamble, J. A. (2008). *A developmental evaluation primer.* Montreal, Canada: J. W. McConnell Family Foundation.

Gallant, M., & Maticka-Tyndale, E. (2004). School-based HIV prevention programmes for African youth. *Social Science & Medicine, 58,* 1337–1351.

Gamson, W. A., & Sifry, M. L. (2013). The #Occupy Movement: An introduction. *The Sociological Quarterly, 54*(2), 159–163.

Garb, H. N. (2005). Clinical judgment and decision making. *Annual Review of Clinical Psychology, 1*, 67–89.

Garb, H. N. (2010). The social psychology of clinical judgment. In J. E. Maddux & J. P. Tangney (Eds.), *Social psychological foundations of clinical psychology* (pp. 297–311). New York, NY: Guilford Press.

Gardner, D. E., Light-Shields, D. L., Bredemeier, B. J., & Bostrom, A. (1996). The relationship between perceived coaching behaviors and team cohesion among baseball and softball players. *Sport Psychologist, 10*, 367–381.

Gardner, R., Ostrom, E., & Walker, J. (1990). The nature of common-pool resource problems. *Rationality & Society, 2*, 335–358.

Gardner, R. M., & Dalsing, S. (1986). Misconceptions about psychology among college students. *Teaching of Psychology, 13*, 32–34.

Gatehouse, J. (2003, June 9). The good news about the bad news. *Maclean's*, 20–22.

Gaudiano, B. A., & Herbert, J. D. (2003). Preliminary psychometric evaluation of a new self-efficacy scale and its relationship to treatment outcome in social anxiety disorder. *Cognitive Therapy and Research, 27*, 537–555.

Gaudiano, B. A., Herbert, J. D. (2007). Self-efficacy for social situations in adolescents with generalized social anxiety disorder. *Behavioural and Cognitive Psychotherapy, 35*(2), 209–223.

Geen, R. G. (2001). *Human aggression*. Buckingham, UK: Open University Press.

Gelfand, M., Nishii, L., Holcombe, K., Dyer, N., Ohbuchi, K., & Fukuno, M. (2001). Cultural influences on cognitive representation of conflict: Interpretations of conflict episodes in the United States and Japan. *Journal of Applied Psychology, 86*, 1059–1074.

Gendreau, P., Little, T., & Goggin, C. (1996). A meta-analysis of the predictors of adult offender recidivism: What works! *Criminology, 34*, 575–607.

Genesee, F., & Holobow, N. E. (1989). Change and stability in intergroup perceptions. *Journal of Language and Social Psychology, 8*(1), 17–38.

Gentile, D. A., Anderson, C. A., Yukawa, S., Ihori, N., Saleem, M., Ming, L. K., . . . Sakamoto, A. (2009). The effects of prosocial video games on prosocial behaviors: International evidence from correlational, longitudinal, and experimental studies. *Personality and Social Psychology Bulletin, 35*, 752–763.

Genuis, S. K., Willows, N., Alexander First Nation, & Jardine, C. (2015). Through the lens of our cameras: Children's lived experience with food security in a Canadian Indigenous community. *Child: Care, Health and Development, 41*(4), 600–610.

George, T. R., & Feltz, D. L. (1995). Motivation in sport from a collective efficacy perspective. *International Journal of Sport Psychology, 26*, 98–116.

Gerard, H. B., & Mathewson, G. C. (1966). The effects of severity of initiation on liking for a group: A replication. *Journal of Experimental Social Psychology, 2*, 278–287.

Gerbner, G., Gross, L., Morgan, M., Signorielli, N., & Shanahan, J. (2002). Growing up with television: Cultivation processes. In J. Bryant & D. Zillmann (Eds.), *Media effects: Advances in theory and research* (2nd ed., pp. 43–68). Mahwah, NJ: Erlbaum.

Gergen, K. J. (1985). The social constructionist movement in modern psychology. *American Psychologist, 40*, 266–275.

Gibbons, F. X., Lane, D. J., Gerrard, M., Reis-Bergen, M., Lautrup, C. L., Pexa, N. A., & Blanton, H. (2002). Comparison-level preferences after performance: Is downward comparison theory still useful? *Journal of Personality and Social Psychology, 83*, 865–880.

Gifford, J., & Gifford, R. (2000). FISH 3: A microworld for studying social dilemmas and resource management. *Behavior Research Methods, Instruments, and Computers, 32*(3), 417–442.

Gifford, R. (2007). *Environmental psychology: Principles and practice* (4th ed.). Colville, WA: Optimal Books.

Gifford, R. (2008). Psychology's essential role in climate change. *Canadian Psychology, 49*, 273–280.

Gifford, R. (2011). The dragons of inaction: Psychological barriers that limit climate change mitigation and adaptation. *American Psychologist, 66*, 290–302.

Gifford, R. (2014). *Environmental psychology: Principles and practice* (5th ed.). Colville, WA: Optimal Books.

Gifford, R., & Comeau, L. (2011). Message framing influences perceived climate change competence, engagement, and behavioral intentions. *Global Environmental Change, 21*, 1301–1307.

Gifford, R., & Hine, D. W. (1997). "I'm cooperative, but you're greedy": Some cognitive tendencies in a commons dilemma. *Canadian Journal of Behavioural Science, 29,* 257–265.

Gifford, R., & Martin, M. (1991). A multiple sclerosis centre program and post-occupancy evaluation. In W. F. E. Preiser & J. Vischer (Eds.), *Design innovation: The challenge of cultural change.* New York, NY: Van Nostrand Reinhold.

Gilbert, D. T., & Malone, P. S. (1995). The correspondence bias. *Psychological Bulletin, 117,* 21–38.

Gilbert, D. T., Pelham, B. W., & Krull, D. S. (1988). On cognitive busyness: When person perceivers meet persons perceived. *Journal of Personality and Social Psychology, 54,* 733–740.

Giles, D. (2003). *Media psychology.* Mahwah, NJ: Erlbaum.

Gillespie, B. M., Chaboyer, W., Longbottom, P., & Wallis, M. (2010). The impact of organizational and individual factors on team communication in surgery: A qualitative study. *International Journal of Nursing Studies, 47,* 732–741.

Gillham, J. E. (Ed.). (2000). *The science of optimism and hope: Research essays in honor of Martin E. P. Seligman.* Philadelphia, PA: Templeton Foundation.

Gillham, J. E., Reivich, K. J., Freres, D. R., Chaplin, T. M., Shatté, A. J., Samuels, B. . . . Seligman, M. E. (2007). School-based prevention of depressive symptoms: A randomized controlled study of the effectiveness and specificity of the Penn Resiliency Program. *Journal of Consulting and Clinical Psychology, 75,* 9–19.

Gilmour, H., & Hofmann, N. (2010). H1N1 vaccination. *Statistics Canada Catalogue no. 82-003-XPE Health Reports, 21,* 1–7.

Gilson, L. L., Maynard, M. T., Jones Young, N. C., Vartiainen, M., & Hakonen, M. (2014). Virtual teams research: 10 years, 10 themes, and 10 opportunities. *Journal of Management, 41,* 1313–1337.

Ginsburg-Block, M. D., Rohrbeck, C. A., & Fantuzzo, J. W. (2006). A meta-analytic review of social, self-concept, and behavioral outcomes of peer-assisted learning. *Journal of Educational Psychology, 98,* 732–749.

Glaser, B. G., & Strauss, A. L. (1967). *The discovery of grounded theory: Strategies for qualitative research.* Chicago, IL: Aldine.

Glaze, L. E., & Kaebel, D. (2014). *Correctional populations in the United States, 2013.* Washington, DC: U.S. Department of Justice. Office of Justice Programs. Bureau of Justice Statistics. Retrieved from http://www.bjs.gov/content/pub/pdf/cpus13.pdf

Glick, P., & Fiske, S. T. (1996). The ambivalent sexism inventory: Differentiating hostile and benevolent sexism. *Journal of Personality and Social Psychology, 70*(3), 491–512.

Goddard, M. J. (2011). On being possibly sane in possibly insane places. *Psychiatric Services, 62*(8), 831–832.

Godin, G., & Kok, G. (1996). The theory of planned behavior: A review of applications to health-related behaviors. *American Journal of Health Promotion, 11*(2), 87–98.

Goh, J. X., & Hall, J. A. (2015). Nonverbal and verbal expressions of men's sexism in mixed-gender interactions. *Sex Roles, 72,* 252–261.

Gonzales, M. H., Aronson, E., & Costanzo, M. A. (1988). Using social cognition and persuasion to promote energy conservation: A quasi-experiment. *Journal of Applied Social Psychology, 18,* 1049–1066.

Gonzalez-Navarro, P., Orengo, V., Zornoza, A., Ripoll, P., & Peiro, J. M. (2010). Group interaction style in a virtual context: The effects of group outcomes. *Computers in Human Behavior, 26,* 1472–1480.

Good, J. J., & Sanchez, D. T. (2010). Doing gender for different reasons: Why gender conformity positively and negatively predicts self-esteem. *Psychology of Women Quarterly, 34,* 203–214.

Goodwin, C. J. (2003). *Research in psychology: Methods and design.* Hoboken, NJ: Wiley.

Goodwin, R. (1999). *Personal relationships across cultures.* London, UK: Routledge.

Goodwin, R., & Tang, D. (1991). Preferences for friends and close relationship partners: A cross-cultural comparison. *Journal of Social Psychology, 131,* 579–581.

Gordon, M. E., & Stewart, L. P. (2009). Conversing about performance: Discursive resources for the appraisal interview. *Management Communication Quarterly, 22,* 473–501.

Gottfredson, D. C., Marciniak, E., Birdseye, A. T., & Gottfredson, G. D. (1991). *Increasing teacher expectations for student achievement: An evaluation.* Baltimore, MD: Center for Research on Effective Schooling for Disadvantaged Students.

Gottfredson, N. C., Panter, A. T., Daye, C. E., Allen, W. A., Wightman, L. F., & Deo, M. E. (2008). Does diversity at undergraduate institutions influence student outcomes? *Journal of Diversity in Higher Education, 1,* 80–94.

Gozenbach, W. J. (1996). *The media, the president, and public opinion: A longitudinal analysis of the drug issue, 1984–1991.* Mahwah, NJ: Erlbaum.

Graham, J., Koo, M., & Wilson, T. D. (2011). Conserving energy by inducing people to drive less. *Journal of Applied Social Psychology, 41,* 106–118.

Graham, J. W., Marks, G., & Hansen, W. B. (1991). Social influence processes affecting adolescent substance use. *Journal of Applied Psychology, 7,* 291–298.

Grandpre, J., Alvaro, E. M., Burgoon, M., Miller, C. H., & Hall, J. R. (2003). Adolescent reactance and anti-smoking campaigns: A theoretical approach. *Health Communication, 15,* 349–366.

Grant, J. D. (1980). From "living learning" to "learning to live": An extension of social therapy. In H. Toch (Ed.), *Therapeutic communities in corrections* (pp. 41–49). Westport, CT: Praeger.

Grau, U., Möller, J., & Gunnarsson, J. I. (1988). A new concept of counseling: A systemic approach for counseling coaches in team sports. *Applied Psychology: An International Review, 37,* 65–83.

Greenlees, I. A., Graydon, J. K., & Maynard, I. W. (2000). The impact of individual efficacy beliefs on group goal selection and group goal commitment. *Journal of Sports Sciences, 18,* 451–459.

Greenlees, I. A., Nunn, R. L., Graydon, J. K., & Maynard, I. W. (1999). The relationship between collective efficacy and pre-competitive affect in rugby players: Testing Bandura's model of collective efficacy. *Perceptual and Motor Skills, 89,* 431–440.

Greitemeyer, T., & Osswald, S. (2010). Effects of prosocial games on prosocial behavior. *Journal of Personality & Social Psychology, 98,* 211–221.

Grieve, F. G., Whelan, J. P., & Meyes, A. W. (2000). An experimental examination of the cohesion-performance relationship in an interactive team sport. *Journal of Applied Sport Psychology, 12,* 219–235.

Griffin, M. A., Neal, A., & Parker, S. K. (2007). A new model of work role performance: Positive behavior in uncertain and interdependent contexts. *Academy of Management Journal, 50,* 327–347.

Griffiths, C. T., & Cunningham, A. C. (2000). *Canadian corrections.* Scarborough, ON: Nelson.

Gross, A. E. (1983). *Date selection: The all-important first meeting.* Unpublished manuscript.

Gruman, J. A., Lumley, M. N., & Gonzalez-Morales, G. (2016). Incorporating balance: Challenges and opportunities for positive psychology. Manuscript submitted for publication. Research

Guay, F., Marsh, H. W., & Boivin, M. (2003). Academic self-concept and academic achievement: Developmental perspectives on their causal ordering. *Journal of Educational Psychology, 95,* 124–136.

Gunter, B. (2002). *Media sex: What are the issues?* Mahwah, NJ: Erlbaum.

Gurung, R. A. R. (2014). *Health psychology: A cultural approach* (3rd ed.). Belmont, CA: Wadsworth Cengage Learning.

Gutkowski, S., Ginath, Y., & Guttman, F. (1992). Improving psychiatric environments through minimal architectural change. *Hospital and Community Psychiatry, 43,* 920–923.

Hackett, R. D., & Guion, R. M. (1985). A reevaluation of the absenteeism-job satisfaction relationship. *Organizational Behavior and Human Decision Processes, 35,* 340–381.

Hackman, J. R., & Oldham, G. R. (1976). Motivation through the design of work: Test of a theory. *Organizational Behavior and Human Performance, 16,* 250–279.

Hackman, J. R., & Oldham, G. R. (1980). *Work redesign.* Reading, MA: Addison-Wesley.

Hagger, M. S., Chatzisarantis, N. L. D., Barkoukis, V., Wang, J. C. K., Hein, V., Pihu, M., Soos, I., & Karsai, I. (2007). Cross-cultural generalizability of the theory of planned behavior among young people in a physical activity context. *Journal of Sport and Exercise Psychology, 29,* 1–20.

Haines, M. P. (1996). *A social norms approach to preventing binge drinking at colleges and universities* (Publication No. ED/OPE/96-18). Newton, MA: The Higher Education Centre for Alcohol and Other Drug Prevention.

Haines, M. P. (2003). The Northern Illinois University experiment: A longitudinal case study of the social norms approach. In H. W. Perkins (Ed.), *The social norms approach to preventing school and college age substance abuse: A handbook for educators, counselors, and clinicians* (pp. 21–34). San Francisco, CA: Jossey-Bass.

Hald, G. M., Malamuth, N. M., & Yuen, C. (2010). Pornography and attitudes supporting violence against women: Revisiting the relationship in non-experimental studies. *Aggressive Behavior, 36,* 14–20.

Halpern-Felsher, B. L., & Millstein, S. G. (2002). The effects of terrorism on teens' perceptions of dying: The new world is riskier than ever. *Journal of Adolescent Health, 30*, 308–311.

Hamermesh, D. S., & Biddle, J. E. (1994). Beauty and the labor market. *American Economic Review, 84*, 1174–1195.

Hamermesh, D. S., & Parker, A. M. (2005). Beauty in the classroom: Instructors' pulchritude and putative pedagogical productivity. *Economics of Education Review, 24*, 369–376.

Hamon, R. R., & Ingoldsby, B. B. (Eds.). (2003). *Mate selection across cultures.* Thousand Oaks, CA: SAGE.

Ham-Rowbottom, K. A., Gifford, R., & Shaw, K. T. (1999). Defensible space theory and the police: Assessing the vulnerability of residencies to burglary. *Journal of Environmental Psychology, 19,* 117–129.

Han, H., Hsu, L., & Sheu, C. (2010). Application of the theory of planned behavior to green hotel choice: Testing the effect of environmental friendly activities. *Tourism Management, 31*(3), 325–334.

Haney, C., Banks, W. C., & Zimbardo, P. (1973). Interpersonal dynamics in a simulated prison. *International Journal of Criminology and Penology, 1*, 69–97.

Haney, C., & Zimbardo, P. G. (2009). Persistent dispositionalism in interactionist clothing: Fundamental attribution error in explaining prison abuse. *Personality and Social Psychology Bulletin, 35*, 807–814.

Hanin, Y. (1992). Social psychology and sport: Communication processes in top performance teams. *Sport Science Review, 1*, 13–28.

Hansen, S., Meissler, K., & Ovens, R. (2000). Kids together: A group play therapy model for children with ADHD symptomatology. *Journal of Child and Adolescent Group Therapy, 10*, 191–211.

Hanze, M., & Berger, R. (2007). Cooperative learning, motivational effects, and student characteristics: An experimental study comparing cooperative learning and direct instruction in 12th grade physics classes. *Learning and Instruction, 17*, 29–41.

Harackiewicz, J. M., Barron, K. E., & Elliott, A. J. (1998). Rethinking achievement goals: When are they adaptive for college students and why? *Educational Psychologist, 33*, 1–21.

Harackiewicz, J. M., Barron, K. E., Pintrich, P. R., Elliott, A. J., & Thrash, T. M. (2002a). Revision of achievement goal theory: Necessary and illuminating. *Journal of Educational Psychology, 94*, 638–645.

Harackiewicz, J. M., Barron, K. E., Tauer, J.M., & Elliott, A. J. (2002b). Predicting success in college: A longitudinal study of achievement goals and ability measures as predictors of interest and performance from freshman year through graduation. *Journal of Educational Psychology, 94*, 562–575.

Hardeman, W., Johnston, M., Johnston, D. W., Bonetti, D., Wareham, N. J., & Kinmonth, L. (2002). Application of the theory of planned behaviour in behaviour change interventions: A systematic review. *Psychology and Health, 17*(2), 123–158.

Hardin, G. (1968). The tragedy of the commons. *Science, 162*, 1243–1248.

Harmon-Jones, E., & Mills, J. (Eds.). (1999). *Cognitive dissonance: Progress on a pivotal theory in social psychology.* Washington, DC: American Psychological Association.

Harrison, K., & Cantor, J. (1999). Tales from the screen: Enduring fright reactions to scary media. *Media Psychology, 1,* 97–116.

Hart, K. E., & Sasso, T. (2011). Mapping the contours of contemporary positive psychology. *Canadian Psychology, 52,* 82–92.

Harter, S. (1982). The perceived competence scale for children. *Child Development, 53*(1), 87–97.

Harvey, M. L., Loomis, R. J., Bell, P. A., & Marino, M. (1998). The influence of museum exhibit design on immersion and psychological flow. *Environment and Behavior, 30,* 601–627.

Hasel, L. E., & Kassin, S. M. (2009). On the presumption of evidentiary independence: Can confessions corrupt eyewitness identifications? *Psychological Science, 20*, 122–126.

Haslam, S. A., Reicher, S. D., & Birney, M. E. (2014). Nothing by mere authority: Evidence that in an experimental analogue of the Milgram paradigm participants are motivated not by orders but by appeals to science. *Journal of Social Issues, 70*, 473–488.

Hass, R. G., Katz, I., Rizzo, N., Bailey, J., & Eisenstadt, D. (1991). Cross-racial appraisal as related to attitude ambivalence and cognitive complexity. *Personality and Social Psychology Bulletin, 17*, 83–92.

Hatfield, E., & Sprecher, S. (1986). *Mirror, mirror . . . The importance of looks in everyday life.* Albany: State University of New York Press.

Hazlett, A., Molden, D., & Sackett, A. M. (2011). Hoping for the best or preparing for the worst? Regulatory focus and preferences for optimism and pessimism in predicting personal outcomes. *Social Cognition, 29*, 74–96.

Hearold, S. (1986). A synthesis of 1,043 effects of television on social behavior. In G. Comstock (Ed.), *Public communication and behavior* (Vol. 1, pp. 66–135). Beverly Hills, CA: SAGE.

Heerwegh, D., & Loosveldt, G. (2008). Face-to-face versus web surveying in a high-Internet-coverage population: Differences in response quality. *Public Opinion Quarterly, 72*, 836–846.

Hegelson, V. S., & Cohen, S. (1996). Social support and adjustment to cancer: Reconciling descriptive, correlational, and intervention research. *Health Psychology, 15*, 135–148.

Heiman, G. W. (2002). *Research methods in psychology* (3rd ed.). Boston, MA: Houghton Mifflin.

Heine, S. J., & Lehman, D. R. (1997). Culture, dissonance, and self-affirmation. *Personality and Social Psychology Bulletin, 23*, 389–400.

Heinrichs, N., Rapee, R. M., Alden, L. A., Bogels, S., Hofmann, S. G., Oh, K. J., & Sakano, Y. (2006). Cultural differences in perceived social norms and social anxiety. *Behaviour Research and Therapy, 44*(8), 1187–1197.

Hendricks, B., Marvel, M. K., & Barrington, B. L. (1990). The dimensions of psychological research. *Teaching of Psychology, 17*, 76–82.

Henggeler, S. W., Schoenwald, S. K., Borduin, C. M., Rowland, M. D., & Cunningham, P. B. (2009). *Multisystemic therapy for antisocial behavior in children and adolescents* (2nd ed.). New York, NY: Guilford Press.

Hennessey, B. A., & Zbikowski, S. M. (1993). Immunizing children against the negative effects of reward: A further examination of intrinsic motivation training techniques. *Creativity Research Journal, 6*, 297–307.

Hennessy, J., & West, M. A. (1999). Intergroup behaviour in organizations: A field test of social identity. *Small Group Research, 30*, 361–382.

Hennigan, K. M., Del Rosario, M. L., Heath, L., Cook, T., Wharton, J. D., & Calder, B. J. (1982). Impact of the introduction of television on crime in the United States: Empirical findings and theoretical implications. *Journal of Personality and Social Psychology, 42*, 461–477.

Hennigan, K. M., Flay, B. R., & Cook, T. D. (1980). "Give me the facts": Some suggestions for using social science knowledge in national policy-making. In R. F. Kidd & M. J. Saks (Eds.), *Advances in applied social psychology* (Vol. 1, pp. 113–145). Hillsdale, NJ: Erlbaum.

Henry, D. B. (2001). Classroom context and the development of aggression: The role of normative processes. In F. Columbus (Ed.), *Advances in psychology research* (Vol. 6, pp. 193–213). Huntington, NY: Nova Science.

Henry, S. (2009). School violence beyond Columbine: A complex problem in need of an interdisciplinary analysis. *American Behavioral Scientist, 52*, 1246–1265.

Hensley, T. R., & Griffin, G. W. (1986). Victims of groupthink. *Journal of Conflict Resolution, 30*, 497–531.

Herzberg, P. Y., Glaesmer, H., & Hoyer, J. (2006). Separating optimism and pessimism: A robust psychometric analysis of the Revised Life Orientation Test (LOT-R). *Psychological Assessment, 18*, 433–438.

Herzog, T. A. (2008). Analyzing the transtheoretical model using the framework of Weinstein, Rothman, and Sutton (1998): The example of smoking cessation. *Health Psychology 27*(5), 548–556.

Heuze, J. P., & Fontayne, P. (2002). A French language instrument for measuring team cohesion. *Journal of Sport and Exercise Psychology, 24*, 42–67.

Hicks, D. J. (1965). Imitation and retention of film-mediated aggressive peer and adult models. *Journal of Personality and Social Psychology, 2*, 97–100.

Hill, C., Memon, A., & McGeorge, P. (2008). The role of confirmation bias in suspect interviews: A systematic evaluation. *Law and Criminological Psychology, 13*, 357–371.

Hill, D. M., & Shaw, G. (2013). A qualitative examination of choking under pressure in team sport. *Psychology of Sport and Exercise, 14*, 103–110.

Hilt, L. M. (2003). Attribution retraining for therapeutic change: Theory, practice, and future directions. *Imagination, Cognition, & Personality, 23*, 289–307.

Hilton, J. L., & von Hipple, W. (1996). Stereotypes. *Annual Review of Psychology, 47*, 237–271.

Hine, D. W., & Gifford, R. (1996). Attributions about self and others in commons dilemmas. *European Journal of Social Psychology, 26*, 429–445.

Hine, D. W., & Gifford, R. (1997). What harvesters really think about in commons dilemma simulations:

A grounded theory analysis. *Canadian Journal of Behavioural Science, 29,* 179–193.

Hinsz, V. B., Tindale, R. S., & Vollrath, D. A. (1997). The emerging conceptualization of groups as information processors. *Psychological Bulletin, 121*(1), 43–64.

Hirt, E. R., & Markman, K. D. (1995). Multiple explanation: A consider-an-alternative strategy for debiasing judgments. *Journal of Personality and Social Psychology, 69,* 1069–1086.

Hirt, E. R., McCrea, S. M., & Kimble, C. E. (2000). Public self-focus and sex differences in behavioral self-handicapping: Does increasing self-threat still make it "just a man's game"? *Personality and Social Psychology Bulletin, 26,* 1131–1141.

Hitsch, G., & Ariely, D. (2007, October). *What makes you click? Mate preferences and matching outcomes in the Internet age.* Paper presented at the meeting of the Society for Experimental Social Psychology, Chicago, IL.

Hobden, K. L., & Olson, J. M. (1994). From jest to antipathy: Disparagement humor as a source of dissonance-motivated attitude change. *Basic and Applied Social Psychology, 15,* 239–249.

Hochschild, A. (1989). *The second shift: Working parents and the revolution at home.* New York, NY: Viking Penguin.

Hodges, L., & Carron, A. V. (1992). Collective efficacy and group performance. *International Journal of Sport Psychology, 23,* 48–59.

Hodges, S. D., Klaaren, K. J., & Wheatley, K. (2000). Talking about safe sex: The role of expectations and experience. *Journal of Applied Social Psychology, 30,* 330–349.

Hodgins, S., Kratzer, L., & McNeil, T. F. (2002). Are pre- and postnatal factors related to the development of criminal offending? In R. R. Corrado, R. Roesch, S. D. Hart, & J. K. Gierowski (Eds.), *Multi-problem violent youth* (pp. 58–80). Amsterdam, Netherlands: IOS Press.

Hoekstra, S. J., Harris, R. J., & Helmick, A. L. (1999). Autobiographical memories about the experience of seeing frightening movies in childhood. *Media Psychology, 1,* 117–140.

Hofstede, G. (1991). *Cultures and organizations: Software of the mind.* London, UK: McGraw-Hill.

Hofstede, G. (1997). *Cultures and organizations: Software of the mind.* New York, NY: McGraw-Hill.

Hofstede, G. (2001). *Culture's consequences* (2nd ed.). Beverly Hills, CA: SAGE.

Hofstede, G. (2010). The GLOBE debate: Back to relevance. *Journal of International Business Studies, 41,* 1339–1346.

Hoge, R. D. (2001). *The juvenile offender: Theory, research, and application.* Boston, MA: Kluwer.

Høigaard, R., Säfvenbom, R., & Tønnessen, F. E. (2006). The relationship between group cohesion, group norms, and perceived social loafing in soccer teams. *Small Group Research, 37,* 217–232.

Holahan, C. J. (1972). Seating patterns and patient behavior in an experimental dayroom. *Journal of Abnormal Psychology, 80,* 115–124.

Holahan, C. J. (1983). Interventions to reduce environmental stress: Enhancing social support and personal control. In E. Siedman (Ed.), *Handbook of social interventions* (pp. 542–560). Beverly Hills, CA: SAGE.

Holmes, T. H., & Rahe, R. H. (1967). The social readjustment rating scale. *Journal of Psychosomatic Research, 11,* 213–218.

Holton, A., Weberling, B., Clarke, C. E., & Smith, M. J. (2012). The blame frame: Media attribution of culpability about the MMR-autism vaccination scare. *Health Communication, 27*(7), 690–701.

Homan, A. C., Buengeler, C., Eckhoff, R. A., van Ginkel, W. P., & Voelpel, S. C. (2015). The interplay of diversity training and diversity beliefs on team creativity in nationality diverse teams. *Journal of Applied Psychology, 100*(5), 1456–1467.

Hooper, J., & Reid, D. H. (1985). A simple environmental re-design for improving classroom performance of profoundly retarded students. *Education and Treatment of Children, 8,* 25–39.

Horn, T., Byrd, M., Martin, E., & Young, C. (2012). Perceived motivational climate and team cohesion in adolescent athletes. *Sport Science Review, 21*(3–4), 25–48.

Horselenberg, R., Merckelbach, H., Smeets, T., Franssens, D., Peters, G.-J. Y., & Zeles, G. (2006). False confessions in the lab: Do plausibility and consequence matter? *Psychology, Crime, and Law, 12*(1), 61–75.

Hoshino-Browne, E., Zanna, A. S., Spencer, S. J., Zanna, M. P., Kitayama, S., & Lackenbauer, S. (2005). On the cultural guises of cognitive dissonance: The case of Easterners and Westerners. *Journal of Personality and Social Psychology, 89,* 294–310.

House, R. J. (1971). A path-goal theory of leader effectiveness. *Administrative Science Quarterly, 16,* 321–338.

Houston, D. A., & Doan, K. (1999). Can you back that up? Evidence (or lack thereof) for the effects of negative and positive political communication. *Media Psychology, 1,* 191–206.

Houston, D. A., Doan, K., & Roskos-Ewoldsen, D. R. (1999). Negative political advertising and choice conflict. *Journal of Experimental Psychology: Applied, 5,* 3–16.

Houston, D. A., & Roskos-Ewoldsen, D. R. (1998). The cancellation-and-focus model of choice and preferences for political candidates. *Basic and Applied Social Psychology, 20,* 305–312.

Hovland, C. I., Janis, I. L., & Kelly, H. H. (1953). *Communication and persuasion: Psychological studies of opinion change.* New Haven, CT: Yale University Press.

Howard, D. J., Gengler, C. E., & Jain, A. (1997). The name remembrance effect: A test of alternative explanations. *Journal of Social Behaviour and Personality, 12,* 801–810.

Howard, J. L., & Ferris, G. R. (1996). The employment interview context: Social and situational influences on interviewer decisions. *Journal of Applied Social Psychology, 26*(2), 112–136.

Howell, A. J., & Watson, D. C. (2007). Procrastination: Associations with achievement goal orientation and learning strategies. *Personality and Individual Differences, 43,* 167–178.

Hoyt, J. L. (1970). Effect of media violence "justification" on aggression. *Journal of Broadcasting, 14,* 455–464.

Huang, W., & Li, D. (2007). Opening up the black box in GSS research: Explaining group decision outcome with group processes. *Computers in Human Behavior, 23,* 58–78.

Hudley, C., Graham, S., & Taylor, A. (2007). Reducing aggressive behavior and increasing motivation in school: The evolution of an intervention to strengthen school adjustment. *Educational Psychology, 42,* 251–260.

Huesmann, L. R., Eron, L. D., Klein, R., Brice, P., & Fischer, P. (1983). Mitigating the imitation of aggressive behaviors by changing children's attitudes about media violence. *Journal of Personality and Social Psychology, 44,* 899–910.

Huesmann, L. R., Moise-Titus, J., Podolski, C. L., & Eron, L. D. (2003). Longitudinal relations between children's exposure to TV violence and their aggressive and violent behavior in young adulthood: 1977–1992. *Developmental Psychology, 39,* 201–221.

Huguet, P., Dumas, F., Monteil, J. M., & Genestoux, N. (2001). Social comparison choices in the classroom: Further evidence for students' upward comparison tendency and its beneficial impact on performance. *European Journal of Social Psychology, 31,* 557–578.

Hui, C-M, & Hui, N. H-H. (2009). The mileage from social axioms: Learning from the past and looking forward. In K. Leung, & M. Bond (Eds.), *Psychological aspects of social axioms: Understanding global belief systems.* New York, NY: Springer.

Hulin, C. L., & Judge, T. A. (2003). Job attitudes. In W. C. Borman, D. R. Ilgen, & R. J. Klimoski (Eds.), *Handbook of psychology* (Vol. 12, pp. 255–276). Hoboken, NJ: Wiley.

Hunt, M. E. (1985). Enhancing a building's imageability. *Journal of Architectural and Planning Research, 2,* 151–168.

Hunt, M. E. (1991). The design of supportive environments for older people. Special Issue: Congregate housing for the elderly: Theoretical, policy, and programmatic perspectives. *Journal of Housing for the Elderly, 9,* 127–140.

Hyde, J. S. (1991). *Half the human experience: The psychology of women* (4th ed.). Toronto, ON: Heath.

Iaffaldano, M. T., & Muchinsky, P. M. (1985). Job satisfaction and job performance: A meta-analysis. *Psychological Bulletin, 97,* 251–273.

Ilies, R., & Judge, T. A. (2003). On the heritability of job satisfaction: The mediating role of personality. *Journal of Applied Psychology, 88*(4), 750–759.

Imada, T., & Kitayama, S. (2010). Social eyes and choice justification: Culture and dissonance revisited. *Social Cognition, 28,* 589–608.

Inbau, F. E., Reid, J. E., Buckley, J. P., & Jayne, B. C. (2013). *Criminal interrogation and confessions* (5th ed.). Burlington, MA: Jones & Bartlett Learning.

Inciardi, J. A., Martin, S. S., & Butzin, C. A. (2004). Five-year outcomes of therapeutic community treatment of drug-involved offenders after release from prison. *Crime & Delinquency, 50,* 88–107.

Innocence Project. (2016). *The causes of wrongful conviction.* Retrieved from http://www.innocenceproject.org/

Intons-Peterson, M. J., & Roskos-Ewoldsen, B. (1989). Mitigating the effects of violent pornography. In S. Gubar & J. Hoff (Eds.), *For adult users only: The dilemma of violent pornography.* Bloomington, IN: University Press.

Intons-Peterson, M. J., Roskos-Ewoldsen, B., Thomas, L., Shirley, M., & Blut, D. (1989). Will educational materials reduce negative effects of exposure to sexual violence? *Journal of Social and Clinical Psychology, 8,* 256–275.

Isen, A. M., & Baron, R. A. (1991). Positive affect as a factor in organizational behavior. *Research in Organizational Behavior, 13,* 1–53.

Ivory, J. D., & Kalyanaraman, S. (2007). The effects of technological advancement and violent content in video games on players' feelings of presence, involvement, physiological arousal, and aggression. *Journal of Communication, 57,* 532–555.

Iyengar, S. (1991). *Is anyone responsible? How television frames political issues.* Chicago, IL: University of Chicago Press.

Iyengar, S., & Kinder, D. R. (1987). *News that matters.* Chicago, IL: University of Chicago Press.

Iyengar, S., & Ottati, V. (1994). Cognitive perspectives on political psychology. In R. S. Wyer, Jr., & T. K. Srull (Eds.), *Handbook of social cognition* (2nd ed., Vol. 2, pp. 143–187). Mahwah, NJ: Erlbaum.

Iyengar, S., & Simon, A. (1993). News coverage of the Gulf Crisis and public opinion: A study of agenda-setting, priming, and framing. *Communication Research, 20,* 365–383.

Jackson, K. M., & Aiken, L. S. (2000). A psychosocial model of sun protection and sunbathing in young women: The impact of health beliefs, attitudes, norms, and self-efficacy for sun protection. *Health Psychology, 19,* 469–478.

Jacobs, J. (1961). *The death and life of great American cities.* New York, NY: Random House.

James, J. R., & Tetrick, L. E. (1986). Confirmatory analytic tests of three causal models relating job perceptions to job satisfaction. *Journal of Applied Psychology, 71,* 77–82.

Jane, J. S., Oltmanns, T. F., South, S. C., & Turkheimer, E. (2007). Gender bias in diagnostic criteria for personality disorders: An item response theory analysis. *Journal of Abnormal Psychology, 116*(1), 166–175.

Janis, I. L. (1983). *Groupthink: Psychological studies of policy decisions and fiascoes* (2nd ed.). Boston, MA: Houghton Mifflin.

Janis, I. L. (1996). Groupthink. In J. Billsberry (Ed.), *The effective manager: Perspectives and illustrations* (pp. 166–178). London, UK: SAGE.

Janis, I. L. (2007). Groupthink. In R. P. Vecchio (Ed.), *Leadership: Understanding the dynamics of power and influence in organizations* (2nd ed., pp. 157–169). Notre Dame, IN: University of Notre Dame Press.

Janz, N. K., & Becker, M. H. (1984). The health belief model: A decade later. *Health Education Quarterly, 11,* 1–47.

Jason, L. A., & Rose, T. (1984). Influencing the passage of child passenger restraint legislation. *American Journal of Community Psychology, 12*(4), 485–495.

Jenkins-Hall, K., & Sacco, W. P. (1991). Effect of client race and depression on evaluations by white therapists. *Journal of Social and Clinical Psychology, 10,* 322–333.

Johns, G., & Saks, A. M. (2001). *Organizational behaviour: Understanding and managing life at work* (5th ed.). Toronto, Canada: Addison Wesley Longman.

Johnson, J. G., Han, Y. S., Douglas, C. J. Johannet, C. M., & Russell, T. (1998). Attributions for positive life events predict recovery from depression among psychiatric inpatients: An investigation of the Needles and Abramson model of recovery from depression. *Journal of Consulting and Clinical Psychology, 66,* 369–376.

Johnson-Cartee, K. S., & Copeland, G. A. (1991). *Negative political advertising.* Mahwah, NJ: Erlbaum.

Johnston, A. C., Worrell, J. L., Di Gangi, P. M., & Wasko, M. (2013). Online health communities: An assessment of the influence of participation and patient empowerment outcomes. *Information Technology & People, 26*(2), 213–235.

Johnston, L. D., O'Malley, P. M., & Bachman, J. G. (1999). *National survey results on drug use from the Monitoring the Future study, 1975–1998: Vol. 2. College students and young adults* (NIH Publication No. 99-4661). Washington, DC: U.S. Government Printing Office.

Joiner, T. E., Steer, R. A., Abramson, L. Y., Metalsky, G. I., & Schmidt, N. B. (2001). Hopelessness depression as a distinct dimension of depressive symptoms among clinical and non-clinical samples. *Behaviour Research and Therapy, 39,* 523–526.

Joinson, C. (1999, May). Teams at work. *HR Magazine, 44*(5), 30–36.

Jones, C. J., Smith, H., & Llewellyn, C. (2014). Evaluating the effectiveness of health belief model interventions: A systematic review. *Health Psychology Review, 8*(3), 253–269.

Jones, E. E. (1998). Major developments in five decades of social psychology. In D. T. Gilbert, S. T. Fiske, & G. Lindzey (Eds.), *The handbook of social psychology* (4th ed., Vol. 1, pp. 3–57). Boston, MA: McGraw-Hill.

Jones, E. E., & Harris, V. A. (1967). The attribution of attitudes. *Journal of Experimental Social Psychology, 3,* 1–24.

Jones, E. E., & Nisbett, R. E. (1972). The actor and the observer: Divergent perceptions of the causes of behavior. In E. E. Jones, D. E. Kanouse, H. H. Kelley, R. E. Nisbett, S. Valins, & B. Weiner (Eds.), *Attribution: Perceiving the causes of behavior* (pp. 79–94). Morristown, NJ: General Learning Press.

Jones, J. M. (1997). *Prejudice and racism* (2nd ed.). New York, NY: McGraw-Hill.

Jones, L. M., & Foley, L. A. (2003). Educating children to decategorize racial groups. *Journal of Applied Social Psychology, 33,* 554–564.

Jones, M. (1953). *The therapeutic community: A new treatment method in psychiatry.* New York, NY: Basic Books.

Josephson, W. L. (1987). Television violence and children's aggression: Testing the priming, social script, and disinhibition predictions. *Journal of Personality and Social Psychology, 53,* 882–890.

Joshi, A. (2006). The influence of organizational demography on the external networking behavior of teams. *The Academy of Management Review, 31,* 583–595.

Jowett, S., & Chaundy, V. (2004). An investigation into the impact of coach leadership and coach-athlete relationship on group cohesion. *Group Dynamics: Theory, Research, and Practice, 8*(4), 302–3011.

Joy, L. A., Kimball, M. M., & Zabrack, M. L. (1986). Television and children's aggressive behavior. In T. M. Williams (Ed.), *The impact of television: A natural experiment in three communities* (pp. 303–360). New York, NY: Academic Press.

Judge, T. A., & Bono, J. E. (2001). Relationship of core self-evaluation traits, self-esteem, generalized self-efficacy, locus of control, and emotional stability with job satisfaction and job performance: A meta-analysis. *Journal of Applied Psychology, 86,* 80–92.

Judge, T. A., Heller, D., & Mount, M. K. (2002). Five-factor model of personality and job satisfaction. *Journal of Applied Psychology, 87,* 530–541.

Judge, T. A., Thoresen, C. J., Bono, J. E., & Patton, G. K. (2001). The job satisfaction-job performance relationship: A qualitative and quantitative review. *Psychological Bulletin, 127*(3), 376–407.

Jussim, L., & Harber, K. D. (2005). Teacher expectations and self-fulfilling prophecies: Knowns and unknowns, resolved, and unresolved controversies. *Personality and Social Psychology Review, 9,* 131–155.

Kahneman, D., & Tversky, A. (1972). Subjective probability: A judgment of representativeness. *Cognitive Psychology, 3,* 430–454.

Kahneman, D., & Tversky, A. (1982). The psychology of preferences. *Scientific American, 39,* 341–350.

Kalokerinos, E. K., von Hipple, C., & Zacher, H., (2014). Is stereotype threat a useful construct for Organizational Psychology research and practice? *Industrial and Organizational Psychology, 7,* 381–402.

Kane, T. D., Marks, M. A., Zaccaro, S. J., & Blair, V. (1996). Self-efficacy, personal goals, and wrestlers' self-regulation. *Journal of Sport & Exercise Psychology, 18,* 36–48.

Kanner, A. D., Coyne, J. C., Schaefer, C., & Lazarus, R. S. (1981). Comparison of two modes of stress measurement: Daily hassles and uplifts versus major life events. *Journal of Behavioral Medicine, 4,* 1–39.

Karasawa, M. (1991). Toward an assessment of social identity: The structure of group identification and its effects on in-group evaluations. *British Journal of Social Psychology, 30*(4), 293–307.

Kashima, Y., Siegal, M., Tanaka, K., & Kashima, E. S. (1992). Do people believe behaviours are consistent with attitudes? Towards a cultural psychology of attribution processes. *British Journal of Social Psychology, 31,* 111–124.

Kassin, S. M. (2015). The social psychology of false confessions. *Social Issues and Policy Review, 9*(1), 25–51.

Kassin, S. M., Bogart, D., & Kerner, J. (2012). Confessions that corrupt: Evidence from the DNA exoneration case files. *Psychological Science, 23,* 41–45.

Kassin, S. M., Drizin, S. A., Grisso, T., Gudjonsson, G. H., Leo, R. A., & Redlich, A. D. (2010). Police-induced confessions: Risk factors and recommendations. *Law and Human Behavior, 34,* 3–38.

Kassin, S. M., Dror, I., & Kukucka, J. (2013). The forensic confirmation bias: Problems, perspectives, and proposed solutions. *Journal of Applied Research in Memory and Cognition, 2,* 42–52.

Kassin, S. M., & Kiechel, K. L. (1996). The social psychology of false confessions: Compliance, internalization, and confabulations. *Psychological Science, 7,* 125–128.

Katz, D., & Kahn, R. L. (1966). *The social psychology of organizations.* New York, NY: Wiley.

Kawakami, K., & Dion, K. L. (1995). Social identity and affect as determinants of collective action: Toward an integration of relative deprivation and social identity theories. *Theory and Psychology, 5*(4), 551–577.

Kazdin, A. E. (2009). Psychological science's contributions to a sustainable environment. *American Psychologist, 64*(5), 339–356.

Keil, L. J., McClintock, C. G., Kramer, R., & Platow, M. J. (1990). Children's use of social comparison standards in judging performance and their effects on self-evaluation. *Contemporary Educational Psychology, 15,* 75–91.

Kelley, H. H. (1973). The process of causal attribution. *American Psychologist, 28,* 107–128.

Kelly, H. K., & Thibault, J. W. (1978). *Interpersonal relationships: A theory of interdependence.* New York, NY: Wiley.

Kelly, S., & Collett, J. L. (2008). From C. P. Ellis to school integration: The social psychology of conflict reduction. *Sociology Compass, 2,* 1638–1634.

Kennedy, D. (1991). The young child's experience of space and child care center design: A practical meditation. *Children's Environments Quarterly, 8,* 37–48.

Kennedy, D. M., Vozdolska, R. R., & McComb, S. A. (2010). Team decision making in computer supported cooperative work: How initial computer-mediated or face-to-face meetings set the stage for later outcomes. *Decision Sciences, 41,* 933–954.

Kenrick, D. T., & Funder, D. C. (1988). Profiting from controversy: Lessons from the person-situation debate. *American Psychologist, 43,* 23–34.

Kerman, S., Kimball, T., & Martin, M. (1980). *Teacher expectations and student achievement: Coordinator manual.* Bloomington, IN: Phi Delta Kappa.

Kerr, S. K., Walker, W. R., Warner, D. A., & McNeill, B. W. (2004). Counselor trainees' assessment and diagnosis of lesbian clients with dysthymic disorder. *15,* 11–26.

Killion, C. M., & Wang, C. C. (2000). Linking African American mothers across life stage and station through Photovoice. *Journal of Health Care for the Poor and Underserved, 11*(3), 310–325.

Kim, N. S., & Ahn, W. (2002). Clinical psychologists' theory-based representations of mental disorders predict their diagnostic reasoning and memory. *Journal of Experimental Psychology, 131*(4), 451–476.

Kim, R. K., & Seo, E. H. (2015). The relationship between procrastination and academic performance: A meta-analysis. *Personality and Individual Differences, 82,* 26–33.

Kim, Y. K., & Lee, H. R. (2009). Airline employee's service behavior toward different nationalities. *International Journal of Hospitality Management, 28*(3), 454–465.

Kimmel, A. J. (2004). Ethical issues in social psychology research. In C. Sansone, C. C. Morf, & A. T. Panter (Eds.), *The SAGE handbook of methods in social psychology* (pp. 45–70). Thousand Oaks, CA: SAGE.

Kingston, D. A., Malamuth, N. M., Fedoroff, P., & Marshall, W. L. (2009). The importance of individual differences in pornography use: Theoretical perspectives and implications for treating sexual offenders. *Journal of Sex Research, 46,* 216–232.

Kingston, K. M., & Hardy, L. (1997). Effects of different types of goals on processes that support performance. *Sport Psychologist, 11,* 277–293.

Kipnis, D. (1997). Ghosts, taxonomies, and social psychology. *American Psychologist, 52,* 205–212.

Kirby, B. J. (1999). Income source and race effects on new-neighbor evaluations. *Journal of Applied Social Psychology, 29,* 1497–1511.

Kitayama, S., Snibbe, A. C., Markus, H. R., & Suzuki, T. (2004). Is there any "free" choice? Cognitive dissonance in two cultures. *Psychological Science, 15,* 527–533.

Klare, M. (2001). *Resource wars: The new landscape of global conflict.* New York, NY: Henry Holt.

Klassen, R. M., Krawchuk, L. L., & Rajani, S. (2008). Academic procrastination of undergraduates: Low self-efficacy to self-regulate predicts higher levels of procrastination. *Contemporary Educational Psychology, 33,* 915–931.

Klaver, J. R., Lee, Z., & Rose, V. G. (2008). Effects of personality, interrogation techniques and plausibility in an experimental false confession paradigm. *Legal and Criminological Psychology, 13,* 71–88.

Kluemper, D. H., Little, L. M., & DeGroot, T. (2009). State or trait: Effects of state optimism on job-related outcomes. *Journal of Organizational Behavior, 30,* 209–231.

Kneidinger, L. M., Maple, T. L., & Tross, S. A. (2001). Touching behavior in sport: Functional components, analysis of sex differences, and ethological considerations. *Journal of Nonverbal Behavior, 25,* 43–62.

Knox, R. E., & Inkster, J. A. (1968). Post-decision dissonance at post time. *Journal of Personality and Social Psychology, 8,* 319–323.

Knox, S., Schlosser, L. Z., Pruitt, N. T., & Hill, C. E. (2006). A qualitative examination of graduate advising relationships: The advisor perspective. *The Counselling Psychologist, 34,* 489–518.

Koch, H. (1970). *The panic broadcast.* Boston, MA: Little, Brown.

Köhnken, G. (1996). Social psychology and the law. In G. R. Semin & K. Fiedler (Eds.), *Applied social psychology* (pp. 257–281). Thousand Oaks, CA: SAGE.

Komorita, S. S., & Parks, C. D. (1994). *Social dilemmas.* Madison, WI: Brown & Benchmark.

Kondowe, E. B., & Mulera, D. (1999). *A cultural approach to HIV/AIDS prevention and care: Malawi's experience.* UNESCO: The United Nations Educational, Scientific, and Cultural Organization.

Konovsky, M. A., & Organ, D. W. (1996). Dispositional and contextual determinants of organizational citizenship behavior. *Journal of Organizational Behavior, 17,* 253–266.

Kowalski, R. M., Giumetti, G. W., Schroeder, A. N., & Lattanner, M. R. (2014). Bullying in the digital age: A critical review and meta-analysis of cyberbullying research among youth. *Psychological Bulletin, 140,* 1073–1137.

Kowalski, R. M., & Limber, S. P. (2007). Electronic bullying among middle school students. *Journal of Adolescent Health, 41,* S22–S30.

Kozub, S. A., & McDonnell, J. F. (2000). Exploring the relationship between cohesion and collective efficacy in rugby teams. *Journal of Sport Behavior, 23,* 120–129.

Kraus, S. J. (1997). Attitudes and the prediction of behavior: A meta-analysis of the empirical literature. *Personality and Social Psychology Bulletin, 21,* 58–75.

Kraut, R., Patterson, M., Lundmark, V., Kiesler, S., Mukopadhyay, T., & Scherlis, W. (1998). Internet paradox: A social technology that reduces social involvement and psychological well-being? *American Psychologist, 53,* 1017–1031.

Kristoff, A. L. (1996). Person-organization fit: An integrative review of its conceptualizations, measurement, and implications. *Personnel Psychology, 49,* 1–49.

Krone, K. J., Jablin, F. M., & Putnam, L. L. (1987). Communication theory and organizational communication: Multiple perspectives. In F. M. Jablin, L. L. Putnam, K. H. Roberts, & L. W. Porter (Eds.), *Handbook of organizational communication: An interdisciplinary perspective* (pp. 18–40). Thousand Oaks, CA: SAGE.

Krosnick, J. A., & Brannon, L. A. (1993). The impact of the Gulf War on the ingredients of presidential evaluations: Multidimensional effects of political involvement. *American Political Science Review, 87,* 963–975.

Krueger, J. I., & Funder, D. C. (2004). Toward a balanced social psychology: Causes, consequences and cures for the problem-seeking approach to social behavior and cognition. *Behavioral and Brain Sciences, 27,* 313–376.

Krueger, J., Ham, J. J., & Linford, K. M. (1996). Perceptions of behavioral consistency: Are people aware of the actor-observer effect? *Psychological Science, 7,* 259–264.

Krupat, E., & Kubzansky, P. E. (1987). Designing to deter crime. *Psychology Today, 21,* 58–61.

Kubiak, S. P. (2009). Assessing the therapeutic environment in hybrid models of treatment: Prisoner perceptions of staff. *Journal of Offenders Rehabilitation, 48,* 85–100.

Kubisch, A. C., Auspos, P., Brown, P., & Delwar, T. (2010). *Voices from the field: Lessons and challenges from two decades of community change efforts.* Washington, DC: The Aspen Institute.

Kukucka, J., & Kassin, S. M. (2014). Do confessions taint perceptions of handwriting evidence? An empirical test of the forensic confirmation bias. *Law and Human Behavior, 38,* 56–70.

Kunda, Z. (1999). *Social cognition: Making sense of people.* Cambridge, MA: The MIT Press.

Kuo, B. C. H., Kwantes, C. T., Towson, S., & Nanson, K. (2006). Generalized social beliefs as determinants of attitudes toward seeking professional psychological help among ethnically-diverse university students, *Canadian Journal of Counselling, 40*(4), 224–241.

Kurlychek, M. C. (2010). Transforming attitudinal change into behavioral change: The missing link. *Criminology & Public Policy, 9,* 119–125.

Kwak, H., Zinkhan, G. M., & Dominick, J. R. (2002). The moderating role of gender and compulsive buying tendencies in the cultivation effects of TV shows and TV advertising: A cross cultural study between the United States and South Korea. *Media Psychology, 4,* 77–111.

Kwantes, C. T. (2003). Organizational citizenship and withdrawal behaviors in the U.S.A. and India: Does commitment make a difference? *International Journal of Cross-Cultural Management, 3,* 5–26.

Kwantes, C. T., Karam, C. M., Kuo, B. C. H., & Towson, S. (2008). Organizational citizenship behaviours: The influence of culture. *International Journal of Intercultural Relations, 32,* 229–243.

Kyllo, L. B., & Landers, D. M. (1995). Goal setting in sport and exercise: A research synthesis to resolve the controversy. *Journal of Sport and Exercise Psychology, 17,* 117–137.

Ladd, G. W., Price, J. M., & Hart, C. H. (1988). Predicting preschoolers' peer status from their playground behaviors and peer contacts. *Child Development, 59,* 986–992.

Lafreniere, K. D., Ledgerwood, D. M., & Docherty, A. L. (1997). Influences of leaving home, perceived family support, and gender on the transition to university. *Guidance and Counselling, 12,* 14–18.

La Greca, A. M., & Stone, W. L. (1993). Social Anxiety Scale for Children—Revised: Factor structure and concurrent validity. *Journal of Clinical Child Psychology, 22*(1), 17–27.

Lamb, M. E., Orbach, Y., Hershkowitz, I., Esplin, P. W., & Horowitz, D. (2007). A structured forensic interview protocol improves the quality and informativeness of investigative interviews with children: A review of research using the NICHD Investigative Interview Protocol, *Child Abuse & Neglect, 31,* 1201–1231.

Lambert, W. E. (1992). Challenging established views on social issues: The power and limitations of research. *American Psychologist, 47*(4), 533–542.

Lane, D. J., & Gibbons, F. X. (2007). Social comparison and satisfaction: Students' reactions after exam feedback predict future academic performance. *Journal of Applied Social Psychology, 37,* 1363–1384.

Langdon, P. E., Cosgrave, N., & Tranah, T. (2004). Social climate within an adolescent medium-security facility. *International Journal of Offender Therapy and Comparative Criminology, 48,* 504–515.

Langlois, J. H., Kalakanis, L., Rubenstein, A. J., Larson, A., Hallam, A., & Smoot, M. (2000). Maxims or myths of beauty? A meta-analytic and theoretical review. *Psychological Bulletin, 126,* 390–423.

Lansing, J. B., & Marans, R. W. (1969). Evaluation of neighborhood quality. *Journal of the American Institute of Planners, 35,* 195–199.

Lapidot-Lefler, N., & Dolev-Cohen, M. (2015). Comparing cyberbullying and school bullying among school students: Prevalence, gender, and grade level differences. *Social Psychology of Education, 18,* 1–6.

Lassiter, G. D., Ware, L. J., Ratcliff, J. J., & Irvin, C. R. (2009). Evidence of the camera perspective bias in authentic videotaped interrogations: Implications for emerging reform in the criminal justice system. *Legal and Criminological Psychology, 14,* 157–170.

Latané, B., & Nida, S. (1981). Ten years of research on group size and helping. *Psychological Bulletin, 89,* 308–324.

Latham, G. P., & Pinder, C. C. (2005). Work motivation theory and research at the dawn of the twenty-first century. *Annual Review of Psychology, 56*(1), 485–516.

Lau, R. R., Jacobs Quadrel, M., & Hartman, K. A. (1990). Development and change of young adults' preventive health beliefs and behavior: Influence from parents and peers. *Journal of Health and Social Behavior, 31,* 240–259.

Lausic, D., Tennebaum, G., Eccles, D., Jeong, A., & Johnson, T. (2009). Intrateam communication and performance in doubles tennis. *Research Quarterly for Exercise and Sport, 80,* 281–290.

Lawler, E. E., III, & Porter, L. W. (1967). The effect of performance on job satisfaction. *Industrial Relations, 7,* 20–28.

Lawrence, J. S., Crocker, J., & Dweck, C. S. (2005). Stereotypes negatively influence the meaning students give to academic settings. In G. Downey, J. S. Eccles, & C. M. Chatman (Eds.), *Navigating the future: Social identity, coping, and life tasks* (pp. 23–43). New York, NY: Russell Sage Foundation.

Lazarus, R. S., & Folkman, S. (1984). Stress, appraisal, and coping. New York, NY: Springer.

Lazarus, R. S., & Launier, R. (1978). Stress-related transactions between person and environment. In L. A. Pervin & M. Lewis (Eds.), *Perspectives in interactional psychology* (pp. 287–327). New York, NY: Plenum Press.

Leary, M. R., & Atherton, S. C. (1986). Self-efficacy, social anxiety and inhibition in interpersonal encounters. *Journal of Social and Clinical Psychology, 4*, 256–267.

Leary, M. R., & Kowalski, R. M. (1995). *Social anxiety: Emotions and social behavior.* New York, NY: Guilford Press.

Leary, M. R., & Miller, R. S. (1986). *Social psychology and dysfunctional behavior: Origins, diagnosis and treatment.* New York, NY: Springer-Verlag.

Lee, F., Hallahan, M., & Herzog, T. (1996). Explaining real-life events: How culture and domain shape attributions. *Personality and Social Psychology Bulletin, 22*, 732–741.

Lee, R. (2000). *Unobtrusive methods in social research.* Buckingham, UK: Open University Press.

Leigh, T. W., & Summers, J. O. (2002). An initial evaluation of industrial buyer's impressions of salesperson's nonverbal cues. *Journal of Personal Selling and Sales Management, 22*, 41–53.

Leippe, M. R., & Eisenstadt, D. (1994). Generalization of dissonance reduction: Decreasing prejudice through induced compliance. *Journal of Personality and Social Psychology, 67*, 395–413.

Lenhart, A., Kahne, J., Middaugh, E., Macgill, E. R., Evans, C., & Vitak, J. (2008, September 16). *Teens, video games, and civics.* Washington, DC: Pew Internet & American Life Project.

Leo, R. A. (2008). *Police interrogation and American justice.* Cambridge, MA: Harvard University Press.

Leo, R. A. (2014). The justice gap and the promise of criminological research. *Criminology, Criminal Justice, Law & Society, 15*(3), 1–37.

Lepper, M. R., Greene, D., & Nisbett, R. E. (1973). Undermining children's intrinsic interest with extrinsic reward: A test of the "overjustification" hypothesis. *Journal of Personality and Social Psychology, 28*, 129–137.

Lepper, M. R., & Henderlong, J. (2000). Turning "play" into "work" and "work" into "play": 25 years of research on intrinsic versus extrinsic motivation. In C. Sansone & J. M. Harackiewicz (Eds.), *Intrinsic and extrinsic motivation: The search for optimal motivation and performance* (pp. 257–307). San Diego, CA: Academic Press.

Lepper, M. R., Ross, L., & Lau, R. R. (1986). Persistence of inaccurate beliefs about the self: Perseverance effects in the classroom. *Journal of Personality and Social Psychology, 50*, 482–491.

Leung, K. (1988). Theoretical advances in justice behavior: Some cross-cultural inputs. In M. H. Bond (Ed.), *The cross-cultural challenge to social psychology* (pp. 218–229). Newbury Park, CA: SAGE.

Leung, K., Bond, M. H., de Carrasquel, S. R., Munoz, C., Hernandez, M., Murakami, F., Yamaguchi, S., Bierbrauer, G., & Singelis, T. M. (2002). Social axioms: The search for universal dimensions of general beliefs about how the world functions. *Journal of Cross-Cultural Psychology, 33*, 286–302.

Levine, J. M., & Moreland, R. L. (1998). Small groups. In D. Gilbert, S. Fiske, & G. Lindzey (Eds.), *The handbook of social psychology* (Vol. 2, 4th ed., pp. 415–469). Boston, MA: McGraw-Hill.

Levine, J. M., & Thompson, L. (1996). Intragroup conflict. In E. T. Higgins & A. W. Kruglanski (Eds.), *Social psychology: Handbook of basic principles* (pp. 745–776). New York, NY: Guilford Press.

Levine, M. (1981). *The history and politics of community mental health.* New York, NY: Oxford University Press.

Levine, M., & Levine, A. (1970). *A social history of helping services.* New York, NY: Oxford University Press.

LeVine, R. A., & Campbell, D. T. (1972). *Ethnocentrism: Theories of conflict, ethnic attitudes, and group behaviour.* New York, NY: Wiley.

Levy, L. H. (2000). Self-help groups. In J. Rapport & E. Seidman (Eds.), *Handbook of community psychology* (pp. 591–614). New York, NY: Plenum.

Levy, P. E. (2003). *Industrial/organizational psychology: Understanding the workplace.* Boston, MA: Houghton Mifflin.

Lewandowsky, S., Stritzke, W. G. K., Oberauer, K., & Morales, M. (2005). Memory for fact, fiction, and misinformation: The Iraq War 2003. *Psychological Science, 16*, 190–195.

Lewin, K. (1936). *A dynamic theory of personality.* New York, NY: McGraw-Hill.

Lewin, K. (1946). Action research and minority problems. *Journal of Social Issues, 2*(4), 34–46.

Lewin, K. (1951). *Field theory in social science.* New York, NY: Harper. (Original work published in 1944)

Lewin, K. (1951). Problems of research in social psychology. In D. Cartwright (Ed.), *Field theory in social science* (pp. 155–169). New York, NY: Harper & Row.

Lewin, K., Lippitt, R., & White, R. K. (1939). Patterns of aggressive behavior in experimentally created "social climates." *Journal of Social Psychology, 10*, 271–301.

Lichacz, F. M., & Partington, J. T. (1996). Collective efficacy and true team performance. *International Journal of Sport Psychology, 27,* 146–158.

Liden, R. C., Martin, C. L., & Parsons, C. K. (1993). Interviewer and applicant behaviors in employment interviews. *Academy of Management Journal, 36*(2), 372–386.

Lieberman, J. D., & Arndt, J. (2000). Understanding the effects of limiting instructions: Social psychological explanations for the failures of instructions to disregard pretrial publicity and other inadmissible evidence. *Psychology, Public Policy, and Law, 6,* 677–711.

Lilienfeld, S. O., Lynn, S. J., Ruscio, J., & Beyerstein, F. L. (2010). *50 great myths of popular psychology: Shattering widespread misconceptions about human behavior.* Malden, MA: Wiley-Blackwell.

Lindskold, S. (1978). Trust development, the GRIT proposal, and the effects of conciliatory acts on conflict and cooperation. *Psychological Bulletin, 85*(4), 772–793.

Link, B. G., Phelan, J. C., Bresnahan, M., Stueve, A., & Pescosolido, B. A. (1999). Public conceptions of mental illness: Labels, causes, dangerousness, and social distance. *American Journal of Public Health, 89,* 1328–1333.

Linley, P. A., Joseph, S. Harrington, S., & Wood, A, M. (2006). Positive psychology: Past, present and (possible) future. *The Journal of Positive Psychology, 1,* 3–16.

Linville, P. W., Fischer, G. W., & Salovey, P. (1989). Perceived distributions of the characteristics of in-group and out-group members: Empirical evidence and a computer simulation. *Journal of Personality and Social Psychology, 57,* 165–188.

Linz, D. (1989). Exposure to sexually explicit materials and attitudes toward rape: A comparison of study results. *Journal of Sex Research, 26,* 50–84.

Linz, D. G., Donnerstein, E., & Penrod, S. (1988). Effects of long-term exposure to violent and sexually degrading depictions of women. *Journal of Personality and Social Psychology, 55,* 758–768.

Lipnevich, A. A., MacCann, C., Krumm, S., Burrus, J., & Roberts, R. D. (2011). Mathematics attitudes and mathematics outcomes of U.S. and Belarusian middle school students. *Journal of Educational Psychology, 103,* 105–118.

Lippmann, W. (1922). *Public opinion.* New York, NY: Macmillan.

Lipton, D. S. (1998). Therapeutic community: Treatment programming in corrections. *Psychology, Crime and Law, 4,* 213–263.

Litt, A., & Tormala, Z. L. (2010). Fragile enhancement of attitudes and intentions following difficult decisions. *Journal of Consumer Research, 37,* 584–598.

Littell, J. H., & Girvin, H. (2002). Stages of change: A critique. *Behavior Modification, 26,* 223–273.

Livingstone, S., & Smith, P. K. (2014). Annual Research Review: Harms experienced by child users of online and mobile technologies: The nature, prevalence, and management of sexual and aggressive risks in the digital age. *Journal of Child Psychology and Psychiatry, 55*(6), 635–654.

Lloyd, W. F. (1968). *Lectures on population, value, poor laws and rent.* New York, NY: August M. Kelley. (Original work published in 1837)

Locke, E. A. (1976). The nature and causes of job satisfaction. In M. D. Dunnette (Ed.), *Handbook of industrial and organizational psychology* (pp. 1297–1350). Chicago, IL: Rand-McNally.

Locke, E. A., & Latham, G. P. (1985). The application of goal setting to sports. *Journal of Sport Psychology, 7,* 205–222.

Lodzinski, A. (1995). Linking program design and evaluation: Five guiding questions for program designers. In A. J. Love (Ed.), *Evaluation methods sourcebook* (pp. 30–38). Ottawa, ON: Canadian Evaluation Society.

Lodzinski, A. (2003). *Effective human service program design and in-house evaluation* (5th ed.). Toronto, ON: Author.

Lodzinski, A. (2012). *In-house program evaluation: A practical guide.* Toronto, Canada: Author.

Loftus, E. F., & Palmer, J. C. (1974). Reconstruction of automobile destruction: An example of the interaction between language and memory. *Journal of Verbal Learning and Verbal Behavior, 13,* 585–589.

Lomas, T. (2015). Positive social psychology: A multilevel inquiry into sociocultural well-being initiatives. *Psychology, Public Policy and Law, 21,* 338–347.

Longman, J. (2000). *The girls of summer: The U.S. women's soccer team and how it changed the world.* New York, NY: HarperCollins.

Lowenberg, G., & Conrad, K. A. (1998). *Current perspectives in industrial/organizational psychology.* Boston, MA: Allyn & Bacon.

Lu, V. (1999, August 15). Rising sick days cost billions. *The Toronto Star,* pp. A1, A10.

Lyons, P. A., Kenworthy, J. B., & Popan, J. R. (2010). Ingroup identification and group-level narcissism as predictors of U.S. citizens' attitudes and behavior toward Arab immigrants. *Personality and Social Psychology Bulletin, 36,* 1267–1280.

Lytton, H. (1990). Child and parent effects in boys' conduct disorder: A reinterpretation. *Developmental Psychopathology, 26,* 683–697.

MacDonald, G., & Jensen-Campbell, L. A. (2010). *Social pain: Neuropsychological and health implications of loss and exclusion.* Washington, DC: American Psychological Association.

Macdonald, J. E., & Gifford, R. (1989). Territorial cues and defensible space theory: The burglar's point of view. *Journal of Environmental Psychology, 9,* 193–205.

Macias, C., Aronson, E., Hargreaves, W., Weary, G., Barreira, P. J., Harvey, J., . . . Fisher, W. (2009). Transforming dissatisfaction with services into self-determination: A social psychological perspective on community program effectiveness. *Journal of Applied Social Psychology, 39,* 1835–1859.

MacKenzie, D. L., Wilson, D. B., & Kider, S. B. (2001). Effects of correctional boot camps on offending. *Annals of the American Academy of Political and Social Sciences, 578,* 126–143.

Mackinnon, A., Amott, N., & McGarvey, C. (2006). *Mapping change: Using a theory of change to guide planning and evaluation.* New York, NY: Ford Foundation, GrandCraft.

Maddux, J. E., & Tangney, J. P. (2010). *Social psychological foundations of clinical psychology.* New York, NY: Guilford Press.

Madill, A., & Gough, B. (2008). Qualitative research and its place in psychological science. *Psychological Methods, 13,* 254–271.

Madon, S. (1997). What do people believe about gay males? A study of stereotype content and strength. *Sex Roles, 37*(9–10), 663–685.

Madon, S., Jussim, L., & Eccles, J. (1997). In search of the powerful self-fulfilling prophecy. *Journal of Personality and Social Psychology, 72,* 791–809.

Maguire, P. (1987). *Doing participatory research: A feminist approach.* Amherst: University of Massachusetts.

Magyar, T. M., Feltz, D. L., & Simpson, I. P. (2004). Individual and crew level determinants of collective efficacy in rowing. *Journal of Sport and Exercise Psychology, 26,* 136–154.

Maier, M. A., Elliot, A. J., & Lichtenfeld, S. (2008). Mediation of the negative effect of red on intellectual performance. *Personality and Social Psychology Bulletin, 34,* 1530–1540.

Main, M., Kaplan, N., & Cassidy, J. (1985). Security in infancy, childhood, and adulthood: A move to the level of representation. *Monographs of the Society for Research in Child Development, 50*(1–2), 66–104.

Malamuth, N. M. (1981). Rape proclivity among males. *Journal of Social Issues, 37,* 138–157.

Malamuth, N. M., & Huppin, M. (2007). Drawing the line on virtual child pornography: Bringing the law in line with the research evidence. *NYU Review of Law & Social Change, 31,* 773–827.

Mallet, P., & Rodriguez-Tome, G. (1999). Social anxiety with peers in 9- to 14-year-olds: Developmental process and relations with self-consciousness and perceived peer acceptance. *European Journal of Psychology of Education, 14,* 387–402.

Manning, J. C. (2006). The impact of Internet pornography on marriage and the family: A review of the research. *Sexual Addiction and Compulsion, 13,* 131–165.

Manning, J. (2014). Construction of values in online and offline dating discourses: Comparing presentational and articulated rhetorics of relationship seeking. *Journal of Computer-Mediated Communication, 19,* 309–324.

Manning, R., Levine, M., & Collins, A. (2007). The Kitty Genovese murder and the social psychology of helping: The parable of 38 witnesses. *American Psychologist, 62,* 555–562.

Mannix, E., & Neale, M. A. (2005). What differences make a difference: The promise and reality of diverse teams in organizations. *Psychological Science in the Public Interest, 6*(2), 31–55.

Mantler, J., Schellenberg, E. G., & Page, S. (2003). Attributions for serious illness: Are controllability, responsibility, and blame different constructs? *Canadian Journal of Behavioural Science, 35*(2), 142–152.

Mantsios, G. (2000). Media magic: Making class invisible. In T. Ore (Ed.), *The social construction of difference and inequality: Race, class, gender, and sexuality.* Mountain View, CA: Mayfield.

Maoz, I. (2002). Is there contact at all? Intergroup interaction in planned contact interventions between Jews and Arabs in Israel. *International Journal of Intercultural Relations Special Issue: Jewish-Arab Inter-Group Relations: The Case of Israel, 26,* 185–197.

Marion, S. B., Kukucka, J., Collins, C., Kassin, S., & Burke, T. M. (2015). Lost proof of innocence: The impact of confessions on alibi evidence. *Law and Human Behavior, 39*(5).

Mark, M. M., & Bryant, F. B. (1984). Potential pitfalls of a more applied social psychology: Review and recommendations. *Basic and Applied Social Psychology, 5,* 231–253.

Marks, M. (1999). A test of the impact of collective efficacy in routine and novel performance environments. *Human Performance, 12,* 295–309.

Marsella, A. (1998). Toward a global community psychology: Meeting the needs of a changing world. *American Psychologist, 53,* 1282–1292.

Marsh, H. W., Trautwein, U., Lüdtke, O., Köller, O., & Baumert, J. (2005). Academic self-concept, interest, grades, and standardized test scores: Reciprocal effects models of causal ordering. *Child Development, 76,* 397–416.

Martens, R., Landers, D. M., & Loy, J. W. (1972). *Sport cohesiveness questionnaire.* Washington, DC: AAHPERD (American Alliance for Health, Physical Education, Recreation and Dance).

Martin, A. J., Marsh, H. W., Williamson, A., & Debus, R. R. (2003). Self-handicapping, defensive pessimism, and goal orientation: A qualitative study of university students. *Journal of Educational Psychology, 95,* 617–628.

Martin, J. A. (2014). Agenda setting, elections, and the impact of information technology. In T. J. Johnson (Ed.), *Agenda setting in a 2.0 world: New agendas in communication* (pp. 28–52). New York, NY: Routledge.

Martinie, M.-A., Olive, T., & Milland, L. (2010). Cognitive dissonance induced by writing a counterattitudinal essay facilitates performance on simple tasks but not on complex tasks that involve working memory. *Journal of Experimental Social Psychology, 46,* 587–594.

Masip, J., Barba, A., & Herrero, C. (2012). Behavioral Analysis Interview and common sense: A study with novice and experienced officers. *Psychiatry, Psychology, and Law, 19,* 21–34.

Maslow, A. H. (1943). A theory of human motivation. *Psychological Review, 50,* 370–396.

Maslow, A. H. (1970). *Motivation and personality* (2nd ed.). New York, NY: Harper & Row.

Massey, S. G., & Barreras, R. E., (2013). Introducing 'Impact Validity.' *Journal of Social Issues, 69,* 615–632.

Matarazzo, J. D. (1980). Behavioral health and behavioral medicine: Frontiers for a new health psychology. *American Psychologist, 35,* 807–817.

Maticka-Tyndale, E., & Brouillard-Coyle, C. (2006). The effectiveness of community interventions targeting HIV and AIDS prevention in young people in developing countries. In D. A. Ross, B. Dick, & J. Ferguson (Eds.), *Preventing HIV/AIDS in young people: A systematic review of the evidence from developing countries.* Geneva, Switzerland: World Health Organization.

Matsumoto, D., & Juang, L. (2004). *Culture and psychology* (3rd ed.). Belmont, CA: Wadsworth.

Mayo, C., & La France, M. (1980). Toward an applicable social psychology. In R. F. Kidd & M. J. Saks (Eds.), *Advances in applied social psychology* (Vol. 1, pp. 81–96). Hillsdale, NJ: Erlbaum.

Mazur, A. (1977). Interpersonal spacing on public benches in "contact" and "noncontact" cultures. *Journal of Social Psychology, 101,* 53–58.

McAlinden, A. M. (2011). 'Transforming justice': Challenges for restorative justice in an era of punishment-based corrections. *Contemporary Justice Review, 14,* 383–406.

McAlister, A. L., Perry, C., & Maccoby, N. (1980). Pilot study of smoking, alcohol and drug abuse prevention. *American Journal of Public Health, 70,* 719–721.

McAllister, H. A. (1996). Self-serving bias in the classroom: Who shows it? Who knows it? *Journal of Educational Psychology, 88,* 123–131.

McChesney, R. W. (1999). *Rich media, poor democracy: Communication politics in dubious times.* New York, NY: The New Press.

McCombs, M. (2014). *Setting the agenda* (2nd ed.). Malden, MA: Polity Press.

McCombs, M., & Stroud, N. J. (2014). Psychology of agenda-setting effects: Mapping the paths of information processing. *Review of Communication Research, 2*(1), 68–93.

McGuire, T. W., Kiesler, S., & Siegel, J. (1987). Group and computer-mediated discussion effects in risk decision making. *Journal of Personality and Social Psychology, 52,* 917–930.

McGuire, W. J. (1964). Inducing resistance to persuasion: Some contemporary approaches.

In L. Berkowitz (Ed.), *Advances in experimental social psychology* (Vol. 1, pp. 191–229). New York, NY: Academic Press.

McKenna, K. Y. A., Green, A. S., & Gleason, M. E. J., (2002). Relationship formation on the Internet: What's the big attraction? *Journal of Social Issues, 58*(1), 9–31.

McKown, C., & Weinstein, R. (2002). Modeling the role of child ethnicity and gender in children's differential response to teacher expectations. *Journal of Applied Social Psychology, 32,* 159–184.

McLeod, P. L., Lobel, S. A., & Cox, T. H. (1996). Ethnic diversity and creativity in small groups. *Small Group Research, 27,* 248–264.

McMillan, D. W., & Chavis, D. M. (1986). Sense of community: Definition and theory. *Journal of Community Psychology, 14,* 6–23.

McNulty, J. K., & Fincham, F. D. (2011). Beyond positive psychology? Toward a contextual view of psychological processes and well-being. *American Psychologist, 67,* 101–110.

Mednick, S. A., Moffitt, T. E., Gabrielli, W., & Hutchings, B. (1986). Genetic influences in criminal behavior: A review. In D. Olweus, J. Block, & M. Radke-Yarrow (Eds.), *Development of antisocial and prosocial behavior* (pp. 33–50). New York, NY: Academic.

Meehl, P. E. (1960). The cognitive activity of the clinician. *American Psychologist, 15,* 19–27.

Meeks, S. (1990). Age bias in the diagnostic decision-making behavior of clinicians. *Professional Psychology: Research and Practice, 21,* 279–284.

Mehrabian, A., & Diamond, S. G. (1971). The effects of furniture arrangement, props and personality on social interaction. *Journal of Personality and Social Psychology, 20,* 18–30.

Mehrabian, A., & Ferris, S. R. (1967). Inference of attitudes from nonverbal communication in two channels. *Journal of Consulting Psychology, 31,* 248–252.

Mello-Goldner, D., & Jackson, J. (1999). Premenstrual syndrome (PMS) as a self-handicapping strategy among college women. *Journal of Social Behavior and Personality, 14,* 607–616.

Merry, S. E. (1981). *Urban danger: Life in a neighborhood of strangers.* Philadelphia, PA: Temple University Press.

Merton, R. (1948). The self-fulfilling prophecy. *Antioch Review, 8,* 193–210.

Metzger, M. (2007). Making sense of credibility on the web: Models for evaluating online information and recommendations for future research. *Journal of the American Society for Information Science and Technology, 58*(13), 2078–2091.

Michelson, W. (1976). *Man and his urban environment: A sociological approach.* Don Mills, ON: Addison-Wesley.

Milam, J. E., Richardson, J. L., Marks, G., Kemper, C. A., & McCutchan, A. J. (2004). The roles of dispositional optimism and pessimism in HIV disease progression. *Psychology and Health, 19,* 167–181.

Milgram, S. (1970). The experience of living in cities. *Science, 167,* 1461–1468.

Milgram, S. (1974). *Obedience to authority: An experimental approach.* New York, NY: Harper & Row.

Miller, A. G., & Lawson, T. (1989). The effect of an informational option on the fundamental attribution error. *Personality and Social Psychology Bulletin, 15*(2), 194–204.

Miller, G. A. (1969). Psychology as a means of promoting human welfare. *American Psychologist, 24,* 1063–1075.

Miller, J. G. (1984). Culture and the development of everyday social explanation. *Journal of Personality and Social Psychology, 46,* 961–978.

Miller, R. S., & Perlman, D. (2009). *Intimate relationships* (5th ed.). Boston, MA: McGraw-Hill.

Mills, J. F., Kroner, D. G., & Forth, A. E. (2002). Measures of Criminal Attitudes and Associates (MCAA): Development, factor structure, reliability, and validity. *Assessment, 9,* 240–253.

Mincy, R. B. (2000). The underclass: Concept, controversy, and evidence. In K. Rosenblum & T. C. Travis (Eds.), *The meaning of difference: American constructions of race, sex and gender, social class, and sexual orientation.* Boston, MA: McGraw-Hill.

Minkler, M., & Wallerstein, N. (2003). Introduction to community-based participatory research. In M. Minkler & N. Wallerstein (Eds.), *Community-based participatory research for health* (pp. 3–26). San Francisco, CA: Jossey-Bass.

Mirolli, K., Henderson, P., & Hills, D. (1998). *Coworkers' influence on job satisfaction.* Paper presented at the 19th annual Graduate Student Conference in Industrial/Organizational Psychology and Organizational Behavior, San Diego, CA.

Mitchell, T., & Kalb, L. (1981). Effects of outcome knowledge and outcome valence on supervisor's evaluations. *Journal of Applied Psychology, 66,* 604–612.

Mitchell, T., & Wood, R. (1980). Supervisors' responses to subordinate poor performance: A test of an attributional model. *Organizational Behavior and Human Decision Processes, 25,* 123–138.

Moffitt, T. E. (1993). Adolescence-limited and life-course-persistent antisocial behavior: A developmental taxonomy. *Psychology Review, 100,* 674–701.

Moffitt, T. E., Caspi, A., Dickson, N., Silva, P., & Stanton, W. (1996). Childhood-onset versus adolescent-onset antisocial conduct problems in males: Natural history from ages 3 to 18 years. *Development and Psychopathology, 8,* 399–424.

Moghaddam, F. M. (1998). *Social psychology: Exploring universals across cultures.* New York, NY: W. H. Freeman.

Moghaddam, F. M., Taylor, D. M., & Wright, S. C. (1993). *Social psychology in cross-cultural perspective.* New York, NY: W. H. Freeman.

Molloy, L. E., Gest, S. D., & Rulison, K. L. (2011). Peer influences on academic motivation: Exploring multiple methods of assessing youths' most "influential" peer relationships. *Journal of Early Adolescence, 31,* 13–40.

Montano, D. E., & Taplin, S. H. (1991). A test of an expanded theory of reasoned action to predict mammography participation. *Social Science and Medicine, 32*(6), 733–741.

Monto, M. A., Newcomb, M. D., Rabow, J., & Hernandez, A. C. (1992). Social status and drunk-driving intervention. *Journal of Studies on Alcohol, 53,* 63–68.

Moorman, R. H. (1991). Relationship between organizational justice and organizational citizenship behaviors: Do fairness perceptions influence employee citizenship? *Journal of Applied Psychology, 76*(6), 845–855.

Moos, R. H. (1973). Conceptualization of human environments. *American Psychologist, 28,* 652–665.

Moos, R. H. (1981). Social-ecological perspectives on health. In G. Stone, F. Cohen, & N. E. Adler (Eds.), *Health psychology: A handbook* (pp. 523–547). San Francisco, CA: Jossey-Bass.

Moos, R. H. (1987). *Correctional Institutions Environment Scale manual.* Palo Alto, CA: Consulting Psychologists Press.

Morawski, J. G. (2000). Social psychology a century ago. *American Psychologist, 55,* 427–430.

Moreland, R. L., & Zajonc, R. B. (1982). Exposure effects may not depend on stimulus recognition. *Journal of Personality and Social Psychology, 37,* 1085–1089.

Morgan, M. (1990). International cultivation effects. In N. Signorielli & M. Morgan (Eds.), *Cultivation analysis: New directions in media effects research* (pp. 225–247). Thousand Oaks, CA: SAGE.

Morgan, M., Shanahan, J., & Signorielli, N. (2009). Growing up with television: Cultivation processes. In J. Bryant & M. B. Oliver (Eds.), *Media effects: Advances in theory and research* (3rd ed., pp. 34–49). New York, NY: Routledge.

Moriano, J. A., Gorgievski, M., Laguna, M., Stephan, U., & Zarafshani, K. (2012). A cross-cultural approach to understanding entrepreneurial intention. *Journal of Career Development, 39*(2), 162–185.

Morrison, M., Epstude, K., & Roese, N. J. (2012). Life regrets and the need to belong. *Social Psychological and Personality Science, 3*(6), 675–681.

Moskowitz, J. (1989). The primary prevention of alcohol problems: A critical review of the research literature. *Journal of Studies on Alcohol, 50,* 54–88.

Mount, M. K., Harter, J. K., Barrick, M. R., & Colbert, A. (2000). *Does job satisfaction moderate the relationship between conscientiousness and job performance?* Paper presented at the meeting of the Academy of Management, Toronto, Ontario.

Moy, P., & Pfau, M. (2000). *With malice toward all? The media and public confidence in democratic institutions.* Westport, CT: Praeger.

Moya, E. M., Chávez-Baray, S., & Martinez, O. (2014). Intimate partner violence and sexual health: Voices and images of Latina immigrant survivors in Southwestern United States. *Health Promotion Practice, 15*(5), 881–893.

Mulac, A., Jansma, L. L., & Linz, D. G. (2002). Men's behavior toward women after viewing sexually explicit films: Degradation makes a difference. *Communication Monographs, 69,* 311–328.

Mulkana, S. S., & Hailey, B. J. (2001). The role of optimism in health-enhancing behavior. *American Journal of Health Behavior, 25,* 388–395.

Mullen, B., & Copper, C. (1994). The relation between group cohesiveness and performance: An integration. *Psychological Bulletin, 115,* 210–227.

Mullin, C. R., & Linz, D. (1995). Desensitization and resensitization to violence against women: Effects of exposure to sexually violent films on judgments of domestic violence victims. *Journal of Personality and Social Psychology, 69,* 449–459.

Mumma, G. H. (2002). Effects of three types of potentially biasing information on symptom severity judgments for major depressive episode. *Journal of Clinical Psychology, 58*(10), 1327–1345.

Münsterberg, H. (1908). *On the witness stand: Essays on psychology and crime.* New York, NY: McClure.

Murphy, J. (1998). Using social psychology. In R. Sapsford, A. Still, D. Miell, R. Stevens, & M. Wetherell (Eds.), *Theory and social psychology* (pp. 161–190). Thousand Oaks, CA: SAGE.

Murphy, K. R., & Anhalt, R. L. (1992). Is halo error a property of the rater, ratees, or the specific behaviors observed? *Journal of Applied Psychology, 77*(4), 494–500.

Murray, C. B., & Warden, M. R. (1992). Implications of self-handicapping strategies for academic achievement: A reconceptualization. *Journal of Social Psychology, 132,* 23–37.

Murray, H. A. (1938). *Explorations in personality.* New York, NY: Oxford University Press.

Myers, D. G., & Spencer, S. J. (2004). *Social psychology* (2nd Canadian ed.). Toronto, ON: McGraw-Hill Ryerson.

Myers, D. G., Spencer, S. J., & Jordon, C. (2009). *Social psychology* (4th Canadian ed.). Toronto, Canada: McGraw-Hill.

Myers, N. D., Feltz, D. L., & Short, S. E. (2004). Collective efficacy and team performance: A longitudinal study of collegiate football teams. *Group Dynamics: Theory, Research and Practice, 8,* 126–138.

Narchet, F. M., Meissner, C. A., & Russano, M. B. (2011). Modeling the influence of investigator bias on the elicitation of true and false confessions. *Law & Human Behavior, 35*(6), 452–465.

Nathanson, A. I. (2004). Factual and evaluative approaches to modifying children's responses to violent television. *Journal of Communication, 54,* 321–336.

Nathanson, A. I., & Cantor, J. (2000). Reducing the aggressive-promoting effect of violent cartoons by increasing children's fictional involvement with the victim: A study of active mediation. *Journal of Broadcasting & Electronic Media, 44,* 125–142.

Nathanson, C. A., & Becker, M. H. (1986). Family and peer influence on obtaining a method of contraception. *Journal of Marriage and the Family, 48,* 513–525.

National Center for Health Statistics. (2008). *Prevalence of overweight, obesity, and extreme obesity among adults: United States, trends 1960–62 through 2005–2006.* NCHS Health E-Stat.

National Institute of Justice. (2003). *Correctional boot camps: Lessons from a decade of research.* Washington, DC: U.S. Department of Justice.

Naughton, F., Eborall, H., & Sutton, S. (2013). Dissonance and disengagement in pregnant smokers: A qualitative study. *Journal of Smoking Cessation, 8,* 24–32.

Needles, D. J., & Abramson, L. Y. (1990). Positive life events, attributional style, and hopefulness: Testing a model of recovery from depression. *Journal of Abnormal Psychology, 99,* 156–165.

Nelson, T. D. (2002). *The psychology of prejudice.* Boston, MA: Allyn & Bacon.

Nemeth, C. J. (1986). Differential contributions of majority and minority influence. *Psychological Review, 93,* 23–32.

Nemme, H. E., & White, K. M. (2010). Texting while driving: Psychosocial influences on young people's texting intentions and behaviour. *Accident Analysis and Prevention, 42,* 1257–1265.

Nes, L. S., Evans, D. R., & Segerstrom, S. C. (2009). Optimism and college retention: Mediation by motivation, performance, and adjustment. *Journal of Applied Social Psychology, 39,* 1887–1912.

New Scientist. (2015). *The rise of on-body cameras and how they will change how we live.* Retrieved from https://www.newscientist.com/article/mg22730314-500-the-rise-of-on-body-cameras-and-how-they-will-change-how-we-live/

Newman, O. (1972). *Defensible space.* New York, NY: Macmillan.

Newman, O. (1980). *Community of interest.* New York, NY: Anchor Press/Doubleday.

Nigbur, D., Lyons, E., & Uzzell, D. (2010). Attitudes, norms, identity and environmental behaviour: Using an expanded theory of planned behaviour to predict participation in a kerbside recycling programme. *British Journal of Social Psychology, 49,* 259–284.

Nisbett, R. D., & Wilson, T. D. (1977). The halo effect: Evidence for unconscious alteration of judgments. *Journal of Personality and Social Psychology, 35,* 250–256.

Nisbett, R. E., & Cohen, D. (1996). *Culture of honor.* Boulder, CO: Westview Press.

No Child Left Behind Act of 2001. (2002, January 8). Pub. L. 107–110, 115 Stat. 1425.

Norem, J. K., & Chang, E. C. (2002). The positive psychology of negative thinking. *Journal of Clinical Psychology, 58,* 993–1001.

Norem, J., & Illingsworth, S. (2004). Mood and performance among defensive pessimists and strategic optimists. *Journal of Research in Personality, 38,* 351–366.

Norem, J. K., & Smith, S. (2006). In L. J. Sanna & E. C. Chang (Eds.), *Judgments over time: The interplay of thoughts, feelings, and behaviors* (pp. 34–46). Oxford, UK: Oxford University Press.

Norman, P., Conner, M., & Bell, R. (1999). The theory of planned behavior and smoking cessation. *Health Psychology, 18,* 89–94.

Norton, M. I., Frost, J. H., & Ariely, D. (2007). Less is more: The lure of ambiguity, or why familiarity breeds contempt. *Journal of Personality and Social Psychology, 92,* 97–105.

Nutbeam, D. (2000). Health literacy as a public goal: A challenge for contemporary health education and communication strategies into the 21st century. *Health Promotion International, 15*(3), 259–267.

Obst, P., & Stafurik, J. (2010). Online we are all able bodied: Online psychological sense of community and social support found through membership of disability-specific websites promotes wellbeing for people living with a physical disability. *Journal of Community and Applied Social Psychology, 20*(6), 525–531.

O'Doherty, K. C., Gauvin, F.-P., Grogan, C., & Friedman, W. (2012). Implementing a Public Deliberative Forum. *Hastings Center Report, 42*(2), 20-23.

Office of Management and Budget. (2015). *Fiscal year 2016 budget of the U.S. government.* Retrieved from https://www.whitehouse.gov/sites/default/files/omb/budget/fy2016/assets/budget.pdf

Ofori-Dankwa, J. C., & Julian, J. D. (2002). Toward diversity and similarity curves: Implication for theory, research, and practice. *Human Relations, 55,* 199–224.

Ogilvie, M. (2010, July 16). Summer program inspires future doctors. *The Toronto Star.* Retrieved from http://www.thestar.com

Ojala, M. (2008). Recycling and ambivalence: Quantitative and qualitative analyses of household recycling among young adults. *Environment and Behavior, 40,* 777–797.

Okdie, B. M., Ewoldsen, D. R., Muscanell, N. L., Guadagno, R. E., Eno, C. A., Velez, J., Dunn, A., O'Mally J., & Reichart, L. (2014). Missed programs (There is no TiVo for this one): Why psychologists should study the media. *Perspectives on Psychological Science, 9,* 180–195.

Okilwa, N. S. A., & Shelby, L. (2010). The effects of peer tutoring on academic performance of students with disabilities in Grades 6 through 12: A synthesis of the literature. *Remedial and Special Education, 31,* 450–463.

O'Neill, P. (1989). Responsible to whom? Responsible for what? Some ethical issues in community intervention. *American Journal of Community Psychology, 17,* 323–341.

O'Neill, P. (1998). Communities, collectivities, and the ethics of research. *Canadian Journal of Community Mental Health, 17,* 67–78.

Organ, D. W. (1988). *Organizational citizenship behavior.* Lexington, MA: Lexington Books.

Organ, D. W. (1990). The subtle significance of job satisfaction. *Clinical Laboratory Management Review, 4,* 94–98.

Organizational Research Services. (2004). *Theory of change: A practical guide for action, results, and learning.* Seattle, WA: Author.

Osgood, C. E. (1962). *An alternative to war or surrender.* Urbana: University of Illinois Press.

Oskamp, S. (1991). *Attitudes and opinions.* Englewood Cliffs, NJ: Prentice Hall.

Oskamp, S. (2000). A sustainable future for humanity: How can psychology help? *American Psychologist, 55,* 509–515.

Oskamp, S., & Schultz, P. W. (1997). *Applied social psychology* (2nd ed.). Upper Saddle River, NJ: Prentice Hall.

Oswald, C. A., Prorock, C., & Murphy, S. M. (2014). The perceived meaning of the video game experience: An exploratory study. *Psychology of Popular Media Culture, 3,* 110–126.

Out, J. W., & Lafreniere, K. D. (2001). Baby Think It Over®: Using role-play to prevent teen pregnancy. *Adolescence, 36,* 571–582.

Owen, K. (2008). The nature of confirmatory strategies in the initial assessment process. *Journal of Mental Health Counseling, 30*(4), 362–374.

Oyserman, D., & Lee, S. W. S (2008). Does culture influence what and how we think? Effects of priming individualism and collectivism. *Psychological Bulletin, 134*(2), 311–342.

Padgett, V. R., Brislin-Slütz, J. A., & Neal, J. A. (1989). Pornography, erotica, and attitudes toward women: The effects of repeated exposure. *Journal of Sex Research, 26,* 479–491.

Page, S. (1981). Social responsiveness toward mental patients: The general public and others. *Canadian Journal of Psychiatry, 15*(2), 34–37.

Page, S. (1997). An unobtrusive measure of racial behavior in a public cafeteria. *Journal of Applied Social Psychology, 27,* 2172–2177.

Page, S. (2000). Community research: The lost art of unobtrusive measures. *Journal of Applied Social Psychology, 30,* 2126–2136.

Page, S., & Day, D. (1990). Acceptance of the mentally ill in Canadian society: Reality and illusion. *Canadian Journal of Community Mental Health, 9,* 51–62.

Paik, H., & Comstock, G. (1994). The effects of television violence on antisocial behavior: A meta-analysis. *Communication Research, 21,* 516–546.

Paladino, M., & Castelli, L. (2008). On the immediate consequences of intergroup categorization: Activation of approach and avoidance motor behavior toward ingroup and outgroup members. *Personality and Social Psychology Bulletin, 34,* 755–768.

Parker, D., Manstead, A. S. R., Stradling, S.G., Reason, J. T., & Baxter, J. S. (1992). Intention to commit driving violations: An application of the theory of planned behavior. *Journal of Applied Psychology, 77,* 94–101.

Paskevich, D. M., Brawley, L. R., Dorsch, K. D., & Widmeyer, W. N. (1999). Relationship between collective efficacy and team cohesion: Conceptual and measurement issues. *Group Dynamics: Theory, Research and Practice, 3,* 210–222.

Patterson, G. R., DeBaryshe, B. D., & Ramsey, E. (1989). A developmental perspective on antisocial behavior. *American Psychologist, 44,* 329–335.

Patterson, M. L. (1975). Personal space—Time to burst the bubble? *Man-Environment Systems, 5,* 67.

Patton, M. (1990). *Qualitative evaluation and research methods* (2nd ed.). London, UK: SAGE.

Patton, M. Q. (1994). Developmental evaluation. *Evaluation Practice, 15,* 311–319.

Patton, M. Q. (2011). *Developmental evaluation: Applying complexity concepts to enhance innovation and use.* New York, NY: Guilford Press.

Pavlik, J. V., & McIntosh, S. (2011). *Converging media: A new introduction to mass communication.* New York, NY: Oxford University Press.

Pavlou, P. A., & Chai, L. (2002). What drives electronic commerce across cultures? A cross-cultural investigation of the theory of planned behavior. *Journal of Electronic Commerce Research, 3*(4), 240–253.

Pearson, C. A. L., & Chong, J. (1997). Contributions of job content and social information on organizational commitment and job satisfaction: An exploration in a Malaysian nursing context. *Journal of Occupational and Organizational Psychology, 70,* 357–374.

Penley, L. E., Alexander, E. R., Jernigan, I. E., & Henwood, C. I. (1991). Communication abilities of managers: The relationship to performance. *Journal of Management, 17,* 57–76.

Pennington, N., & Hastie, R. (1986). Evidence evaluation in complex decision making. *Journal of Personality and Social Psychology, 51,* 242–258.

Perillo, J. T., & Kassin, S. M. (2011). Inside interrogation: The lie, the bluff, and false confessions. *Law and Human Behavior, 35,* 327–337.

Perkins, H. W. (2003). The emergence and evolution of the social norms approach to substance abuse prevention. In H. W. Perkins (Ed.), *The social norms approach to preventing school and college age substance abuse: A handbook for educators, counselors, and clinicians* (pp. 21–34). San Francisco, CA: Jossey-Bass.

Perkins, H. W., Haines, M., & Rice, R. (2005). Misperceiving the college drinking norm and related problems: A nationwide study of exposure to prevention information, perceived norms, and student alcohol misuse. *Journal of Studies on Alcohol, 66,* 470–478.

Perry, D. K. (2007). Does television kill? Testing a period-characteristic model. *Media Psychology, 9,* 567–594.

Perry, R. P., Hechter, F. J., Menec, V. H., & Weinberg, L. E. (1993). Enhancing achievement motivation and performance in college students: An attributional retraining perspective. *Research in Higher Education, 34,* 687–723.

Peter, J., & Valkenburg, P. M. (2008). Adolescents' exposure to sexually explicit internet material, sexual uncertainty, and attitudes toward uncommitted sexual exploration: Is there a link? *Communication Research, 35,* 579–601.

Peterson, C. (2000). The future of optimism. *American Psychologist, 55,* 44–55.

Peterson, C., & Chang, E. C. (2003). Optimism and flourishing. In C. L. M. Keyes, & J. Haidt (Eds.),

Flourishing: Positive psychology and the life well-lived (pp. 55–79). Washington, DC: American Psychological Association.

Peterson, C., Maier, S. F., & Seligman, M. E. P. (1995). *Learned helplessness: A theory for the age of personal control.* New York, NY: Oxford University Press.

Peterson, C., & Seligman, M. E. P. (1984). Causal explanations as a risk factor for depression: Theory and evidence. *Psychological Review, 91,* 347–374.

Peterson, C., & Vaidya, R. S. (2001). Explanatory style, expectations, and depressive symptoms. *Personality and Individual Differences, 31,* 1217–1223.

Peterson-Badali, M., & Koegl, C. J. (2002). Juveniles' experiences of incarceration: The role of correctional staff in peer violence. *Journal of Criminal Justice, 30,* 41–49.

Petrosino, A., Turpin-Petrosino, C., & Buehler, J. (2002). *"Scared Straight" and other juvenile awareness programs for preventing juvenile delinquency.* Cochrane Database of Systematic Reviews, 2–3.

Petty, R. E., & Wegener, D. T. (1998). Attitude change: Multiple roles for persuasion variables. In D. T. Gilbert, S. T. Fishe, & G. Lindzey (Eds.), *Handbook of social psychology* (4th ed., Vol. 1, pp. 323–390). Boston, MA: McGraw-Hill.

Pfeffer, J., Cialdini, R. B., Hanna, B., & Knopoff, K. (1998). Faith in supervision and the self-enhancement bias: Two psychological reasons why managers don't empower workers. *Basic and Applied Social Psychology, 20,* 313–321.

Pfeiffer, A. M., Whelan, J. P., & Martin, J. M. (2000). Decision-making bias in psychotherapy: Effects of hypothesis source and accountability. *Journal of Counseling Psychology, 47,* 429–436.

Pillow, D. R., Zautra, A. J., & Sandler, I. (1996). Major life events and minor stressors: Identifying mediational links in the stress process. *Journal of Personality and Social Psychology, 70,* 381–394.

Pinquart, M., Feubner, C., & Ahnert, L. (2013). Meta-analytic evidence for stability in attachments from infancy to early adulthood. *Attachment & Human Development, 15*(2), 189–218.

Piquero, A., Farrington, D., & Blumstein, A. (2003). The criminal career paradigm. In M. Tonry (Ed.), *Crime and justice: A review of research* (Vol. 30, pp. 359–506). Chicago, IL: University of Chicago Press.

Platt, J. (1973). Social traps. *American Psychologist, 28,* 641–651.

Police Executive Research Forum. (2013). *A national survey of eyewitness identification procedures in law enforcement agencies.* Retrieved from https://www.ncjrs.gov/App/Publications/abstract.aspx?ID=264692

Policy. [Def. 5]. (2016). *In Merriam Webster Online.* Retrieved from http://www.merriam-webster.com/dictionary/policy?show=0&t=1314051181

Pollock, T. G., Whitbred, R. C., & Contractor, N. (2000). Social information processing and job characteristics: A simultaneous test of two theories with implications for job satisfaction. *Human Communication Research, 26*(2), 292–330.

Pomazal, R. J., & Jaccard, J. J. (1976). An informational approach to altruistic behavior. *Journal of Personality and Social Psychology, 33*(3), 317–326.

Ponterotto, J. G. (2005). Qualitative research in counselling psychology: A primer on research paradigms and philosophy of science. *Journal of Counselling Psychology, 52,* 126–136.

Porter, L. W., & Steers, R. M. (1973). Organization, work, and personal factors in employee turnover and absenteeism. *Psychological Bulletin, 80,* 151–176.

Posavac, E. J., & Carey, R. G. (2007). *Program evaluation: Methods and case studies* (7th ed.). Upper Saddle River, NJ: Prentice Hall.

Potter, W. J. (2003). *The 11 myths of media violence.* Thousand Oaks, CA: SAGE.

Prapavessis, H., & Carron, A. V. (1997). Cohesion and work output. *Small Group Research, 28,* 294–301.

Prasad, J. (1950). A comparative study of rumours and reports in earthquakes. *British Journal of Psychology, 46,* 129–144.

Preiser, W. P. E., & Taylor, A. (1983). The habitability framework: Linking human behavior and physical environment in a special education. *EEQ: Exceptional Education Quarterly, 4,* 1–15.

Prentice, D. A., & Miller, D. T. (1993). Pluralistic ignorance and alcohol use on campus: Some consequences of misperceiving the social norm. *Journal of Personality and Social Psychology, 64,* 243–256.

Price, J. L., & Mueller, C. W. (1986). *Handbook of organizational measurement.* Marshfield, MA: Pitman.

Price, M. (2008). New system ranks HIV/AIDS interventions. *Monitor on Psychology, 39*(5), 12–13.

Prilleltensky, I. (2008). The role of power in wellness, oppression, and liberation: The promise of psychopolitical validity. *Journal of Community Psychology, 36*, 116–136.

Prochaska, J. O., & DiClemente, C. C. (1983). Stages and processes of self-change of smoking: Toward an integrative model of change. *Journal of Consulting and Clinical Psychology, 51*, 390–395.

Prochaska, J. O., & DiClemente, C. C. (1986). Toward a comprehensive model of change. In W. R. Miller & N. Heather (Eds.), *Treating addictive behaviors: Processes of change* (pp. 3–27). New York, NY: Plenum Press.

Prochaska, J. O., DiClemente, C. C., & Norcross, J. C. (1992). In search of how people change: Applications to addictive behaviors. *American Psychologist, 47*, 1102–1114.

Prochaska, J. O., DiClemente, C. C., Velicer, W. F., & Rossi, J. S. (1993). Standardized, individualized, interactive, and personalized self-help programs for smoking cessation. *Health Psychology, 12*, 399–405.

Prohaska, V. (1994). "I know I'll get an A": Confident overestimation of final course grades. *Teaching of Psychology, 21*, 141–143.

Pulakos, E. D., & Wexley, K. N. (1983). Relationship among perceptual similarity, sex, performance, and ratings in manager-subordinate dyads. *Academy of Management Journal, 26*, 129–139.

Putnam, R. (1995). Bowling alone: America's declining social capital. *Journal of Democracy, 6*, 65–78.

Rabbie, J. M., & Horwitz, M. (1969). Arousal of ingroup-outgroup bias by a chance win or loss. *Journal of Personality and Social Psychology, 13*, 269–277.

Ragin, D. F. (2015). Health psychology: An interdisciplinary approach to health (2nd ed.). New York, NY: Routledge.

Rahim, A., & Bonoma, T. V. (1979). Managing organizational conflict: A model for diagnosis and intervention. *Psychological Reports, 44*, 1323–1344.

Rand, G. (1984). Crime and environment: A review of the literature and its implications for urban architecture and planning. *Journal of Architecture and Planning Research, 1*, 3–19.

Rapoport, A. (1969). *House form and culture.* Englewood Cliffs, NJ: Prentice Hall.

Rappaport, J. (2000). Community narratives: Tales of terror and joy. *American Journal of Community Psychology, 28*(1), 1–24.

Redmond, M. V. (2000). Cultural distance as a mediating factor between stress and intercultural communication competence. *International Journal of Intercultural Relations, 24*(1), 151–159.

Reeve, J. (2004). Self-determination theory applied to educational settings. In E. L. Deci & R. M. Ryan (Eds.), *Handbook of self-determination research* (pp. 183–203). Rochester, NY: University of Rochester Press.

Reeve, J., Ryan, R., Deci, E. L., & Jang, H. (2008). Understanding and promoting autonomous self-regulation: A self-determination theory perspective. In D. H. Schunk & B. J. Zimmerman (Eds.), *Motivation and self-regulated learning: Theory, research, and applications* (pp. 223–244). New York, NY: Erlbaum.

Refuerzo, B. J., & Verderber, S. (1990). Dimensions of person-environment relationships in shelters for victims of domestic violence. *Journal of Architectural and Planning Research, 7*, 33–52.

Regan, P. R. (2003). *The mating game: A primer on love, sex, and marriage.* Thousand Oaks, CA: SAGE.

Reich, J. W. (1981). An historical analysis of the field. In L. Bickman (Ed.), *Applied social psychology* (pp. 45–70). Beverly Hills, CA: SAGE.

Reich, S. M. (2010). Adolescents' sense of community on MySpace and Facebook: A mixed-methods approach. *Journal of Community Psychology, 38*(6), 688–705.

Reichardt, C. S., & Mark, M. M. (1998). Quasi-experimentation. In L. Bickman & D. J. Rog (Eds.), *Handbook of applied social research methods* (pp. 193–228). Thousand Oaks, CA: SAGE.

Reicher, S. D., Haslam, S. A., & Miller, A. G. (2014). What makes a person a perpetrator? The intellectual, moral, and methodological arguments for revisiting Milgram's research on the influence of authority. *Journal of Social Issues, 70*, 393–408.

Reid, F. J., Ball, L. J., Morley, A. M., & Evans, B. T. (1997). Styles of group discussion in computer-mediated decision making. *British Journal of Social Psychology, 36*, 241–262.

Reis, H. T., Maniaci, M. R., Caprariello, P. A., Eastwick, P. W., & Finkel, E. J. (2011). Familiarity does indeed promote attraction in live interaction. *Journal of Personality and Social Psychology, 101*, 557–570.

Reivich, K. J., Gillham, J. E., Chaplin, T. M., & Seligman, M. E. P. (2005). From helplessness to optimism: The role of resilience in treating and preventing depression in youth. In S. Goldstein & R. B. Brooks (Eds.), *Handbook of resilience in children* (pp. 223–237). New York, NY: Kluwer Academic/Plenum.

Renick M. J., & Harter, S. (1989). Impact of social comparisons on the developing self-perceptions of learning disabled students. *Journal of Educational Psychology, 81*, 631–638.

Rentsch, J. R., & Steel, R. P. (1992). Construct and concurrent validation of the Andrews and Withey job satisfaction questionnaire. *Educational and Psychological Measurement, 52*, 357–367.

Rheingold, H. (1993). *The virtual community: Homesteading on the electronic frontier.* Reading, MA: Addison-Wesley.

Rhodewalt, F. (1990). Self-handicappers: Individual differences in the preference for anticipatory, self-protective acts. In R. L. Higgins (Ed.), *Self-handicapping: The paradox that isn't* (pp. 69–106). New York, NY: Plenum.

Rhodewalt, F., Sanbonmatsu, D. M., Tschanz, B., Feick, D. L., & Waller, A. (1995). Self-handicapping and interpersonal trade-offs: The effects of claimed self-handicaps on observers' performance evaluations and feedback. *Personality and Social Psychology Bulletin, 21*, 1042–1050.

Rideout, V. J., Foehr, U. G., & Roberts, D. F. (2010). *Generation M²: Media in the lives of 8- to 18-year-olds.* Menlo Park, CA: Kaiser Family Foundation.

Riess, M., & Schlenker, B. R. (1977). Attitude change and responsibility avoidance as modes of dilemma resolution in forced-compliance situations. *Journal of Personality and Social Psychology, 35*, 21–30.

Riger, S. (1989). The politics of community intervention. *American Journal of Community Psychology, 17*, 379–383.

Riketta, M. (2008). The causal relation between job attitudes and performance: A meta-analysis of panel studies. *Journal of Applied Psychology, 93*(2), 472–481.

Riksheim, E. C., & Chermak, S. M. (1993). Causes of police behaviour revisited. *Journal of Criminal Justice, 21*, 353–382.

Riley, D. A. (1997). Using local research to change 100 communities for children and families. *American Psychologist, 52*(4), 424–433.

Rind, B., & Strohmetz, D. (2001). Effect on restaurant tipping of presenting customers with an interesting task and of reciprocity. *Journal of Applied Social Psychology, 31*, 1379–1384.

Ritscher, J. B., & Phelan, J. C. (2004). Internalized stigma predicts erosion of morale among psychiatric outpatients. *Psychiatry Research, 129*, 257–265.

Robbins, S. P., & Langton, N. (2001). *Organizational behaviour: Concepts, controversies, applications.* Toronto, ON: Pearson Education Canada.

Roberge, M., & van Dick, R. (2010). Recognizing the benefits of diversity: When and how does diversity increase group performance? *Human Resource Management Review, 20*(4), 295–308.

Roberson, L., & Kim, R. (2014). Stereotype threat research hits the sweet spot for organizational psychology. *Industrial and Organizational Psychology, 7*(3), 450–452.

Robert, C., Probst, T. M., Martocchio, J. J., Drasgow, F., & Lawler, J. J. (2000). Empowerment and continuous improvement in the United States, Mexico, Poland, and India: Predicting fit on the basis of the dimensions of power distance and individualism. *Journal of Applied Psychology, 85*, 643–658.

Robertson, K., McNeill, L., Green, J., & Roberts, C. (2012). Illegal downloading, ethical concern, and illegal behavior. *Journal of Business Ethics, 108*, 215–227.

Robinson, M. B., & Robinson, C. E. (1997). Environmental characteristics associated with residential burglaries of student apartment complexes. *Environment and Behavior, 29*, 657–675.

Robinson, S. (2012, February 1). New rules for radicals: 10 ways to spark change in a post-occupy world. *AlterNet.* Retrieved from http://www.alternet.org

Robinson, T. L., & Howard-Hamilton, M. F. (2000). *The convergence of race, ethnicity, and gender.* Upper Saddle River, NJ: Prentice Hall.

Rodriguez, C. M. (2009). The impact of academic self-concept, expectations and the choice of learning strategy on academic achievement: The case of business students. *Higher Education Research and Development, 28*, 523–539.

Roethlisberger, F. J., & Dickson, W. J. (1939). *Management and the worker.* Cambridge, MA: Harvard University Press.

Rogers, E. M. (1994). *A history of communication study: A biographical approach.* New York, NY: Free Press.

Rogers, P. N., & Schoenig, S. E. (1994). A time series evaluation of California's 1982 driving-under-the-influence legislative reforms. *Accident Analysis & Prevention, 26*, 63–78.

Roloff, M. E. (1981). *Interpersonal communication: The social exchange approach.* Beverly Hills, CA: SAGE.

Romer, D., Jamieson, K. H., & Aday, S. (2003). Television news and the cultivation of fear of crime. *Journal of Communication, 53,* 88–104.

Rosenhan, D. L. (1973). On being sane in insane places. *Science, 179,* 250–258.

Rosenstock, I. M. (1974). Historical origins of the health belief model. *Health Education Monographs, 2,* 328–335.

Rosenthal, R., & Jacobson, L. (1968). *Pygmalion in the classroom: Teacher expectation and pupils' intellectual development.* New York, NY: Holt, Rinehart & Winston.

Roskos-Ewoldsen, B., Davies, J., & Roskos-Ewoldsen, D. R. (2004). Implications of the mental models approach for cultivation theory. *Communications, 29,* 345–363.

Roskos-Ewoldsen, D. R. (1997). Attitude accessibility and persuasion: Review and a transactive model. In B. Burleson (Ed.), *Communication Yearbook 20* (pp. 185–225). Beverly Hills, CA: SAGE.

Roskos-Ewoldsen, D. R., Klinger, M. R., & Roskos-Ewoldsen, B. (2007). Media priming: A meta-analysis. In R. W. Press, M. Allen, B. M. Gayle, & N. Burrell (Eds.), *Media effects research: Advances through meta-analysis* (pp. 53–80). Mahwah, NJ: Erlbaum.

Roskos-Ewoldsen, D. R., Roskos-Ewoldsen, B., & Carpentier, F. R. D. (2009). Media priming: An updated synthesis. In J. Bryant & M. B. Oliver (Eds.), *Media effects: Advances in theory and research* (3rd ed., pp. 73–93). New York, NY: Routledge.

Ross, L. (1977). The intuitive psychologist and his shortcomings: Distortions in the attribution process. In L. Berkowitz (Ed.), *Advances in experimental social psychology* (Vol. 10, pp. 174–221). New York, NY: Academic Press.

Ross, L., Greene, D., & House, P. (1977). The "false consensus effect": An egocentric bias in social perception and attribution processes. *Journal of Experimental Social Psychology, 13,* 279–301.

Ross, L., Lepper, M., & Ward, A. (2010). History of social psychology: Insights, challenges, and contributions to theory and application. In S. T. Fiske, D. T. Gilbert, & G. Lindzey (Eds.), *Handbook of social psychology* (5th ed., Vol. 1, pp. 3–50). Hoboken, NJ: Wiley.

Ross, L., & Nisbett, R. E. (1991). *The person and the situation: Perspectives of social psychology.* New York, NY: McGraw-Hill.

Rosser, S., Issakidis, C., & Peters, L. (2003). Perfectionism and social phobia: Relationship between the constructs and impact on cognitive behavior therapy. *Cognitive Therapy and Research, 27,* 143–151.

Rothman, A. J., Haddock, G., & Schwarz, N. (2001). How many partners is too many? Shaping perceptions of personal vulnerability. *Journal of Applied Social Psychology, 31,* 2195–2214.

Rovio, E., Eskola, J., Kozub, S. A., Duda, J. L., & Lintunen, T. (2009). Can high group cohesion be harmful? A case study of a junior ice-hockey team. *Small Group Research, 40,* 421–435.

Royse, D., Thyer, B. A., Padgett, D. K., & Logan, T. K. (2006). *Program evaluation: An introduction* (4th ed.). Belmont, CA: Thomson Brooks/Cole.

Rubie-Davies, C., Hattie, J., & Hamilton, R. (2006). Expecting the best for students: Teacher expectations and academic outcomes. *British Journal of Educational Psychology, 76,* 429–444.

Rudkin, J. (2003). *Community psychology.* Upper Saddle River, NJ: Prentice Hall.

Runciman, W. G. (1972). *Relative deprivation and social justice.* Middlesex, UK: Penguin Books.

Russano, M. B., Meissner, C. A., Narchet, F. M., & Kassin, S. M. (2005). Investigating true and false confessions within a novel experimental paradigm. *Psychological Science, 16*(6), 481–486.

Russo, N. F., & Denious, J. E. (2001). Violence in the lives of women having abortions: Implications for practice and public policy. *Professional Psychology: Research and Practice, 32*(2), 142–150.

Russo, N. F., & Zierk, K. L. (1992). Abortion, childbearing, and women's well-being. *Professional Psychology: Research and Practice, 33*(4), 269–280.

R. v. Butler [1992], 1 S.C.R. 452. File No.: 22191. 1991: June 6; 1992: February 27.

R. v. Henry (2010), B.C.J. No. 2072; 2010 BCCA 462 (British Columbia Court of Appeal).

R. v. Mariani (2007), O.J. No. 1715, 2007 ONCA 329, 223 O.A.C. 308, 220 C.C.C. (3d) 74 (Ontario Court of Appeal).

R. v. Parks (1993), 24 C.R. (4th) 81, C.C.C. (3d) 353, 15 O.R. (3d) 324, 65 O.A.C. 122.

Ryan, R. M., & Deci, E. L. (2000). Intrinsic and extrinsic motivations: Classic definitions and new directions. *Contemporary Educational Psychology, 25,* 54–67.

Ryan, R. M., & Deci, E. L. (2004). Overview of self-determination theory: An organismic dialectical perspective. In E. L. Deci & R. M. Ryan (Eds.), *Handbook of self-determination research* (pp. 3–33). Rochester, NY: University of Rochester Press.

Ryhammer, L., & Smith, G. J. W. (1999). Creative and other personality functions as defined by percept-genetic techniques and their relation to organizational conditions. *Creativity Research Journal, 12*, 277–286.

Ryska, T. A., Yin, Z., Cooley, D., & Ginn, R. (1999). Developing team cohesion: A comparison of cognitive-behavioral strategies of U.S. and Australian sport coaches. *The Journal of Psychology, 133*(5), 523–539.

Sadava, S. W. (1997). Applied social psychology: An introduction. In S. Sadava & D. McCreary (Eds.), *Applied social psychology* (pp. 1–9). Upper Saddle River, NJ: Prentice Hall.

Sagiv, L., & Schwartz, S. H. (1995). Value priorities and readiness for out-group social contact. *Journal of Personality and Social Psychology, 69*(3), 437–448.

Saks, M. J., & Marti, M. W. (1997). A meta-analysis of the effects of jury size. *Law and Human Behavior, 21*, 451–467.

Salancik, G. R., & Pfeffer, J. (1978). A social information processing approach to job attitudes and task design. *Administrative Science Quarterly, 23*(2), 224–253.

Salmivalli, C., & Poskiparta, E. (2012). Making bullying prevention a priority in Finnish schools: The KiVa antibullying program. *New Directions for Youth Development, 133*, 41–53.

Salovey, P., Rothman, A. J., & Rodin, J. (1998). Health behavior. In D. T. Gilbert, S. T. Fiske, & G. Lindzey (Eds.), *The handbook of social psychology* (Vol. 2, 4th ed., pp. 633–683). New York, NY: McGraw-Hill.

Sang, Y., Lee, J., Kim, Y., & Woo, H. (2015). Understanding the intentions behind illegal downloading: A comparative study of American and Korean college students. *Telematics and Informatics, 32*, 333–343.

Santandreu Calonge, D., & Safiullin (Eugene Lee), A. F. (2015). Can culturally, disciplinarily and educationally diverse (D3) teams function and be creative? A case study in a Korean University. *Educational Studies, 41*(4), 369–392.

Sapsford, R., & Dallos, R. (1998). Resisting social psychology. In R. Sapsford, A. Still, D. Miell, R. Stevens, & M. Wetherell (Eds.), *Theory and social psychology* (pp. 191–208). London, UK: SAGE.

Sarafino, E. P. (1998). *Health psychology: Biopsychosocial interactions* (3rd ed.). New York, NY: Wiley.

Sarafino, E. P. (2002). *Health psychology: Biopsychosocial interactions* (4th ed.). New York, NY: Wiley.

Savage, D., & Miller, T. (Eds.). (2011). *It gets better: Coming out, overcoming bullying, and creating a life worth living.* New York, NY: Penguin.

Schachter, S. (1959). *The psychology of affiliation: Experimental studies of the sources of gregariousness.* Stanford, CA: Stanford University Press.

Scharff, M. M. (2005). Understanding WorldCom's accounting fraud: Did groupthink play a role? *Journal of Leadership & Organization Studies, 11*, 109–118.

Scheepers, D., Spears, R., Doosje, B., & Manstead, A. S. R. (2006). The social functions on ingroup bias: Creating, confirming, or changing social reality. *European Review of Social Psychology, 17*, 359–396.

Scheier, M. F., & Carver, C. S. (1992). Effects of optimism on psychological and physical well-being: Theoretical overview and empirical update. *Cognitive Therapy and Research, 16*, 201–228.

Schein, E. H. (2006). So how can you assess your corporate culture? In J. Gallos (Ed.), *Organization development: A Jossey-Bass reader* (pp. 614–633). San Francisco, CA: Jossey-Bass.

Schellenberg, E. G., & Bem, S. L. (1998). Blaming people with AIDS: Who deserves to be sick? *Journal of Applied Biobehavioral Research, 3*(2), 65–80.

Schermerhorn, J. R., Hunt, J. G., & Osborn, R. N. (2005). *Organizational behavior.* Hoboken, NJ: Wiley.

Schiff, A. (2014). Reaching a mutual agreement: Readiness theory and coalition building in the Aceh peace process. *Negotiation and Conflict Management Research, 7*(1), 57–82.

Schifter, D. E., & Ajzen, I. (1985). Intention, perceived control, and weight loss: An application of the theory of planned behavior. *Journal of Personality and Social Psychology, 49*(3), 843–851.

Schindler-Zimmerman, T. (1993). Systems family therapy with an athlete. *Journal of Family Psychotherapy, 4*(3), 29–37.

Schindler-Zimmerman, T., & Protinsky, H. (1993). Uncommon sports psychology: Consultation using family therapy theory and techniques. *The American Journal of Family Therapy, 21,* 161–174.

Schindler-Zimmerman, T., Washle, W., & Protinsky, H. (1990). Strategic intervention in an athletic system. *Journal of Strategic and Systemic Therapies, 9*(2), 1–7.

Schneekloth, L. H., & Shibley, R. G. (1993). The practice of placemaking. *Architecture et Comportement*[*Architecture and Behavior*]*, 9,* 121–144.

Schneider, F. W., Pilon, P., Horrobin, B., & Sideris, M. (2000). Contributions of evaluation research to the development of community policing in a Canadian city. *Canadian Journal of Program Evaluation, 15,* 101–129.

Schneider, S. K., & Northcraft, G. B. (1999). Three social dilemmas of workforce diversity in organizations: A social identity perspective. *Human Relations, 11,* 1445–1467.

Schramm, W., & Carter, R. F. (1959). Effectiveness of a political telethon. *Public Opinion Quarterly, 23,* 121–127.

Schruijer, S. G. L., & Mostert, I. (1997). Creativity and sex composition: An experimental illustration. *European Journal of Work & Organizational Psychology Special Issue: Group Diversity, 6*(2), 175–182.

Schuller, R. A., & Ogloff, J. R. P. (2001). An introduction to psychology and law. In R. A. Schuller & J. R. P. Ogloff (Eds.), *Introduction to psychology and law: Canadian perspectives* (pp. 3–28). Toronto, ON: University of Toronto Press.

Schuller, R. A., & Yarmey, M. (2001). The jury: Deciding guilty and innocence. In R. A. Schuller & J. R. P. Ogloff (Eds.), *Introduction to psychology and law: Canadian perspectives* (pp. 3–28). Toronto, ON: University of Toronto Press.

Schultz, P. W. (1998). Changing behavior with normative feedback interventions: A field experiment on curbside recycling. *Basic and Applied Social Psychology, 21,* 25–36.

Schultz, P. W., Nolan, J., Cialdini, R., Goldstein, N., & Griskevicius, V. (2007). The constructive, destructive, and reconstructive power of social norms. *Psychological Science, 18,* 429–434.

Schulz, R., & Beach, S. R. (1999). Caregiving as a risk factor for mortality: The caregiver health effects study. *Journal of the American Medical Association, 282,* 2215–2219.

Schulz-Hardt, S., Frey, D., Lüthgens, C., & Moscovici, S. (2000). Biased information search in group decision making. *Journal of Personality and Social Psychology, 78*(4), 655–669.

Schultz-Hardt, S., Giersiepen, A., & Mojzisch, A. (2016). Preference-consistent information repetitions during discussion: Do they affect subsequent judgments and decisions? *Journal of Experimental Social Psychology, 64,* 41–49.

Schulz-Hardt, S., Jochims, M., & Frey, D. (2002). Productive conflict in group decision making: Genuine and contrived dissent as strategies to counteract biased information seeking. *Organizational Behavior and Human Decision Processes, 88,* 563–586.

Schwartz, S. H. (1992). Universals in the content and structure of values: Theory and empirical tests in 20 countries. In M. Zanna (Ed.), *Advances in experimental social psychology* (Vol. 25, pp. 1–65). New York, NY: Academic Press.

Schwartz, S. H., Lehmann, A., & Roccas, S. (1999). Multimethod probes of basic human values. In J. Adamopoulos & Y. Kashima (Eds.), *Social psychology and cultural context* (pp. 107–124). Thousand Oaks, CA: SAGE.

Schwartz, S. H., Sagiv, L., & Boehnke, K. (2000). Worries and values. *Journal of Personality, 68,* 309–346.

Scott, K. A., Heathcote, J., & Gruman, J. A. (2011). The diverse organization: Finding gold at the end of the rainbow. *Human Resource Management, 50,* 735–755.

Sears, D. O. (1988). Symbolic racism. In P. Katz & D. Taylor (Eds.), *Towards the elimination of racism: Profiles in controversy* (pp. 53–84). New York, NY: Plenum.

Segerstrom, S. C. (2005). Optimism and immunity: Do positive thoughts always lead to positive effects? *Brain, Behavior, and Immunity, 19,* 195–200.

Segerstrom, S. C. (2007). Optimism and resources: Effects on each other and on health over 10 years. *Journal of Research in Personality, 41,* 772–786.

Seiter, J. S., & Weger, H., Jr. (2010). The effect of generalized compliments, sex of server, and size of dining party on tipping behavior in restaurants. *Journal of Applied Social Psychology, 40,* 1–12.

Sejwacz, D., Ajzen, I., & Fishbein, M. (1980). Predicting and understanding weight loss: Intentions, behaviors, and outcomes. In I. Ajzen & M. Fishbein (Eds.), *Understanding attitudes and* predicting *social behavior* (pp. 101–112). Englewood Cliffs, NJ: Prentice-Hall.

Seligman, M. E. P. (1975). *Helplessness: On depression, development and death.* San Francisco, CA: Freeman.

Seligman, M. E. P. (1999). The president's address. *American Psychologist, 54,* 559–562.

Seligman, M. E. P. (2011). *Flourish: A visionary new understanding of happiness and well-being.* New York, NY: Free Press.

Seligman, M. E. P., & Csikszentmihalyi, M. (2000). Positive psychology: An introduction. *American Psychologist, 55,* 1–14.

Semin, G. R. (2007). Grounding communication. In A. W. Kruglanski & E. T. Higgins (Eds.), *Social psychology: Handbook of basic principles* (2nd ed., pp. 630–649). New York, NY: Guilford Press.

Senécal, J., Loughead, T. M., & Bloom, G. A. (2008). A season-long team-building intervention: Examining the effect of team goal setting on cohesion. *Journal of Sport & Exercise Psychology, 30,* 186–199.

Senko, C., Hulleman, C. S., & Harackiewicz, J. M. (2011). Achievement goal theory at the crossroads: Old controversies, current challenges, and new directions. *Educational Psychologist, 46,* 26–47.

Shapira, L. B., & Mongrain, M. (2010). The benefits of self-compassion and optimism exercises for individuals vulnerable to depression. *The Journal of Positive Psychology, 5,* 377–389.

Shaver, P. R., & Hazan, C. (1994). Attachment. In A. L. Weber & J. H. Harvey (Eds.), *Perspectives on close relationships* (Ch. 6, pp. 110–130). Boston, MA: Allyn & Bacon.

Shaver, P. R., Hazan, C., & Bradshaw, D. (1988). Love as attachment: The integration of three behavioral systems. In R. J. Sternberg & M. L. Barnes (Eds.), *The psychology of love* (pp. 68–99). New Haven, CT: Yale University Press.

Shaw, K. T., & Gifford, R. (1994). Residents' and burglars' assessment of burglary risk form defensible space cues. *Journal of Environmental Psychology, 14,* 177–194.

Shaw, M. E., & Costanzo, P. R. (1982). *Theories of social psychology* (2nd ed.). New York, NY: McGraw-Hill.

Shaw Taylor, L., Fiore, A. T., Mendelsohn, G. A., & Cheshire, C. (2011). "Out of my league": A real-world test of the matching hypothesis.

Personality and Social Psychology Bulletin, 37(7), 942–954.

Shehata, A. (2010). Unemployment on the agenda: A panel study of agenda-setting effects during the 2006 Swedish national election campaign. *Journal of Communication, 60,* 182–203.

Shehata, A., & Stromback, J. (2013). Not (yet) a new era of minimal effects: A study of agenda setting at the aggregate and individual levels. *International Journal of Press/Politics, 18,* 234–255.

Sherif, M. (1966a). *Group conflict and cooperation.* London, UK: Routledge & Kegan Paul.

Sherif, M. (1966b). *In common predicament: Social psychology of intergroup conflict and cooperation.* Boston, MA: Houghton Mifflin.

Sherif, M., Harvey, O. J., White, B. J., Hood, W. E., & Sherif, C. W. (1961). *Intergroup conflict and cooperation: The Robber's Cave experiment.* Norman: University of Oklahoma Book Exchange.

Sherif, M., & Sherif, C. W. (1953). *Groups in harmony and tension.* New York, NY: Harper Brothers.

Sherif, M., & Sherif, C. W. (1969). *Social psychology.* New York, NY: Harper & Row.

Shields, S. A. (1975). Functionalism, Darwinism, and the psychology of women: A study in social myth. *American Psychologist, 30,* 739–754.

Shipler, D. K. (2004). *The working poor: Invisible in America.* New York, NY: Knopf.

Shoda, Y. (2004). Individual differences in social psychology: Understanding situations to understand people, understanding people to understand situations. In C. Sansone, C. Morf, & A. Panter (Eds.), *The Sage handbook of methods in social psychology* (pp. 117–141). Thousand Oaks, CA: SAGE.

Shrum, L. J. (1999). The relationship of television viewing with attitude strength and extremity: Implications for the cultivation effect. *Media Psychology, 1,* 3–25.

Shrum, L. J. (2009). Media consumption and perceptions of social reality: Effects and underlying processes. In J. Bryant & M. B. Oliver (Eds.), *Media effects: Advances in theory and research* (3rd ed., pp. 50–73). New York, NY: Routledge.

Shultz, T. R., Léveillé, E., & Lepper, M. R. (1999). Free choice and cognitive dissonance revisited: Choosing "lesser evils" versus "greater goods." *Personality and Social Psychology Bulletin, 25,* 40–48.

Shura, R., Siders, R. A., & Dannefer, D. (2011). Culture change in long-term care: Participatory action research and the role of the resident. *The Gerontologist, 51,* 212–225.

Shuter, R. (1976). Proxemics and tactility in Latin America. *Journal of Communication, 26,* 46–52.

Sideridis, G. D., & Padeliadu, S. (2001). The motivational determinants of students at risk of having reading difficulties. *Remedial and Special Education, 22,* 268–279.

Siegel, P. A., Scillitoe, J., & Parks-Yancy, R. (2005). Reducing the tendency to self-handicap: The effect of self-affirmation. *Journal of Experimental Social Psychology, 41,* 589–597.

Signorielli, N. (1990). Television's mean and dangerous world: A continuation of the cultural indicators perspective. In N. Signorielli & M. Morgan (Eds.), *Cultivation analysis: New directions in media effects research* (pp. 85–106). Newbury Park, CA: SAGE.

Sikorski, J. F., Rich, K., Saville, B. K., Buskist, W., Drogan, O., & Davis, S. F. (2002). Student use of introductory texts: Comparative survey findings from two universities. *Teaching of Psychology, 29,* 312–313.

Simon, L., Greenberg, J., & Brehm, J. (1995). Trivialization: The forgotten mode of dissonance reduction. *Journal of Personality and Social Psychology, 68,* 247–260.

Simpson, D. D. (2005). Using social psychology to ameliorate the human condition: An inspirational student-friendly introduction and guide. [Review of the book *Applied social psychology: Understanding and addressing social and practical problems*]. *PsycCritiques, 50*(19).

Sinclair, H. C., Hood, K. B., & Wright, B. L. (2014). Revisiting the Romeo and Juliet Effect (Driscoll, Davis, & Lipetz, 1972): Reexamining the links between social network opinions and romantic relationship outcomes. *Social Psychology, 45*(3), 170–178.

Singh, K., Granville, M., & Dika, S. (2002). Mathematics and science achievement: Effects of motivation, interest, and academic engagement. *Journal of Educational Research, 95,* 323–332.

Slavin, R. E. (1990). *Cooperative learning: Theory, research, and practice.* Englewood Cliffs, NJ: Prentice Hall.

Sledge, M. (2011, November 10). Reawakening the radical imagination: The origins of Occupy Wall Street. *The Huffington Post.* Retrieved from http://www.huffingtonpost.com

Slum surgery in St. Louis. (1951). *Architectural Forum, 94,* 128–136.

Smith, A. (1976). *The wealth of nations: Book 1.* Chicago, IL: University of Chicago Press. (Original work published in 1776)

Smith, A. M., & Cutler, B. L. (2013). Identification procedures and conviction of the innocent. In B. L. Cutler (Ed.), *Reform of eyewitness identification procedures* (pp. 3–21). Washington, DC: American Psychological Association Press.

Smith, J. A., & Rhodes, J. E. (2015). Being depleted and being shaken: An interpretative phenomenological analysis of the experiential features of a first episode of depression. *Psychology and Psychotherapy: Theory, Research, and Practice, 88,* 197–209.

Smith, S. H., & Whitehead, G. I., III. (1984). Attributions for promotion and demotion in the United States and India. *Journal of Social Psychology, 124,* 27–34.

Smith, S. L., & Wilson, B. J. (2002). Children's comprehension of and fear reactions to television news. *Media Psychology, 4,* 1–26.

Smith, S. L., Wilson, B. J., Kunkel, D., Linz, D., Potter, W. J., Colvin, C. M., et al. (1998). Violence in television programming overall: University of California, Santa Barbara study. In *National television violence study* (Vol. 3, pp. 5–194.). Thousand Oaks, CA: SAGE.

Smits, J. A. J., Rosenfield, D., McDonald, R., & Telch, M. J. (2006). Cognitive mechanisms of social anxiety reduction: An examination of specificity and temporality. *Journal of Consulting and Clinical Psychology, 74*(6), 1203–1212.

Snyder, C. J., Lassiter, G. D., Lindberg, M. J., & Pinegar, S. K. (2009). Videotaped interrogations and confessions: Does a dual-camera approach yield unbiased and accurate evaluations? *Behavioral Sciences and the Law, 27,* 451–466.

Snyder, C. R. (2002). Hope theory: Rainbows of the mind. *Psychological Inquiry, 13,* 249–275.

Snyder, C. R., & Lopez, S. J., & Pedrotti, J. T. (2011). *Positive psychology: The scientific and practical explorations of human strengths.* Thousand Oaks, CA: SAGE.

Snyder, M., & Ickes, W. (1985). Personality and social behavior. In G. Lindzey & E. Aronson (Eds.), *Handbook of social psychology* (3rd ed., pp. 883–947). New York, NY: Random House.

Solomon, A. (1992). Clinical diagnosis among diverse populations: A multicultural perspective. *Families in Society, 73,* 371–377.

Sommer, R. (1972). *Design awareness*. New York, NY: Holt, Rinehart, & Winston.

Sommer, R. (1983). *Social design*. Englewood Cliffs, NJ: Prentice Hall.

Sommer, R. (1987). Crime and vandalism in university residence halls: A confirmation of defensible space theory. *Journal of Environmental Psychology, 7*, 1–12.

Sommer, R., & Olsen, H. (1980). The soft classroom. *Environment and Behavior, 12*, 3–16.

Sommers, S. R. (2006). On racial diversity and group decision-making: Identifying multiple effects of racial composition on jury deliberations. *Journal of Personality and Social Psychology, 90*(4), 597–612.

Sommers, S. R. (2007). Race and the decision making of juries. *Legal and Criminological Psychology, 12*, 171–187.

Sorensen, N., Nagda, B. A., Gurin, P., & Maxwell, K. E. (2009). Taking a "hands on" approach to diversity in higher education: A critical-dialogic model for effective intergroup interaction. *Analyses of Social Issues and Public Policy, 9*, 3–35.

Sørensen, K., Van den Broucke, S., Fullam, J., Doyle, G., Pelikan, J., Slonska, Z., & Brand, H. (2012). Health literacy and public health: A systematic review and integration of definitions and models. *BMC Public Health, 12*, 80.

Souza, K. A., & Dhami, M. K. (2008). A study of volunteers in community-based restorative justice programs. *Canadian Journal of Criminology and Criminal Justice, 50*, 31–57.

Spink, K. S. (1990a). Collective efficacy in the sport setting. *International Journal of Sport Psychology, 21*, 380–395.

Spink, K. S. (1990b). Group cohesion and collective efficacy in volleyball teams. *Journal of Sport & Exercise Psychology, 12*, 301–311.

Sporer, S. L., & Schwandt, B. (2007). Moderators of nonverbal indicators of deception: A meta-analytic synthesis. *Psychology, Public Policy, and Law, 13*(1), 1–34.

Sports Illustrated. (2002, August 5). Business as Usual. Retrieved November 15, 2002, from http://sportsillustrated.cnn.com/baseball/news/2002/08/05/dominating_braves_ap/

Spoth, R. L., Redmond, C., Trudeau, L., & Shin, C. (2002). Longitudinal substance initiation outcomes for a universal preventive intervention combining family and school programs. *Psychology of Addictive Behaviors, 16*, 129–134.

Sprecher, S. (1989). The importance to males and females of physical attractiveness, earning potential, and expressiveness in initial attraction. *Sex Roles, 21*, 501–607.

Sprecher, S., & Chandak, R. (1992). Attitudes about arranged marriages and dating among men and women from India. *Free Inquiry in Creative Sociology, 20*, 59–69.

Stahlberg, D., Eller, F., Maass, A., & Frey, D. (1995). We knew it all along: Hindsight bias in groups. *Organizational Behavior and Human Decision Processes, 63*, 46–58.

Stamler, L. L., Thomas, B., & Lafreniere, K. (2000). Working women identify influences and obstacles to breast health practices. *Oncology Nursing Forum, 27*, 835–842.

Stamps, A. (1989). Are environmental aesthetics worth studying? *Journal of Architectural and Planning Research, 6*, 344–356.

Statistics Canada. (2010). *Internet use by individuals, by location of access, by province*. Retrieved from http://www40.statcan.ca/l01/cst01/comm36a-eng.htm

Staw, B. M., Bell, N. E., & Clausen, J. A. (1986). The dispositional approach to job attitudes: A lifetime longitudinal test. *Administrative Science Quarterly, 31*, 437–453.

Steblay, N., Dysart, J. E., & Wells, G. L. (2011). Seventy-two tests of the sequential lineup superiority effect: A meta-analysis and policy discussion. *Psychology, Public Policy, and Law, 17*, 99–139.

Steblay, N., Hosch, H. M., Culhane, S. E., & McWethy, A. (2006). The impact on juror verdicts of judicial instruction to disregard inadmissible evidence: A meta-analysis. *Law and Human Behavior, 30*, 469–492.

Steblay, N. K., Wells, G. L., & Douglass, A. B. (2014). The eyewitness post identification feedback effect 15 years later: Theoretical and policy implications. *Psychology, Public Policy, and Law, 20*(1), 1–18.

Steel, P. (2007). The nature of procrastination: A meta-analytic and theoretical review of quintessential self-regulatory failure. *Psychological Bulletin, 133*, 65–94.

Steel, R. P., & Ovalle, N. K. (1984). A review and meta-analysis of research on the relationship between behavioral intentions and employee turnover. *Journal of Applied Psychology, 69*, 673–686.

Steele, C. M. (1997). A threat in the air: How stereotypes shape intellectual identity and performance. *American Psychologist, 52,* 613–629.

Steele, C. M., & Aronson, J. (1995). Stereotype threat and the intellectual test performance of African Americans. *Journal of Personality and Social Psychology, 69,* 797–811.

Steele, F. I. (1973). *Physical settings and organizational development.* Don Mills, ON: Addison-Wesley.

Steers, R. M., & Porter, L. W. (Eds.). (1991). *Motivation and work.* New York, NY: McGraw-Hill.

Steg, L., & Vlek, C. (2009). Encouraging pro-environmental behaviour: An integrative review and research agenda. *Journal of Environmental Psychology, 29,* 309–317.

Stein, L. M., & Memon, A. (2006). Testing the efficacy of the cognitive interview in a developing country. *Applied Cognitive Psychology, 20,* 597–605.

Steuer, F. B., Applefield, J. M., & Smith, R. (1971). Televised aggression and the interpersonal aggression of preschool children. *Journal of Experimental Child Psychology, 11,* 442–447.

Stevens, C. A. (2010). Lessons from the field: Using Photovoice with an ethnically diverse population in a HOPE VI evaluation. *Family and Community Health, 33*(4), 275–284.

Stevens, D. E., & Bloom, G. A. (2003). The effect of team building on cohesion. *Avante, 9,* 43–54.

Stice, E., Chase, A., Stormer, S., & Appel, A. (2001). A randomized trial of an eating disorder prevention program. *International Journal of Eating Disorders, 29,* 247–262.

Stice, E., Marti, N., Spoor, S., Presnell, K., & Shaw, H. (2008). Dissonance and healthy weight eating disorder prevention programs: Long-term effects from a randomized efficacy trial. *Journal of Consulting and Clinical Psychology, 76,* 329–340.

Stice, E., Mazotti, L., Weibel, D., & Agras, W. S. (2000). Dissonance prevention program decreases thin-ideal internalization, body dissatisfaction, dieting, negative affect, and bulimic symptoms: A preliminary experiment. *International Journal of Eating Disorders, 27,* 206–217.

Stice, E., Shaw, H., Burton, E., & Wade, E. (2006). Dissonance and healthy weight eating disorder prevention programs: A randomized efficacy trial. *Journal of Consulting and Clinical Psychology, 74,* 263–275.

Stice, E., Shaw, H., & Marti, C. N. (2007). A meta-analytic review of eating disorder prevention programs: encouraging findings. *Annual Review of Clinical Psychology, 3,* 207–231.

Stice, E., Trost, A., & Chase, A. (2003). Healthy weight control and dissonance-based eating disorder prevention programs: Results from a controlled trial. *International Journal of Eating Disorders, 33,* 10–21.

Stockemer, D., & Praino, R. (2015). Blinded by beauty? Physical attractiveness and candidate selection in the U.S. House of Representatives. *Social Science Quarterly, 96,* 430–443.

Stokes, J., Fuerher, A., & Childs, L. (1984). Group members' self-disclosure: Relation to team cohesion. *Small Group Behavior, 14,* 63–76.

Stoliker, B. E., & Lafreniere, K. D. (2015). The influence of perceived stress, loneliness, and learning burnout on university students' educational experience. *College Student Journal, 49*(1), 146–159.

Stone, J., Aronson, E., Crain, A. L., Winslow, M. P., & Fried, C. B. (1994). Inducing hypocrisy as a means of encouraging young adults to use condoms. *Personality and Social Psychology Bulletin, 20,* 116–128.

Stoner, J. A. F. (1961). *A comparison of individual and group decisions involving risk.* Unpublished master's thesis, Massachusetts Institute of Technology, Cambridge, Massachusetts.

Stouffer, S. A., Suchman, E. A., DeVinney, L. C., Star, S. A., & Williams, R. M., Jr. (1949). *The American soldier: Adjustment during army life.* Princeton, NJ: Princeton University Press.

Strauss, S. G., & McGrath, J. E. (1994). Does the medium matter? The interaction of task type and technology on group performance and member reactions. *Journal of Applied Psychology, 79,* 87–97.

Streng, J. M., Rhodes, S. D., Ayala, G. X., Eng, E., Arceo, R., & Phipps, S. (2004). Realidad Latina: Latino adolescents, their school, and university use Photovoice to examine and address the influence of immigration. *Journal of Interprofessional Care, 18*(4), 403–415.

Streufert, S., & Streufert, S. C. (1969). Effects of conceptual structure, failure, and success on attribution of causality and interpersonal attitudes. *Journal of Personality and Social Psychology, 11,* 138–147.

Streufert, S., & Suedfeld, P. (1982). A decade of applied social psychology. *Journal of Applied Social Psychology, 12,* 335–342.

Strong, S. R., Welsh, J. A., Corcoran, J. L., & Hoyt, W. T. (1992). Social psychology and counseling psychology: The history, products, and promise of an interface. *Journal of Counseling Psychology, 39*(2), 139–157.

Struthers, C. W., Weiner, B., & Allred, K. (1998). Effects of causal attributions on personnel decisions: A social motivation perspective. *Basic and Applied Social Psychology, 20*, 155–166.

Sue, S., Zane, N., Nagayama-Hall, G. J., & Berger, L. K. (2009). The case for cultural competency in psychotherapeutic interventions. *Annual Review of Psychology, 60*, 525–548.

Sullivan, P. A. (1993). Communication skills for interactive sports. *The Sport Psychologist, 7*, 79–91.

Sullivan, P. J. (1995). *The relationship between communication and cohesion in inter-collegiate rugby players.* Unpublished master's thesis, University of Windsor, Windsor, Ontario, Canada.

Sullivan, P. J., & Feltz, D. L. (2003). The preliminary development of the Scale for Effective Communication in Sports Teams (SECTS). *Journal of Applied Social Psychology, 33*, 1693–1715.

Sum, S., Mathews, R. M., Pourghasem, M., & Hughes, I. (2009). Internet use as a predictor of sense of community in older people. *CyberPsychology & Behavior, 12*(2), 235–239.

Sumi, K. (2006). Correlations between optimism and social relationships. *Psychological Reports, 99*, 938–940.

Sungur, S., & Tekkaya, C. (2006). Effects of problem-based learning and traditional instruction on self-regulated learning. *Journal of Educational Research, 99,* 307–317.

Suspected SUV bomber held without bail. (2004, March 18). *CBC News.* Retrieved from http://www .cbc.ca/stories/print/2004/03/18/world/suv_bombings040318

Sussman, N. M., & Rosenfeld, H. M. (1982). Influence of culture, language, and sex on conversational distance. *Journal of Personality and Social Psychology, 42*, 66–74.

Swim, J. K., & Hyers, L. L. (1999). Excuse me—what did you just say? Women's public and private responses to sexist remarks. *Journal of Experimental Social Psychology, 35,* 68–88.

Sypher, B. D., & Zorn, T. E. (1986). Communication-related abilities and upward mobility: A longitudinal investigation. *Human Communication Research, 12*(3), 420–431.

Szabo, Z. (2006). The influence of attributional retraining on career choices. *Journal of Cognitive and Behavioral Psychotherapies, 6*, 89–103.

Tajfel, H., & Billig, M. (1974). Familiarity and categorization in intergroup behaviour. *Journal of Experimental Social Psychology, 10*, 159–170.

Tajfel, H., & Turner, J. C. (1986). The social identity theory of intergroup behaviour. In S. Worchel & W. G. Austin (Eds.), *Psychology of intergroup relations* (2nd ed., pp. 33–47). Chicago, IL: Nelson-Hall.

Talley, R. C., & Crews, J. E. (2007). Framing the public health of caregiving. *American Journal of Public Health, 97*(2), 224–228.

Tang, S., & Hall, V. C. (1995). The overjustification effect: A meta-analysis. *Applied Cognitive Psychology, 9*, 365–404.

Tangney, J. P., Miller, R. S., Flicker, L., & Barlow, D. H. (1996). Are shame, guilt and embarrassment distinct emotions? *Journal of Personality and Social Psychology, 70*, 1256–1269.

Tashiro, T., & Mortensen, L. (2006). Translational research: How social psychology can improve psychotherapy. *American Psychologist, 61*(9), 959–966.

Taylor, S. E. (2006). Health psychology (6th ed.). New York, NY: McGraw-Hill.

Taylor, S. E., & Sirois, F. M. (2012). *Health psychology* (2nd Canadian ed.). Toronto, ON: McGraw-Hill Ryerson.

Team JIAAP. (2014). Review of Applied Social Psychology. *Journal of the Indian Academy of Applied Psychology, 40*, 157–158

Technical Working Group for Eyewitness Evidence. (1999). *Eyewitness evidence: A guide for law enforcement* [Booklet]. Washington, DC: U.S. Department of Justice, Office of Justice Programs.

Temerlin, M. K. (1968). Suggestion effects in psychiatric diagnosis. *Journal of Nervous and Mental Disease, 147*, 349–353.

Terrier, L., & Marfaing, B. (2015). Using social norms and commitment to promote pro-environmental behavior among hotel guests. *Journal of Environmental Psychology, 44*, 10–15.

Thibaut, J. W., & Kelley, H. H. (1959). *The social psychology of groups.* New York, NY: Wiley.

Thoits, P. A. (1982). Conceptual, methodological, and theoretical problems in studying social support as a buffer against life stress. *Journal of Health and Social Behavior, 23*, 145–159.

Thompson, T. (1994). Self-worth protection: Review and implications for the classroom. *Educational Review, 46*, 259–274.

Thompson-Cannino, J., Cotton, R., & Torneo, E. (2009). *Picking cotton: Our memoir of injustice and redemption.* New York, NY: St. Martin's Griffin.

Thornton, J., & Wahl, O. (1996). Impact of a newspaper article on attitudes toward mental illness. *Journal of Community Psychology, 24*, 17–28.

Tindale, R. S. (1993). Decision errors made by individuals and groups. In N. J. Castellan, Jr. (Ed.), *Individual and group decision making: Current issues* (pp. 109–124). Hillsdale, NJ: Erlbaum.

Toch, H., & Klofas, J. (1984). Pluralistic ignorance, revisited. In G. M. Stephenson & J. H. Davis (Eds.), *Progress in applied social psychology* (Vol. 2, pp. 129–159). New York, NY: Wiley.

Tomes, H. (2004). The case—and the research—that forever connected psychology and policy. *Monitor on Psychology, 35*(6), 28.

Topolski, D. (1989). *True blue: The story of the Oxford boat race mutiny.* London, UK: Bantam Books.

Topping, K. J. (2005). Trends in peer learning. *Educational Psychology, 25,* 631–645.

Tran, H. (2014). Online agenda setting: A new frontier for theory development. In T. J. Johnson (Ed.), *Agenda setting in a 2.0 world: New agendas in communication* (pp. 205–229). New York, NY: Routledge.

Travis, J. (1995, May 2). *Criminal justice research and public policy in the United States.* Speech given at the Ninth United Nations Congress on the Prevention of Crime and the Treatment of Offenders, Cairo, Egypt. Retrieved from http://www.nij.gov/nij/about/speeches/past-directors/unspeech.htm

Tredoux, C. G. (2002). A direct measure of facial similarity and its relation to human similarity perceptions. *Journal of Experimental Psychology: Applied, 8,* 180–193.

Trevino, L. K., Daft, R. L., & Lengel, R. H. (1990). Understanding managers' media choices: A symbolic interactionist perspective. In J. Fulk & C. Steinfeld (Eds.), *Organizations and communication technology* (pp. 71–94). Newbury Park, CA: SAGE.

Triandis, H. C. (1994). *Culture and social behavior.* New York, NY: McGraw-Hill.

Triandis, H. C. (1995). *Individualism & collectivism.* Boulder, CO: Westview Press.

Triandis, J., C., Kurowski, L. L., & Gelfand, M. J. (1994). Workplace diversity. In H. C. Triandis, M. Dunnette, & L. Hough (Eds.), *Handbook of industrial and organizational psychology* (Vol. 4, pp. 769–827). Boston, MA: Nicholas Brealey.

Tripodi, T., Fellin, P., & Epstein, I. (1971). *Social program evaluation.* Itasca, IL: Peacock.

Turban, D. B., & Jones, A. P. (1988). Supervisor-subordinate similarity: Type, effects, and mechanisms. *Journal of Applied Psychology, 73*(2), 228–234.

Turkle, S. (1984). *The second self.* New York, NY: Simon & Schuster.

Turner, C. W., Layton, J. F., & Simons, L. S. (1975). Naturalistic studies of aggressive behavior: Aggressive stimuli, victim visibility, and horn honking. *Journal of Personality and Social Psychology, 31,* 1098–1107.

Turner, D. C. (1996). The role of culture in chronic illness. *American Behavioral Scientist, 39,* 717–728.

Turner, J. C., Midgley, C., Meyer, D. K., Gheen, M., Anderman, E. M., Kang, Y., & Patrick, H. (2002). The classroom environment and students' reports of avoidance strategies in mathematics: A multimethod study. *Journal of Educational Psychology, 94,* 88–106.

Turner, M. E., Pratkanis, A. R., Probasco, P., & Leve, C. (1992). Threat, cohesion, and group effectiveness: Testing a social identity maintenance perspective in groupthink. *Journal of Personality and Social Psychology, 63,* 781–796.

Tversky, A., & Kahneman, D. (1973). Availability: A heuristic for judging frequency and probability. *Cognitive Psychology, 5,* 207–232.

Tversky, A., & Kahneman, D. (1974). Judgment under uncertainty: Heuristics and biases. *Science, 185,* 1124–1131.

TV Parental Guidelines. (2011, January 8). *Understanding the TV ratings.* Retrieved from http://www.tvguidelines.org/ratings.htm

Union of Concerned Scientists. (1993). *World scientists warning to humanity* [statement]. Cambridge, MA: Author.

United Nations Global Report. (2010). *UNAIDS Report on the Global AIDS Epidemic 2010.* Retrieved from http://www.unaids.org/globalreport/Global_report.htm

United Nations Human Development Reports. (2014). *International human development indicators: Build your own index.* Retrieved from http://www.hdr.undp.org/en/data/build

University of Toronto (n.d.). Office of Health Professions Student Affairs (OHPSA): Summer Mentorship Program. Retrieved from http://www.ohpsa.utoronto.ca/smp

Unrau, Y. A., Gabor, P. A., & Grinnell, R. M., Jr. (2001). *Evaluation in the human services.* Itasca, IL: Peacock.

Urdan, T. (2004). Predictors of academic self-handicapping and achievement: Examining achievement goals, classroom goal structures, and culture. *Journal of Educational Psychology, 96,* 251–264.

Urdan, T., & Midgley, C. (2001). Academic self-handicapping: What we know, what more there is to learn. *Educational Psychology Review, 13,* 115–138.

Urdan, T., Midgley, C., & Anderman, E. M. (1998). The role of classroom goal structure in students' use of self-handicapping strategies. *American Educational Research Journal, 35,* 101–122.

Urdan, T., & Schoenfelder, E. (2006). Classroom effects on student motivation: Goal structures, social relationships, and competence beliefs. *Journal of School Psychology, 44,* 331–349.

U.S. Census Bureau. (2011). *Household Internet usage by type of Internet connection and state: 2009* (Table 1155; Statistical Abstract of the United States). Retrieved from http://www.census.gov/compendia/statab/2011/tables/11s1156.pdf

U.S. Department of Education. (2013). *Digest of education statistics.* Retrieved from http://nces.ed.gov/pubsearch/pubsinfo.asp?pubid=2015011

U.S. Department of Energy. (2009). *U.S. Energy Information Administration: Emissions of greenhouse gases report.* Retrieved from http://205.254.135.24/oiaf/1605/ggrpt/carbon.html

U.S. Department of Justice. (n.d.). *Prisons and Detention Fact Sheet.* Retrieved from http://www.justice.gov/sites/default/files/jmd/legacy/2013/09/07/prisons-detention.pdf

U.S. Department of Justice. (1986, July). *Attorney General's commission on pornography: Final report.* Washington, DC: Author.

Valacich, J. S., Sarker, S., Pratt, J., & Groomer, M. (2009). Understanding risk-taking behavior in groups: "A decision analysis" perspective. *Decision Support Systems, 46,* 902–912.

Vallerand, R. J., Fortier, M. S., & Guay, F. (1997). Self-determination and persistence in a real-life setting: Toward a motivational model of high school dropout. *Journal of Personality and Social Psychology, 72,* 1161–1176.

van Boven, L., White, K., Kamada, A., & Gilovich, T. (2003). Intuitions about situational correction in self and others. *Journal of Personality and Social Psychology, 85,* 249–258.

Vancouver, J. B., Thompson, C. M., Tischner, E. C., & Putka, D. J. (2002). Two studies examining the negative effect of self-efficacy on performance. *Journal of Applied Psychology, 87,* 506–516.

Vandello, J. A., & Cohen, D. (1999). Patterns of individualism and collectivism across the United States. *Journal of Personality and Social Psychology, 77,* 279–292.

Van der Kliej, R., Schraagen, J. M., Werkhoven, P., & De Dreu, C. K. W. (2009). How conversations change over time in face-to-face and video-mediated communication. *Small Group Research, 40,* 355–381.

van der Voordt, T. J. M., & van Wegen, H. B. R. (1990). Testing building plans for public safety: Usefulness of the Delft checklist. *Housing and Environmental Research, 5,* 129–154.

Vandevelde, S., Broekaert, E., Yates, R., & Kooyman, M. (2004). The development of the therapeutic community in correctional establishments: A comparative retrospective account of the "democratic" Maxwell Jones TC and the hierarchical concept-based TC in prison. *International Journal of Social Psychiatry, 50,* 66–79.

Van De Ven, M. O. M., Engels, R. C. M. E., Otten, R., & Van Den Eijnden, R. J. J. M. (2007). A longitudinal test of the theory of planned behavior predicting smoking onset among asthmatic and non-asthmatic adolescents. *Journal of Behavioral Medicine, 30*(5), 435–445.

van Knippenberg, D., & Schippers, M. C. (2007). Work group diversity. *Annual Review of Psychology, 58,* 515–541.

Vansteenkiste, M., Simons, J., Lens, W., Sheldon, K. M., & Deci, E. L. (2004). Motivating learning, performance, and persistence: The synergistic effects of intrinsic goal contents and autonomy-supportive contexts. *Journal of Personality and Social Psychology, 87,* 246–260.

Van Straaten, I., Engels, R. C. M. E., Finkenauer, C., & Holland, R. W. (2009). Meeting your match: How attractiveness similarity affects approach behavior in mixed-sex dyads. *Personality and Social Psychology Bulletin, 35,* 685–697.

Van Voorhis, P. (2012). On behalf of women offenders: Women's place in the science of evidence-based practice. *Criminology & Public Policy, 11,* 111–145.

Vaughan, E. D. (1977). Misconceptions about psychology among introductory psychology students. *Teaching of Psychology, 4,* 138–141.

Vazin, T., & Reile, P. (2006). Collaborative learning: Maximizing students' potential for success. In W. Buskist & S. F. Davis (Eds.), *Handbook of the teaching of psychology* (pp. 65–69). Malden, MA: Blackwell.

Velez, J. A. (2015). Extending the theory of Bounded Generalized Reciprocity: An explanation of the social benefits of cooperative video game play. *Computers in Human Behavior, 48,* 481–491.

Velez, J., & Ewoldsen, D. R. (2013). Helping behaviors in video game play. *Journal of Media Psychology, 25,* 190–200.

Velez, J., Mahood, C., Ewoldsen, D. R., & Moyer-Guse, E. (2014). Ingroup versus outgroup conflict in the context of violent video game play: The effect of cooperation on increased helping and decreased aggression. *Communication Research, 41,* 607–626.

Velez, J., Whitaker, J., Greitemeyer, T., Ewoldsen, D. R., & Bushman, B. (in press). Violent video games and reciprocity: The attenuating effects of cooperative game play on subsequent aggression. *Communication Research.*

Vennig, A., Kettler, L., Eliot, J., & Wilson, A. (2009). The effectiveness of Cognitive-Behavioral Therapy with hopeful elements to prevent the development of depression in young people: A systematic review. *International Journal of Evidence Based Healthcare, 7,* 15–33.

Véronneau, M.-H., & Vitaro, F. (2007). Social experiences with peers and high school graduation: A review of theoretical and empirical research. *Educational Psychology, 27,* 419–445.

Véronneau, M.-H., Vitaro, F., Brendgen, M., Dishion, T. J., & Tremblay, R. E. (2010). Transactional analysis of the reciprocal links between peer experiences and academic achievement from middle childhood to early adolescence. *Developmental Psychology, 46,* 773–790.

Vidmar, N., & Schuller, R. A. (2001). The jury: Selecting twelve impartial peers. In R. A. Schuller & J. R. P. Ogloff (Eds.), *Introduction to psychology and law: Canadian perspectives* (pp. 126–156). Toronto, ON: University of Toronto Press.

Vis, A. A., Dijkstra, A., & Slop, M. (1992). Safety effects of 30 Km/H zones in the Netherlands. *Accident Analysis and Prevention, 24,* 75–86.

Voelz, Z. R., Haeffel, G. J., Joiner, T. E., & Wagner, K. D. (2003). Reducing hopelessness: The interaction of enhancing and depressogenic attributional styles for positive and negative life events among youth psychiatric inpatients. *Behaviour Research and Therapy, 41,* 1183–1198.

Vorauer, J. D., & Ratner, R. K. (1996). Who's going to make the first move? Pluralistic ignorance as an impediment to relationship formation. *Journal of Social and Personal Relationships, 13,* 483–506.

Wahl, O., & Lefkowits, J. (1989). Impact of a television film on attitudes toward mental illness. *American Journal of Community Psychology, 17,* 521–528.

Walgrave, M., Heirman, W., & Hallam, L. (2014). Under pressure to sext? Applying the theory of planned behaviour to adolescent sexting. *Behaviour and Information Technology, 33,* 85–97.

Walker, E. L. (1969). Experimental psychology and social responsibility. *American Psychologist, 24,* 862–868.

Wallace, P. (1999). *The psychology of the Internet.* Cambridge, UK: Cambridge University Press.

Waller, M. J., Huber, G. P., & Glick, W. H. (1995). Functional background as a determinant of executives' selective perception. *Academy of Management Journal, 38,* 943–974.

Walsh-Bowers, R. (1998). Community psychology in the Canadian psychological family. *Canadian Psychology, 39*(4), 280–287.

Walster, E., Aronson, V., Abrahams, D., & Rottmann, L. (1966). Importance of physical attractiveness in dating behavior. *Journal of Personality and Social Psychology, 4,* 508–516.

Wandersman, A., & Nation, M. (1998). Urban neighborhoods and mental health: Psychological contributions to understanding toxicity, resilience, and interventions. *American* Psychologist, *53*(6), 647–656.

Wang, C. C., & Burris, M. (1994). Empowerment through photo novella: Portraits of participation. *Health Education Quarterly, 21,* 171–186.

Wang, J., Iannotti, R. J., & Nansel, T. R. (2009). School bullying among adolescents in the United States: Physical, verbal, relational, and cyber. *Journal of Adolescent Health, 45,* 368–375.

Wang, X., & McClung, S. R. (2012). The immorality of illegal downloading: The role of anticipated guilt and general emotions. *Computers in Human Behavior, 28,* 153–159.

Ward, R. M., & Schielke, H. J. (2011). Assessing the predictive ability of the transtheoretical model's heavy episodic drinking constructs among a population of underage students. *Substance Use & Misuse, 46*(9), 1179–1189.

Warner, H. W., Özkan, T., & Lajunen, T. (2009). Cross-cultural differences in drivers' speed choice. *Accident Analysis and Prevention, 41,* 816–819.

Wason, P. C. (1960). On the failure to eliminate hypotheses in a conceptual task. *Quarterly Journal of Experimental Psychology, 12,* 129–140.

Water: Our Thirsty World [Special issue]. (2010, April). *National Geographic, 217.*

Watkins, D. (1982). Causal attributions for achievement of Filipino barrio children. *The Journal of Social Psychology, 118,* 149–156.

Watson, J. B. (1913). Psychology as the behaviorist views it. *Psychological Review, 20,* 158–177.

Watson, O. M., & Graves, T. D. (1966). Quantitative research in proxemic behavior. *American Anthropologist, 68,* 971–985.

Wechsler, H., Davenport, A., Dowdall, G., Moeykens, B., & Castillo, S. (1994). Health and behavioral consequences of binge drinking in college: A national survey of students at 140 campuses. *Journal of the American Medical Association, 272,* 1672–1677.

Wechsler, H., Lee J. E., Kuo, M., & Seibring, M., Nelson, T. F., & Lee, H. (2002). Trends in college binge drinking during a period of increased prevention efforts. *Journal of American College Health, 50,* 203–221.

Wechsler, H., Nelson, T. F., Lee, J. E., Seibring, M., Lewis, C., & Keeling, R. P. (2003). Perception and reality: A national evaluation of social norms marketing interventions to reduce college students' heavy alcohol use. *Journal of Studies on Alcohol, 64,* 484–494.

Wegner, D. M., Coulton, G. F., & Wenzlaff, R. (1985). The transparency of denial: Briefing in the debriefing paradigm. *Journal of Personality and Social Psychology, 49,* 338–346.

Wehrens, M. J. P. W., Kuyper, H., Dijkstra, P., Buunk, A. P., & van der Werf, M. P. C. (2010). The longterm effect of social comparison on academic performance. *European Journal of Social Psychology, 40,* 1158–1171.

Weick, K. E. (1969). Social psychology in an era of social change. *American Psychologist, 24,* 990–998.

Weick, K. E. (1979). *The social psychology of organizing* (2nd ed.). New York, NY: McGraw-Hill.

Weinberg, R. S., & Gould, D. (1999). *Foundations of sport and exercise psychology* (2nd ed.). Champaign, IL: Human Kinetics.

Weiner, B. (1995). Inferences of responsibility and social motivation. In M. Zanna (Ed.), *Advances in experimental social psychology* (pp. 1–47). San Diego, CA: Academic Press.

Weinstein, N. D., Rothman, A. J., & Sutton, S. R. (1998). Stage theories of health behavior: Conceptual and methodological issues. *Health Psychology, 17,* 290–299.

Weiss, R. S. (1975). *Marital separation.* New York, NY: Basic Books.

Wells, G. L., Malpass, R. S., Lindsay, R. C. L., Fisher, R. P., Turtle, J. W., & Fulero, S. M. (2000). From the lab to the police station: A successful application of eyewitness research. *American Psychologist, 55,* 581–598.

Wells, G. L., Memon, A., & Penrod, S. D. (2006). Eyewitness evidence. Improving its probative value. *Psychological Science in the Public Interest, 7*(2), 45–75.

Wells, G. L., & Turtle, J. W. (1986). Eyewitness identification: The importance of linear models. *Psychological Bulletin, 99,* 320–329.

Welsh, B. C., & Farrington, D. P. (2007). Scientific support for early prevention and delinquency and later offending. *Victims and Offenders, 2,* 125–140.

West, S., Jett, S. E., Beckman, T., & Vonk, J. (2010). The phylogenic roots of cognitive dissonance. *Journal of Comparative Psychology, 124,* 425–432.

Westre, K. R., & Weiss, M. R. (1991). The relationship between perceived coaching behaviors and group cohesion in high school football teams. *Sport Psychologist, 5,* 41–54.

Wexler, H. K. (1995). The success of therapeutic communities for substance abusers in American prisons. *Journal of Psychoactive Drugs, 27,* 57–66.

Wexler, H. K., Falkin, G. P., & Lipton, D. S. (1990). Outcome evaluation of a prison therapeutic community for substance abuse treatment. *Criminal Justice and Behavior, 17,* 71–92.

White, M. (2010, April 26). *Why did nobody help? asks mugged man, 79.* The Star. Retrieved from http://www.thestar.com/news/gta/crime/article/800974--armed-citizenry

Wholey, J. S. (1983). *Evaluation and effective public management.* Toronto, ON: Little, Brown.

Whyte, G. (1993). Escalating commitment in individual and group decision-making: A prospect theory approach. *Organizational Behavior and Human Decision Processes, 53,* 430–455.

Whyte, G. (1998). Recasting Janis's groupthink model: The key role of collective efficacy in decision fiascoes. *Organizational Behavior and Human Decision Processes, 73*(2–3), 185–209.

Whyte, W. H. (1980). *The social life of small urban spaces.* New York, NY: The Conservation Foundation.

Wicker, A. W. (1969). Attitudes versus actions: The relationship between verbal and overt behavioral responses to attitude objects. *Journal of Social Issues, 25,* 41–78.

Wicklund, R. A., & Brehm, J. W. (1976). *Perspectives on cognitive dissonance.* New York, NY: Wiley.

Widmeyer, W. N., Brawley, L. R., & Carron, A. V. (1985). *The measurement of cohesion in sport teams: The Group Environment Questionnaire.* London, Ontario: Sport Dynamics.

Widmeyer, W. N., Brawley, L. R., & Carron, A. V. (1990). The effects of group size in sport. *Journal of Sport and Exercise Psychology, 12,* 177–190.

Widmeyer, W. N., Silva, J. M., & Hardy, C. J. (1992). *The nature of group cohesion in sport teams: A phenomenological approach.* Paper presented at the Association for the Advancement of Applied Sport Psychology Conference, Colorado Springs, CO.

Widmeyer, W. N., & Williams, J. (1991). Predicting cohesion in a coacting sport. *Small Group Research, 22,* 548–570.

Wiesner, M., & Capaldi, D. M. (2003). Relations on childhood and adolescent factors to offending trajectories of young men. *Journal of Research in Crime and Delinquency, 40,* 231–262.

Williams, J., & Best, D. (1982). *Measuring sex stereotypes: A thirty-nation study.* Beverly Hills, CA: SAGE.

Williams, J., & Widmeyer, W. N. (1991). The cohesion performance outcome relationship in a coacting sport. *Journal of Sport and Exercise Psychology, 13,* 364–371.

Williams, K. Y., & O'Reilly, C. A. (1998). Demography and diversity in organizations: A review of 40 years of research. *Research in Organizational Behavior, 20,* 77–140.

Williams v. Florida, 399 U.S. 78 (1970).

Williford, A., Elledge, L. C., Boulton, A. J., DePaolis, K. J., Little, T. D., & Salmivalli, C. (2013). Effects of the KiVa antibullying program on cyberbullying and cybervictimization frequency among Finnish youth. *Journal of Clinical Child and Adolescent Psychology, 42,* 820–833.

Wills, T. A. (1981). Downward comparison principles in social psychology. *Psychological Bulletin, 90,* 245–271.

Wilson, B. J., Kunkel, D., Linz, D., Potter, W. J., Donnerstein, E., Smith, S. L., . . . Berry, M. (1998). Violence in television programming overall: University of California, Santa Barbara study. In *National television violence study* (Vol. 2, pp. 3–180). Thousand Oaks, CA: SAGE.

Wilson, B. J., Kunkel, D., Linz, D., Potter, W. J., Donnerstein, E., Smith, S. L., . . . Gray, T. (1997). Violence in television programming overall: University of California, Santa Barbara study. In *National television violence study* (Vol. 1, pp. 3–159). Thousand Oaks, CA: SAGE.

Wilson, B. J., Smith, S. L., Potter, W. J., Kunkel, D., Linz, D., Colvin, C. M., & Donnerstein, E. (2002). Violence in children's television programming: Assessing the risks. *Journal of Communication, 52*(4), 5–35.

Wilson, D. B., MacKenzie, D. L., & Mitchell. F. N. (2008). *Effects of correctional boot camps on offending.* Oslo, Norway: The Campbell Collaboration.

Wilson, R. J., Huculak, B., & McWhinnie, A. (2002). Restorative justice innovations in Canada. *Behavioral Sciences and the Law, 20,* 363–380.

Wilson-Doenges, G. (2000). An exploration of sense of community and fear of crime in gated communities. *Environment and Behavior, 32,* 597–611.

Wilton, L. S., Moss-Racusin, C. A., Good, J. J., & Sanchez, D. T. (2015). Communicating more than diversity: The effect of institutional diversity statements on expectations and performance as a function of race and gender. *Cultural Diversity and Ethnic Minority Psychology, 21*(3), 315–325.

Wimperis, B. R., & Farr, J. L. (1979). The effects of task content and reward contingency upon task performance and satisfaction. *Journal of Applied Social Psychology, 9,* 229–249.

Winzelberg, A. (1997). Analysis of an electronic support group for individuals with eating disorders. *Computers in Human Behavior, 13,* 393–407.

Wisch, A. F., & Mahalik, J. R. (1999). Male therapists' clinical bias: Influence of client gender roles and therapist gender role conflict. *Journal of Counseling Psychology, 46,* 51–60.

Wise, J. A., & Wise, B. K. (1985). *Bank interiors and bank robberies: A design approach to environmental security.* Rolling Meadows, IL: Bank Administration Institute.

Wolfgang, M. E., & Ferracuti, F. (1981). *The subculture of violence.* Beverly Hills, CA: SAGE.

Wollin, D. D., & Montagne, M. (1981). College classroom environment: Effects of sterility versus amiability on student and teacher performance. *Environment and Behavior, 13,* 707–716.

Wong, C. Y., Sommer, R., & Cook, R. (1992). The soft classroom 17 years later. *Journal of Environmental Psychology, 12,* 337–343.

Wong, J. (1999, November 20). Jan Wong's last word: What do we tell our kids if a pal is attacked? Stand by him? Or is it everyone for himself? *Globe and Mail,* p. A32.

Wood, D., Kaplan, R., & McLoyd, V. C. (2007). Gender differences in the educational expectations of urban, low-income African-American youth: The role of parents and the school. *Journal of Youth and Adolescence, 36,* 417–427.

Wright, A. M., & Alison, L. (2004). Questioning sequences in Canadian police interviews: Constructing and confirming the course of events? *Psychology, Crime, & Law, 10*(2), 137–154.

Wright, B. L., & Loving, T. J. (2011). Health implications of conflict in close relationships. *Social and Personality Psychology Compass, 5*(8), 552–562.

Yalom, I. D. (1995). *The theory and practice of group psychotherapy* (4th ed.). New York, NY: Basic Books.

Yang, S., Kadouri, A., Revah-Levy, A., Mulvey, E. P., & Falissard, B. (2009). Doing time: A qualitative study of long-term incarceration and the impact of mental illness. *International Journal of Law and Psychiatry, 32,* 294–303.

Yaniv, I. (2011). Group diversity and decision quality: Amplification and attenuation of the framing effect. *International Journal of Forecasting, 27,* 41–49.

Yarbrough, D. B., Shulha, L. M., Hopson, R. K., & Caruthers, F. A. (2011). *The program evaluation standards: A guide for evaluators and evaluation users* (3rd ed.). Thousand Oaks, CA: SAGE.

Yoon, J. S., & Barton, E. (2008). The role of teachers in school violence and bullying prevention. In T. W. Miller (Ed.), *School violence and primary prevention* (pp. 249–275). New York, NY: Springer.

Young, S. G., Hugenberg, K., Bernstein, M. J., & Sacco, D. F. (2012). Perception and motivation in face recognition: A critical review of theories of the cross-race effect. *Personality and Social Psychology Review, 16*(2), 116–142.

Younge, G. (2003, January 27). America is a class act. *The Guardian.* Retrieved from http://www.guardian.co.uk/comment/story/0,3604,882935,00.html

Youssef, C. M., & Luthans, F. (2007). Positive organizational behavior in the workplace: The impact of hope, optimism, and resilience. *Journal of Management, 33,* 774–800.

Yox, S. (2003, April 9). Cultural responsiveness improves healing. *Medscape Medical News.* Retrieved from http://www.medscape.com/viewarticle/452137

Yukl, G. A. (2006). *Leadership in organizations.* Upper Saddle River, NJ: Pearson/Prentice Hall.

Zaidel, D., Hakkert, A. S., & Pistiner, A. H. (1992). The use of road humps for moderating speeds on urban streets. *Accident Analysis and Prevention, 24,* 45–56.

Zajonc, R. B. (1965). Social facilitation. *Science, 149,* 269–274.

Zajonc, R. B. (1968). Attitudinal effects of mere exposure. *Journal of Personality and social psychology, 9*(2, Part 2), 1–27.

Zajonc, R. B. (2001). Mere exposure: A gateway to the subliminal. *Current Directions in Psychological Science, 10,* 224–228.

Zhang, Y. (2015, June). Functional diversity and group creativity: The role of group longevity. *The Journal of Applied Behavioural Science,* 1–27.

Zheng, Z., Paterson, C., Ledgerwood, K., Hogg, M., Dip, G., Arnold, C. A., & Xue, C. C. L. (2013). Chaos to hope: A narrative of healing. *Pain Medicine, 14,* 1826–1838.

Zhu, D. H. (2013). Group polarization on corporate boards: Theory and evidence on board decisions about acquisition premiums. *Strategic Management Journal, 34,* 800–822.

Zillmann, D. (1994). Erotica and family values. In D. Zillman, J. Bryant, & A. C. Huston (Eds.), *Media, children, and the family: Social scientific, psychodynamic, and clinical perspectives* (pp. 199–213). Mahwah, NJ: Erlbaum.

Zillmann, D., & Bryant, J. (1982). Pornography, sexual callousness, and the trivialization of rape. *Journal of Communication, 32,* 10–21.

Zillmann, D., & Bryant, J. (1984). Effects of massive exposure to pornography. In N. M. Malamuth & E. Donnerstein (Eds.), *Pornography and sexual aggression* (pp. 115–138). Orlando, FL: Academic Press.

Zillmann, D., & Bryant, J. (1986). Shifting preferences in pornography consumption. *Communication Research, 13,* 560–578.

Zillmann, D., & Bryant, J. (1988a). Effects of prolonged consumption of pornography on family values. *Journal of Family Issues, 9,* 518–544.

Zillmann, D., & Bryant, J. (1988b). Pornography's impact on sexual satisfaction. *Journal of Applied Social Psychology, 18,* 438–453.

Zimbardo, P. G. (1969). The human choice: Individuation, reason, and order versus deindividuation, impulse, and chaos. In W. J. Arnold & D. Levine (Eds.), *Nebraska symposium on motivation* (Vol. 17, pp. 237–307). Lincoln: University of Nebraska.

Zimbardo, P. G. (2002a). Going forward with commitment. *Monitor on psychology, 33*(1), 5.

Zimbardo, P. G. (2002b). Psychology in the public service. *American Psychologist, 57,* 431–433.

Zuckerman, M., Kieffer, S. C., & Knee, C. R. (1998). Consequences of self-handicapping: Effects on coping, academic performance, and adjustment. *Journal of Personality and Social Psychology, 74,* 1619–1628.

AUTHOR INDEX

Cron, W. L., 270
Crouse, E. M., 89
Crowell, D. H., 291
Csikszentmihalyi, M., 108, 110, 455, 460, 461, 465, 471
Cuddy, A. C., 399
Culhane, S. E., 309
Cunha, M. Jr., 35
Cunningham, A. C., 310, 312
Cunningham, I. J., 146
Cunningham, J., 230
Cunningham, P. B., 296
Cutler, B. L., 305

Dabbs, J. M., 291
Daft, R. L., 271, 273
Dale, G. A., 146
D'Alessio, S., 377
Dallos, R., 10
Dalsing, S., 442
Dalton, J., 322, 324, 325
Dannefer, D., 16
Danzinger, P. R., 123
Darcy, K., 105
Darley, J. M., 30, 61, 289, 328
Das, E., 7
Dasgupta, N., 444
Davenport, A., 80
Davies, J., 170
Davila, J., 105
Davis, J. H., 278
Davis, S. F., 447
Davison, K., 332
Dawe, S. W. L., 136
Dawes, R. M., 354, 355
Dawson, J. A., 275
Day, D., 336
Daye, C. E., 413
Deacon, Z., 343
DeAngelis, T., 75, 413
Dearing, J. W., 180, 181, 182
DeBaryshe, B. D., 294
Debus, R. R., 228
De Carrasquel, S. R., 391
Deci, E. L., 230, 231, 232, 234, 450
DeCoster, J., 161
De Dea, C., 7
De Dreu, C., 405
DeForge, B. R., 121

DeGroot, T., 464
DeLeon, P. H., 89
Del Rosario, M. L., 159
Delwar, T., 88
Demaine, L. J., 262
Denious, J. E., 345
Dennis, A. R., 283
Deo, M. E., 413
DePaolis, K. J., 248
DePaulo, B. M., 257, 298
DePaulo, P., 276
DeSanctis, G., 277
Desforges, D. M., 410
DeShong, H., 424
Deshpande, S., 205
DeSteno, D., 444
Deutsch, M., 12, 247, 279, 405
Devellis, B. M., 42
Devine, D., 469
DeVinney, L. C., 406
De Visser, R. O., 85, 86
Devos-Comby, L., 196
De Vries, H., 42
Diamond, S. G., 375
Diamond, S. S., 307
DiBerardinis, J. D., 145, 146
Dickerson, C., 37, 45, 65, 67
Dickerson, S., 332
Dickson, N., 294
Dickson, W. J., 268
DiClemente, C. C., 208, 209, 210
Diefenbach, D., 337
Dietz, J., 408
DiFonzo, N., 359
Di Gangi, P. M., 331
Dijkstra, A., 376
Dijkstra, M., 42, 405
Dijkstra, P., 235, 236
Dillman, D. A., 48
DiMatteo, M. R., 193, 195, 197
Dion, K. K., 424
Dion, K. L., 393
Dishion, T. J., 241, 242, 294, 295, 296
Doan, K., 186
Docherty, A. L., 214, 215
Dodd, P., 332, 333
Dolan, E., 307
Dolan, F. J., 307
Dolev-Cohen, M., 246, 247

SUBJECT INDEX

Note: In page references, f indicates figures and t indicates tables.

ABOUT THE EDITORS

Jamie A. Gruman, (PhD, University of Windsor) earned his doctorate in Applied Social Psychology with a specialization in organizational psychology. He is currently an Associate Professor of Organizational Behavior at the University of Guelph in Ontario, Canada, and has previously taught in both the psychology departments and business schools at the University of Toronto and the University of Windsor. An award-winning researcher, he has published articles in such journals as *Basic and Applied Social Psychology, Human Resource Management*, the *Journal of Vocational Behavior, Industrial and Organizational Psychology, Human Resource Management Review, Human Resource Development Quarterly*, and the *Journal of Managerial Psychology*. His current research interests pertain largely to positive organizational psychology, and his point of entry into this topic is often the organizational socialization process. He is also the founding Chair of the Canadian Positive Psychology Association.

Frank W. Schneider (PhD, University of Florida) is Professor Emeritus of Psychology, University of Windsor. He is a cofounder of the doctoral program in Applied Social Psychology at the University of Windsor. He coauthored a textbook on differential psychology and has published articles related to a variety of topics, including policing, group dynamics, organizational effectiveness, evaluation research, social psychology of education, gender roles, domestic violence, helping behavior, race relations, nonverbal communication, attribution theory, and adjustment of the elderly. His current research interests are in the areas of community policing and police organization effectiveness.

Larry M. Coutts (PhD, University of Windsor) is the president of L. M. Coutts & Associates, an organizational and human resource management consulting firm, and he teaches part-time in the Sprott School of Business, Carleton University. Larry is a former Director of Research and Development for the human resource consulting company EPSI Inc., and a former Assistant Professor in the Applied Social Psychology division at the University of Windsor. He also has held positions with the Royal Canadian Mounted Police as director of the Organizational Design and Job Evaluation Branch, and as a senior research principal with both the Personnel Research Branch and the Canadian Police College. His research interests include industrial and organizational psychology, specifically personnel selection (assessment centers, simulation exercises, structured interviews, and testing), and organizational change and development. Much of his published research has focused around law enforcement settings (personnel selection in law enforcement, police hiring and promotion, senior police executive development, etc.).

CONTRIBUTORS

Louise R. Alexitch, PhD
Associate Professor
Culture, Health, and Human
    Development Program
Psychology Department
University of Saskatchewan
Saskatoon, Saskatchewan

Sherry Bergeron, PhD
Program Evaluation Specialist
Corporate Services Division
Windsor-Essex County Health Unit
Windsor, Ontario

Greg A. Chung-Yan, PhD
Associate Professor
Applied Social Psychology Program
Department of Psychology
University of Windsor
Windsor, Ontario

Kenneth M. Cramer, PhD
Professor
Applied Social Psychology Program
Department of Psychology
University of Windsor
Windsor, Ontario

David M. Day, PhD
Professor
Department of Psychology
Ryerson University
Toronto, Ontario

Lori Dithurbide, MA
Doctoral student
Program in Psychosocial Aspects of Sport and
    Physical Activity
Department of Kinesiology
Michigan State University
East Lansing, Michigan

Jennifer Dobson, PhD
Postdoctoral researcher
Department of Psychology
University of Guelph
Guelph, Ontario

David R. Ewoldsen, PhD
Professor
Department of Media & Information
Michigan State University
East Lansing, Michigan

Deborah L. Feltz, PhD
Professor
Program in Psychosocial Aspects of Sport and
    Physical Activity
Department of Kinesiology
Michigan State University
East Lansing, Michigan

Robert Gifford
Professor
Environmental Psychology Lab
Department of Psychology
University of Victoria
Victoria, British Columbia

Kenneth E. Hart, PhD
Associate Professor
Clinical Psychology Program
Department of Psychology
University of Windsor
Windsor, Ontario

Phillip A. Ianni
Doctoral student
Psychology Department
University of Windsor
Windsor, Ontario

Ritu Kaushal, PhD
Organizational Development Consultant
Private Practice
Toronto, Ontario

Michelle A. Krieger
Doctoral student
Psychology Department
University of Windsor
Windsor, Ontario

Catherine T. Kwantes, PhD
Professor
Applied Social Psychology Program
Department of Psychology
University of Windsor
Windsor, Ontario

Kathryn D. Lafreniere, PhD
Professor
Applied Social Psychology Program
Department of Psychology
University of Windsor
Windsor, Ontario

Adam C. Lodzinski, PhD
Organizational Development and Program
    Design/Evaluation Consultant
Dr. Adam Lodzinski & Associates
Toronto, Ontario

Stéphanie B. Marion, PhD
Postdoctoral Fellow
Faculty of Social Science and Humanities
Forensic Psychology
University of Ontario Institute of Technology
Oshawa, Ontario

Michiko S. Motomura, PhD
Independent consultant
Guelph, Ontario

Stewart Page, PhD
Professor Emeritus
Applied Social Psychology Program
Department of Psychology
University of Windsor
Windsor, Ontario

Beverly Roskos, PhD
Associate Professor
Cognitive Psychology Concentration
Department of Psychology
University of Alabama
Tuscaloosa, Alabama

Charlene Y. Senn, PhD
Professor
Applied Social Psychology Program
Department of Psychology/Women's and
    Gender Studies
University of Windsor
Windsor, Ontario

Randolph A. Smith, PhD
Adjunct Professor
Department of Psychology
Moravian College
Bethlehem, Pennsylvania

Philip J. Sullivan, PhD
Associate Professor
Department of Kinesiology
Brock University
St. Catherines, Ontario

Shelagh M. J. Towson, PhD
Associate Professor
Applied Social Psychology Program
Department of Psychology
University of Windsor
Windsor, Ontario

Ann L. Weber, PhD
Professor of Psychology, Emerita
University of North Carolina at Asheville
Asheville, North Carolina